Criminal Law and Procedure for the Paralegal

Aspen College Series

Criminal Law and Procedure for the Paralegal

Edward C. Carter, III

Second Edition

Published by Wolters Kluwer in New York.

Wolters Kluwer Legal & Regulatory US serves customers worldwide with CCH, Aspen Publishers, and Kluwer Law International products. (www.WKLegaledu.com)

To contact Customer Service, e-mail customer.service@wolterskluwer.com, call 1-800-234-1660, fax 1-800-901-9075, or mail correspondence to:

Wolters Kluwer
Attn: Order Department
PO Box 990
Frederick, MD 21705

Printed in the United States of America.

1 2 3 4 5 6 7 8 9 0

ISBN 978-1-4548-7352-5

Library of Congress Cataloging-in-Publication Data

Names: Carter, Edward C., 1953- author.
Title: Criminal law and procedure for the paralegal / Edward C. Carter, III.
Description: Second edition. | New York : Wolters Kluwer, [2016]
Identifiers: LCCN 2016012200 | ISBN 9781454873525
Subjects: LCSH: Criminal law-United States. | Criminal procedure-United States.
Classification: LCC KF9219.85 .C37 2016 | DDC 345.73-dc23
LC record available at http://lccn.loc.gov/2016012200

About Wolters Kluwer Legal & Regulatory US

Wolters Kluwer Legal & Regulatory US delivers expert content and solutions in the areas of law, corporate compliance, health compliance, reimbursement, and legal education. Its practical solutions help customers successfully navigate the demands of a changing environment to drive their daily activities, enhance decision quality and inspire confident outcomes.

Serving customers worldwide, its legal and regulatory portfolio includes products under the Aspen Publishers, CCH Incorporated, Kluwer Law International, ftwilliam.com and MediRegs names. They are regarded as exceptional and trusted resources for general legal and practice-specific knowledge, compliance and risk management, dynamic workflow solutions, and expert commentary.

This book is dedicated to my wife Angela who,
without complaint, sacrificed all that I asked
and then had to sacrifice more than any person should.

Summary of Contents

Contents

Section II: CRIMINAL LAW AND CRIMINAL PROCEDURE 59

CHAPTER 5 THE DISTINCTION BETWEEN CRIMINAL LAW AND CRIMINAL PROCEDURE 61

Section III: SUBSTANTIVE CRIMINAL LAW 69

CHAPTER 6 PRINCIPLES OF CRIMINAL JURISDICTION RECOGNIZED BY CUSTOMARY INTERNATIONAL LAW 71

CHAPTER 7   THE AMERICAN FEDERAL SYSTEM AND CRIMINAL JURISDICTION   87

CHAPTER 10   CATEGORIES AND TYPES OF CRIMINAL OFFENSES

CHAPTER 11   HOW CRIMINAL OFFENSES ARE DEFINED   193

CHAPTER 17   CRIMINAL PROCEDURE DURING THE INVESTIGATIVE STAGE—PRIVILEGE AGAINST SELF-INCRIMINATION AND OTHER RIGHTS   415

CHAPTER 18 CRIMINAL PROCEDURE AT THE CHARGING STAGE 455

CHAPTER 21   CRIMINAL PROCEDURE DURING THE POST-TRIAL STAGE—SENTENCING AND BEYOND   559

Preface to the Second Edition

In this Second Edition of *Criminal Law and Procedure for the Paralegal*, the law has been updated where necessary, the examination of certain subjects has been deepened or expanded by the addition of new material, and some of the chapters have been reorganized either in response to changes in the law or to enhance analytic clarity and student understanding. The changes are described more specifically below.

Chapters 3 and 4 have been updated with the most recent statistics available about law enforcement agencies and federal and state prosecutions.

Chapter 6 has undergone extensive change. The law has been updated, the chapter has been expanded by the addition of new material, and the chapter has been reorganized.

New introductory paragraphs at the beginning of the chapter introduce the terms "legislative jurisdiction" and "adjudicative jurisdiction" and explain that one refers to the substantive element of criminal jurisdiction (the subject of Chapter 6) and the other refers to the procedural element of criminal jurisdiction (the subject of a later chapter). Those terms are new to both the chapter and the textbook. The new introductory paragraphs also make explicit what was only implicit in Chapter 6 of the First Edition: that a sovereign can exercise legislative jurisdiction under either customary international law or its own domestic law and still have a valid verdict.

As reorganized, Section A now examines how legislative jurisdiction is established under customary international law. Section B examines the domestic law alternative to establishing legislative jurisdiction through customary international law as that alternative is explicated in *United States v. Yunis*[1], a case which is reproduced in edited form in the body of the textbook.

The discussion of customary international law as it relates to legislative jurisdiction has been updated with new decisions and has been deepened by the addition of an examination of customary international law's reasonableness limitation.

The law in Chapter 7 has been updated and the chapter has been expanded by the addition of two subjects. First, recognizing the importance of the *Vilar*[2] decision, a brief discussion of the presumption against extra-territorial application of federal criminal statutes has been added. Second, a brief examination of the limits that the Fifth Amendment's due process clause places on the exercise of extra-territorial jurisdiction by the federal government has also been added.

Chapter 8 has been expanded, its treatment of certain subjects deepened, and its law updated. It has been expanded, and its discussion of the limits the equal protection clause imposes on the power of the federal government and the states to enact criminal laws has been deepened by the addition of a brief discussion about the application of the disparate impact doctrine to facially neutral criminal statutes. The chapter has also been expanded and its examination of the due process based void for vagueness doctrine has been deepened by the addition of a discussion of that doctrine in relation to jurisdictional statutes.

The law in Chapter 9 has been updated and the Eye on Ethics sidebar relating to the no contact rule has been edited and expanded to reflect developments in the law surrounding that rule since the First Edition of the textbook was published. The original sidebar explained that the no contact rule is case specific. The edited sidebar uses recent court decisions to explain in more detail what that means. A new section of the sidebar examines the "authorized by law exception" that is now found in versions of the no contact rule adopted by some states or which appears in comments that accompany a revised version of the rule adopted in other states. That new section of the sidebar also uses recent decisions to explain the limits of the authorized by law exception.

The law in Chapter 10 has been updated and its discussion of the offenses of Mail Fraud and Forgery has been edited. In the case of both offenses the changes were made for the purpose of enhancing analytic clarity and student understanding. In the case of Mail Fraud and the other federal scheme statutes referred to in connection with the discussion of that offense the changes also reflect recent decisions relating to them.

Chapter 11 was expanded by the addition of a recent court decision to the body of the textbook. That decision, *State v. Kenny*,[3] provides an easy to understand explanation in a factually simple case of the principle of cause in fact and illustrates how that principle operates to relieve a defendant of criminal responsibility for results that his actions bring about.

In Chapter 13, the sidebar relating to the cultural background defense has been updated and expanded by a brief discussion of the International Convention of Civil and Political Rights and whether that convention creates a right to such a defense in the United States.

The law in Chapter 16 has been updated and the chapter has been edited and expanded to reflect the Supreme Court's teaching in the 2012 *Jones*[4] decision. The chapter now includes a discussion of the concept of a Fourth Amendment search, as explicated in *Jones* and reflects the holding of *Jones* that the *Katz*[5] expectation of privacy test does not supplant the pre-*Katz*, textually based, enumerated areas/trespass analysis. The chapter now also reflects the holding of *Jones* that the *Katz* expectation of privacy test is to be used only when government agents intrude into areas not specifically mentioned in the Fourth Amendment.

In Chapter 18, the section that examines the right to counsel has been reorganized and updated with the addition of several post-*Rothgery*[6] decisions.

Chapter 19 has been expanded by the addition of a brief examination of the concept of adjudicatory jurisdiction (an addition necessitated by the expanded examination of criminal law jurisdiction in Chapter 6 where the term "adjudicatory jurisdiction" is introduced) and how, in criminal law, that element of jurisdiction is established by acquiring *in personam* jurisdiction over the defendant.

Chapter 20 was expanded by the addition of a brief discussion of an alternate closing argument procedure used in some jurisdictions.

The law in Chapter 21 has been updated and the section of the chapter that discusses how and by whom a sentence in a criminal case is determined has been reorganized and deepened. As reorganized, that section now more clearly delineates the difference between the sentencing procedure in capital cases, a procedure that is fairly uniform among the states with a death penalty statute and the sentencing procedure in non-capital cases, a procedure in which there is substantially less uniformity among the states. The reorganized section has also been deepened to provide a fuller discussion of the process by which a death sentence is imposed and, as it relates to the death penalty, it: 1) incorporates the Supreme Court's January 2016 decision in *Hurst v. Florida*[7] and 2) replaces the portion of the now repealed Illinois death penalty that appeared in the First Edition of the textbook with a statutorily equivalent section of the Idaho death penalty statute.

ENDNOTES

1. 924 F.2d 1086 (D.C. Cir. 1991).
2. *United States v. Vilar*, 729 F.3d 62 (2nd Cir. 2013).
3. 116 So.3d 992 (Ct. Of App. of La. 4th Dist. 2013).
4. *United States v. Jones*, 565 U.S. _____ (2012).
5. *Katz v. United States*, 389 U.S. 347 (1967).
6. *Rothgery v. Gillespie County, Texas*, 554 U.S. 191 (2008).
7. 557 U.S. _____ (2016).

Preface to the First Edition

Criminal Law and Procedure for the Paralegal takes a practical approach to teaching paralegal students about the criminal justice system, criminal law and procedure, the role of paralegals in the criminal justice system, and how to perform tasks that paralegals can reasonably expect to be assigned while working in the field.

Organization of the Textbook

The textbook is divided into four sections each of which covers a broad subject area. Each section contains a brief introduction to its subject and a brief description of the topics of each chapter in the section. At the beginning of each chapter there is a statement of chapter objectives. That statement tells the student what he or she is expected to learn from the chapter. Each chapter also has at least one introductory paragraph that explains what the chapter will cover thereby reinforcing for the students what they should expect to learn. When a new legal term or possibly unfamiliar nonlegal term is introduced, it is defined in the margin of the page on which the term first appears. In most instances, legal terms are also discussed within the body of text. Those terms then appear at the end of the chapter in a list called "Chapter Terms." At appropriate points there is a discussion of the role paralegals often play in relation to the chapter's subject.

Most chapters also contain cases. In most instances the cases provide examples of the legal principles discussed in the body of the text and often provide further explanation for or discussion of those principles. In some instances a case is included to provide historical context to a legal principle discussed in the text, and in other instances a case is included to illustrate a competing legal principle that the court considered or had previously adopted. Each case is followed by a "Case Focus" text box that contains questions aimed at focusing the students' attention on the point or points the case was included to illustrate. The cases do not introduce new subjects. Thus, instructors who do not want to assign cases for reading can do so without forfeiting coverage of any subject.

Many chapters also contain sidebars, two of which recur in various chapters. One of the recurring sidebars is the "Eye on Ethics" sidebar. The Eye on Ethics sidebars discuss ethical issues that relate to a subject discussed in a particular chapter. The other recurring sidebar is the "Historical Perspective" sidebar. The Historical Perspective sidebar provides students with historical background to the development of some legal principle or legal institution discussed in a chapter. Non-recurring sidebars provide more depth or context to certain subjects.

At the end of each chapter there is a list of questions called "Review Questions." The review questions are tied to the chapter objectives and are designed to test whether the student has achieved those objectives. Many chapters also contain a section called "Additional Reading" that lists articles, books, and other material for students who are interested in reading more about a subject covered in the chapter.

Introducing Students to the Criminal Justice System

Unless they already work in the criminal justice system it is the author's experience that most paralegal students at best have an imperfect understanding of how the criminal justice system works, who its primary actors are, and the limits imposed on those actors. In particular, students have little understanding of the vast array of law enforcement agencies and prosecuting offices that enforce the criminal laws in the United States. The chapters in Section I introduce the student to the criminal justice system. The first chapter gives the students an overview of the criminal justice process by breaking it into different phases. The students will encounter those phases again in Section IV, which discusses criminal procedure in a phase-by-phase manner. In Chapter 2 the students are introduced to the legal concept of crime and learn the distinction between civil and criminal law. This chapter also provides the students with a brief history of the development of criminal law. The chapter also introduces the students in a general way to some of the different ways in which crimes are classified (e.g., felony/misdemeanor and *malum in se/malum prohibitum*) and explains why understanding those classifications is important.

The third and fourth chapters of Section I introduce students to the different types of law enforcement agencies that investigate crime and the different offices that initiate criminal prosecutions. In conjunction with its examination of the different types of law enforcement agencies at different levels of the American political system, Chapter 3 also examines the different types of investigations they conduct (informal and formal) and introduces the students to the different forms of investigations such agencies conduct. In particular, Chapter 3 introduces the student to the grand jury and explains how grand jury investigations are conducted. Included in Chapter 3 is a discussion of administrative investigations and administrative subpoenas—an important subject given the number of federal and state criminal investigations that are conducted in that manner and the role paralegals often play in them. This is a subject that is often ignored by other criminal law textbooks for paralegals.

Chapter 4 not only introduces the student to the different prosecuting offices found in the American political system, but it also discusses the nature and exercise of prosecutorial discretion and the limiting effect the principle of separation of powers has on the power of the judiciary to investigate and prosecute or to order the investigation and prosecution of crime.

Substantive Law and Procedure

Sections II through IV address the subjects of criminal law and procedure. Section II is a short section that consists of one chapter that examines the distinction between substantive criminal law and criminal procedure. Section III covers the subject of substantive criminal law and Section IV covers the subject of criminal procedure.

Approach of the Textbook in Relation to Criminal Offenses and Affirmative Defenses

Teaching substantive criminal law, even to the limited extent that it is done through a textbook for paralegal students, presents major challenges that are only exacerbated when the book is aimed at a nationwide audience. The existence of more than 51 different criminal codes in the American political system and the uncounted number of different crimes defined in those codes and in other statutes presents instructors with a daunting pedagogical challenge and makes it a nearly Sisyphean task to try to discuss even a substantial minority of offenses in any meaningful way.

Some paralegal textbooks try to meet this challenge by devoting much space to discussion of the Model Penal Code and examining the crimes and legal principles that code defines, usually to the exclusion of any discussion of federal crimes and the Federal Criminal Code. Other textbooks take a catalog-like approach placing criminal statutes into different categories and then briefly describing a large number of the federal and state crimes contained in those categories. To some extent some of the textbooks also put an emphasis on whatever offenses are the "crimes du jour" at the time they were written or revised. A glance at recently revised or released textbooks in the field reveals discussions of terrorism, terrorist crimes, and war crimes. Virtually all of the textbooks supplement their examination of criminal offenses with discussions of crime related issues that are more appropriate to a sociology class or criminal justice class but which have nothing to do with the work of paralegals.

The Model Penal Code approach and the catalog approach both have serious drawbacks and do not serve the needs of paralegal students who may work in the field of criminal law. It makes little sense to place a heavy emphasis on discussing the Model Penal Code and the terms and crimes it defines when that Code has not been adopted in full in any state and to the extent it has been adopted, most of the states adopting it have chosen, to greater and lesser degrees, to use different terminology, define their terms somewhat differently, define their offenses differently, and give their offenses different names. It also makes little sense to ignore federal crimes and the Federal Criminal Code when that code is used across the country in federal criminal prosecutions and is significantly different in structure and approach from that of the Model Penal Code based state criminal codes. At the same time the brief snippet-like discussions of many different crimes found in the books that use the catalog approach provide a paralegal student with little that will help her do her job in a prosecuting or defense attorney's office or to understand what actually constitutes any particular crime.

This textbook takes a different approach to teaching paralegal students about crimes. Instead of following either of the above routes this textbook uses what the author refers to as the elemental analysis approach. The elemental analysis approach does not focus on a particular code or on particular offenses. Instead, it teaches students that all crimes are defined by elements, discusses the fundamental elements that are used to define all crimes in Anglo-American criminal law, and then teaches students how to find and learn about the elements of any criminal offense.

The elemental analysis approach, which the author has used in his classes, eliminates the pedagogical problems inherent in teaching about criminal law in a nation of more than 51 different criminal codes while at the same time teaches students a method which they can use to learn about and understand any type of Anglo-American criminal statute without regard to the jurisdiction, without regard to the type of offense, and without regard to the terminology it uses. The elemental analysis approach thus provides a paralegal student with knowledge that will enable her to perform any type of task given to her that requires her to have some understanding of a criminal statute, even if it is one with which she is wholly unfamiliar or it is one of the many new or recently amended criminal statutes regularly churned out by our many legislative bodies.

The subject of criminal offenses is examined in Chapter 10 and Chapter 11. Chapter 10 provides students with a broad overview of the different types of crimes defined in criminal statutes and uses a commonly recognized system to categorize statutes based on the type of crime they define. To the extent the textbook employs an offense categorization paradigm it does so only as a vehicle to facilitate student understanding of the categories of conduct at which the criminal statutes are aimed and not as an end in itself. The textbook employs an eight category paradigm and uses as examples to illustrate the type of conduct to which the statutes in each of those categories apply, offenses whose names (e.g., incest, arson, perjury, and treason) capture, albeit in a non-technical way, the gist of the crimes they define.

The textbook does not completely forego a discussion of specific crimes. In connection with providing its overview of the different types of offenses, Chapter 10 discusses in a general way a few important, frequently prosecuted, and sometimes highly technical or widely misunderstood offenses. Consistent with the elemental approach to teaching about criminal offenses, each offense discussed is discussed in relation to the elements that define it. The following specific offenses are discussed:

- Each of the three anticipatory offenses is discussed. These are highly technical offenses which can be confusing and are difficult for students to understand.

- The offense of theft is examined. Theft in its various forms and under different names is one of the most frequently charged general property crimes. In many statutory forms it contains two *mens rea* elements and consists of multiple alternate elements which themselves often have multiple alternate definitions thereby making theft a highly technical offense. Theft is also an offense in connection with which most paralegals in prosecutors' offices will frequently be given some form of assignment. In its examination of the offense of theft the textbook notes three acts which theft statutes usually condemn and examines two of those acts.[1] The textbook includes a perfunctory discussion of theft's historical antecedents: the common law crimes of larceny, embezzlement, and false pretenses,[2] but spends no time discussing those crimes or the hyper-technical differences that distinguish them from each other. The author sees little value in devoting time to examining common law crimes that no longer exist and whose technical aspects today are of little interest to anyone other than law school academics and legal historians.

- The text includes a discussion of the statutes that define the homicidal crimes of murder and manslaughter, first degree murder and second degree murder, and felony murder. Few students are aware that there are two distinctly different approaches to defining crimes involving the intentional killing of a human being and virtually none are aware that there are important differences between how, under each approach, those forms of homicide are defined. Moreover, it is the rare paralegal student who has heard of the crime of felony murder or has any idea what the crime is. For all of those reasons and because of the seriousness of those offenses the author considered it important to include a discussion of them.

● There is also a brief discussion of the offense of forgery. That discussion examines the modern form of the offense which, in many jurisdictions, is broadly defined to include the making or delivery of a document that is false in any material way. The book also examines how in many jurisdictions the offense has been updated for the digital age by defining the term "document" to include electronic documents and the term "signature" to include electronic signatures. Because the breadth of the offense of forgery is widely misunderstood by the public as well as by many prosecutors and defense attorneys and because of how the offense has been updated for the digital age it was considered important to include a discussion of it.

● The text also contains a somewhat lengthy discussion of the crime of mail fraud and of the scheme element of that offense. (The scheme can be a scheme to defraud, a scheme to deprive someone of honest services, or a scheme to obtain money or property by means of false pretenses or representations.) Paralegal texts virtually ignore any discussion of this offense. Examination of the offense and particularly of its scheme element is important for a number of reasons: First, mail fraud is one of the most wide sweeping and, with the possible exception of drug offenses, one of the most frequently charged of all federal crimes; it is used to prosecute simple fraud schemes, public corruption, and sophisticated business frauds and because prosecutions of the offense usually involve large volumes of documents, overhear tapes, video recordings, and digital evidence it is one of the crimes in relation to which paralegals in federal prosecutors' offices are most frequently assigned to work. For those reasons alone a paralegal should have some understanding of the offense and of its scheme element. Secondly, mail fraud's scheme element has been imported into other important federal crimes such as wire fraud, bank fraud, and securities fraud. That makes an understanding of that element even more important, particularly for paralegals who may work in federal prosecutors' offices or in federal regulatory agencies such as the FDIC, Federal Reserve, SEC, or FTC. Thirdly, many states have adopted criminal statutes which either contain a scheme element as part of the offense they define[3] or are state level statutory clones of a federal scheme statute.[4] Given the widespread use of the scheme element in so many federal and state statutes it is a gross disservice to paralegal students not to examine it and show how it is used in a particular criminal statute.[5]

Building on the introduction to the concept of elements provided by the discussion of the above offenses in Chapter 10, Chapter 11 provides students with an introduction to and extended discussion of the fundamental elements that are used to define all crimes in American criminal law.

In keeping with the philosophy that it disserves students to ignore the Federal Criminal Code, the discussion of fundamental elements is done with reference to that code, the Model Penal Code, and the common law concepts on which the terms used in both codes are based. The text devotes significant space to the discussion of *mens rea* and explains the fundamental difference between the approach taken to that concept in the Federal Criminal Code and the approach taken to it by the Model Penal Code and by the states that have patterned their criminal codes after it.

Building on that foundation the textbook proceeds to discuss how to find the elements of an offense and how to determine the meaning of those elements. In connection with that latter discussion the book examines the use of terms in the definitions of offenses that themselves are defined in a definitions section of a criminal code that then carry that meaning wherever those terms are used in it and the use of special or limited definitions that are applicable only when a term is used in the definition of a particular offense or in relation to a particular category of offenses. The Illinois theft statute is used to illustrate how to go about finding and learning the meaning of the elements of an offense. The book then employs a hypothetical prosecution referral to illustrate how a paralegal would combine the factual information contained in the referral with the law as explicated in the Illinois theft statute to prepare a report that will assist a prosecutor in making a charging decision or which a prosecutor can use as the basis of a prosecution memorandum, if his office uses them, or which a defense attorney can use in evaluating a client's case.

Chapters 12 through 15 cover affirmative defenses. On its face it may seem incongruous to devote more space to discussing affirmative defenses than to criminal offenses, but because there are far fewer affirmative defenses than criminal offenses, a somewhat greater degree of uniformity in their definitions, and because most of them apply to multiple offenses and some, such as the constitutionally based defenses apply to all offenses, a more thorough discussion is not only possible, but useful and warranted.

The first section of Chapter 12 provides the students with a general introduction to the concept of defenses in criminal law. That section discusses simple defenses and affirmative defenses and distinguishes between them. That section also provides a general discussion of affirmative defenses that tells students what such defenses are and examines the three burdens (assertion, production, and persuasion) that are associated with all affirmative defenses. That section also introduces students to a five category system for classifying different types of affirmative defenses. That system is then used as a framework for discussing affirmative defenses in that and the remaining affirmative defense chapters. The classification system employed in the textbook uses the following categories: 1) excuse defenses; 2) justification defenses; 3) failure of proof defenses; 4) offense modification defenses; and 5) non-exculpatory public policy defenses. The author recognizes that the category titles may not be what some instructors are accustomed to seeing and that some instructors may not be accustomed to considering certain concepts contained in those categories as defenses. While any classification system may to some extent be arbitrary, the system employed in the textbook represents a modern classification system that is used in at least one major treatise and is recognized by many courts.[6]

The first section of Chapter 12 also explains that as is the case with criminal offenses: 1) affirmative defenses are defined differently in different states and 2) different states may give some of the defenses different names. Also as with the chapter that discusses criminal offenses, the affirmative defense chapters urge students to look at the criminal code of their own jurisdiction to see what affirmative defenses their jurisdiction's code recognize and how their jurisdiction's code defines them. Continuing the elemental approach taken with respect to criminal offenses, all the chapters dealing with affirmative defenses focus the students on the elements of each defense.

The instructor should be aware that the textbook does not purport to catalog and examine all of the affirmative defenses. Instead, each affirmative defense chapter discusses the important affirmative defenses contained in the affirmative defense category or categories to which the chapter relates. In the same vein, the textbook does not purport to provide a comprehensive analysis of the defenses it examines. Instead, the textbook examines the broad contours of the defenses and a few of the major variations in those contours that exist in different jurisdictions.

Approach of the Textbook in Relation to Criminal Procedure

Section IV of the book covers criminal procedure and examines that subject differently than most textbooks. Instead of focusing on the specific procedural rights the textbook focuses on the different stages of the criminal justice process and examines both what occurs at each stage and what rights are applicable at that stage. One result of that approach is that some rights, albeit different aspects of those rights are discussed in more than one chapter. An example of one such right is the privilege against self-incrimination. The chapters in Section IV examine the criminal justice process chronologically starting with the investigative stage and concluding with the post-trial stage. It is the author's belief that this organization helps the student to understand not only the flow of the criminal justice process but also how the procedural rights operate.

Textbook Resources

The companion website for *Criminal Law and Procedure for the Paralegal* at aspenparalegaled.com/books/crimlaw_crimpro includes additional resources for students and instructors, including:

- Study aids to help students master the key concepts for this course. Visit the site to access interactive StudyMate exercises such as flash cards, matching, fill-in-the-blank, and crosswords. These activities are also available for download to an iPod or other hand-held device.

- Instructor resources to accompany the text

- Links to helpful websites and updates

Text comes packaged with four months of prepaid access to Loislaw's online legal research database, at http://www.loislawschool.com. Blackboard and eCollege course materials are available to supplement this text. This online courseware is designed to streamline the teaching of the course, providing valuable resources from the book in an accessible electronic format.

Instructor resources to accompany this text include a comprehensive Instructor's Manual, Test Bank, and PowerPoint slides. All of these materials are available on a CD-ROM or for download from our companion website.

Acknowledgments

I would like to thank the following reviewers for their helpful insights:

Laura Barnard, Lakeland CC

Janine Ferraro, Nassau CC

Shawn Friend, Daytona State College

Victoria Green, Baker College

Mark Gruwell, Iowa Lakes Community College

Deborah Howard, University of Evansville

Russell J. Ippolito, SUNY/Westchester Community College

Kathryn Myers, St. Mary-of-the-Woods College

Tom Ogas, California State University—East Bay

Marcy Trew, Brown Mackie College

ENDNOTES

1. The discussion of theft examines unauthorized control theft and theft by deception, but because its meaning is fairly self evident, does not examine theft of property through a threat of force.

2. The author realizes that some states continue to call offenses by these names. Despite the use of those names, the offenses to which the names are attached are, for the most part, based on Model Penal Code offense definitions and as such they do not carry the technical baggage of the common law offenses from which their names were taken.

3. *See, e.g.*, the Illinois offense of Computer Fraud: *A person commits the offense of computer fraud when he knowingly: (1) Accesses or causes to be accessed a computer or any part thereof, or a program or data, for the purpose of devising or executing any scheme to defraud, or as part of a deception,* 720 ILCS § 5/16D-5(a) and the Florida offense of Fraudulent Transactions: *(1) It is unlawful and a violation of the provisions of this chapter for a person (a) in connection with the rendering of any investment advice or in connection with the . . . sale . . . of any investment or security (1) To employ any device, scheme, or artifice to defraud,* Fla. Stat. Ann. § 517.301.

4. *See, e.g.*, the Illinois offense of Financial Institution Fraud: *A person commits the offense of financial institution fraud when the person knowingly executes or attempts to execute a scheme or artifice: (1) to defraud a financial institution,* 720 ILCS § 5/16H-25(1), which is virtually identical to 18 USC § 1344 and the Kentucky offense of Securities Fraud: *It is unlawful for any person, in connection with the offer, sale, or purchase of any security, directly or indirectly, (a) To employ any device, scheme, or artifice to defraud,* Ky. Rev. Stat. § 292.320 which is virtually identical to 15 USC § 77(q)(a)(1).

5. It has been the author's experience that many students find discussion of the corruption and economic crimes prosecuted with the mail and wire fraud statutes interesting. That is particularly true with economic crimes such as the two mail fraud cases contained in the text which introduce them to concepts which at best most paralegal students only vaguely understood when they signed up to take the course.

6. The author also recognizes that there is some debate about whether certain defenses should be included in one category or another. To a large extent that is a function of how the defense is defined. Entrapment is an example of such a defense. Some states define entrapment subjectively which logically puts it in the excuse category while other states define it objectively which logically places it in the failure of proof category. The text does not burden the students with these type of distinctions and instead places such defenses in the category where based on the definition used in a majority of the states it logically should be placed. The text discusses the different forms of the defense there and simply notes that under the alternative definition the defense would be in a different category. The author also recognizes that depending on the jurisdiction some defenses may fit into two categories. Intoxication which can either be a defense or simply negate the specific intent element of a crime is one such defense. Again, the text does not burden the students with that level of technical information and simply explains the defense while noting its additional application.

Criminal Law and Procedure for the Paralegal

Introduction to the Criminal Justice System

The criminal justice system is the system that investigates crime, initiates charges against those persons who evidence suggests there is probable cause to believe have committed a crime, and places those persons on trial. This section consists of four chapters that will introduce you to the criminal justice system. Chapter 1 discusses the criminal justice process, Chapter 2 discusses what constitutes a crime, Chapter 3 discusses the investigation of crime, and Chapter 4 discusses the prosecution of crime.

Chapter 1
The Criminal Justice Process

Chapter Objectives

After reading this chapter, you should be able to

- Identify the different phases of the criminal justice process
- Explain what occurs during each phase of the criminal justice process
- Understand what law enforcement agents attempt to do during the investigative phase of the criminal justice process
- Explain when in the criminal justice process arresting and charging decisions are made

> . . . [I]n taking cognizance of all wrongs, or unlawful acts, the law has a double view: *viz.* not only to redress the party injured . . . but also to secure to the public the benefit of society, by preventing or punishing every breach and violation of those laws, which the sovereign power has thought proper to establish, for the government and tranquility of the whole. —Blackstone, *Commentaries on the Laws of England*, Book 4, Chapter 1

Society addresses the problem of crime through the criminal justice process. The criminal justice process consists of a number of distinct phases. The process begins when a crime is committed or begun and ends when a defendant is either acquitted of committing that crime or is convicted of it and sentenced. This chapter will introduce you to the different phases of the criminal justice process and will briefly explain what occurs during each of those phases. Before proceeding further you should be aware that while the phases of the criminal justice process described below are generally the same in

The student should be aware that this is the first of what will be a recurring refrain: that criminal law and procedure differs significantly from state to state and that it is important for the student to make herself aware of what the practice in her jurisdiction is.

every state, because there is no uniform criminal justice procedure in the United States, what occurs during any particular phase of that process may differ significantly both from state to state and from what is described here.

The first phase of the criminal justice process is the crime phase. The crime phase begins when a crime is committed or, in the case of criminal enterprises and schemes, it begins when the criminal enterprise or scheme is started and continues until that enterprise or scheme is abandoned by its perpetrators or halted by law enforcement agents.

The second phase of the criminal justice process is the investigation phase. The investigation phase usually begins after a crime is committed. For example, James is shot in an alley and dies immediately. The crime is complete when the shooting occurs and the investigation phase begins at that time. In the case of criminal enterprises and schemes the investigation stage often begins while the criminal enterprise or scheme is still operating. For example, Kevin is operating an investment fraud scheme and during the investigation of the scheme Kevin continues to solicit investor-victims.

During the investigation phase law enforcement agents, often with the assistance of prosecutors and forensics experts, gather evidence for the purpose of establishing several things: (1) that the event or enterprise they are investigating was or is criminal; (2) that if what occurred was criminal, the specific crime that was committed; and (3) the identity of the perpetrator. For example, law enforcement agents respond to a call of shots fired in an alley. When the law enforcement agents arrive on the scene they find that James has a gunshot wound and is dead but find no gun. During the investigation phase of the shooting law enforcement agents and forensics experts will attempt to determine through the evidence they gather whether James's death was caused by a criminal act. (James may have shot himself and a passerby stole the gun or James may have died from a heart attack and was shot by a robber who, not realizing James was already dead, thought James was sleeping, shot James, and robbed him.) If they determine James's shooting was a crime they will also try to determine who killed him and whether the killing was murder or some less serious form of homicide.

The investigative phase ends when, based on the evidence they are able to obtain, law enforcement agents either determine that no crime was committed and close their investigation or determine that a specific crime has been committed and either arrest the person they have identified as the perpetrator or refer the case to the prosecutor and recommend that the suspected perpetrator be charged with certain offenses.

The third phase of the criminal justice process is the charging phase. The charging phase begins when the prosecutor receives reports (and in some cases evidence) from law enforcement agents and must decide whether to initiate prosecution of the person identified by law enforcement as the perpetrator of a crime and if so, what charges to bring against her. In later chapters we will examine who prosecutes criminal cases, the legal principles that are the basis of the criminal law to which prosecutors must refer when deciding whether to initiate a criminal prosecution, and some nonlegal factors that can affect a prosecutor's charging decision.

The prosecutor may receive the reports from law enforcement agents either before or after the suspect is arrested. When a law enforcement agent actually sees a crime being committed or when there is otherwise a need to make an immediate arrest, law enforcement agents arrest perpetrators and suspected perpetrators before any reports are sent to the prosecutor, without consulting the prosecutor, and without obtaining an arrest warrant. In such cases the arrested individual is taken to a facility, usually a police station, where he is "booked."

During the booking process law enforcement agents record the name and personal identifying information of the individual arrested, the date and time of the arrest, and the crime for which the individual was arrested. As part of the booking process the individual will also be fingerprinted and photographed. Once the booking process is complete the individual is placed in a holding cell. In the case of minor crimes many jurisdictions have a preset bond that the arrested individual is allowed to post at the facility to which he was taken when he was arrested.

At some point after the booking process is complete reports from the arresting law enforcement agents will be transmitted to the prosecutor's office. The prosecutor must then decide whether to initiate prosecution of the arrested individual and, if so, whether the prosecution will be for the offense for which the individual was arrested or for some other offense. If, after reviewing the police reports and any evidence provided to him by law enforcement agents, the prosecutor decides the evidence is insufficient to charge, he will decline prosecution. If the prosecutor declines to prosecute, the individual is released from law enforcement custody. If the prosecutor decides to initiate prosecution, the individual will be brought before a judge, informed of the charges, and given a bond hearing.

When there is no immediate need to make an arrest, law enforcement agents often bring their reports to the prosecutor to review and consult with him before making an arrest. At that time the prosecutor will decide whether there is sufficient evidence to charge and what charges will be sought. In many large urban areas law enforcement agents and the prosecutor's office have established a pre-arrest review process for cases where there is no immediate need to make an arrest. That process, which is called by different names in different jurisdictions ("felony review" in many jurisdictions), requires law enforcement agents to consult with a prosecutor and obtain the prosecutor's approval before making an arrest.

The charging phase of the criminal justice process ends when the prosecutor initiates a criminal prosecution of the individual who law enforcement agents have identified as the perpetrator of specific crimes. At that point the individual is transformed from being merely a person suspected of committing a crime to a defendant in a criminal case formally accused of committing one. As you will learn in later chapters the initiation of a criminal prosecution against an individual is a significant point in the criminal justice process that gives rise to important constitutional rights.

The fourth phase of the criminal justice process is the pre-trial phase. The pre-trial phase begins with a defendant's initial appearance before a judge and, unless the prosecutor dismisses the case, continues until the defendant either pleads guilty or trial begins. During the pre-trial phase of the criminal justice process the defense has an opportunity to see and examine the evidence against the defendant and has its first chance to judge the strength of the prosecution's case.

During the pre-trial phase the defense also has an opportunity to review how law enforcement agents conducted their investigation and form an opinion about whether the agents violated any of the defendant's constitutional rights. If the defense concludes that law enforcement agents in some way may have violated a constitutional right of the defendant, it is during this phase of the criminal justice process that the defense may file (and in some jurisdictions is required to file) motions alleging those violations and asking the court to impose sanctions on the prosecution for them. What those sanctions are is discussed in a later chapter.

The pre-trial phase of the criminal justice process is also the phase during which plea negotiations are usually engaged in by the defense and the prosecution. Plea negotiations can range from a quick informal exchange between the prosecutor and defense attorney in the courtroom just before court opens or during a court recess to formal meetings at the prosecutor's office between the prosecutor assigned to the case and the defense attorney.

The fifth phase of the criminal justice process is the trial phase. The trial phase begins when the defendant's trial gets under way and ends either when the defendant is found guilty or is acquitted. Depending on the type of trial, the judge may or may not have the job of determining the defendant's guilt. If the trial is what is called a **bench trial** it is the judge who decides whether or not the defendant is guilty of the crimes charged. If the trial is a jury trial, the jury makes that determination.

Bench trial in a criminal case is a trial in which a judge and not the a jury decides whether a defendant is guilty or not guilty.

Phases of the Criminal Justice Process

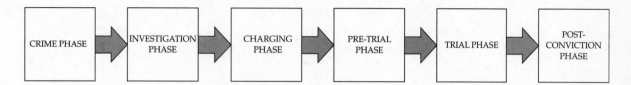

CRIME PHASE → INVESTIGATION PHASE → CHARGING PHASE → PRE-TRIAL PHASE → TRIAL PHASE → POST-CONVICTION PHASE

The sixth and final phase of the criminal justice process is the post-trial stage. The post-trial stage begins after the defendant is found guilty and continues through sentencing and, if they are pursued by the defendant, to appeal and through an application for a pardon or some other form of clemency.

CHAPTER TERM

Bench trial

REVIEW QUESTIONS

1. What are the phases of the criminal justice process?
2. During the investigation phase of the criminal justice process what three things do law enforcement agents try to do?
3. When does the investigation phase of the criminal justice process end?
4. What occurs during the booking process?
5. Do law enforcement agents always arrest suspects without consulting a prosecutor? If not, when do they make arrests without consulting the prosecutor and when do they consult a prosecutor before making an arrest?
6. What are three things that occur during the pre-trial phase of the criminal justice process?

ADDITIONAL READING

Steve Bogira, *Courtroom 302: A Year Behind the Scenes in an American Criminal Courthouse* (2005).

Chapter 2
The Nature of Crime

Chapter Objectives

After reading this chapter, you should be able to

- Understand what is meant by the term "crime"
- Understand how the criminal law we have today developed and what institutions played a role in developing it
- Explain the ways that crimes are classified and why classification is important
- Understand the difference between criminal law and civil law

> A crime . . . consist[s] in the Committing (by Deed or Word) of that which the Law forbiddeth, or the Omission of what it hath commanded. —Thomas Hobbes, *Leviathan*, Chapter XXVII

When we say that conduct is criminal or that certain conduct is a crime, what exactly do we mean by the term "crime?" In other words, what makes certain conduct a crime? The term "crime" embraces a vast range of different forms of misconduct. Are there some ways of classifying crimes and is classification important? Frequently the conduct that constitutes a crime also constitutes a civil wrong that is litigated in the civil justice system either instead of or in addition to prosecution in the criminal justice system. How does the criminal law differ from the civil law? This chapter will examine: (A) what crime is; (B) the different ways that crimes can be classified and why that classification can be significant; and (C) the differences between the criminal law and civil law.

A. What Is Crime?

Crime is any conduct that is forbidden by law to be performed and for engaging in which the law prescribes a penalty. Thus, it is not a crime to engage in conduct that is not forbidden by law, and it is not a crime to engage in forbidden conduct for which the law prescribes no punishment. Today we can look at statutes passed by legislative bodies that tell us what conduct is forbidden and what the punishment is for engaging in that conduct. Legislative bodies have not always played such a prominent role in determining what conduct constitutes a crime.

Historically, most offenses were created and defined through decisions of English common law courts and not by legislators.[1] That means that historically it was judges and not legislators who determined what conduct was prohibited and what elements defined particular offenses. English common law judges created and defined many offenses, such as murder, burglary, robbery, arson, and rape, that continue, in modified form, to be offenses today. When the English settled the original 13 colonies they brought English common law with them, including common law crimes, and made the common law the law of the colonies.

After the American Revolution the newly independent 13 states retained the common law as well as common law crimes. Those states, however, quickly began to modify the common law crimes and add to them through statutes adopted by their legislatures. As new states were added many of those new states also adopted English common law, including common law crimes. Even today many states have a statute or constitutional provision that expressly adopts English common law as the law of the state when there is no applicable state statutory or decisional law. In some of the states the incorporation statute adopts the common law as it existed in 1607, the year Jamestown, the first English settlement in America, was founded, while in other states their incorporation statutes adopt the common law as it existed in 1775, the year the American colonies broke away from England.

In the nineteenth century states began to enact comprehensive criminal codes. While those codes represented an advancement in that they codified many offenses, they were for the most part incomplete in their coverage and disorganized.[2] In many cases some of the most significant crimes, such as murder, were not even defined.[3] In the early 1960s the American Law Institute (ALI) unveiled the first version of what it called the Model Penal Code. That code, which has gone through a number of revisions since it first appeared, seeks to provide an organized and comprehensive set of penal laws and commentary that identifies what its authors feel are the major issues that should be considered by legislators. In the commentary, the Code examines alternative methods of dealing with problems in criminal law as a way of informing legislators of important issues. Many states have adopted the Model Penal Code either in whole or in part.

When the states began to adopt criminal codes they were faced with a problem of what to do with the common law crimes. Many states chose to abolish the common law crimes, but a few states have chosen to retain them as a supplement to their criminal laws. On the federal level as a matter of constitutional law, the U.S. Supreme Court has held that there are no federal common law crimes, and unless certain conduct is made criminal by Congress, that conduct is not a crime.[4]

Mossew v. United States

United States Court of Appeals for the Second Circuit
(1920) 266 F. 18

MANTON, J. This indictment was presented by the grand jury on the 10th day of June, 1919. The first count of the indictment charges that the plaintiff in error, within the jurisdiction of the District Court, was engaged as a retail grocer, doing business in the city of Binghamton, state and Northern district of New York, and was there handling and selling certain necessities of life, including granulated sugar;

"That at all the said times herein mentioned the fair, just, reasonable, and controlling rate, charge, and price in handling and dealing in granulated sugar to the retail trade in said city of Binghamton was and is from 10 to 11 cents per pound, which said fair, just, and reasonable rate and charge in handling and dealing in granulated sugar to the retail trade had theretofore been fixed according to law by the proclamation of the President of the United States and the rules and regulations promulgated by the President of the United States and the United States Food Administrator, pursuant to the provisions of the National Defense Act approved August 10, 1917, and the amendments thereto.

"That on the 8th day of July, 1919, the said defendant, in the said city of Binghamton, did unlawfully, knowingly, and feloniously, for the purpose of gain and profit, handle, sell, and distribute to one Margaret Donovan three pounds of granulated sugar, for which said defendant did then and there exact from and charge to the said Margaret Donovan 15 cents per pound for the said sugar, which said rate and charge was then and there unfair, unjust, and unreasonable in handling and dealing in said granulated sugar, contrary to the form of the statute in such case made and provided and against the peace and dignity of the United States." * * *

This indictment is intended to be an accusation against the plaintiff in error for a violation of an act of Congress passed August 10, 1917, relating to conservation of supply and control of disposition of necessities. It is intended to guard against waste and a monopolizing or hoarding of necessities—to guard against unfair and unjust practices. It is also aimed at unjust and unreasonable charges in regard to such necessities. * * *

Section 5 of the act (section 3115 1/8g) provides for licensing dealers, and imposes a penalty for violation of this section. It provides that its provisions shall not apply to retail dealers. Section 6 (section 3115 1/8gg) defines hoarding, and provides a penalty for violation of its provisions; but charging an excessive or unreasonable price is not within the definition of hoarding. Section 9 (section 3115 1/8i) provides a penalty for conspiracy in regard to necessities.

On August 12, 1919, the plaintiff in error pleaded not guilty, but thereafter withdrew this plea and pleaded guilty. He was sentenced to pay a fine of $200 * * *. The fine was paid the same day.

Section 4 declares it unlawful to make any unjust or unreasonable rate or charge in handling or dealing in necessaries, but there is no provision for punishment of this particular act thus made unlawful. As to other offenses which are denounced by the act, for the doing of which acts the section makes it unlawful, a penalty is prescribed; but nowhere in the act is a penalty prescribed for doing any of the acts made unlawful by this section, and there is no general provision in the act announcing a penalty or prescribing punishment for a violation of these provisions, where no specific penalty or punishment is provided. It further appears that this alleged indictment charges certain acts as unlawful, that is to say, making an unreasonable and unjust charge for sugar; but no penalty or punishment for a violation of the statute is prescribed by a valid statute.

We are of the opinion that no crime is charged in this indictment. Therefore the conviction, even though upon plaintiff in error's plea of guilty, is void. Payment of the fine cannot be deemed to be a voluntary contribution to the government, and has been held not to be a bar in a suit to recover. U.S. v. Rothstein, 187 Fed. 269, 109 C.C. A. 521; Durr v. Howard, 6 Ark. 461; Devlin v. United States, 12 Ct. Cl. 266. * * *

In Tennessee v. Davis, 100 U.S. 257, 25 L. Ed. 648, it was said:

Congress "must first make an act a crime, affix a punishment to it, and prescribe what courts have jurisdiction of such an indictment, before any federal tribunal can determine the guilt or innocence of the supposed offender." Citing U.S. v. Hudson et al., 7 Cranch 32, 3 L. Ed. 259.

And in the same case it was further said (100 U.S. at page 279 [25 L. Ed. 648]):

"Since that decision the law has been considered as settled that the Circuit Courts have no jurisdiction to try and sentence an offender, unless it appears that the offense charged is defined by an act of Congress, and that the act defining the offense, or some other act, prescribes the punishment to be imposed, and specifies the court that shall have jurisdiction of the offense."

In United States v. Hudson et al., 7 Cranch, 32, 3 L. Ed. 259, it was said:

"The only question which this case presents is whether the Circuit Courts of the United States can exercise a common-law jurisdiction in criminal cases. * * * The only ground on which it has ever been contended that this jurisdiction could be maintained is that, upon the formation of any political body, an implied power to preserve its own existence and promote the end and object of its creation necessarily results to it. * * * If it may communicate certain implied powers to the general government, it would not follow that the courts of that government are vested with jurisdiction over any particular act done by an individual in supposed violation of the peace and dignity of the sovereign power. The legislative authority of the Union must first make an act a crime, affix a punishment to it, and declare the court that shall have jurisdiction of the offense. Certain implied powers must necessarily result to our courts of justice, from the nature of their institution. But jurisdiction of crimes against the state is not among those powers; * * *."

By failure to provide a penalty for an infraction of this statute, or to prescribe a punishment, the statute does not denounce the unlawful act as criminal.

We think the writ of error should be sustained, and the judgment reversed.

Case Focus

● Did the defendant engage in the conduct prohibited by the statute?
● What was the defect in the statute that caused the court to reverse the defendant's conviction?

● ● ● ● ● ● ● ●

Today, every state as well as the federal government has an organized criminal code. Those codes, however, do not contain all criminal laws enacted by those jurisdictions. In addition to the offenses contained in those criminal codes, other crimes are defined in other statutes. For example, federal tax crimes are not contained in the U.S. Criminal Code (Title 18). They are instead found in the Internal Revenue Code (Title 26). Thus, even today's criminal codes do not represent a comprehensive collection of all criminal offenses.

B. Classification of Crimes

There are a number of different ways in which crimes can be classified, and because the classification of a crime can have important legal or practical consequences, it is important to understand how the classes of crime are defined. This section examines several different ways in which crimes are classified and explains why those classifications are important.

1. *Felony and Misdemeanor Classification*

Felony is an offense for which a sentence of death or a term of imprisonment for one or more years may be imposed. *See, e.g.,* 720 ILCS 5/2-7.

Misdemeanor is an offense for which a term of imprisonment for less than one year may be imposed. *See, e.g.,* 720 ILCS 5/2-11.

Because of the significant legal consequences that flow from it, one of the most important methods of classifying crimes is as a **felony** or **misdemeanor**. The classification of a crime as one of those types of offenses is determined by the sentence that may be imposed for committing it. A felony is any offense for which the perpetrator can be sentenced to a year or more in prison and, in those jurisdictions that have the death penalty, includes any offense for which a sentence of death may be imposed.[5] A misdemeanor is an offense for which the offender can be sentenced to a term of imprisonment for less than a year.[6] Offenses called petty offenses and business offenses are simply different types of misdemeanor offenses; in some jurisdictions defendants in these cases may not be entitled to all of the constitutional rights that are accorded to defendants in other types of misdemeanor cases.

The distinction between felony and misdemeanor offenses is important both at the charging stage and upon conviction. In almost all jurisdictions a felony prosecution can only be started after a preliminary hearing or upon indictment by a grand jury, whereas a misdemeanor prosecution can be started with the filing of a complaint by a police officer, a private citizen, or a prosecutor.[7] Upon conviction of a felony, in some states, the defendant will lose the right to vote, lose the right to possess firearms, and may be barred from obtaining certain government licenses. In the case of government employees and public officials, a felony conviction that is job related can also result in the loss of their government pension.

2. Malum in Se *and* Malum Prohibitum *Classification*

Malum in se offense is an offense that involves conduct that, without regard to the existence of a statute, is inherently wrong. *People v. Treen,* 33 Misc. 2d 571 (N.Y. Co. Ct. 1962).

Malum prohibitum offense is an offense that involves conduct that is not inherently wrong, but is made so because it is prohibited by statute. *People v. Boxer,* 24 N.Y.S.2d 628 (N.Y. Sp. Sess. 1940).

Another way in which offenses are classified is as either *malum in se* or *malum prohibitum*. While this classification of offenses is an ancient one, classifying offenses as being in either category is not easy. *Malum in se* offenses are offenses that involve conduct that, without regard to the existence of a statute, is said to be inherently wrong. Offenses included in that category are murder, robbery, rape, and arson. *Malum prohibitum* offenses are offenses involving conduct which it is said is not inherently wrong, but which is prohibited by statute. An example of a *malum prohibitum* offense is counterfeiting. While there are exceptions, in general the offenses created at common law are considered to be *malum in se* and statutory offenses not based on common law offenses are considered to be *malum prohibitum*.

The classification of offenses as *malum in se* and *malum prohibitum* is of little current importance in criminal law except in the area of manslaughter and battery. Some legal scholars suggest that because of the difficulty in classifying offenses in this manner, this form of classification should be abandoned.

3. Crimes of Moral Turpitude

Turpitude means contrary to justice, honesty, or good morals. *Heron v. State Bar of California*, 24 Cal. 2d 53 (1944).

Yet another way in which crimes are classified is as crimes involving moral **turpitude** and as crimes not involving moral turpitude. Generally the distinction between crimes that involve and do not involve moral turpitude is made in the same way as the distinction between crimes that are *malum in se* and *malum prohibitum*. However, distinguishing between crimes that involve moral turpitude and crimes that do not is important. For an alien, conviction of a crime involving moral turpitude can result in her deportation or in barring her from acquiring American citizenship. For persons with professional licenses or those who wish to obtain such licenses, conviction of a crime of moral turpitude can lead to the loss of that license or their disqualification from obtaining one.

4. White Collar Crime and Street Crime

White collar crime a crime in which the illegal act is characterized by deceit, concealment, or a violation of trust and which is not dependent upon the application or threat of physical force or violence.

Street crime a crime usually directed at a person in public such as robbery or mugging.

The classifications of crimes we have examined so far are important because of the legal consequences that flow from a conviction. The classification of crime as either **white collar crime** or **street crime** is important not because of the legal consequences that flow from a conviction of one instead of the other, but because of the different investigative and legal challenges these different forms of crime present to investigators, prosecutors, and defense attorneys.

The distinction between street crime and white collar crime is a relatively recent development in criminal law and it has generated some controversy about exactly how the category of offenses called white collar crime should be defined. The FBI takes an offense-based approach and defines white collar crime as those illegal acts that are characterized by deceit, concealment, or violation of trust that are not dependent upon the application or threat of physical force or violence. By contrast, street crime is crime in which the threat or use of force is employed to commit the offense.

The distinction between white collar crime and street crime is important for several reasons. From an investigative standpoint the distinction is important because of the different investigative problems the two forms of crime present. In most street crime investigations the identification of the perpetrator (i.e., identifying who committed the crime) is usually one of the most important if not the sole investigative issue. In contrast, with

The History of the Concept of White Collar Crime

The concept of white collar crime was first introduced in 1939 by the American sociologist Edwin H. Sutherland. Sutherland, however, did not define white collar crime by reference to the offense. Instead he defined white collar crime as crimes committed by persons of high social status during the course of their employment. Sutherland's definition suffers from at least two problems. First, it is vague because the term "high social status" itself is vague. Does that term refer to a person's wealth or prestige or some combination of both? The more serious problem is that the definition does not include crimes all would consider to be "white collar" crimes. For example, a bookkeeper who embezzles money from her employer would be considered by almost all people to be committing a white collar crime, yet under Sutherland's definition her crime would not be a white collar crime because a bookkeeper, whether viewed by income or by profession, is not a person of high social status.

Since Sutherland first articulated the concept of white collar crime, a debate has raged among experts on just how to define it. In addition to those who still adhere to Sutherland's definition, some define white collar crime in terms of organizational culture while others define it to include corporate crimes such as environmental law violations and safety law violations. The FBI has chosen to define white collar crime in terms of the offense. Whether or not that is the best way to define the category of crime now referred to as white collar crime, the FBI uses that definition when collecting and categorizing crime data, and for that reason it is a useful definition to know and understand.

white collar crime, except for certain types of cybercrimes, the identity of the suspected perpetrator is usually known, and significant identification issues are seldom part of these investigations.

Another difference between the investigation of white collar crime and street crime is that, other than in the small number of cases in which self-defense or consent may be an issue, in most street crime investigations there is usually little dispute about the fact that what happened was a crime. In many white collar crime cases it is not clear at the outset that the conduct is criminal, and frequently law enforcement agents incorrectly tell victims that no crime has been committed and that the matter is civil, not criminal.

From both an investigative and trial standpoint another important difference is that with street crime, once it is shown that a particular person engaged in the criminal act, there is seldom any serious question

Mens rea means guilty mind. *Herd v. State,* 125 Md. App. 77 (1999). The guilty mind refers to the mental state element of a criminal offense that the perpetrator of the offense must have when he commits the offense. The mental state element which the perpetrator must have when he commits an offense is usually intent, knowledge, or recklessness.

about whether he also acted with the *mens rea* specified in the criminal statute. By contrast, with white collar crime one of the most important investigative issues (and one of the most litigated trial issues) is whether the person who is alleged to have engaged in the criminal act did so with the *mens rea* prescribed in the statute.

Thus, the focus in street crime investigations is usually on who committed the crime, whereas the focus in white collar crime investigations is often on whether the conduct was criminal and on the somewhat ephemeral question of whether the perpetrator possessed the mental state specified in the statute when she engaged in the criminal act.

One other important distinction between street crime and white collar crime is that the prosecution of street crime is usually preceded by little grand jury investigation, while the prosecution of white collar crime is usually preceded by significant grand jury investigation that may take months and in some cases years to complete[8] and that frequently results in litigation before any charges are even filed. From the standpoint of the prosecutor and defense attorney that distinction means that before a white collar crime prosecution is initiated they will confront important legal and strategic issues that will significantly affect the case once prosecution is begun.

From a legal standpoint, another significant difference between white collar crime and street crime is that white collar crime is usually accompanied by significant civil consequences that must be considered, primarily by the defense but also by the prosecutor. For example, what are the consequences for a medical doctor's professional license if, instead of answering questions during a grand jury investigation of whether he engaged in an illegal referral scheme that resulted in him receiving kickbacks from labs for ordering unnecessary tests, he refuses to answer questions because the answers may incriminate him? What civil action might insurance companies file against the physician to recoup the money he defrauded them out of should he plead guilty to having engaged in such a scheme?

C. Distinction Between Criminal Law and Civil Law

Tort is a legal wrong other than a breach of contract that causes harm for which courts will impose civil liability. 1 Daniel Dobbs, *The Law of Torts* 1 (2000).

Criminal law and civil law have much in common and share many legal concepts.[9] Of the different areas of civil law the law of **torts** is more closely related to the criminal law than any other.[10] Indeed, most criminal conduct also constitutes a tort, and many torts are also crimes. Despite the similarities between civil and criminal law, historically it has always been understood that there is a difference between them, the most important being in their objectives. The general objective of the criminal law is to punish, whereas the general objective of civil law is to adjust disputes and inequities.[11] While some legal scholars assert that the distinction between civil and criminal law is disappearing,[12] important differences between the two remain. This section will briefly examine those differences.

To help understand the differences between criminal law and civil law it is helpful to understand the purpose of the criminal law. The broad aim of the criminal law is to prevent harm by punishing those who have done harm and those who would do harm to others.[13] The harm to society can range from physical harm (such as death by murder) to harm to property (such as the loss of a home through arson) to intangible harm (such as the outrage a person feels after being subjected to indecent exposure).[14]

To the extent that the purpose of the criminal law is to deter conduct that is harmful to society, it is similar to the law of torts, because one of the purposes of the law of torts is to discourage conduct that causes or may cause injury to others. How those two areas of law try to achieve that goal represents one of the most significant differences between criminal law and civil law in general and between criminal law and

Purposes of Punishment Imposed by the Criminal Law

The punishment that the criminal law metes out is supposed to accomplish a number of things: (1) deter the criminal from committing further crimes by giving him an unpleasant experience; (2) remove the criminal from society so that he is unable to commit further crimes against it; (3) reform the prisoner by giving him treatment or providing him with job skills; (4) provide an example through punishment of the defendant so that others will be deterred from committing crimes; (5) educate the public about what conduct is criminal and the costs of engaging in criminal conduct; and (6) exaction of revenge against the criminal for committing the crime.

The criminal law provides no guidance in how important any of those things are and provides no guidance about how they should be weighed when deciding on an appropriate punishment. Indeed there is a certain degree of disconnect between legal scholars and the public on at least one of the goals of punishment. Societal revenge is one of the oldest justifications for punishing criminals and enjoys widespread support from the public, and thus from the public's view that should be an important element of punishment. In contrast, most theorists argue that revenge is morally indefensible and should not be one of the goals of punishment.

tort law in particular. As pointed out above, the criminal law seeks to deter harmful conduct through punishment. With the exception of those relatively few tort cases where punitive damages may be assessed, the purpose of tort law is not to punish, but to reimburse victims for the damages they suffer from a defendant's tortious conduct.

In tort law, particularly in the law of negligence, the defendant's act is usually not seen as inherently bad. Instead, it is usually the way the defendant performed the tortious act that is viewed as bad. For example, driving a car is not inherently bad, but driving it negligently is. Tort law generally tries to balance the benefits of the defendant's act against the social cost that results from the tortious manner in which he acted. Those social costs are measured by the damages the act causes. Thus, tort law is often described as creating a pricing structure in which the social costs of a defendant's tortious activity are extracted from him.

By contrast, the criminal law engages in no such calculation. Except in the cases of certain traditional defenses such as self-defense and necessity (these and other defenses are discussed in Section III), with respect to that conduct which the criminal law condemns, the criminal law is generally unconcerned with the possible utility of the defendant's actions and metes out punishment to some degree for performing the prohibited act or for causing a prohibited result.

Another distinction between the criminal law and civil law is that the criminal law is concerned with punishment or deterrence through the threat of punishment and generally is not concerned with restitution to the victim. Certainly, judges in criminal cases frequently order convicted perpetrators to pay restitution to their victims and sentencing statutes give judges authority to do so, but judges are not obligated to enter such orders, and prosecutors may determine such an order is an empty exercise and recommend incarceration instead of restitution. The civil law, however, is concerned almost exclusively with reimbursing plaintiffs for the damages they suffered at the hands of the defendant.

Yet a further distinction is that tort law is entirely private: The victim must bring a lawsuit in order to obtain economic redress, and decisions about what civil actions to bring and which ones of those to proceed to trial on are decisions made exclusively by the plaintiff and his attorney. By contrast, the criminal law is enforced by the government. It is a government agent who decides whether to bring charges, what charges to bring, and which ones to proceed upon, and it is a government agent who decides whether or not to discontinue a prosecution. While the government may consider the wishes of the victim, ultimately it is the government agent who manages all aspects of criminal cases.

Historically, one factor that was seen to most distinguish criminal law from civil law was the social stigma that attaches to criminal conduct that does not attach to civil wrongs such as torts.[15] At least one legal scholar has argued that because of that distinction, the criminal law should not be used to create crimes from conduct that does not deserve moral condemnation.[16] The rise of what might be termed technical offenses, such as traffic offenses and failing to keep certain records required by regulatory laws, has to a large extent erased that historic distinction.

CHAPTER TERMS

Felony	Misdemeanor	White collar crime
Malum in se	Street crime	
Malum prohibitum	Tort	
Mens rea	Turpitude	

REVIEW QUESTIONS

1. Early in the development of criminal law, how were crimes created and defined?
2. What are the two elements that are necessary to define a criminal offense?
3. How are offenses determined to be misdemeanors or felonies?
4. What are the possible consequences of committing a crime of moral turpitude?
5. What determines whether a crime is a white collar crime or a street crime?
6. Why is the distinction between white collar crime and street crime important?
7. What is the aim of the criminal law?
8. What are the purposes of the punishment that the criminal law specifies for criminal conduct?
9. How does the criminal law differ from the law of civil wrongs?

ADDITIONAL READING

Cynthia Barnett, *The Measurement of White Collar Crime Using Uniform Crime Reporting (UCR) Data* (2005).

Susan Chandler. *Personalities in Abundance at Black Trial,* Chicago Tribune (March 11, 2007), sec. 5, p.1.

James Helmkamp, Richard Ball, & Kitty Townsend, eds., *Definitional Dilemma: Can and Should There Be a Universal Definition of White Collar Crime?* National White Collar Crime Ctr. (1996).

ENDNOTES

1. William LaFave & Austin Scott, Jr., *Criminal Law* 58 (1972).
2. *Id.* at 3.
3. *Id.* at 3.
4. *United States v. Hudson*, 11 U.S. 32 (1812).
5. *See, e.g.,* 720 ILCS 5/2-7.
6. *See, e.g.,* 720 ILCS 5/2-11.
7. *See, e.g.,* 725 ILCS 5/111-2.
8. Pamela Bucy, *Bucy's White Collar Practice: Cases and Materials* 2 (3d ed. 2004).
9. LaFave & Scott, *supra* n.1 at 11.
10. *Id.*
11. *Foster v. Alex*, 213 Ill. App. 3d 1001 (5th Dist. 1991).
12. John C. Coffee, *Does "Unlawful" Mean "Criminal"?: Reflections on the Disappearing Tort/Crime Distinction in American Law*, 71 B.U. L. Rev. 201 (1991).
13. LaFave & Scott, *supra* n.1 at 9.
14. *Id.*
15. *Id.* at 11.
16. Henry M. Hart, Jr., *The Aims of the Criminal Law*, 23 Law & Contemp. Probs. 401 (1958).

Chapter 3
Investigation of Crime in the United States

Chapter Objectives

After reading this chapter, you should be able to

- Explain the difference between various types of law enforcement agencies
- Understand the jurisdiction of different types of law enforcement agencies
- Understand what a sting operation is
- Understand the difference between an informal and formal criminal investigation
- Explain the legal tools used to conduct formal criminal investigations
- Explain what a grand jury is and its role in investigating crime

> The grand jury can investigate merely on suspicion that the law is being violated, or even just because it wants assurance that it is not. —*United States v. R. Enterprises*, 498 U.S. 292 (1991)

In the United States crime is investigated by law enforcement agencies at the federal, state, and local levels and by various law enforcement agencies at each of those levels. The level of government at which a crime is investigated, the agency that conducts the investigation, the primary investigative issues faced, and the type of investigation conducted are determined by whether the offense is a federal or state crime, the nature of the offense, and the place or places where the crime is committed. The purpose of this chapter is to give an overview of: (A) the different types of law enforcement agencies that investigate crime in the United States and (B) the different types of investigations they conduct.

A. Different Types of Law Enforcement Agencies

In the United States there are more than 18,000 federal and non-federal law enforcement agencies, which combined employ more than 900,000 sworn law enforcement officers. Most of those law enforcement agencies are local police departments that in total employ more than half of all American law enforcement officers. Local police departments have general law enforcement authority and investigate the vast majority of crime committed in the United States.

Local police departments, with a few minor exceptions, are limited to investigating only those crimes that occur within the geographical borders of the municipality under whose authority they operate. Thus, for example, with some limited exceptions, the Chicago Police Department investigates only those crimes that occur within the corporate limits of the city of Chicago. Local police departments have general law enforcement authority and the power to investigate criminal violations of all state laws and of local ordinances. At the county or parish level, sheriffs' offices also enforce state laws. The power of a sheriff is often limited to investigating and making arrests for crimes committed within those areas of the county or parish that are not part of any incorporated municipality.

Local and county or parish-level law enforcement agencies are supplemented on the state level by law enforcement agencies that have statewide **jurisdiction** to investigate criminal violations of state law. These law enforcement agencies have different names in different states but frequently are referred to as the State Police or the State Department of Law Enforcement. These statewide law enforcement agencies may investigate crimes that cross county lines (such as drug conspiracies

Jurisdiction refers to the power to act. As to agencies of government, it is the power to administer and enforce the law, *Carroll Voc. Inst. v. United States*, 211 F.2d 539 (5th Cir. 1954), and as to courts, it is the power to hear and decide a case. *Davis v. Cleveland, C., C. & St. L. Ry. Co.*, 217 U.S. 157 (1910).

STATE AND LOCAL POLICE AGENCIES AND SWORN OFFICERS, SEPTEMBER 2008		
Police Agency	**Number of Agencies**	**Number of Full-Time Sworn Officers**
Local police	12,501	461,063
Sheriff	3,063	182,979
Primary state	50	60,772
Special jurisdiction	1,733	56,968
Constable-marshal	638	3,464
Total	17,985	765,246

Source: Brian Reaves, *Census of State and Local Law Enforcement Agencies, 2008*, BUREAU OF JUSTICE STATISTICS BULLETIN, July 2011

or large-scale fraud schemes) or may, at the request of a sheriff or local police department, investigate a wholly local crime. Sheriffs and local police often request investigative assistance when they lack the expertise or resources to conduct an investigation themselves or when one of their officers is or may be suspected of being involved in criminal activity.

State-level police officers as well as county, parish, and local law enforcement officers have no authority to investigate or make arrests for federal crimes unless specifically authorized by a state statute or local ordinance, and the federal government cannot compel them to enforce federal law.[1]

On the federal level, the Federal Bureau of Investigation (FBI) has nationwide jurisdiction and investigates a broad range of federal crimes. The FBI and other federal law enforcement agencies have no authority on their own to investigate and make arrests for criminal violations of state law, but can and often do provide assistance to state and local police when requested. General law enforcement agencies such as the FBI, state police, and large local police departments that are responsible for investigating a broad range of criminal activity are usually divided into separate divisions or units that investigate a single type or a discrete group of offenses (such as homicide, sex crimes, and terrorism) and have their own internal investigations division that investigates wrongdoing by their agency's employees.

At the state and federal levels there are also specialized law enforcement agencies that focus solely on or whose law enforcement powers are statutorily limited to certain types of crimes. These specialized law enforcement agencies usually are a part of some government agency that is charged with administering certain statutes or a certain government

FEDERAL LAW ENFORCEMENT AGENTS

Function	Full-Time Federal Officers*
Criminal investigation/enforcement	44,832
Police response and patrol	28,132
Inspections/Non-criminal investigations	18,435
Corrections/detention	17,088
Court operations	5,692
Security/protection	6,096
Other	73
Total	120,348

* Non-military federal officers authorized to carry firearms and make arrests. Excludes officers in foreign countries, the Central Intelligence Agency, and Transportation Security Administration Federal Air Marshals.
Source: Brian Reaves, *Federal Law Enforcement Officers, 2008*, BUREAU OF JUSTICE STATISTICS BULLETIN, June 2012.

program. An example of one of these specialized law enforcement agencies on the federal level is the United States Department of Housing & Urban Development's Office of Inspector General, which investigates criminal fraud in the agency's low-income housing assistance program and fraud in the agency's Federal Housing Administration (FHA) mortgage loan program. An example of a specialized law enforcement agency on the state level is the law enforcement arm of a state's tax agency (such as the Illinois Department of Revenue's Criminal Investigations Division), whose law enforcement powers, by statute, are limited to criminal violations of the state's tax laws.[2] The non-uniformed criminal investigators who work in these specialized law enforcement agencies are usually referred to as special agents, inspectors, or investigators.

The offenses that the specialized law enforcement agencies investigate are usually both more technical and complex than those that sheriffs' offices and local police agencies investigate.

When a police officer investigates a crime he usually only needs to reference the state criminal code to determine whether the conduct he is investigating is criminal. By contrast, when a special agent investigates an offense he frequently will need to look at and apply the legal concepts of the regulatory statute his agency administers together with the criminal provisions contained within that statute and frequently will also need to look at his jurisdiction's general criminal code.

For example, before being able to conclude whether a financial advisor has committed a crime under the securities laws (such as the offense of engaging in a course of business in connection with the sale of securities that works a fraud on the purchaser[3]), the special agent must determine that the financial product that was sold by the advisor was a security within the meaning of the securities law, he must determine what representations were made by the advisor, he must determine what facts the advisor failed to disclose, and then he must determine whether those representations and omissions were material as that term is used in his jurisdiction's securities laws. As a result special agents not only develop expertise in investigating certain types of offenses, just as homicide detectives, for example, develop expertise in investigating murders, they also develop expertise with respect to both the criminal statutes they enforce and the regulatory concepts upon which those statutes draw for meaning.

B. Types of Criminal Investigations

In the United States crimes can be investigated either informally or formally. In this section we will examine both types of criminal investigations.

1. Informal Investigations

An informal investigation is one that does not use any type of formal legal process to acquire evidence. Most police investigations are informal investigations[4] of street crimes that can be investigated effectively without resort to formal legal process, because the victims and witnesses are usually eager to help investigators and often have valuable evidence.

Informal investigations rely on the collection of evidence from the crime scene and on the voluntary cooperation of others. When conducting an informal investigation, law enforcement agents rely on consensual interviews with and on the consensual production of bodily fluids, handwriting exemplars, and business and other records by victims, witnesses, suspects, and ultimately the **target**. Because no one is required to cooperate with law enforcement by answering questions or producing evidence, suspects, targets, witnesses, and other third parties can refuse to answer questions of law enforcement agents and can refuse law enforcement requests to produce other types of evidence. In such instances the investigation will turn into a formal investigation if law enforcement agents want their questions answered or if they want to obtain the other types of evidence they are seeking.

Target is a person as to whom the prosecutor or the grand jury has substantial evidence linking him to a crime and who in the judgment of the prosecutor is a putative defendant. *United States Attorney's Manual,* §9-11.151.

2. Formal Investigations

A formal investigation is an investigation in which some type of legal process (such as a subpoena or search warrant) is used to gather evidence. Formal investigations are usually necessary for white collar crimes, such as those involving public integrity and financial fraud, and in cases involving drugs, gambling, prostitution, and child pornography. In most white collar crimes the victim is either not identifiable (e.g., in public integrity and tax fraud cases the victim is the public) or often has little useful information, and in drug and other so-called vice cases there is seldom a complaining victim. Often the only sources of evidence in such cases are the perpetrators themselves, and usually the only way to obtain evidence from them is through the use of some type of legal process to extract it.

There are two types of formal investigations: administrative investigations and judicial process investigations. In this section we will examine both types of investigations.

a. Administrative Investigations

Administrative investigations are conducted by the law enforcement arm of government agencies that have been given subpoena power by

Congress or a state legislature. An agency does not need probable cause to open a criminal investigation and can open one merely because it wants to satisfy itself that the law has been complied with.[5] The fact that the agency may be on what is frequently referred to as a "fishing expedition" does not prevent the agency from investigating.[6]

Agencies that have subpoena power issue subpoenas that in most jurisdictions are called administrative subpoenas. Administrative subpoenas can require the person or entity to which they are directed to appear before a specified agency official and produce records or other types of evidence and give testimony. If the person to whom the subpoena is directed fails to appear or appears and refuses to produce the evidence demanded or to answer the questions asked, the agency can go to court and ask the court to enforce the subpoena through what is called an enforcement proceeding.[7]

In order to obtain judicial enforcement of one of its subpoenas the issuing agency must show several things. First, it must show that the investigation is being conducted for a legitimate purpose. That generally means that the agency must show that it is investigating a matter that it has the statutory power to regulate or administer. So, for example, in an enforcement proceeding filed by the Internal Revenue Service, the agency would have to show that it was investigating a federal tax matter. In addition to showing that the investigation is being conducted for a legitimate purpose, the agency must show that the information sought in the subpoena is relevant to that purpose, and that the agency does not already have possession of the information it is seeking.[8]

Department of Revenue v. Continental Illinois Bank & Trust Co.

Illinois Appellate Court, First District, 1975
27 Ill. App. 3d 326

Mc Namara, J. This appeal is from an order of the circuit court of Cook County directing a bank to comply with an administrative subpoena duces tecum issued by the Illinois Department of Revenue commanding the bank to produce certain records relating to the financial affairs of one of its customers.

On August 22, 1972, the Illinois Department of Revenue (hereinafter "the Department") issued a subpoena duces tecum commanding Continental Illinois Bank and Trust Company (hereinafter "Continental") to appear at a hearing in the office of the Department at a specified date with certain books and records of Continental relating to the State income tax liability of Julius W. Butler for the years 1969-1971.

The records described in the subpoena were "[a]ll signature cards, ledger sheets, deposit tickets, credit memos, debit memos, transfer of fund advices, microfilms of checks charged or deposited; and any and all other records relative to the commercial and savings accounts of Julius W. Butler, and all records of the

Hinsdale Golf Club Trust, known as Trust Number 31-57214-1, for the years of 1969, 1970, and 1971." Upon being served with the subpoena, Continental notified Butler, who in turn informed Continental that its voluntary compliance with the subpoena would be at the risk of a lawsuit brought by him. Continental thereupon refused to voluntarily comply with the subpoena, and the Department filed suit on September 28, 1972, seeking judicial enforcement of its subpoena. [Following a hearing the court below ordered Continental to comply with the subpoena.]

Butler alone prosecutes this appeal. * * *

Butler * * * argues that he was denied due process by the actions taken by the trial court. The thrust of this position is that since the trial court struck two paragraphs from the amended complaint, the amended complaint contained less information than the previously struck original complaint, and therefore the amended complaint must be conclusively deemed insufficient as a matter of law.

Without passing on the correctness of the trial court's order striking two paragraphs of the amended complaint, we find the amended complaint, as struck, states a valid cause of action. It alleges that Butler had a duty to pay State income taxes; that Continental had the necessary records to establish Butler's proper tax liability for 1969, 1970, and 1971; that these records were in the hands of Continental; that an administrative subpoena duces tecum, attached to the complaint, had been served on Continental; that no voluntary production of the records had been made by Continental; and that a judicial order was necessary to enforce the administrative subpoena.

On its face, the complaint charges that the investigation is being conducted pursuant to a legitimate purpose, that the inquiry may be relevant to that purpose, that the information is not in the Department's possession, and that the proper statutory administrative steps have been followed. These conditions, set out in *United States v. Powell* (1964), 379 U.S. 48, as the prerequisites that the Commissioner of the Internal Revenue Service must show to obtain enforcement of his summons, should apply equally, we believe, to our State revenue administrative subpoenas. (See *Illinois Crime Investigating Com. v. Buccieri* (1967), 36 Ill. 2d 556, 224 N.E.2d 236, *cert. denied* (1967), 389 U.S. 848.) The amended complaint states a valid cause of action. * * *

Accordingly, the judgment of the circuit court of Cook County is affirmed.

Affirmed.

Case Focus

- What are the requirements that must be satisfied to obtain enforcement of an administrative subpoena?
- On what evidence in this case was the court able to conclude that those requirements were satisfied?

An administrative agency can use its subpoena power to conduct a purely civil investigation, parallel civil and criminal investigations, or solely to conduct a criminal investigation.[9] Once the agency makes what is called a criminal referral (i.e., when it refers a report to a prosecutor in which it recommends or asks for the prosecution of a particular person or entity), the agency can no longer use its subpoena power to gather evidence for the criminal case. The agency remains free, however, to continue to use its subpoena power to gather evidence for a civil case against the target identified in the criminal referral.

A **privilege** excuses a witness from disclosing evidence. *Bank of Dearborn v. Saxon*, 244 F. Supp. 394 (E.D. Mich. 1965). An **evidentiary privilege** is a privilege created by the law of evidence (e.g., the attorney-client privilege) and a **constitutional privilege** is a privilege created by the United States Constitution or the constitution of a state (e.g., the Fifth Amendment's privilege against self-incrimination).

Most government agencies that administer government programs have subpoena power. A paralegal working for one of those agencies may assist an agency investigation by preparing administrative subpoenas and by preparing any schedules that will be attached to them. Schedules that are attached to subpoenas are used to describe the various types of documents or other things the agency is demanding to be produced. A paralegal working at the law firm representing the subpoenaed witness may be responsible for obtaining the subpoenaed materials from the client and organizing them for the attorney so he can determine what materials are responsive to the subpoena and what materials might be protected by an **evidentiary** or **constitutional privilege**.

b. Judicial Process Investigations

Unlike the law enforcement arms of certain regulatory agencies, police departments and other general law enforcement agencies such as the FBI do not have subpoena power. To obtain evidence from persons who refuse to provide it voluntarily, such law enforcement agencies must resort to a second type of formal investigation that is often called a judicial process investigation. Judicial process investigations use one or more of several different types of legal process to gather evidence. To obtain any of those types of process, law enforcement agents must usually go to the prosecutor's office and ask the prosecutor to obtain it for them.

At the federal level and in those states that have retained them, one way that evidence is gathered from targets or suspects and reluctant or uncooperative witnesses is through the institution known as the grand jury. In the American criminal justice system the grand jury plays a dual role: one as an investigative body that the prosecutor can use to gather evidence and the second as an accusatory body that the prosecutor can use to initiate criminal prosecutions. In this section we will examine how the grand jury performs its investigative function, and in a later chapter we will examine how the grand jury performs its accusatory function.

In its investigatory role the function of the grand jury is to inquire into all information until it has identified an offense that has been

Historical Perspective

Grand Jury History and Operation

The grand jury is a creation of medieval English law. Its roots can be traced back at least to the early twelfth century when the grand jurors consisted of knights and other freeman.[10] Initially the grand jury performed only an accusatory or charging function, but by the seventeenth century it had also acquired its investigatory function. The institution of the grand jury was exported to America where all of the colonies made them part of their criminal justice systems.[11] In the American colonies, as it had in England, the grand jury came to be viewed as one of the important safeguards against malicious and unfounded criminal charges,[12] a view of the grand jury that continues today.[13]

When the U.S. Constitution was submitted to the states for ratification it did not contain any provision for grand juries. During the ratification debates that followed its submission to the states, the Constitution was criticized for not containing a grand jury provision and several states recommended that one be added by amendment.[14] In response to that and certain other criticisms leveled against the Constitution during the ratification process, when the first Congress convened it drew up ten amendments which it submitted to the states for ratification. Among those was one that has become known as the Fifth Amendment, which contains a provision that provides that in certain types of cases prosecution must be begun by a grand jury.

As a matter of federal law the grand jury is considered to be separate from the courts and to belong to no branch of the federal government.[15] While the grand jury usually meets in a courthouse under judicial auspices, courts generally exercise no supervisory judicial authority over them.[16] To the extent courts exercise control over an investigatory grand jury, that control is usually limited to refusing to compel a witness to answer questions or produce evidence when the witness asserts an applicable evidentiary or constitutional privilege[17] or can establish that the subpoena issued by the grand jury is over broad.[18]

In federal practice, grand juries are called at the request of the prosecutor and require no authorization from the courts to initiate an investigation[19] or prosecution.[20] Federal grand juries can consist of between 16 and 23 citizens with 16 being the number of persons who must be present to constitute a quorum to conduct business. Unlike with petit or trial juries whose decisions must be unanimous, the grand jury can act by simple majority vote.

At the state level, some states have abolished the grand jury and less than half still require that a grand jury initiate prosecutions of serious crimes.[21] Some states give the prosecutor the option of using the grand jury to initiate prosecutions or of using an alternate procedure.[22] Most states, including those that have eliminated the grand jury as a charging body, have retained it as an investigative body.[23] In those states that have retained the grand jury, as in federal practice, the prosecutor has the power to call the grand jury and the grand jury does not need judicial pre-approval to investigate or charge. Some states allow citizens to petition a court to call a grand jury. Some states have also altered the size of the grand jury by reducing the number of required grand jurors from the traditional 23 persons to some smaller number.[24]

committed or satisfied itself that no crime has occurred.[25] The grand jury performs its investigatory function by issuing subpoenas (called grand jury subpoenas because they are issued by or in the name of that body instead of by authority of a court) to witnesses for testimony and for the production of other types of evidence, such as books and records, handwriting exemplars, and bodily fluids. The grand jury can investigate on suspicion or merely because it wants to satisfy itself that the law has not been broken.[26] The grand jury does not need probable cause to begin an investigation or to issue subpoenas because the purpose of a grand jury investigation is to discover whether probable cause exists.[27] In a grand jury investigation the identity of the offender and the nature of the offense, if one was committed, is developed at the conclusion of the investigation, not the beginning.[28]

In federal grand jury practice, and in the practice of most states that have retained grand juries, the prosecutor, usually in concert with the investigator, selects the witnesses the grand jury will hear and the evidence the grand jury will see, and the prosecutor issues subpoenas in the name of the grand jury to those witnesses and for that evidence. In some jurisdictions the prosecutor does not have authority to issue subpoenas in the grand jury's name. In those jurisdictions the prosecutor must ask the grand jury either to issue the subpoenas itself or to give him the authority to issue them in its name.

Grand jury subpoenas require witnesses to appear before the grand jury at a specific date and time and to answer questions posed to them by the prosecutor and the grand jurors themselves. Grand jury witnesses have no constitutional right to an attorney and must face the prosecutor's questions without the presence of counsel.[29] Grand jury subpoenas may include attached schedules that list any documents or other things the witness is required to bring to the grand jury and any evidence the witness will be required to produce for it, such as handwriting, voice, or bodily fluid samples.

Prosecutors often ask subpoenaed witnesses to voluntarily come to the prosecutor's office prior to their scheduled appearance before the grand jury for the purpose of discussing their testimony. Subpoenaed witnesses are free to accept the prosecutor's invitation or decline it. While asking subpoenaed grand jury witnesses to come to the prosecutor's office to discuss their testimony is not considered an abuse of the grand jury, it is an abuse of the grand jury for the prosecutor to issue grand jury subpoenas simply as a means of bringing witnesses to the prosecutor's office for questioning.[30] Paralegals who work in prosecutors' offices frequently prepare grand jury subpoenas for witnesses, prepare any schedules that must be attached to them, and schedule time with the grand jury for the prosecutor.

While it is usually the prosecutor who decides what witnesses to subpoena before the grand jury, the grand jury has the power to refuse to hear them[31] and can decide to hear other witnesses. If a witness to whom a grand jury subpoena has been issued fails to appear before the grand jury or appears and refuses to answer the questions asked or produce the evidence subpoenaed, it is usually the prosecutor who decides whether to ask a court to use its power to compel the witness to appear, answer the questions, or produce the material demanded.

Courts can compel a witness to comply with a grand jury subpoena by issuing an arrest warrant for a witness who does not appear and by jailing a witness who refuses to answer questions or refuses to produce subpoenaed material until the witness answers the questions or produces that material. In some instances, before a court will consider the prosecutor's request to enforce a grand jury subpoena, the court will require that the grand jury expressly authorize the prosecutor to seek enforcement.[32]

Grand jury investigations are secret. As a result, the grand jurors and the law enforcement agents and prosecutors assisting in the investigation are prohibited from divulging matters that occur before the grand jury. Prosecutors and law enforcement agents may, however, disclose evidence obtained through the grand jury to experts for forensic or other analysis, the results of which will be reported back to the grand jury, but which are otherwise secret.

Witnesses, however, are not bound by grand jury secrecy and are free to disclose the contents of their own testimony to third parties, including the news media.[33] Often the prosecutor will ask a witness to refrain for some specific period of time from disclosing the fact that he was subpoenaed and from disclosing the contents of his testimony. Such requests, while not binding, are permitted[34] and are usually made by means of a letter from the prosecutor that is given to the witness when a grand jury subpoena is served. If a prosecutor feels that silence of the witness is necessary to protect the integrity of a grand jury investigation, he can ask a court to order the witness not to disclose the fact he was subpoenaed, the questions he was asked, and the contents of his testimony.[35]

Other tools of a formal investigation that may supplement a grand jury investigation or that may be used independently of one are search warrants and orders to surreptitiously monitor and record conversations.

Search warrants, which will be discussed more fully in Chapter 16, are orders issued by judges that command law enforcement agents and, at times, civilians who are assisting them to search certain described premises, vehicles, and computers and other types of electronic storage devices for the fruits, instrumentalities, and evidence of specified crimes.

Orders that allow law enforcement agents to surreptitiously monitor and record conversations are referred to by different names (commonly called eavesdrop orders and overhear orders) in different jurisdictions. Federal agents and law enforcement officials in many states are allowed to use eavesdropping devices without a court order as long as one party to the conversation consents to the monitoring. Those types of overhears are called consensual overhears. In some states law enforcement agents must obtain court authorization even for consensual overhears. Federal agents as well as law enforcement agents in all states must obtain court orders for nonconsensual overhears.

Overhears are a valuable law enforcement tool and can be used by law enforcement agents to passively monitor a target's conversations or as part of a proactive covert operation, usually referred to as a "sting operation." Sting operations can be conducted without employing overhears, but without the use of surreptitious monitoring and recording, the extent and value of sting operations is significantly limited. By themselves, sting operations are not a formal investigative tool because court approval is not needed to engage in them.

In most sting operations, law enforcement agents pose as agents of some criminal enterprise for the purpose of gathering evidence against and recording incriminating conversations with the targets of their investigation. Sting operations are frequently associated in the public mind with investigations involving child pornography, child predators, and sales of controlled substances (such as narcotics). Sting operations are used just as widely and in much more sophisticated ways in cases involving terrorism[36] and various types of white collar crimes (such as public corruption). One of the most complex and long-running sting operations and one that made extensive use of consensual overhears was called Operation Greylord. Operation Greylord was a massive investigation into corruption in the Cook County (the Illinois county in which Chicago is located) Illinois court system that spanned more than three years. The investigation resulted in the conviction of 17 judges, 48 lawyers, 8 policemen, 10 deputy sheriffs, 8 court officials, and 1 state legislator.[37]

Two of Operation Greylord's most important undercover operatives were civilians: Brocton Lockwood who was a judge and Terry Hake who was a lawyer. Judge Lockwood was an honest judge who was so outraged by the judicial corruption he saw that he contacted the FBI and agreed to wear an eavesdropping device to gather evidence. Judge Lockwood kept the eavesdropping device in the cowboy boots he wore to court and used it to record in-chambers conversations with corrupt attorneys and court officials who offered him bribes.

As part of the investigation, undercover FBI agents committed low-level crimes against each other so that one of them could be arrested and charged with a crime. Once charged, the undercover-agent defendants were "represented" by Terry Hake, a former county prosecutor who posed as a corrupt defense attorney and wore an eavesdropping device to capture conversations he had with judges while bribing them to dismiss charges against his undercover FBI agent clients.

United States v. Devine

United States Court of Appeals for the Seventh Circuit, 1986 787 F.2d 1086

CAMPBELL, J. Defendant John J. Devine was convicted of knowingly and willfully devising and participating in a scheme to defraud in violation of 18 U.S.C. §§1341, 1951 and 1962(c). Judge Susan Getzendanner of the Northern District of Illinois sentenced him to numerous concurrent 15-year terms of imprisonment. For the reasons set forth below, we affirm.

Defendant, a former Cook County Associate Judge, was convicted of orchestrating deals with attorneys to fix cases for monetary payments. At trial two attorneys, Martin Schachter and Arthur Cirignani, testified they paid defendant to secure favorable results and to be "court-appointed" to represent defendants in future "deals." Devine usually requested one-third of the attorneys' fees for a fixed case. The attorneys usually secured their fees from clients' bond money. In addition to the testimony of the two attorneys mentioned above there was the testimony of F.B.I. agent/informant Terrence Hake who worked "undercover" in defendant's courtroom as part of the now famous Operation Greylord investigation. He verified defendant Devine accepted money from him. A third attorney, Howard Shaffner, testified he personally had an encounter with defendant and believed defendant was trying to "shake him down."

Additionally, Chicago police officer Joseph Trunzo testified he witnessed an attorney named Harry Klepper leave defendant's courtroom upset one day because defendant demanded he be paid additional dollars to secure the result Klepper desired. We believe there is little need to detail other testimony at the trial. In sum, we find no paucity of evidence from which defendant could have been found guilty as charged.

Defendant claims reversible error occurred because the district court refused to allow a linguist, Dr. Robert Shuy, to testify concerning difficult to hear sections of a "body bug" tape produced by F.B.I. agent Hake. Hake produced such tapes while "dealing" with defendant and his courtroom personnel. Defendant claims that since the government was allowed to present transcripts of its version of the conversations to the jury, the exclusion of Dr. Shuy's testimony denied him his right to a fair trial and his Sixth Amendment right to present an adequate defense. Defendant adds Dr. Shuy's testimony was reliable and helpful and therefore should have been presented to the jury under Rule 702 of the Federal Rules of Evidence. We note that Dr. Shuy testified during defendant's offer of proof and stated, contrary to defendant's assertions, that if defense counsel were allowed to play the tapes to the jury and present its argument it would have the same effect as any transcripts given to them. The tapes were played. Shuy also rejected defendant's argument that he would be using his expertise in understanding the context and dynamics of conversations in analyzing the tape. Shuy claimed he would rely instead on auditory and phonetic indicia, i.e., listening skills. The district court concluded Shuy's testimony would "not have given the jury significant help in understanding the evidence or in determining a fact in issue, and understanding what is said in a tape recorded conversation is not outside the average person's understanding." (D. Ct. Op. of Dec. 17, 1984 at 3.) We agree. "We will reverse the court's ruling on the admissibility of expert testimony only upon a clear showing of abuse of discretion." *Spray-Rite Service Corp. v. Monsanto Co.*, 684 F.2d 1226, 1241 (7th Cir. 1982) See also *Contractor Utility Sales Co. v. Certain-Teed Corp.*, 748 F.2d 1151, 1155 (7th Cir. 1984). We see no clear abuse of discretion here. We also reject defendant's argument he was unable to present his version of what the tapes said. Defendant's counsel cross-examined Agent Hake for three days. The tapes were played during this cross-examination on equipment identical to that used by Dr. Shuy. Portions of the tapes contested by defendant were deleted when given to the jury in transcript form during deliberations. We see no reversible error.

* * *

We close by stating we leave this case with the impression that the evidence presented against defendant Devine at trial was very strong. Testimony from several reliable, credible and independent sources indicates defendant Devine was properly convicted of conduct so despicable we will not engage in a battle of adjectives in an attempt to describe it. The evidence speaks for itself.

For the reasons set forth above, the decision of the district court is hereby AFFIRMED.

Case Focus

● How did the government obtain evidence against the judge in this case?
● What was the role of Terry Hake and what evidence did he obtain to corroborate his testimony?
● What do you think about gathering evidence through surreptitious recording of conversations?

● ● ● ● ● ● ● ●

While sting operations have become a valuable tool for law enforcement, it is a tool that has its critics. Some say that law enforcement should not be involved in illegal activity and that such operations pose dangers for innocent people. Despite these criticisms, neither Congress nor any state legislature has prohibited law enforcement from engaging in them.

CHAPTER TERMS

Constitutional privilege   Jurisdiction
Evidentiary privilege   Target

REVIEW QUESTIONS

1. What are the different types of law enforcement agencies in the United States?
2. What types of offenses do local police departments and sheriffs' offices investigate?
3. How do specialized law enforcement agencies differ from local police departments and sheriffs' offices?
4. Describe the different types of criminal investigations.
5. What are some of the investigative tools used in formal criminal investigations?

ADDITIONAL READING

John Fletcher, *Charge to a Grand Jury*, 18 F.R.D. 211 (Cir. Ct. Md. 1955).
Brocton Lockwood with Harland H. Mendenhall, *Operation Greylord: Brocton Lockwood's Story* (1989).

James Tuohy & Rob Warden, *Justice Chicago Style* (1989).

ENDNOTES

1. *Printz v. United States*, 521 U.S. 898 (1997).
2. *See, e.g.*, 20 ILCS 2505-305, which limits the peace officer powers of Illinois Department of Revenue investigators to enforcement of state tax laws administered by the Department of Revenue and the Illinois Gaming Board.
3. Engaging in a course of business in connection with the sale of a security is a federal offense, 15 U.S.C. §77q(a)(3) and is an offense in many states. *See, e.g.*, 815 ILCS 5/12(F). Under federal law and under the law of some states the offense is a felony.
4. Sara Beal et al., 1 *Grand Jury Law & Practice* §6:1 (2d ed. 2008).
5. *United States v. Powell*, 379 U.S. 48 (1964).
6. *In re Keegan*, 18 F. Supp. 786 (S.D.N.Y. 1937).
7. *See, e.g.*, 35 ILCS 5/916(c).
8. *Powell*, 379 U.S. at 48.
9. *Kitner v. United States*, 568 F. Supp. 809 (D. Or. 1983).
10. Irving Kaufman, *The Grand Jury—Its Role and Its Powers*, 17 F.R.D. 331 (1955). Prior to the twelfth century the origins of the grand jury are murky. Some historians believe the grand jury developed from Saxon law, while others believe it developed from Norman law and was brought to England by William the Conqueror.
11. Sara Beal et al., 1 *Grand Jury Law & Practice*, §1:3 (2d ed. 2008).
12. *Id.* at §1:4.
13. *Impounded*, 241 F.3d 308 (3d Cir. 2001).
14. Sara Beal et al., 1 *Grand Jury Law & Practice* at §1:4.
15. *United States v. Williams*, 504 U.S. 36 (1992).
16. *Id.*
17. *Branzburg v. Hayes*, 408 U.S. 665 (1972).
18. *United States v. R. Enterprises*, 498 U.S. 292 (1991). Whether a subpoena is over broad is for the most part determined by the Fourth Amendment and its prohibition against unreasonable searches and seizures. That subject is examined in Chapter 15.
19. *United States v. Williams*, 504 U.S. at 36.
20. *Id.*
21. Sara Beal et al., 1 *Grand Jury Law & Practice* at §1:1.
22. *See, e.g.*, 720 ILCS 5/111-2.
23. Sara Beal et al., 1 *Grand Jury Law & Practice* at §1:1. Many of the states that have eliminated the grand jury as an investigative body have conferred its investigative and subpoena powers on judges and require the prosecutor to go before a judge to obtain investigative subpoenas. *See, e.g., Mich. Comp. Law Ann.* §767.3.
24. *See, e.g.*, 725 ILCS 5/112-2, which provides that grand juries shall consist of 16 persons, 12 of whom are necessary to constitute a quorum.
25. *United States v. R. Enterprises*, 498 U.S. 292 (1991).
26. *Id.*
27. *Id.*
28. *Blair v. United States*, 250 U.S. 273 (1919).
29. *United States v. McKenna*, 327 F.3d 830 (9th Cir. 2003). Witnesses are allowed to step outside the grand jury room to consult with their attorney. Some states have created a statutory right to be accompanied by an attorney.
30. *Durbin v. United States*, 221 F.2d 520 (D.C. Cir. 1954).
31. *In re Grand Jury Proceedings (John Doe)*, 790 F. Supp. 422 (E.D.N.Y. 1992).
32. *Id.*
33. *In re Grand Jury Subpoena*, 626 F. Supp. 1057 (D.P.R. 1986).
34. *In re Grand Jury Subpoena*, 626 F. Supp. at 1057.
35. *In re Swearingen Aviation Corp.*, 486 F. Supp. 9 (D. Md. 1979).
36. In one sting operation involving FBI agents and law enforcement agents of two other countries eight persons were arrested for trying to obtain Russian-made surface-to-air missiles, missile launchers, and AK-47s for the Tamil Tigers terrorist organization in Sri Lanka. The eight were charged in federal court in Brooklyn. *See* Lea Terhune, *FBI Sting Operation Nets Suspects in Sri Lanka. http://usinfo.state.gov.* Site last visited December 20, 2006.
37. Federal Bureau of Investigation, *Operation Greylord. http://www.fbi.gov/page2/march04/greylord031504.htm.* Site last visited December 11, 2006.

Chapter 4
Prosecution of Crime in the United States

Chapter Objectives

After reading this chapter, you should be able to

- Understand which officials prosecute crimes on the federal and state level
- Explain how those officials are selected
- Identify the branch of government in which those officials work
- Explain what prosecutorial discretion is
- Understand the separation of powers principle and how it applies to prosecutorial discretion
- Explain factors that are used in reaching a decision to prosecute

After he ordered the imprisonment of a group of fanatics called "Prophets" for seditious language, Lord Holt was visited by Lacy, one of their friends ... [who] told Lord Holt, "I come to you a prophet from the Lord God, who has sent me to thee, and would have thee grant a *nolle prosequi* for John Atkins, his servant, whom thou has cast into prison." Lord Holt replied, "Thou art a false prophet, and a lying knave. If the Lord God had sent thee it would have been to the Attorney General, for He knows that it belongth not to the Chief Justice to grant a *nolle prosequi*. ... " —2 *Campbell's Lives of the Chancellors* 173

In the United States, crime is prosecuted by both the federal government and the states. The vast majority of criminal prosecutions in the United States are done by the criminal justice systems of the states. The federal criminal justice system is responsible for less than 2 percent of the total prosecutions brought in the United States each year and accounts for less than 6 percent of all felony prosecutions.[1]

The U.S. Constitution and the constitutions and laws of the states lodge the prosecuting power of their respective governments in different prosecuting officials. Those prosecuting officials are part of particular branches of the governments that employ them, and due in part to the constitutional principle of separation of powers, they are given great discretion in the discharge of their prosecutorial duties. This chapter examines: (A) what officials are charged with prosecuting crime in the United States; (B) the branch of government of which those prosecuting officials are a part; and (C) the nature and exercise of prosecutorial discretion.

A. Officials That Are Charged with Prosecuting Crime in the United States

The American political system is a federal system in which power is allocated between the federal government and the states. Within their respective spheres each government has the power to define criminal offenses. Just as the power to define criminal offenses is divided, the power to prosecute is also divided. Federal prosecutors are responsible for prosecuting federal offenses and state prosecutors are responsible for prosecuting state offenses. Federal and state prosecutors are selected in different ways. This section examines what officials are responsible for prosecuting crime for the federal and state governments and how those officials are selected.

1. Prosecution at the Federal Level

The federal officials charged with prosecuting federal crimes are United States Attorneys, who are appointed by the President with the advice and consent of the Senate and serve for a term of four years. Despite the fact that U.S. Attorneys have a four-year term, they may be dismissed by the President at any time.

The United States is divided into a number of judicial districts with one United States Attorney for and at least one federal courthouse in each district (Figure 4-1). States containing large populations are divided into two or more districts, and states with a small population constitute one district. Thus, for example, the state of Illinois is divided into three federal districts, the Northern District, the Central District, and the Southern District, each with its own U.S. Attorney and at least one federal courthouse, while the state of Wyoming is a single federal district called the District of Wyoming, with a single U.S. Attorney. Sometimes a

Figure 4-1 U.S. Courts of Appeals and United States District Courts

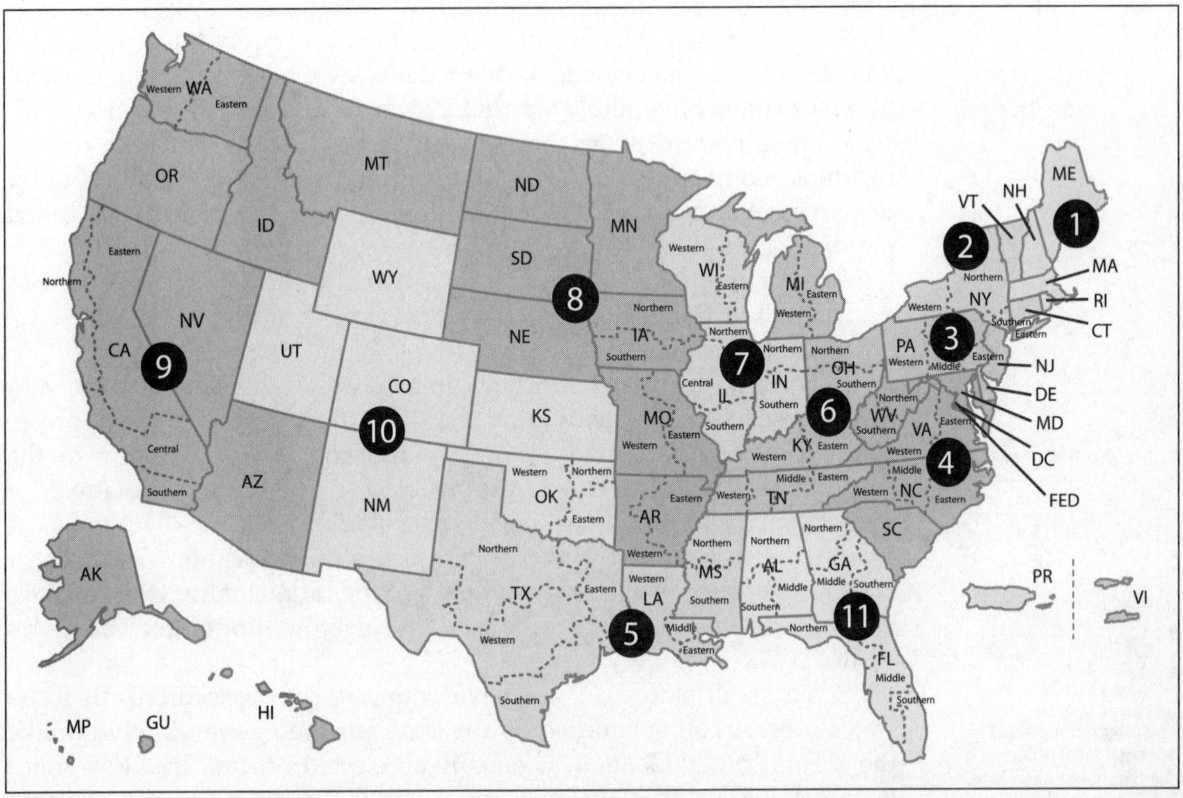

Source: Administrative Office of the United States Courts. *http://www.uscourts.gov/images/circuitMap.pdf.Court_Locater.aspx*

federal district is divided into different geographical divisions. Each division is staffed by federal prosecutors hired and supervised by the U.S. Attorney in whose district the division is located.

With a few exceptions[2], United States Attorneys are responsible for the prosecution of all federal crimes that occur within their districts. Each U.S. Attorney's office is staffed by a U.S. Attorney and Assistant U.S. Attorneys. The number of Assistant U.S. Attorneys in an office varies from a few assistants in small districts to over 100 assistants in districts that include densely populated urban areas, such as the Southern District of New York. When a case arises in which the U.S. Attorney for a district may have a conflict (as, for example, when a member of his staff is the target of a criminal investigation) or when a prosecution requires expertise or a level of staff resources that the U.S. Attorney's office for the district does not have, the prosecution will be handled by attorneys from the Criminal Division of the U.S. Department of Justice in Washington, D.C., who will travel to the district to prosecute the case.

2. Criminal Prosecution in the States

Understanding the allocation of the power to prosecute on the state level is not quite as easy as on the federal level because to some extent different states have allocated that power to and among different officials, and different states have given those officials different names. In almost every state the power to prosecute crime is vested in a county- or parish-level prosecutor who, depending on the state, may be called the district attorney, the county prosecutor, or the state's attorney. (For the sake of simplicity only the term "district attorney" will be used to describe all of these officials.) District attorneys, unlike U.S. Attorneys, are elected officials.

In addition to district attorneys, in most states there are also city and town prosecutors. Depending on the state, these municipal-level prosecutors may be referred to as the city attorney, city prosecutor, or the corporation counsel and are responsible for prosecuting violations of their municipality's ordinances. In some states municipal-level prosecutors may also have the power to prosecute misdemeanor violations of state law that occur within the borders of the municipality that employs them. Municipal-level prosecutors are usually appointed and not elected.

The **attorney general** is the chief legal officer of a state, *Environmental Protection Agency v. Pollution Control Bd.*, 69 Ill. 2d 394 (1977), and chief legal officer of the federal government. *United States v. San Jacinto Tin Co.*, 125 U.S. 273 (1888). State attorneys general represent state officials and state agencies in court and provide them with advice. In states that do not have county prosecutors the Attorney General also handles state criminal prosecutions.

Some small states do not have county-level prosecutors. In those states prosecution is handled by the state **attorney general**, who, unlike the U.S. Attorney General, is usually an elected official. In a few states (Georgia, for example) one prosecutor handles prosecutions for an entire circuit, which, depending upon the population, may consist of a single county or multiple counties. These circuit prosecutors are usually referred to as district attorneys and, like their county-level counterparts in other states, are elected.

Other than in those states in which the power to prosecute is vested exclusively in the state attorney general, all of the states also vest some prosecuting power in an officer who has statewide jurisdiction and who, in effect, is available to supplement the work done by the district attorney. In most states the power to prosecute statewide is vested in the state attorney general who, in most states, is an elected official. In some states (Florida, for example) the power to prosecute statewide is vested in an officer called the statewide prosecutor, who is appointed by the Attorney General.

Other than in those states with no district attorneys, the extent of the attorney general's and statewide prosecutor's jurisdiction to prosecute is different in different states. In some states the attorney general provides merely a supportive service, assisting the district attorney in large cases that are beyond the expertise or resource level of the district attorneys' offices and also prosecutes cases when the district attorney has a conflict or if the crime involves victims in more than one county. In other states the attorney general or statewide prosecutor has the power to initiate prosecutions in certain statutorily defined types of cases or with the consent of the district attorney.[3] The jurisdiction of the statewide prosecuting officer may be set out in a statute, such as is done in Florida, or may be determined by a provision of the state constitution and the decisional law that has developed around it.

B. The Branch of Government of Which the Prosecutor Is a Part

The U.S. Constitution divides the power of the federal government among the legislative, executive, and judicial branches. The Constitution vests the executive power in the President and provides that the President shall "take Care that the Laws be faithfully executed."[4] Thus, the enforcement of federal criminal law is given to the executive branch, and it is the President who is constitutionally responsible for investigation and prosecution of federal crimes. The President discharges that responsibility through the various federal investigative agencies, the U.S. Attorney General, and the U.S. Attorneys.

As appointees of the President, U.S. Attorneys are part of the executive branch of the federal government. As a part of that branch, federal prosecutors exercise the prosecutorial powers that are constitutionally vested in the President and to the extent that those vested powers are discretionary powers they exercise that discretion. U.S. Attorneys, like all attorneys, are also officers of the court. As an incident of the separation of power principle (discussed below), notwithstanding that the U.S. Attorneys are officers of the court, the judiciary is forbidden to interfere with or regulate their exercise of discretionary executive branch power.

Whether a district attorney is a part of the executive branch of state government is a matter of state law that is usually determined by reference to a state's constitution. In many states the state constitutional provision that creates the district attorney's office is found within the judicial article of that document.[5] That has led to the conclusion in some of those states that the district attorney is part of the judicial branch of state government, even though he exercises what are otherwise executive branch powers.[6] In other states, notwithstanding that the provision creating the district attorney's office is found within the state constitution's judicial article, the district attorney is considered to be part of the executive branch of state government.[7] In virtually all states the state attorney general is considered to be part of the executive branch of government.

C. Nature and Exercise of Prosecutorial Discretion

The U.S. Constitution's division of power between the legislative, executive, and judicial branches has given rise to the separation of powers principle, which is a principle of federal constitutional law, even though it is not expressly stated in that document.[8] That principle is followed in the states as a matter of state constitutional law and is expressly stated in some state constitutions.[9]

Under the separation of powers principle one branch of government is forbidden from exercising the powers granted to another branch of government. An important corollary of that principle is that the judiciary is forbidden to interfere with the exercise of a discretionary power given to the executive branch by the Constitution.[10] Under the doctrine of **judicial review** courts will strike down statutes that violate the separation of powers principle by purporting to confer the power of one branch of government on another branch. Courts will also curb exercises of judicial power that interfere with the exercise of the executive branch's **discretionary power**.

An incident of the President's constitutional duty to take care that the laws of the United States be faithfully executed is that the power to investigate crime is an executive branch function that is considered to be discretionary. Because U.S. Attorneys and federal law enforcement agents are part of the executive branch, they have the discretion to choose whether or not to investigate a crime. The judicial branch does not have the power to order the executive branch to conduct a criminal investigation nor does it have the power to conduct such an investigation on its own. In virtually all of the states criminal investigation is also considered to be an executive branch function that is not shared by the judicial branch, and in some states the duty to investigate is actually imposed on the prosecutor.[11]

Judicial review is the power of the judiciary to determine whether acts of the other two branches of government are void because those acts violate the Constitution. *State v. LaFrance,* 124 N.H. 171 (1983).

Discretionary power is the power to do or refrain from doing a certain thing. *Bennett v. Norton,* 171 Pa. 221 (1895).

In Re United States

United States Court of Appeals for the Seventh Circuit (2005)
398 F.3d 615

PER CURIAM. Unnecessary medical procedures performed at Edgewater Hospital in order to obtain payments from insurers (including the federal government's health-care programs) led to criminal prosecutions for fraud. Peter Rogan, a principal at one of Edgewater's management companies, was not among the criminal defendants, but the United States filed a civil suit against him seeking compensatory damages and penalties under the False Claims Act.

In this capacity Rogan obtained materials that had been gathered by the grand jury that issued the indictments. The estate of Albert Okoro, who had died during one of Edgewater's unnecessary procedures, also sought grand jury materials for use in civil litigation against Rogan and others. Persuaded that Okoro's estate should have some (though not all) of the materials already in Rogan's possession, the United States Attorney for the Northern District of Illinois applied to the district court for an order under Fed. R. Crim. P. 6(e)(3)(E)(I) permitting their release. The application [was] made *ex parte** * *[,] presented to Chief Judge Kocoras and granted. [Judge Kocoras's order] authorized the United States to give Okoro's estate whatever grand jury materials the prosecutor saw fit to release.

After learning that Okoro's estate had acquired grand jury materials for use in the pending suit, Rogan protested to Chief Judge Kocoras. This led to his recusal—for his son is a partner at Winston & Strawn, which represents Rogan. * * * Under local practice, Rogan's motion was transferred to Judge Holderman * * *. The United States Attorney acknowledged that the grant of discretion to determine which materials to hand over was not best practice, and it volunteered to retrieve the materials so that any dispute about the extent of the estate's access could be decided with Rogan's participation. Judge Holderman vacated Chief Judge Kocoras's order in light of this undertaking. At that point, however, consideration of the estate's request for information came to a halt. Judge Holderman decided not to address it until he learned why the United States had made the *ex parte* request to Chief Judge Kocoras. He deemed *ex parte* action, and the grant of discretion to an Assistant United States Attorney, so irregular that he threatened to hold the Assistant in criminal contempt of court, and he demanded to know who within the United States Attorney's Office participated in the decision to file such a request and why they had approved it. * * *

The United States now asks us to issue a writ of mandamus to accomplish Judge Holderman's recusal, on the ground that his impartiality reasonably may be questioned by objective and informed observers. See 28 U.S.C. §455(a); *Liteky v. United States*, 510 U.S. 540, 127 L. Ed. 2d 474, 114 S. Ct. 1147 (1994) * * *. Mandamus is the right—indeed, we have held, see *United States v. Boyd*, 208 F.3d 638, 645 (7th Cir. 2000) * * *, the only—means to this end. Yet many of the petition's arguments deal more with what is being done (an investigation of decision-making within the U.S. Attorney's Office) than with which judge is doing the investigation. One form of relief fairly comprised within the petition's scope is a halt to the inquest. We conclude that the inquiry is inappropriate and must cease; this makes it unnecessary to decide whether someone other than Judge Holderman is the right person to preside.

When Rogan's protest sparked Chief Judge Kocoras's recusal and landed the matter in Judge Holderman's lap, he concluded (as his response in this court states): "It was hard for me to believe that Chief Judge Kocoras would sign such an erroneous order unless he were misled." Judge Holderman thought that the United States had "cited inapplicable subsections of Rule 6(e)" and failed to alert Chief Judge Kocoras to decisions of this circuit that disparaged *ex parte* applications under Rule 6(e). To quote again from Judge Holderman's response: "I wondered why . . . better procedures had not been employed? Was it by neglect or design? That was the key question that I needed to have answered."

The judge threatened to have Assistant United States Attorney Jacqueline Stern, who had signed the application, prosecuted for criminal contempt of court. Instead of leading to the information the judge sought, however, the threat caused Stern to retain a lawyer. The judge then asked that Stern be given immunity from prosecution in order to induce her cooperation. It is not clear that the Executive Branch *can* foreclose a charge of criminal contempt, see *Young v. United States,* 481 U.S. 787, 799, 95 L. Ed. 2d 740, 107 S. Ct. 2124 (1987), but at all events immunity is not bestowed lightly (or quickly). Thus the judge asked for information from other attorneys in the Office, only to find that they were less than forthcoming given the threat to prosecute whoever turned out to be responsible; and when the Office did not provide as much information (and as fast) as the judge sought, he insisted that everyone, right up to the United States Attorney, be investigated by the Department of Justice's Office of Professional Responsibility, which the judge wanted to report back to him with its findings.

The fundamental problem with this inquiry is that the United States Attorney is not answerable to a judge for the deliberations among his staff. The intra-office conversations and memoranda that the judge wants to see are covered by multiple privileges. See, e.g., *United States v. Zingsheim*, 384 F.3d 867 (7th Cir. 2004), which holds that federal judges may not insist that prosecutors reveal deliberative or pre-decisional materials. A federal court must evaluate lawyers' final submissions—that is, must review outputs rather than inputs. How the United States reaches its litigating positions, who said what to whom within the prosecutor's office, and so on, are for the Attorney General and the President to evaluate. The Judicial Branch is limited to assessing counsel's public deeds.

Judges often are tempted to seek a larger role in the conduct of litigants that appear frequently before them. See also, e.g., *In re United States*, 345 F.3d 450 (7th Cir. 2003). Temptation may be especially strong for a judge who spent many years as a prosecutor before donning the robe. (Judge Holderman served for six years as an Assistant United States Attorney in the Northern District of Illinois.) But temptation must be resisted in order to maintain separation between executive and judicial roles, and between the formulation and evaluation of positions in litigation. In the rare situations when a prima facie case of criminal contempt has been made out, and the contempt is not committed in the judge's presence (and thus amenable to summary disposition), the judge must turn the matter over to a prosecutor rather than assume an inquisitorial role inappropriate to the Judicial Branch.

None of the papers that the United States tendered to Chief Judge Kocoras is objectively frivolous. There is accordingly no basis for civil sanctions, let alone criminal proceedings, against any member of the United States Attorney's Office. The United States did not release any grand jury material without judicial approval; it sought and obtained authorization before acting. Nor did it hide from Chief Judge Kocoras the fact that Rogan had not been notified. To the contrary, the application alerted the Chief Judge to its *ex parte* nature. If that was a problem, the Chief Judge could have denied the application and ordered service on Rogan's lawyers. Likewise the application showed that the United States sought discretion to decide which materials to hand over, and the Chief Judge bestowed that power on the prosecutor's office. Perhaps he should not have done so, but it cannot be thought a form of criminal contempt to ask the court and then proceed with its approval.* * *

[T]he United States is entitled to file an application *ex parte*, after which the judge must decide whether to order an interested private party to be notified. * * *[W]hen the United States Attorney's Office makes a mistake and seeks inappropriate relief, the judiciary's proper course is to deny the motion, not to threaten criminal prosecution or seek privileged pre-decisional materials. Our legal system does not contemplate an inquisitorial role for federal judges.

The petition for a writ of mandamus is granted, and the district court is directed to close its investigation into the proceedings that occurred before Chief Judge Kocoras in December 2003. The Office of Professional Responsibility is free to proceed as it chooses, but it need not investigate at the behest of the Judicial Branch—nor are its findings (if it conducts an investigation voluntarily) to be reported to the Judicial Branch. This is a matter for the Executive Branch to handle internally using its own judgment. Because we have halted the district court's inquest, we need not discuss any of the other issues on which the U.S. Attorney, the civil litigants, and the district judge have exchanged opposing views.

Case Focus

- In this case what did the judge do that resulted in the initiation of suit by the United States Attorney?
- What did the court say about the judge initiating a criminal investigation and about the court's power to order such an investigation?

• • • • • • • •

On the federal level, whether or not to initiate a criminal prosecution is also a discretionary power of the executive branch that flows from the President's Article II "take care" power. As a result, U.S. Attorneys have the power to refuse to prosecute and cannot be ordered by the judicial branch to initiate a prosecution. That rule is followed in most of the states, though in some states the prosecutor must provide a court with the reasons she has declined to prosecute and if the court disagrees with her decision it can order the prosecution to proceed.[12]

Nolle prosequi in a criminal case is a formal statement by the prosecutor that he will not proceed with the prosecution of either all charges or some charges. *Commonwealth v. Dascalakis,* 246 Mass. 12 (1923). The effect of a prosecutor's *nolle prosequi* is to terminate the proceedings on the charges to which the action relates, and if it is to all charges it releases the defendant. *State ex rel. Norwood v. Drumm,* 691 S.W.2d 238 (Mo. 1985).

As a part of the executive branch the prosecutor also has discretion on what charges to bring. That means, for example, that if two people engage in the same conduct and that conduct constitutes a violation of a felony statute and also a violation of a misdemeanor statute, the prosecutor can decide to charge one of those persons with the felony and the other with the misdemeanor, or the prosecutor can decide to charge one person with the felony and not charge the other person with any crime and the judiciary has no power to compel the prosecutor to do otherwise.

The prosecutor also has discretionary power to terminate a prosecution through a motion to *nolle prosequi*. The prosecutor can use that power to dismiss some charges against a defendant and go forward on other pending charges, he can decide to move for a *nolle prosequi* of all charges, and he can move for a *nolle prosequi* against one defendant but not against a codefendant. The motion for a *nolle prosequi* is a motion that must be granted by the judge before whom the case is pending. Except in an instance where the prosecutor is harassing a defendant by repeatedly initiating a prosecution and then dismissing it, a judge has no power to refuse to grant the prosecutor's motion to *nolle prosequi*.

In Re United States

United States Court of Appeals for the Seventh Circuit (2003) 345 F.3d 450

POSNER, J. Kenneth Bitsky, the defendant in the case that gives rise to the government's petition for mandamus, was indicted on one count of violating 18 U.S.C. §242 (deprivation of civil rights under color of law) and two counts of violating 18 U.S.C. §1512(b)(3) (obstruction of justice). According to the indictment, Bitsky, a Wisconsin police officer, had assaulted an arrested person and had then tried to induce another officer to write a false arrest report justifying Bitsky's use of force and had threatened another officer in an effort to prevent her from informing on him. The government and Bitsky made a plea agreement under which he would plead guilty to one of the obstruction of justice counts and the government would dismiss the other two counts. At the sentencing hearing the district judge asked the prosecutor why the civil rights count, for which the sentencing range was 24 to 30 months, had been dropped, when the sentencing range for the count to which Bitsky had agreed to plead guilty was only 6 to 12 months. * * * The prosecutor explained that his main aim was to get a felony conviction, which would bar Bitsky from remaining in law enforcement, without the risk of a trial, which might result in Bitsky's being acquitted. The judge rejected the plea agreement on the ground that the one count of which Bitsky would be convicted if the agreement were accepted did not reflect the gravity of his actual offense. * * *

Bitsky decided to go ahead and plead guilty even though he no longer had the protection of a plea agreement. The judge accepted his plea and, * * * sentenced him to 16 months in prison * * *. The government then filed a motion to dismiss the other two counts. The district court dismissed the other obstruction of justice count, but refused to dismiss the civil rights count and instead appointed a private lawyer to prosecute that count. The government asks us to issue a writ of mandamus commanding the district judge to dismiss that count as well and to rescind the appointment of the prosecutor. The judge has responded, stating as his reason for refusing to dismiss the civil rights count and for appointing a private lawyer to prosecute it that the government was trying to circumvent his sentencing authority because it considered the sentence that he would have imposed had Bitsky been convicted of the civil rights violation excessive. * * *

The historic and still the central function of mandamus is to confine officials within the boundaries of their authorized powers * * * and in our system of criminal justice, unlike that of some foreign nations, the authorized powers of federal judges do not include the power to prosecute crimes. *Wayte v. United States*, 470 U.S. 598, 607, 84 L. Ed. 2d 547, 105 S. Ct. 1524 (1985) * * *. "A judge in our system does not have the authority to tell prosecutors which crimes to prosecute or when to prosecute them." *United States v. Giannattasio*, 979 F.2d 98, 100 (7th Cir. 1992). There is an exception for criminal contempts of court, *Young v. United States ex rel. Vuitton et Fils S.A.*, 481 U.S. 787, 800-01, 95 L. Ed. 2d 740, 107 S. Ct. 2124 (1987) * * *, but it is irrelevant to this case. * * *

It is true that Rule 48(a) of the Federal Rules of Criminal Procedure requires leave of court for the government to dismiss an indictment, information, or complaint—or, we add, a single count of such a charging document. *United States v. Delagarza,* 650 F.2d 1166, 1167 (10th Cir. 1981) (per curiam); 3A Charles Alan Wright, *Federal Practice and Procedure* §811 (2d ed. 1982). But the purpose, at least the principal purpose, is to protect a defendant from the government's harassing him by repeatedly filing charges and then dismissing them before they are adjudicated. *Rinaldi v. United States*, 434 U.S. 22, 29 n. 15, 54 L. Ed. 2d 207, 98 S. Ct. 81 (1977) (per curiam) * * *. In such a case the judge might rightly condition dismissal on its being with prejudice. *United States v. Derr*, 726 F.2d 617, 619 (10th Cir. 1984) * * *. There is no issue of that sort here. The government wants to dismiss the civil rights count with prejudice, and that is what Bitsky wants as well. The district judge simply disagrees with the Justice Department's exercise of prosecutorial discretion. As he explained in his response to the petition for mandamus, he thinks the government has exaggerated the risk of losing at trial: "the evidence was strong and conviction extremely likely." The judge thus is playing U.S. Attorney. It is no doubt a position that he could fill with distinction, but it is occupied by another person. * * *

We are mindful of speculations in some judicial opinions that a district judge could properly deny a motion to dismiss a criminal charge even though the defendant had agreed to it. These opinions say that such a motion should be denied if it is in bad faith or contrary to the public interest, as where "the prosecutor appears motivated by bribery, animus towards the victim, or a desire to attend a social event rather than trial." *In re Richards, supra*, 213 F.3d at 787. * * * We are unaware, however, of any appellate decision that actually upholds a denial of a motion to dismiss a charge on such a basis. That is not surprising. The Constitution's "take Care" clause (art. II, §3) places the power to prosecute in the executive branch, just as Article I places the power to legislate in Congress. A judge could not properly refuse to enforce a statute because he thought the legislators were acting in bad faith or that the statute disserved the public interest; it is hard to see, therefore, how he could properly refuse to dismiss a prosecution merely because he was convinced that the prosecutor was acting in bad faith or contrary to the public interest.

The Constitution does place judicially enforceable limits on the powers of the nonjudicial branches of the government—for example, the government may not make its prosecutorial decisions on racially discriminatory grounds—but they are the limits found in the Constitution and thus do not include "bad faith" and "against the public interest." Custom, limited prosecutorial resources that compel prioritizing prosecutions, federal criminal statutes that overlap with each other and with state criminal statutes, plea bargaining, and the federal sentencing guidelines themselves combine to lodge enormous charging discretion in the Justice Department, to the occasional frustration of judges—yet without giving rise to any judicial remedy. See, e.g., *United States v. Batchelder*, 442 U.S. 114, 123-124, 60 L. Ed. 2d 755, 99 S. Ct. 2198 (1979) * * *.

Paradoxically, the plenary prosecutorial power of the executive branch safeguards liberty, for, in conjunction with the plenary legislative power of Congress, it assures that no one can be convicted of a crime without the concurrence of all three branches (again, criminal contempt of judicial orders constitutes a limited exception). When a judge assumes the power to prosecute, the number shrinks to two.

Even if a federal judge could properly deny, on the basis of bad faith or contravention of the public interest, a motion to dismiss a criminal charge, it would not follow that he could appoint a prosecutor. Presumably an assistant U.S. attorney who accepts a bribe, wants to go on vacation rather than conduct a trial, etc., is acting alone rather than at the direction or with the approval of the Justice Department, and a different assistant U.S. attorney would continue with the prosecution. In any event, a judge could not possibly win a confrontation with the executive branch over its refusal to prosecute, since the President has plenary power to pardon a federal offender, U.S. Const. art. II, §2, cl. 1—even before trial or conviction. *Ex parte Garland*, 71 U.S. (4 Wall.) 333, 380, 18 L. Ed. 366 (1866).

The government's petition for mandamus is granted and the district judge is ordered to grant the government's motion to dismiss the civil rights count against Bitsky, and to vacate the appointment of the special prosecutor.

> ### Case Focus
>
> ● What action by the federal judge prompted the United States Attorney to file this suit?
> ● What did the court say about the power of a federal judge to tell a federal prosecutor what crimes to prosecute? What reasons did the court give?
> ● Can a federal judge refuse a prosecutor's motion to dismiss a criminal charge? Why or why not?
> ● How does lodging the power to prosecute in the executive branch safeguard defendants?

• • • • • • • •

The only legal limit on the exercise of discretion by the prosecutor is that he cannot base his exercise of discretionary power on the defendant's race, religion, or some other invidious classification or on the defendant's exercise of some constitutional right such as freedom of speech.[13] A defendant who believes that a prosecutor has improperly exercised her discretion can file a motion to dismiss the prosecution with the court before which his case is pending.

An incident of the enormous discretionary power vested in the prosecutor is the expectation that the prosecutor will establish policies that will guide him and his staff in exercising that discretion. Whatever policies a prosecutor establishes, he is free to change them at any time, and they are neither subject to review by the judiciary nor are they generally held to create a right that the judiciary can enforce. In the case of district attorneys the prosecutor's policies are in effect subject to review only by the voters who elect him; if the voters do not like the policies he establishes they may vote him out of office at the next election. In the case of U.S. Attorneys their policies are to some extent dictated by the U.S. Justice Department and to some extent are set by each U.S. Attorney. These policies are subject to review by the U.S. Attorney General, the President, and Congress through its oversight powers.

Leone v. Fanelli

Supreme Court, Special Term, Westchester County (1949)
194 Misc. 826

FLANNERY, J. The application for an order to compel the respondent as District Attorney of the County of Westchester to fully and faithfully perform his duties as District Attorney and forthwith and diligently to prosecute the indictments against one Frank Smith and John Smith alleging felonious and malicious mischief, and felonious assault, must be denied. The office of District Attorney is a constitutional office, New York Constitution, Art. 9, §5, but apparently his powers and duties are set forth in no single statute or single place, Matter of Knight (People v. Neff), 191 N.Y. 286, 288, 84 N.E. 63, 64; Matter of Turecamo Contracting Co., Inc., 260 App. Div. 253, 257, 21 N.Y.S.2d 270, 274, and although until the adoption of the County Law in 1892 the Revised Statutes required him to attend the Courts of oyer and terminer and jail delivery, and general sessions in his county and conduct all prosecutions for crimes and offenses in those Courts, the statute was repealed by the County Law of 1892 and nothing substituted therefor. County Law, §200, however, indicates quite clearly that it is his duty to prosecute crimes within the county for which he is elected.

This duty, although not judicial and purely executive, is one calling for the exercise of discretion and the pursuit of some fixed enforcement policy which it is not the function of the Courts to supervise. A specific act which the District Attorney might by law be required to perform involving no special exercise of discretion and necessary for the satisfaction of some personal right of a petitioner could, undoubtedly, be required. But the general duty to prosecute all crimes or the special duty to prosecute a particular crime may not be required or supervised.

Submit order.

Case Focus

● Does a court have the power to supervise the establishment or implementation of a prosecution policy in a prosecutor's office? Why?

● ● ● ● ● ● ● ●

One of the challenges facing a prosecutor's office is to develop policies that allow the prosecutor to make the best use of the discretionary powers that the law gives him. Other than large district attorneys' offices, most district attorneys' offices have simple prosecution policies. Many large district attorney's offices, state attorneys general offices, and the U.S. Justice Department have detailed prosecution policies that require consideration of multiple factors before making a charging decision.

Prosecutors' offices generally use a three-part analysis for determining when to prosecute and as a basis for developing prosecution policy: (1) There must be admissible evidence on each element of the offense; (2) the evidence must establish guilt beyond a reasonable doubt; and (3) the case must be one on which it is appropriate to expend scarce prosecutorial resources. As can be seen, in this analytical model the first two elements are in the nature of technical legal matters; it is in the last element that the nontechnical policy decisions, sometimes called judgment calls or political decisions (political because the answer is not one that can be derived from legal principles) of the prosecutor play a decisive role.

In determining a policy for the allocation of prosecutorial resources the prosecutor will consider a number of factors, including the law enforcement needs of the community, the resources of the prosecutor's office, the resources of the law enforcement agencies with which the prosecutor works, and whether justice will be served by the prosecution.

In assessing the law enforcement needs of the community the prosecutor will usually look at the type of crimes being committed in it. Violent crime will almost always warrant the expenditure of prosecution resources. Crimes not involving violence may or may not warrant an expenditure of resources. Thus, for example, occasional acts of vandalism or a low level of prostitution that does not involve solicitation of customers on the street may not be significant enough problems in a prosecutor's community to warrant allocating prosecutors to prosecute those offenses, when the commission of other offenses that present a more significant threat to the community are being committed and therefore warrant vigorous prosecution. But a sudden surge in one type of crime could be viewed as a change in the law enforcement needs of the community that requires vigorous prosecution of those cases both to try to take the perpetrators of that offense off the street and to deter others from engaging in that type of misconduct.

In establishing prosecution policies the prosecutor may determine that while there are serious crimes occurring in his community, law enforcement does not have enough police resources to spend time investigating all crimes and that he does not have enough prosecutors to prosecute all cases. In that situation, which is the most common one, the prosecutor may establish prosecution thresholds, such as not prosecuting thefts of property with a value of less than $500 or not prosecuting illegal possession of hypodermic needles. That type of policy frees law enforcement agents and prosecutors to pursue more serious crimes.

The prosecutor will also consider mitigating factors in determining whether to expend prosecution resources on a case. Thus, for example, the prosecutor might decide as a matter of policy that thefts in which the perpetrator pays back the victim before prosecution is initiated will not be prosecuted, or that gun registration violations will not be used to prosecute homeowners who use unregistered firearms to kill burglars who break into a home, or not to prosecute zero-loss loan fraud cases (such as ones where the borrower falsely overstates his income on the loan application, but the loan is not in default).

Arthur Andersen and the Corporate Death Sentence

The prosecution of Arthur Andersen LLP provides an example of the effects that the prosecution of an entity can have and why prosecution policies for entities must take into account many more factors than prosecution policies for violent crimes and for crimes committed by natural persons.

Arthur Andersen LLP was one of the largest accounting firms in the world. Among the services it provided to its publicly held clients was auditing of their quarterly and annual earnings reports. Those reports are relied upon by individual and institutional investors when making investment decisions. The United States Securities & Exchange Commission (SEC) requires that the statements be audited by outside accountants who certify that the audits are performed in accordance with generally accepted accounting principles. In 2001, one of Andersen's clients, Enron Corp., a Texas-based energy trading company, collapsed resulting in millions of dollars of losses to investors.

In the wake of Enron's collapse the government decided to prosecute Andersen. In the indictment the government charged Andersen with obstructing the SEC's investigation of Enron by ordering the mass destruction of audit papers and supporting documents. Andersen was alleged to have destroyed the documents to protect itself and Enron. The government's decision to prosecute Andersen came against a backdrop of earlier Andersen misconduct. Early in 2001, Andersen had agreed to pay a $7 million fine levied by the SEC for issuing false and misleading statements that its audit of Waste Management, Inc., a publicly held corporation, had been conducted in accordance with generally accepted accounting principles when, in fact, it had not. Prior to that, Andersen was implicated in helping to conceal huge losses at the Arizona-based Baptist Foundation, the collapse of which caused investors, many of whom were retirees who had invested their retirement savings with the Foundation, to lose a total of $570 million.

The government convicted Andersen. One consequence of the conviction was that Andersen had to dissolve because the conviction barred it from auditing the earnings statements of publicly held corporations, work that represented a large portion of its business. As a result, 28,000 Andersen employees, all but a few of which had no role in Andersen's misconduct, lost their jobs. The conviction also meant that Andersen's professional malpractice policy would not cover any losses suffered by

Enron's shareholders, money that could otherwise be used to at least partially reimburse them. Andersen's dissolution also meant that the already small number of accounting firms that audited publicly held corporations was reduced, thereby reducing competition. Ultimately, the U.S. Supreme Court reversed the conviction because the trial judge had given the jury an incorrect instruction. The government chose not to re-try the case. The Supreme Court's decision came two years after Andersen dissolved and too late to resurrect the firm or help the innocent employees who lost their jobs.

In cases involving white collar crime and artificial entities additional considerations are taken into account in determining whether or not a case warrants the expenditure of prosecutorial resources. One important consideration with white collar crimes, particularly when the amount of money involved is not large, is the availability of civil redress. If the perpetrator of a fraud or embezzlement has money or other assets, if the amount stolen is not large, or if the victim is a business entity such as a corporation or partnership that has insurance to cover the loss and trial of the case would be time consuming and expensive, the prosecutor may decide not to prosecute.

In determining whether or not to use prosecutorial resources to prosecute a business entity such as a corporation or partnership, the prosecutor will usually consider some factors other than or in addition to those described above. One of those factors will be the effect of a conviction on the entity; specifically, whether a conviction will be tantamount to a death sentence for the entity. In some instances a conviction will bar the entity from engaging in the type of work that is its primary business. In those cases a conviction will almost always result in the dissolution of the entity.

Where a conviction will result in a corporate death sentence the prosecutor will need to consider the economic impact that a prosecution will have, what alternatives there are to a criminal prosecution, and whether the need to prosecute sufficiently outweighs the economic impact of a conviction. Some considerations affecting that decision would be the number of people who will be put out of work, how widespread the misconduct is within the entity (is it only management that is involved or is the misconduct endemic to the organization), and the macroeconomic effects of a conviction, such as whether prosecution will result in the dissolution of the only business entity in the community that provides a specific product or service or will have the effect of handing a competing entity a de facto monopoly.

Prosecutors can also establish initiatives against certain types of crime. These types of initiatives can range from things as simple as responding to community complaints about prostitutes soliciting on streets to responding to complaints from an industry about an upsurge in some form of criminal activity (such as mortgage fraud) that can have economic effects throughout the community or the United States. In these instances prosecutors can work with law enforcement to concentrate investigatory assets and dedicate prosecutors to assist law enforcement with investigations and ultimately prosecute the cases that such initiatives develop.

Because crime rates fluctuate and the rate at which certain types of crimes are committed change from time to time, prosecution policies are not static creations, but instead change as different types of criminal activity ebb and flow and different forms of crime evolve.

CHAPTER TERMS

Attorney general

Discretionary power

Judicial review

Nolle prosequi

REVIEW QUESTIONS

1. Who are the primary prosecutors of federal crimes and how are those prosecutors chosen?
2. What is the role of district attorneys in the American judicial system and how are they selected?
3. Who besides district attorneys prosecute crimes on a state level?
4. By what branch of government are prosecutors on the federal and state level usually employed?
5. What is the usual geographic jurisdiction of district attorneys?
6. What is prosecutorial discretion?
7. What is the principle of separation of powers?

OUTSIDE ASSIGNMENTS

1. What is the title of the person who prosecutes state crimes in the state where you live and what is that official's territorial jurisdiction?
2. How many federal districts are there in the state where you live and what are the names of those districts?

3. Are the federal districts in your state divided into divisions and, if they are, what are the names and locations of those divisions?

ADDITIONAL READING

Greg Farrell, *A Posthumous Victory*, U.S.A. Today (June 1, 2005), p.1B.

ENDNOTES

1. Wayne R. LaFave, Jerold Israel, Nancy J. King, and Orin Kerr, 1 *Criminal Procedure* §1.2(e) (3d Ed. Database Updated December 2014).
2. The U.S. Justice Department in Washington, D.C. has primary responsibility for prosecuting a limited group of offenses, primarily antitrust, civil rights, and environmental crimes. *Id.* at §1.4(e).
3. *See People v. Massarella*, 72 Ill. 2d 531 (1978).
4. *U.S. Const.*, Art. II, Sec. 3.
5. *See, e.g., Illinois Constitution (1970)*, Art. VI, Sec. 19.
6. *State v. Wharfield*, 41 Idaho 14 (1925).
7. *People ex rel. Daley v. Moran*, 94 Ill. 2d 41 (1983).
8. *Miller v. French*, 530 U.S. 327 (2000).
9. *See, e.g., Illinois Constitution (1970)*, Art. III, Sec. 2.
10. *United States v. Edmondson*, 792 F.2d 1492 (9th Cir. 1986).
11. *People v. Nohren*, 283 Ill. App. 3d 753 (4th Dist. 1996).
12. *See State ex rel. Clyde v. Lauder*, 11 N.D. 136 (1902).
13. *United States v. Roberson*, 474 F.3d 432 (7th Cir. 2007).

Criminal Law and Criminal Procedure

All law is either substantive or procedural. The chapter in this section examines the distinction between those two forms of law in the context of criminal law and criminal procedure.

Chapter 5
The Distinction Between Criminal Law and Criminal Procedure

Chapter Objectives

After reading this chapter, you should be able to

- Understand the importance of the distinction between substantive criminal law and criminal procedure
- Explain what substantive criminal law is
- Explain what criminal procedure is
- Explain the difference between substantive criminal law and criminal procedure

> The real significance of crime is in its being a breach of faith with the community of mankind.
> —Joseph Conrad,
> English Novelist

All law is either substantive or procedural and in the field of criminal justice both substantive criminal law and the law of criminal procedure play important roles. Substantive criminal law and criminal procedure are examined in depth in the next two sections of this textbook. Before examining either subject, however, it is useful to understand the difference between those two areas of law. This chapter examines that difference. Understanding the distinction between substantive criminal law and criminal procedure is important because whether a statute is substantive or procedural may, in some instances, determine whether it is constitutional or unconstitutional.

The ex post facto clause[1] of the U.S. Constitution prohibits the adoption of certain types of **ex post facto laws**. In particular, the clause prohibits the adoption of ex post facto substantive criminal laws, but does not bar the adoption of ex post facto procedural laws.[2] So, for example, if a statute is adopted that defines a new crime, that statute can only make it a crime to engage in the newly prohibited conduct from that point forward. The Constitution bars the adoption of a statute that makes it a crime to have engaged in certain conduct prior to its adoption. As a result, the ex post facto clause may, in the proper circumstance, be asserted as a defense to a criminal prosecution. (The assertion of the ex post facto clause as a defense is discussed more fully in Chapter 13.) In contrast, the legislature may adopt a statute that makes a change in criminal procedure that will be applicable both to the trial of cases involving crimes committed prior to the statute's enactment and the trial of cases involving crimes committed after the statute is adopted.

Ex post facto law is a law that (1) punishes conduct that was innocent when performed; (2) makes more burdensome the punishment for a crime, after its commission; (3) deprives one charged with a crime of any defense available at the time the act was committed; or (4) alters the legal rules of evidence to require less or different evidence to convict that the law required at the time the act was committed. *In re U.G.V.*, 193 S.W.3d 1 (Tex. App.—El Paso 2005).

A. Substantive Criminal Law

Generally, substantive law creates duties, rights, and obligations. In the field of criminal law, **substantive criminal law** declares what forms of conduct are crimes and states what the punishment is for engaging in that conduct.[3] In addition to declaring and defining what conduct constitutes a crime, substantive criminal law also defines the general legal principles that are applicable throughout the field of criminal law. For example, substantive criminal law uses terms such as "intent," "knowledge," and "willful" in the definition of almost every crime. Substantive criminal law provides the meaning of these terms as they are used in the definitions of criminal offenses and also defines defenses that nullify elements of offenses and that justify or excuse its commission, assuming an offense was committed.[4]

Substantive criminal law is the law that declares what forms of conduct are crimes and states what the punishment is for engaging in that conduct. *State v. Elmore*, 179 La. 1057 (1934).

B. Criminal Procedure

Generally, procedural law provides a method of enforcing and protecting the duties, rights, and obligations created by substantive law.[5] The body of law relating to **criminal procedure** consists of legal rules that govern the course of the proceedings that bring defendants into court and the course of the proceedings thereafter.[6]

Stated another way, the law of criminal procedure regulates the methods by which a criminal investigation is performed and how a

Criminal procedure is the body of legal rules that govern the course of the proceedings that bring defendants into court and the course of the proceedings thereafter. *State v. Elmore*, 179 La. 1057 (1934).

criminal prosecution is conducted. Thus, criminal procedure sets out rules that regulate the investigation of a crime, the charging of a person with the commission of a crime, the trial of a defendant after being charged, and, if convicted, the imposition of the sentence authorized by the substantive criminal law.

In the area of criminal investigation, criminal procedure specifies such things as: (1) the quantity of evidence that the police need before they can stop and question a person; (2) what the police need to do to be able to search private property; (3) the amount of evidence the police need to obtain a judicial order to conduct a search of private property; (4) the method by which a person who does not want to speak to the police may be compelled to answer law enforcement's questions; and (5) the rights of persons being questioned to refuse to answer incriminating questions.

As it relates to formally accusing someone of committing a crime, criminal procedure specifies: (1) the methods by which a criminal prosecution may be begun; (2) the time period, if any, within which a prosecution must be started; (3) the quantity of evidence needed to initiate a criminal prosecution; and (4) the quantity of evidence needed to make an arrest if the police decide to arrest without a warrant.

Once a person is charged with a crime, criminal procedure sets out the rules: (1) that regulate whether he will be allowed to remain free prior to trial; (2) that determine what disclosures must be made by the prosecution to the defense and by the defense to the prosecution prior to trial; (3) that specify the method by which the defendant's guilt is determined; (4) about who has the burden of proof at trial; and (5) about the extent to which the prosecution's evidence must convince the judge or jury of the defendant's guilt.

Upon conviction, criminal procedure determines: (1) how the judge will decide what sentence to impose; (2) what evidence the judge can consider in deciding on the sentence to impose; and (3) the rules relating to when and how an appeal from a conviction must be filed.

Today, most criminal procedure is determined by the provisions of the Fourth, Fifth, Sixth, and Eighth Amendments to the U.S. Constitution. Those and other procedural rights are examined in depth in Section IV of this book. To the extent that criminal procedure is not dictated by federal constitutional law and is instead regulated by statute, the legislative branch of government is free to change those procedures at any time. Such changes can affect the investigation and trial of and execution of sentences for crimes that were committed prior to the adoption of the new procedural statute. So, for example, the legislature can pass a statute that lengthens the **statute of limitations** for crimes that have been committed but for which the current statute of limitations has not yet expired[7] or pass a statute that changes the method by which a sentence may be carried out and have it apply to past crimes and previously imposed sentences.[8]

Statute of limitations in criminal law is a statute that establishes a fixed period of time following the occurrence of a criminal act within which a person may be prosecuted. *United States v. Ratcliff*, 245 F.3d 1246 (11th Cir. 2001). An act of grace through which the sovereign surrenders its right to prosecute. *People v. Ross*, 325 Ill. 417 (1927).

United States v. Knipp

United States Court of Appeals for the Sixth Circuit, 1992
963 F.2d 839

MILBURN, **Circuit Judge.** Defendants Barry L. Knipp and Vernon L. Hamilton appeal their jury convictions on one count of conspiracy (a) to defraud a federally insured financial institution and (b) to misapply the monies, funds, credits and securities of a federally insured financial institution in violation of 18 U.S.C. §371, and six related counts of aiding and abetting each other in devising a scheme to defraud federally insured financial institutions in violation of 18 U.S.C. §2 and §1344. On appeal, the issue * * * [is] whether Congress' extension of the statute of limitations from five years to ten years violates the Ex Post Facto Clause of the United States Constitution * * *. For the reasons that follow, we affirm. * * *

Defendant Barry L. Knipp was president of the People's Bank of Olive Hill, Kentucky ("PBOH"), and his co-defendant, Vernon L. Hamilton, was president of Hamilton Hardwood Lumber Company, Inc. ("HHLC"), a lumber business in Carter County, Kentucky. HHLC maintained a checking account at PBOH. Hamilton also maintained a checking account in the name of Hamilton Farms at the First National Bank of Grayson, Kentucky ("FNBG"). Both banks were insured by the FDIC.

In 1983 and early 1984, HHLC borrowed $1,200,000 from PBOH and also established a $750,000 ready reserve account that functioned as a demand loan to cover overdrafts up to $750,000. Defendant Knipp was the bank's account officer for all these loans. By November 1984, the ready reserve account established for HHLC had reached its $750,000 limit, but Hamilton continued to write checks on the account which drove it into an overdraft status. By March 1985, the HHLC account had been over drafted to the extent of $552,153.06. Because PBOH was at its legal lending limits with HHLC, and in order to disguise the overdraft status of the account, a check kiting system was set up by defendant Hamilton to cycle checks between the HHLC account at PBOH and the Hamilton Farms account at FNBG.

According to various employees of PBOH, the kite was operated by the daily transfer of checks, drawn on uncollected funds, between the two banks. On instructions from defendant Knipp, employees of PBOH kept a daily watch on HHLC's checking account for overdrafts beyond the $750,000 ready reserve fund. When an overdraft check was presented, payment of it was delayed while a telephone call was placed to defendant Hamilton to advise him of the amount of the deposit he would be required to make to cover the overdraft. Hamilton would then deposit at PBOH one or more checks drawn on the Hamilton Farms account at FNBG. As the amount of the overdrafts spiraled upward, Hamilton was required to come to PBOH daily and deposit checks drawn on the Hamilton Farms account at FNBG to cover HHLC's overdrafts. He kept the Hamilton Farms account stocked with checks written on the HHLC account at PBOH. * * *

Matters began coming to a head in February 1985 when FNBG installed a new computer system that could track floats on items being deposited in that bank. The Hamilton Farms account immediately appeared on that new report with a large uncollected balance in excess of $200,000. In investigating the Hamilton Farms account, FNBG's controller determined that 3, 4, or 5 checks, all for different amounts, and totaling between $230,000 and $250,000, were being written and deposited back and forth between the Hamilton Farms account at FNBG and the HHLC account at PBOH on a daily basis. The same number of checks in the same amounts were being deposited each day. * * *

Both defendants argue that the district court should have granted their motions to dismiss this case because it was brought in violation of the Ex Post Facto provisions of Article 1, Section 9, of the United States Constitution. * * * The date of the last offense mentioned in the indictment is April 30, 1985, and the statute of limitations in effect on that date was the five-year limitations period established by 18 U.S.C. §2382. On August 9, 1989, before the five-year statute of limitations ran as to this case, Congress enacted 18 U.S.C. §3293, which extended the limitations period applicable to the offense as charged from five years to ten years. Defendants were indicted on July 24, 1990. Therefore, the old five-year statute of limitations had run, but the new ten-year statute had not. * * *

Pleading an expired limitations period is certainly a defense in the general sense that it is a defensive measure. More particularly, however, it is a matter in bar of prosecution and as such is distinguishable from a "pure" defense, which defeats one or more of the elements of the crime. This distinction was noted and strongly reinforced by the Court in *Youngblood* when the Court, after an extended analysis, decided to overrule *Kring v. Missouri*, 107 U.S. 221 (1883), because in *Kring* it had erred in confusing procedural defenses with defenses to the elements of the crime. Focusing on the meaning of the word "defense" as used in the quotation from *Beazell* and applying it to *Kring*, the Court said:

> But the use of the word "defense" carries a meaning quite different from that which appears in the quoted language from *Beazell*, where the term was linked to the prohibition on alterations in "the legal definition of the offense" or "the nature or amount of the punishment imposed for its commission." *Beazell*, 269 U.S., at 169-170. The "defense" available to *Kring* under earlier Missouri law *was not one related to the definition of the crime*, but was based on the law regulating the effect of guilty pleas. Missouri had not changed any of the elements of the crime of murder, or the matters which might be pleaded as an excuse or justification for the conduct underlying such a charge; it had changed its law respecting the effect of a guilty plea to a lesser included offense.

Youngblood, 110 S. Ct. at 2723 (emphasis added).

Thus, "defense" as used in *Beazell* means a defense related to the definition or elements of the crime. It does not have the much broader meaning assigned to it by defendants, because a plea in bar is not related to the definition of a crime and is not pleaded as a nullification of one or more of its elements or as an excuse or justification for its commission. Accordingly, defendants' reliance on *Youngblood* is entirely misplaced.

Moreover, the courts of appeals considering this issue have held that the extension of a limitations period before that period has run does not violate the Ex Post Facto Clause. In *United States ex rel. Massarella v. Elrod,* 682 F.2d 688, 689 (7th Cir. 1982), *cert. denied,* 460 U.S. 1037, 103 S. Ct. 1426, 75 L. Ed. 2d 787 (1983), the Seventh Circuit held that the extension of a period of limitations was procedural only and did not implicate the Ex Post Facto Clause. * * *

The Second Circuit in *Falter v. United States,* 23 F.2d 420, 425 (2d Cir.), *cert. denied,* 277 U.S. 590 (1928), and the Ninth Circuit in *Clements v. United States,* 266 F.2d 397, 399 (9th Cir.), *cert. denied,* 359 U.S. 985 (1959), also concluded that extensions of limitations periods do not implicate the Ex Post Facto Clause. Although this circuit has not directly decided this issue, it has stated that "a change in the law which is procedural is not *ex post facto* even though it may work to the disadvantage of the defendant." *United States v. Prickett,* 790 F.2d 35, 37 (6th Cir. 1986).

The defensive use of a statute of limitations is a procedural defense in the nature of a plea in bar. Because it has nothing to do with the internal structure of the crime or its elements, it is not the kind of "defense" that the Supreme Court was referring to in *Beazell* when it stated that the Ex Post Facto Clause was violated if a defendant was later deprived of a defense that had been available to him at the time he committed the crime in question. Instead, the defensive use of a statute of limitations is merely a procedural matter, and it follows that Congress' extension of the statute of limitations in this case did not violate the Ex Post Facto Clause. * * *

For the foregoing reasons, the judgment of the district court is *AFFIRMED.*

Case Focus

1. Why is a change to a defense to a criminal prosecution such as the statute of limitations not subject to the ex post facto clauses of the U.S. Constitution?
2. In this case how did the court distinguish a procedural law from a substantive law?

● ● ● ● ● ● ● ●

CHAPTER TERMS

Criminal procedure   Statute of limitations
Ex post facto law   Substantive criminal law

REVIEW QUESTIONS

1. Why is the distinction between substantive criminal law and criminal procedure important?
2. What type of laws are considered to be substantive criminal law?

3. What type of laws are considered to be procedural?

ENDNOTES

1. *U.S. Const.*, Art. I, Sec. 10.
2. *Dobbert v. Florida*, 432 U.S. 282 (1977).
3. *State v. Elmore*, 179 La. 1057 (1934).
4. *United States v. Knipp*, 963 F.2d 839 (6th Cir. 1992).
5. *Elmore*, 179 La. at 1057.
6. *Id.*
7. *Knipp*, 963 F.3d at 839.
8. *Malloy v. South Carolina*, 237 U.S. 180 (1901).

Substantive Criminal Law

Substantive criminal law is concerned with six broad subjects: (1) the power of a sovereign to apply its criminal law to persons engaged in conduct that sovereign has defined to be criminal; (2) the limits on the power of a government to enact criminal law; (3) the definition and punishment of criminal offenses; (4) the definition of general principles applicable throughout the criminal law; (5) the establishment of principles that make a person accountable under the law for criminal conduct in which he or another has engaged; and (6) the definition of defenses that can prevent a finding of guilt in a criminal case. The chapters contained in this section examine those subjects.

Chapter 6
Principles of Criminal Jurisdiction Recognized by Customary International Law

Chapter Objectives

After reading this chapter, you should be able to

- Understand the substantive law concept of legislative jurisdiction and how it applies in criminal law
- Understand the two ways by which legislative jurisdiction may be established
- Explain the principles of legislative jurisdiction recognized by customary international law
- Understand what admiralty jurisdiction is
- Understand the two aspects of the territorial principle of legislative jurisdiction

Under domestic law, statutes supersede customary international law and no enactment of Congress can be challenged on the ground that it violates customary international law. —*Oliva v. U.S. Department of Justice*, 433 F.3d 229 (2d Cir. 2005)

In criminal practice, jurisdiction has a substantive aspect, which is the subject of this chapter, and a procedural aspect. The substantive aspect of jurisdiction is called **legislative jurisdiction** and refers to the power

71

of a sovereign to apply its law to prescribe or regulate conduct.[1] The procedural aspect of jurisdiction is called **adjudicative jurisdiction** and refers to the power of a court to subject a particular person or thing to the judicial process.[2] Adjudicative jurisdiction is examined in Chapter 19. The most frequently litigated jurisdictional issues in criminal cases are issues of legislative jurisdiction.

Historically, legislative jurisdiction was seldom an issue in criminal prosecutions because the *actus reus* of criminal offenses was almost always committed and took effect in the prosecuting jurisdiction. That changed with the creation of the Internet and the rise in the late twentieth century of transnational terrorism. The Internet has made it easy for perpetrators of fraud schemes and criminal acts directed at networks and servers to initiate their crimes thousands of miles from where those schemes and acts take effect. At the same time, the phenomenon of transnational terrorism has given rise to targeted attacks planned in one nation and perpetrated against another nation's citizens and interests abroad as well as within that other nation's borders.

Nations establish legislative jurisdiction over the perpetrators of transnational and other crimes through either A) principles of customary international law or B) their own domestic law. The extent to which a nation can exercise legislative jurisdiction and the manner in which that power is allocated within a nation's political system is determined by the nation's domestic statutory and constitutional law. For example, a nation's legislative branch may choose to exercise legislative jurisdiction under only one of the several jurisdictional principles recognized by customary international law or a nation's constitution may impose limits on the exercise of legislative jurisdiction under any of those principles and on any statutory assertion of legislative jurisdiction not connected to them. This chapter examines the two methods of establishing legislative jurisdiction. How the power to exercise legislative jurisdiction is allocated in the American political system and the constitutional limits on its exercise is examined in Chapter 7.

A. Customary International Law as a Basis of Legislative Jurisdiction

Customary international law recognizes five different principles under which a sovereign can exercise legislative jurisdiction. Those five principles can be divided into two broad categories: (1) territorial principles and (2) non-territorial principles. The distinction between the territorial and non-territorial jurisdictional principles is important. A principle of American law which is applicable to criminal statutes

What Is Customary International Law?

Customary international law is one of the two major sources of international law. (The other major source is treaties.) A practice of nations develops into a rule of customary international law when: (1) there is a general and consistent practice of nations following the principle and (2) nations follow the principle from a sense of legal obligation. *Restatement (Third) of Foreign Relations Law*, §102(2) (1987). There is no agreement on the number of nations that must consistently follow a practice to transform it into a rule of customary international law. Instead of a specific number, it has been said that to transform a practice into a rule, the practice of nations should be "both extensive and virtually uniform in the sense of the provision invoked." *The North Sea Continental Shelf Case (Judgment)*, 1969 I.C.J. 12. In addition, before a practice can become recognized as a rule of customary international law, within the relevant nations the will has to be formed that the practice will become law. *Committee of United States Citizens Living in Nicaragua v. Reagan*, 859 F.2d 929 (D.C. Cir. 1988). The result is that customary international law is continuously evolving and there is no clear-cut point at which a practice of nations becomes a rule of law.

is that unless a contrary intent appears, Congressional legislation is meant to apply only within the territorial jurisdiction of the United States.[3] When a statute is applied under a territorial principle, even if it is being applied to extra-territorial conduct, it is not being applied extra-territorially[4] and thus, there is no need to examine Congressional intent as to its extra-territorial application.[5]

1. *Territorial Principle*

The territorial principle of customary international law is based on the premise that a sovereign has the power to make conduct that occurs or produces effects within his borders criminal. The territorial principle also has application to questions of admiralty jurisdiction. There are two aspects of the territorial principle: (1) the subjective aspect and (2) the objective aspect.

a. Subjective Aspect

Under the subjective aspect of the territorial principle a sovereign is recognized as having the power to apply his criminal laws to persons who commit crimes within his borders. Criminal conduct occurs within a sovereign's borders, without regard to where the defendant was when he performed the act proscribed by the statute, when the *actus reus* of the offense takes effect there. For example, under this aspect of the territorial principle the sovereign has the power to apply his criminal law to a person within his borders who shoots and kills another person who is also within the sovereign's borders and to a person who from outside of the sovereign's borders fires a shot that strikes and kills a person within the sovereign's borders.

b. Objective Aspect

The objective aspect of the territorial principle provides that a sovereign has jurisdiction to apply his criminal law to a person who commits a crime wholly outside of the sovereign's borders that has or is intended to have a substantial and detrimental effect within the sovereign's territory.[6] The substantial effect element of this aspect of the principle is liberally construed.

For example, when a woman on a cruise ship that was owned by a Panamanian corporation and registered in Liberia was sexually assaulted by a non-U.S. national while the ship was in international waters, the United States could exercise jurisdiction to prosecute the perpetrator because the victim, who was a resident of the United States, needed to undergo psychiatric counseling that would be done in the United States, and because the FBI had to conduct an investigation of the offense when the ship docked.[7]

The objective aspect of the territorial principle has proven to be particularly useful as a basis for prosecuting persons who from outside a state or the United States devise schemes to defraud Americans in the United States and for prosecuting those persons who launch cyberattacks or release computer viruses from outside the United States on servers and computers located within the United States, because such schemes and acts have substantial negative effects within a state or the United States. That principle has also been useful in prosecuting conspiracies to distribute controlled substances in the United States even when no act in furtherance of the conspiracy has been performed here.

The objective aspect of the territorial principle can also be the basis of applying American criminal statutes to terrorists outside the United States who conspire to commit terrorist acts against American citizens or property located within the United States, even if the act in furtherance of the conspiracy is committed outside of American borders. For example, when in connection with a conspiracy to launch an agroterrorist attack on the United States, a member of the conspiracy obtains equipment in the Middle East with which to culture hoof and mouth disease and also obtains a culture of the disease from the same general area for the purpose of breeding it and releasing it in the United States, the United States has jurisdiction to prosecute the members of the conspiracy because the crime is intended to produce substantial negative effects in the United States, notwithstanding that none of the members of the conspiracy ever entered the United States and notwithstanding that none of the acts in furtherance of the conspiracy were committed here.

c. Application of the Territorial Principle to Admiralty Jurisdiction

Admiralty jurisdiction involves a special application of the territorial principle. Ships of a sovereign are considered to be part of the sovereign's territory while the ships are on the high seas.[8] Therefore, under the principles of admiralty jurisdiction a sovereign is considered to have the power to apply his criminal laws to those who commit crimes on the sovereign's ships while they are on the high seas. Thus, the existence of a sovereign's admiralty jurisdiction is determined by whether his ship is on the high seas.

For purposes of criminal law, the term "high seas" includes the seas and the waters that are tributary to them to the extent that those waters are navigable.[9] So, for example, when a murder was committed on an American ship that was docked 250 miles up the Congo River from the sea, the United States had the power to prosecute the perpetrator of the crime under its admiralty jurisdiction despite the fact the ship was within the territorial waters of another nation.[10]

United States v. Davis

Circuit Court, D. Massachusetts, 1837 25 Fed. Cases 786

Indictment against James Davis for manslaughter of a person, whose name was unknown, against the act of 1790, c. 36, §12 (1 Story's Laws, 84 [1 Stat. 115, c. 9]). There were two counts, one stating the offence to be committed on the high seas; the other containing a special statement of all the circumstances as to locality, &c. Plea, not guilty.

At the trial, it appeared in evidence from the testimony of the mate, that the defendant (Davis), was master of the ship Rose, an American whale ship. The ship sailed on the voyage in August, 1833. In the course of the voyage, the ship arrived at the island of Raiatea, one of the Society Islands, where she lay for ten or twelve days to recruit, and to cooper her oil. While lying there, a schooner came alongside, which belonged to some persons, who were residents of one of the islands, and was tied to the ship. The deceased was one of the crew of that schooner. Some difficulty having occurred with an Irishman who did not belong to the ship, but was employed on board; and the defendant (Davis) ordered him to be tied up and flogged, which was accordingly done by the mate. The deceased at that time came on board of the ship, and said to the defendant, Captain Davis, do not strike the man across the loins. The defendant told him to go out of the ship, and he immediately left the ship and went on board of the schooner. The Irishman was then put in irons. Sometime after, the * * * crew of the * * * Rose came on board and refused to do duty, while the Irishman remained in irons. The defendant told them to go to work. They still refused, and one of them (a blackman) took up a handspike. The defendant had previously sent for his gun below, and then had it in his hands; and the blackman having the handspike, said to him; 'Shoot straight, if you do not shoot me I will kill you.' The defendant then ordered the mate to put the blackman in irons; and while the mate was doing it, the gun, then in the captain's hands, went off, and the mate, upon looking up, saw the deceased was shot, and fall instantly dead on the deck of the schooner. How the gun went off, whether purposely or not, did not appear. The defendant then went below. The deceased had not taken any part in his affray, and was all the time on board of the schooner until he was shot. An examination was afterwards had before the American consul at the island, and the defendant was sent home for trial. From the testimony it further appeared, that the deceased was not an American but was a foreigner, and was believed to be an Englishman. From the testimony and other evidence, it farther appeared, that the island of Raiatea is surrounded or in a great part surrounded by a coral reef, which forms a fine harbor, a half mile wide from the reef to the island. * * * The ship and schooner, at the time of the occurrence, lay within the reef about one hundred and fifty yards from the shore of the island, about two miles from one of the entrances. The place was commonly called a harbor or port.

Upon this evidence obtained from the witness for the government; Choate for the defendant, without going into any evidence on his side, cited 3 Murray, Enc. Geography, art. Raiatea, p. 159, and 2 Malte Brun, Geography, p. 294, and contended, that upon the government's own evidence, the court had no jurisdiction of the case. He said, that he was prepared to show, that no offence had been committed; but that the defendant had good reason to suppose, that his gun was not loaded, and only pointed it for intimidation; and that he had been tried before the king of the Society Islands, and had been acquitted. But, as he thought, the offence, if any, was not within the jurisdiction of the court. He cited *U.S. v. McGill*, 4 Dall. [4 U.S.] 426. * * *

Mr. Mills, Dist. Atty., said he was willing to submit the case upon the evidence, to the court and jury.

Story, Circuit Justice.

We are of opinion, that under the circumstances established in evidence, there is no jurisdiction in this cause. The crimes act of 1790 (chapter 36, §12), on which this indictment is founded, gives to this court jurisdiction of the crime of manslaughter only when committed 'on the high seas.' [We need not decide whether the place where the offense was committed was the high seas.] * * *

What we found ourselves upon in this case, is, that the offence, if any, was committed, not on board of the American ship Rose; but on board of a foreign schooner belonging to inhabitants of the Society Islands, and of course, under the territorial government of the king of the Society Islands, with which kingdom we have trade, and friendly intercourse, and which our government may be presumed (since we have a consul there) to recognize as entitled to the rights and sovereignty of an independent nation, and of course entitled to try offences committed within its territorial jurisdiction. I say the offence was committed on board of the schooner; for although the gun was fired from the ship Rose, the shot took effect and the death happened on board of the schooner; and the act was, in contemplation of law, done where the shot took effect. So the law was settled in the case of *Rex v. Coombes*, 1 Leach. 388, where a person on the high seas was killed by a shot fired by a person on shore, and the offence was held to be committed on the high seas, and to be within the admiralty jurisdiction. Of offences committed on the high seas on board of foreign vessels (not being a piratical vessel,) but belonging to persons under the acknowledged government of a foreign country, this court has no jurisdiction under the act of 1790 (chapter 36, §12). That was the doctrine of the supreme court in *U.S. v. Palmer*, 3 Wheat. [16 U.S.] 610, * * * . We lay no stress on the fact that the deceased was a foreigner. Our judgment would be the same, if he had been an American citizen. We decide the case wholly on the ground, that the schooner was a foreign vessel, belonging to foreigners, and at the time under the acknowledged jurisdiction of a foreign government. We think, that under such circumstances, the jurisdiction over the offence belonged to the foreign government, and not to the courts of the United States under the act of congress.

The jury immediately returned a verdict of not guilty.

Case Focus

1. Where did the court decide the crime alleged in this case occurred? What reason did the court give for that decision?
2. The shot that killed the victim was fired from the American ship, *Rose*, by one of the ship's officers. Why did the U.S. government not have jurisdiction to prosecute the defendant for the alleged crime?

• • • • • • • •

2. Non-Territorial Principles of Jurisdiction

Customary international law also recognizes four non-territorial principles of criminal jurisdiction. Under those principles a sovereign has the power to apply his criminal law to conduct that occurs outside of his territory even if the conduct does not take effect in or produce negative effects within the sovereign's territory. Exercise of jurisdiction under the non-territorial principles may be based on the nationality of the perpetrator, the nature or nationality of the victim, or, in some instances, the nature of the offense itself.

One of the non-territorial jurisdiction principles recognized by customary international law is called the protective principle, under which a sovereign may apply his criminal statutes to a person outside of his borders when the conduct of that person affects the sovereign himself. For example, under the protective principle the United States can prosecute persons who make false representations at an American embassy in a foreign country for the purpose of obtaining a visa to enter the United States[11] or can prosecute the persons who blew up the American embassies in Tanzania and Kenya.[12] The protective principle has also been used to prosecute persons who engage in espionage against the United States.

United States v. Zehe

United States District Court, D. Mass (1985) 601 F. Supp. 196

NELSON, J. The United States government brings this criminal prosecution under the Espionage Act (the Act), 18 U.S.C. §§792-799, against Alfred Zehe, an East German citizen, for alleged acts of espionage against the United States committed in Mexico and the German Democratic Republic. Zehe moves for dismissal of the indictment, contending that the Act fails to confer jurisdiction over acts of espionage committed outside of this country's territorial boundaries by persons who are not citizens of the United States. [This jurisdictional inquiry arguably is only pertinent to the Counts Two through Eight because these counts allege substantive offenses occurring wholly outside United States territory.] This Court on January 2, 1985 denied the defendant's motion and now offers this Memorandum Opinion in support of that ruling.

The Espionage Act proscribes various acts of collecting and disclosing national defense information to a foreign nation. The defendant is charged under §§793(b), 794(a) and 794(c) of the Act in eight counts alleging that he (1) unlawfully sought and obtained information regarding this country's national defense, (2) delivered that information to the German Democratic Republic, and (3) conspired to deliver such information, all with the intent that the information be used to the injury of the United States or to the advantage of the German Democratic Republic. * * * These sections do not, nor does the Act elsewhere, define the territorial scope of the Act.

There is no question, nor does Zehe contest, that the Act applies to extra-territorial acts of espionage committed by citizens. Although no provision of the Act explicitly so states, the courts have consistently inferred such extraterritorial application to citizens when the proscribed offense tended to impair important governmental functions and when the United States government was vulnerable to the offense regardless of where it was committed. *See United States v. Bowman*, 260 U.S. 94, 98, 67 L. Ed. 149, 43 S. Ct. 39 (1922) (fraud against a government corporation); *United States v. Cotten*, 471 F.2d 744, 749-51 (9th Cir. 1973) (theft of government property); *United States v. Birch*, 470 F.2d 808, 811-12 (4th Cir. 1972) (forgery or false use of government documents). In these three cases, the courts expressly relied upon the nature of the offenses, and not just upon the citizenship of the defendants, in order to apply other criminal statutes extraterritorially to citizens. Because espionage is an offense threatening the national security of the United States, regardless of where it occurs, the Court readily concludes that the Espionage Act was meant to apply extraterritorially to citizens. * * *

Nor is there any dispute that Congress has the power to prosecute both citizens and non-citizens for espionage committed outside of this country's territorial limits. The defendant concedes that under principles of international law recognized by United States courts, Congress is competent to punish criminal acts, wherever and by whomever committed, that threaten national security or directly obstruct governmental functions. *See, e.g., United States v. Bowman*, 260 U.S. at 98 * * *. [The defendant also acknowledges that the protective principle, though rarely used, has been a part of the jurisprudence of this country both before 1961 and in 1961, when Congress enacted the statutory amendment at issue here. Under international law, the "protective principle" gives a country the jurisdiction to prescribe a rule of law attaching legal consequences to conduct outside its territory that threatens its security as a state or the operation of its governmental functions, provided the conduct is generally recognized as a crime under the law of states that have a reasonably developed legal system.] * * *

The defendant, while agreeing that the Espionage Act has extraterritorial application to citizens and that Congress is empowered to assert extraterritorial jurisdiction over non-citizens as well as citizens, nonetheless contends that the Act was not meant to apply to non-citizens acting entirely outside of the United States. [Under the defendant's reading of the Act, courts could assert extraterritorial jurisdiction over non-citizens in just two situations: 1) in cases where a non-citizen while abroad had conspired with a citizen to collect or disseminate defense information of the United States, even if no act occurred within this country, and 2) in cases where a non-citizen while abroad had conspired with another non-citizen who committed over acts in the United States.]

Zehe asserts that in order to apply a criminal statute to acts committed by non-citizens beyond this country's territorial boundaries, there must be a strong and clear showing of congressional intent. In the case of the Espionage Act, the defendant maintains that the legislative history behind the repeal of §791's territorial language unmistakably supports the conclusion that Congress intended to reach only the extraterritorial actions of citizens. * * *

The defendant relies on various references in the legislative record to argue that Congress did not intend to assert jurisdiction over actions of non-citizens while abroad. * * *

The Court does not find the defendant's legislative evidence persuasive. * * *

The Court finds that the Act may be applied extraterritorially to both citizens and non-citizens because of the threat to national security that espionage poses. It is for the foregoing reasons that this Court denied the defendant's motion to dismiss for lack of subject matter jurisdiction.

Case Focus

1. The defendant in this case was not a U.S. citizen and the crime he committed was committed from outside the United States. On what jurisdictional principle was the application of American criminal law to him based?

2. Explain how that principle was applicable in the case against Zehe.

• • • • • • • •

A second non-territorial jurisdiction principle recognized by customary international law is the nationality principle, under which a sovereign can enact criminal laws that make certain conduct engaged in by his nationals overseas a crime. Under the nationality principle, for example, Congress has made it a crime for American nationals to pay bribes to foreign government officials outside of the United States.[13]

A third non-territorial jurisdiction principle recognized by customary international law is called the passive personal principle, under which a sovereign may apply his criminal law to persons who commit crimes outside of the sovereign's territory against a person who is a national of the sovereign.[14] The passive personal principle dates back at least 200 years but has been infrequently used and is somewhat controversial. In fact it is only recently that the United States has recognized the passive personal principle and chosen to exercise power under it.[15]

The fourth non-territorial principle of criminal jurisdiction recognized by customary international law is the universal principle, under which a sovereign has the power to enact criminal laws and apply them, without regard to the nationality of the perpetrator or victim, to any persons who violate those laws anywhere in the world. For example, under this principle, if Congress passes a law making piracy a federal crime,[16] and if the U.S. Navy were to capture a ship of Somali pirates in the Indian Ocean who had engaged in piratical actions solely against Japanese and Indian merchant ships, those pirates could be tried for violating American piracy laws despite the fact that the pirates committed no crimes against American citizens, were not American citizens themselves, and the crimes had no effect within the United States.

Traditionally, universal jurisdiction has been limited to such matters of universal concern as piracy and engaging in the slave trade. In recent years the universal principle has been extended to include airline hijacking, genocide, and to some acts of terrorism.[17]

Customary international law imposes an important limitation on the ability of a sovereign to exercise legislative jurisdiction under any of the five principles just examined. Assuming one of the bases for exercising legislative jurisdiction under customary international law exists, a sovereign cannot exercise jurisdiction to prescribe law with respect to a person or activity having a connection with another sovereign when it would be unreasonable to do so.[18] Customary international law looks at various factors considered to be relevant to determining reasonableness. There are two clear cases in which it is not unreasonable to exercise legislative jurisdiction over a person or activity having a connection to another sovereign: 1) when the condemned conduct or condemned result is universally condemned[19], and 2) when the condemned conduct or condemned result is condemned by all sovereigns that could assert jurisdiction.[20]

B. Domestic Law as a Basis of Legislative Jurisdiction

The principles of customary international law examined above purport to define the extent to which a nation has the power to apply its criminal laws to regulate conduct or a result. Customary international law, however, does not trump a nation's domestic law. A nation's domestic law decides whether the nation will recognize the limits of customary international law. Thus, when pursuing the prosecution of a defendant for a crime, a nation can ignore the principles of customary international law and for purposes of its domestic law still render a valid verdict.[21] Accordingly, a nation may use its domestic law as a basis for exercising legislative jurisdiction when legislative jurisdiction under customary international law is not possible.

United States v. Yunis

United States Court of Appeals, District of Columbia Circuit, 1991 924 F.2d 1086

Mɪᴋᴠᴀ, **Chief Judge**. Appellant Fawaz Yunis challenges his convictions on conspiracy, aircraft piracy, and hostage-taking charges stemming from the hijacking of a Jordanian passenger aircraft in Beirut, Lebanon. He appeals from orders of the district court denying his pretrial motion relating to jurisdiction * * *.

Although this appeal raises novel issues of domestic and international law, we reject Yunis' objections and affirm the convictions.

I. BACKGROUND

On June 11, 1985, appellant and four other men boarded Royal Jordanian Airlines Flight 402 ("Flight 402") shortly before its scheduled departure from Beirut, Lebanon. They wore civilian clothes and carried military assault rifles, ammunition bandoleers, and hand grenades. Appellant took control of the cockpit and forced the pilot to take off immediately. The remaining hijackers tied up Jordanian air marshals assigned to the flight and held the civilian passengers, including two American citizens, captive in their seats. The hijackers explained to the crew and passengers that they wanted the plane to fly to Tunis, where a conference of the Arab League was under way. The hijackers further explained that they wanted a meeting with delegates to the conference and that their ultimate goal was removal of all Palestinians from Lebanon.

After a refueling stop in Cyprus, the airplane headed for Tunis but turned away when authorities blocked the airport runway. Following a refueling stop at Palermo, Sicily, another attempt to land in Tunis, and a second stop in Cyprus, the plane returned to Beirut, where more hijackers came aboard. These reinforcements included an official of Lebanon's Amal Militia, the group at whose direction Yunis claims he acted. The plane then took off for Syria, but was turned away and went back to Beirut. There, the hijackers released the passengers, held a press conference reiterating their demand that Palestinians leave Lebanon, blew up the plane, and fled from the airport.

An American investigation identified Yunis as the probable leader of the hijackers and prompted U.S. civilian and military agencies, led by the Federal Bureau of Investigation (FBI), to plan Yunis' arrest. After obtaining an arrest warrant, the FBI put "Operation Goldenrod" into effect in September 1987. Undercover FBI agents lured Yunis onto a yacht in the eastern Mediterranean Sea with promises of a drug deal, and arrested him once the vessel entered international waters. The agents transferred Yunis to a United States Navy munitions ship and interrogated him for several days as the vessel steamed toward a second rendezvous, this time with a Navy aircraft carrier. Yunis was flown to Andrews Air Force Base from the aircraft carrier, and taken from there to

Washington, D.C. In Washington, Yunis was arraigned on an original indictment charging him with conspiracy, hostage taking, and aircraft damage. A grand jury subsequently returned a superseding indictment adding additional aircraft damage counts and a charge of air piracy. * * *

Yunis admitted participation in the hijacking at trial but denied parts of the government's account and offered the affirmative defense of obedience to military orders, asserting that he acted on instructions given by his superiors in Lebanon's Amal Militia. The jury convicted Yunis of conspiracy, 18 U.S.C. §371 (1988), hostage taking, 18 U.S.C. §1203 (1988), and air piracy, 49 U.S.C. App. §1472(n) (1988) [and acquitted him of the other charged offenses]. * * * The district court imposed concurrent sentences of five years for conspiracy, thirty years for hostage taking, and twenty years for air piracy. Yunis appeals his conviction and seeks dismissal of the indictment.

II. ANALYSIS

Yunis argues that the district court lacked subject matter * * * jurisdiction to try him on the charges of which he was convicted.

A. Jurisdictional Claims

Yunis appeals first of all from the district court's denial of his motion to dismiss for lack of subject matter * * * jurisdiction. *See United States v. Yunis,* 681 F. Supp. 896 (D.D.C. 1988). Appellant's principal claim is that, as a matter of domestic law, the federal hostage taking and air piracy statutes do not authorize assertion of federal jurisdiction over him. Yunis also suggests that a contrary construction of these statutes would conflict with established principles of international law, and so should be avoided by this court.

1. Hostage Taking Act

The Hostage Taking Act provides, in relevant part: (a) [W]hoever, whether inside or outside the United States, seizes or detains and threatens to kill, to injure, or to continue to detain another person in order to compel a third person or a governmental organization to do or to abstain from any act . . . shall be punished by imprisonment by any term of years or for life. (b)(1) It is not an offense under this section if the conduct required for the offense occurred outside the United States unless—(A) the offender or the person seized or detained is a national of the United States; (B) the offender is found in the United States; or (c) the governmental organization sought to be compelled is the Government of the United States. 18 U.S.C. §1203.

Yunis claims that this statute cannot apply to an individual who is brought to the United States by force, since those convicted under it must be "found in the United States." But this ignores the law's plain language. Subsections (A), (B), and (C) of section 1203(b)(1) offer *independent* bases for jurisdiction where "the offense occurred outside the United States." Since two of the passengers on Flight 402 were U.S. citizens, section 1203(b)(1)(A), authorizing assertion of U.S. jurisdiction where "the offender or the person seized or detained is a national of the United States," is satisfied. The statute's jurisdictional requirement has been met regardless of whether or not Yunis was "found" within the United States under section 1203(b)(1)(B).

Appellant's argument that we should read the Hostage Taking Act differently to avoid tension with international law falls flat. Yunis points to no treaty obligations of the United States that give us pause. Indeed, Congress intended through the Hostage Taking Act to execute the International Convention Against the Taking of Hostages, which authorizes any signatory state to exercise jurisdiction over persons who take its nationals hostage "if that State considers it appropriate." International Convention Against the Taking of Hostages, *opened for signature* Dec. 18, 1979, art. 5, para. 1, 34 U.N. GAOR Supp. (No. 39), 18 I.L.M. 1456, 1458. *See* H.R. CONF. REP. No. 1159, 98th Cong., 2d Sess. Page 1091 418 (1984), *reprinted in* 1984 U.S. CODE CONG. & ADMIN.NEWS 3182, 3710, 3714.

Nor is jurisdiction precluded by norms of customary international law. The district court concluded that two jurisdictional theories of international law, the "universal principle" and the "passive personal principle," supported assertion of U.S. jurisdiction to prosecute Yunis on hijacking and hostage-taking charges. *See Yunis,* 681 F. Supp. at 899-903. * * *

Relying primarily on the RESTATEMENT, Yunis argues that hostage taking has not been recognized as a universal crime and that the passive personal principle authorizes assertion of jurisdiction over alleged hostage takers only where the victims were seized because they were nationals of the prosecuting state. Whatever merit appellant's claims may have as a matter of international law, they cannot prevail before this court. Yunis seeks to portray international law as a self-executing code that trumps domestic law whenever the two conflict. That effort misconceives the role of judges as appliers of international law and as participants in the federal system. Our duty is to enforce the Constitution, laws, and treaties of the United States, not to conform the law of the land to norms of customary international law. *See* U.S. CONST. art. VI. As we said in *Committee of U.S. Citizens Living in Nicaragua v. Reagan,* 859 F.2d 929 (D.C. Cir. 1988): "Statutes inconsistent with principles of customary international law may well lead to international law violations. But within the domestic legal realm, that inconsistent statute simply modifies or supersedes customary international law to the extent of the inconsistency." *Id.* at 938. *See also Federal Trade Comm'n v. Compagnie de Saint-Gobain-Pont-a-Mousson,* 636 F.2d 1300, 1323 (D.C. Cir. 1980) (U.S. courts "obligated to give effect to an unambiguous exercise by Congress of its jurisdiction to prescribe even if such an exercise would exceed the limitations imposed by international law").

To be sure, courts should hesitate to give penal statutes extraterritorial effect absent a clear congressional directive. *See Foley Bros. v. Filardo,* 336 U.S. 281,

285, 69 S. Ct. 575, 577, 93 L. Ed. 680 (1949); *United States v. Bowman,* 260 U.S. 94, 98, 43 S. Ct. 39, 41, 67 L. Ed. 149 (1922). Similarly, courts will not blind themselves to potential violations of international law where legislative intent is ambiguous. *See Murray v. The Schooner Charming Betsy,* 6 U.S. (2 Cranch) 64, 118, 2 L. Ed. 208 (1804) ("[A]n act of congress ought never to be construed to violate the law of nations, if any other possible construction remains. . . ."). But the statute in question reflects an unmistakable congressional intent, consistent with treaty obligations of the United States, to authorize prosecution of those who take Americans hostage abroad no matter where the offense occurs or where the offender is found. Our inquiry can go no further. * * *

III. CONCLUSION

For the foregoing reasons, the convictions are
   Affirmed.

Case Focus

1. If there is a conflict between customary international law and American domestic law, which law must an American court follow?
2. What reasons does the court give for following American domestic law when it conflicts with customary international law?

• • • • • • • •

CHAPTER TERMS

Adjudicative jurisdiction   Legislative jurisdiction

REVIEW QUESTIONS

1. In what way or ways can a nation establish legislative jurisdiction?
2. What are the five recognized principles of customary international law under which a nation can exercise legislative jurisdiction?

3. What are the two aspects of territorial jurisdiction?
4. How does the principle of territorial jurisdiction apply in admiralty?

5. How does the protective principle of jurisdiction differ from the objective aspect of the territorial principle?

6. What type of criminal laws does the passive personal principle allow a sovereign to enact?

7. What type of criminal laws does the nationality principle allow a sovereign to enact?

8. Do principles of customary international law impose limits on the power of Congress to assert legislative jurisdiction?

ENDNOTES

1. *Restatement (Third) of Foreign Relations Law of the United States*, §401 (1987).
2. *Id.* §401(b)-(c).
3. *United States v. Vilar*, 729 F.3d 62 (2nd Cir. 2013).
4. *United States v. Philip Morris USA, Inc.*, 566 F.3d 1095 (D.C. Cir. 2009).
5. *United States v. Ivanov*, 175 F. Supp. 2d 367 (D. Conn. 2001).
6. *United States v. Roberts*, 1 F. Supp. 2d 601 (E.D. La. 1998).
7. *Id.*
8. *United States v. Flores*, 289 U.S. 137 (1933).
9. *Id.*
10. *Id.*
11. *United States v. Rodriguez*, 182 F. Supp. 479 (S.D. Cal. 1960).
12. The indictment in the embassy bombings was brought in the Southern District of New York and is captioned *United States v. Bin Laden et al.*, 98 CR 1023. Of the 21 persons charged in the indictment, four have been convicted and are serving sentences of life without parole, three have been held in the U.K. since at least late 1998, two are being held in the Guantanamo Bay detention camp, three, including Osama Bin Laden, have been killed, and the rest are at large.
13. 15 U.S.C. §§78dd-2(g), 78dd-3(e), 78ff(c).
14. *Roberts*, n.1.
15. *United States v. Bin Laden*, 92 F. Supp. 2d 189 (S.D.N.Y. 2000).
16. *See* 18 U.S.C. §1651 et seq.
17. *United States v. Yunis*, 924 F.2d 1086 (D.C. Cir. 1991).
18. *United States v. Vasquez-Velasco*, 15 F.3d 833 (9th Cir. 1994)
19. *Id.*
20. *United States v. Nippon Paper Industries*, 109 F.3d 1 (1st Cir. 1997)
21. *United States v. Yunis*, 924 F.2d at 1086.

Chapter 7
The American Federal System and Criminal Jurisdiction

Chapter Objectives

After reading this chapter, you should be able to

- Understand the difference between the power of the federal government and the states to apply their criminal laws
- Understand the power of the federal government to enact criminal law applicable in American territories
- Understand the power of the federal government to enact criminal laws applicable within the states
- Understand the power of state governments to enact criminal law
- Explain the doctrines of concurrent jurisdiction and preemption

The federal system established by our Constitution preserves the sovereign status of the States in two ways. First it reserves to them a substantial portion of the Nation's primary sovereignty . . . The States form distinct and independent portions of supremacy no more subject, within their respective spheres, to the general authority than the general authority is subject to them within its own sphere. —*Alden v. Maine*, 527 U.S. 706 (1999)

In the previous chapter we examined the power of a sovereign nation to apply its criminal laws to conduct engaged in within its borders and to conduct engaged in outside of its borders. In that chapter we also learned that while internationally accepted principles of criminal jurisdiction recognize that sovereign nations have the power to apply their criminal laws domestically (and in some cases extra-territorially), the domestic law of a nation can limit the exercise of that power and can divide and allocate it to different bodies within a nation's political system. This chapter examines how in the United States the American political system divides, allocates, and limits the sovereign power to apply criminal law.

The American political system is a federal system in which sovereign power is divided between the federal government and the states. Under the U.S. Constitution certain powers have been given to the federal government and all the powers not allocated to it are retained by the states. The division of power between the federal government and the states has important effects on their power to apply their criminal laws domestically and extra-territorially. This chapter examines: (A) the power of the federal government to apply federal criminal law within and outside of the United States; (B) the power of the states to apply their criminal laws within and outside of their borders; (C) the limitations domestic law imposes on the exercise of extra-territorial jurisdiction; and (D) the principle of concurrent jurisdiction.

A. The Power of the Federal Government to Apply Federal Criminal Law Inside and Outside the United States

The power of the federal government to apply federal criminal laws to illegal conduct is best understood by reference to the place where the federal government seeks to apply them. The power of the federal government is broader when it seeks to apply its criminal laws outside the states than when it seeks to apply them inside the states. This section examines the power of the federal government to apply its criminal laws in each of those geographic areas and also discusses how that power is different in each of them.

1. *Power to Apply Federal Criminal Law Outside Territorial Jurisdiction of the States*

Police power is the power inherent in government to enact laws to protect the order, safety, health, morals, and general welfare of society. *Lees v. Bay Area Air Pollution Control Board,* 238 Cal. App. 2d 850 (1st Dist. 1965).

Outside the territorial jurisdiction of the states the federal government has the power to enact a full criminal code and apply it under what is sometimes called the government's **police power**. The source of this power differs based upon the type of territory in which its application is being made. It is now generally agreed that Congress acts under Article IV, Section 3 of the U.S. Constitution when it is legislating for American territories (such as American Samoa or Guam). Under that provision Congress is given the power to enact criminal laws for U.S.

territories. Congress has also used that provision of the Constitution as a basis for enacting laws applicable to territories controlled by the United States but that are not American possessions. Those territories are called trust territories, which the United States administers under a resolution of the United Nations and includes territories such as the Northern Mariana Islands and Palau.

Congress also has the power to enact criminal laws for federal enclaves within the states such as forts, naval bases, post offices, and national parks. That power is specifically provided for in Article I, Section 8 of the U.S. Constitution. Despite the fact that Congress has the power to enact a criminal code for federal enclaves, it has chosen instead to enact a statute called the Assimilative Crimes Act,[1] which adopts for federal enclaves the criminal law that at the time the crime is committed is in force in the state, territory, or district in which the enclave is located.

Outside of the United States and U.S. and U.S. trust territories, the United States, like any sovereign, has the power to exercise extra-territorial jurisdiction under the principles of customary international law examined in the previous chapter and as explained there can exercise such jurisdiction in ways that might violate customary international law. With the exception of criminal statutes aimed at protecting the government itself, such as one designed to protect U.S. personnel engaged in the performance of their duties from assault or interference, because of the presumption against extra-territorial application of laws, Congress must show its intent that a criminal statute be given extra-territorial effect.[2] Congress usually expresses that intent in the criminal statute itself.

More generally, Congress has also asserted that intent under the special maritime and territorial jurisdiction statute.[3] Under that statute, Congress has defined federal jurisdiction as including the high seas and any waters within the admiralty and maritime jurisdiction of the United States that are also outside the jurisdiction of any state. By providing that the special maritime and territorial jurisdiction of the federal government does not include high seas and territorial waters within the jurisdiction of a state, Congress has ceded substantial and important jurisdiction to the states because that gives them jurisdiction over crimes committed on all vessels (including those owned by the federal government) when those vessels are within a state's territorial waters.

Under the special maritime and territorial jurisdiction statute Congress has also asserted jurisdiction over any vessel outside of state waters that belongs in whole or part to any U.S. citizen or to any corporation created under the laws of the United States or under the laws of any state, territory, or district. Under that statute, Congress has also asserted jurisdiction over any aircraft belonging to a U.S. citizen or corporation organized under American law while the plane is in flight over the high seas or other waters within the admiralty and maritime jurisdiction of the United States and outside the jurisdiction of a state.

People v. Schurman

Supreme Court of New York, Appellate Division Second Department (1950)
277 A.D. 897

Memorandum Opinion

Judgment of the County Court, Richmond County, convicting defendant of the crime of burglary in the third degree, unanimously affirmed. The jury could find that the defendant had broken and entered into the room of a nurse on the army transport docked at a pier in Richmond County, in the city of New York, with intent to commit a larceny of the personal property of said nurse. The pier was within the jurisdiction of the State of New York and the army transport docked there was on waters within the jurisdiction of this State. (*United States v. Bevans*, 3 Wheat. [U.S.] 336.) The power of Congress to exclude from the jurisdiction of the several States burglaries committed on vessels of the United States tied to docks in the States, does not appear to have been exercised by the provisions of the United States Code (tit. 18, Crimes and Criminal Procedure). Section 7 declares that the special maritime and territorial jurisdiction of the United States shall include any vessel belonging to the United States when such vessel is "out of the jurisdiction of any particular State." Undoubtedly, Congress had the "enlightened purpose" to inter-fere as little as possible with the authority of States in the punishment of crime. (*United States v. Press Pub. Co.*, 219 U.S. 1, 9.) International comity permits the application of foreign local law to crimes committed on United States vessels when the peace of the locality is disturbed by the act. (*United States v. Flores*, 289 U.S. 137, 153.) It would seem that because of the relation of the States to the Federal Government, Congress, by limitation of Federal jurisdiction to vessels out of the jurisdiction of any State, desired not to interfere with the jurisdiction of the States of crimes that can disturb the peace of the States. In the absence of a distinct manifestation of intention to exclude the States from jurisdiction of crimes commit-ted on vessels within the territorial jurisdiction of the States, the defendant was indictable in the county of Richmond (Penal Law, §§400, 404). We find no error in the admission of evidence or in the charge which warrants a reversal of the con-viction. Present—NOLAN, P. J., CARSWELL, JOHNSTON, SNEED and MACCRATE, JJ.

Case Focus

1. The crime in this case was committed on a U.S. Army transport ship while it was docked in New York. Why did the State of New York and not the federal government have jurisdiction to prosecute the perpetrator?

• • • • • • • •

Under the special maritime and territorial jurisdiction statute, Congress also has asserted jurisdiction over objects and vehicles designed for flight in space while those vehicles are in flight. In more terrestrial matters, under that statute Congress has asserted jurisdiction over crimes committed against American nationals while outside the jurisdiction of any nation. Finally, in response to terrorist attacks on American embassies, Congress has asserted jurisdiction over crimes committed in American diplomatic missions overseas, including crimes committed in buildings and residences used by American personnel.

As a sovereign nation the United States also has the power to exercise extra-territorial jurisdiction under the nationality principle, the passive protective principle, and the universal principle. Historically, Congress exercised power under those principles sparingly, but beginning in the late 1970s with the Foreign Corrupt Practices Act, Congress began to exercise its powers under those principles with increasing frequency.

2. *Jurisdiction to Apply Federal Criminal Law Within the States*

The power of Congress to adopt statutes that apply to criminal conduct within the states is much more limited than its power to do so within American territories and in federal enclaves. Congress can only apply federal criminal law within the states when the criminal statute is based upon a specific grant of power to the federal government that is contained in the U.S. Constitution. For example, Congress has the power to enact a statute for Guam that makes murder of a private citizen in that territory a federal crime, but because the Constitution does not give it jurisdiction over all crimes committed in the states, it does not have the power to pass a statute that the makes murder of a private citizen in the states a federal crime.

There are two sources of constitutional power under which Congress can enact a criminal statute applicable to conduct within the states. One of those sources of power is where the Constitution expressly gives Congress the power to enact a criminal law. The Constitution contains few such express grants. One expressly granted power to enact criminal statutes is the power given to Congress to enact criminal laws relating to the counterfeiting of U.S. currency and federally issued securities.[4]

A second basis for enacting criminal statutes applicable within the states is under the necessary and proper clause of the Constitution.[5] Under that provision, Congress is empowered to enact all laws that are "necessary and proper" for carrying into execution the powers granted to the federal government by the Constitution. Most, but not all, power granted to the federal government is found in Article I, Section 8 of the Constitution.

Under the necessary and proper clause, Congress has the power to enact criminal laws to make its exercise of the powers granted to the federal government by the Constitution effective. For example, under the Sixteenth Amendment Congress is given the power to enact an income tax; to make the income tax laws effective, Congress has the power under the necessary and proper clause to enact criminal laws relating to the filing of income tax returns. Congress also has the power to enact laws to protect federal interests, federal employees, and federal property, including statutes that make it a crime to assault or murder federal officers or employees while they are on federal business, engage in conduct that obstructs the operation of the federal government, commit crimes against federal property, defraud the federal government, and engage in certain types of conduct directed against federally chartered entities (such as federal banks).

One of the largest grants of power to the federal government in the Constitution is under what is called the commerce clause,[6] which gives Congress the power to regulate interstate commerce, foreign commerce, and commerce with Indian tribes. Over the years the Supreme Court has read the commerce clause as giving Congress the power to regulate commerce and anything that substantially affects commerce. Under the commerce clause, Congress is able to enact criminal laws that make it a federal crime to engage in conduct within the states that affects interstate commerce or affects or involves the use of the channels of interstate commerce.

United States v. Lopez

Supreme Court of the United States (1995) 514 U.S. 549

CHIEF JUSTICE REHNQUIST delivered the opinion of the Court.

In the Gun-Free School Zones Act of 1990, Congress made it a federal offense "for any individual knowingly to possess a firearm at a place that the individual knows, or has reasonable cause to believe, is a school zone." 18 U.S.C. §922(q)(1)(A) (1988 ed., Supp. V). The Act neither regulates a commercial activity nor contains a requirement that the possession be connected in any way to interstate commerce. We hold that the Act exceeds the authority of Congress "to regulate Commerce . . . among the several States . . ." U.S. Const., Art. I, §8, cl. 3. * * *

A federal grand jury indicted respondent on one count of knowing possession of a firearm at a school zone, in violation of §922(q). Respondent moved to dismiss his federal indictment on the ground that §922(q) "is unconstitutional as

it is beyond the power of Congress to legislate control over our public schools."
The District Court denied the motion, concluding that §922(q) "is a constitutional exercise of Congress' well-defined power to regulate activities in and affecting commerce, and the 'business' of elementary, middle and high schools . . . affects interstate commerce." App. to Pet. for Cert. 55a. Respondent waived his right to a jury trial. The District Court conducted a bench trial, found him guilty of violating §922(q), and sentenced him to six months' imprisonment and two years' supervised release.

On appeal, respondent challenged his conviction based on his claim that §922(q) exceeded Congress' power to legislate under the Commerce Clause. The Court of Appeals for the Fifth Circuit agreed and reversed respondent's conviction. * * * Because of the importance of the issue, we granted certiorari, 511 U.S. 1029 (1994), and we now affirm.

We start with first principles. The Constitution creates a Federal Government of enumerated powers. See Art. I, §8. As James Madison wrote, "the powers delegated by the proposed Constitution to the federal government are few and defined. Those which are to remain in the State governments are numerous and indefinite." The Federalist No. 45, pp. 292-293 (C. Rossiter ed. 1961). This constitutionally mandated division of authority "was adopted by the Framers to ensure protection of our fundamental liberties." *Gregory v. Ashcroft*, 501 U.S. 452, 458, 115 L. Ed. 2d 410, 111 S. Ct. 2395 (1991) (internal quotation marks omitted). "Just as the separation and independence of the coordinate branches of the Federal Government serve to prevent the accumulation of excessive power in any one branch, a healthy balance of power between the States and the Federal Government will reduce the risk of tyranny and abuse from either front." *Ibid.*

The Constitution delegates to Congress the power "to regulate Commerce with foreign Nations, and among the several States, and with the Indian Tribes." Art. I, §8, cl. 3. The Court, through Chief Justice Marshall, first defined the nature of Congress' commerce power in *Gibbons v. Ogden*, 22 U.S. 1, 9 Wheat. 1, 189-190, 6 L. Ed. 23 (1824):

> "Commerce, undoubtedly, is traffic, but it is something more: it is intercourse. It describes the commercial intercourse between nations, and parts of nations, in all its branches, and is regulated by prescribing rules for carrying on that intercourse."

The commerce power "is the power to regulate[." *Id.*] The *Gibbons* Court, however, acknowledged that limitations on the commerce power are inherent in the very language of the Commerce Clause.

"Comprehensive as the word 'among' is, it may very properly be restricted to that commerce which concerns more States than one. . . . The enumeration presupposes something not enumerated; and that something, if we regard the language, or the subject of the sentence, must be the exclusively internal commerce of a State." *Id.*, at 194-195. * * *

[I]n the watershed case of *NLRB v. Jones & Laughlin Steel Corp.*, 301 U.S. 1, 81 L. Ed. 893, 57 S. Ct. 615 (1937), the Court upheld the National Labor Relations

Act against a Commerce Clause challenge * * * [saying] * * * intrastate activities that "have such a close and substantial relation to interstate commerce that their control is essential or appropriate to protect that commerce from burdens and obstructions" are within Congress' power to regulate. *Id.*, at 37. * * *

In *Jones & Laughlin Steel*, the Court warned that the scope of the interstate commerce power "must be considered in the light of our dual system of government and may not be extended so as to embrace effects upon interstate commerce so indirect and remote that to embrace them, in view of our complex society, would effectually obliterate the distinction between what is national and what is local and create a completely centralized government." 301 U.S. at 37[.] * * *

Consistent with this structure, we have identified three broad categories of activity that Congress may regulate under its commerce power. * * * First, Congress may regulate the use of the channels of interstate commerce. ("The authority of Congress to keep the channels of interstate commerce free from immoral and injurious uses has been frequently sustained, and is no longer open to question" (quoting *Caminetti v. United States*, 242 U.S. 470, 491, 61 L. Ed. 442, 37 S. Ct. 192 (1917)). Second, Congress is empowered to regulate and protect the instrumentalities of interstate commerce, or persons or things in interstate commerce, even though the threat may come only from intrastate activities. See, *e.g.,* * * * *Southern R. Co. v. United States*, 222 U.S. 20, 56 L. Ed. 72, 32 S. Ct. 2 (1911) (upholding amendments to Safety Appliance Act as applied to vehicles used in intrastate commerce); *Perez v. United States*, 402 U.S. 146, 150 (1971) ("For example, the destruction of an aircraft (18 U.S.C. §32), or . . . thefts from interstate shipments (18 U.S.C. §659)"). Finally, Congress' commerce authority includes the power to regulate those activities having a substantial relation to interstate commerce, *Jones & Laughlin Steel*, 301 U.S. at 37, *i.e.*, those activities that substantially affect interstate commerce. * * *

Within this final category, admittedly, our case law has not been clear whether an activity must "affect" or "substantially affect" interstate commerce in order to be within Congress' power to regulate it under the Commerce Clause. * * * We conclude, consistent with the great weight of our case law, that the proper test requires an analysis of whether the regulated activity "substantially affects" interstate commerce.

We now turn to consider the power of Congress, in the light of this framework, to enact §922(q). The first two categories of authority may be quickly disposed of: §922(q) is not a regulation of the use of the channels of interstate commerce, nor is it an attempt to prohibit the interstate transportation of a commodity through the channels of commerce; nor can §922(q) be justified as a regulation by which Congress has sought to protect an instrumentality of interstate commerce or a thing in interstate commerce. Thus, if §922(q) is to be sustained, it must be under the third category as a regulation of an activity that substantially affects interstate commerce.

First, we have upheld a wide variety of congressional Acts regulating intrastate economic activity where we have concluded that the activity substantially affected interstate commerce. Examples include the regulation of intrastate coal mining; intrastate extortionate credit transactions, restaurants utilizing substantial interstate supplies, inns and hotels catering to interstate guests, and production and consumption of homegrown wheat, *Wickard v. Filburn*, 317 U.S. 111, 87 L. Ed. 122, 63 S. Ct. 82 (1942). These examples are by no means exhaustive, but the pattern is clear. Where economic activity substantially affects interstate commerce, legislation regulating that activity will be sustained. * * *

Section 922(q) is a criminal statute that by its terms has nothing to do with "commerce" or any sort of economic enterprise, however broadly one might define those terms. Section 922(q) is not an essential part of a larger regulation of economic activity, in which the regulatory scheme could be undercut unless the intrastate activity were regulated. It cannot, therefore, be sustained under our cases upholding regulations of activities that arise out of or are connected with a commercial transaction, which viewed in the aggregate, substantially affects interstate commerce. * * *

The Government's essential contention, *in fine*, is that we may determine here that §922(q) is valid because possession of a firearm in a local school zone does indeed substantially affect interstate commerce. Brief for United States 17. The Government argues that possession of a firearm in a school zone may result in violent crime and that violent crime can be expected to affect the functioning of the national economy in two ways. First, the costs of violent crime are substantial, and, through the mechanism of insurance, those costs are spread throughout the population. See *United States v. Evans*, 928 F.2d 858, 862 (CA9 1991). Second, violent crime reduces the willingness of individuals to travel to areas within the country that are perceived to be unsafe. Cf. *Heart of Atlanta Motel*, 379 U.S. at 253. The Government also argues that the presence of guns in schools poses a substantial threat to the educational process by threatening the learning environment. A handicapped educational process, in turn, will result in a less productive citizenry. That, in turn, would have an adverse effect on the Nation's economic well-being. As a result, the Government argues that Congress could rationally have concluded that §922(q) substantially affects interstate commerce.

We pause to consider the implications of the Government's arguments. The Government admits, under its "costs of crime" reasoning, that Congress could regulate not only all violent crime, but all activities that might lead to violent crime, regardless of how tenuously they relate to interstate commerce. See Tr. of Oral Arg. 8-9. Similarly, under the Government's "national productivity" reasoning, Congress could regulate any activity that it found was related to the economic productivity of individual citizens: family law (including marriage, divorce, and child custody), for example. Under the theories that the Government presents in support of §922(q), it is difficult to perceive any limitation on federal power, even in areas such as criminal law enforcement or education where States historically have been sovereign. Thus, if we were to accept the Government's arguments, we are hard pressed to posit any activity by an individual that Congress is without power to regulate. * * *

Admittedly, a determination whether an intrastate activity is commercial or noncommercial may in some cases result in legal uncertainty. But, so long as

Congress' authority is limited to those powers enumerated in the Constitution, and so long as those enumerated powers are interpreted as having judicially enforceable outer limits, congressional legislation under the Commerce Clause always will engender "legal uncertainty." *Post*, at 630. As Chief Justice Marshall stated in *McCulloch v. Maryland*, 17 U.S. 316, 4 Wheat. 316, 4 L. Ed. 579 (1819):

> "The [federal] government is acknowledged by all to be one of enumerated powers. The principle, that it can exercise only the powers granted to it . . . is now universally admitted. But the question respecting the extent of the powers actually granted, is perpetually arising, and will probably continue to arise, as long as our system shall exist." *Id.*, at 405. * * *

In *Jones & Laughlin Steel*, 301 U.S. at 37, we held that the question of congressional power under the Commerce Clause "is necessarily one of degree." To the same effect is the concurring opinion of Justice Cardozo in *Schechter Poultry:*

> "There is a view of causation that would obliterate the distinction between what is national and what is local in the activities of commerce. Motion at the outer rim is communicated perceptibly, though minutely, to recording instruments at the center. A society such as ours 'is an elastic medium which transmits all tremors throughout its territory; the only question is of their size.'" 295 U.S. at 554 (quoting *United States v. A.L.A. Schechter Poultry Corp.*, 76 F.2d 617, 624 (CA2 1935) (L. Hand, J., concurring)).

These are not precise formulations, and in the nature of things they cannot be. But we think they point the way to a correct decision of this case. The possession of a gun in a local school zone is in no sense an economic activity that might, through repetition elsewhere, substantially affect any sort of interstate commerce. Respondent was a local student at a local school; there is no indication that he had recently moved in interstate commerce, and there is no requirement that his possession of the firearm have any concrete tie to interstate commerce.

To uphold the Government's contentions here, we would have to pile inference upon inference in a manner that would bid fair to convert congressional authority under the Commerce Clause to a general police power of the sort retained by the States. Admittedly, some of our prior cases have taken long steps down that road, giving great deference to congressional action. See *supra*, at 556-558. The broad language in these opinions has suggested the possibility of additional expansion, but we decline here to proceed any further. To do so would require us to conclude that the Constitution's enumeration of powers does not presuppose something not enumerated, cf. *Gibbons v. Ogden, supra*, at 195, and that there never will be a distinction between what is truly national and what is truly local, cf. *Jones & Laughlin Steel, supra*, at 30. This we are unwilling to do.

For the foregoing reasons the judgment of the Court of Appeals is
Affirmed.

Case Focus

1. What did the Court say about why the constitutional division of power
   between the federal government and the states is important and
   about why that division must be respected?
2. What did the Court say the commerce power is?
3. What three areas of activity does the commerce power allow Congress to regulate?
4. On what basis does the Court conclude that the Gun-Free School
   Zones Act is beyond Congress's power to legislate?
5. What reason does the Court give for rejecting the government's "cost
   of crime" and "national productivity" arguments?

• • • • • • • • •

It is important to keep in mind that while the necessary and proper
clause gives Congress the power to enact those laws that are necessary
and proper to make effective the exercise of powers granted to the
federal government by the Constitution, that clause does not give Congress the power to enact statutes that Congress simply deems to be
necessary and proper for the good of the nation. Thus, the enactment
of laws under the necessary and proper clause must be related to a
specific power granted to the federal government by the Constitution.
Criminal laws that are enacted by Congress and that are not based on
one of the powers granted to it by the Constitution are null and void and
will be struck down by the courts under their power of judicial review.
Both federal and state courts have the power to strike down both federal
and state statutes that are unconstitutional.

The nature of the federal system also limits the power of law enforcement officers. For example, federal law enforcement agents are limited to
enforcing federal criminal law and absent a state statute or some local
regulation that allows state law enforcement officials to enforce federal
law, state law enforcement agents are limited to enforcing state criminal
law. The federal government does not have the power to require that
state law enforcement officers enforce federal criminal law, and states
cannot require federal law enforcement officers to enforce state law.[7] For
example, Congress cannot pass a law that requires local sheriffs and
police departments to enforce federal law.

B. The Power of the States to Apply State Criminal Law Inside and Outside of Their Borders

In contrast to the federal government, the states have broad power to define crimes and apply their criminal laws within their borders. Unlike the federal government, which is limited to the exercise of those powers specifically granted to it by the Constitution, the states need not look to specific grants of power upon which to base their criminal laws. As a result, states generally have the power to define as crimes and apply their criminal laws to any conduct they choose, subject only to the specific limits contained in their respective constitutions and in the U.S. Constitution. As sovereign entities themselves, subject only to limits imposed by the U.S. Constitution or by proper federal statute, the states can exercise legislative jurisdiction to the fullest extent permitted by customary international law.[8] Thus, states can exercise legislative jurisdiction under both the territorial and the non-territorial jurisdictional principles.

When acting under the territorial principle of jurisdiction the states have the power to apply their criminal laws to criminal conduct that has its situs within the state. In order to determine the situs of a crime it is necessary to look at the particular statute to see whether it criminalizes certain conduct or the result of certain conduct and then determine whether either have occurred within a state's borders.

For example, if Alphonse is standing in Texas and shoots a bullet that strikes and kills Barry, who is standing in Oklahoma, the conduct that results in the murder occurred in Texas and the result of that conduct takes effect in Oklahoma. Depending on their respective laws either Texas or Oklahoma or both may have jurisdiction over the crime. Which state actually has jurisdiction or whether both have jurisdiction is a matter of how each state defines the crime of murder and how each state has chosen to exercise its criminal jurisdiction.

In contrast, if states A and B make it a crime to devise a scheme to defraud and a person in state A devises such a scheme and then goes to state B where he perpetrates it, he has violated that statute in state A, but he has not violated the statute in state B. He did not violate the statute in state B because he did not devise the scheme there. That person may, however, be prosecuted in state B for some other crime (such as theft by deception) if his conduct falls within the definition of that offense when he defrauds a citizen of that state.

In the case of crimes that are committed by failure to perform a required duty, the crime is considered committed in the place where the duty is to be performed. For example, if a person who is a resident of state A has earned income in state B and so is required to file a state income tax return in state B and he willfully fails to do so, assuming the returns are required to be filed with the tax agency in the state capital of state B, the crime of failing to file a tax return is committed where the state capital is located.[9]

As sovereign entities, the states retain their power to exercise jurisdiction under the non-territorial principles and, in fact, have long exercised power under them. For example, states have exercised their power under the nationality principle and made it a crime for their citizens to commit certain crimes outside of their borders,[10] under the protective principle to make it a crime for persons outside the state to forge deeds that could affect title to land within the state,[11] and under the objective aspect of the territorial principle have made it a crime for persons outside of the state to commit crimes that produce adverse effects within the state.[12]

State v. Stepansky

Supreme Court of Florida (2000) 761 So. 2d 1027

PARIENTE, J.

We have on appeal *Stepansky v. State*, 707 So. 2d 877 (Fla. 5th DCA 1998), a decision of the Fifth District Court of Appeal declaring section 910.006(3)(d), Florida Statutes (1995), to be unconstitutional as an intrusion "upon the exclusive province of [the United States] Congress and the President as delineated by Article I, section 10 of the United States Constitution." *Stepansky*, 707 So. 2d at 879. (That statute provides in relevant part: *The special maritime criminal jurisdiction of the state extends to acts or omissions on board a ship outside of the state under the following circumstances . . . (d) The act or omission during a voyage on which over half of the revenue passengers on board the ship originally embarked and plan to finally disembark in this state, without regard to intermediate stopovers.*) * * * For the reasons expressed in this opinion, we reverse the decision of the Fifth District and find that section 910.006(3)(d), which is part of Florida's "special maritime criminal jurisdiction" statute, is constitutional as applied in this case.

FACTS

Matthew Stepansky, a United States citizen, was charged in Brevard County, Florida with burglary and attempted sexual battery of a thirteen-year-old American citizen that allegedly occurred on board a cruise ship, the M/V Atlantic. The cruise ship departed from and returned to Port Canaveral, which is located in Brevard County. At the time of the alleged crime, the cruise ship was approximately 100 nautical miles from the Atlantic coastline of Florida. Stepansky and the complainant are both United States citizens but neither one is a Florida resident. The M/V Atlantic is registered in Liberia but owned by Premier Cruise Lines, Ltd. of the British West Indies. * * *

Stepansky moved to dismiss the charge on the grounds that the State lacked jurisdiction because the crime occurred outside the territorial jurisdiction of Florida and because the prosecution was precluded by the Supremacy Clause of the United States Constitution. * * * The trial court denied the motion, and Stepansky sought a writ of prohibition from the Fifth District. The Fifth District issued the writ, holding that the Florida Legislature was without constitutional authority to enact section 910.006(3)(d) because the statute intruded upon the exclusive province of Congress and the President under the United States Constitution, specifically Article I, Section 10. *See Stepansky*, 707 So. 2d at 879.

ANALYSIS

Section 910.006(3)(d) of the special maritime criminal jurisdiction statute that is the subject of the constitutional attack in this case extends the ability of this State to prosecute crimes to criminal acts committed on cruise ships sailing outside the State's territorial waters if the "act or omission occurs during a voyage on which over half of the revenue passengers on board the ship originally embarked and plan to finally disembark" in Florida. * * *

A. Principles of Federalism

The Tenth Amendment to the United States Constitution specifically provides that all "powers not delegated to the United States by the Constitution" are reserved to the states. Indeed, "it is fundamental in our federal structure that states have vast residual powers. Those powers, unless constrained or displaced by the existence of federal authority or by proper federal enactments, are often exercised in concurrence with those of the national government." *United States v. Locke*, 146 L. Ed. 2d 69, 120 S. Ct. 1135, 1148 (2000) * * *.

The United States Supreme Court has observed that "the States under our federal system have the principal responsibility for defining and prosecuting crimes." *Abbate v. United States*, 359 U.S. 187, 195, 3 L. Ed. 2d 729, 79 S. Ct. 666 (1959) * * *[.] Nonetheless, if federal law has preempted state law, either expressly or impliedly, the Supremacy Clause requires state law to yield. *See, e.g., Barnett Bank of Marion County, N.A. v. Nelson*, 517 U.S. 25, 30, 134 L. Ed. 2d 237, 116 S. Ct. 1103 (1996) * * *.

Thus, in *Skiriotes v. Florida*, 313 U.S. 69, 85 L. Ed. 1193, 61 S. Ct. 924 (1941), the United States Supreme Court concluded that Florida could prosecute one of its citizens for violating state laws regulating the taking of commercial sponges, even if the crime occurred outside of Florida's territorial waters. *Id.* In determining that the State's exercise of extraterritorial jurisdiction was proper, the Court examined whether any conflict with federal law existed. *See id.* at 74-75. Because there was no conflict with federal law and the State had an interest in the proper maintenance of its sponge fishery, the Court found that the State continued to exercise its traditional police powers. *See id.*

With this constitutional framework in mind, we examine whether * * * the prosecution is within the State's police powers. * * *

B. The State's Sovereign Authority—the Effects Doctrine

Finding that the exercise of jurisdiction in this case does not conflict with the constitution or federal law, our inquiry turns to whether the State's exercise of jurisdiction is within the State's traditional police powers. The State asserts that the "effects" doctrine provides a proper basis for the State to assert jurisdiction in this case although the criminal acts were committed outside the State's territorial waters.

As Justice Holmes, writing for the United States Supreme Court, recognized, "Acts done outside a jurisdiction, but intended to produce and producing detrimental effects within it, justify a State in punishing the cause of the harm as if he had been present at the effect, if the State should succeed in getting him within its power." *Strassheim v. Daily*, 221 U.S. 280, 285, 55 L. Ed. 735, 31 S. Ct. 558 (1911); *see also Hartford Fire Ins. Co. v. California*, 509 U.S. 764, 125 L. Ed. 2d 612, 113 S. Ct. 2891 (1993) (applying effects doctrine to allow states to bring a Sherman Act claim in federal court against foreign defendants). The Restatement of Foreign Relations provides that a state may exercise its jurisdiction over criminal acts committed outside its territorial boundaries * * * if the acts have significant effects within the state. *See* Restatement, *supra*, §402. Likewise, the Supreme Court of Alaska has relied upon the principles incorporated in the effects doctrine to exercise criminal jurisdiction in the waters outside the geographical boundaries of that state. *See State v. Sieminski*, 556 P.2d 929 (Alaska 1976); *see also State v. Bundrant*, 546 P.2d 530, 555-556 (Alaska 1976).

In fact, the Fifth District acknowledged the effects doctrine as a basis for asserting jurisdiction beyond the state's geographic boundaries. *See Stepansky*, 707 So. 2d at 878. As properly explained by the Fifth District, "The state may . . . exercise criminal jurisdiction over acts committed beyond this three mile limit, at least where such acts have an effect in this state and there is no conflict with federal law and no foreign nation has criminal jurisdiction over said acts." *Id.* at 877-878. Accordingly, we conclude that Florida's sovereign authority includes the ability to exercise criminal jurisdiction over acts committed outside the territorial limits of the State under the effects doctrine as long as the exercise of jurisdiction does not conflict with federal law and the exercise of jurisdiction is a reasonable application of the effects doctrine. * * *

Federal courts have recognized that a criminal act having a similar adverse effect on the United States will justify the exercise of federal jurisdiction over crimes on cruise ships that would otherwise go unprosecuted. *See Roberts*, 1 F. Supp. 2d at 608; *Pizdrint*, 983 F. Supp. at 1113. In those cases, the federal courts found a significant effect on the United States because the cruise lines conducted substantial business in the United States, the cruises began and ended in the United States, and federal law enforcement agents were required to become involved in prosecution. *See Roberts*, 1 F. Supp. 2d at 608; *Pizdrint*, 983 F. Supp. at 1113.

Similarly, in this case the Legislature has determined that the State of Florida is a "major center for international travel and trade by sea" and that the "state has an interest in ensuring the protection of persons traveling to or from Florida by sea."§910.006(1)(a), (c). Florida's tourism industry could be significantly affected if crimes that occur on board cruise ships where a majority of the fare-paying passengers embark and disembark in Florida were to go unprosecuted. We emphasize that pursuant to this statute the State exercises limited jurisdiction by operating only where the crime has not been prosecuted by any other government entity, including the federal government or the foreign country in which the ship is registered. * * *

We reverse the decision of the Fifth District Court of Appeal and remand for proceedings consistent with this opinion.

It is so ordered.

SHAW, ANSTEAD, LEWIS and QUINCE, JJ., concur.

WELLS, J., dissents with an opinion in which HARDING, C.J., concurs.

Case Focus

1. What reasons does the defendant give for why he believes the Florida statute is unconstitutional?
2. What is the basis on which the court finds that Florida's exercise of non-territorial jurisdiction is constitutional?
3. On what principle of non-territorial jurisdiction is the Florida statute based?

• • • • • • • •

C. Constitutional Limits on the Power of the Federal Government and States to Exercise Legislative Jurisdiction Extra-Territorially

The due process clause of the Fifth Amendment to the U.S. Constitution limits the extent to which the United States can exercise legislative jurisdiction.[13] That clause requires that before legislative jurisdiction can be exercised, there be a sufficient nexus between the defendant and the United States.[14] Typically, nexus is not an issue when the crime charged is not extra-territorial.[15] Under the due process clause, a sufficient nexus exists when the aim of a defendant's activity is to cause harm inside the United States or to U.S. citizens or interests.[16] The due process clause would require the same nexus to exist between a defendant and a state before a state could exercise legislative jurisdiction over a defendant.

D. Concurrent Federal and State Jurisdiction

It is important to understand that while the Constitution divides the power to legislate and enact criminal laws on certain subjects between the federal government and the states, the mere allocation of power to the federal government to legislate on a particular subject does not by itself prohibit the states from applying their criminal laws to conduct related to that subject. Under the principle of concurrent jurisdiction, generally applicable state criminal laws can be applied to conduct that also violates federal law. Under that same principle, assuming it relates to a matter over which the Constitution gives the federal government the power to legislate, the federal government can apply its criminal law to conduct that violates state law. As a result a person can be prosecuted by both a state and the federal government for the same criminal act.

For example, the federal government can and has made it a federal crime to rob a federally chartered bank, and the states can and have made it a crime to rob banks (because state governments are not governments of specified powers, they can make it a crime to rob any bank, including federally chartered banks, within their borders). A bank robber who robs a federal bank can be prosecuted for the bank robbery by the federal government or by the state in which the bank is located or by both.

The doctrine of concurrent jurisdiction is based on the principle that the federal government and the states are each separate sovereigns that derive their power from different organic documents. The federal government derives its power from the U.S. Constitution and the state governments derive their power from their respective state constitutions.

With respect to matters within the jurisdiction of the federal government, Congress can preempt state criminal statutes. When Congress chooses to preempt state criminal laws applicable to matters assigned to the federal government by the Constitution, that action has the effect of barring the application of state law to that conduct and barring state prosecution. Until Congress preempts state law, states can apply their criminal laws to conduct within federal jurisdiction. For example,

Congress could choose to preempt the application of all state bank robbery statutes to robberies committed against federally chartered or federally insured banks, thereby prohibiting states from prosecuting robberies of those institutions, but until it does, states can apply their own criminal statutes to those robberies.

It is important to keep in mind that Congress can only preempt a state statute that relates to a subject over which the Constitution gives Congress the power to legislate. Congress cannot preempt a state statute on a subject that is exclusively a state matter.

Federal preemption of state statutes is done either expressly or implicitly. The courts have consistently held that Congress does not preempt a state criminal statute merely by legislating in a field over which the Constitution has given jurisdiction to the federal government. Express preemption occurs when Congress expressly mandates the preemption of state law. Implicit preemption occurs either where a federal statute is so comprehensive that Congress's intent to preempt state statutes can be inferred or where the federal statute conflicts with a state statute. As a result, because Congress has neither expressly nor implicitly preempted state criminal law, in many fields of federal jurisdiction state criminal law can be and is used to prosecute conduct that ordinarily might be thought to involve areas of exclusive federal interest, such as the filing of false federal income tax returns[17] and criminal violations related to federal programs and federal regulatory statutes.

People v. Lewis

Illinois Appellate Court, Second District, 1998 295 Ill. App. 3d 587

JUSTICE McLAREN delivered the opinion of the court:

Defendant, Gregory P. Lewis, was charged by indictment with two counts of theft (720 ILCS 5/16-1(a)(1), 16-1(a)(2) (West 1996)) for filing a fraudulent unemployment benefits claim with the United States Railroad Retirement Board. Defendant moved to dismiss the charges, arguing that section 359(a) of the Railroad Unemployment Insurance Act (45 U.S.C.A. §359(a) (West 1986)), which imposes a penalty for fraudulently obtaining benefits, preempts state criminal prosecutions for the same conduct. The trial court denied defendant's motion. After a jury trial, defendant was convicted of both counts and was sentenced to 24 months' probation. On appeal, defendant argues only that the trial court erred in denying his motion to dismiss. We affirm.

When faced with a preemption question, we begin by reminding ourselves of the basic structure of our federal system, in which the states and the federal government are separate political communities. *United States v. Wheeler*, 435 U.S. 313 (1978). State and federal governments derive their power from different sources, each from the organic law that established it. *Wheeler,* 435 U.S. at 320. Each has the power, inherent in any sovereign, to determine independently what shall be an offense against its authority and to punish such offenses, and in doing so each is exercising its own sovereignty, not that of the other. *Wheeler,* 435 U.S. at 320.

Of course, the supremacy clause of the United States Constitution gives Congress the power to limit the states' exercise of their sovereignty. The supremacy clause provides that "the Laws of the United States * * * shall be the supreme Law of the Land *** any Thing in the Constitution or Laws of any State to the Contrary notwithstanding." U.S. Const., art. VI, §2. The extent to which federal legislation preempts state law is a question of congressional intent. *Gade v. National Solid Wastes Management Ass'n,* 505 U.S. 88 (1992). If Congress, when acting within constitutional limits, explicitly mandates the preemption of state law within a stated situation, we need not proceed beyond the statutory language to determine that state law is preempted. *Gade,* 505 U.S. at 98. In the absence of an explicit preemption, we may infer an intent to preempt state law, and that inference may take one of two forms: (1) field preemption, "where the scheme of the federal regulation is 'so pervasive as to make reasonable the inference that Congress left no room for the States to supplement it' [citation]" (*Gade,* 505 U.S. at 98); or (2) conflict preemption, where either compliance with both federal and state law is a physical impossibility or state law stands as an impediment to the accomplishment and execution of the full purposes and objectives of Congress. *Gade,* 505 U.S. at 98.

Where the field that Congress is said to have preempted traditionally has been occupied by the states, we start with the assumption that the historic police powers of the states were not to be superseded by the federal act unless that was Congress's clear and manifest purpose. *Jones v. Rath Packing Co.,* 430 U.S. 519, 525 (1977); *People v. Chicago Magnet Wire Corp.,* 126 Ill. 2d 356, 366-367 (1989). Certainly, the power to prosecute criminal conduct traditionally has been regarded as properly within the scope of state superintendence. *Chicago Magnet,* 126 Ill. 2d at 367. Thus, absent a clear and manifest intent by Congress, we will not find that a federal act preempts a state's power to enforce a generally applicable criminal statute. See *Chicago Magnet,* 126 Ill. 2d at 367.

With these principles in mind, we turn to the issue at hand, namely, whether defendant's theft prosecution was preempted by the penalty provision contained in section 359(a) of the Railroad Unemployment Insurance Act. Because the prohibition of theft is a generally applicable criminal law, we will not find preemption unless that was Congress's clear and manifest purpose. See *Jones,* 430 U.S. at 525; *Chicago Magnet,* 126 Ill. 2d at 367.

Found in section 359(a), the Railroad Unemployment Insurance Act's penalty provision states, in relevant part:

> "Any employee * * * who shall knowingly make or aid in making or cause to be made any false or fraudulent statement or claim for the purpose of causing benefits or other payment to be made or not to be made under this chapter, shall be

punished by a fine of not more than $10,000 or by imprisonment not exceeding one year, or both." 45 U.S.C.A. §359(a) (West 1986).

Defendant argues that, by enacting section 359(a), Congress created the exclusive remedy for benefits fraud and thereby expressed a manifest intent to preempt the enforcement of generally applicable state laws against the same conduct. We disagree.

First, although the Railroad Unemployment Insurance Act contains an explicit preemption clause (see 45 U.S.C.A. §363(b) (West 1986)), we are convinced that defendant's theft prosecution does not fall within it. * * *

By its own terms, section 363(b) precludes the states only from providing unemployment insurance benefits to employees covered by the Railroad Unemployment Insurance Act. Here, the State has attempted no such thing. Rather, the State indicted defendant under its generally applicable theft statute for conduct that, while prohibited by and punishable under section 359(a), also is a crime in the State of Illinois. Nothing in section 363(b) explicitly precludes the State from pursuing that prosecution. Thus, we conclude that defendant's theft prosecution does not fall within section 363(b)'s express preemption.

Having concluded that defendant's theft prosecution is not explicitly preempted by section 363(b), our next task is to determine whether it is implicitly preempted by the Railroad Unemployment Insurance Act as a whole. We conclude that it is not.

First, we are not persuaded that the Railroad Unemployment Insurance Act regulates benefits fraud so pervasively "as to make reasonable the inference that Congress left no room for the States to supplement it" (*Gade,* 505 U.S. at 98). It is well established that, in general, an act denounced by both federal and state law is an offense against the peace and dignity of both and may be punished by both. See *Wheeler,* 435 U.S. at 316-318 (1978). In numerous cases, courts have recognized that states may prosecute criminal conduct even though that same conduct also is punishable under federal law. For example, even though the applicable federal statute prohibits and makes punishable the very same conduct, states are not preempted from prosecuting the following: * * * the filing of a fraudulent claim for federal Social Security benefits (*Commonwealth v. Morris,* 394 Pa. Super. 185 (1990)); the forging of federal income tax documents (*State v. Radzvilowicz,* 47 Conn. App. 1 (1997)); the counterfeiting of United States' currency (*State v. McMurry,* 184 Ariz. 447 (Ariz. App. Div. 1 1995)) * * *.

As these cases make clear, the mere fact that the same conduct constitutes a crime under both state and federal law is insufficient reason to presume that Congress intended to preclude the states from enforcing their generally applicable criminal laws against that conduct. Here, although section 359(a) makes punishable the filing of a fraudulent benefits claim, nothing in the Railroad Unemployment Insurance Act in any way suggests that Congress intended that punishment to be the only punishment. We therefore conclude that the Railroad

Unemployment Insurance Act does not so pervasively regulate the field of benefits fraud as to preempt defendant's theft prosecution.

We likewise conclude that conflict preemption is not present in this case. Again, conflict preemption arises where either compliance with both federal and state law is a physical impossibility or state law stands as an impediment to the accomplishment and execution of the full purposes and objectives of Congress. *Gade,* 505 U.S. at 98. Thus, in this case, for conflict preemption to be present, either (1) compliance with both section 359(a) and the Illinois theft statute must be a physical impossibility, or (2) the State's prosecution of defendant for theft must stand as an impediment to the accomplishment and execution of Congress's full purposes and objectives in enacting the Railroad Unemployment Insurance Act. Neither of these conditions is present here.

First, section 359(a) prohibits and punishes the filing of fraudulent benefits claims. The Illinois theft statute (720 ILCS 5/16-1(a)(1), (a)(2) (West 1996)) prohibits and punishes the obtaining of property with the intent to deprive its owner permanently of its use or benefit. Compliance with both of these statutes is not a physical impossibility. * * *

Second, we are confident that the State's prosecution of defendant for theft of federal unemployment benefits does not operate as an impediment to Congress's purposes and objectives in prohibiting benefits fraud. On the contrary, we strongly suspect it furthers those purposes and objectives. Every time a defendant is convicted of theft, the number of persons defrauding the federal government is decreased by one. * * * Finally, because the federal government and the State of Illinois are separate jurisdictions, defendant's theft prosecution in no way precludes the federal government from prosecuting defendant for violating section 359(a). See *Wheeler,* 435 U.S. at 316-318.

Before concluding, we wish to address one final argument. Defendant contends that, even if the Railroad Unemployment Insurance Act does not preempt defendant's theft prosecution *per se,* the trial court nevertheless lacked subject matter jurisdiction over that prosecution because it required the trial court to interpret federal law. Contrary to defendant's assumption that the state courts are powerless to interpret federal law, the United States Supreme Court consistently has held that state courts have inherent authority, and thus are presumed competent, to adjudicate claims arising under the laws of the United States. See *Tafflin v. Levitt,* 493 U.S. 455, 458-459 (1990). According to the Supreme Court, nothing in the concept of our federal system prevents the state courts from enforcing rights created under federal law, and exclusive federal jurisdiction over cases arising under federal law is the exception rather than the rule. *Tafflin,* 493 U.S. at 459. * * *

For the foregoing reasons, the judgment of the circuit court of Kane County is affirmed.

Affirmed.

INGLIS and HUTCHINSON, JJ., concur.

Case Focus

1. According to the court, when does Congress have the power to preempt state law?

2. In the absence of preemption by Congress, why does the state have the power to convict a person of a crime for conduct that violates both federal and state law?

3. What are the three different ways in which a state law can be preempted by a federal law?

4. Does a state court have the power to interpret federal law?

• • • • • • • •

CHAPTER TERM

Police power

REVIEW QUESTIONS

1. Why is the federal government called a government of limited powers?

2. When enacting a criminal statute that is to be applicable within the states, on what, (if anything), must Congress base the statute, and if Congress must base a statute on something, what is the consequence if Congress enacts a statute that is not based on it?

3. What is an American territory and what is a federal enclave?

4. When enacting a criminal statute applicable to people within a federal territory or enclave, is Congress's power the same as when it is enacting a criminal statute applicable to people within the states, and if it is not, how is it different?

5. How does the power of an American state to enact a criminal statute applicable to people within its borders differ from the power of the federal government to enact a criminal statute?

6. Do the states have the power to enact statutes under the same principles of extraterritorial jurisdiction that sovereign nations are recognized as having the power to use?

7. Explain the doctrine of concurrent jurisdiction and how the doctrine of preemption applies to it. Can state criminal law be applied to criminal conduct that is related to matters assigned to the federal government by the U.S. Constitution?

ADDITIONAL READING

The Federalist Nos. 18, 41-46.
Leonard D. White, *The Federalists* (1956).

Printz v. United States, 521 U.S. 898 (1997).

ENDNOTES

1. 18 U.S.C. §13.
2. *United States v. Vilar*, 729 F.3d 62 (2d Cir. 2013).
3. 18 U.S.C. §7.
4. *U.S. Const.*, Art. I, Sec. 8.
5. The necessary and proper clause reads as follows: *The Congress shall have the power. . . . To make all Laws which shall be necessary and proper for carrying into Execution the foregoing Powers, and all other Powers vested by this Constitution in the Government of the United States, or in any Department or Officer thereof. U.S. Const.*, Art. I, Sec. 8.
6. The commerce clause reads as follows: *The Congress shall have the power . . . To regulate Commerce with foreign Nations, and among the several states, and with the Indian tribes. U.S. Const.*, Art. I, Sec. 8.
7. *Printz v. United States*, 521 U.S. 898 (1997).
8. *State v. Flores*, 218 Ariz. 407 (2009).
9. *People v. Wolfe*, 86 Ill. App. 3d 1134 (4th Dist. 1980).
10. *Skiriotes v. Florida*, 313 U.S. 69 (1941).
11. *Hanks v. State*, 13 Tex. App. 289 (1882).
12. *State v. Stepansky*, 761 So. 2d 1027 (2000).
13. *United States v. Mostafa*, 965 F. Supp. 2d 451 (S.D.N.Y. 2013).
14. *Id.*
15. *United States v. Hayes*, 99 F. Supp. 3d 409 (S.D.N.Y. 2015).
16. *United States v. Al Kassar*, 660 F.3d 108 (2d Cir. 2011).
17. *State v. Radzvilowicz*, 47 Conn. App. 1 (1997).

Chapter 8

Constitutional Limits on the Power to Define Crimes

Chapter Objectives

After reading this chapter, you should be able to

- Understand what an ex post facto law is and why its enactment is prohibited
- Understand what a bill of attainder is and why its enactment is prohibited
- Know what the equal protection clause is and how it restricts enactment of certain statutes
- Know the concepts embodied in the due process clause and how they prohibit the enactment of certain statutes
- Understand how various provisions of the Bill of Rights prohibit the enactment of certain laws

> It will be of little avail to the people that the law is made by men of their own choice, if the law be so voluminous that they cannot be read, or so incoherent that they cannot be understood; if they be repealed or revised before they are promulgated, or undergo such incessant changes that no man who knows what the law is today can guess what it will be tomorrow. —James Madison
> *Federalist* No. 62

The previous chapter examined the jurisdictional limits on the power of the federal and state governments to enact and apply criminal law. As you saw in that chapter many of those jurisdictional limits are based on the constitutional allocation of power between the

111

These constitutional limits can be asserted as defenses by defendants in criminal prosecutions. The use of these non-jurisdictional constitutional limits as defenses are discussed in Chapter 13, which examines non-exculpatory criminal defenses.

federal government and the states. The U.S. Constitution and the constitutions of the states also place a number of important non-jurisdictional limits on the power of federal and state legislative bodies to enact criminal laws. In this chapter we will examine five constitutional provisions that impose such limits: (A) the bar on enacting ex post facto laws; (B) the bar on enacting bills of attainder; (C) the equal protection clause; (D) the due process clause; and (E) the Bill of Rights.

A. The Bar on Enacting Ex Post Facto Laws

No . . . ex post facto *Law shall be passed. U.S. Const.* Art. I, Sec. 9.

No State shall . . . pass any . . . ex post facto *Law . . . , U.S. Const.,* Art. I, Sec. 10.

In separate clauses the U.S. Constitution bars the federal government from enacting ex post facto laws and also prohibits the states from enacting them. The ban on ex post facto laws in the Constitution stems from the excesses of the American colonial rulers, who used retroactive legislation as a means of political warfare and retribution.[1] The constitutions of all of the states also contain a prohibition against the enactment of ex post facto laws. The ban on enacting ex post facto laws is a narrow one, limited to criminal laws,[2] is applicable only to statutes,[3] and does not apply to judicial decisions.[4]

There are four different forms of ex post facto laws, the enactment of which is prohibited by the ex post facto clauses of the U.S. Constitution.[5] The most commonly recognized form of ex post facto law (one that is almost never seen) is a law that makes certain conduct criminal and that applies retroactively to conduct that occurred before the statute was adopted.

A second form of ex post facto law is one that increases the penalty for an offense after the offense has been committed. The ex post facto clause does not, however, bar a retroactive change in the manner in which a sentence is executed as long as the penalty is not increased. For example, if when a defendant commits a crime he is subject to the death penalty, it does not violate the ex post facto clause and prohibit carrying out a sentence of death if after he commits the murder the state changes the method by which defendants are executed.[6]

A third form of ex post facto law is one that, after the offense is committed, retroactively eliminates a defense or changes the definition of an offense to make a conviction for committing that offense easier.

The fourth type of ex post facto law is one that after the offense is committed, alters the legal rules so that less or different evidence is needed to convict the defendant than at the time the crime was committed.[7] For example, if at the time a defendant committed a sex crime the statute required that to be able to obtain a conviction there must be both testimony of the victim and evidence that corroborates the victim's testimony, but after the defendant committed the crime the legislature changed the statute to allow conviction based on the uncorroborated testimony of the victim alone, application of the new statute to the defendant's case would violate the ex post facto clause.

The date when an offense is committed is the critical date for analyzing any ex post facto question. The date when the prosecution is initiated and the date when a defendant is placed on trial are irrelevant.

Usually there is little serious question about when a crime was committed, but when a substantial period of time elapses between the criminal act and the effect of a criminal act, it raises the question of when the crime was committed and whether application of a statute that changed the law during that interval would bring the statute within the definition of an ex post facto law. For example, a defendant shoots her husband and he lingers in a coma for a period of months before dying. During the period after the shooting, but prior to the husband's death, the legislature increases the maximum sentence for murder from life in prison to death. Does it violate the ex post facto clause to sentence the defendant to death under the new law? In such cases the courts have held that the date of the criminal act (the shooting) is the date when the crime is committed, and application of a statute enacted after the criminal act is committed but before the act has its effect (the victim's death) would violate the ex post facto prohibition.

State v. Detter

Supreme Court of North Carolina (1979) 298 N.C. 604

COPELAND, J. Defendant was charged in an indictment, proper in form, with first-degree murder in the death of her husband, Don Gene Detter. The primary evidence for the State was presented through the testimony of five lay witnesses and four doctors.

Joan Ladale Brooks, a friend and neighbor of the Detter family, visited the Detters in their home at 5301 Prince Charles Drive, Kernersville, in January, 1977. During the visit, defendant mentioned how cruel her husband was to the family and stated that she had had something done to the brakes of her husband's car "to either hurt him or harm him." In late January or early February, 1977, Brooks went with the defendant to the Crown Drug Store. There, the defendant gave Brooks some money and asked her to purchase a bottle of Terro Ant Killer for her which Brooks did. Dr. McBay, Chief Toxicologist of North Carolina, testified that one bottle of Terro Ant Killer contains 300 milligrams of arsenic. A lethal dose of arsenic is between 100 milligrams and 300 milligrams.

During this same period of time, Brooks accompanied the defendant to the home of James Thomas Holly, Jr. During the visit the defendant asked Holly "what lead or lead poisoning would do to someone" and "where she could get some." Holly advised the defendant that lead "would most likely kill somebody." After returning home, Brooks observed the defendant go to a storage area, get some lead weights from a fishing tackle box, place them in a cooking pot half full of water, boil it down so that there was only a few drops of water left, and then observed the defendant pour the drops of water into a liquor bottle. Other evidence disclosed that the deceased was a heavy drinker and that he consumed three to four fifths of liquor per week.

Approximately one week later, Brooks observed the defendant pour the contents of a bottle of Terro Ant Killer into a glass of ice tea which defendant then gave to her husband which he drank. On her next visit to the Detter's house, Brooks heard the defendant remark that she "had asked her husband for a divorce and he wouldn't give her one . . . and she would be glad when everything was over and she wouldn't have to put up with Mr. Detter anymore."

In late March or early April, 1977, Brooks accompanied the defendant's son, Ted, to the Crown Drug Store, where he purchased two bottles of Terro Ant Killer which he then took home and gave to his mother. On several occasions in the latter half of March, 1977, Brooks observed the defendant place Terro Ant Killer in ice tea and give it to the deceased. On one occasion, Brooks observed the defendant pour Terro Ant Killer over a dish of ice cream and give the ice cream to the deceased.

In February, 1977, defendant and her son, Ted, visited Holly and defendant asked Holly if he "would be interested in killing her husband for Five Thousand Dollars." Holly declined the offer. On a later occasion Ted bought some "PCP" which is also known as "Angel Dust" from Holly. Two weeks later defendant accused Holly of "ripping her off." She stated that she put the drugs in her husband's food but they "did nothing but make him happy." Defendant advised Holly that she wanted the drugs "to kill her husband." Holly also sold the defendant some cocaine and some "acid." Holly's wife testified that defendant asked Holly "how could she kill somebody with a needle and air?" Holly told the defendant that "an air bubble . . . in your vein . . . could kill you instantly." On a later occasion defendant told Holly that the drugs were not working and she did not understand why because she had placed the "PCP," cocaine and "acid" in her husband's food and in his liquor. Defendant stated that she was going to the Magic Market to meet someone "who could help her" and Holly did not see the defendant again.

In January, 1977, the defendant talked to Gregory Wayne Boyd and showed him a plastic bag which contained a pale brown powder. Defendant asked Boyd if he thought the powder would kill her husband. Defendant asked Boyd if he knew anybody who would kill her husband for five thousand dollars, and defendant offered to pay Boyd five thousand dollars if he would kill her husband.

In November or December, 1976, defendant met her hairdresser, Pamela Christy, at a restaurant in Kernersville for lunch. During lunch defendant asked

Christy if she or her husband could "get some dope" for her; that she wanted the dope "to kill her husband." In January and February, 1977, defendant told Christy that she had put "some stuff" in her husband's food and he ate it but it didn't do anything to him.

The deceased was hospitalized from 30 March 1977 until 13 April 1977 and from 17 May 1977 until his death on 9 June 1977. During the first period of hospitalization, Dr. William Joseph Spencer tested deceased's urine for heavy metal poisoning and the results were negative. Dr. Spencer's diagnosis was that deceased was suffering from "peripheral neuropathy resulting from excessive alcohol intake." During the second period of hospitalization, Dr. Spencer noticed white lines across deceased's fingernails and he noticed a thickening of the skin over deceased's hands for which the medical term is hyperkeratosis, both symptoms of arsenic poisoning. A test for heavy metal poisoning was positive and deceased was treated with British Anti-Lewisite, a drug to combat arsenic poisoning. Dr. Spencer testified that arsenic poisoning is also a cause of peripheral neuropathy and in his opinion, as an expert in internal medicine, deceased died as a result of arsenic poisoning.

Dr. James Alvis McCool performed the autopsy on deceased on the day of his death. Samples of hair, fingernails, bile, liver, blood, kidney, urine, stomach content and small bowel content were taken by Dr. McCool and mailed to Dr. Arthur J. McBay, Chief Toxicologist for the State of North Carolina. Test results at the State Laboratory showed that these specimens from deceased's body contained approximately ten times the normal amount of arsenic. In response to a hypothetical question, Dr. McBay stated that in his opinion deceased died of arsenic poisoning.

Defendant testified that neither she nor her son asked Brooks to purchase Terro Ant Killer or purchased any themselves. On one occasion, Brooks and her son did go to the drugstore to pick up a prescription for her. She never talked to Brooks about poisoning or wanting to kill her husband. * * *

Several witnesses acquainted with the defendant testified that they had never heard her talk of wanting to or trying to kill her husband and that they had never seen her put any poisons in her husband's food. Also, several witnesses testified that the defendant had a good reputation in her community and in her church.

At the guilt-determination phase of the trial, the jury found the defendant guilty of first-degree murder. At the sentencing phase, the jury * * * recommended the death sentence and pursuant to G.S. 15A-2002, the trial judge imposed that sentence. Defendant appealed to this Court. * * *

By her twenty-fourth assignment of error, defendant contends that imposition of the death penalty in this case violates the proscription against *ex post facto* laws contained in the United States and North Carolina constitutions. We agree; therefore, the death sentence imposed in this case must be and is vacated and the case is remanded to the Superior Court of Forsyth County for imposition of a life sentence.

Article 1, §10 of the United States Constitution forbids any state to pass an *ex post facto* law. Article 1, §16 of the North Carolina Constitution forbids *ex post facto* laws in this State. The prohibition against *ex post facto* legislation includes the prohibition against passage of a law that changes the punishment for a crime, and inflicts a greater punishment than the law annexed to the crime when committed. *Calder v. Bull*, 3 U.S. 386, 1 L. Ed. 648 (1798). * * *

Here, defendant committed all of her efforts to kill her husband in January, February and March, 1977. At that time, the penalty in this State for first-degree murder was life imprisonment as a result of the United States Supreme Court's decision in *Woodson v. North Carolina*, 428 U.S. 280, 49 L. Ed. 2d 944, 96 S. Ct. 2978 (1976) which declared G.S. 14-17 (1974) (automatic death penalty for first-degree murder) unconstitutional. The deceased died on 9 June 1977. Our new death penalty statute, G.S. 15A-2000 *et seq.* became effective 1 June 1977. As of that date, the punishment for first-degree murder became death or life imprisonment as determined in accordance with G.S. 15A-2000. G.S. 14-17 (Cum. Supp. 1977) * * *. As part of that legislation, 1977 N.C. Sess. Laws, Ch. 406, s. 8 provides: "The provisions of this act shall apply to murders committed on or after the effective date of this act."

Therefore, the question presented is whether this murder was committed when the murderous acts were performed so that the punishment is life imprisonment or whether this murder was committed when death resulted so that the sentence of death imposed pursuant to G.S. 15A-2002 is constitutionally permissible under the *ex post facto* provisions of the United States and North Carolina constitutions. It is true that the definition of murder includes the unlawful killing of a human being with malice aforethought by means of poisoning, in which case premeditation and deliberation are presumed. G.S. 14-17 (Cum. Supp. 1977); *State v. Dunheen*, 224 N.C. 738, 32 S.E. 2d 322 (1944). Therefore, murder is a crime requiring both an act and a result. * * *

[F]or purposes of this decision and application of the prohibition against *ex post facto* legislation, we hold that the date the murderous acts were performed is the date the murder was committed. All of the murderous acts here were committed before 1 June 1977 at a time when the maximum punishment for first degree murder was life imprisonment. Therefore, imposition of the sentence of death under G.S. 15A-2002 in this case violates the prohibition against imposition of an *ex post facto* punishment and the sentence is therefore, vacated. The legislature has provided that when application of the death penalty to a defendant is declared unconstitutional for any reason, then the punishment is life imprisonment. 1977 N.C. Sess. Laws, Ch. 406, s. 6.

Accordingly, this case is remanded to the Superior Court of Forsyth County with directions (1) that the presiding judge, without requiring the presence of defendant, enter judgment imposing life imprisonment for the first-degree murder of which defendant has been convicted, and (2) that, in accordance with this judgment, the clerk of the superior court issue commitment in substitution for the commitment heretofore issued. * * *

Guilt determination phase: No error.

Sentencing phase: Death sentence vacated; case remanded for imposition of life sentence.

Case Focus

1. For purposes of the ex post facto clause, when a period of time elapses between an act and a prohibited result caused by that act, when is the crime considered to be committed?

2. If during the period between the act and the prohibited result the substantive law relating to the crime changes, under which version of the law can the perpetrator of the crime be prosecuted?

3. How, if at all, does the constitutional provision barring enactment of ex post facto laws apply to sentencing laws?

• • • • • • • • •

However, when the defendant's criminal conduct begins before a statute makes that conduct a crime or before the sentence for a crime is increased, and the conduct continues for some period of time after the statute making the conduct a crime or increasing the penalty is enacted, application of the new statute to the defendant's conduct does not violate the ex post facto clause. For example, if a defendant joins a conspiracy to distribute controlled substances in January and the conspiracy continues to operate through May, and in April the legislature increases the sentence for engaging in conspiracies to distribute controlled substances, the application of the new enhanced sentencing statute to the defendant does not violate the ex post facto clause.[8]

B. Prohibition Against Bills of Attainder

Bill of attainder is a legislative act that inflicts punishment on a person or an easily identifiable group of persons without a judicial trial. *United States v. Lovett*, 328 U.S. 303 (1946).

The same clauses of the U.S. Constitution that prohibit the enactment of an ex post facto law also prohibit legislative bodies from passing bills of attainder. A **bill of attainder** is a legislative act that inflicts punishment on a person or an easily identifiable group of persons without a judicial trial.[9] For example, if a legislative body were to pass a statute that provides that any government official who by a two-thirds vote of that body is found guilty of violating the law will be imprisoned and fined, an action taken under that statute would constitute a bill of attainder and would be unconstitutional.[10]

C. Limitations Imposed by the Equal Protection Clause

The equal protection clause of the Fourteenth Amendment provides that no state shall deny any person within its jurisdiction the equal protection of the laws. In the field of criminal law the equal protection clause prohibits two things: 1) the adoption of criminal laws that make arbitrary classifications, and 2) the arbitrary enforcement of the criminal law by the executive branch.[11] A statute is enforced arbitrarily when it is neutral on its face but enforced only against one racial group. The strictness of the application of the equal protection clause to a statute that makes classifications depends upon the subject to which the statute's classification relates.

[. . . nor shall any State] deny to any person within its jurisdiction the equal protection of the laws. U.S. Const., Amend. XIV, Sec. 1.

When the statutory classification relates to business activity the courts give wide discretion to the legislature and only require that the statute bear a rational relationship to the evil at which the statute is aimed. In such cases courts will concede every circumstance that will make the classification reasonable and not arbitrary. For example, if the legislature decides it wants to protect the public from the danger posed by untrained physicians, it can restrict the practice of medicine to persons who have a license to practice issued by the state, make it a crime to practice medicine without a license, and restrict the issuance of licenses to the class of persons who have both obtained a medical degree and passed a state medical licensing exam. In practice, the courts seldom invalidate an economic regulation on equal protection grounds.

When a criminal statute uses race as the basis of a classification or as part of the definition of an offense, the statute is subject to strict scrutiny and is rebutably presumed to be unconstitutional.[12] Indeed, such statutes are almost always struck down as unconstitutional. For example, a statute that makes it a crime for a black man and white woman or white man and black woman to live together is subject to strict scrutiny because race is used in defining the crime and, absent a compelling state interest for such a statute, it is unconstitutional.[13] Classifications based on sex are subject to something less than the strict scrutiny that is given to racial classifications, but to more scrutiny than is given to statutes that regulate economic matters.

In some instances a criminal statute may be neutral on its face, but in application it may fall disproportionately (disparate impact) on certain racial or national minorities. Such a statute violates the equal protection clause only if it can be shown that it was enacted for a discriminatory purpose.[14] When no discriminatory intent is shown, such statutes are subject only to rational basis review.[15]

The equal protection clause's strict scrutiny test is also applied to those statutes that categorize certain forms of constitutionally protected activity and then impose punishment for engaging in one form of that activity but not in another form. For example, if a statute allows picketing in a residential neighborhood if it is related to a labor dispute, but bars picketing in a residential neighborhood for any other reason, absent a showing of a compelling state interest that justifies the differing treatment of the two forms of constitutionally protected activity, such a statute violates the equal protection clause and is unconstitutional.

By its terms the equal protection clause of the Fourteenth Amendment applies only to the states and not to the federal government. The U.S. Supreme Court has held, however, that the due process clause of the Fifth Amendment, which applies to the federal government, also imposes equal protection restraints on it.[16] As a result, the federal government is also constitutionally barred from enacting criminal statutes that violate the principles embodied in the equal protection clause.

D. Limitations Imposed by Due Process Clauses

No person . . . [shall] be deprived of life, liberty, or property without due process of law. U.S. Const., Amend. V.

. . . nor shall any State deprive any person of life, liberty, or property, without due process of law. U.S. Const., Amend. XIV, Sec. 1.

The U.S. Constitution contains a due process clause in the Fifth Amendment that (as discussed above) applies to the federal government and a due process clause in the Fourteenth Amendment that applies to the states. The concept of due process embodied in each of the two due process clauses has two major aspects: a procedural aspect, which is examined in Section IV relating to criminal procedure, and a substantive aspect, which is examined here. Not completely fitting into either category is a third aspect of due process that creates standards for the drafting of criminal statutes under what is called the void for vagueness rule. That aspect of due process is examined here as well.

1. Substantive Due Process

The concept of substantive due process first appeared in Supreme Court decisions in the late nineteenth century when the states and Congress began to pass statutes to regulate the then-emerging industrial economy. In that early period the Supreme Court frequently used the doctrine of substantive due process to strike down those statutes. Originally, substantive due process was understood as limiting the power of legislative bodies to the enactment of statutes that had a real or substantial relationship to the government's police powers. Statutes that the courts viewed as going beyond those powers were struck down as being violative of substantive due process.

Beginning in the middle 1930s that formulation of the concept of substantive due process was jettisoned and the court all but abandoned it as a principle with which to strike down economic legislation. Starting in the 1950s the Supreme Court resurrected the principle, redefined it, and began to use it as a basis to strike down criminal and other statutes that regulated certain forms of private conduct. As reformulated by the Supreme Court, the concept of substantive due process today protects fundamental rights and liberties that are objectively and deeply rooted in the history and tradition of the United States and bars the enactment of criminal laws that transgress on those rights and liberties.[17]

2. *Void for Vagueness*

Criminal statutes may be vague either as to the conduct or result they define as illegal or as to the persons who are subject to prosecution. Due process requires that criminal statutes be drafted in such way that they give notice of what they forbid.[18] A criminal statute that is vague in defining what it forbids violates the void for vagueness principle of due process and is unconstitutional.[19] Statutes that employ terms used in the common law are seldom held to be vague because those terms are considered to have developed a specific and known meaning. Due process, however, does not require that defendants be able to understand that they could be subject to prosecution in the United States.[20]

E. Limitations Imposed by the Bill of Rights

The **Bill of Rights** refers to the first ten amendments to the *United States Constitution*. Amendments I through VIII place limits on substantive criminal law and specify much of criminal procedure.

Today the **Bill of Rights** is held to place certain limits on the power of both the federal and state governments to enact substantive criminal law, regulate criminal procedure, and enact other types of laws. The Bill of Rights was not always seen as applicable to the states. Beginning with *Barron v. Baltimore*, 32 U.S. 243 (1833) and continuing through *Twining v. New Jersey*, 211 U.S. 78 (1908) and *Wolf v. Colorado*, 338 U.S. 25 (1949), the Supreme Court consistently held that the Bill of Rights applied only to the federal government and not to the states.

Starting in the 1950s and continuing into the 1960s, using various theories, the Supreme Court began to selectively incorporate different provisions of the Bill of Rights into the due process clause of the Fourteenth Amendment and through that apply them to the states. As a result, today, with the exception of the Fifth Amendment's requirement that felony prosecutions be initiated by grand jury indictment, the Bill of Rights has been made applicable to the states. This section examines how the Bill of Rights limits the enactment of criminal statutes.

1. The First Amendment

The First Amendment proscribes the enactment of laws that abridge freedom of expression and religion. The Amendment also includes proscriptions against the enactment of laws relating to freedom of the press and the right to assemble. The discussion in this section relating to limits placed on the enactment of statutes by the free speech provision of the Amendment is generally applicable to the press and assembly provisions to the extent they protect free expression.

The First Amendment paints a broad swath of free speech protection and prohibits the enactment of statutes that limit many kinds of speech, including speech that teaches or advocates violence. On its face the First Amendment appears to be a complete bar to the enactment of statutes that punish any form of speech. The courts, however, have never read the free expression provisions of the Amendment in an absolute sense. The courts have held that the right to free expression does not extend to libelous statements, obscenity, fighting words, speech that itself involves the commission of a crime (such as an oral agreement between two or more persons to engage in criminal conduct), or to speech in which the speaker disseminates information with the specific intent that the information be used to commit a crime of violence. As a result, while the federal government and the states are prohibited from enacting criminal laws that regulate and punish most forms of speech, both are free to enact criminal statutes relating to libel, obscenity, fighting words, speech which itself involves the commission of a crime, and words spoken with the intent that the information the speech conveys be used to commit a crime of violence.

Congress shall make no law respecting an establishment of religion, or prohibiting the free exercise thereof; or abridging the freedom of speech, or of the press . . . U.S. Const., Amend. I.

United States v. Coronado

United States District Court, Southern District of California (2006)
461 F. Supp. 2d 1209

MILLER, **District Judge.** Defendant Rodney Adam Coronado ("Coronado") moves to dismiss the indictment charging him with violation of 18 U.S.C. §842(p)(2)(A), Distribution of Information Relating to Explosives, Destructive Devices and Weapons of Mass Destruction, on grounds that the statute is impermissibly overbroad * * *. The Government opposes the motion. For the reasons set forth below, the court denies the motion to dismiss the indictment.

BACKGROUND

On February 15, 2006, Coronado was charged in a single count indictment with violation of 18 U.S.C. §842(p)(2)(A), Distribution of Information Relating to

Explosives, Destructive Devices and Weapons of Mass Destruction. The indictment alleges that on August 1, 2003, Coronado "did teach and demonstrate the making and use of a destructive device and did distribute by any means, information pertaining to, in whole or in part, the manufacture of a destructive device, with the intent that the teaching, demonstration, and information be used for, and in furtherance of, an activity that constitutes a federal crime of violence, to wit, arson."

The parties identify the following events and background information. * * * Coronado is a self-characterized radical animal and environmental rights activist. In 1992 Coronado participated in an action that destroyed fur-industry research facilities involved in animal testing at Michigan State University. Coronado pled guilty and was sentenced to 57 months incarceration.

On August 1, 2003 Coronado gave a lecture on militant animal and earth liberation rights at the Lesbian Gay Bisexual Transgender Center located in the Hillcrest area of San Diego, California. The flyer promoting the lecture indicated that Coronado was an individual who "lives by the principles of direct action. Rod Coronado talks beyond theory." * * * The flyer also represented that Coronado participated in an action that "sunk two illegal whaling ships off the coast of Iceland." The advertisement also touted Coronado's experience as a "hunt saboteur" defending threatened species. Coronado's speech attracted media attention because, on the day before the lecture, an apartment structure in the University Town Center area of San Diego had been destroyed by arson, causing as estimated loss of $50 million. At the scene of the fire, investigators found a large banner reading "IF YOU BUILD IT—WE WILL BURN IT. THE ELF'S (sic) ARE MAD" (ELF is the acronym for Earth Liberation Front. The Government asserts that ELF is the name of a group of loosely organized cells of individuals dedicated to using illegal means to pursue a radical environmentalist agenda (Oppo. at p.2, fn.1)).

During the speech, recorded by FBI agents present at the meeting, Coronado spoke about his experiences and beliefs in direct action in support of animals and the environment against human exploitation. After his prepared remarks, Coronado fielded questions from the audience. One unidentified attendee asked, according to Coronado, "tell us about the device you used at the Michigan State arson." (Motion at p.3:28). The Government, in contrast, represents that the attendee asked how she could "make a bomb for an action." (Oppo. at p.5:7). In response to the question, Coronado explained that he did not use a bomb, but an incendiary device. He then approached the food table, picked-up a plastic one-gallon apple juice container, and described how he made the device. Coronado also commented that he "wouldn't be surprised if investigators found a device similar to this at the fire scene last night," a reference to the $50 million arson fire in the University Town Center the previous day. (Oppo. at p.5:15-16).

Coronado is currently serving a ten-month federal sentence in the District of Arizona for a conviction for conspiracy to interfere with an officer, in relation to his attempts to sabotage a mountain lion hunt.

DISCUSSION

The Statute and Brief Legislative History

Defendant is charged with violating 18 U.S.C. §842(p)(2)(A), which provides in pertinent part:

It is unlawful for any person—

(A) to teach or demonstrate the making or use of an explosive, a destructive device, or a weapon of mass destruction, or to distribute by any means information pertaining to, in whole or in part, the manufacture or use of an explosive, destructive device, or weapon of mass destruction, with the intent that the teaching demonstration, or information be used for, or in furtherance of, an activity that constitutes a Federal crime of violence. * * *

Facial Overbreadth

Coronado raises a facial challenge to §842(p)(2)(A) contending that the statute is overbroad because it punishes a substantial amount of constitutionally protected speech. In the area of First Amendment expression, "an overbroad regulation may be subject to facial review and invalidation, even though its application in the case under consideration may be constitutionally unobjectionable." *Forsyth County v. Nationalist Movement*, 505 U.S. 123, 129, 112 S. Ct. 2395, 120 L. Ed. 2d 101 (1992). A party may

challenge an ordinance under the overbreadth doctrine in cases where every application creates an impermissible risk of suppression of ideas, such as an ordinance that delegates overly broad discretion to the decision maker, . . . and in cases where the ordinance sweeps too broadly penalizing a substantial amount of speech that is constitutionally protected.

Id. at 129-130. Overbroad statutes "may have such a deterrent effect on free expression that they should be subject to challenge even by a party whose own conduct may be unprotected." *City Council of Los Angeles v. Taxpayers for Vincent*, 466 U.S. 789, 798, 104 S. Ct. 2118, 80 L. Ed. 2d 772 (1984).

The scope of the First Amendment overbreadth doctrine must be "carefully tied to the circumstances in which facial invalidation of a statute is truly warranted." *New York v. Ferber*, 458 U.S. 747, 768, 102 S. Ct. 3348, 73 L. Ed. 2d 1113 (1982). Striking down a statute under facial attack is employed "with hesitation and then 'only as a last resort.'" *Id.* (quoting *Broderick v. Oklahoma*, 413 U.S. 601, 613, 93 S. Ct. 2908, 37 L. Ed. 2d 830 (1973)). Consequently, where conduct and not merely speech is involved, a statute may be stricken only where the overbreadth is "substantial," *Ferber*, 458 U.S. at 768, and justified by "weighty countervailing policies." *Id.* at 770 (quoting *United States v. Raines*, 362 U.S. 17, 22-23, 80 S. Ct. 519, 4 L. Ed. 2d 524 (1960)). Finally, "[o]verbreadth scrutiny is less rigid when the questioned legislation regulates 'conduct in the shadow of the First Amendment, but do[es] so in a neutral, noncensorial manner.'" *United States v. Gilbert*, 813 F.2d 1523, 1530 (9th Cir. 1986) (quoting *Broderick*, 413 U.S. at 614).

Applying these principles to the facial overbreadth challenge, the court concludes that the statute is not substantially overbroad. To the extent Coronado argues the statute is too broad because it could be applied to individuals who may innocently teach or demonstrate the construction of a destructive device, or otherwise provide such information, this "argument does not identify a constitutional defect." *Hill v. Colorado*, 530 U.S. 703, 730-731, 120 S. Ct. 2480, 147 L. Ed. 2d 597 (2000). The specific focus of the statute is not on mere teaching, demonstrating, or disseminating information on how to construct a destructive device, but upon teaching, demonstrating, or disseminating information with the specific intent that the knowledge be used to commit a federal crime of violence. Moreover, as *Hill* teaches, where conduct and not merely speech is implicated the overbreadth of a statute must be judged in relation to its legitimate sweep. *Id*. at 732.

While the conduct at issue (i.e., the teaching or demonstration of the making of a destructive device with specific intent to commit arson) falls within the shadow of the First Amendment in the sense that such conduct involves speech, the First Amendment has never been held to immunize conduct "merely because the conduct was in part initiated, evidenced, or carried out by means of language, either spoken, written or printed." *Giboney v. Empire Storage & Ice Co.*, 336 U.S. 490, 498, 69 S. Ct. 684, 93 L. Ed. 834 (1949) * * * The statute does not seek to censor the mere teaching or demonstration of a destructive device. It is only when the teaching or demonstration of a destructive device is coupled with specific intent to commit a federal crime of violence that an individual runs afoul of the statute. See *Hill*, 530 U.S. at 730-732. * * *

The essence of Coronado's argument is that he was simply engaged in protected speech when he demonstrated how he constructed the incendiary device he employed to destroy fur-industry research facilities at Michigan State University. Arguing these facts * * * he concludes that his speech or demonstration is protected under *Brandenburg v. Ohio*, 395 U.S. 444, 89 S. Ct. 1827, 23 L. Ed. 2d 430 (1969). In *Brandenburg* the Supreme Court considered an as applied challenge to the constitutionality of the Ohio Criminal Syndicalism Act which criminalized "advocating . . . the duty, necessity or propriety of crime, sabotage, violence, or unlawful methods of terrorism as a means of accomplishing industrial or political reform and for voluntarily assembling with any society, group or assemblage or persons formed to teach or advocate the doctrines of criminal syndicalism." *Id*. at 444-445. Brandenburg, leader of a Ku Klux Klan group, was shown on film—accompanied by about 12 hooded Klansmen— making derogatory comments about African-Americans and Jews. He was found guilty and sentenced to one to ten years imprisonment.

The Supreme Court began its analysis by noting that

the constitutional guarantees of free speech and free press do not permit a State to forbid or proscribe advocacy of the use of force or of law violation except where such advocacy is directed to inciting or producing imminent lawless action and is likely to incite or produce such action, . . . the mere abstract teaching of the moral propriety or even moral necessity for a resort to force and violence is not the same as preparing a group for violent action and steeling it to such action. A statute which fails to draw this distinction impermissibly intrudes upon the freedoms guaranteed by the First and Fourteenth Amendments. It sweeps within its condemnation speech which our Constitution has immunized from governmental control.

Id. at 447-448 (citations omitted). * * *

Coronado contends that the Government may not proscribe constitutionally protected speech under *Brandenburg* unless it is likely to incite others to imminent lawless action. Coronado argues that because the indictment does not allege that the complained of conduct was likely to incite imminent lawless action, the indictment must be dismissed. This argument fails for three reasons. First, the argument ignores fundamental differences between the Ohio Criminal Syndicalism Act at issue in *Brandenburg*, and the statute at bar. As set forth above, the statute at bar does not target abstract advocacy, teaching, or speech as criminalized by the Ohio Criminal Syndicalism Act. Consequently, for purposes of a facial challenge, *Brandenburg* and its progeny cannot serve as the template by which the subject statute is analyzed. Second, the argument fails to appreciate that the issues addressed by the Supreme Court in *Brandenburg* arose in the context of an as applied analysis. The focus of the present facial attack is on the statute, the indictment, and well-established overbreadth principles. Coronado's proffered factual arguments are more properly addressed to an as applied analysis, which at the very least must await the development of an evidentiary record. Third, the argument makes particularly apt the following insight from [*United States v.*] *Featherston*[, 461 F.2d 1119 (5th Cir. 1972)]:

The words "clear and present danger" do not require that the government await the fruition of planned illegal conduct of such nature as is here involved. . . . "[T]he words cannot mean that before the Government may act, it must wait until the putsch is about to be executed, the plans have been laid and the signal is awaited. . . ."

Featherston, 461 F.2d at 1122 (citations omitted). * * *

Coronado further contends that the following statutory language is facially overbroad: ". . . the distribut[ion] by any means [of] information pertaining to, in whole or in part, the manufacture or use of an explosive [or] destructive device . . ." 18 U.S.C. §842(p)(2)(A). As the language criminalizing the "distribution of information by any means, in whole or in part" is imprecise, id., Coronado argues the statute is therefore overbroad. This challenged phrase is taken out of context as a whole. As set forth above, the reach of the statute is directed not to the expressive principles of teaching alone, but to conduct or a call for action where the teaching or demonstration of such destructive devices is committed with the specific intent that such teaching or demonstration be used to carry out a federal crime of violence. While there may be certain circumstances under which the statute may be overbroad as applied, any overbreadth that may exist will only be apparent after the presentation of evidence at the time of trial. At that time, any perceived overbreadth may be cured by appropriate jury instructions. * * *

In sum, the motion to dismiss the indictment is denied.

IT IS SO ORDERED.

Case Focus

1. On what basis did the court conclude that the statute did not violate the right to free speech guaranteed by the First Amendment?

• • • • • • • •

The First Amendment's clause relating to freedom of religion prohibits the states and the federal government from enacting laws that would compel a religious belief or that would punish any forms of religious belief. Thus, the First Amendment bars the passage of criminal or any other laws that would punish religious belief.

When it comes to religious practices, however, the First Amendment is not absolute. The First Amendment does not prohibit the enactment of a generally applicable criminal law that is not aimed at a religious practice, even if that law has the effect of making some aspect of that practice illegal. As a result, the First Amendment does not exempt adherents of a religion from prosecution for engaging in conduct that violates a generally applicable criminal law, even if the practice is based on their religious belief or is a ritual practice of their religion.[21] If, however, the law is neutrally phrased but is aimed at a particular religious practice, it will be unconstitutional. For example, if a city ordinance that bans the killing of animals is enacted after a group that believes in animal sacrifice moves into a community, that ordinance, though neutrally written, will be seen not as a law of general application, but as one aimed at a religious practice. That law violates the First Amendment.[22]

In contrast, a law that simply outlaws the possession of certain controlled substances does not violate the First Amendment when applied to a religious group that uses those substances as part of its religious ritual, and the fact that its use is part of a religious ritual does not prevent prosecution of persons who use it during such ritual.

Employment Division v. Smith

Supreme Court of the United States (1990)
494 U.S. 872

JUSTICE SCALIA delivered the opinion of the Court.

This case requires us to decide whether the Free Exercise Clause of the First Amendment permits the State of Oregon to include religiously inspired peyote use within the reach of its general criminal prohibition on use of that drug, and thus permits the State to deny unemployment benefits to persons dismissed from their jobs because of such religiously inspired use.

I

Oregon law prohibits the knowing or intentional possession of a "controlled substance" unless the substance has been prescribed by a medical practitioner. Ore. Rev. Stat. §475.992(4) (1987). The law defines "controlled substance" as a drug classified in Schedules I through V of the Federal Controlled Substances Act * * *. Ore. Rev. Stat. §475.005(6) (1987). Persons who violate this provision by possessing a controlled substance listed on Schedule I are "guilty of a Class B felony." §475.992(4)(a). * * * Schedule I contains the drug peyote, a hallucinogen derived from the plant *Lophophora williamsii Lemaire*. Ore. Admin. Rule 855-80-021(3)(s) (1988).

Respondents Alfred Smith and Galen Black (hereinafter respondents) were fired from their jobs with a private drug rehabilitation organization because they ingested peyote for sacramental purposes at a ceremony of the Native American Church, of which both are members. When respondents applied to petitioner Employment Division (hereinafter petitioner) for unemployment compensation, they were determined to be ineligible for benefits because they had been discharged for work-related "misconduct." The Oregon Court of Appeals reversed that determination, holding that the denial of benefits violated respondents' free exercise rights under the First Amendment.

On appeal to the Oregon Supreme Court, petitioner argued that the denial of benefits was permissible because respondents' consumption of peyote was a crime under Oregon law. The Oregon Supreme Court reasoned, however, that the criminality of respondents' peyote use was irrelevant to resolution of their constitutional claim—since the purpose of the "misconduct" provision under which respondents had been disqualified was not to enforce the State's criminal laws but to preserve the financial integrity of the compensation fund, and since that purpose was inadequate to justify the burden that disqualification imposed on respondents' religious practice. Citing our decisions in [in two earlier cases] the court concluded that respondents were entitled to payment of unemployment benefits. *Smith v. Employment Div., Dept.*

of Human Resources, 301 Ore. 209, 217-219 (1986). We granted certiorari. 480 U.S. 916 (1987).

Before this Court in 1987, petitioner continued to maintain that the illegality of respondents' peyote consumption was relevant to their constitutional claim. We agreed, concluding that "if a State has prohibited through its criminal laws certain kinds of religiously motivated conduct without violating the First Amendment, it certainly follows that it may impose the lesser burden of denying unemployment compensation benefits to persons who engage in that conduct." *Employment Div., Dept. of Human Resources of Oregon v. Smith*, 485 U.S. 660, 670 (1988) (*Smith I*). We noted, however, that the Oregon Supreme Court had not decided whether respondents' sacramental use of peyote was in fact proscribed by Oregon's controlled substance law * * * [and b]eing "uncertain about the legality of the religious use of peyote in Oregon," we determined that it would not be "appropriate for us to decide whether the practice is protected by the Federal Constitution." *Id.*, at 673. Accordingly, we vacated the judgment of the Oregon Supreme Court and remanded for further proceedings. *Id.*, at 674.

On remand, the Oregon Supreme Court held that respondents' religiously inspired use of peyote fell within the prohibition of the Oregon statute [and] * * * then considered whether that prohibition was valid under the Free Exercise Clause, and concluded that it was not. The court therefore reaffirmed its previous ruling that the State could not deny unemployment benefits to respondents for having engaged in that practice.

We again granted certiorari. 489 U.S. 1077 (1989).

II

Respondents' claim for relief rests on our decisions in *Sherbert v. Verner,* 374 U.S. 398 (1963), *Thomas v. Review Bd. of Indiana Employment Security Div.,* 450 U.S. 707 (1981), and *Hobbie v. Unemployment Appeals Comm'n of Florida*, 480 U.S. 136 (1987), in which we held that a State could not condition the availability of unemployment insurance on an individual's willingness to forgo conduct required by his religion. As we observed in *Smith I*, however, the conduct at issue in those cases was not prohibited by law. We held that distinction to be critical, for "if Oregon does prohibit the religious use of peyote, and if that prohibition is consistent with the Federal Constitution, there is no federal right to engage in that conduct in Oregon" * * *. Now that the Oregon Supreme Court has confirmed that Oregon does prohibit the religious use of peyote, we proceed to consider whether that prohibition is permissible under the Free Exercise Clause.

A

The Free Exercise Clause of the First Amendment, which has been made applicable to the States by incorporation into the Fourteenth Amendment, see

Cantwell v. Connecticut, 310 U.S. 296, 303 (1940), provides that "Congress shall make no law respecting an establishment of religion, or *prohibiting the free exercise thereof* . . . ." U.S. Const., Amdt. 1 (emphasis added). The free exercise of religion means, first and foremost, the right to believe and profess whatever religious doctrine one desires. Thus, the First Amendment obviously excludes all "governmental regulation of religious *beliefs* as such." *Sherbert v. Verner, supra*, at 402. The government may not compel affirmation of religious belief, see *Torcaso v. Watkins*, 367 U.S. 488 (1961), punish the expression of religious doctrines it believes to be false, *United States v. Ballard*, 322 U.S. 78, 86-88 (1944), impose special disabilities on the basis of religious views or religious status, see *McDaniel v. Paty*, 435 U.S. 618 (1978); *Fowler v. Rhode Island*, 345 U.S. 67, 69 (1953); cf. *Larson v. Valente*, 456 U.S. 228, 245 (1982), or lend its power to one or the other side in controversies over religious authority or dogma, see *Presbyterian Church in U.S. v. Mary Elizabeth Blue Hull Memorial Presbyterian Church*, 393 U.S. 440, 445-452 (1969) * * *.

But the "exercise of religion" often involves not only belief and profession but the performance of (or abstention from) physical acts: assembling with others for a worship service, participating in sacramental use of bread and wine, proselytizing, abstaining from certain foods or certain modes of transportation. * * *

Respondents in the present case * * * contend that their religious motivation for using peyote places them beyond the reach of a criminal law that is not specifically directed at their religious practice, and that is concededly constitutional as applied to those who use the drug for other reasons. They assert, in other words, that "prohibiting the free exercise [of religion]" includes requiring any individual to observe a generally applicable law that requires (or forbids) the performance of an act that his religious belief forbids (or requires). As a textual matter, we do not think the words must be given that meaning. It is no more necessary to regard the collection of a general tax, for example, as "prohibiting the free exercise [of religion]" by those citizens who believe support of organized government to be sinful, than it is to regard the same tax as "abridging the freedom . . . of the press" of those publishing companies that must pay the tax as a condition of staying in business. It is a permissible reading of the text, in the one case as in the other, to say that if prohibiting the exercise of religion (or burdening the activity of printing) is not the object of the tax but merely the incidental effect of a generally applicable and otherwise valid provision, the First Amendment has not been offended. * * *

Our decisions reveal that the latter reading is the correct one. We have never held that an individual's religious beliefs excuse him from compliance with an otherwise valid law prohibiting conduct that the State is free to regulate. On the contrary, the record of more than a century of our free exercise jurisprudence contradicts that proposition. As described succinctly by Justice Frankfurter in *Minersville School Dist. Bd. of Ed. v. Gobitis*, 310 U.S. 586, 594-595 (1940): "Conscientious scruples have not, in the course of the long struggle for religious toleration, relieved the individual from obedience to a general law not aimed at the promotion or restriction of religious beliefs. The mere possession of religious convictions which contradict the relevant concerns of a political society does not relieve the citizen from the discharge of political responsibilities (footnote omitted)." We first had occasion to assert that principle in *Reynolds v. United States*, 98 U.S. 145 (1879), where we rejected the claim that criminal laws against polygamy could not be constitutionally applied to those whose religion commanded the practice. "Laws," we said, "are made for the government of actions, and while they cannot interfere with mere religious belief and opinions, they may with practices. . . . Can a man excuse his practices to the contrary because of his religious belief? To permit this would be to make the professed doctrines of religious belief superior to the law of the land, and in effect to permit every citizen to become a law unto himself." *Id.*, at 166-167.

Subsequent decisions have consistently held that the right of free exercise does not relieve an individual of the obligation to comply with a "valid and neutral law of general applicability on the ground that the law proscribes (or prescribes) conduct that his religion prescribes (or proscribes)." *United States v. Lee*, 455 U.S. 252, 263, n.3 (1982) (STEVENS, J., concurring in judgment) * * * In *Gillette v. United States*, 401 U.S. 437, 461 (1971), we sustained the military Selective Service System against the claim that it violated free exercise by conscripting persons who opposed a particular war on religious grounds. * * *

The only decisions in which we have held that the First Amendment bars application of a neutral, generally applicable law to religiously motivated action have involved not the Free Exercise Clause alone, but the Free Exercise Clause in conjunction with other constitutional protections, such as freedom of speech and of the press, see *Cantwell v. Connecticut*, 310 U.S., at 304-307 (invalidating a licensing system for religious and charitable solicitations under which the administrator had discretion to deny a license to any cause he deemed nonreligious). * * *

The present case does not present such a hybrid situation, but a free exercise claim unconnected with any communicative activity or parental right. Respondents urge us to hold, quite simply, that when otherwise prohibitable conduct is accompanied by religious convictions, not only the convictions but the conduct itself must be free from governmental regulation. We have never held that, and decline to do so now. There being no contention that Oregon's drug law represents an attempt to regulate religious beliefs, the communication of religious beliefs, or the raising of one's children in those beliefs, the rule to which we have adhered ever since *Reynolds* plainly controls. "Our cases do not at their farthest reach support the proposition that a stance of conscientious opposition relieves an objector from any colliding duty fixed by a democratic government." *Gillette v. United States, supra*, at 461.

B

Respondents argue that even though exemption from generally applicable criminal laws need not automatically be extended to religiously motivated actors, at least the claim for a religious exemption must be evaluated under the balancing test set forth in *Sherbert v. Verner*, 374 U.S. 398 (1963). Under the *Sherbert* test, governmental actions that substantially burden a religious practice must be justified by a compelling governmental interest. See *id.*, at 402-403; * * *.

Even if we were inclined to breathe into *Sherbert* some life beyond the unemployment compensation field, we would not apply it to require exemptions from a generally applicable criminal law. * * *

[W]e have sometimes used the *Sherbert* test to analyze free exercise challenges to [certain] * * * laws, see *United States v. Lee, supra*, at 257-260; *Gillette v. United States, supra*, at 462, we have never applied the test to invalidate one. We conclude today that the sounder approach, and the approach in accord with the vast majority of our precedents, is to hold the test inapplicable to such challenges. The government's ability to enforce generally applicable prohibitions of socially harmful conduct, like its ability to carry out other aspects of public policy, "cannot depend on measuring the effects of a governmental action on a religious objector's spiritual development." *Lyng, supra*, at 451. To make an individual's obligation to obey such a law contingent upon the law's coincidence with his religious beliefs, except where the State's interest is "compelling"—permitting him, by virtue of his beliefs, "to become a law unto himself," *Reynolds v. United States*, 98 U.S., at 167—contradicts both constitutional tradition and common sense.

The "compelling government interest" requirement seems benign, because it is familiar from other fields. But using it as the standard that must be met before the government may accord different treatment on the basis of race, see, *e.g.*, *Palmore v. Sidoti*, 466 U.S. 429, 432 (1984), or before the government may regulate the content of speech, see, *e.g.*, *Sable Communications of California v. FCC*, 492 U.S. 115, 126 (1989), is not remotely comparable to using it for the purpose asserted here. What it produces in those other fields—equality of treatment and an unrestricted flow of contending speech—are constitutional norms; what it would produce here—a private right to ignore generally applicable laws—is a constitutional anomaly. * * *

If the "compelling interest" test is to be applied at all, then, it must be applied across the board, to all actions thought to be religiously commanded. * * * Any society adopting such a system would be courting anarchy, but that danger increases in direct proportion to the society's diversity of religious beliefs, and its determination to coerce or suppress none of them. * * * The rule respondents favor would open the prospect of constitutionally required religious exemptions from civic obligations of almost every conceivable kind—ranging from compulsory military service, see, *e.g.*, *Gillette v. United States*, 401 U.S. 437 (1971), to the payment of taxes, see, *e.g.*, *United States v. Lee, supra*; to health and safety regulation such as manslaughter and child neglect laws, see, *e.g.*, *Funkhouser v. State*, 763 P.2d 695 (Okla. Crim. App. 1988), compulsory vaccination laws, see, *e.g.*, *Cude v. State*, 237 Ark. 927 (1964), [and] drug laws, see, *e.g.*, *Olsen v. Drug Enforcement Administration*, 279 U.S. App. D.C. 1, 878 F.2d 1458 (1989) * * * to social welfare legislation such as minimum wage laws, see *Tony and Susan Alamo Foundation v. Secretary of Labor*, 471 U.S. 290 (1985) * * * and animal cruelty laws, see, *e.g., Church of the Lukumi Babalu Aye Inc. v. City of Hialeah*, 723 F. Supp. 1467 (S.D. Fla. 1989) * * * and laws providing for equality of opportunity for the races, see, *e.g., Bob Jones University v. United States*, 461 U.S. 574, 603-604 (1983). The First Amendment's protection of religious liberty does not require this. * * *

Just as a society that believes in the negative protection accorded to the press by the First Amendment is likely to enact laws that affirmatively foster the dissemination of the printed word, so also a society that believes in the negative protection accorded to religious belief can be expected to be solicitous of that value in its legislation as well. It is therefore not surprising that a number of States have made an exception to their drug laws for sacramental peyote use. See, *e.g.*, Ariz. Rev. Stat. Ann. §§13-3402(B)(1)-(3) (1989); Colo. Rev. Stat. §12-22-317(3) (1985); N.M. Stat. Ann. §30-31-6(D) (Supp. 1989). But to say that a nondiscriminatory religious-practice exemption is permitted, or even that it is desirable, is not to say that it is constitutionally required, and that the appropriate occasions for its creation can be discerned by the courts. It may fairly be said that leaving accommodation to the political process will place at a relative disadvantage those religious practices that are not widely engaged in; but that unavoidable consequence of democratic government must be preferred to a system in which each conscience is a law unto itself or in which judges weigh the social importance of all laws against the centrality of all religious beliefs.

Because respondents' ingestion of peyote was prohibited under Oregon law, and because that prohibition is constitutional, Oregon may, consistent with the Free Exercise Clause, deny respondents unemployment compensation when their dismissal results from use of the drug. The decision of the Oregon Supreme Court is accordingly reversed.

It is so ordered.

Case Focus

1. What are the two aspects of religious exercise the Court identifies?
2. Which of those two aspects may be subject to regulation by the government through criminal laws?
3. Under the holding of the Court, what type of criminal laws can be applied to the exercise of religion?
4. What reason does the Court give for allowing such regulation by government?

• • • • • • • • •

2. *The Second Amendment*

A well regulated Militia, being necessary to the security of a free State, the right of the people to keep and bear Arms, shall not be infringed. U.S. Const., Amend. II.

The Second Amendment's right to keep and bear arms creates an individual right of citizens to possess weapons for self defense.[23] While the right is not unlimited, the Second Amendment bars the enactment of statutes that make it a crime for all citizens to possess any firearm.[24]

3. *The Fifth Amendment*

[No person] shall be compelled in any criminal case to be a witness against himself. U.S. Const., Amend. V.

The Fifth Amendment's privilege against self-incrimination which is discussed in depth in Chapter 17, also places limits on the power of the federal and state government to enact statutes. The privilege against self-incrimination prohibits the federal government and the states from enacting regulatory statutes that require licensing of and record-keeping by those who are engaged in illegal activity. For example, under the guise of a tax law Congress cannot enact a statute that requires gamblers to keep certain records and to produce them on demand to the government.[25] The privilege against self-incrimination does not, however, prohibit the enactment of records-keeping statutes as part of a regulatory or tax scheme that is aimed at legal activity.

4. *The Fourth Amendment*

The right of the people to be secure in their persons, houses, papers, and effects, against unreasonable searches and seizures, shall not be violated, and no Warrants shall issue, but upon probable cause, supported by Oath or affirmation and particularly describing the place to be searched, and the persons or things to be seized. U.S. Const., Amend. IV.

The Fourth Amendment's prohibition on unreasonable searches also places a limit on the power to enact criminal laws. For example, the Fourth Amendment prohibits the government from enacting a statute that makes it a crime for a homeowner to refuse to allow a building inspector into his home without a warrant.[26]

CHAPTER TERMS

Bill of attainder   Bill of Rights

REVIEW QUESTIONS

1. What four types of statutes do the ex post facto clauses of the U.S. Constitution prohibit the federal government and the states from enacting?

2. Menendez administered poison to Smith by sprinkling it on a steak that Smith was eating. Smith became violently ill shortly after ingesting the meat, but did not die until four months later. During the four months that Smith lay dying the state legislature increased the penalty for murder from life imprisonment to death. Menendez is charged with Smith's murder three weeks after the new statute goes into effect. If Menendez is convicted of murdering Smith, can he be sentenced to death? If at the time Menendez administered the poison to Smith the crime of murder carried a penalty of death by electrocution, and sometime after Smith died the state changed the method by which executions were to be carried out to lethal injection, and Menendez is convicted of Smith's murder, would that change in the statute prohibit the imposition of the death penalty on Menendez on ex post facto grounds?

3. What is a bill of attainder?

4. Does the equal protection clause of the Fourteenth Amendment prohibit the enactment of all criminal statutes that compose any type of classifications? Explain.

5. When deciding whether a statute violates the Fourteenth Amendment's equal protection clause, do courts look at criminal statutes that regulate or classify economic activity differently from those criminal statutes that use race? If so, describe that difference.

6. What type of non-procedural limits, if any, does the due process clause of the Fifth and Fourteenth Amendments impose on Congress and the state legislatures when they enact criminal laws?

7. Does the First Amendment prohibit the enactment of all criminal statutes that punish any type of speech, or can the federal government or a state enact criminal statutes that punish certain types of speech? If so, what types of speech may be made criminal?

8. Islam permits the practice of polygamy. Wyoming has a statute that makes polygamy a crime. Ahmed, a devout Muslim, moves to Wyoming and while there, following the tenants of his religion, he takes four wives. The State of Wyoming initiates a criminal prosecution of Ahmed charging him with the crime of polygamy. Since Ahmed's polygamy is connected with his religious beliefs and with his religion, does that fact act as a defense to the polygamy prosecution?

9. Does the Second Amendment prohibit the enactment of statutes that make it a crime for private citizens to own or possess firearms?

10. Money laundering is a crime. A senator from California proposes a bill that would impose a tax on money launderers based on the volume of money they launder. If passed the bill would require money launderers to keep certain records relating to the places where and the quantities of money they launder each year. The statute would require money launderers to make such records available for inspection by the Internal Revenue Service. If enacted into law, would such a statute violate any provision of the Bill of Rights?

ENDNOTES

1. *People v. Frazer*, 21 Cal. 4th 737 (1999).
2. *Galvan v. Press*, 347 U.S. 522 (1954).
3. *Rogers v. Tennessee*, 532 U.S. 451 (2003).
4. *Id.*
5. *Carmell v. Texas*, 529 U.S. 513 (2000).
6. *Malloy v. South Carolina*, 237 U.S. 180 (1901).
7. *Id.*
8. *United States v. Fazio*, 914 F.2d 950 (7th Cir. 1990).
9. *United States v. Lovett*, 328 U.S. 303 (1946).
10. *See Jones v. Slick*, 56 So. 2d 459 (Fla. 1952).
11. *Yick Wo v. Hopkins*, 118 U.S. 356 (1886).
12. *McLaughlin v. Florida*, 379 U.S. 184 (1964).
13. *Id.*
14. *United States v. Rafle*, 2012 WL 1424438 (S.D. Ind. 2012).
15. *Id.*
16. *Bolling v. Sharpe*, 347 U.S. 497 (1954).
17. *Washington v. Glucksberg*, 521 U.S. 702 (1997).
18. *United States v. Al Kassar*, 660 F.3d 108 (2d Cir. 2011).
19. *Id.*
20. *United States v. Hayes*, 99 F. Supp. 3d 409 (2015).
21. *Employment Division v. Smith*, 494 U.S. 872 (1990).
22. *Church of the Lukumi Babalu Aye, Inc. v. Hialeah*, 508 U.S. 520 (1993).
23. *McDonald v. City of Chicago*, 561 U.S. 742 (2010).
24. *District of Columbia v. Heller*, 128 S. Ct. 2783 (2008).
25. *Marchetti v. United States*, 390 U.S. 39 (1968).
26. *Camera v. Municipal Court*, 387 U.S. 523 (1967).

Chapter 9
Accountability for Criminal Conduct

Chapter Objectives

After reading this chapter, you should be able to

- Name the different types of accomplices recognized by the common law and understand the differences between them
- Understand how modern statutes make a person accountable for crimes committed by others
- Explain the extent of a person's accountability for a crime
- Understand when a corporation will be responsible for a crime committed by one of its agents
- Explain when an officer or director of a corporation will be responsible for the criminal acts of a corporate agent

The last point of enquiry is, how accessories are to be treated . . . [T]he general rule of the ancient law (borrowed from the Gothic constitutions) is this, accessories shall suffer the same punishment as their principals: if one be liable to death, the other is also liable: as by the law of Athens, delinquents and their abettors were to receive the same punishment. —Blackstone, *Commentaries on the Law of England*

The law of accountability determines when a person will be held responsible for criminal conduct. As such the law of accountability does not itself define any crime, but is merely a mechanism through which a criminal conviction may be obtained.[1] Under the law of accountability a person is responsible for criminal conduct either when he performs that conduct or when he is an

An **accomplice** is a person who, intending to promote the commission of a crime, encourages or requests another to commit it or agrees or provides aid to another in its commission. *Scales v. United States*, 367 U.S. 203 (1961).

accomplice to criminal conduct performed by another person. If under the law of accountability a person is an accomplice to a crime, then he is guilty of that crime (no matter how small his role was as an accomplice) and generally is subject to the same potential penalty as the person who actually performed the criminal act.[2] An accomplice can be convicted of a crime even if the actual perpetrator of the criminal act is not charged or is acquitted.

Closely related to the law of accountability are the principles of corporate responsibility and of vicarious responsibility of corporate officers and directors for crimes committed by corporate agents. This chapter examines both the law of accountability and the principles of corporate and corporate officer and director responsibility.

A. Principles of Accountability

The common law recognized that there could be different parties to a crime and that each of those parties could play a distinct role in its commission. The common law developed rules that identified and differentiated between those parties, determined what conduct of those parties would result in making them accountable for the commission of a crime, and determined the extent to which any of those parties would be held accountable for the criminal acts of another party to a crime. This section examines five subjects related to accountability: (1) the common law's system of classifying parties to a crime and the statutory alternative to it; (2) the type of conduct that makes a person accountable as an accomplice for the criminal conduct of another; (3) the effect of an accomplice's incapacity to commit a crime on his accountability for its commission; (4) the extent of an accomplice's accountability for the criminal acts of his confederates; and (5) termination of accountability.

1. Common Law Parties to a Crime and Their Elimination by Some Statutes

The common law identified and defined different categories of actors who, despite their differing conduct in relation to the commission of a crime, were considered to be parties to and held accountable for its commission. While some states have adopted accountability statutes that have eliminated the common law party classifications and replaced them with simple accountability rules, other states have retained and continue to use those classifications.[3] For that reason understanding how the common law classified the different parties to a crime continues to be important. This section (a) identifies and examines the different parties to a crime recognized by the common law and examines how the common law differentiated between them and (b) examines the modern statutory principles of accountability that in many states have replaced the common law classification system.

a. Types of Accomplices Under the Common Law

The common law identified and differentiated between four different possible parties to a crime: (1) principals in the first degree, (2) principals in the second degree, (3) accessories before the fact, and (4) accessories after the fact. Under the common law, principals in the second degree and all accessories were accountable for and could be convicted of crimes committed by a principal in the first degree, and all four were subject to the same potential penalties.

Principal in the first degree is the person who either actually performs the criminal act, *Lake v. State*, 100 Fla. 373 (1930), or causes an innocent person to perform it. *Bailey v. Commonwealth*, 229 Va. 258 (1985).

Under common law principles, a **principal in the first degree** was the person who actually engaged in the criminal act.[4] For example, if Carl gives a check that he knows is forged to a car dealer to pay for a car, assuming that delivery of a forged document constitutes a form of the crime of forgery, Carl is a principal in the first degree to the crime of forgery.

The common law also treated a person who caused an innocent agent to engage in a criminal act for him as a principal in the first degree.[5] In the above example, instead of taking the forged check to the car dealer himself, Carl gives Yvonne the forged check and asks her to deliver it for him to the car dealer to pay for the car. Yvonne, not knowing and having no reason to suspect that the check is forged, delivers it to the car dealer. Carl is considered to be a principal in the first degree even though he did not actually perform the physical act of delivery.

Constructive presence occurs when, without regard to his physical proximity to the place where a crime will be committed, a person places himself where he can render assistance to the perpetrator of the crime if needed. *United States v. Peichev*, 500 F.2d 917 (9th Cir. 1974).

A person who causes another to commit a criminal act is called a "causer" and under the common law a causer was said to be **constructively present** at the situs of the crime. The concept of constructive presence is important because it gives a jurisdiction the power to prosecute a causer who from outside of its borders causes one who is within its borders to commit a crime.

Principal in the second degree is a person who is actually or constructively present at the scene of the crime who does not commit the criminal act, but has agreed to render assistance to one who does. *State v. Sowell*, 353 Md. 713 (1999).

A **principal in the second degree** is a person who is actually or constructively present at the situs of the crime who does not himself commit the criminal act, but who aids, counsels, commands, or encourages the principal in the first degree to commit it. A person is considered to be constructively present at the situs of a crime when he has agreed to render assistance to another who will engage in certain criminal conduct and, without regard to his physical proximity to the place where the crime will be committed, he places himself in a location where he can render that assistance, if needed.[6] For example, an accomplice who is located 500 miles from the actual situs of a crime and who has agreed to render assistance to the perpetrator of a criminal act is considered constructively present at the situs of the crime as long as at that distant location he can render the promised aid to the perpetrator, if needed.

United States v. Peichev

United States Court of Appeals for the Ninth Circuit (1974) 500 F.2d 917

WALLACE, J. The grand jury indicted Peichev on three counts: Aiding and abetting aircraft piracy [18 U.S.C. §2; 49 U.S.C. §1472(I)], conspiracy to commit aircraft piracy [18 U.S.C. §371] and conspiracy to commit extortion by means of aircraft piracy [18 U.S.C. §1951]. Peichev pleaded not guilty and was tried before a jury. After all of the evidence had been submitted, Peichev moved for a judgment of acquittal on count one on the ground that there was insufficient evidence * * *. The court denied [the motion] * * * and the jury returned a verdict of guilty on all counts. The court sentenced Peichev to life on count one and to 20 years on count three, both sentences to run concurrently. The court did not impose sentence on count two. Peichev appeals. [We affirm] on the basis that there was sufficient evidence of aiding and abetting under count one.

* * * Over the weekend of June 16-19, 1972, Peichev and two other men, Michael Azmanoff and Dimitr Alexiev, traveled by car to Washington state, allegedly in search of gold. During this trip they also traveled to Vancouver and to Hope and Puntzi, two remote landing sites, both over 100 miles from Vancouver. While on this trip, plans were made for Azmanoff and Alexiev to hijack an airplane and to fly it to a remote airport in Canada. There, a fourth person would be waiting with a car ready to take the skyjackers to an apartment hide-out in the outskirts of Vancouver. Peichev was to rent a private plane and to meet them at an auxiliary landing strip in case the hijacked plane was unable to land at the preferred airport.

The three men returned to San Francisco and on July 1, 1972, met at the San Francisco International Airport with Illia Shishkoff who agreed to meet Peichev at noon on July 4, at the Vancouver Airport and to rent an apartment in the outskirts of the city. On July 3, Peichev withdrew $1,700 from his bank account and borrowed a gun under the guise of a need to protect himself while hunting for gold. Later the same day he met with Alexiev and Azmanoff at the San Francisco International Airport. They gave him a plane ticket to Seattle and told him to take a bus to Vancouver.

After meeting Shishkoff in Vancouver, Peichev rented two cars and traveled with Shishkoff to Hope airport, approximately 100 miles, and returned to Vancouver. The following day, July 5, Peichev rented a private plane and hired a pilot to fly him to Bella Coola and then to Anaheim Lake. While at Anaheim Lake,

Peichev learned by radio that the hijack attempt had failed. He proceeded to Puntzi airstrip where he spent the night and then returned to Vancouver. In Vancouver he met Shishkoff and arranged for the return of the rental cars and then returned to San Francisco.

On July 5, the same day that Peichev flew to Puntzi airstrip, Azmanoff and Alexiev hijacked a Pacific Southwest Airline flight scheduled to travel from Sacramento to San Francisco. The hijackers demanded $800,000, parachutes and aircharts of Canada, Alaska and the Soviet Union. After the plane landed in San Francisco, an F.B.I. agent, posing as an international pilot, was allowed to board the plane. Gunfire erupted between the hijackers and F.B.I. agents and Azmanoff and Alexiev were killed. Azmanoff killed one passenger and wounded three others. The F.B.I. agents found on the bodies of the hijackers a map of British Columbia, Canada, and a small piece of note paper containing the map coordinates of Puntzi airstrip. * * *

Peichev argues that the evidence was insufficient to support his conviction of aiding and abetting aircraft piracy. Under count one, Peichev was charged with only aiding and abetting aircraft piracy * * *. He concedes for the sake of argument that the evidence was sufficient to show a conspiracy, but argues that the government did not show that he aided and abetted in the perpetration of the crime.

At common law an abettor was one who was either actually or constructively present at the site of the crime and "who, with mens rea, either assist[ed] the perpetrator in the commission of the crime, [stood] by with intent (known to the perpetrator) to render aid if needed, or command[ed], counsel[ed] or otherwise encourage[d] the perpetrator to commit the crime." R. Perkins, *Criminal Law* 645 (1969) (footnotes omitted). *See* W. LaFave & A. Scott, *Criminal Law* 495 (1972). The distinction between an accessory before the fact and an abettor (a principal in the second degree) was the requirement that the abettor be either actually or constructively present at the site of the crime. R. Perkins at 658. A person was deemed constructively present "whenever he [was] cooperating with the perpetrator and '[was] so situated as to be able to aid him, with a view known to the other, to insure success in the accomplishment of the common purpose.'" R. Perkins at 660. * * * The only proximity required was that the person be close enough to render aid as needed. *Rex v. Soares*, 168 Eng. Rep. 664 (1802).

Modern courts in construing 18 U.S.C. §2 have generally followed the common law principles, but have emphasized the requirement that the person actively participate in the criminal venture. The Supreme Court defined the elements of aiding and abetting in *Nye & Nissen v. United States*, 336 U.S. 613, 619 (1949), as follows:

> In order to aid and abet another to commit a crime it is necessary that a defendant "in some sort associate himself with the venture, that he participate in it as in something that he wishes to bring about, that he seek by his action to make it succeed." L. Hand, J., in United States v. Peoni, 2d Cir., 100 F.2d 401, 402.

Subsequently, the Court in *United States v. Williams*, 341 U.S. 58, 64 (1951), stated: "Aiding and abetting means to assist the perpetrator of the crime." * * *

On the authority of these cases we hold that a person is an aider and abettor under 18 U.S.C. §2 if he actively assists in planning and preparing for the perpetration of the crime and assumes a station with the knowledge of the perpetrators where he may be able to assist either in the commission of the crime or in the escape immediately following the perpetration of the crime. Under this standard, the evidence was sufficient to show that Peichev was guilty of aiding and abetting. He traveled to Canada with Azmanoff and Alexiev to look at the landing sites. He was involved in planning the crime and agreed to be a participant. He borrowed a gun and had it with him at the time he expected to become an active participant. He traveled to Canada, rented cars and an airplane to aid the perpetrators in their escape. He was en route to the airstrip planned for a possible rendezvous when he learned that the crime had failed. According to a plan, known to the perpetrators, he was positioning himself so as to assist their escape, an element essential to the successful completion of the crime. His substantial distance from the site of the hijacking is irrelevant so long as he was in a proximity where he could assist the successful completion of the crime. He was in a position to assist the escape from a jet airplane as much as the driver of a get-away car waiting outside of a bank that is being robbed. The fact that the criminal plot was foiled before he could be of assistance is immaterial; he completed his assignment with the expectation that it would result in the successful commission of the crime. We hold that there was ample evidence to support the jury verdict. * * *

[A]s no sentence was imposed on count two and the record reflects no reason why none was imposed, count two should be dismissed. This case is remanded to the district court for proper disposition of count two.

Affirmed in part and remanded in part.

Case Focus

- According to the court why would the defendant be accountable as an accomplice when he was miles away from the scene of the crime?
- Based on this case, can a person be held accountable as an accomplice to a crime if the crime is discovered and the perpetrator is arrested before the person renders assistance?

• • • • • • • •

An **accessory before the fact** is a person who aids, counsels, commands, or encourages the principal in the first degree to commit an offense, but who is not actually or constructively present at the situs of the offense. Thus, whether an accomplice is a principal in the second degree or an accessory before the fact is determined by the actual or constructive location of the accomplice at the time the offense is committed.

An **accessory before the fact** is a person who aids, counsels, commands, or encourages a person to commit a crime, but was not actually or constructively present at the time the crime was committed.

State v. Sowell, 353 Md. 713 (1999).

An **accessory after the fact** is one who, knowing that a person has committed a felony, gives aid to that person for the purpose of hindering that person's apprehension, conviction, or punishment. *Lowe v. People*, 135 Colo. 209 (1957).

An **accessory after the fact** is one who, knowing that a person has committed a felony, gives aid to that person for the purpose of hindering that person's apprehension, conviction, or punishment.[7] It is important to keep in mind that a person is not an accessory after the fact if *before* the offense is committed he agrees to give post-commission assistance. In such a case the accomplice could be either a principal in the second degree or an accessory before the fact, depending upon the actual or constructive location of the accomplice when the crime is committed.

b. Modern Statutory Approach

The common law party classification system gave rise to a number of highly technical jurisdictional and procedural problems. In an effort to eliminate those problems and to simplify the law of accountability some modern statutes, including the Model Penal Code and many of the state codes that are patterned on it, have eliminated reference to and use of the common law party to a crime categories and instead have simply provided that a person is responsible for conduct that constitutes an offense if: (1) it is his own conduct or (2) it is the conduct of another and (a) having the mental state described in the statute he causes that other person to perform the illegal act or (b) having the intent to facilitate the commission of a crime, before or during its commission, he solicits, aids, or abets its planning or commission. The Illinois accountability statute is an example of one such statute:

> When Accountability Exists. A person is legally accountable for the conduct of another when:
> (a) Having a mental state described by the statute defining the offense, he causes another to perform the conduct, and the other person in fact or by reason of legal incapacity lacks such a mental state; or
> (b) The statute defining the offense makes him so accountable; or
> (c) Either before or during the commission of an offense, and with the intent to promote or facilitate such commission, he solicits, aids, abets, agrees or attempts to aid, such other person in the planning or commission of the offense. 720 ILCS 5/5-2.

Virtually all of the modern accountability statutes have completely eliminated the concept of accessory after the fact and in its place many states have adopted statutes that define a crime that in its definition includes the conduct that, under the common law, made a person an accessory after the fact.[8] In some states the crime is called concealing or aiding a fugitive; in others it is included in a more general crime called obstructing justice. An example of one such statute is the following Illinois offense:

> Concealing or Aiding a Fugitive. Every person not standing in the relation of husband, wife, parent, child, brother, or sister to the offender, who, with the intent to prevent the apprehension of the offender, conceals his

knowledge that an offense has been committed or harbors, aids or conceals the offender, commits a Class 4 felony. 720 ILCS 5/31-5.

2. *What Makes a Person Accountable for the Criminal Conduct of Another*

While most modern accountability statutes do not use the common law's party to a crime categories, with the exception of the concept of accessory after the fact, those statutes continue to use the essential concepts upon which common law accountability was based. For example, while most accountability statutes eliminate use of the terms "principal in the second degree" and "accessory before the fact," they retain the common law principle that was shared by both of those types of accomplices and, without regard to a person's actual or constructive presence at the situs of the crime, they impose accountability on him for the criminal conduct of another when he solicits, assists, or attempts to assist that other person in the commission of a criminal offense.

Also, while modern statutes have eliminated use of the term "principal in the first degree," they retain the common law principle of making a person who causes another to commit a criminal act accountable for that other person's act. As a result, whether we are talking about common law accountability or statutory accountability, what constitutes aiding and abetting and what constitutes causing are, with allowance for variations in the specific wording of different state statutes, substantially the same under both the common law and today's accountability statutes.

Pleading Accountability in the Charging Instrument

Under the law of most American jurisdictions the prosecutor is not required to allege in the changing instrument that a particular defendant was an accomplice. The prosecutor can charge the defendant as the person who committed the crime and if the evidence at trial shows that the defendant was an accomplice instead, the defendant can be convicted as an accomplice even though he was not so charged.

The reason accountability does not need to be specifically alleged is because accountability is not a separate crime and all criminal charges are read as if accountability was alleged in them. *United States v. Moore*, 936 F.2d 1508 (7th Cir. 1991).

In this section we will examine the mental state a person must have and the acts she must perform with that mental state to be held accountable for a crime, either by aiding or abetting its commission or by causing another to commit the criminal act.

a. Aiding and Abetting

The specific wording of statutes that impose accountability on persons for what is commonly referred to as aiding and abetting varies widely in different jurisdictions. As a result, in specific cases there can be significant differences between different jurisdictions as to whether a defendant's actions will make him accountable as an aider and abettor. For that reason, it is important for a paralegal to familiarize herself with the accountability provisions of her jurisdiction's criminal code.

The differences in the various aiding and abetting statutes make it difficult to generalize about what conduct will make a person accountable as an aider and abettor. Broadly speaking, however, most accountability statutes make a person accountable as an aider and abettor when that person has an intent to promote or facilitate the commission of an offense and: (1) by acts such as requesting, soliciting, encouraging, or commanding another to commit a crime he induces that other person to commit it; (2) he agrees to provide or provides some type of physical assistance, such as driving a getaway car, acting as a lookout, or supplying weapons or other instrumentalities with which to commit the crime to the person who is committing or will commit it; or (3) with the knowledge of the person who is committing or who will commit a planned crime he provides aid to the perpetrator of the criminal act, but for some reason the aid is not utilized.[9] The following example illustrates the latter: Manny, having agreed to drive a getaway car for George after George robs a certain bank, is in the getaway car outside the bank waiting to drive George away immediately after the robbery. But when George exits the bank after the robbery, instead of getting into the car with Manny he hijacks a car stopped at a stoplight and forces the driver to drive him from the scene. Under those facts Manny will be considered an aider and abettor even though George did not use the assistance Manny was prepared to provide.

It is important to understand that a person does not become accountable as an aider and abettor merely by being present when a crime is committed and, while there are some differences between the states, absent some specific provision in the accountability statute, a person is not accountable for a crime merely because he fails to intervene to thwart its commission.[10]

Commonwealth v. Raposo

Supreme Judicial Court of Massachusetts (1992) 413 Mass. 182

O'CONNOR, J. After a jury-waived trial, a judge in the Superior Court found the defendant guilty of being an accessory before the fact to rape and to indecent assault and battery on a mentally retarded person. After sentencing the defendant to concurrent terms of probation, the judge stayed execution of the sentences and reported the case to the Appeals Court pursuant to Mass. R. Crim. P. 34, 378 Mass. 905 (1979). We transferred the case to this court on our own initiative, and now reverse the convictions and order judgments for the defendant. * * *

In his report, the judge set forth his findings and a series of questions of law. The significant findings were as follows. The defendant is the mother of a mildly retarded daughter, who was seventeen years old at the time of the incidents described below. The defendant's boy friend, Manuel F. Matos, Jr., lived with the defendant and her daughter for about two months before May 22, 1988. Matos told the defendant that he intended to have sexual intercourse with her daughter. In response, the defendant expressed neither encouragement nor discouragement. On one occasion, Matos told the defendant that he was going to have intercourse with her daughter, stating that "she needs a man." The defendant did not respond, although she knew that her daughter did not want to have intercourse with Matos. Matos had intercourse with the daughter from two to four times by force and against her will. At least once, after Matos had entered the daughter's bedroom, the defendant pounded on the closed, unlocked door and told Matos to stop. On May 22, 1988, the defendant took her daughter to a New Bedford police station, where they gave statements about the sexual activity between Matos and the daughter. Prior to this visit at the police station, the defendant made no effort to enlist outside assistance to prevent Matos from engaging in sexual intercourse with her daughter.

The judge's questions, set forth in his report, are as follows.

> "1. Does a parent have any duty to take action to prevent harm to his/her child?
> "2. If such a duty exists, does it include a requirement to take reasonable steps to prevent a sexual assault in the family home on a [seventeen] year old, mildly mentally retarded daughter?
> "3. If the duty exists, is the failure to fulfill it a crime?
> "4. If it is a crime, is it a violation of [G. L. c. 274, §2]?"

We need not answer the four questions separately. It is clear that the basic question that prompted the report is whether a person may be found guilty of being an accessory before the fact * * * to rape * * * and to indecent assault and battery on a mentally retarded person * * * where the victim is a minor, the defendant is the minor's parent, and the defendant failed to take reasonable steps to prevent the sexual attacks by a third person. Stated another way, the question as to each conviction is whether the subsidiary facts found by the judge, on which he clearly based his ultimate guilty findings, support such conclusions.

General Laws c. 274, §2, provides: "Whoever aids in the commission of a felony, or is accessory thereto before the fact by counselling, hiring or otherwise procuring such felony to be committed, shall be punished in the manner provided for the punishment of the principal felon." * * * In order to be found guilty as an accessory before the fact, the evidence must prove beyond a reasonable doubt that the defendant must "in some sort associate himself with the venture, that he participate in it as in something that he wishes to bring about, [and] that he seek by his action to make it succeed." *Commonwealth v. Stout*, 356 Mass. 237, 241 (1969), quoting *United States v. Peoni*, 100 F.2d 401, 402 (2d Cir. 1938). We have held that the plain language of the statute, involving aiding, counselling, hiring or otherwise procuring a principal to commit the crime, requires "something more than mere acquiescence," although not necessarily physical participation, "if there is association with the criminal venture and any significant participation in it." *Commonwealth v. Morrow*, 363 Mass. 601, 609 (1973) * * *. Moreover, "presence at the scene of the [crime], together with the failure to take affirmative steps to prevent it, does not render a person liable as principal." *Commonwealth v. Murphy*, 1 Mass. App. Ct. 71, 76 (1973). A person cannot be found guilty as an accessory before the fact simply because she knows a crime is going to be committed, even when this knowledge is coupled with her subsequent concealment of the completed crime. *Commonwealth v. Perry*, 357 Mass. 149, 151 (1970). *Commonwealth v. Murphy, supra* at 77. Therefore, it is clear that what is required to be convicted as an accessory before the fact is not only knowledge of the crime and a shared intent to bring it about, but also some sort of act that contributes to its happening.

The Commonwealth argues that the case was tried, and the defendant convicted, on the theory that, as the mother of the victim, the defendant had a common law duty to protect her child from harm, and that her failure to take reasonable steps to fulfil this duty is an omission sufficient to make her liable as an accessory. Putting the Commonwealth's contention another way, it is that, in allowing Matos access to her daughter and failing to take reasonable steps to stop his wrongful actions, the defendant "aided" Matos in committing [*186] the crimes and thus became a participant in the criminal activity. The defendant's intent that the underlying crimes be committed, the Commonwealth contends, can be inferred from her knowledge of the crimes and her intentional acts of omission.

Only one case cited by the Commonwealth in support of this theory involves a statute similar to c. 274, §2. In *State v. Walden*, 306 N.C. 466 (1982), the Supreme Court of North Carolina upheld a mother's conviction of aiding and abetting an assault with a deadly weapon by another person on her child. * * * In *Walden*, the evidence showed that the mother witnessed, but made no attempt to stop, another person's lengthy beating of her small child with a belt, which resulted in serious injuries to the child. * * * The *Walden* court created an exception to the general aiding and abetting rule when a parent, who is present, neglects his or her affirmative legal duty to "take all steps reasonably possible to protect the parent's child from an attack by another person" and that such an omission shows the parent's "consent and contribution to the crime being committed." * * * The Commonwealth urges this court to follow the Supreme Court of North Carolina in holding that a parent's failure to take reasonable steps to perform his or her affirmative duty to protect his or her child is a form of consent and participation in the commission of a criminal act against the child.

The Commonwealth bolsters its contention that the defendant's conduct was criminal by analogizing this situation to cases in which this court held that a parent's failure to protect his or her child, knowing there was a high degree of likelihood that the child would be substantially harmed, constituted wanton or reckless conduct sufficient to support a manslaughter conviction. In *Commonwealth v. Gallison*, 383 Mass. 659, 665-666 (1981), this court upheld the manslaughter conviction of a mother where the evidence was sufficient for the jury to believe that she made no effort to obtain medical help for her child who had an extreme fever and became unconscious. This court stated, "[a]s a parent . . . the defendant had a duty to provide for the care and welfare of her child," and found that the jury could have concluded that her inaction in light of the child's obvious illness was a type of intentional conduct which "involves a high degree of likelihood that substantial harm will result" and thus constituted "wanton or reckless" conduct for the purposes of manslaughter. * * *

Other jurisdictions, referred to by the Commonwealth, have reached similar results. See *State v. Zobel*, 81 S.D. 260, 273, 281 (1965) (father's conviction of second-degree manslaughter upheld where the evidence proved that he knowingly exposed his children to cruel and inhuman beatings by his wife, resulting in their deaths). * * *

While it is clear in this and other jurisdictions that a parent's failure to fulfil his or her duty to provide for the safety and welfare of a child may rise to the level of wanton or reckless conduct sufficient to support a manslaughter conviction, we decline to follow the Supreme Court of North Carolina and read into our accessory before the fact law the principle that a mere omission by a parent to take action to protect a child, without more, is the equivalent of intentionally aiding in the commission of a felony against that child. By its very terms, c. 274, §2, requires more than an omission to act. As our case law makes clear, in order to be punished as an accessory before the fact, the defendant must have actually aided in the commission of the felony or counseled, hired, or otherwise procured someone to commit it. See G. L. c. 274, §2; *Commonwealth v. Murphy, supra* at 77. * * *

On the facts reported by the Superior Court judge, the Commonwealth has failed to show beyond a reasonable doubt that the defendant aided, counselled, hired, or procured Matos to commit rape and indecent assault and battery, or that she took any other action which would constitute participation in the commission of these crimes against her daughter. The fact that she knew ahead of time of Matos's intent to commit the criminal acts, and did not report the subsequent crimes to the police immediately, does not make her guilty as an accessory before the fact. *Commonwealth v. Perry, supra* at 151.

We conclude that the convictions must be reversed and that judgments of acquittal are required.

So ordered.[11]

Case Focus

1. As discussed in the case, is there a distinction between breaching a legally imposed duty of protecting an individual from a known harm by taking no action and aiding a person in perpetrating it?

2. On what legal principles of accountability and on what facts did the court rely in concluding that the defendant did not aid or abet the rape of her daughter?

• • • • • • • •

A person may, however, be considered to be an aider and abettor through a communicated promise of passivity if the promised passivity induces commission of a crime and the person making the promise intended to facilitate the commission of the crime with that promise.[12] The following example illustrates how communicated passivity can constitute aiding and abetting: Luis is the chief of the Hooded Cobras street gang and Maurice is the chief of the Insane Unknowns street gang. Both gangs peacefully coexist. Maurice meets with Luis and tells Luis that Hooded Cobra gang member Raul has "disrespected" a member of the Insane Unknowns and needs to pay for doing so. Luis, wanting to kill Raul for other reasons and knowing that if there is no risk of retaliation Maurice will kill Raul for the disrespect Raul showed to the Insane Unknowns gang member, tells Maurice that if Maurice kills Raul, Luis will tell his gang members not to engage in a retaliatory killing, and based on that promise Maurice kills Raul. In that case, despite his passivity Luis will be accountable for Raul's murder.[13]

b. Causing

Just as the common law imposed accountability on a person who caused another to commit a crime, virtually all modern accountability statutes do the same. Most of the modern statutes follow the common law and specifically provide that a person is accountable as an accomplice when he causes an innocent person to commit an offense.[14] The causer accountability statutes of some jurisdictions do not in their terms contain an innocent agent element.[15] Under such statutes the guilt or innocence of the agent is irrelevant.[16] A paralegal should be aware that even when a state's criminal code includes an innocent agent requirement for causer accountability, some offenses, particularly those offenses not contained in the criminal code, may have their own accountability provisions that do not contain an innocent agent element.[17]

United States v. Rapoport

United States Court of Appeals for the Second Circuit (1974) 545 F.2d 802

Hays, J. Appellant, Jerome Rapoport, appeals his conviction by the district court after having been found guilty by a jury of several counts of causing the filing of false applications for loans guaranteed by the Small Business Administration, 18 U.S.C. §§2(b), 1001, 1014, and one count of swearing falsely at a previous jury trial, 18 U.S.C. §1623. Appellant does not attack the sufficiency of the evidence supporting his conviction but nonetheless urges several grounds for reversal. We find no merit in Rapoport's arguments and accordingly we affirm the conviction. * * *

III

The Government did not charge that Rapoport himself made the false statements in the loan applications. Rather, the Government charged that Rapoport was liable as a principal because he "willfully cause[d] an act to be done which if directly performed by him or another would be an offense against the United States. . . ." 18 U.S.C. §2(b). Rapoport does not contend that the evidence was not sufficient to establish that he caused the loan applicants to omit reference to him in their applications. Rather, appellant advances the novel theory that, because the Government failed to prove that the persons who actually made the loan applications were innocent of the substantive crime with which Rapoport was charged and the Government even produced evidence tending to establish their guilt, Rapoport could not be prosecuted under section 2(b). Rapoport argues that 18 U.S.C. §2(a) punishes as a principal one who assists a *guilty* accomplice in committing an offense. He contends that if section 2(b) were also interpreted to include the situation where the accomplice was guilty, the statute would be redundant, a circumstance Congress could not have intended.

Rapoport's argument is simply untenable. Section 2(b) merely "removes all *doubt* that one who puts in motion or assists in the illegal enterprise or causes the commission of an indispensable element of the offense by an innocent agent or instrumentality, is guilty . . . ." Revisor's Note, 18 U.S.C. §2 (emphasis supplied). The statute makes it "*unnecessary* that the intermediary who commits the forbidden act have a criminal intent." *United States v. Kelner*, 534 F.2d 1020, 1023 (2d Cir.). * * * Though it removes any requirement that the intermediary be guilty, section 2(b) contains no express requirement that the intermediary actually be innocent.

While Rapoport suggests that logic supports the incorporation of such a requirement by construction, the opposite is true. It may frequently be a matter of doubt whether the intermediary is guilty or innocent of the crime with which the defendant is charged pursuant to section 2(b). Since the guilt or innocence of the intermediary is irrelevant to the moral culpability of the defendant, the sound administration of criminal justice would not be served by requiring judges to determine the validity of the myriad personal defenses and immunities which the intermediary might possess. Moreover, the construction advocated by appellant would force upon prosecutors a hazardous election between proving a defendant's guilt by means of section 2(a) which under appellant's theory would require that the jury be satisfied of the intermediary's guilt, or by means of section 2(b) which would require satisfaction of the jury that the intermediary was innocent. We believe that Congress recognized as much when it enacted section 2(b) and accordingly we reject Rapoport's contention.

We have considered carefully appellant's other claims of error and find that they do not merit further discussion.

Affirmed.

Case Focus

1. In this case the defendant argued that he could not be convicted of causing another to commit a crime because the government failed to prove that the person who performed the criminal act was innocent. How did the court rule and what reasons did the court give to support its decision?

• • • • • • • •

3. *Extent of Accessory's Accountability*

Assuming that a defendant is an accomplice to a crime, there is a question about the extent to which the accomplice-defendant will be held accountable for crimes committed by the person who actually performed the criminal acts. Clearly, for example, if Manny agrees to act as a getaway driver for Fred when Fred robs a bank and Manny accompanies Fred to the bank in a car, waits behind the wheel of the car while Fred robs the bank, and when after completing the robbery Fred enters the car and Manny drives away, Manny is going to be accountable as an aider and abettor of that robbery.

The problem that arises is when the actual perpetrator of the criminal act commits some crime that was not discussed between him and his accomplice or to the commission of which the accomplice never expressly agreed. Using the above example, if when Fred enters the bank to rob it he shoots and wounds a bank guard, something that was not discussed between Manny and Fred prior to the robbery and a crime toward the commission of which Manny never expressly agreed to provide assistance, will Manny be accountable for the attempted murder of the guard by Fred?

The law of accountability generally holds that when a person aids another in the planning or commission of an offense he is legally accountable for the conduct of the person to whom he provides assistance and that accountability includes any criminal act done in furtherance of the planned and intended crime[18] without regard to whether the accomplice actually agreed to assist in the commission of that other offense.[19] As a result, Manny in the above example will be accountable for the crime of attempted murder committed by Fred notwithstanding that Manny never agreed to assist Fred in committing that offense and that they never discussed committing it.

People v. Kessler

Supreme Court of Illinois (1974) 57 Ill. 2d 493

DAVIS, J. In a jury trial in the circuit court of Winnebago County, defendant, Rudolph Louis Kessler, was convicted on one count of burglary and two counts of attempted murder. The appellate court affirmed the burglary conviction and reversed the attempted-murder convictions (11 Ill. App. 3d 321), and we allowed the People's petition for leave to appeal. The facts are stated in the opinion of the appellate court and will be restated here only to the extent necessary to more fully delineate the issues. Defendant waited in an automobile outside a tavern while his two unarmed companions entered the building to commit the burglary. While inside the tavern, they were surprised by the owner, and one of the burglars shot and wounded him with a gun taken during the burglary. Later, while defendant's companions were fleeing on foot, one of them fired a shot at a pursuing police officer. At that time defendant was sitting in the automobile.

The evidence established that on the day before the burglary in question, the defendant went to Chicago to see Ronald Mass, who introduced him to Rodney Abney. The three men went to a restaurant and drank coffee, where the defendant heard Mass ask another person about obtaining a pistol. The person stated he could not obtain a pistol, but would get a sawed-off shotgun by 8 o'clock that evening.

Later Kessler, Mass and Abney went to a store where Mass purchased a screwdriver while Abney simultaneously shoplifted one. Mass indicated that he had to "put his hands on" $1800. Kessler told Mass that he recalled seeing quantities of cash at the Anchor Tap, where he had previously been employed.

The three men left Chicago about 8 p.m. and arrived at the Anchor Tap in Rockford about 10:30 p.m. Mass and Abney went into the Tap, had a drink, * * * returned to Kessler, who had remained in the car[,] * * * went to another bar for a drink and then returned to the Anchor Tap.

Just as they parked the car there, Louis Cotti, a co-owner of the Tap, came out to go home. He drove past the parked car as he left and then returned. He testified that he looked around, saw no one at the front of the tavern, then went to the rear of the building, entered the rear door and saw Abney and Mass up at the bar. He then left the building by the rear door and went across the street to a restaurant to call the police and to get help. Thereupon, Cotti and another man from the restaurant returned to the Tap and entered the rear door. Mass, who had found a pistol at the bar, then shot Cotti in the neck. Mass and Abney then fled from the bar and entered the car where Kessler sat. Mass drove the car from the Tap and was pursued by the police. Mass was forced off the road and into a ditch. Mass and Abney ran from the car. Kessler remained seated. Abney started shooting at the police, who had arrived at the scene. After an exchange of gunfire, one police officer ordered the defendant from the car and frisked him. As the defendant climbed from the car, and before being advised of his rights, the defendant said, "I don't know what's going on all the shooting. I was just hitchhiking." The defendant was then advised of his rights and was taken to Rockford in a squad car where he later at the police station made an inculpatory oral and a written statement.

In reversing the attempted-murder convictions, the appellate court held that "The application of the 'common design' principle is not justified by the language of section 5-2 to hold a defendant accountable for crimes committed by an accomplice which the defendant was not shown to have intended." (11 Ill. App. 3d 321, 327.) And, at page 325, the court stated: "* * * the question before us is whether Kessler can be found guilty on accountability principles without proof of his specific intent to commit the attempt murders perpetrated by Mass and Abney." The court further stated that * * * the [Criminal] Code does not impose liability on accountability principles for all consequences and further crimes which could flow from participation in the initial criminal venture, absent a specific intent by the accomplice being held accountable to commit, or aid and abet the commission of, such further crimes. 11 Ill. App. 3d at 325-326.

The People argue "that a person is responsible for all criminal violations actually committed by another if he assists another in the commission of a single criminal violation," and that "if the legislature had intended to limit accomplice liability only to further criminal acts which were specifically intended the word 'conduct' would not have been included in the language of section 5-2."

Sections 5-1 and 5-2 of the Criminal Code provide in pertinent part:

"Sec. 5-1. Accountability for *conduct* of another.

A person is responsible for *conduct* which is an element of an offense if the *conduct* is either that of the person himself, or that of another and he is legally accountable for such *conduct* as provided in Section 5-2 or both.' (Emphasis added.) Ill. Rev. Stat. 1971, ch. 38, par. 5-1.

"Sec. 5-2. When Accountability Exists.

A person is legally accountable for the *conduct* of another when:
    * * *

(b) The statute defining the offense makes him so accountable; or

(c) Either before or during the commission of *an offense* and with the intent to promote or facilitate such commission, he solicits, aids, abets, agrees [**32] or attempts to aid, such other person in the planning or commission of the offense. * * *] (Emphasis added.) (Ill. Rev. Stat. 1971, ch. 38, par. 5-2.)

"*Conduct*" is defined as:

"* * * an act or a series of acts, and the accompanying mental state." Ill. Rev. Stat. 1971, ch. 38, par. 2-4.

The People argue that the appellate court disregarded the plain meaning of legal doctrines applied by this court and by the highest courts of other jurisdictions, *i.e.*, that where two or more persons engage in a common criminal design or agreement, any acts in the furtherance thereof committed by one party are considered to be the acts of all parties to the common design and all are equally responsible for the consequences of such further acts; and that the court made an unsound and unwarranted interpretation of section 5-2 of the Illinois accountability statute (Ill. Rev. Stat. 1971, ch. 38, par. 5-2).

We believe the statute, as it reads, means that where one aids another in the planning or commission of an offense, he is legally accountable for the conduct of the person he aids; and that the word "conduct" encompasses any criminal act done in furtherance of the planned and intended act.

An early application of this rule is found in *Hamilton v. People* (1885), 113 Ill. 34. The defendant and two companions invaded a watermelon patch intending to steal some melons. The owner discovered them and a scuffle or fight ensued during which the owner pinned one of the three to the ground, and when in this position another of the three fired a gun at the owner, but the shot missed the owner and struck the potential watermelon thief, who the owner had thrown to the ground. During this occurrence, the third potential watermelon thief stood by. All three of the putative watermelon thieves were charged and convicted of assault with intent to commit murder. This court, at pages 37 and 38, stated:

The fact is undisputed that the three defendants, one of whom was armed with a pistol, invaded the premises of the prosecuting witness with a criminal purpose. The business upon which the parties had deliberately entered was a hazardous one.

They had a right to expect that in the event they were detected in stealing the melons, it would result in violence endangering life or limb,—as it actually turned out afterwards. That they were all co-conspirators in a dangerous criminal enterprise, is an undisputed fact. Such being the case, whatever was done by one, in contemplation of law was done by all, and all are therefore equally responsible.

In the case at bar, the record shows a common design to commit a robbery or burglary. Kessler, Mass and Abney sat in on the plan, and Kessler led Mass and Abney to the Anchor Tap where he stated the day's receipts were kept. * * *

[T]he burglary was the offense which the defendant, Mass, and Abney had jointly planned and were jointly committing, and each was legally accountable for the conduct of the other in connection therewith. The result was the offense of attempted murder of Louis Cotti, the tap owner, and of State Trooper Max L. Clevenger, who answered a report of the incident and who tried to apprehend the fleeing parties.

For the foregoing reasons, we affirm the part of the appellate court decision which affirmed the burglary conviction of the defendant, and we reverse the part of its decision which reversed the conviction of the defendant for attempted murder, and we affirm the judgment of the circuit court.

Appellate court affirmed in part and reversed in part; circuit court affirmed.

Case Focus

1. In this case the defendant took no part in shooting at either intended victim and there was no joint plan to commit any crime other than a burglary, yet the defendant was held accountable for the attempted murder committed by his confederates. What legal principle did the court use to hold the defendant accountable and what facts supported the application of that principle to the defendant's conduct?

• • • • • • • • •

4. *Legal Incapacity of Accessory to Commit Offense*

A number of crimes are defined in such a way that they can only be committed by certain classes of persons. For example, federal law makes it a crime for any representative of any employees (e.g., a labor union) to accept any money or any thing of value from an employer.[20] Persons who do not represent employees are legally incapable of committing that crime. If a person is outside of the class of people who can commit a crime (in the above example, a person who does not represent employees) and he causes one who is within the class to commit it or he aids or abets a person within the class in committing it, can the accomplice, whether he is a causer or an aider and abettor, be convicted of that crime notwithstanding that if he engaged in the conduct himself, as a matter of law, he could not commit it?

Under the law of accountability the causer takes on the capacity of the intermediary[21] and the aider and abettor takes on the capacity of the person who he aids and abets.[22] As a result, an accomplice can be convicted of a crime notwithstanding that he is legally incapable of committing it. For example, if a statute defines the crime of embezzlement such that it applies only to officers of a corporation who embezzle from their corporation and Steve (who is not an officer of ABC, Inc.) aids and abets John (who is an officer of ABC, Inc.) in embezzling from it, Steve is accountable for and can be convicted of the crime of embezzlement, notwithstanding that he was not a member of the class of persons who could commit the offense and thus is legally incapable of committing it.

5. *Termination of Accountability*

There are several different ways in which an accomplice who aided and abetted before the commission of a crime can avoid being held accountable for it if it is committed. One way an accomplice can end his accountability for a crime he aided or abetted is by engaging in measures before its commission that deprive his pre-commission efforts of their effectiveness. For example, if Rafik and Maurice planned to rob a tavern and Rafik supplied the gun Maurice was going to use to commit the robbery, prior to its commission Rafik could terminate his accountability as an accomplice by destroying the gun or taking it back so that if Maurice does commit the robbery he could not use the gun Rafik supplied. Another way in which an accomplice can terminate his accountability for a crime is by giving a timely warning to law enforcement about the planned but as yet uncommitted crime.[23]

A third way in which an accomplice can terminate his accountability is to withdraw from the anticipated criminal activity before the crime is committed and to communicate that withdrawal to those who the accomplice to that point has aided or abetted.[24] Ceasing to provide assistance before commission of the crime is not, by itself, sufficient to terminate accountability for it.

To effectively terminate accountability for a crime by withdrawal, before the crime is committed the accomplice must both communicate his withdrawal to his confederates and he must in fact withdraw.[25] For example, Albert helped Sam and George to plan a bank robbery and also agreed to drive the getaway car, but on the morning of the robbery Albert decides not to participate in the planned bank robbery and as a result simply does not show up to drive the getaway car. If Sam and George decide to rob the bank without further assistance from

Albert, Albert will still be held accountable (because of his role in help-ing to plan the crime) for the bank robbery. To terminate his account-ability as an accomplice so that he would not be accountable for the robbery, before the robbery Albert must tell Sam and George that he is no longer going to assist them in committing the crime and then, as he did above, he must provide no further assistance to them.[26]

State v. Guptill

Supreme Judicial Court of Maine (1984) 481 A.2d 772

Roberts, J. Reginald L. Guptill appeals from his conviction of burglary, theft, and arson, *17-A M.R.S.A. §§401, 353, & 802* (1983), following a jury trial in the Super-ior Court, Waldo County. He contends on appeal, *inter alia*, (1) that the presiding justice erred in refusing to instruct the jury as to termination of accomplice lia-bility; * * *. We affirm the judgment.

I.

On the night of August 3, 1982, a wooden camp in the town of Monroe was broken into and several items of furniture were stolen. Early on the morning of August 4, Guptill was stopped by a police officer in downtown Belfast while driving a pick-up truck loaded with furniture. He was arrested and detained at the Waldo County Jail for operating under the influence. Later that same morn-ing, Guptill was released on bail provided by one Steven Burchill. Burchill, the owner of the truck, sought the return of his vehicle and produced a fraudulent receipt evidencing ownership of the furniture by Guptill. The Sheriff's Depart-ment released the truck to Burchill but kept the furniture. Later that same day, the camp that had been burglarized was destroyed by fire.

During his trial for burglary, theft, and arson, Guptill admitted that he was present when the burglary and theft were committed by others, but insisted that he was unaware that any crime was being committed. He further testified that after his release on bail he accompanied Steven Burchill to a gas station and waited while Burchill filled a plastic gallon jug with gasoline. Guptill then directed Burchill to the camp, but supposedly asked to be let out of the truck before reach-ing the camp, and waited by the side of the road until Burchill returned. Rejecting Guptill's denial of complicity, the jury found him guilty of all three offenses.

II.

Guptill argues, in reference to his conviction of arson, that the court erred in not instructing the jury as to termination of accomplice liability. The statute govern-ing accomplice liability, *17-A M.R.S.A. §57*, provides that:

Unless otherwise expressly provided, a person is not an accomplice in a crime committed by another person if: . . .

C. He terminates his complicity prior to the commission of the crime by

(1) informing his accomplice that he has abandoned the criminal activity and

(2) leaving the scene of the prospective crime, if he is present thereat.

17-A M.R.S.A. §57(5)(c) (1983). While Guptill was entitled to an instruction on any theory of defense rationally supported by the evidence, *State v. Reed*, 459 A.2d 178, 181 (Me. 1983); *State v. Rowe*, 453 A.2d 134, 138-139 (Me. 1982), the issue of termination of accomplice liability was not generated by the evidence in this case.

It is clear from Guptill's own admission that he aided Burchill by directing him to the camp, thus warranting an instruction as to accomplice liability, *see State v. Lee*, 451 A.2d 313, 315 (Me. 1982); *State v. Ayers*, 433 A.2d 356, 364 (Me. 1981). It is also clear that he did no more than ask to be let out of the truck upon nearing the camp. In his own words, "I told Mr. Burchill if he didn't mind I would get out." We cannot say that this meets the standard of "informing his accomplice that he has abandoned the criminal activity" required under *section 57*. The refusal to give an instruction as to termination of accomplice liability, therefore, was not error. * * *

Judgment affirmed.

Case Focus

1. The defendant in this case clearly assisted the perpetrators in committing the crimes, but ceased providing assistance before the crimes were committed and took no part in committing them yet was held accountable for committing them. According to the court, what should the defendant have done before the crimes were committed to terminate accountability for their commission?

2. As will be discussed later in a later chapter, in jury trials the judge instructs the jury as to the law applicable to the case they heard. In this case the defendant asserted he was not complicit in the crime committed and asked the judge to instruct the jury on the law as it related to terminating accountability for the commission of a crime. What reason did the court give for affirming the judge's refusal to instruct the jury as the defendant asked?

• • • • • • • •

B. Corporate and Corporate Officer Accountability

An **agent** is one who acts on behalf of another person with consent of that other person and subject to the control of that other person. *Yeager v. McManama*, 874 N.E.2d 629 (Ind. App. 2007). Corporations are artificial entities and as such can only act through agents.

Corporations frequently are the targets of criminal investigations and can be held responsible for and convicted of crimes committed by one of their **agents**. Just as a corporation can be prosecuted and convicted of a crime committed by one of its agents, the officers and directors of a corporation also can be held responsible for and convicted of crimes committed by a corporate agent. In this section we will examine the legal principles that determine when a corporation and when an officer or director of a corporation can be held responsible for a crime committed by a corporate agent.

1. Corporate Criminal Responsibility

Generally corporations can be prosecuted and convicted of misdemeanors committed by their agents. There is, however, an important difference between federal law and the law of some states with respect to when a corporation can be convicted of a felony committed by one of its agents.

a. Federal Law

Federal law relating to corporate criminal responsibility does not distinguish between misdemeanors and felonies. As a result, under federal law a corporation can be convicted of a misdemeanor or a felony when four conditions are satisfied: (1) the person who performed the criminal act is an agent of the corporation, (2) the agent acted with the *mens rea* specified in the violated criminal statute, (3) the agent acted for the corporation's benefit, and (4) when the agent committed the criminal act he was acting within the scope of his employment.[27] Under federal law the rank of the agent within the corporate hierarchy is irrelevant.[28] Thus, the corporation can be held accountable whether the agent who performs the criminal act is a salesman[29] or an executive.[30]

Generally, an agent of a corporation is considered to act within the scope of his employment when the act he performs is one the corporation has assigned or authorized him to perform. An agent performs an illegal act within the scope of his employment when he performs the

The No Contact Rule, Corporations, and Corporate Employees

The Rules of Professional Responsibility impose a duty on lawyers not to communicate or cause another to communicate with a person about a subject on which the lawyer knows the person is represented by another lawyer.[31] The rule exists in some form in all American jurisdictions,[32] but with significant variations in its wording. Those variations in wording can have an important effect on determining the applicability of the rule in certain situations.[33] As a result it is important for a paralegal to be familiar with the rule and how it is applied in the jurisdiction in which she works. One common formulation of the rule is:

Rule 4.2. Communication with Person Represented by Counsel

In representing a client, a lawyer shall not communicate about the subject of the representation with a person the lawyer knows to be represented by another lawyer in the matter unless the lawyer has the consent of the other lawyer or is authorized to do so by law or by court order.

Illinois Supreme Court Rules of Professional Conduct Rule 4.2

Rule 4.2 is usually referred to as the "no contact" rule and is applicable to prosecutors and defense attorneys alike. A violation of the rule may result in disciplinary action being taken against the attorney who knowingly violates it and in the case of a violation by the prosecutor may also result in the suppression of statements or other evidence obtained from the represented person through that violation. The possible consequences that can flow from a violation of the no contact rule make it important for a paralegal to notify the lawyer for whom she works as soon as she learns a witness or potential witness is represented by an attorney. For a paralegal in a prosecutor's office the possible consequences of a violation make it critically important that she notify the attorney for whom she works as soon as she learns that a target of an investigation, a defendant, or even a witness is represented by an attorney in relation to the matter in her office and that she never ask an investigator to speak to and that she herself not speak to a target, witness, or defendant who she knows is represented in the matter that will be the subject of the conversation.

By its own terms, the no contact rule has two conditions that must be satisfied before it becomes applicable to a communication by an attorney or his agent with the represented person.

The first condition is that the person to whom the communication is directed must be represented in the matter that is the subject of the communication. The rule is case specific, which means that it applies to the case in which the lawyer is retained to represent the client and not to the set of facts that may give rise to culpability.[34] Consequently, having an attorney, even if it is in a related matter, is not sufficient to effect a bar on any communication on the subject,[35] and having representation in a civil matter, the facts of which are also the basis of a criminal investigation, does not mean that for purposes of Rule 4.2 the person is represented in the criminal investigation.[36] For example a person may have an attorney that he has retained to represent him in a civil tax dispute with the Internal Revenue Service

(IRS). The no contact rule will bar any IRS attorney from communicating with that person about the subject of the civil tax dispute. The no contact rule does not, however, bar contact with that client by an IRS attorney who is conducting a criminal investigation of that person even if the criminal investigation is based on the same facts. The reason Rule 4.2 does not bar the latter communication is that person's attorney was retained to represent and represents him in the civil dispute and does not represent him (at least as of now) in a criminal investigation.

Also, the fact that a defendant is represented in a criminal case does not mean that for purposes of Rule 4.2 she is represented with respect to an investigation based on the same facts, but aimed at obtaining evidence to charge a different offense.[37]

The second condition that must be satisfied is that the contacting attorney must know that the person he is contacting is represented in the matter that is the subject of the contact. If the contacting attorney's paralegal is aware of the representation that attorney will be considered to have knowledge of the representation even if the paralegal fails to inform him and any evidence obtained from the represented party can be suppressed. For that reason it is critically important for a paralegal to ensure that she immediately tells the attorney for whom she works if she receives a notice of representation. If the attorney for the represented party fails to notify another attorney of the representation that other attorney does not violate the rule by speaking to the party about the subject matter of the representation. As a result it is also important that a paralegal who is directed by the attorney for whom she works to send a notice of representation to another attorney that she do so promptly and retain proof of giving such notice.

Application of the no contact rule becomes complicated when the represented person is a corporation and the communication by an attorney is directed to corporate employees. Such a communication frequently occurs when a prosecutor and an investigator make an unannounced after business hours visit to the home of an employee of a represented corporation for the purpose of interviewing him and obtaining evidence. Such contacts raise the question of how far down the corporate ladder the cloak of the no contact rule reaches. Does it cover all of the corporation's employees or only some of them?

In many jurisdictions, representation of the corporation extends, and hence the no contact rule extends, only to the control group of the corporation.[38] The control group consists of corporate managers with responsibility for final decisions and those who advise them.[39] As a result, non-control group employees of the represented corporation are not covered by the no contact rule and, unless those employees have their own lawyer, they can be contacted and interviewed on the subject of the corporation's representation by or at the direction of the prosecutor or some other lawyer. Former employees of a corporation are not covered by the no contact rule and may be contacted even if they were a member of the control group.[40]

A lawyer violates the no contact rule when he speaks to or directs a non-lawyer to speak to a represented person about the matter in which that person is represented. The rule does not apply to investigators who, not acting at the direction of an attorney, contact a represented person.[41] As the U.S. Supreme Court has observed in relation to the American Bar Association's Model Rule 4.2 (2008), the Constitution does not codify the ABA's Model Rules and it does not make investigating police officers lawyers.[42]

The no contact rule has given rise to bitter conflicts between the organized and defense bars on one side and prosecutors on the other.[43] The controversy over the no contact rule arises from pre-indictment covert investigations that prosecutors direct at represented persons. The organized and defense bars have taken the position that such contacts violate the no contact rule and any evidence obtained from such prohibited contacts should be suppressed. Federal appeals courts, with one exception, have rejected the importuning of the organized and defense bars and have held that such contacts do not violate the no contact rule.[44] State courts are split, with some holding that any contact by a prosecutor or his agent violates the rule,[45] while others hold the rule is only violated if the prosecutor himself makes the contact or instructs his agent what to elicit from the represented person.[46]

A number of states have attempted to resolve the conflict by adopting a version of the no contact rule that contains an "authorized by law" exception such as the one contained in Illinois's Rule 4.2 set out above. The authorized by law exception exempts pre-indictment covert contacts with the represented person.[47] Under that exception a prosecutor is allowed to direct informants to contact unindicted represented persons for the purpose of obtaining evidence of either ongoing or past criminal conduct.[48] The authorized by law exception is, however, limited to covert contacts.[49] For example, it is within the authorized by law exception, and hence not a violation of Rule 4.2, for a prosecutor to direct a member of a conspiracy who is cooperating with law enforcement to meet with an uncharged co-conspirator who the prosecutor knows is represented by an attorney in relation to an investigation of that conspiracy to attempt to elicit statements from the co-conspirator that would implicate that co-conspirator as a participant in the conspiracy and to covertly record those statements, but it would be outside of the exception and hence a violation of Rule 4.2 for the prosecutor to direct an FBI agent to openly approach that same co-conspirator to elicit that same evidence.[50]

The no contact rule was devised for the benefit of the lawyer and as a result only the lawyer for the represented party can consent to allowing another lawyer talk to her client.[51] That means if a person is represented, even if she agrees to talk about the subject of the representation or contacts a lawyer for the other side on her own initiative and the other lawyer talks to her about the subject of the representation, the other lawyer violates the no contact rule.

The no contact rule can present a serious obstacle to the investigation of corporate crime. When a corporation retains counsel to represent it in a matter, that action places its control-group members off limits to interviews directed by prosecutors. In such instances, even if a member of the control group wishes to talk to the prosecutor, he cannot do so without the consent of the lawyer representing the corporation. The one exception to the no contact rule is when a person who is represented through corporate counsel approaches the prosecutor and alleges attempts by the corporation's attorney to obstruct a criminal investigation. In that situation the prosecutor is allowed to speak to the represented person without the attorney's prior consent.[52]

assigned or authorized act in an illegal manner.[53] For example, under a description of his duties a corporation's sales manager, Julius, is responsible for selling the products the corporation manufactures and is paid by commission for each sale. If Julius bribes the purchasing agents of several customers by giving those purchasing agents kickbacks on his sales commission so they will purchase his company's products instead of those of a competitor, Julius has committed an offense called commercial bribery. Because selling the corporation's product was one of his duties as sales manager and Julius performed that duty in an illegal manner by paying the kickbacks, Julius would be considered to have acted within the scope of his employment.

In contrast, if the same sales manager instead bribed a health inspector who was inspecting the cleanliness of the cafeteria in the corporation's factory, assuming the sales manager had no duties with respect to the operation of the cafeteria, the payment of the bribe by the sales manager to the health inspector would not be within the scope of his employment.

In order to hold the corporation responsible for the criminal act of its agent, as pointed out above the agent must have performed the illegal act to benefit the corporation. Using the commercial bribery example above, the agent is clearly acting for the benefit of the corporation because his actions are generating sales for the corporation. The fact that paying the bribes may also benefit Julius (because he will earn more commissions from the additional sales) is irrelevant so long as the corporation is also benefitting.

The existence of a corporate policy that prohibits its agents from engaging in the specific illegal acts the agent performed or the fact that the agent's act is contrary to explicit instructions given to him by management does not insulate the corporation from being held criminally responsible for the agent's criminal act[54] nor does the fact that corporate officers are unaware of the agent's illegal conduct insulate the corporation from being held criminally responsible.[55] Finally, a corporation can be convicted of a crime even if the corporate agent who is charged with actually committing the criminal act is acquitted.[56]

b. State Law

The law of corporate responsibility in a number of states and as provided in the Model Penal Code differs significantly from federal law. Under the law of these states a corporation is responsible for a felony committed by one of its agents only when the criminal act was authorized, commanded, or performed by the board of directors or by a high managerial agent who was acting within the scope of his employment.[58] A high managerial agent under these types of statutes is usually defined to be an officer of the corporation or an agent who has a comparable position of authority in and who formulates policy for or supervises subordinate employees of the corporation.[59]

2. *Responsibility of Corporate Officers for Corporate Criminal Conduct*

The agent of a corporation who performs a criminal act for the corporation is always responsible for his own illegal act and is subject to prosecution and conviction for it notwithstanding that he performed it for the corporation. An important question that corporate criminal conduct presents is whether a corporate officer will be held responsible for the criminal conduct of his corporation notwithstanding that he did not perform or direct performance of the criminal act.

In cases not involving a violation of federal food and drug safety laws, a corporate officer who did not perform a criminal act for his corporation is held responsible for the corporation's criminal conduct either when he directs the criminal conduct or when he (1) had knowledge of the illegal conduct; (2) had responsibility and authority to exercise control over the illegal action; and (3) acquiesced in it. The corporate officer's responsibility for and authority over particular corporate functions and personnel is determined by reference to the corporation's bylaws[59] and the power and authority the corporation otherwise confers on its officers.[60]

A corporate officer who knows of criminal conduct performed by an agent of the corporation in connection with a function over which the officer has no supervisory authority will not be responsible for the agent's criminal acts. This can be illustrated using the commercial bribery example above. If the vice president in charge of manufacturing for the corporation has no supervisory authority over or responsibility for sales and the sales staff and learns that sales manager Thomas is paying bribes to purchasing agents to buy the corporation's product, the vice president of manufacturing could not be held responsible for Thomas's criminal acts because he did not have any responsibility for sales or control over Thomas's actions.

People v. International Steel Corp.

Appellate Department Cal. Superior Court (1951)
102 Cal. App. 2d Supp. 935

SHAW, J. The defendants, a corporation and two natural persons, were convicted on charges of violating section 24242 of the Health and Safety Code, which is a part of the law for the formation of air pollution control districts, enacted in 1947 (Stats. 1947, chap. 632, pp. 1640-1651) as an addition to the Health and Safety Code, for the purpose of reducing air contamination, popularly known as "smog." Defendants appeal from the judgments, and in support of the appeals contend that the prohibitory provisions of this law are unconstitutional and void for various reasons, that the evidence does not support the findings of guilt, and that the court erred in rulings on evidence. We have concluded that the control of "smog" is a proper subject of the police power, that the prohibitions of the statute herein mentioned violate none of the constitutional provisions referred to, that the evidence supports the finding of guilt, except as to the secretary of the corporation, defendant Olmstead, that no errors in ruling on evidence appear, and the judgments must be affirmed except as to Olmstead. * * *

As to defendant Hochman and the defendant corporation, we are satisfied that the evidence is sufficient to support the convictions. We come to a different conclusion regarding defendant Olmstead. The place where the smoke was discharged was operated by the defendant corporation and the smoke was discharged in the course of and as a part of its operations in burning automobile bodies, of which it appears defendant Hochman was in charge as an officer and manager. But as to defendant Olmstead, it appears only that he was secretary of the corporation, and that he had a conversation with an inspector of the air pollution control district and wrote him a letter showing that he had knowledge of these burning operations and that the corporation desired and expected to stop these operations soon. There is nothing to show that he had any control over these operations. The secretary of a corporation, merely as such, is a ministerial officer, without authority to transact the business of the corporation upon his independent volition and judgment. (6A Cal. Jur. 1162; and see *Walsh v. American Trust Co*. (1935), 7 Cal. App. 2d 654, 659.) "An officer of a corporation is not criminally answerable for any act of a corporation in which he is not personally a participant." (*People v. Campbell* (1930), 110 Cal. App. Supp. 783, 789; *Otis v. Superior Court* (1905), 148 Cal. 129, 131; to same effect, *People v. Doble* (1928), 203 Cal. 510, 517.)

The judgments against defendants International Steel Corporation and Hochman are affirmed. The judgments against the defendant Olmstead are reversed and the cause is remanded to the municipal court for a new trial as to him.

Case Focus

- Why was the defendant Olmstead, who was an officer of the defendant corporation, not held responsible for the criminal conduct of the corporation even though he knew about it while the corporation was engaging in it?

• • • • • • • •

The federal food and drug safety laws are some of the very few criminal statutes that impose criminal liability without regard to the defendant's knowledge of the criminal conduct. As a result, under these laws a corporate officer who does not perform the acts those statutes condemn can be held responsible for their violation by a corporate agent without regard to the fact that the corporate officer had no knowledge of the agent's criminal conduct.[61]

CHAPTER TERMS

Accomplice

Agent

Aider and abettor

Causer

Constructively present

REVIEW QUESTIONS

1. Explain what the law of accountability does and what crimes, if any, it defines.
2. When a person assists another in the commission of a crime, even if his assistance is as small as merely making a phone call for a burglar to see if someone is at home in a house that the burglar intends to break into and steal from, can that person be convicted of the burglary and is he subject to the same potential sentence as the burglar himself?
3. Who were the different parties to a crime recognized by the common law?
4. Under the common law, what act or acts could or would make a person a principal in the first degree to a crime?
5. Under the common law what was the difference between a principal in the second degree and an accessory before the fact?
6. What was an accessory after the fact under the common law?
7. How do modern accountability statutes differ from the common law?
8. Generally, what are three different forms of conduct that if performed by a person will result in his being held accountable as an aider and abettor of a crime?

9. If a defendant is not charged as an aider and abettor in the indictment that charges him with committing a crime and the evidence at trial shows that he did not commit the criminal act but instead merely assisted in its commission by driving the actual perpetrator to the place where he knew the crime was to be committed, can the defendant be convicted of the crime as an aider and abettor even though he was not charged as being such?
10. Under all the modern statutes that impose accountability on a person who causes another to commit a crime, must the person who the causer causes to commit the crime be innocent?
11. Can an accomplice be convicted of either aiding or abetting or causing the commission of a crime when the crime is one that it was legally impossible for him to commit?
12. What are three ways in which an accomplice can terminate his accountability for a crime prior to its commission?
13. Can a corporation be responsible for the criminal acts of one of its agents when the corporation has a policy that expressly forbids its agents to engage in those acts?

14. How do federal law and the law of some states differ as to when a corporation will be held responsible for the criminal conduct of a corporate agent?

15. Does the no contact rule bar communication by an attorney with a represented party about any matter?

16. Under one of the common interpretations of the no contact rule, if a corporation is represented by an attorney, does that representation apply to all employees of the corporation and thereby prohibit contact of those employees by an opposing attorney?

17. Explain the authorized by law exception to the no contact rule and how, if at all, it treats covert contacts differently than overt contacts.

18. Will the president of a corporation that manufactures keyboards for computers be held responsible for the criminal acts an agent of the corporation performs for its benefit if he had no knowledge of the agent's criminal acts?

19. When will an officer of a corporation be held responsible for the criminal acts of an agent of his corporation?

ADDITIONAL READING

Edward C. Carter, III, *Limits of Judicial Power: Does the Constitution Bar the Application of Some Ethics Rules to Executive Branch Attorneys?* 27 S. Ill. U. L.J. 295 (Winter 2003).

Kurt Eichenwald, *The Informant* (2000).

John Gramlich, *Should Murder Accomplices Face Execution?* (August 13, 2008). *http://www.fadp.org/news/2008082401/*. Site last visited May 26, 2011.

Lewis A. Kaplan, *Some Reflections on Corporate Criminal Responsibility* (October 2007). *http://www.abanet.org/antitrust/at-source/07/10/Oct07-Kaplan10-18f.pdf*. Site last visited August 19, 2008.

Celia Wells, *Corporation and Criminal Responsibility* (2d ed. 2001).

ENDNOTES

1. *People v. Rodriguez*, 229 Ill. 2d 285, 2008 WL 2278886 (2008).
2. *Commonwealth v. Coccioletti*, 493 Pa. 103 (1981).
3. *See, e.g., Mazzell v. Evatt*, 88 F.3d 263 (4th Cir. 1996) (construing South Carolina accountability law).
4. *Lake v. State*, 100 Fla. 373 (1930).
5. *Bailey v. Commonwealth*, 229 Va. 258 (1985).
6. *United States v. Peichev*, 500 F.2d 917 (9th Cir. 1974).
7. *Lowe v. People*, 135 Colo. 209 (1957).
8. *People v. Donelson*, 45 Ill. App. 3d 609 (4th Dist. 1977).
9. *State v. Tazwell*, 30 La. Ann. 884 (1878).
10. *Commonwealth v. Raposo*, 413 Mass. 182 (1992).
11. The accountability section of the Model Penal Code makes a person accountable for the criminal acts of another if that person has a legal duty to prevent the commission of that offense. Model Penal Code §2.06(3)(a)(iii). Many states, including Massachusetts, that patterned their criminal codes on the Model Penal Code, have not included that provision in their accountability law. *See also, e.g., State v. Conde*, 67 Conn. App. 474 (2001). Arguably, inclusion of such a provision would have changed the result in *Raposo*.
12. *State v. Conde*, 67 Conn. App. 474 (2001).
13. *Id.*
14. *See, e.g.,* 720 ILCS 5/5-2(a).
15. *See, e.g.,* 18 U.S.C. §2(b).
16. *United States v. Rapoport*, 545 F.2d 802 (2d Cir. 1976).

17. The Illinois Criminal Code's causer accountability provision contains the equivalent of an innocent agent element, see, e.g., 720 ILCS 5/5-2(a), while the criminal provisions of the Illinois Retailer's Occupation Tax Act contain their own causer accountability provisions, which do not contain an innocent agent element. *See* 35 ILCS 120/13.

18. *People v. Jackson*, 333 Ill. App. 3d 962 (1st Dist. 2002).

19. *People v. Kessler*, 57 Ill. 2d 493 (1974).

20. *United States v. Inciso*, 292 F.2d 374 (7th Cir. 1961).

21. *United States v. Tobon-Builes*, 706 F.2d 1092 (11th Cir. 1983).

22. *Bishop v. State*, 118 Ga. 799 (1903).

23. *See, e.g.*, 720 ILCS 5/5-2(c)(3).

24. *State v. Allen*, 47 Conn. 121 (1879).

25. *People v. Rybka*, 16 Ill. 2d 394 (1959).

26. This method has at least two serious practical problems, which means that while it is theoretically possible to terminate accountability in this manner, it is seldom done this way. One problem is if the accomplice communicates his withdrawal to his confederates, they may kill him to ensure that he does not talk to the police about the planned crime. As a result, an accomplice is unlikely to tell his confederates that he is withdrawing. A second problem for the accomplice is proving that he told his confederates that he would not give them any further assistance. X can testify to the fact he told his confederates he was withdrawing, but he would have little credibility, and because of the privilege against self-incrimination he could not force his confederates to testify, and even if they did, the likelihood that they would tell the truth and be believed is small.

27. *New York Central & Hudson River R.R. v. United States*, 212 U.S. 481 (1909).

28. *United States v. Geo. Fish, Inc.*, 154 F.2d 798 (2d Cir. 1946).

29. *Id.*

30. *United States v. Empire Packing Co.*, 174 F.2d 16 (7th Cir. 1949).

31. *See, e.g., Supreme Court Rules of Prof. Conduct*, Rule 4.2 (Ill. Sup. Ct.).

32. *United States v. Ward*, 895 F. Supp. 1000 (N.D. Ill. 1995).

33. See, e.g. *United States v. Koerber*, 966 F. Supp. 2d 1207 (D. Utah 2013).

34. *People v. Santiago*, 236 Ill. 2d 417 (2010).

35. *Miller v. Material Science Corp.*, 986 F. Supp. 1104 (N.D. Ill. 1997).

36. *Santiago*, 236 Ill.2d at 417.

37. *United States v. Mullins*, 613 F.3d 1273 (10th Cir. 2010).

38. *Fair Automotive v. Car X Service Systems*, 128 Ill. App. 3d 763 (2d Dist. 1984).

39. *Id.*

40. *Orlowski v. Dominick's Finer Foods*, 937 F. Supp. 723 (N.D. Ill. 1996).

41. *United States v. Thompson*, 35 F.3d 100 (9th Cir. 1993).

42. *Montejo v. Louisiana*, 556 U.S. 778 (2009).

43. *See, e.g.*, Roger C. Cramton & Lisa K. Udell, Syposium: *State Ethics Rules and Federal Prosecutors: The Controversies Over the Anti-Contact and Subpoena Rules*, 53 U. Pitt. L. Rev. 291 (1992).

44. *In re Grand Jury Subpoena to Carter*, 1998 U.S. Dist. LEXIS 19497 (D.D.C. 1998).

45. *People v. Sharp*, 150 Cal. App. 3d 13 (1st Dist. 1983).

46. *People v. White*, 209 Ill. App. 3d 844 (5th Dist. 1991).

47. *United States v. Brown*, 595 F.3d 498 (3d Cir. 2010).

48. *United States v. Binday*, ___F.3d ___, 2015 WL 6444932 (2d Cir. 2015).

49. *Koerber*, 966 F. Supp.2d at 1207.

50. *Id.*

51. *United States v. Lopez*, 4 F.3d 1455 (9th Cir. 1993).

52. *United States v. Talao*, 222 F.3d 1133 (9th Cir. 2000).

53. *United States v. Hilton Hotels*, 467 F.2d 1000 (9th Cir. 1973).

54. *Dollar S.S. Co. v. United States*, 101 F.2d 638 (9th Cir. 1939).

55. *United States v. Matlack, Inc.* 149 F. Supp. 814 (D. Md. 1957).

56. *United States v. General Motors Corp.*, 121 F.2d 376 (7th Cir. 1941).

57. *See, e.g.*, 720 ILCS 5/5-4(a).

58. *See, e.g.*, 720 ILCS 5/5-4(b).

59. *United States v. New England Grocers Supply Co.*, 488 F. Supp. 230 (D.C. Mass. 1980).

60. *O'Brien v. DeKalb County*, 256 Ga. 757 (1987).

61. *United States v. Dotterweich*, 320 U.S. 277 (1943).

Chapter 10
Categories and Types of Criminal Offenses

Chapter Objectives

After reading this chapter, you should be able to

- List the different categories of crimes and name examples of offenses in each category
- Understand the different ethical duties imposed on defense attorneys and prosecutors
- Understand what anticipatory offenses are and name them
- Understand what constitutes crimes against persons
- Understand the different types of property crimes
- Explain what scheme statutes are and name some common scheme offenses
- Understand and explain what constitutes honest services fraud
- Name and identify the different types of property that property offenses are designed to protect

[A] person who acquires special knowledge by virtue of a confidential or fiduciary relationship * * * is not free to exploit that knowledge to his own personal benefit.
—*Diamond v. Oreamuno*, 24 N.Y.2d (1969)

The previous chapters in this section examined the power of a sovereign to apply its criminal laws to prescribe or regulate conduct, the limits placed on the power of American jurisdictions to define offenses, and accountability for the commission of crimes. In this chapter we will examine the different categories of criminal offenses and the types of offenses included in each category.

To facilitate your understanding of the different types of criminal statutes this section divides criminal offenses into eight categories. The first category consists of those offenses in which some step was taken toward committing an offense, but the offense toward the commission of which that step was taken was not completed. The other seven categories of offenses are defined by the focus of the criminal activity that the crimes contained in each of them condemn.[1] For example, when a person engages in deception for the purpose of obtaining money or property (a form of theft under most modern statutes) and the mails are used to further the fraud (a conventional fraud under the federal mail fraud statute[2]), those crimes would be placed in the crimes against property category.

The eight categories of offenses examined in this chapter are: (1) anticipatory offenses; (2) offenses against the person; (3) offenses against morals; (4) offenses against structures; (5) offenses against property; (6) offenses against public peace and public welfare; (7) offenses against public authority and government function; and (8) offenses involving foreign relations and international law. The different categories of criminal offenses and some of the crimes that are contained in each of those categories are illustrated in the following table.

A CLASSIFICATION SYSTEM FOR CRIMINAL OFFENSE

Anticipatory Offenses	Offenses Against the Person	Offenses Against Morals	Offenses Against Structures
Attempt	Murder	Adultery	Burglary
Solicitation	Manslaughter	Bigamy	Arson
Conspiracy	Felony Murder	Incest	Home Invasion
	Rape	Prostitution	
	Battery	Sodomy	
	Assault	Obscenity	
	Kidnapping	Transportation for Illegal Sexual Activity	
		Gambling	
		Possession of Controlled Substance	
		Distribution of Controlled Substances	

Offenses Against Property	Offenses Against Public Peace and Welfare	Offenses Against Public Authority and Government Function	Offenses Involving Foreign Relations & International Law
Theft	Breach of Peace	Obstructing Justice	War Crimes
Receiving Stolen Property	Nuisance	Perjury	Piracy
Robbery	Riot	Bribery	Military Expedition Against a Friendly Nation
Forgery	Libel	Sedition	
Mail Fraud	Mob Action	Treason	
Wire Fraud	Commercial Bribery	Counterfeiting of Currency	
Bank Fraud	Terrorism	Tax Evasion	
Continuing Financial Crimes Enterprise	Possession and Manufacture of Biological Weapons	Filing Fraudulent Tax Returns	
Insurance Fraud	Possession and Manufacture of Chemical Weapons	Escape	
Securities Fraud	Money Laundering	Bail Jumping	
Economic Espionage		Official Misconduct	
Theft of Trade Secrets		Visa Fraud	
Trademark Counterfeiting		Espionage	
Telemarketing Fraud		Bankruptcy Fraud	
Insurance Fraud		Obstruction of the Mail	
Identity Theft		Theft of Mail	
Wrecking Trains		Sabotage	
Interstate Transportation of Stolen Property		Making False Statement to a Federal Official	

In addition to providing an overview of the types of criminal offenses contained in each category of criminal offenses, this section will briefly examine a few of the important criminal offenses contained in some of those categories. This section does not attempt to provide a complete catalog of American criminal offenses or attempt to provide an in-depth discussion of offenses. It is important to realize that to have any hope of understanding a criminal offense it is essential to look at how that offense is defined by the laws of your jurisdiction or, in the case of federal offenses, how it is defined in the United States Code.

EYE ON ETHICS

Ethical Responsibilities of Defense Attorneys and Prosecutors

The Rules of Professional Responsibility apply to all attorneys, but they contain certain rules that apply to attorneys who are not prosecutors and certain rules that apply only to prosecutors. Those rules impose different duties on each type of attorney. A paralegal who works in a prosecutor's office or in a defense attorney's office must have a basic understanding of the different duties those rules impose.

Defense Attorneys Have a Duty to Represent Clients Zealously

A defense attorney is expected to zealously defend his client within the bounds of the law[3] and to use the law for the fullest benefit of his client.[4] The defense attorney's sole duty of loyalty is to his client and he is under no duty to seek truth.[5] That means, without regard to the defendant's guilt or innocence, the defense attorney must always try to obtain an acquittal and failing that imposition of the least serious sanction on his client.[6]

In pursuing those goals the defense attorney is expected to file motions to suppress evidence notwithstanding that if they are granted it will result in the acquittal of a guilty person,[7] may seek to place the entire blame for a crime on a codefendant,[8] and is expected to rigorously cross-examine a witness, even if the defense attorney believes the witness is telling the truth. As Justice White observed:

> If [defense counsel] can confuse a witness, even a truthful one, or make him appear at a disadvantage, unsure, or indecisive, that will be his normal course. Our interest in not convicting the innocent permits counsel to put the State to its proof, to put the State's case in the worst possible light, regardless of what he thinks or what he knows to be the truth. *United States v. Wade*, 388 U.S. 218 (1967) (White, J., dissenting and concurring in part).

A paralegal who works in a defense attorney's office or in a public defender's office will frequently find herself assisting the attorney in the assembly of material for such cross-examination and in the preparation of motions to suppress statements and arrests of defendants who may be or who clearly are guilty of crimes. From a personal standpoint the paralegal who decides to work in a defense attorney's office must be prepared to provide assistance to the attorney so he can fulfill the duty of zealous representation and achieve the goal of acquittal of or imposition of the least serious possible sanction.

There are limits on the defense attorney's advocacy, but they are few and at best are only vaguely captured by the phrase "advocating in good faith."[9] One of the few clear limits placed on a defense attorney's advocacy is that it must be within the bounds of the law. Clearly beyond the limits of the law are actions such as knowingly eliciting perjured testimony from a witness or a defendant, destroying evidence, or hiding evidence. One tactic that falls into a gray area, but one that is nonetheless used by many defense attorneys,[10] is attempting to induce a judge or the prosecutor to commit reversible error. As long as the defense attorney is not trying to corrupt the proceeding, attempting to inject reversible error into it is generally considered to be an acceptable tactic.[11]

An important ethical question arises when a defense attorney comes into or affirmatively takes possession of either the products of his client's crime (e.g., jewels obtained by the client in the robbery of a jewelry store) or the instrumentalities of that crime (e.g., a knife used by the client to commit murder). The defense attorney who comes into or takes possession of either the products or instrumentalities of his client's crime is ethically required to turn them over either to the prosecutor or law enforcement,[12] and before accepting or taking possession of either, the defense attorney must inform his client of that obligation.[13] Violation of either rule can result in the imposition of professional discipline against the attorney.[14] For those reasons a paralegal employed by a defense attorney should always consult the attorney for whom she works before accepting anything from a client that might be the product or instrumentality of the client's crime.

Prosecutor's Duty Is to Do Justice

In contrast to the defense attorney upon whom without regard to truth the rules of professional responsibility impose a duty of zealous representation of his client, the rules of professional responsibility impose upon the prosecutor the duty to do justice.[15] That duty flows from the fact that the prosecutor is a representative of the sovereign who has an obligation to govern impartially and whose interest is served not by winning a case, but by justice.[16] As such the prosecutor's duty is twofold: ensure that the guilty do not escape and ensure that the innocent do not suffer.

To implement those duties, the rules of professional responsibility impose a number of obligations on the prosecutor.[17] One obligation is that the prosecutor not initiate a prosecution when he knows or should know that the charges are not supported by probable cause. A second obligation is that the prosecutor disclose to the defense the existence of any evidence that tends to negate the guilt of the defendant or mitigates the degree of the offense. As will be seen in a later chapter, the due process clause of the U.S. Constitution separately imposes a similar obligation on the prosecutor. For a paralegal who works in a prosecutor's office it is critically important that she notify the prosecutor for whom she works if she becomes aware of such evidence or if she becomes aware that law enforcement agents have such evidence.

The rules also require that the prosecutor refrain from making extra-judicial comments that would have the effect of heightening the public condemnation of the defendant beyond what is necessary to inform the public of the nature and extent of the prosecutor's action. That rule notwithstanding, the prosecutor can publicly distribute the charging instrument contained in the court file because that instrument is public record. The rules do not apply to non-attorneys (such as police and investigators), but they do impose a duty on the prosecutor to exercise reasonable care to prevent law enforcement authorities and his own employees from making such statements. Because of these rules, a paralegal working in a prosecutor's office should not herself or through others make any comments to any members of the media without first discussing with the prosecutor what those comments may or should be.

A. Anticipatory Offenses

The category of offenses called anticipatory offenses (sometimes called inchoate offenses) consists of those offenses that make it a crime to take some step toward committing some other offense. As such, these offenses depend upon the existence of some other criminal statute to make the step toward commission that the anticipatory offenses condemn a crime. In many jurisdictions anticipatory offenses are often treated as less serious offenses than the completed offense toward the commission of which the step was taken.[18] There are three anticipatory offenses: (1) solicitation; (2) attempt; and (3) conspiracy.

1. Solicitation

The crime of solicitation is a crime separate from the crime solicited and is committed when, with the intent that an offense be committed, a person commands, encourages, or requests another to commit that offense.[19] The crime is committed even if the person solicited neither agrees to commit the crime nor takes action toward committing it.[20] For example, if Walid wants to have James killed and approaches Rafik and says to Rafik, "I will pay you $10,000 to kill James," Walid has committed the crime of solicitation. Some jurisdictions have a single generally applicable solicitation statute, some have one solicitation statute for murder and one for other crimes, and a few states have no crime of solicitation.

2. Attempt

The crime of attempt is committed when, with the specific intent to commit a crime, a defendant takes a substantial step toward the commission of that crime.[21] The purpose of punishing attempts is not to deter the commission of completed crimes, but rather to subject to corrective action by the state those individuals who have sufficiently manifested their dangerousness to society.[22]

It is important to note that because an attempt is part of every completed offense, a person may be charged with and convicted of attempt even when the evidence establishes that he actually completed commission of the offense he was charged with merely attempting to commit.[23] Stated another way, failure to consummate an offense is not an element of the offense of attempt. For example, if Tyrone puts a gun in the face of Anna (who is the owner of a liquor store) and demands and receives from her the money in the cash register, Tyrone has committed the offense of armed robbery. Tyrone can be charged with and convicted of the completed offense of armed robbery or with the anticipatory offense of attempted armed robbery. In jurisdictions where attempt is a less serious crime than the completed crime, as part of a plea agreement prosecutors frequently will file a charge of attempt to which in return the defendant will plead guilty and the prosecutor will then dismiss the charge that alleges commission of the more serious completed crime.

United States v. Fleming

District of Columbia Court of Appeals (1966)
215 A.2d 839

Hood, Chief Judge. Appellee was originally brought into court on a charge of sodomy. At the preliminary hearing the sodomy complaint was nol-prossed. Thereupon an information was filed charging that appellant did "attempt to commit the act of Oral Sodomy on the person of Norman J. Landry, an adult male." Appellee pleaded not guilty and demanded trial by jury. Later he moved to dismiss the information "for insufficiency in that it did not allege an overt act." This motion was granted, and with consent of the court an amended information was filed. This last information charged that appellee on a certain date "did then and there attempt to commit the act of oral sodomy on the person of Norman J. Landry, an adult male, to wit: in that he did place the penis of one Norman J. Landry into his mouth."

After pleading not guilty to the second information and demanding trial by jury, appellee moved to dismiss the information on the grounds * * * (3) that if the Government offered evidence of a completed act, the court would have to enter a judgment of acquittal on the charge of attempt, * * *. [The court below granted the motion to dismiss and the Government appealed.] * * *

The real question presented, as we see it, is whether, if the Government's proof at trial establishes a completed act of sodomy, appellee will be entitled to an order of acquittal on the only charge against him, an attempt to commit sodomy.

There are numerous authorities to the effect that failure to consummate the crime is one of the essential elements of an attempt. A logical extension of that rule is that an attempt conviction must be vacated or reversed if it was based upon evidence of a consummated offense. This result, however, presents the anomalous situation of a defendant going free "not because he was innocent, but for the very strange reason, that he was too guilty." [*State v. Shepard*, 7 Conn. 54 (1828).]

In an investigation of the common law origins of criminal attempts, Professor Rollin M. Perkins has recommended the "complete abandonment of any thought of failure as an element of criminal attempt." * * *

Professor Perkins points out that the rule of no conviction for attempt when shown to be successful was due to the general English doctrine of merger and not to any unusual requirement in the law of attempt. * * *

The English doctrine of merger of offenses has never been fully accepted in this country, particularly in modern times. In *Williams v. State*, 205 Md. 470, 109 A.2d 89, 92 (1954), after pointing out that the doctrine of merger is not favored today, the court observed:

> Historically, there was justification for the doctrine of merger, which included the fact that the incidents of a trial for a felony were so different from those of a trial for a misdemeanor that it was unfair to permit the prosecution to interchange them.

Our conclusion is that the rule that a defendant charged with an attempt must be acquitted if shown to have committed the full offense has today no reasonable basis and should be rejected. We agree with the following statement from *People v. Baxter*, 245 Mich. 229, 222 N.W. 149, 150 (1928): "If an information admits of conviction of an attempt to commit a felony, an accused may be found guilty of the attempt, though the evidence shows a completed offense."

Reversed.

Case Focus

1. Can a person be convicted of an attempt to commit a crime when the evidence shows that he has completed the offense?

● ● ● ● ● ● ● ●

It is important to note that some crimes are defined such that the completed crime and the attempted crime are simply alternate forms of one offense and carry the same potential sentence. The Illinois crime of insurance fraud is an example of such a statute:

> A person commits the offense of insurance fraud when he or she knowingly obtains, *attempts* to obtain, or causes to be obtained, by deception, control over property of an insurance company . . . intending to deprive an insurance company . . . permanently of the use and benefit of that property. *Illinois Compiled Statutes*, Chapter 720, Section 5/46-1(a) (emphasis added).

As can be seen in the above statute, the crime of insurance fraud is committed either by obtaining property of an insurance company by deception or by attempting to obtain property from an insurance company by deception.

3. Conspiracy

The third anticipatory offense is the offense of conspiracy. The crime of conspiracy is committed when, with the intent that an offense be committed, two or more people agree to commit an offense and one of them engages in an overt act in furtherance of that agreement.[24] The offense that the conspirators agree to commit is called the "object offense." The conspiracy may involve an agreement to commit one object offense or multiple object offenses.

The crime of conspiracy is a highly technical offense that is committed both by those who enter into an agreement to commit a crime and perform some overt act in furtherance of it and by those who entered into the agreement but who did not themselves commit any overt act. For example, if Anton, Franklin, and Marty agree to rob a bank and in furtherance of that agreement Anton purchases masks for each of them to wear during the robbery, assuming purchasing the masks is an act in furtherance of the conspiracy, not only can Anton be convicted of conspiracy, but so can Franklin and Marty, notwithstanding that they themselves have not committed any overt act in furtherance of the conspiracy.

There are general conspiracy statutes and special conspiracy statutes. A general conspiracy statute is one that makes it a crime to conspire to commit any criminal offense and often carries a lesser potential sentence than the offense the conspirators conspired to commit. A special conspiracy statute is one that makes it a crime to conspire to commit only certain specified offenses. Instead of carrying a lesser potential sentence than the object offense, special conspiracy statutes usually carry the same (or in some instances a greater) potential sentence.[25] The paralegal should be aware that while such special conspiracy statutes may be placed in the criminal code in the same section as the general conspiracy statute, many states instead place them with the criminal statute that defines the object offense to which the special conspiracy statute relates.

B. Offenses Against the Person

Offenses against the person consist of those crimes in which the criminal act itself is directed at a person. Crimes in this category include the homicidal crimes of murder, felony murder, and manslaughter (usually divided into voluntary and involuntary manslaughter), and the non-homicidal crimes of battery, assault, kidnapping, and rape (in many jurisdictions called criminal sexual assault).[26]

The crime of murder is usually defined as either intentionally or knowingly causing the death of another human being or intentionally and knowingly engaging in conduct that manifests a depraved indifference to the value of human life and causes the death of another and under some forms of the crime may also include intentionally or knowingly causing another to commit suicide.[27]

The offense of voluntary manslaughter, like murder, includes in its definition an intent to kill but usually requires that intent to have been formed in response to some type of provocation.[28] The rationale behind the voluntary manslaughter statutes is that the law has some tolerance for a death-causing act that is powered by a justifiable passion, but none when that act is powered by a malicious heart.[29] As one court characterized it, "homicide in the heat of passion reasonably provoked is manslaughter, not because the law supposes that the passion stripped the killing of an intent to commit it, but because it presumes that the passion disturbed the sway of reason." [30] The provocation that will result in a homicide being considered voluntary manslaughter instead of murder is that provocation that would cause a reasonable person to lose his normal self-control. Whether a particular provocation is of that magnitude is determined by a judge in a bench trial or by a jury in a jury trial.

The crime of involuntary manslaughter is committed when, under circumstances known to the defendant, his act creates a high degree of risk of death or serious bodily harm and the act causes the death of the victim.

Many jurisdictions do not classify the intentional killing of a human being as murder or manslaughter. In those states that do not use that form of classification such killings are classified as either first degree murder or second degree murder.

Typically, in jurisdictions that classify murder by degree, the crime of first degree murder is defined differently than the crime of murder. The crime of first degree murder is usually defined such that it requires an intent to kill and also requires proof of some additional element, which (depending on the jurisdiction) may be that the defendant killed without lawful justification,[31] that there was some premeditation or deliberation by the defendant before he killed his victim,[32] or that the defendant acted with malice aforethought.[33] In those states that require premeditation, the interval between the premeditation and the act of killing can be brief. All that is required is that there be sufficient time for the act of killing to follow formation of the thought of killing.[34]

The crime of second degree murder is very similar to the crime of voluntary manslaughter. The crime of second degree murder is usually committed when the crime of first degree murder is committed and either: (1) at the time of the killing the defendant acted under a sudden and intense passion caused by a serious provocation from the person killed or (2) at the time the defendant killed the victim the defendant believed facts existed that would constitute a justification defense.[35]

The crime of felony murder, which is classified as a form of murder in states with intent to kill murder statutes and a form of first degree murder in states with murder by degree statutes, has a long history. Under the common law form of the crime, a person was guilty of felony murder when, without regard to the dangerousness or likelihood that death might result during the commission or attempted commission of a felony, he caused the death of another.

Though defined in various ways in different states, the crime of felony murder continues to exist today but has been expanded in some ways and limited in others. The most important limitation has been on the type of felonies that may be a predicate offense for the crime. At common law, any felony could be a predicate offense for felony murder. Today, the predicate felony is often limited to felony offenses that are dangerous to human life, such as armed robbery or arson[36] or to crimes that were felonies under the common law.[37]

The expansion of the offense has taken place with respect to when the defendant will be held responsible under the felony murder rule for a death that occurs. Today, assuming the commission of one of the specified predicate felonies, a defendant will be responsible for murder under the felony murder rule for any death that might reasonably be foreseen from the felonious conduct. For example, Tyrone holds up a liquor store with a gun and as he is running from the store he sees a policeman and shoots at him. The policeman returns fire missing Tyrone, but hitting and killing innocent bystander Agnes. Tyrone will be guilty of the murder of Agnes because it is reasonably foreseeable that the police would return fire.[38]

C. Offenses Against Morals

Offenses categorized as crimes against morals are those offenses that are often (but sometimes incorrectly characterized as) consensual. These offenses are also sometimes said to be victimless. Crimes in this category include the offenses of adultery, bigamy, incest, prostitution, sodomy, obscenity, gambling, transportation for illegal sexual activity, possession of controlled substances, and distribution of controlled substances. With these offenses there are seldom complaining witnesses, and to the extent there is investigation of them, the investigation is usually done through proactive undercover police operations.

D. Offenses Against Structures

All property is **real** or **personal** property. *In re Paulson*, 276 F.3d 389 (8th Cir. 2002). **Real property** is land and anything permanently affixed to the land such as a building. 1 Cunningham et al., *The Law of Property* §1.4 (2d ed. 1993). All property that is not real is **personal property**. *Austin v. Housing Authority of the City of Hartford*, 143 Conn. 338 (1956).

The offenses that are characterized as offenses against structures include the crimes of burglary, arson, and home invasion. The crimes of burglary and arson both had their origins in the common law. The crime of burglary was originally limited to dwellings and the crime of arson was limited to buildings not owned by the arsonist. Both offenses have been statutorily expanded so that today both offenses include conduct aimed at any structures. As a result, today in most jurisdictions burglary can be perpetrated against an office or commercial structure and arson can be committed against structures such as warehouses, barns, and other buildings owned by the defendant and often includes the burning or destruction by explosives of **personal property** as well.[39]

E. Offenses Against Property

In terms of the sheer number of offenses, one of the largest categories of offenses is called offenses against property. This category consists of offenses in which the object of the criminal act is to obtain money, property, or economic gain and includes general criminal statutes such as theft, robbery, and forgery; special criminal statutes that define crimes with respect to certain types of property such as trade secrets (economic espionage), trademarks (trademark counterfeiting), personal identifying information (identity theft), and trains (train wrecking); and scheme statutes such as mail fraud, bank fraud, and computer fraud that contain as one of their elements a scheme of some specified type.

The special criminal statutes and the scheme statutes were developed for different reasons. Some were developed in response to certain criminal acts that, while they may fit within a general criminal statute such as theft, are considered to be serious enough to be defined separately and carry a higher possible sentence. Some were developed to address particular types of misconduct peculiar to a single industry (such as the banking industry) or aimed at certain types of property (such as **intellectual property**), while others were developed to provide a jurisdictional hook to allow federal prosecution of conduct that would otherwise be solely within state jurisdiction.

Intellectual property is property that is derived from the work of the mind, Jay Dratler, Jr. & Stephen McJohn, *Intellectual Property Law: Commercial, Creative, and Intellectual Property* §1.01 (2009), and includes such things as trademarks, formulas, data, and patents.

Of the general property crimes, the offense of theft is probably the most important and certainly one of the widest sweeping and most frequently charged. Today's theft statutes are derived from the common law crimes of embezzlement, larceny, and false pretenses, which had facially simple definitions and highly technical distinctions that

Tangible personal property is property that is visible and corporeal and has substance and body. *Navistar International Transportation Corp. v. State Board of Equalization*, 8 Cal. 4th 868 (1994).

Intangible personal property has no physical existence, *Adams v. Great American Lloyd's Insurance Co.*, 891 S.W.2d 769 (Tex. Ct. of App.—Austin, 1995), and is generally defined as a right. *Navistar* at 8 Cal. 4th 868. Intangible rights may be evidenced by or represented in physical objects such as a stock certificate or promissory note, *Id.*, or they can be in electronically stored data. *United States v. Ivanov*, 175 F. Supp. 2d 367 (D. Conn. 2001).

frequently were difficult to understand and difficult to apply. The modern theft statutes have eliminated those problems. The common law precursors of the modern theft statutes applied only to **tangible personal property** and not to **intangible personal property** or real property. Today, in most jurisdictions, the theft statutes apply to all forms of property.[40]

Most of the modern theft statutes condemn at least three different types of acts, any one of which, when combined with other elements of the offense, constitute a form of theft: (1) exertion of unauthorized control over property of the owner; (2) obtaining control over property of the owner by deception; and (3) obtaining control over property of the owner by threat.

Unauthorized control involves those situations in which the defendant was given or allowed to have custody of property by its owner subject to certain instructions that limit what the defendant may do with it or that had the effect of making the property subject to certain legal restrictions on its use, and the defendant acted inconsistently with those instructions or legal restrictions. An example of the former would be: Enrico is a financial adviser who also sells securities. Enrico tells Doris that certain securities he is selling are a sound investment. Doris gives Enrico $50,000, telling him to use the money to purchase the securities for her. If instead of using the money to purchase the securities, Enrico uses the money to take his girlfriend on a three-week vacation to the French Riviera, Enrico has exerted unauthorized control over the money. An example of the latter would be: Cornelius gives property to Harold and tells him to hold it in trust for the benefit of Penelope. Assuming that is sufficient to create a trust, the law of trusts places restrictions on what Harold can do with the property. If Harold performs acts with respect to the trust property that are not allowed by the law of trusts, he exerts unauthorized control over the property.

A defendant obtains property by deception when he creates in another an impression that he knows to be untrue. Using the above example, if Enrico tells Doris that the securities are a sound investment when Enrico knows the issuer has lost money for the past two years and is contemplating filing for bankruptcy, and in reliance on Enrico's representation Doris gives Enrico $50,000 and tells him to purchase the securities, Enrico obtained the money by deception.

The offense of forgery is another important general property crime. The offense originally related to the genuineness of documents,[41] but has statutorily evolved and in many states it has been expanded in different ways. As a result, the offense of forgery now includes much more than imitating someone's signature on a document without that person's consent. In many jurisdictions forgery is now a broadly defined offense that includes creating any document that is capable of defrauding another.[42] In most states the crime still relates to the genuineness of documents,[43] but in some states the offense has been expanded such that a document is a forgery if it is false in any material way. In those states a document can be a forgery either if it is not genuine or notwithstanding that the document is genuine it contains a false statement of a material fact.[44] In many states the term "document" has now been defined to include electronic documents, and the term "signature" has now been defined to include electronic signatures.

The scheme statutes, many of which are found in the Federal Criminal Code, represent some of the broadest and most important types of criminal statutes. Common to all of the scheme statutes is the element of devising or participating in a scheme or artifice either to defraud or to obtain money or property by a false representation or pretense. These statutes make it a crime either to further the scheme by certain means (e.g., in the case of the offense of wire fraud, to further the scheme through use of the electronic communications systems)[45] or to execute it against certain persons (e.g., in the case of the offense of financial institution fraud, to execute the scheme against a bank or against a bank's property).[46]

The oldest and most important of the scheme statutes and the one after which all the others are patterned is the federal offense of mail fraud.[47] The crime of mail fraud and its electronic communications cognate, the crime of wire fraud,[48] are wide-sweeping criminal statutes that are used to prosecute criminal conduct ranging from conventional fraud schemes in which money or property is obtained through false representations, to public corruption and sophisticated business frauds such as manipulation of currency markets by manipulating the London Inter Bank Rate (LIBOR) for Yen.[49]

By examining the offense of mail fraud it is possible to see the wide range of fraudulent activity reached by the scheme statutes.[50] The offense of mail fraud makes it a crime to devise or participate in a scheme condemned by the statute and to use the mail for the purpose of furthering that scheme.[51] In the scheme statutes, a scheme is a pattern or course of conduct.[52] As with most of the scheme statutes, the schemes condemned in the mail fraud statute are (1) schemes to defraud and (2) schemes to obtain money or property by means of false pretenses or representations. The scheme to defraud that is condemned in the scheme statutes is a fraud scheme whose object is money or property.[53] By statute, the concept of scheme to defraud includes schemes to defraud someone of honest services.[54] A scheme to defraud can exist even if no money or property is obtained[55] and no false representation is made.[56] In contrast, in a scheme to obtain money or property by false pretenses, some false representation must be made.

Honest services fraud, which is a scheme to defraud someone of another's honest services, is frequently the basis for prosecuting public

Honest services fraud occurs when a public official or public or private employee receives a bribe to perform his official duty or receives a kickback for performing his official duty. *See Skilling v. United States,* 561 U.S. 358 (2010).

officials who accept bribes or kickbacks[57] for performing or in connection with performing an official act. Honest services fraud by a public officer occurs when, without regard to whether the public officer is an honest bribe taker (one who performs the act that he was bribed to perform) or a dishonest bribe taker (one who takes the bribe and does his job honestly or fails to perform the act that he accepted the bribe to perform), he accepts a bribe to perform or not perform an official act, or when through a kickback a public officer secretly profits from an official act.[58] An example of the latter is when a government official's duties include making recommendations to the municipality that employs him about companies from which the municipality should purchase a service, he recommends that the municipality purchase the service from a company, and the company secretly pays him some percentage of the amount it bills to the municipality for the service it provides.[59]

Honest services fraud is also used to prosecute employees of private businesses who accept bribes or kickbacks from third parties to perform an act that their employer hired them to perform or who in connection with performing some act for their employer (such as purchasing products) receive a payment from some third person for performing that act without the knowledge of their employer.[60]

In honest services fraud cases, the gain the defendant receives need not necessarily be from the person or entity to whom the honest services were owed. As long as the public official, corporate officer, or employee uses his position to obtain a bribe or kickback, that is sufficient to constitute honest services fraud even if that gain comes from some third party instead of from the government body or corporation by whom he is employed.

United States v. Cantrell

United States Court of Appeals for the Seventh Circuit (2010) 617 F.3d 919

Evans, J. During his lifetime, which spans almost 70 years, Robert Cantrell accomplished many things. In a brief on this appeal, his attorney writes that "Cantrell is an Indiana legend and hero." That brief goes on (for many pages) noting that Cantrell was a college baseball and basketball star, * * * a longtime teacher, a decorated war veteran, a beloved husband, father, and grandfather, a mentor to needy students, and a well-known public servant in Indiana. Unfortunately, during the past decade, Cantrell also got into some serious trouble. Specifically, a jury found that he committed honest services fraud, using his position in public office to steer contracts to a third party in exchange for kickbacks (a cut from the proceeds of the contracts), in violation of 18 U.S.C. §§1341 and 1346. * * *

Although this is primarily a sentencing appeal, we begin briefly addressing Cantrell's preserved argument regarding his §1346 conviction. * * * [While this case was pending on appeal the Supreme Court decided *Skilling v. United States*, 561 U.S. ___ (2010) and there held that the honest services fraud statute, §1346, encompasses only bribery and kickback schemes.]

The indictment charged Cantrell with using his position as a public official of North Township of Lake County, Indiana to secure contracts for Addiction and Family Care, Inc, a counseling company owned by an acquaintance, Nancy Fromm, in exchange for a share of the proceeds from the contracts. By failing to fairly, honestly, and candidly award contracts [i.e., by receiving kickbacks for awarding them,] Cantrell defrauded North Township and its citizens of their right to his honest services. This was clearly a kickback scheme, so §1346 — even as pared down by *Skilling* — applies to Cantrell. As he presents no other challenge to his convictions, they will not be disturbed.

For these reasons the judgment of the district court is AFFIRMED.

Case Focus

1. How did the defendant in the above case engage in honest services fraud?

• • • • • • • •

Other than in cases involving honest services fraud, the schemes to which the mail fraud and other scheme statutes apply are schemes to obtain money or property. Under the statute the term "property" includes both tangible property (such as diamonds) and intangible property (such as proprietary information that a business compiles) or property rights (such as the voting rights associated with shares of stock). Proprietary information developed by a business embodies two forms of intangible property: the information itself and the right to control the use of that information. As a result, a scheme that is calculated to deprive a business of either is a scheme to deprive the business of property.

Assuming there is a scheme, the crime of mail fraud is not committed unless the mail is used to further or execute the scheme. For the mail to be considered used to further the scheme it is not necessary that any false representation be sent through the mail. It is sufficient that the mail somehow be used to advance the scheme. The mail is considered to have been used if the defendant, through false representations to the victim, induces the victim to use the mail or if it is foreseeable that the mail will be used by the victim for that or some other purpose that advances the scheme. For example, insurance companies usually mail claim payment checks to their insureds. If an insured devises a scheme to defraud the insurance company through a false claim and makes the claim in person at one of the insurer's local offices, and if the insurance company mails the insured a check in payment of that false claim, the mail will be considered to have been used to further the scheme because it was foreseeable to the defendant that the insurance company would mail him the settlement check.

The mail will also be considered to have been used to further the scheme if after the defendant obtains the money or property from the victim he sends the defendant lulling "letters." For example, if the defendant sells a victim an investment in a nonexistent oil-well-drilling company through in-person representations and is handed a check by the victim, and two months later the defendant mails the victim a report that falsely states that drilling is proceeding and that positive signs have been found that indicate the presence of oil at a greater depth, that communication is considered a lulling letter and constitutes a mailing in furtherance of the scheme to defraud.

Carpenter v. United States

Supreme Court of the United States (1987) 484 U.S. 19

Justice White delivered the opinion of the Court.

Petitioners Kenneth Felis and R. Foster Winans were convicted of violating §10(b) of the Securities Exchange Act of 1934, and Rule 10b-5, [promulgated under that Act.] Carpenter, Winans' roommate, was convicted for aiding and abetting. With a minor exception, the Court of Appeals for the Second Circuit affirmed, 791 F.2d 1024 (1986); we granted certiorari, 479 U.S. 1016 (1986).

I

In 1981, Winans became a reporter for the Wall Street Journal (the Journal) and in the summer of 1982 became one of the two writers of a daily column, "Heard on the Street." That column discussed selected stocks or groups of stocks, giving positive and negative information about those stocks and [took a point of view with respect to investment in the stocks it reviewed.] * * * Because of the "Heard" column's perceived quality and integrity, it had the potential of affecting the price of the stocks which it examined. The District Court concluded on the basis of testimony presented at trial that the "Heard" column "does have an impact on the market, difficult though it may be to quantify in any particular case."

The official policy and practice at the Journal was that prior to publication, the contents of the column were the Journal's confidential information. Despite the rule Winans entered into a scheme in October 1983 with Peter Brant and petitioner Felis, both connected with the Kidder Peabody brokerage firm in New York City, to give them advance information as to the timing and contents of the "Heard" column. This permitted Brant and Felis and another conspirator, David Clark, a client of Brant, to buy or sell based on the probable impact of the column on the market. Profits were to be shared. The conspirators agreed that the scheme would not affect the journalistic purity of the "Heard" column, and the District Court did not find that the contents of any of the articles were altered to further the profit potential of petitioners' stock-trading scheme. Over a 4-month period, the brokers made prepublication trades on the basis of information given them by Winans about the contents of some 27 "Heard" columns. The net profits from these trades were about $690,000.

In November 1983, correlations between the "Heard" articles and trading in the Clark and Felis accounts were noted at Kidder Peabody and inquiries began. * * * Later, the Securities and Exchange Commission began an investigation. Questions were met by denials both by the brokers at Kidder Peabody and by Winans at the Journal. As the investigation progressed, the conspirators quarreled, and on March 29, 1984, Winans and Carpenter went to the SEC and revealed the entire scheme. This indictment and a bench trial followed. Brant, who had pleaded guilty under a plea agreement, was a witness for the Government.

The District Court found, and the Court of Appeals agreed, that Winans had knowingly breached a duty of confidentiality by misappropriating prepublication information regarding the timing and contents of the "Heard" column, information that had been gained in the course of his employment under the understanding that it would not be revealed in advance of publication and that if it were, he would report it to his employer. It was this appropriation of confidential information that underlay both the securities laws and mail and wire fraud counts. * * *

In affirming the mail and wire fraud convictions, the Court of Appeals ruled that Winans had fraudulently misappropriated "property" within the meaning of the mail and wire fraud statutes and that its revelation had harmed the Journal. It was held as well that the use of the mail and wire services had a sufficient nexus with the scheme to satisfy §§1341 and 1343. The petition for certiorari challenged these conclusions. * * *

For the reasons that follow, we also affirm the judgment with respect to the mail and wire fraud convictions.

II

Petitioners assert that their activities were not a scheme to defraud the Journal within the meaning of the mail and wire fraud statutes [The mail and wire fraud statutes share the same language in relevant part, and accordingly we apply the same analysis to both sets of offenses here.]; and that in any event, they did not obtain any "money or property" from the Journal, which is a necessary element of the crime under our decision last Term in *McNally v. United States*, 483 U.S. 350 (1987). We are unpersuaded by either submission and address the latter first.

We held in *McNally* that the mail fraud statute does not reach "schemes to defraud citizens of their intangible rights to honest and impartial government," *id.*, at 355, and that the statute is "limited in scope to the protection of property rights." *Id.*, at 360.[*] Petitioners argue that the Journal's interest in prepublication confidentiality for the "Heard" columns is no more than an intangible consideration outside the reach of §1341 * * *. This is not a case like *McNally*, however. The Journal, as Winans' employer, was defrauded of much more than its contractual right to his honest and faithful service, an interest too ethereal in itself to fall within the protection of the mail fraud statute, which "had its origin in the desire to protect individual property rights." *McNally, supra*, at 359, n.8. Here, the object of the scheme was to take the Journal's confidential business information—the publication schedule and contents of the "Heard" column—and its intangible nature does not make it any less "property" protected by the mail and wire fraud statutes. *McNally* did not limit the scope of §1341 to tangible as distinguished from intangible property rights.

Both courts below expressly referred to the Journal's interest in the confidentiality of the contents and timing of the "Heard" column as a property right, 791 F.2d, at 1034-1035; 612 F. Supp., at 846, and we agree with that conclusion. Confidential business information has long been recognized as property. See *Ruckelshaus v. Monsanto Co.*, 467 U.S. 986, 1001-1004 (1984); *Dirks v. SEC*, 463 U.S. 646, 653, n.10 (1983); *Board of Trade of Chicago v. Christie Grain & Stock Co.*, 198 U.S. 236, 250-251 (1905); cf. 5 U.S.C. §552(b)(4). "Confidential information acquired or compiled by a corporation in the course and conduct of its business is a species of property to which the corporation has the exclusive right and benefit, and which a court of equity will protect through the injunctive process or other appropriate remedy." 3 W. Fletcher, Cyclopedia of Law of Private Corporations §857.1, p.260 (rev. ed. 1986) (footnote omitted). The Journal had a property right in keeping confidential and making exclusive use, prior to publication, of the schedule and contents of the "Heard" column. *Christie Grain, supra*. As the Court has observed before:

> "[N]ews matter, however little susceptible of ownership or dominion in the absolute sense, is stock in trade, to be gathered at the cost of enterprise, organization, skill, labor, and money, and to be distributed and sold to those who will pay money for it, as for any other merchandise." *International News Service v. Associated Press*, 248 U.S. 215, 236 (1918).

Petitioners' arguments that they did not interfere with the Journal's use of the information or did not publicize it and deprive the Journal of the first public

---

[*] Congress overruled McNally by enacting §1346, the honest services fraud statute. *Skilling v. United States*, 561 U.S. 358 (2010).

use of it, see Reply Brief for Petitioners 6, miss the point. The confidential information was generated from the business, and the business had a right to decide how to use it prior to disclosing it to the public. Petitioners cannot successfully contend based on *Associated Press* that a scheme to defraud requires a monetary loss, such as giving the information to a competitor; it is sufficient that the Journal has been deprived of its right to exclusive use of the information, for exclusivity is an important aspect of confidential business information and most private property for that matter.

We cannot accept petitioners' further argument that Winans' conduct in revealing prepublication information was no more than a violation of workplace rules and did not amount to fraudulent activity that is proscribed by the mail fraud statute. Sections 1341 and 1343 reach any scheme to deprive another of money or property by means of false or fraudulent pretenses, representations, or promises. As we observed last Term in *McNally*, the words "to defraud" in the mail fraud statute have the "common understanding" of "'wronging one in his property rights by dishonest methods or schemes,' and 'usually signify the deprivation of something of value by trick, deceit, chicane or overreaching.'" 483 U.S., at 358 (quoting *Hammerschmidt v. United States*, 265 U.S. 182, 188 (1924)). The concept of "fraud" includes the act of embezzlement, which is "the fraudulent appropriation to one's own use of the money or goods entrusted to one's care by another." *Grin v. Shine*, 187 U.S. 181, 189 (1902).

The District Court found that Winans' undertaking at the Journal was not to reveal prepublication information about his column, a promise that became a sham when in violation of his duty he passed along to his co-conspirators confidential information belonging to the Journal, pursuant to an ongoing scheme to share profits from trading in anticipation of the "Heard" column's impact on the stock market. In *Snepp v. United States*, 444 U.S. 507, 515, n.11 (1980) (*per curiam*), although a decision grounded in the provisions of a written trust agreement prohibiting the unapproved use of confidential Government information, we noted the similar prohibitions of the common law, that "even in the absence of a written contract, an employee has a fiduciary obligation to protect confidential information obtained during the course of his employment." As the New York courts have recognized: "It is well established, as a general proposition, that a person who acquires special knowledge or information by virtue of a confidential or fiduciary relationship with another is not free to exploit that knowledge or information for his own personal benefit but must account to his principal for any profits derived therefrom." *Diamond v. Oreamuno*, 24 N.Y.2d 494, 497, 248 N.E.2d 910, 912 (1969); see also Restatement (Second) of Agency §§388, Comment *c*, 396(c) (1958).

We have little trouble in holding that the conspiracy here to trade on the Journal's confidential information is not outside the reach of the mail and wire fraud statutes, provided the other elements of the offenses are satisfied. The Journal's business information that it intended to be kept confidential was its property; the declaration to that effect in the employee manual merely removed any doubts on that score and made the finding of specific intent to defraud that much easier. Winans continued in the employ of the Journal, appropriating its confidential business information for his own use, all the while pretending to perform his duty of safeguarding it. In fact, he told his editors twice about leaks of confidential information not related to the stock-trading scheme, 612 F. Supp., at 831, demonstrating both his knowledge that the Journal viewed information concerning the "Heard" column as confidential and his deceit as he played the role of a loyal employee. Furthermore, the District Court's conclusion that each of the petitioners acted with the required specific intent to defraud is strongly supported by the evidence. *Id.*, at 847-850.

Lastly, we reject the submission that using the wires and the mail to print and send the Journal to its customers did not satisfy the requirement that those mediums be used to execute the scheme at issue. The courts below were quite right in observing that circulation of the "Heard" column was not only anticipated but an essential part of the scheme. Had the column not been made available to Journal customers, there would have been no effect on stock prices and no likelihood of profiting from the information leaked by Winans.

The judgment below is
Affirmed.

Case Focus

1. What was the *Wall Street Journal* defrauded of?
2. Was that property and if so what type of property was it?
3. How were the mails and wires used to execute the scheme?
4. Who actually used the mail and wires to execute the scheme and why was that considered to be a use of those means of communication that constituted use of the mail and wires to execute the scheme?

• • • • • • • •

F. Offenses Against Public Peace and Public Welfare

The offenses in this category are offenses that generally are not committed against a specific individual or to obtain money or property but instead are offenses that when committed have their effects against society as a whole or affect the public welfare in some way. Some of the important offenses contained in this category are money laundering, mob action, terrorism, possession or manufacture of chemical or biological weapons, and crimes affecting the environment.

G. Offenses Against Public Authority and Government Function

The offenses in this category are offenses that are designed to protect the government itself or to protect the functions of government. Offenses of the former type include treason, sedition, espionage, and sabotage. Offenses of the latter type include perjury, bribery, bankruptcy fraud, making false statements to federal officers, tax evasion, and visa fraud.

H. Offenses Involving Foreign Relations or International Law

The offenses in this category include war crimes, piracy, and engaging in a military expedition against a friendly nation. Crimes in this category are federal crimes and found in the federal criminal code.

CHAPTER TERMS

Honest services fraud
Intangible personal property
Intellectual property

Object offense
Personal property
Real property

Tangible personal property

REVIEW QUESTIONS

1. What are the different categories of criminal offenses?
2. What are anticipatory offenses?
3. What are the anticipatory offenses?
4. Why can a person who has committed an offense be convicted of attempting to commit it?
5. What are the two different statutory schemes for classifying homicide and how do they differ?

6. What are the different types of property to which property offenses often relate?
7. What are scheme statutes and what types of schemes are criminal?
8. What is honest services fraud and in what types of statutes is that form of fraud often found?

ADDITIONAL READING

Paul H. Robinson & Markus D. Dubber, *The American Model Penal Code: A Brief Overview*, 10 New Crim. L. Rev. 319. (2007).

ENDNOTES

1. There are a number of different systems for classifying the different forms of crime. No one system is correct or incorrect. Common to all of the systems, however, is an effort to place distinct families of offenses into logically discrete and separate categories. Such organization not only facilitates learning about the offenses but also facilitates comparison and analysis of them by lawyers, judges, and legislators.
2. *See United States v. Black*, 530 F.3d 596 (7th Cir. 2008).
3. Wolfram, *Modern Legal Ethics* §10.3 (1986).
4. *Model Rules of Professional Conduct*, Rule 3.1, Comment 1.
5. *United States v. Wade*, 388 U.S. 218 (1967) (White, J., dissenting and concurring in part).
6. Wolfram at §10.5.3.
7. *Id.*§10.5.2.
8. *State v. Brown*, 644 S.W.2d 418 (Tenn. Ct. App. 1982).
9. Wolfram at §10.5.3.
10. *Ratner v. Young*, 465 F. Supp. 386 (D.C. Virgin Islands 1979).
11. *Id.*
12. *Morrell v. State*, 575 P.2d 1200 (Alaska 1978); *Oregon Ethics Opinion*, 1991-105 (Oregon St. Bar Assn. 1991).
13. *California Ethics Opinion*, 1984-76 (Cal. St. Bar Comm. Prof. Resp. 1984).
14. *See, e.g., In re Ryder*, 263 F. Supp. 360 (D.C. Va. 1967).
15. *See, e.g., Supreme Court Rules of Professional Conduct*, Rule 3.8 (Ill. S. Ct. 2000).
16. *Berger v. United States*, 295 U.S. 78 (1935).
17. *Supreme Court Rules of Professional Conduct*, Rule 3.8 (Ill. S. Ct. 2000).
18. Stuart P. Green, *Moral Ambiguity in White Collar Criminal Law*, 18 Notre Dame J.L. Ethics & Pub. Pol'y 501 (2004).
19. *See, e.g.*, 720 ILCS 5/8-1(a).
20. *State v. Flores*, 218 Ariz. 407 (2008).
21. *See, e.g.*, 720 ILCS 5/8-4(a).
22. Wayne R. LaFave, *Substantive Criminal Law* §11.2 (2007).
23. *People v. Wallee*, 57 Ill. 2d 285 (1974).
24. *See, e.g.*, 720 ILCS 5/8-2 (a).
25. *E.g.*, 720 ILCS 5/46-3 (Conspiracy to Commit Insurance Fraud). Conspiracy to commit insurance fraud is a Class 2 felony when the object offense is the offense of Insurance Fraud. The offense of insurance fraud, depending upon the amount of money involved, can range from a misdemeanor to a Class 1 felony. (In Illinois the least serious felony is a Class 4 felony and the most serious numbered felony is a Class 1 felony.)
26. *See, e.g.*, 720 ILCS 5/12-13.
27. *See, e.g.*, 17-A Maine Revised Statutes Annotated §201(1).
28. *Commonwealth v. Colandro*, 231 Pa. 343 (1911).
29. *Commonwealth v. Flax*, 331 Pa. 145 (1938).
30. *Smith v. State*, 83 Ala. 26 (1888).
31. *See, e.g.*, §720 ILCS 5/9-1(a).
32. *See, e.g.*, Colo. Rev. Stat. 18-3-102.
33. *See, e.g.*, Cal. Pen. Code §187.
34. *Sandoval v. People*, 117 Colo. 588 (1948).
35. *See, e.g.*, 720 ILCS 5/9-2(a)(1)-(2). As to what constitutes a justification defense, see Chapter 13, Affirmative Defenses—Justification.
36. *See, e.g.*, 720 ILCS §5/9-1(a)(3).
37. *Commonwealth v. Exler*, 243 Pa. 155 (1914).
38. *See Commonwealth v. Almeida*, 362 Pa. 596 (1949).
39. *See, e.g.*, 720 ILCS 5/20-1.
40. *See, e.g., People v. Perry*, 224 Ill. 2d 312 (2007).
41. *State v. Entringer*, 246 Wis. 2d 839 (2001).
42. *See, e.g., People v. Young*, 19 Ill. App. 3d 455 (4th Dist. 1974).
43. *Entringer*, 246 Wis.2d at 839.
44. *People v. Mau*, 377 Ill. 199 (1941); *Capitol Bank of Chicago v. Fidelity and Cas. Co. of New York*, 414 F.2d 986 (7th Cir. 1969); *See, e.g.* 720 ILCS §5/17-3(c-5).

45. *See, e.g.,* 18 U.S.C. §1343.
46. *See, e.g.,* 720 ILCS 5/17-10.6(c). An important distinction between Mail Fraud and Wire Fraud on the one hand and Bank Fraud on the other is the act the statutes specify as the criminal act. *United States v. Molinaro,* 11 F.3d 858 (9th Cir. 1993). The Mail Fraud and Wire Fraud statutes make it a crime to further or execute the scheme, respectively, through the use of the mail or the electronic communications system while the Bank Fraud statute, 18 USC §1344 and 720 ILCS §5/17-10.6(c), only make it a crime to execute a scheme. *United States v. Lemons,* 941 F.2d 309 (5th Cir. 1991). The distinction between an act in furtherance and an execution is highly technical and beyond the scope of this textbook.
47. 18 U.S.C. §1341.
48. 18 U.S.C. §1343.
49. *E.g. United States v. Hayes,* 2015 WL 4620254 (S.D.N.Y. 2015).
50. Scheme to defraud means the same thing in Mail Fraud, Wire Fraud, and Bank Fraud. *United States v. Doherty,* 969 F.2d 425 (7th Cir. 1992).
51. *United States v. Lilly,* 983 F.2d 300 (1st Cir. 1992).
52. *United States v. Goldblatt,* 813 F.2d 619 (3rd Cir. 1987).
53. *United States v. Carpenter,* 2015 WL 9305638 (D. Conn. 2015).
54. 18 U.S.C. §1346.
55. *United States v. Ajayi,* 2015 WL 8538025 (7th Cir. 2015).
56. *United States v. Steffan,* 678 F.3d 1104 (8th Cir. 2012).
57. *E.g., Skilling v. United States,* 561 U.S. 358 (2010).
58. *E.g., United States v. Cantrell,* 617 F.3d 919 (7th Cir. 2010).
59. *United States v. Bush,* 522 F.2d 641 (7th Cir. 1975).
60. *United States v. George,* 477 F.2d 508 (7th Cir. 1973). Paying a bribe to an employee of a private company also constitutes the separate offense of commercial bribery, and if it is an employee of a financial institution it is a more serious offense. Compare the offense of Commercial Bribery, a misdemeanor, 720 ILCS 5/29A-1 and 5/29A-2, with the offense of Commercial Bribery Involving a Financial Institution, which is a felony, 720 ILCS 5/§17-10.6(b).

Chapter 11
How Criminal Offenses Are Defined

Chapter Objectives

After reading this chapter, you should be able to

- Name the five elements that are used to define all criminal offenses
- Understand the role of *mens rea* and *actus reus* in criminal law
- Explain what a voluntary act is
- Find the elements of any criminal offense
- Analyze and understand any criminal offense
- Read and analyze a police report and determine if a crime has been committed and whether it contains sufficient evidence to charge
- Understand the significance of the elements that are used to define criminal offenses

> In the first place, we must deal with those elements which occur in every case of crime; . . . the absence of [any] of which excludes the act from the category of crimes. —Seymour Harris, *Principles of the Criminal Law*, 1884

Different American jurisdictions frequently define crimes that criminalize the same or similar conduct differently, frequently give similar offenses different names, often use different terms to describe the same legal concept, and sometimes give the same name to different legal concepts. All of those variations combined with the shear number of criminal offenses defined in the laws of the 50 states and in the United States Code make it impossible to examine specific offenses in any meaningful way.

Without regard to how differently American jurisdictions may define crimes and how differently they may label them, in the United

States all crimes are defined against a background of English common law, which developed and refined five fundamental elements that are used in defining all crimes in Anglo-American law. In the United States all crimes are defined by using at least one (and usually more than one) of those five fundamental elements or by using one of their multiple alternate forms. When defining criminal offenses, the legislative branch selects not only which elements to include in the definition of an offense, but also which forms of those elements are to be included in that definition.

The five fundamental elements used in defining all American crimes are: (a) mental state, which is frequently referred to as *mens rea*, scienter, or criminal intent; (b) forbidden act or result, which is usually referred to as the *actus reus*; (c) concurrence; (d) causation; and (e) circumstances. In this chapter we will examine each of those elements, and in Section F we will see how to use those elements to analyze a report from a law enforcement agent to determine whether a crime has been committed and whether there is sufficient evidence to prove that a specific individual committed it.

A. *Mens Rea*

This section examines the *mens rea* element of criminal offenses. The term *mens rea* means guilty mind and is one of the most complicated concepts in criminal law. That complexity results partly from the fact that frequently different terms have been used to describe the same *mens rea* concept and that sometimes the same term has been used to describe different *mens rea* concepts. The problems caused by such terminological confusion are compounded by definitional imprecision. Historically, *mens rea* terms were not always precisely defined and as a result there often appeared to be (and often were) overlaps between the concepts to which the *mens rea* terms referred.

Early in its history the common law did not include a *mens rea* element in offenses. By the 1600s, however, common law judges had added *mens rea* elements to most common law crimes. Thus, the *mens rea* concepts of modern criminal law are the result of a slow judicial evolution in which, until relatively recently, the legislative branch played no role. The concepts of *mens rea* developed by the common law continue to be important today.

In the United States, criminal codes take one of two different approaches to *mens rea*. In one approach the criminal code contains no comprehensive list of the mental states it employs in defining crimes or definitions of the mental states that it employs. In those codes the individual criminal statutes usually contain a specific *mens rea* term, but leave the meaning of that term to be developed by the judiciary. In those types of criminal codes the judiciary determines the meaning of the *mens rea* term by reference to legislative intent and the term's common law definition. As a result, in jurisdictions with those types of codes the common law definitions of the different forms of *mens rea* continue to be important. The Federal Criminal Code is an important example of such a code.

The Model Penal Code represents a different approach and one that also reduces the role of the judiciary in interpreting the different forms of *mens rea*. The Model Penal Code contains a section of general applicability that includes a comprehensive list of all the mental states used in the Code and specifically and carefully defines the meaning of each of those mental states. Most states have followed the pattern of the Model Penal Code. As a result, most state criminal codes contain a comprehensive list of well-defined mental states that are used in the definition of the crimes those codes define. Even in those states that have followed the pattern of the Model Penal Code, some have merely codified the common law mental states.[1] Consequently, in those states, as under federal law, the common law definitions of the different types of *mens rea* continues to be important.

This section examine five different *mens rea*-related subjects: (1) *mens rea* at common law; (2) *mens rea* in the Model Penal Code; (3) other forms of *mens rea*; (4) motive and *mens rea*; and (5) offenses without mental states.

1. *Mens Rea at Common Law*

At common law crimes were generally classified as either specific intent crimes or general intent crimes.[2] While that distinction has been criticized by some legal scholars and has been rejected in the criminal codes of some American jurisdictions, it has nevertheless been codified in the criminal codes of many American states.[3] The distinction between specific intent crimes and general intent crimes is important because of the different types of evidence needed to prove their respective mental state elements. One important point to keep in mind is that with specific intent crimes the *mens rea* cannot be inferred from the prohibited act alone and additional evidence is needed to establish it. In contrast, with general intent crimes the *mens rea* may be inferred solely from the performance of the statutorily prohibited act.

a. Specific Intent

A specific intent crime is one in which the act is committed voluntarily and purposely with the specific intent to do something the law forbids.[4]

The meaning of the term specific intent differs depending upon whether the crime that incorporates it into its definition condemns an act or a result. If the criminal statute condemns an act, the concept of specific intent requires that the defendant have engaged in the condemned act with the specific design to engage in conduct of that nature.[5] For example, the crime of burglary is defined such that for conviction it must be shown that the defendant entered a structure with the intent to steal. If the criminal statute condemns a result and has a specific intent *mens rea* element, it must be proved that the defendant engaged in some conduct with the specific design to bring about the condemned result.[6] For example, with intent to kill murder it must be proved that the defendant engaged in some conduct with the specific design to bring about the death of a person. Specific intent crimes generally do not require that the defendant know that he was violating the law when he acted.[7]

Intent to kill murder is a form of murder that is defined as being committed when a person has an intent to kill another and by his conduct causes the death of that person. *See, e.g.,* 17-A Maine Rev. Stat. §201(1)(A).

b. General Intent

A general intent crime is one in which an act is done voluntarily and intentionally and not because of mistake or accident.[8] The heart of the distinction between the concept of specific intent and the concept of general intent is that specific intent requires some intent beyond the intent to do the physical act.[9]

Just as the meaning of the concept of specific intent differs depending upon whether the statute that incorporates it into the definition of a crime condemns an act or a result, the definition of the concept of general intent also differs based upon that distinction. General intent requires only that the defendant intended to engage in the physical act the law condemns or that the defendant committed a physical act and that there was a high risk that a result condemned by a criminal statute would follow from that act. With general intent crimes, as long as the result was substantially certain to follow from an act, it can be inferred that the defendant intended the result; whether or not the defendant actually wanted to achieve that result is immaterial.

c. Transferred Intent

Incorporated into the concepts of specific and general intent is the doctrine of transferred intent. Under that doctrine, if the defendant intended to commit a particular crime against a particular person or property and through mistake or otherwise he ends up committing it against a different person or property, the defendant is deemed to have intended to commit the crime against that other person or property. With the concept of transferred intent it is frequently said that the intent follows the bullet. For example, if Jermaine intends to kill Susan and carefully aims his gun and shoots at Susan, but misses her and hits and kills Sophia instead, Jermaine is considered to have intended to kill Sophia even though he had no intention to harm Sophia and may have even liked her. The doctrine of transferred intent is limited to the type of crime that was intended and does not apply if a different crime results from the act. So, in the above example, if instead of the bullet hitting and killing Sophia (which would have constituted the crime of intent to kill murder), the bullet from the gun fired by Jermaine hits and kills Sophia's dog, the doctrine of transferred intent does not impute to Jermaine the intent to destroy Sophia's property (the crime of criminal damage to property).

Regina v. Pembilton

Court of Criminal Appeal (1874) 12 Cox Cr. Cases 607

Case stated for the opinion of this Court by the Recorder of Wolverhampton.

At a Quarter Session of the Peace held at Wolverhampton on the 8th day of January instant Henry Pembilton was indicted [charging] that he "unlawfully and maliciously did commit damage, injury, and spoil upon the window in the house of Henry Kirkham" contrary to the provision of the stat. 24 & 25 Vict. C. 97, s. 51. This section of the statute enacts:

> Whosoever shall unlawfully and maliciously commit any damage, injury, or spoil to or upon any real or personal property whatsoever either of a public or private nature for which no punishment is hereinbefore provided, the damage, injury, or spoil being to an amount exceeding £5, shall be guilty of a misdemeanor, and being convicted thereof shall be liable, at the discretion of the court, to be imprisoned for any term not exceeding two years with or without hard labour, and in case any such offense shall be committed between the hours of nine of the clock in the evening and six of the clock in the next morning, he shall be liable at the discretion of the Court to be kept in penal servitude for any term not exceeding five years and not less than three, or to be imprisoned for any term not exceeding two years without hard labour.

On the night of the 6th day of December, 1873, the prisoner was drinking with others at a public-house called "The Grand Turk" kept by the prosecutor. About eleven o'clock p.m. the whole party were turned out of the house for being disorderly, and they then began to fight in the street and near the prosecutor's window, where a crowd of from 40 to 50 persons collected. The prisoner, after fighting some time with persons in the crowd, separated himself from them, and removed to the other side of the street where he picked up a large stone and threw it at the persons he had been fighting with. The stone passed over the heads of those persons and struck a large plate glass window in the prosecutor's house, and broke it, thereby doing damage to the extent of £7. 12*s. 8d*.

The jury, after hearing evidence on both sides, found that the prisoner threw the stone which broke the window, but that he threw it at the people he had been fighting with, intending to strike one or more of them with it, but not intending to break the window, and they returned a verdict of "guilty" whereupon I respited the sentence, and admitted the prisoner to bail, and pray the judgment of the Court for Crown Cases Reserved, whether upon the facts stated and the finding of the jury, the prisoner was rightly convicted or not.

(Signed) John J. Powell.

Recorder of Wolverhampton

* * *

LORD COLERIDGE, C.J. I am of the opinion that this conviction must be quashed. * * * The jury found that the prisoner threw the stone at the people he had been fighting with, intending to strike one or more of them with it, but not intending to break the window. The question is whether under the indictment for unlawfully and maliciously committing an injury to the window in the house of the prosecutor the proof of these facts alone, coupled with finding of the jury, will do? Now I think that is not enough. The indictment is framed under the 24 & 25 Vict. C. 97, s. 51. The Act is an Act relating to malicious injuries to property, and sect. 51 enacts that whosoever shall unlawfully and maliciously commit any damage, &c., to or upon any real or personal property * * * to an amount exceeding £5, shall be guilty of a misdemeanor. There is also the 58th section which deserves attention. "Every punishment and forfeiture by this Act imposed on any person maliciously committing any offence, whether the same be punishable upon indictment or upon summary conviction, shall equally apply and be enforced whether the offence shall be committed from malice conceived against the owner of the property in respect which it shall be committed, or otherwise." It seems to me on both these sections that what was intended to be provided against by the Act is wilfully doing an unlawful Act, and that the Act must be wilfully and intentionally done on the part of the person doing it, to render him liable to be convicted. Without saying that, upon these facts, if the jury had found the prisoner had been guilty of throwing the stone recklessly, knowing that there was a window near which it might probably hit, I should not have been disposed to interfere with the conviction, yet as they have found that he threw the stone at the people he had been fighting with intending to strike them and not intending to break the window, I think his conviction must be quashed. I do not intend to throw any doubt on the case which have been cited and which show this sufficient to constitute malice in the case of murder. They rest on the principles of the common law, and have no application to a statutory offence created by an Act in which the words are carefully studied.

BLACKBURN, J. I am of the same opinion, and I quite agree that it is not necessary to consider what constitutes wilful malice aforethought to bring a case with the common law crime of murder, when we are construing this statute. * * * A person may be said to act maliciously when he wilfully does an unlawful act without lawful excuse. The question here is can the prisoner be said, when he not only threw the stone unlawfully but broke the window unintentionally to have unlawfully and maliciously broke the window, if they had found that the prisoner was aware that the natural and probable consequence of his throwing the stone was that it might break the glass window, on the principle that a man may be taken to intend what is the natural and probable consequence of his acts. But the jury have not found that the prisoner threw the stone knowing that, on the other side of the crowd he was throwing at, there was a glass window and that he was reckless as to whether he did or did not break the window. On the contrary, they found that he did not intend to break the window. I think therefore that the conviction must be reversed.

PIGOTT, B. I am of the same opinion.

LUSH, J. I also think that on this finding of the jury we have no alternative but to hold the conviction must be quashed. The word "maliciously" means an act done either actually or constructively with a malicious intent. The jury might have found that he did intend actually to break the window or constructively to do so, as that he knew that the stone might probably break it when he threw it. But they have not so found.

CLEASBY, B. Concurred.

Conviction quashed.

Case Focus

1. What *mens* rea did the jury find?
2. On what basis did the court determine that the defendant's conviction for unlawfully and maliciously breaking the window should be reversed?

• • • • • • • •

2. Mens Rea *in the Model Penal Code*

The Model Penal Code, which has been adopted in whole or part in many states, has attempted to bring organization and precision to the subject of *mens rea*. The Code recognizes four mental states, any one or more of which may be used to define crimes: (1) purpose, (2) knowledge, (3) recklessness, and (4) negligence. It is important to remember that states that have adopted the Model Penal Code have not all adopted its *mens rea* terminology or necessarily adopted all of its *mens rea* definitions.

Under the Model Penal Code approach a person acts purposely when it is his conscious object to engage in conduct of that nature or to cause the result that followed from his act. In a general sense the Code's concept of purpose corresponds to the common law concept of specific intent.[10] With respect to the mental state called knowledge, the Code provides that a person acts knowingly when he is consciously aware of the nature of his conduct, that a particular result is practically certain to be caused by his conduct, or that certain circumstances exist. That concept of knowledge corresponds generally to the common law concept of general intent.[11]

Under the Code a person acts recklessly when he consciously disregards a substantial and unjustifiable risk that a result will follow, and the risk is of such nature and degree that, considering the circumstances known to the person, its disregard is a gross deviation from the standard of conduct that a law-abiding person would observe in the situation. A person acts negligently when he fails to be aware of a substantial and unjustifiable risk that circumstances exist or a result will follow that is described in a criminal statute, and failing to be aware of either constitutes a substantial deviation from the standard of care that a reasonable person would exercise in the situation.

3. *Other Forms of* Mens Rea

Some of the criminal statutes of many jurisdictions contain terms other than those discussed above to describe their mental state element. Those terms (such as "corruptly," "fraudulently," and "maliciously") have various meanings, and the only way to determine the sense in which they are used in a criminal statute of a particular jurisdiction is to look at how that jurisdiction's courts have construed that term in that statute. Of those various other *mens rea* terms, two of the most commonly used are the terms "willfully" and "maliciously."

The term "willfully" is one of the more chameleon-like terms in criminal law. Depending upon the statute the term may be used with the meaning of specific intent and may or may not include a requirement that the person have actual knowledge of the law, or it may be used with the meaning of general intent or knowledge. For example, "willful" as used in the criminal provisions of the Internal Revenue Code means an intentional violation of a known legal duty, whereas the same term used in the criminal provisions of some state tax codes only means knowledge. The only way to determine the sense in which willfulness is used in a statute of a particular jurisdiction is to look at how that jurisdiction's courts have construed that term in that statute. The Model Penal Code has addressed the concept of "willfulness" and provides that the term means "knowledge."[12]

The term "malice" or "maliciously" also can be a term of different meanings. At common law "malice" meant that a person acted either with: (1) an actual intent to commit the act condemned by the criminal statute or (2) a heedless disregard that the prohibited harm is a plain and strong likelihood.[13] As with willfulness, the only way to determine what the term means in a jurisdiction's statute is to see how the courts in that jurisdiction have construed it in that statute.

4. *Motive and* Mens Rea

One concept that is frequently associated with *mens rea* issues is the concept of motive, which refers to the reason why a defendant engaged in particular criminal conduct. Motive is not an element of any criminal offense and as a result need never be proved by the prosecutor, notwithstanding that motive often plays an important role in criminal prosecutions.

Motive is important because it can be used as evidence of intent. As a result, a prosecutor can introduce evidence relating to motive to prove the defendant's *mens rea*. For example, a defendant who needs money and knows his wealthy father has written a will leaving him a substantial sum of money may kill his father so that he can inherit it. If the defendant is charged with intent to kill murder and the prosecutor has evidence showing the defendant's need for the money and that the defendant knew that upon his father's death he would inherit money from him, the prosecutor can use those facts to establish a motive and thereby argue that that motive is evidence that when the defendant killed his father it was his intent to do so.

Motive can also play an important role prior to the defendant being charged with or after he has been convicted of a crime. If when a defendant commits an offense he acted for a good purpose, the prosecutor may rely on that good motive as a reason to decline prosecution or to charge a less serious crime. A judge can also take motive into account when sentencing a convicted defendant and impose a lighter sentence if the defendant acted with a good motive or a harsher sentence if the defendant acted with a bad motive.

5. *Offenses Without Mental States*

Crimes without a *mens rea* element are called strict liability offenses. A person can be guilty of a strict liability offense merely upon proof that he committed the act condemned by a criminal statute or that he brought about the result that a criminal statute condemns. It is important to keep in mind that an offense is not a strict liability offense just because the statute defining an offense does not contain a *mens rea* element. Courts use different methods by which to determine whether an offense whose statutory definition does not contain a *mens rea* element is a strict liability offense. Generally, if a criminal statute contains no *mens rea* element and it is a minor offense, courts will construe it as a strict liability offense. With more serious offenses courts will consider the offense itself and look at the legislative purpose and try to determine from those if the legislature intended to create a strict liability offense.[14]

If a criminal statute does not contain a *mens rea* element and a court determines that a *mens rea* element was intended, that presents the court with the question of what *mens rea* element to read into that offense. Until definitively construed by a court, offenses that by their terms do not contain a *mens rea* element also pose an identical problem for the prosecutor when he charges that offense: Does the crime defined by the statute have a *mens rea* element and, if so, what *mens rea* should be alleged when charging that offense? For a paralegal who is tasked with drafting a charging instrument for the violation of a statute whose terms do not contain a *mens rea* element it is essential that she determine whether the courts of her jurisdiction have nonetheless determined that the offense has a *mens rea* element and determine what that *mens rea* element is.

Many criminal codes contain a default statute that provides that, if a criminal statute does not have a *mens rea* element in its definition and the crime it defines is not a strict liability offense, any of certain listed mental states may be considered as the *mens rea* element.[15] In such instances, until a court definitively decides what the mental state element of the offense is, the prosecutor may select a mental state from that list when charging the offense.

People v. Sevilla

Supreme Court of Illinois (1989) 132 Ill. 2d 113

MORAN, C.J. The defendant, Leota L. Sevilla, was indicted by a grand jury in Cook County for knowingly failing to file a retailers' occupation tax return for January 1985 where the amount due was $300 or more * * * The indictment charged the defendant with knowingly failing to act, even though the statute did not indicate that the offense included a mental state element. * * *

A jury found the defendant guilty of knowingly failing to file the return where the amount due was under $300. * * * After a sentencing hearing in which the parties introduced evidence in aggravation and mitigation, the circuit court sentenced the defendant to a 14-month term of imprisonment. The defendant appealed. * * *

At issue is whether the offense of failing to file a retailers' occupation tax return includes a mental state element. If so, it must be determined: (1) whether "knowledge" is the mental state element implied under the Act; * * *

The following facts were adduced at the defendant's trial. The defendant was the sole proprietor of a retail business known as "Lee's Creative Designs." In January 1985, the defendant collected retailers' occupation taxes in an amount under $300. The defendant failed to file the monthly return [was] * * * due. * * *

I

The first issue to be addressed is whether the offense of failing to file a retailers' occupation tax return includes a mental state element. In *People v. Player* (1941), 377 Ill. 417, 422, the court, addressing the identical issue, held that the offense of failing to file a return did not include a mental state element. The State argues that *Player* is still controlling; therefore, the language in the indictment charging the defendant with "knowingly" failing to file the return was mere surplusage. The defendant argues that *Player* is no longer controlling because the legislature has made certain amendments to the Act which affect the holding of that case. We agree with the defendant.

The purpose of the Act is to levy a tax on the retailer for the privilege of operating a business in the State. (*Reif v. Barrett* (1933), 355 Ill. 104, 109.) Section 3 of the Act imposes a duty on the retailer to file a retailers' occupation tax return and to remit the tax payment. (Ill. Rev. Stat. 1985, ch. 120, par. 442.) To ensure compliance the Act contains a detailed registration and enforcement scheme. (See Ill. Rev. Stat. 1985, ch. 120, pars. 440 through 451.) Section 13 of the Act makes the failure to file a return, among other things, a criminal offense. (Ill. Rev. Stat. 1985, ch. 120, par. 452.) Section 13 provides in pertinent part:

> "When the amount due is under $300, any person engaged in the business of selling tangible personal property at retail in this State who *fails to file a return*, or who files a fraudulent return, or any officer or agent of a corporation engaged in the business of selling tangible personal property at retail in this State who signs a fraudulent return filed on behalf of such corporation, or any accountant or other agent who knowingly enters false information on the return of any taxpayer under this Act, *is guilty of a Class 4 felony*." (Emphasis added.) (Ill. Rev. Stat. 1985, ch. 120, par. 452.)

The section does not indicate whether mental state is an element of the offense of failing to file a return; the words "knowingly" and "fraudulent" as used in this section do not refer to the alleged violation.

Section 4-9 of the Criminal Code of 1961, which became effective January 1962, governs absolute liability. The section provides:

> "A person may be guilty of an offense without having, as to each element thereof, one of the mental states described in Sections 4-4 through 4-7 if the offense is a misdemeanor which is not punishable by incarceration or by a fine exceeding $500, or *the statute defining the offense clearly indicates a legislative purpose to impose absolute liability for the conduct described*." (Emphasis added.) (Ill. Rev. Stat. 1985, ch. 38, par. 4-9.)

This section applies to all criminal penalty provisions, including those outside of the Criminal Code of 1961. *People v. Valley Steel Products Co.* (1978), 71 Ill. 2d 408, 424.

* * *

The committee comments to section 4-9 reveal that the legislature intended to limit the scope of absolute liability. The comments provide in pertinent part:

> "This section is intended to establish, as an expression of general legislative intent, *rather strict limitations upon the interpretation that mental state is not an element of an offense*, although the express language of the provision defining the offense fails to describe such an element. * * *
>
> * * *
>
> The first part of section 4-9 recognizes the type of offense which carries so little culpability that incarceration is not a part of the penalty, and the fine is less than $500. * * * In view of the difficulty of enforcing such provisions if mental state must be proved in each instance, the assumption seems proper that in these instances the omission of such a requirement is intended to create absolute liability. * * *
>
> * * * [T]he second part of section 4-9 expresses the policy that *in other offenses not including a mental state in the definition only a clearly indicated legislative intent to create absolute liability should be recognized, and in all other instances, a mental-state requirement should be implied as an application of the general rule that an offense consists of an act accompanied by a culpable mental state* * * *." (Emphasis added.) Ill. Ann. Stat., ch. 38, par. 4-9, Committee Comments, at 226-228 (Smith-Hurd 1989). * * *

Absent either a clear indication that the legislature intended to impose absolute liability or an important public policy favoring it, this court has been unwilling to interpret a statute as creating an absolute liability offense. See *People v. Valley Steel Products Co.* (1978), 71 Ill. 2d 408, 423-424 (certain offenses involving filing requirements under the Motor Fuel Tax Law include a mental state element); *People v. Nunn* (1979), 77 Ill. 2d 243, 249-251 (offense of leaving the scene of an accident includes knowledge of the accident as an element); *People v. Whitlow* (1982), 89 Ill. 2d 322, 332-333 (certain offenses involving securities law include a *scienter* element). * * *

[W]e hold that the offense includes a mental state element. The section does not indicate a clear legislative purpose for imposing absolute liability and there is not an important public policy which favors absolute liability, especially in light of the civil penalty provisions available to the Department of Revenue as a means of collecting unpaid and overdue taxes.

II

As we have concluded that the offense of failing to file a retailers' occupation tax return includes a mental state element, we must address the remaining questions: whether "knowledge" is the mental state element implied under the Act and whether the circuit court erred in denying the defendant the opportunity to introduce evidence in support of her mistake of law defense.

A

Where a statute neither prescribes a particular mental state nor creates an absolute liability offense, then either intent, knowledge or recklessness applies. (Ill. Rev. Stat. 1985, ch. 38, par. 4-3(b).) Both the State and the defendant maintain that if the statute in the present case does not create an absolute liability offense, knowledge is the mental state element implied under the Act. We agree. * * *

The language of section 13, which establishes criminal sanctions for violations of the Act, compels a finding that the legislature intended knowledge to be the requisite mental state element. With the exception of those violations involving fraudulent acts, the section designates the mental state accompanying the particular criminal act as either willfulness or knowledge. Conduct performed willfully is performed knowingly or with knowledge. (Ill. Rev. Stat. 1985, ch. 38, par. 4-5.) The section does not designate intent or recklessness as the mental state accompanying any criminal act. Further support for this finding comes from the language of the parallel provision of the Illinois Income Tax Act (Ill. Rev. Stat. 1985, ch. 120, par. 13-1301), which establishes criminal sanctions for failing to file an income tax return. The section provides in pertinent part:

> "Any person * * * who *willfully* fails to file a return * * * [is] guilty of a Class 4 felony for the first offense and a Class 3 felony for each subsequent offense." (Emphasis added.) (Ill. Rev. Stat. 1985, ch. 120, par. 13-1301.)

In light of the language of section 13 of the Act and the language of the parallel section of the Income Tax Act, we hold that knowledge is an element of the offense of failing to file a retailers' occupation tax return.

B

Knowledge generally refers to an awareness of the existence of the facts which make an individual's conduct unlawful. (21 Am. Jur. 2d *Criminal Law* §136 (1981).) Section 4-5 of the Criminal Code defines knowledge:

> "A person knows, or acts knowingly or with knowledge of:
>
> (a) The nature or attendant circumstances of his conduct, described by the statute defining the offense, when he is consciously aware that his conduct is of such nature or that such circumstances exist. Knowledge of a material fact includes awareness of the substantial probability that such fact exists.
>
> (b) The result of his conduct, described by the statute defining the offense, when he is consciously aware that such result is practically certain to be caused by his conduct." Ill. Rev. Stat. 1985, ch. 38, par. 4-5.

The indictment charged the defendant with knowingly failing to file a monthly return. At trial, the State introduced evidence tending to prove that the defendant had knowledge of the circumstances surrounding her failure to file the return. The defendant sought to raise a mistake of law defense, but the circuit court did not allow the defendant the opportunity to introduce evidence in support of that defense. At the close of the evidence, a jury found the defendant guilty of knowingly failing to file the monthly return. * * *

For the reasons stated above, the judgment of the appellate court, reversing the judgment of the circuit court and remanding the cause for a new trial, is reversed, and the judgment of the circuit court of Cook County is affirmed.

Appellate court reversed; circuit court affirmed.

Case Focus

1. The terms of the statute did not contain a mental state element; notwithstanding that, did the court determine that the offense the statute defined actually had a mental state?
2. What *mens rea* element did the court determine the offense contained?
3. How did the court decide what the *mens rea* element of the offense should be?

• • • • • • • •

B. *Actus Reus*

So far we have examined the mental state element of criminal offenses. However, a fundamental principle of Anglo-American criminal law is that bad thoughts, no matter how evil, do not a crime make. The bad act element of a crime is called the *actus reus*. The *actus reus* of an offense is the specific act or result that the law, whether common law or statute, condemns. An example of a specific bad act that the law condemns in an offense is making a document that is apparently capable of defrauding another. (The *actus reus* of the offense of forgery.) An example of a result that the law condemns in an offense is death in the crime of murder. Note that in the former the law condemns a specific type of act whereas in the latter it condemns bringing about a result without specifying any particular act by which that result is achieved.

In Anglo-American criminal law, for there to be a crime the *actus reus* must have been voluntarily performed. This section examines what the terms voluntary and act mean in criminal law.

1. *Voluntariness*

What constitutes voluntariness as that term is used in criminal law has long been a matter of much debate. One definition that is used in the criminal codes of many states and that captures the core understanding of what voluntary means as that term is applied to criminal acts is: an act performed consciously as a result of effort or determination.[16] As can be seen from that definition a voluntary act requires a conscious effort by the defendant. As a result acts done unconsciously, as a reflex, or caused by another are not voluntary acts. For example, if Alan pushes against Ronald's arm, causing Ronald to fire the gun he had in his hand, Ronald has not committed a voluntary act because the act of firing the gun was not the result of Ronald's conscious effort.

It is important to distinguish the term voluntariness used in connection with an act from the defense of duress, which is discussed later in this textbook. Voluntariness as used in connection with a criminal act refers to a conscious physical movement. One who acts under duress is consciously engaging in a movement, albeit for some reason that the law may excuse. The distinction between voluntariness and duress is important because while the prosecution must prove that a defendant's criminal act is voluntary in the sense that the term "voluntary" is used in connection with a criminal act, the defendant has the burden of proving that he acted under duress.

Fain v. Commonwealth

Supreme Court of Kentucky (1879) 78 Ky. 183

COFER, J. The appellant was indicted and tried for the murder of Henry Smith, a porter at the Veranda Hotel at Nicholasville. He was found guilty of manslaughter, and sentenced to confinement in the penitentiary for two years. From that judgment he prosecutes this appeal.

The prisoner and his friend George Welch went to the Veranda Hotel after dark on an evening in February. The weather was cold, and there was snow upon the ground. They sat down in the public room and went to sleep. In a short time Welch awoke, and, finding the deceased in the barber's shop, in the next room, called for a bed for himself and the prisoner, to pay for which he handed the deceased a bill. Welch attempted to awaken the prisoner by shaking him, but failed. He then told the deceased to wake him up. The deceased shook him for some time, and failing to wake him, said he believed he was dead. Welch said no, he is not; wake him up. The deceased shook him harder and harder until the prisoner looked up and asked what he wanted. The deceased said he wanted him to go to bed. The prisoner said he would not, and told the deceased to go away and let him alone. The deceased said it was getting late, and he wanted to close the house, and still holding the prisoner by the coat, the latter either raised or was lifted up, and, as he arose, he threw his hand to his side as if to draw a weapon. A bystander said to him, don't shoot; but without noticing or giving any sign that he heard what was said, he drew a pistol and fired. The deceased instantly grappled him to prevent him from shooting again, but a second shot was fired almost immediately, and a third soon followed. After the third shot was fired the prisoner was thrown down and held by the deceased. The prisoner, while being held on the floor, hallooed *hoo-wee* very loud two or three times, and called for Welch. He asked the deceased to let him get up; but the deceased said. "If I do, you will shoot me again." The prisoner said he would not, and the deceased released his hold and allowed him to get up. Upon getting up the prisoner went out of the room with his pistol in his hand. His manner was that of a frightened man. He said to a witness, "Take my pistol and defend me;" said he had shot some one, but did not know who it was, and upon being told who it was, expressed sorrow for what he had done.

It did not appear that the prisoner knew or had ever seen the deceased before. There was not the slightest evidence of a motive on his part to injure the deceased, nor does there appear to have been anything in what the deceased did or the manner of doing it which, the facts being understood, was calculated to excite anger, much less a desire to kill him. At that time the prisoner was about thirty-three years of age, and he introduced evidence to show that he had been a man of good character and of peaceable and orderly habits.

He also offered to prove that he had been a sleep-walker from his infancy; that he had to be watched to prevent injury to himself; that he was put to sleep in a lower room, near that of his parents, and a servant-man was required to sleep in the room to watch him; that frequently, when aroused from sleep, he seemed frightened, and attempted violence as if resisting an assault, and for some minutes seemed unconscious of what he did or what went on around him; that sometimes, when partly asleep, he resisted the servant who slept in the room with him, as if he supposed the servant was assaulting him.

He also offered to prove by medical experts that persons asleep sometimes act as if awake; that they walk, talk, answer questions, and do many other things, and yet are unconscious of what they do; that with many persons there is a period between sleeping and waking in which they are unconscious, though they seem to be awake; that loss of sleep, and other causes which produce nervous depression or mental anxiety, may produce such a state of unconsciousness between sleep and waking; and that for some days previous his children had been afflicted with a dangerous disease, and he had, in consequence, lost much sleep.

He likewise offered to prove that his life had been threatened by a person living near where he had been on business during the day, and that he had on that morning borrowed the pistol with which he shot the deceased, and had stated at the time that he was required to go near to where the person lived who had threatened him, and he wanted the pistol to defend himself in case he was attacked.

The court rejected all this proffered evidence, and the prisoner excepted.

All the modern medico-legal writers to whose writings we have had access, recognize a species of mental unsoundness connected with sleep, which they commonly treat of under the general head of *Somnambulism*.

In speaking of this peculiar affection, Dr. Ray says:

"Not only is the power of locomotion enjoyed, as the etymology of the term signifies, but the voluntary muscles are capable of executing motions of the most delicate kind. Thus, the somnambulist will walk securely on the edge of a precipice, saddle his horse, and ride off at a gallop; walk on stilts over a swollen torrent; practice airs on a musical instrument; in short, he may read, write, run, leap, climb, and swim, as well as, and sometimes even better than, when fully awake." (Ray's Med. Jur., sec. 495; Wharton & Stille, Taylor, and Brown announce similar views; Wharton & Stille on Med. Jur., sec. 149 *et seq.*; Taylor's Med. Jur., page 176; Med. Jur. of Insanity, sec. 328 *et seq.*) * * *

Ray says: "As the somnambulist does not enjoy the free and rational exercise of his understanding, and is more or less unconscious of his outward relations, none of his acts during the paroxysms can rightfully be imputed to him as crimes." (Med. Jur., sec. 508.)

Brown, and Wharton & Stille express substantially the same views.

But we are not under the necessity of relying wholly upon writers on medical jurisprudence as authority upon this point. It is one of the fundamental principles of the criminal law that there can be no criminality in the absence of criminal intention; and when we ascertain from medical experts or otherwise that there is such a thing in nature as somnolentia and somnambulism, the task of the jurist is ended, so far as relates to the right of one accused of crime to offer evidence conducing to prove that he committed the act imputed to him as a crime while in a paroxysm of somnolentia or somnambulism. In criminal trials, the jury must try every pertinent question of fact the evidence conduces to prove. When evidence is offered, the sole question for the court is, will it conduce to prove any fact material in the case? and if the law gives an affirmative response, the evidence must be admitted. If, as claimed, the appellant was unconscious when he fired the first shot, it cannot be imputed to him as a crime. Nor is he guilty if partially conscious, if, upon being partially awakened, and finding the deceased had hold of him and was shaking him, he imagined he was being attacked, and believed himself in danger of losing his life or of sustaining great bodily injury at the hands of his assailant, he shot in good faith, believing it necessary to preserve his life or his person from great harm. In such circumstances, it does not matter whether he had reasonable grounds for his belief or not. He had been asleep, and could know nothing of the surrounding circumstances. In his condition he may have supposed he was assailed for a deadly purpose, and if he did, he is not to be punished because his half-awakened consciousness deceived him as to the real facts, any more than if, being awake, the deceased had presented a pistol to his head with the apparent intention to shoot him, when in fact he was only jesting, or if the supposed pistol, though sufficiently resembling a deadly weapon to be readily mistaken for one, was but an inoffensive toy.

The evidence conducing to prove that the appellant's children had been sick, and that he had recently lost considerable sleep, should have been admitted as conducing to show that, at the moment of being aroused, he may have been unconscious, or partly so, and, therefore, unable readily to understand the real circumstances of his situation.

The physicians introduced would have proved, as the appellant avowed, that loss of sleep and mental anxiety each has a tendency to develop a predisposition to *somnolentia*, or sleep drunkenness, as it is otherwise called, and in this they would but corroborate the opinions of medical jurists.

We are also of the opinion that the offered evidence in regard to the alleged threats against the prisoner should have been admitted.

The central position of the defense was, that the prisoner fired the fatal shots while partially or wholly unconscious, under the false impression that he was being assaulted by the deceased.

His effort was to show that he was subject to a peculiar affection which made him imagine, when suddenly aroused from sleep, that he was being assaulted by the person arousing him, and that under that impression he was accustomed to make unconsciously violent resistance; that at such times he mistook the mere creatures of his imagination for real facts and circumstances.

If he had been threatened, it was natural, or at least not unnatural, especially while near to the person who had threatened him, that the threat should make such an impression on his mind as would contribute to develop with more than ordinary force the predisposition to imagine himself assaulted and to make resistance, and particularly so when, on being aroused, he found himself in the hands of a stranger, by whom he was being persistently and violently shaken. * * *

As the case must go back for a new trial, and it is, in some of its features, one of first impression, we will, at the risk of being prolix, consider the law applicable to it somewhat in detail.

There are several phases in which the case presents itself, all of which should be submitted to the jury.

1. If the prisoner, when he shot the deceased, was unconscious, or so nearly so that he did not comprehend his own situation and the circumstances surrounding him, or that he supposed he was being assailed, and that he was merely resisting an attempt to take his life or do him great bodily injury, he should be acquitted—in one case, because he was not legally responsible for any act done while in that condition, and in the other, because he is excusable on the ground of self-defense; for although it is clear that he was not in danger, and had no reasonable grounds to believe he was, yet if, through derangement of his perceptive faculties, it appeared to him that he was in danger, he is as free from punishable guilt as if the facts had been as he supposed them to be.

2. If he was so far unconscious when he fired the first shot, or the first and second, that he supposed he was defending himself against a dangerous assault, and regained consciousness before he fired the second or third shot, the question of guilt or innocence will depend upon whether he then believed in good faith that he was in danger of losing his life or of sustaining great bodily injury.

It was not necessary, under the circumstances, that he should have reasonable grounds to believe he was in danger. In the view we are now taking of the case we are supposing he was unconscious or partly so when he fired the first shot. If so, when he regained consciousness and found himself seized and held by a stranger who was struggling to overpower him, it would be unreasonable to expect him to wait until he could discover the purpose or apparent purpose of his antagonist, as it might have appeared to those who, in the full possession of their faculties and senses, had witnessed the whole affair.

But if he fired after he became conscious, and did not at the time in good faith believe he was in danger of loss of life or great personal injury, he is guilty of either murder or manslaughter—murder if he was actuated by malice, manslaughter if he acted without malice.

3. Although he may have been so far conscious when he fired the first shot as to understand what he was doing, yet, if he did not understand the purpose of his assailant, and believed he was attempting to inflict on him great personal injury, he should be acquitted, for, as already remarked, if, in consequence of a derangement of his perceptive faculties, or from being suddenly aroused from sleep and finding the deceased holding and shaking him, he believed he was in great danger of losing his life or suffering great personal injury, although there was in fact no danger, and, those who had witnessed the affair, had no reason to apprehend danger, he is no more guilty than if there had been actual danger. Such a case admits of no other test than the good faith of the prisoner, to be judged of by the jury.

4. If the prisoner was conscious of what he was himself doing, and that the purpose of the deceased was merely to wake him up, and the prisoner shot him simply because he did so, he is guilty of either murder or manslaughter: murder if the shooting was malicious, manslaughter if without malice.

If the prisoner is and has been afflicted in the manner claimed, and knew, as he no doubt did, his propensity to do acts of violence when aroused from sleep, he was guilty of a grave breach of social duty in going to sleep in the public room of a hotel with a deadly weapon on his person, and merits, for that reckless disregard of the safety of others, some degree of punishment, but we know of no law under which he can be punished. Our law only punishes for overt acts done by responsible moral agents. If the prisoner was unconscious when he killed the deceased, he cannot be punished for that act, and as the mere fact that he had the weapon on his person and went to sleep with it there did no injury to any one, he cannot be punished for that.

Instructions two and three, given by the court, are inconsistent with the foregoing views, and should not have been given.

For the errors indicated, the judgment is reversed, and the cause is remanded for a new trial upon principles not inconsistent with this opinion.

Case Focus

1. The defendant in this case shot and killed an individual. The court reversed the defendant's conviction for two separate reasons related to the defendant's condition. What were those reasons?
2. How are the two reasons different, and does one describe an involuntary act by the defendant?

• • • • • • • •

2. Act

As used in criminal law the term act includes not only positive acts, such as making a false document, but also omissions to act and possession. An omission to perform an act is only a criminal act when the law imposes a duty to act and the defendant had the ability to perform it.[17] In the absence of a legal duty to act, a person has no duty to act, even if, under the circumstances, he might have a moral duty to do so. As a result, absent a legal duty a person has no obligation to assist another, even if by doing so he can save the life of that other person at no risk to himself.

The law imposes a duty to act in only a limited number of situations, one of which is where a statute imposes a duty to do so. For example, the Internal Revenue Code imposes a duty on persons who receive a certain amount of income in a year to file a federal income tax return. Another situation in which the law imposes a duty to act is when there is a familial relationship to minor children or some type of business relationship between one person and another. For example, parents have a duty to aid their minor children,[18] an employer has a duty to aid an endangered employee when the danger arises in connection with the employer's business,[19] and ship captains have a duty to come to the aid of crewmen and passengers.[20]

A duty to act also arises from the marital relationship. As a result, the law imposes a duty on spouses to aid each other.[21] For example, a man who stands by while another man rapes his wife will, along with the actual rapist, be held legally responsible for the crime.[22] Absent a marital relationship it is somewhat unclear how far the law will go today to impose such a duty where there is merely a family-like relationship, such as in a domestic partnership. In the absence of a family-like relationship, a mere romantic or sexual relationship does not give rise to a duty to give assistance.

People v. Beardsley

Supreme Court of Michigan (1907) 150 Mich. 206

McALVAY, C.J. Respondent was convicted of manslaughter before the circuit court for Oakland county, and was sentenced to the State prison at Jackson for a minimum term of one year and a maximum term not to exceed five years. He was a married man living at Pontiac, and at the time the facts herein narrated occurred, he was working as a bartender and clerk at the Columbia Hotel. He lived with his wife in Pontiac, occupying two rooms on the ground floor of a house. Other rooms were rented to tenants, as was also one living room in the basement. His wife being temporarily absent from the city, respondent arranged with a woman named Blanche Burns, who at the time was working at another hotel, to go to his apartments with him. He had been acquainted with her for some time. They knew each other's habits and character. They had drunk liquor together, and had on two occasions been in Detroit and spent the night together in houses of assignation. On the evening of Saturday, March 18, 1905, he met her at the place where she worked, and they went together to his place of residence. They at once began to drink and continued to drink steadily, and remained together, day and night, from that time until the afternoon of the Monday following, except when respondent went to his work on Sunday afternoon. There was liquor at these rooms, and when it was all used they were served with bottles of whiskey and beer by a young man who worked at the Columbia Hotel, and who also attended respondent's fires at the house. He was the only person who saw them in the house during the time they were there together. Respondent gave orders for liquor by telephone. On Monday afternoon, about one o'clock, the young man went to the house to see if anything was wanted. At this time he heard respondent say they must fix up the rooms, and the woman must not be found there by his wife, who was likely to return at any time. During this visit to the house the woman sent the young man to a drug store to purchase, with money she gave him, camphor and morphine tablets. He procured both articles. There were six grains of morphine in quarter-grain tablets. She concealed the morphine from respondent's notice, and was discovered putting something into her mouth by him and the young man as they were returning from the other room after taking a drink of beer. She in fact was taking morphine. Respondent struck the box from her hand. Some of the tablets fell on the floor, and of these, respondent crushed several with his foot. She picked up and swallowed two of them, and the young man put two of them in the spittoon. Altogether it is probable she took from three to four grains of morphine. The young man went away soon after this. Respondent called him by telephone about an hour later, and after he came to the house requested him to take the woman into the room in the basement which was occupied by a Mr. Skoba. She was in a stupor and did not rouse when spoken to. Respondent was too intoxicated to be of any assistance and the young man proceeded to take her downstairs. While doing this Skoba arrived, and together they put her in his room on the bed. Respondent requested Skoba to look after her, and let her out the back way when she waked up. Between nine and ten o'clock in the evening Skoba became alarmed at her condition. He at once called the city marshal and a doctor. An examination by them disclosed that she was dead.

Many errors are assigned by respondent, who asks to have his conviction set aside. The principal assignments of error are based upon the charge of the court, and refusal to give certain requests to charge, and are upon the theory that under the undisputed evidence in the case, as claimed by the people and detailed by the people's witnesses, the respondent should have been acquitted and discharged. In the brief of the prosecutor his position is stated as follows:

"It is the theory of the prosecution that the facts and circumstances attending the death of Blanche Burns in the house of respondent were such as to lay upon him a duty to care for her, and the duty to take steps for her protection, the failure to take which, was sufficient to constitute such an omission as would render him legally responsible for her death. * * * There is no claim on the part of the people that the respondent * * * was in any way an active agent in bringing about the death of Blanche Burns, but simply that he owed her a duty which he failed to perform, and that in consequence of such failure on his part she came to her death."

Upon this theory a conviction was asked and secured.

The law recognizes that under some circumstances the omission of a duty owed by one individual to another, where such omission results in the death of the one to whom the duty is owing, will make the other chargeable with manslaughter. 21 Cyc. p.770 et seq., and cases cited. This rule of law is always based upon the proposition that the duty neglected must be a legal duty, and not a mere moral obligation. It must be a duty imposed by law or by contract, and the omission to perform the duty must be the immediate and direct cause of death. * * * Clark & Marshall on Crimes (2d ed.), p.379(e), and cases cited.

Although the literature upon the subject is quite meager and the cases few, nevertheless, the authorities are in harmony as to the relationship which must exist between the parties to create the duty, the omission of which establishes legal responsibility. One authority has briefly and correctly stated the rule, which the prosecution claims should be applied to the case at bar, as follows:

"If a person who sustains to another the legal relation of protector, as husband to wife, parent to child, master to seaman, etc., knowing such person to be in peril of life, willfully or negligently fails to make such reasonable and proper efforts to rescue him as he might have done without jeopardizing his own life or the lives of others, he is guilty of manslaughter at least, if by reason of his omission of duty the dependent person dies.

"So one who from domestic relationship, public duty, voluntary choice, or otherwise, has the custody and care of a human being, helpless either from imprisonment, infancy, sickness, age, imbecility, or other incapacity of mind or body, is bound to execute the charge with proper diligence and will be held guilty of manslaughter, if by culpable negligence he lets the helpless creature die." 21 Am. & Eng. Enc. Law (2d ed.), p.197, notes and cases cited. * * *

Seeking for a proper determination of the case at bar by the application of the legal principles involved, we must eliminate from the case all consideration of mere moral obligation, and discover whether respondent was under a legal duty towards Blanche Burns at the time of her death, knowing her to be in peril of her life, which required him to make all reasonable and proper effort to save her; the omission to perform which duty would make him responsible for her death. This is the important and determining question in this case. If we hold that such legal duty rested upon respondent it must arise by implication from the facts and circumstances already recited. The record in this case discloses that the deceased was a woman past 30 years of age. She had been twice married. She was accustomed to visiting saloons and to the use of intoxicants. She previously had made assignations with this man in Detroit at least twice. There is no evidence or claim from this record that any duress, fraud, or deceit had been practiced upon her. On the contrary it appears that she went upon this carouse with respondent voluntarily and so continued to remain with him. Her entire conduct indicates that she had ample experience in such affairs.

It is urged by the prosecutor that the respondent "stood towards this woman for the time being in the place of her natural guardian and protector, and as such owed her a clear legal duty which he completely failed to perform." The cases cited and digested establish that no such legal duty is created based upon a mere moral obligation. The fact that this woman was in his house created no such legal duty as exists in law and is due from a husband towards his wife, as seems to be intimated by the prosecutor's brief. Such an inference would be very repugnant to our moral sense. Respondent had assumed either in fact or by implication no care or control over his companion. Had this been a case where two men under like circumstances had voluntarily gone on a debauch together and one had attempted suicide, no one would claim that this doctrine of legal duty could be invoked to hold the other criminally responsible for omitting to make effort to rescue his companion. How can the fact that in this case one of the parties was a woman, change the principle of law applicable to it? Deriving and applying the law in this case from the principle of decided cases, we do not find that such legal duty as is contended for existed in fact or by implication on the part of respondent towards the deceased, the omission of which involved criminal liability. We find no more apt words to apply to this case than those used by Mr. Justice Field in *United States v. Knowles,* supra.

"In the absence of such obligations, it is undoubtedly the moral duty of every person to extend to others assistance when in danger; * * * and if such efforts should be omitted by any one when they could be made without imperiling his own life, he would, by his conduct, draw upon himself the just censure and reproach of good men; but this is the only punishment to which he would be subjected by society."

Other questions discussed in the briefs need not be considered. The conviction is set aside, and respondent is ordered discharged.

MONTGOMERY, OSTRANDER, HOOKER, AND MOORE, JJ., concurred.

Case Focus

1. Based on this case, when is an individual responsible for assisting another individual who is in danger?
2. Why was the defendant in this case not required by law to provide assistance to Ms. Burns?

• • • • • • • •

A duty to act can also arise from a contractual obligation. For example, a lifeguard has a duty imposed by his employment contract to aid persons who are drowning. A lifeguard who fails to come to the aid of a drowning swimmer may, depending on her *mens rea*, be liable for murder or some lesser form of homicide if she fails to go to the aid of a drowning swimmer and the swimmer dies. In contrast, if the lifeguard observes a man beating a woman on a sidewalk along the beach, assuming the lifeguard's job duties are only to save drowning swimmers, she has no contractual duty to go to the aid of the woman being beaten and can ignore the matter with impunity.

A duty also can arise from assuming responsibility for the care of a helpless or incompetent person or a minor child. A person has no duty to provide assistance to the helpless or incompetent or to a minor child with whom he does not have a family relationship, but once a person undertakes to provide assistance to such a person, he becomes obligated to continue to provide it.

Finally, if a person places another in danger, she has the duty to rescue that person from the danger she created.

In order to hold a person responsible for failing to perform a duty it must be shown that he knew the facts that gave rise to the duty. For example, a sleeping husband who did not know that his wife had become intoxicated and went outside their home during a blizzard where she passed out and died cannot be held responsible for failing to assist her because he did not know the facts that gave rise to the duty act.

A more difficult question is whether a person also needs to know that the law imposes a duty on him to act. The answer generally depends upon whether or not the *mens rea* element of the offense requires such knowledge. For example, if the *mens rea* element for the offense of failing to file an income tax return requires as its *mens rea* element an intentional violation of a known legal duty, to convict a defendant of the crime of failing to file an income tax return it must be shown that the defendant knew the law imposed a legal duty on him to file a return.[23] If, however, the offense is defined simply as a general intent crime, knowledge that the law imposed a legal duty to file is irrelevant and need not be proved.[24]

Finally, in order to be held criminally responsible for not performing a legal duty, it must be shown that the defendant had the ability to act. For example, if on April 15 Sonia is unconscious in the hospital, she does not commit the offense of failing to file an income tax return because she was not capable of doing so on that date.

In criminal law possession also constitutes an act. In order for possession to be a culpable act it must be established that the defendant had conscious possession of the object whose possession the law forbids.

C. Concurrence Between *Mens Rea* and *Actus Reus*

When a crime is defined in such a way that it contains a mental state element, for the defendant to be guilty of that crime not only must the defendant have committed the *actus reus* and have the *mens rea*, but there must have been a concurrence between the defendant's *mens rea* and the *actus reus*. The *mens rea* and *actus reus* are considered to concur when the *mens rea* actuates the condemned act or actuates the act that brings about the condemned result. Consequently, if the condemned act is committed before the mental state is formed, the offense is not committed. For example, Paul was in an accident and unconscious on April 15 and as a result does not file his income tax return on that date. When Paul regains consciousness on April 20 he decides not to file his income tax return. He has not committed the offense of failing to file an income tax return because on April 15 his failure to file was not actuated by a conscious decision not to file, and on April 20 when he did make the conscious decision not to file, the condemned act had already been committed.

Wilson v. State

Supreme Court of Arkansas (1910) 96 Ark. 148

McCulloch, C.J. Appellant was convicted of the crime of grand larceny in stealing a bull alleged to be the property of one Chapman. He took the bull from the range, claiming it to be his own which had strayed away, and kept it several months in his son's pasture. Chapman heard of the bull being in his pasture, and laid claim to it, but appellant refused to give it up. Appellant afterwards sold it to a butcher, who killed it, and this prosecution was begun against appellant for stealing the bull.

At the trial of the case, appellant and Chapman both introduced testimony tending to establish their respective claims of ownership. The testimony was sufficient to have warranted a finding of the jury either way on that issue, and also that the appellant took the bull from the range, and afterwards converted it to his own use under an honest belief that it was his own property. The court gave, over appellant's objection, the following instruction No. 6:

> "If he took it honestly believing it was his, and learning afterwards that it was not his property, and converted it to his own use with the felonious intent to deprive the owner of it, when he knew it was not his own property, he would be guilty."

If a person takes property in good faith, under an honest belief that he is the owner, it does not constitute larceny, for the felonious intent is lacking. The felonious intent must, in order to constitute larceny, exist at the time of the taking;

and a subsequent formation of such an intent is not sufficient. So, if the taking is under an honest belief of ownership, there being no felonious intent to steal at that time, the fact that such an intent is formed after ascertaining that another person is the true owner does not make it larceny. Rapalje on Larceny and Kindred Offenses, §23; *People v. Miller,* 4 Utah 410, 11 P. 514; *Beckham v. State,* 100 Ala. 15, 14 So. 859; *Beatty v. State,* 61 Miss. 18; *Billard v. State,* 30 Tex. 367; *Lamb v. State,* 40 Neb. 312, 58 N.W. 963.

By some courts it has been held that, if the original taking was a trespass, followed subsequently by a wrongful conversion of the thing taken, the intent to steal need not, in order to make it larceny, have existed at the time of the taking, because, in contemplation of law, as it is said, "a tortious taking does not divest the possession of the owner, but a subsequent conversion by the taker has such effect, and will, therefore, constitute larceny when accompanied by a felonious intent." Conceding this to be the correct rule, it cannot be extended so as to apply to one who takes property in good faith under an honest belief of ownership, for in this there is no element of a wilful trespass, even though there be a subsequent conversion with knowledge of the true ownership.

It follows, therefore, that the court erred in its instruction, and for this reason the judgment should be reversed, and the cause remanded for new trial. It is so ordered.

Case Focus

1. The defendant in this case took possession of a bull that belonged to another and sometime after taking possession had it slaughtered. Why was the defendant's conviction for stealing the bull reversed?

• • • • • • • •

Similarly, if the *mens rea* to perform an act for the purpose of bringing about a condemned result is abandoned before the defendant performs an act to achieve that result, the fact that the defendant later commits an act that brings about the result he no longer wishes to bring about, there is no concurrence. For example, James wanted to kill Zelda and planned on doing so for a month, but after a month James concludes his hatred of Zelda is irrational and abandons the desire to kill her. Several days later James is driving recklessly down the street and hits and kills Zelda. James has not committed intent to kill murder because at the time James acted he had abandoned the desire to kill Zelda.

A person may sometimes act with the *mens rea* specified in criminal statute, but after the physical act takes effect and before the condemned result is achieved he changes his mind about bringing about the condemned result. In such cases concurrence will still be considered to exist between the *mens rea* and *actus reus*. For example, Moe wants to kill Mel and with that intent shoots Mel. Mel does not die immediately but instead lingers for a month before succumbing to the wound. Despite the fact that a week after the shooting Moe changes his mind about desiring Mel's death and pays to fly a specialist in to treat Mel, when Mel dies from the wound the law still considers there to be a concurrence of Moe's mental state with his act.

In crimes such as murder, which condemn a result and not an act, a problem arises when, with the required *mens rea* a defendant performs an act that he mistakenly believes has accomplished the condemned result he desired and then, believing he had accomplished that result, with a different *mens rea* performs a different act that, without his knowledge, accomplishes the result he thought he had accomplished with the first act. In that situation what, if any, crime has been committed? For example, Mohammad decides to kill Andrew and to accomplish that end gives Andrew poison in a cocktail, which Andrew drinks and then passes out. Mohammad, then mistakenly believing Andrew to be dead throws him into a lake for the purpose of hiding the body and as a result Andrew dies by drowning. Has Mohammad committed intent to kill murder? The answer to that question is unclear, with different jurisdictions reaching different answers.

Some jurisdictions hold that under those facts Mohammad committed intent to kill murder notwithstanding that when he threw Andrew into the lake he no longer had an intent to kill Andrew. Courts reaching that result have simply held that the defendant's original intent carries through to the subsequent act. In other jurisdictions, courts have held that Mohammad did not commit intent to kill murder because when he committed the act that killed Andrew, he did not have the intent to kill. A third approach to the above problem, and one that has been recognized as being the better of the three, is to look at the act that Mohammad committed when he had the intent to kill Andrew and if that act would have been fatal to Andrew, to hold Mohammad responsible for the intent to kill murder of Andrew, and if it would not have been fatal to hold that Mohammad did not engage in the intent to kill murder, but may have committed some other crime such as attempted murder.

Queen v. Khandu

High Court at Bombay (1890) 15 Indian Law Rep. (Bombay Series) 194

The accused struck his father-in-law three blows on the head with a stick, with the intention of killing him. He fell down senseless on the ground. The accused thinking that he was dead, put under his head a box of firewood, and set fire to the hut in which he was lying with the intention of removing all evidence of the crime.

The accused made the following confession:

"Seven days ago my wife Sai ran away from my house for five days. She went to Wake. On the day following the day on which my wife had run away from my house I went to my father-in-law's at Pimpalgaon Mor. I asked the father-in-law whether my wife had run away to him. He assaulted me. He beat me on the ears and the back with stick. I then returned to my house at Somaj. After eating my food I again started for Pimpalgaon Mor at 3 o'clock in the night. There is a vadi of watermelons in the jungle of Pimpalgaon. He was watching this vadi. He sat near a hut. No one else was present near him at that time. Somaj is one mile Pimpalgaon. I went to Pimpalgaon with the same stick as is now before the Court. I gave him (my father-in-law) three blows with the stick with force, one on the back and two on his ears—one on each ear. My father-in-law sat at the door of the hut. Immediately after I dealt him three blows he died and fell down on the ground. I kept under his head a box of firewood which was lying in the hut, and setting the hut on fire, I returned. I got fire near the hut for rekindling. When I returned I took with me one brass *thali* (pot) and a small bundle of bread which were in the hut. Both these articles were thrown by me into the *doha* (deep part), named Sehrad, of the river near Somaj. * * *

"My wife has been in the habit of running away from my house for five years since. Whenever I go to fetch her, her father and brother beat me. As my father-in-law beat me when I bring her, I got angry and killed him. I dealt him three blows with the stick, with the intention of killing."

The accused adhered to this confession during the preliminary enquiry before the committing Magistrate, but retracted it before the Court of Sessions.

The Session Judge convicted the accused of murder under section 302 of the Indian Penal code, passed a sentence of death, subject to its confirmation by the High Court.

The accused appealed to the High Court.

On the 19th of August 1890 the High Court (Birdwood and Candy, JJ.) Made the following order for examination of the Civil Surgeon:

The accused has admitted in the confession made by him to the Second Class Magistrate, that he struck the deceased three blows with a stick. He adds: "Immediately after I dealt him three blows, he died and fell down to the ground. I kept under his head a box of firewood which was lying in the hut. And setting the hut on fire I returned." This statement contains the only statement on the record of the circumstances connected with the death of the deceased, there having been no one present at the time but the deceased and the accused. There appears to be no sufficient ground for holding that this confession was wrongly induced; and we are of the opinion that it can be safely used as evidence against the accused. It shows that he attacked the deceased with intention of killing him and that he believed that he had killed him with three blows which he struck with a stick. It shows, further, that when the accused thought that his father-in-law was dead, he placed him, with his head on a box, in the hut in which he used to live, and then set fire to the hut and left. He thought the deceased was already dead when the hut was set fire to. The object was apparently to remove evidence of the crime—not to make the deceased's death certain, if by any chance he should have been stunned only and not killed by the blows on the back and ears. If this statement of the deceased could be accepted as strictly correct in all its details, there could be no question as to his having caused the deceased's death, "by doing an act with the intention of causing death." The Acting Civil Surgeon has, however, expressed his belief, in his deposition before the committing Magistrate, that the deceased's death was due to burning and not to the wound on the back of his head. The Civil Surgeon was not examined in the Court of Sessions; but we think that he ought to have been examined fully as to the nature of the wound described by him and as to his reasons for thinking that it could not be fatal. If the blows stuck by the accused were not likely to cause the deceased's death, and did not, as a matter of fact, cause his death, but only stunned him, then in striking the blows he would not have committed murder, but would have been guilty only of an attempt murder. We, therefore, direct that the Civil Surgeon's evidence be taken with reference to the foregoing matters.

The Civil Surgeon was accordingly examined; his evidence was to the following effect:

> On June 1st the dead body of an old man was sent to me for examination. I examined it. It was the body of an old man. I can't give his age. It was much decomposed when I received it. I found on the left side beneath the arm an opening in the body communicating with the abdomen through which some of the viscera were protruding. The skin was much charred and extensively decomposed, and I cannot consequently state how this wound was caused. There was an incised wound, two inches long, extending to the bone on the occipital region. The skin itself was not injured. I did not open the head. The back of the trunk was extensively charred, as also the skin on the back of the legs and buttocks. I did not open the body. I have heard the statements of the accused. The wound on the head was from a dangerous blow, but would not, I think, have been likely to cause death. I only found the wound on the head. The opening in the side did not look like the result of a blow from a stick. I thought it resulted partly from the charred state of the skin and partly from the decomposed body. *The injury to the head would not, in my opinion, have caused death if the hut had not been set fire to. I think the burning caused death and did not merely accelerate it.* The blow on the head would probably have caused concussion of the brain. The injuries caused by the burning are such as would have caused death. Deceased would have been likely to have fallen senseless from the bow on the head, the mark of which I saw.
>
> "Cross-examined: I don't think that deceased died immediately after receiving the blow."

On receipt of this evidence the case was further argued, and the following judgments were delivered:

BIRDWOOD, J. We have now received the medical evidence called for in our order of the 19th August. It is to the effect that the death of the deceased was not caused by the blows struck by the accused, and that those blows, moreover, were not likely to cause death. They probably, however, stunned the deceased. Death was really caused by the injuries from burning, when the accused set fire to the deceased's shed.

It was not murder. The accused believed he had killed his victim and believed the victim to be dead at the time he set the fire. The accused set the fire to destroy evidence of the crime, not to ensure that the victim was dead. There was no concurrence of the prisoner's intent with his action. The accused should have been convicted of attempt murder under Section 307 and should be sentenced to transportation for life.

Parsons, J. My learned colleague holds that the accused is not guilty of murder, because when he set fire to the hut he thought that his father-in-law was dead, and his object in setting fire to the hut was apparently to remove evidence of the crime, and not to make the deceased's death certain. Assuming that this mistake of fact, if it existed, would be a valid plea in defence of the accused, I am of the opinion that the evidence on the record is insufficient to warrant any supposition of change of intention. It is true that the accused says that immediately after he dealt the three blows, his father-in-law died and fell down on the ground, but he does not say dead or even that he thought that he was dead, still less does he say that his intention in setting fire to the hut was to conceal his crime. He does not say what his intention was. This being so, I think the presumption of the law is that in all that he did he was actuated throughout by one and the same intention. There is no evidence of proof of any change therein. There is then the intention of the accused to cause death and there are two acts committed by him which together have caused death—acts so closely following upon and so intimately connected with each other that they cannot be separated and assigned the one to one intention and the other to another, but must both be ascribed to the original intention which prompted the commission of those acts and without which neither would have been done. In my opinion, the accused in committing those acts is guilty of murder. The murder was a very deliberate, cold-blooded and brutal one, and I would confirm the sentence of death. As, however, we differ as to the actual offence of which the accused ought legally to be convicted, the case must be laid before another Judge. I may add that if the offence is held to be only attempt to murder, I agree with the sentence which my colleague proposes to pass for that offence.

In consequence of this difference of opinion the case was referred to Sargent, C.J.

Sargent, C.J. It is to be regretted that the attention of the Civil Surgeon was not drawn to the statement of the prisoner that he struck the deceased three blows, two of which were on the ears, and that he was only questioned as to the probable consequences of the wound on the back of the head. Having called for and seen the stick with which the blows were struck, I think there is but very little reason for doubt, more especially as the deceased was a leper in a feeble state, that the blows proved fatal, as the accused himself says was the case. But, assuming the evidence from the Civil Surgeon establishes that the deceased would not have died from the effect of the blows, I agree with Mr. Justice Birdwood that as the accused undoubtedly believed he had killed his victim, there would be difficulty regarding what occurred from first to last as one continuous act done with the intention of killing the deceased. Under the circumstances the offence should be held to have been only the attempt to murder, and the sentence should be transportation for life under section 307.

Case Focus

1. The defendant in this case killed his father-in-law and was charged with murder. Why was the defendant not convicted of murder?
2. Why, despite the fact that the defendant killed his father-in-law, did the court decide he should have been convicted of attempted murder?

• • • • • • • •

One other situation frequently encountered is where the harm that results is different from the harm that was intended. Where the offense is one that condemns a result and the harm that occurs is different from what was intended, there is no concurrence between the *mens rea* and *actus reus*.

D. Causation

With crimes that condemn a result there is always an element of causation; that is, did the defendant's act cause the condemned result? There are two aspects to causation: (1) cause in fact and (2) proximate or legal cause.

1. Cause in Fact

The principle of cause in fact simply asks whether the condemned result would not have occurred without the defendant's act. If the result would not have occurred without the defendant's act, then there is cause in fact. This is sometimes referred to as a "but for" test. In other words, but for the defendant's act the result would not have occurred.

State v. Kenny

Court of Appeal of Louisiana, Fourth District (2013)
116 So. 3d 992

LANDRIEU, J. Appellant, James J. Kenny, Jr., was convicted of vehicular homicide in violation of Louisiana Revised Statute 14:32.1. He was sentenced to five years at hard labor, without benefit of parole, probation, or suspension of sentence, and fined $2,000.00. For the reasons that follow, we reverse Mr. Kenny's conviction. * * *

A bench trial was held on July 18 and August 5, 2011. The trial court found Mr. Kenny guilty as charged of vehicular homicide. In accordance with Louisiana Revised Statute 14:33.1(B), the court sentenced Mr. Kenny to five years at hard labor, without benefit of parole, probation, or suspension of sentence, and fined him $2,000.00. Mr. Kenny timely filed the instant appeal. * * *

By this assignment of error, Mr. Kenny asserts that the evidence was insufficient to sustain his conviction for negligent homicide. The standard of review for the sufficiency of the evidence is "whether, after viewing the evidence in a light most favorable to the prosecution, any rational trier of fact could have found the essential elements of the crime beyond a reasonable doubt." *Jackson v. Virginia*, 443 U.S. 307, 319, 99 S. Ct. 2781, 2789, 61 L. Ed. 2d 560 (1979). * * *

The crime of vehicular homicide is defined by Louisiana Revised Statute 14:32.1, which provides in pertinent part:

> A. Vehicular homicide is the killing of a human being caused proximately or caused directly by an offender engaged in the operation of, or in actual physical control of, any motor vehicle, ... whether or not the offender had the intent to cause death or great bodily harm, whenever any of the following conditions exists and such condition was a contributing factor to the killing:
> (1) The operator is under the influence of alcoholic beverages as determined by chemical tests administered under the provisions of R.S. 32:662.
> (2) The operator's blood alcohol concentration is 0.08 percent or more by weight based upon grams of alcohol per one hundred cubic centimeters of blood.
> * * *
> (4) The operator is under the influence of alcoholic beverages.

In the instant case, Mr. Kenny's argument on sufficiency of evidence is twofold. He urges that the State not only failed to prove that he was intoxicated but also failed to establish that any alleged intoxication caused the accident.

According to the record before us, the evidence introduced at trial of Mr. Kenny's alleged intoxication when he struck the victim was Officer Wahl's testimony that Mr. Kenny smelled strongly of alcohol at the time of the accident and that he was nervous and upset; Mr. Tran's testimony that Mr. Kenny's blood alcohol level was 0.16 gram percent[.] * * *

In order to convict a defendant under the vehicular homicide statute, the State must prove that an offender's unlawful blood alcohol concentration, combined with his operation of a vehicle, caused the death of a human being. *State v. Taylor*, 463 So. 2d 1274, 1274-1275 (La. 1985). "It is insufficient for the state to prove merely that the alcohol consumption 'coincides' with the accident." *State v. Archer*, 619 So. 2d 1071, 1074 (La. App. 1st Cir. 1993).

The Louisiana Supreme Court has determined that a causal relation between the defendant's conduct and the harm for which the prosecutor seeks to impose criminal sanctions is an essential element of every crime. Causation is a question of fact which has to be considered in the light of the totality of circumstances surrounding the ultimate harm and its relation to the actor's conduct. *State v. Kalathakis*, 563 So. 2d 228, 231 (La. 1990). A defendant should not be held responsible for remote and indirect consequences which a reasonable person could not have foreseen as likely to have flowed from his conduct or from those consequences which would have occurred regardless of his conduct. *Id*.

In the instant case, the State offered only circumstantial evidence of causation. Even though there was evidence that the victim was standing on the neutral ground with other people just prior to the accident, none of these witnesses were called or came forward to testify. Mr. Jones, who was across the street, testified that he did not actually witness the accident. He only witnessed the sudden appearance of a vehicle, but at all times that he observed the vehicle, it was in the lane closest to the neutral ground. He testified that he looked up when he heard what he believed to be the sound of the car hitting the victim. Testimony regarding the point of impact between Mr. Kenny's car and the victim is scant, but at best, supports a finding that the impact between the car and the victim was on the front left corner of Mr. Kenny's vehicle, indicating that the victim had just stepped off of the neutral ground when he was struck. There was no competent evidence that Mr. Kenny was driving erratically or speeding. And, the evidence established that the victim and his companions were attempting to cross the street in the middle of the block, not at a crosswalk or at an intersection.[6]

Testimony from Officer Wahl established that it was very dark on the night of the accident, that he did not know whether Mr. Kenny's car had its headlights on, and that he did not check to see if they were working. Although Officer Wahl testified that he turned Mr. Kenny over to a First District Unit for field sobriety testing, no one testified as to the results of this testing.

Mr. Kenny presented the testimony of an accident reconstruction expert, Mr. Sunseri. Based on his analysis, Mr. Sunseri opined that pedestrian error caused the accident. He conducted a reconstruction of the accident using two people, a state trooper and a female, and placed them on the neutral ground at the scene. In this reconstruction, Mr. Sunseri determined that it was "almost impossible to see a pedestrian until you were right up on them." He further testified that a vehicle travelling at 35 mph would travel about 51.3 feet per second. The lag time between when a driver recognizes a pedestrian and moves his foot from the gas pedal to the brake is approximately three seconds. Thus, at 35 mph, the vehicle would travel almost 154 feet before the driver could "begin to do anything." He opined that there was not enough information to determine Mr. Kenny's speed but there was sufficient information to conclude that he was travelling less than 50 mph. Based on his reconstruction analysis, Mr. Sunseri opined that "anybody, drinking or not, would have hit that person stepping out in front of them ... whether or not they [sic] had alcohol."

Mr. Kenny contends that the State's evidence does not establish, beyond a reasonable doubt, a causal relationship between his purported intoxication and the accident. We agree.

Where the State relies on circumstantial evidence as the basis of the conviction, such evidence must consist of proof of collateral facts and circumstances from which the existence of the main fact may be inferred according to reason and common experience. The elements must be proven such that every reasonable hypothesis of innocence is excluded. La. R.S. 15:439; [State v.] Huckabay, [809 So. 2d 1093] * * * [(La. App. 4 Cir. 2002)]. On the record before us, viewing the evidence in the light most favorable to the State, there is no question that the victim stepped into the lane of travel on a dark night, in the middle of the block, in front of oncoming traffic. The only question is whether Mr. Kenny's apparent intoxication prevented him from avoiding striking the victim. We find that the State failed to prove, beyond a reasonable doubt, that Mr. Kenny's intoxication was the cause of the victim's death. Louisiana Revised Statute 14:32.1, the statute under which Mr. Kenny was convicted, "is not aimed at persons involved in vehicular fatalities whose alcohol consumption does not cause but merely coincides with such an accident." [State v.] Taylor, 463 So. 2d [1274] * * * [(La. 1985)].

DECREE

For the foregoing reasons, we reverse Mr. Kenny's conviction and vacate his sentence and pretermit the consideration of Mr. Kenny's remaining assignments of error. We adjudicate him not guilty and order him discharged from custody on this charge. See, [State v Hearold. 603 So. 2d [731] * * * [(La. 1992)].

REVERSED

Case Focus

1. The evidence established that the defendant's blood alcohol level was twice the legal limit when, while driving, he struck and killed a pedestrian. Why did the court say the defendant's alcohol consumption did not cause the accident?

2. *Proximate Cause*

Proximate cause (sometimes called legal cause) is a limiting principle that determines when a person will no longer be held responsible for a result that is caused by his act. The principle of proximate cause represents a policy decision not to hold persons criminally liable for the results of their conduct because the connection between their act and the result has become too attenuated.[25] Questions of proximate cause arise in two broad situations: (1) when because of a pre-existing condition unknown to a defendant the defendant's act brings about a condemned result and (2) when some type of intervening act brings about a condemned result.

A defendant is considered to take his victim as he finds him and if because of the victim's pre-existing condition the defendant's act causes an unanticipated result in the victim, his act will still be deemed to be the proximate cause of that result, even if the defendant was not aware of that condition. For example, unknown to Alvin, Louis has hemophilia. Alvin strikes Louis and the blow causes a cut that would not be fatal to a person without hemophilia, but because Louis has hemophilia he bleeds to death. Alvin will be considered to have caused Louis's death. What type of crime Alvin has committed depends, however, on Alvin's *mens rea* when he committed the act that resulted in Louis's death.

In some instances acts intervene in the chain of events that a defendant's act set in motion and bring about the condemned result. Whether the defendant's act will then be considered to have caused that result depends on the intervening act. If an act of nature intervenes and causes the condemned result the defendant will not be deemed to have caused it. For example, Arthur is looking for Calvin for the purpose of fighting him because Calvin had seduced Arthur's wife. Calvin knows that and knowing that Arthur is waiting for him on a certain road decides to take a different road home. While traveling on that road Calvin is struck by lightning and killed. Arthur is not considered to have caused Calvin's death.

Where the condemned result is caused by the act of a third party, the defendant, depending on the facts, may be deemed to have caused the result. For example, if Rafik intends to kill Chester, aims a gun at him and shoots but only wounds him, but due to negligent medical treatment Chester dies of the wound, Rafik will be considered to have caused Chester's death because the possibility of medical negligence is considered foreseeable. If, however, the physician was grossly negligent in treating Chester and Chester dies as a result, Rafik will not be considered to be the cause of Chester's death, because the possibility of gross negligence is not considered foreseeable.

A third situation is where the victim himself brings about the condemned result. For example, if Anton, intending to kill Joseph, shoots Joseph and wounds him, and Joseph for religious reasons refuses treatment that would have saved his life, in most jurisdictions Anton will not be considered to have caused Joseph's death.

The common law, which developed in an era of primitive medical care, promulgated what is called the year and a day rule. Under that rule, if a victim does not die within a year and a day of the time when the criminal act was inflicted upon him but dies sometime thereafter, the person who perpetrated that act is not considered to have caused the death. Despite advances in medical science most jurisdictions continue to follow that rule, though some have increased the time period to more than a year and a day.[26]

E. Circumstances

Certain crimes are defined in such a way that they require the existence of certain circumstances. For example, the crime of perjury is defined such that for a person to be guilty of committing it not only must he have knowingly made a false statement, but at the time the false statement was made the following circumstances must have existed: (1) the person was under oath and (2) the false statement was made in a proceeding where an oath is required.

How Elements Are Used to Define Offenses

When a legislative body defines an offense, it does so by selecting different elements from the five fundamental elements of offenses discussed in this chapter. Looking at the Illinois offense of forgery you can see how the legislature used some forms of those elements to define that offense. One form of the offense of forgery is called "forgery by making." That offense is defined as follows:

A person commits forgery when, with the intent to defraud, he knowingly makes or alters any document apparently capable of defrauding another. *People v. Young*, 19 Ill. App. 3d 455 (4th Dist. 1974); 720 ILCS 5/17-3(a)(1).

Looking at the above statute you can see that the legislature selected several forms of the fundamental elements discussed in this section to define the making form of the offense of forgery:

1. *Mens rea.* The legislature defined the offense so that it contains two *mens rea* elements, an intent to defraud and knowledge.

2. *Actus reus.* The legislature defined the offense so that it actually contains two alternative forms of an *actus reus*: (1) making a document apparently capable of defrauding another and (2) altering any document so as to render it capable of defrauding another.

3. Concurrence. Because the legislature defined the offense so that it has both a *mens rea* element and an *actus reus* element, the offense necessarily contains the element of concurrence, which means that for a defendant to be guilty of the offense of forgery his *mens rea* must have actuated his act of creating a document that is apparently capable of defrauding another or actuated his act of altering the document in that manner.

The accompanying chart illustrates how the elements are used to define the offense.

Elements of Criminal Offenses

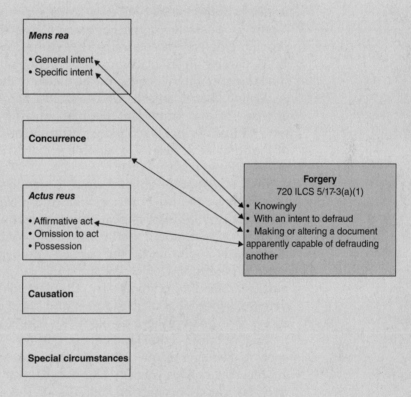

The above chart illustrates how an offense can be defined by selecting and combining components of the elements of criminal offenses.

F. Analysis of Criminal Offenses

As shown in the preceding section, all criminal offenses are defined by elements. Only when there is evidence to prove each element of the crime with which the defendant is charged can he be guilty of that offense. If there is no evidence to prove even one element of an offense that a defendant is charged with committing, he has not committed that crime, even if he performed the *actus reus* that the statute condemns.

For a paralegal finding, knowing, and having some understanding of the elements of an offense is critically important. Paralegals in prosecutors' offices frequently will be tasked with: (a) reviewing police or investigator's reports to determine if a case is ready to charge or if additional investigation is necessary; (b) victim intake, part of which includes obtaining information from a crime victim about what occurred; and (c) drafting an information or indictment to charge a street crime or other simple crime. Similarly, a paralegal in a defense attorney's office may be tasked with reviewing evidence contained in a police or investigator's report to determine if the government has the evidence necessary to prove the defendant committed the crime charged.

A paralegal cannot competently perform any of those tasks unless she knows and understands the elements of the offenses with which she is dealing. Being able to find and identify the elements of criminal offenses is also important because as you will see in Chapter 15, which discusses non-exculpatory affirmative defenses, the applicability of the affirmative defense of double jeopardy is determined by elements of the offense analysis.

In this part of the chapter we will examine how to find the elements of an offense and how to learn what those elements mean. In addition, this section will illustrate how to analyze an investigator's prosecution referral to determine if a crime has been committed. One point that is particularly important for the paralegal student to keep in mind is that, with the exception of a few attorneys who limit their practice to a particular field of criminal law, the vast majority of prosecutors and defense attorneys consult statutes and court decisions when handling a new case, and you, as a paralegal, should be prepared to do so as well.

In American criminal law, except for common law crimes, the specific elements of offenses are almost always explicitly stated in the statute that defines them.[27] The elements of common law crimes can only be found through an analysis of the court decisions that over time have defined those offenses. Criminal statutes do not, however, always contain all the elements that define a particular crime. Courts sometimes read an element into the definition of a crime that the legislature did not expressly include in the statute that defines it. An example of that can be seen in the federal offense of mail fraud.[28] By its terms, the statute that defines that offense does not require that the false representation on which a prosecution is based be a material misrepresentation. The Supreme Court has held, however, that notwithstanding the terms of the statute, a false representation must be material.[29]

As can be seen from the above, when trying to determine what elements define a particular offense, looking at the statute that defines it is a critical first step, but it should not be the only step. At a minimum, one further step must be taken to ensure that the statutory elements alone define the crime and that some additional element has not been judicially added. In the United States, every jurisdiction has some type of annotated code in which court decisions interpreting a particular statute are assembled and put into a logical order. With criminal statutes, if a court or courts have stated what the elements of an offense are, the annotated code will list those cases under a topic heading called "Elements" or some similar term. At a minimum, it is necessary to look at the annotated statutes and read the two or three sentence summaries of the cases listed under the "Elements" topic heading to determine whether or not some element not expressly stated in the statute has been judicially added.

In order to understand an offense, it is frequently necessary to go beyond the mere listing of its elements in the statute that defines it and see if the terms used in that definition have been given a particular or special meaning. Most criminal codes contain a section that lists and defines certain terms and provides that whenever those terms are used in the code they have those meanings. For example, the Wyoming Criminal Code contains a section of definitions that, *inter alia*, gives the term "person" a particular meaning whenever that term is used in it:

As used in W.S. 6-1-101 through 6-10-203 unless otherwise defined:

(vii) "Person" includes an individual, partnership, corporation, joint stock company or any other association or entity, public or private. *Wyoming Statutes*, 6-1-104 (vii).

In addition, subdivisions of codes that contain a related group of offenses frequently contain definitions of terms that are applicable only when those terms are used in offenses contained in that subdivision. Finally, in many codes a particular criminal statute may contain special definitions of terms that are applicable only when those terms are used in the context of defining that particular criminal offense. An example of such a statute is the Illinois forgery statute. The statute defines the offense of forgery as:

A person commits forgery when, with the intent to defraud, he knowingly: makes or alters any document apparently capable of defrauding another . . . 720 ILCS 5/17-3(a)(1).

The statute then defines the terms "intent to defraud" and "document":

> An intent to defraud means an intention to cause another to assume, create, transfer, alter or terminate any right, obligation, or power with reference to any person or property. As used in this Section, "document" includes, but is not limited to, any document, representation, or image produced manually, electronically, or by computer. 720 ILCS 5/17-3(b).

In many instances, a term used in a criminal statute may not be given a definition in the code. In that case the term may derive its meaning from a number of possible sources. Those sources include: court decisions; a civil law concept such as the limits the law of agency place on an agent's authority to deal with the principal's property; and sometimes even the victim, such as when the victim gives money to a person with instructions to use the money to buy him groceries and instead of using the money to buy groceries for the victim, the person uses the money to buy illegal drugs for himself. In other instances, the meaning of a term may be defined in the code, but that meaning is further refined by court decisions.

To illustrate this, look at the Illinois theft statute. The Illinois crime of theft is defined, *inter alia*, as follows:

> A person commits theft when he knowingly obtains or exerts unauthorized control over property of the owner and intends to permanently deprive the owner of the use or benefit of the property. 720 ILCS 5/16-(a)(1).[30]

The Illinois crime of unauthorized control theft thus consists of the following elements:

1. Knowingly
2. Obtains or exerts
3. Unauthorized control
4. Over property
5. Of the owner
6. With the intent to permanently deprive the owner of the use or benefit of the property

The Illinois Criminal Code defines some of the terms used in the elements of the offense of unauthorized control theft and does not define others. To the extent it defines terms used in the definition of the offense, some are definitions that are applicable whenever the term is used in the Code and others are special definitions of limited application:

1. **Knowingly**—A person knows or acts knowingly or with knowledge of the nature or attendant circumstances of his conduct described by the statute defining the offense, when he is consciously aware that his

conduct is of such nature or that such circumstances exist . . . 720 ILCS 5/4-5(a). (This is a generally applicable definition of the term that appears in the section of the Code that defines the *mens rea* terms for all Illinois crimes.)

2. **Obtain**—In relation to property means to bring about a transfer of interest or possession whether to the offender or another . . . 720 ILCS 5/15-7(a). (This is a special definition that appears in the section that relates and applies only to offenses directed against property.)

3. **Property**—Means anything of value. 720 ILCS 5/15-1. (This is a special definition that appears in the section that relates and applies only to offenses directed against property.)

4. **Owner**—Means a person other than the offender who has possession or any interest in the property involved without whose consent the offender has no authority to exert control over the property. 720 ILCS 5/15-2. (This is a special definition that appears in the section that relates and applies only to offenses directed against property.)

5. **Permanent deprivation**—Means, *inter alia*, to deprive the owner permanently of the beneficial use of the property or to sell, give, or transfer any interest in the property to a person other than the owner. 720 ILCS 5/15-3(b). (This is a special definition that appears in the section that relates and applies only to offenses directed against property.)

The Illinois Criminal Code does not define the term "unauthorized control." That is an example of a term whose meaning is determined from some other legal concept or from the victim. For example, on the one hand, if Andrew gives Raul property to hold in trust for Bertina, the question about whether what Raul did with the property is unauthorized is determined by reference to the law of trusts. On the other hand, if Andrew employs Raul and authorizes Raul to collect payments from customers at Andrew's water park, Raul's authority to deal with the cash receipts is determined by Andrew.

How a paralegal may be required by her job to deal with such a statute is illustrated by the following example:

> Pauline Paralegal works in an Illinois prosecutor's office. One of the prosecutors for whom she works has given her a prosecution referral their office received from the State Police. The referral consists of a number of documents: (1) a summary report written by the investigator; (2) memoranda memorializing interviews of the witness and the target; (3) a report from a computer forensics expert; and (4) a bank account analysis. Pauline Paralegal is asked to review the referral and determine if the crime of theft was committed, whether there is sufficient evidence to charge, and if not, what additional investigation is needed.

The summary report states in part as follows: *Global Engineering P.C. is a professional corporation owned by Robert Mitchell. Mitchell called the State Police to report that Global was the victim of a theft of proprietary engineering data.*

The report contains a memorandum that summarizes an interview of Mitchell that was conducted by the investigator. The memorandum of interview contains, in part, the following: *Mitchell advised the investigator that in addition to himself, Global employs two engineers, an officer manager named LaToya Smith, and two other employees. Mitchell also said that he believes that certain proprietary engineering data that belonged to Empire State Motor Manufacturing, Inc. of Albany, New York and which Global had in its custody had been stolen. Mitchell related that Global had been given possession of the data to use in connection with designing certain parts for a new high efficiency electric motor Empire was developing and planned to manufacture at its North Carolina factory. Mitchell further stated that just recently the manufacture of a virtually identical motor was begun by an electric motor manufacturer in Beijing, China. Mitchell asserted that he suspected the theft of data when Empire's vice president of product development showed him the Chinese motor. Mitchell also related that other than himself and the two other engineers employed by Global, no one at Global was authorized to access or download from its server or any of its computers any file named "Engineering Designs" or "Engineering Data" and that all employees, other than the two engineers, were told that when they were hired. Mitchell put the value of the data at $4,000,000.*

The referral also contains a report from a computer forensics expert who analyzed Global's computer network. That report states, in part: *On January 21, 20 ___ at 8:55 p.m. the file named "Engineering Data" was accessed and certain subfiles in it were downloaded from a computer at Global's office. That computer is identified to LaToya Smith.*

The summary report also indicates that a prosecutor obtained a grand jury subpoena for Smith's bank records for the last three years. The referral contains an analysis of those records done by the investigator which in relevant part states: *A review of Smith's bank records for the three years prior to February 28, 20 ___ showed that during that entire period Smith's account balance was low and frequently negative. The records show multiple withdrawals from ATMs. ATM records show the withdrawals were made late at night and during early morning hours at ATMs near two casinos. The analysis also states that Smith's bank records show that a few days after January 21 Smith made a deposit of $50,000 into her account and that deposit was in the form of a cashier's check that showed the remitter as "The Rosenberg Group, Inc."*

Finally, the referral contains a memorandum memorializing an interview of Smith that the investigator did one evening at Smith's home. The memorandum of interview contains, in part, the following: *Smith initially denied any knowledge of engineering data and denied accessing and downloading it. When confronted with a copy of the cashier's check from the Rosenberg Group, Inc., Smith admitted to receiving the check from someone named Moy. She said she was approached by Moy and offered $50,000 merely to copy some engineering* *data. Smith admitted to downloading certain subfiles from what she found in Global's server in the file called "Engineering Data." Smith admitted to giving those files to Moy. When confronted with a list of the subfiles, Smith admitted to downloading some of them, but claimed she could not remember others. Smith said that while she downloaded files, she did not remove any actual data from Global's server. Smith also admitted that when she was hired, she was expressly told that she was never to access or download the contents of any electronic files called "Engineering Designs" or "Engineering Data" from Global's server or any computer at Global. When asked why she did it, Smith said, "I needed the money."*

To perform the tasks assigned to her, Pauline Paralegal would first go to the Illinois Theft statute to determine what the elements of the offense of theft are and then look and see if the Illinois courts have judicially added any elements. She would then need to look at the definitions section of the Illinois Criminal Code and at the property-crimes part of the Code to see if there were any special definitions of terms used to define the offense of theft.

At this point Pauline Paralegal may want to create a checklist that lists the elements of the offense of theft and then review the referral and note the facts it contains in its various component parts that prove each element. Pauline Paralegal might then use that checklist to prepare a brief memo to the prosecutor. To see how the statute and the information contained in the investigator's prosecution referral might be used in a memo to the prosecutor, read the following excerpt from Pauline Paralegal's memo:

The investigator's report contains information that, if true, indicates that the crime of unauthorized control theft was committed by LaToya Smith. No additional investigation is necessary. The crime of Theft is committed when a person knowingly exerts unauthorized control over property of the owner and intends to permanently deprive the owner of the use or benefit of the property. 720 ILCS 5/16-1.

The evidence to support the charge is as follows: (1) Smith exerted unauthorized control over engineering data. Mitchell said only he and two other Global Engineers were authorized to access and download the data from the file called "Engineering Data." During an interview Smith admitted both to accessing that file and downloading subfiles contained in it. She also identified the names of some of the subfiles she downloaded; (2) Smith knowingly exerted unauthorized control because during the interview of Mitchell he said that at the time employees were hired they were told they were not to access the file named "Engineering Data." Further evidence of knowledge by Smith came out during her interview when she admitted to the investigator that she knew she was not supposed to access that file; (3) The engineering data was property because property is anything of value and Mitchell said the data was worth at least $4,000,000; (4) Global and Empire were the owners of the data. Empire was the actual owner of the data and while Global merely had custody of it,

Global was also the owner within the meaning of the theft statute because Global had possession of it and Smith could not access it or download it without Global's consent; (5) Smith obtained the property because she brought about its transfer to Moy; and (6) Smith intended to permanently deprive Global and Empire of the beneficial use of the data because by transferring it to Moy she permanently deprived Global and Empire of the exclusive use and benefit of it.

Drafting Charging Instruments

Paralegals working in prosecutors' offices are sometimes asked to prepare charging instruments such as indictments or informations. Most state prosecutors' offices have fill-in-the-blank forms, and the paralegal obtains the necessary information from the police report or an investigator's prosecution referral and inserts it into the appropriate place of the charging instrument. Most violent crimes and many simple property crimes can easily be charged using such basic charging instruments. Crimes such as conspiracy, securities fraud, and perjury and crimes involving fraud schemes and organized criminal enterprises usually require much more detail in the charging instrument and frequently will consist of multiple counts with multiple paragraphs of allegations in each count. Such indictments can consist of many pages and in very complex criminal cases may run in excess of 100 pages. Paralegals seldom have much role in drafting these types of complex charges, but may be tasked with proofreading them and ensuring that the factual allegations are accurate.

Whether the crimes alleged are simple or complex, all charging instruments must contain certain things: (1) the name of the defendant, if known, and if not known then by a description through which the defendant can be identified with reasonable certainty (Today, if the name of the defendant is unknown and the statute of limitations is close to barring prosecution, if law enforcement has a DNA sample, some indictments use the DNA profile to describe the defendant.); (2) the name of the offense; (3) citation to the statute alleged to have been violated; (4) the elements of the offense; and (5) an allegation as to the county (or, in the case of a federal prosecution, the federal district) in which the offense was committed.

Of those requirements one of the most important is to ensure that the charging instrument states all the elements of the offense it charges. In many jurisdictions a charge that does not contain all of the elements of the offense is subject to dismissal at any time, even after trial or while on appeal. In many jurisdictions, if an indictment contains such an error, that deficiency cannot be cured through an amendment by the prosecutor. Instead, a new indictment that contains all of the elements of the offense must be sought from the grand jury.

The accuracy of the allegation of the date when the offense occurred is not usually important unless there is a question about whether the statute of limitations may bar prosecution. In drafting a charge the paralegal should still do her best to ensure it accurately states the date of the offense. When the exact date is unknown or when an offense is committed on multiple occasions over a period of time, it is usually alleged that the offense occurred between on or about one date and on or about a second date. For example, if as part of a single intention and design, X commits theft by deception from Y on January 6, 2001, February 1, 2001, and February 27, 2001, the charging instrument might allege: "That between January 5, 2001, and February 28, 2001, the defendant committed the offense of Theft by Deception."

If the charging instrument is an indictment, in many jurisdictions the indictment must be signed by the foreperson of the grand jury and in some jurisdictions it must be signed by the prosecutor. In most jurisdictions the indictment or some other document used in the grand jury must contain the name and address of the witness or witnesses who testified before the grand jury when the indictment was obtained. If the charging instrument is an information, the charge is brought in the name of the prosecutor and is signed by the prosecutor. The practice in many states is to indicate on the charging instrument whether the offense is a misdemeanor or felony, together with the grade of the misdemeanor or felony it charges.

A sample indictment and a sample information using the facts from the LaToya Smith/Global Engineering example discussed above appears on the next two pages. The fill-in parts are underlined. Note that in the sample charging instruments it is alleged that the value of the property exceeds a certain dollar amount. Under Illinois law, the value of the property is not an element of the offense, but must be alleged because value determines the seriousness of the offense of theft and in a jury trial must be found by the jury. Many jurisdictions follow that pattern.

IN THE CIRCUIT COURT OF
THE SECOND JUDICIAL CIRCUIT
FRANKLIN COUNTY, ILLINOIS

PEOPLE OF THE STATE OF ILLINOIS,   )
)
             Plaintiff   )
)
                v.   )
LATOYA SMITH,   )
)
            Defendant   )

BILL OF INDICTMENT
COUNT I

The Grand Jurors chosen, selected, and sworn, in and for the County of Franklin, in the State of Illinois, in the name and by the authority of the People of the State of Illinois, upon their oaths present that on or about <u>January 21, 20</u> at and within Franklin County,

LATOYA SMITH

committed the offense of **THEFT**

in that <u>she</u> knowingly <u>exerted unauthorized control</u> over property of <u>Global Engineering, P.C. a professional corporation organized under the laws of the State of Illinois and Empire State Motor Manufacturing, Inc., a corporation organized under the laws of the State of New York,</u> the owners, to wit: <u>on or about the said date she accessed and downloaded certain engineering data belonging to the owners from a computer which she knew she did not have authority to access or download;</u> that <u>she</u> intended to permanently deprive the owners of the use and benefit of the said property; and that the value of the property is in excess of <u>$100,000,</u> in violation of Illinois Compiled Statutes, Chapter 720, Section <u>5/16-1(a)(1),</u> and contrary to the peace and dignity of the same People of the State of Illinois

Class 1 Felony

A TRUE BILL

_____
Foreperson of the Grand Jury

Witness:
John Doe
Special Agent
Illinois State Police
XXXX State Street 4th Floor
City, Illinois

IN THE CIRCUIT COURT OF THE SECOND JUDICIAL CIRCUIT
FRANKLIN COUNTY, ILLINOIS

PEOPLE OF THE STATE OF ILLINOIS,	)
	)
Plaintiff	)
	)
v.	)
LATOYA SMITH,	)
	)
Defendant	)

INFORMATION

COUNT I

The State's Attorney of Franklin County of Illinois charges that on or about
<u>January 21, 20</u> at and within Franklin County,

LATOYA SMITH

committed the offense of **THEFT**

in that <u>she</u> knowingly <u>exerted unauthorized control</u> over property of <u>Global
Engineering, P.C. a professional corporation organized under the laws of the State
of Illinois and Empire State Motor Manufacturing, Inc., a corporation organized
under the laws of the State of New York</u>, the owners, to wit: <u>on or about the said
date she accessed and downloaded certain engineering data belonging to the owners
from a computer which she knew she did not have authority to access or download;</u>
that <u>she</u> intended to permanently deprive the owners of the use and benefit of the said
property; and that the value of the property is in excess of <u>$100,000,</u> in violation of
Illinois Compiled Statutes, Chapter 720, Section <u>5/16-1(a)(1),</u> and contrary to the
peace and dignity of the same People of the State of Illinois

Class 1 Felony

> Robert Roe
> Assistant State's Attorney
> XXXX Lincoln Street
> Benton, Illinois 62746
> Ph: XXX-XXX-XXXX

STATE OF ILLINOIS	)
	) ss
COUNTY OF FRANKLIN	)

Robert Roe, Assistant State's Attorney, after first being duly sworn states upon
oath that he has read the foregoing Information and to the best of his knowledge and
belief the allegations contained therein are true.

> Robert Roe, Assistant State's Attorney

Subscribed and sworn to before me
this _____ day of _____, 20 _____

_____
Judge or Notary Public

REVIEW QUESTIONS

1. What were the forms of *mens rea* recognized by the common law and how did those forms of *mens rea* differ?
2. What are the forms of *mens rea* recognized in the Model Penal Code and how do they differ from one other?
3. In a criminal statute, what does the term "willfulness" or "willful" mean when it is used as a *mens rea* element? Does the term have more than one meaning? If so, what are those meanings?
4. What is the doctrine of transferred intent?
5. What is a strict liability offense?
6. When the statute defining a criminal offense does not contain a *mens rea* element, does that mean that the offense is a strict liability offense?
7. In criminal law, to what does the concept of motive refer and why is evidence of motive important?
8. What is the *actus reus* element of a criminal offense and what are components of that element?
9. With respect to the criminal law concept of *actus reus*, is an act voluntary when it is performed under duress? Why or why not?
10. In what situations, if any, can a person's failure to act be the *actus reus* of an offense?
11. In criminal law, what does it mean when it is said that there must be concurrence between a defendant's mental state and his act for a crime to have been committed? Does a person commit a crime when he does the act condemned by a criminal statute and after doing that act forms the *mens rea* that is an element of that offense?
12. What is the difference between cause in fact and proximate cause?
13. Is a defendant's act considered to be the proximate cause of a victim's death when, unknown to the defendant at the time he engaged in the act that brought about the victim's death, the victim suffered from a condition that made the act fatal to him, but which if he had not suffered from that condition would not have been fatal to him?
14. What are intervening acts and what role, if any, do they play with respect to proximate cause?
15. What is the "but for" test?

ADDITIONAL READING

Paul H. Robinson & Markus D. Dubber, *The American Model Penal Code: A Brief Overview*, 10 New Crim. L. Rev. 319 (2007).

ENDNOTES

1. *State v. Schouten*, 707 N.W.2d 820 (S.D. 2005).
2. *United States v. Bailey*, 444 U.S. 394 (1980).
3. *See, e.g., State v. Schouten*, n.1.
4. *United States v. Blair*, 54 F.3d 639 (10th Cir. 1995).
5. *Schouten*, n.1.
6. *Id.*
7. *Blair*, n.4.
8. *Id.*
9. *Schouten*, n.1.
10. *Bailey*, n.2.
11. *Id.*
12. *See, e.g.*, Model Penal Code §2.02(8).
13. *People v. Nowack*, 462 Mich. 392 (2000).
14. *See, e.g.*, ILCS 720 5/4-9.
15. *See, e.g.*, ILCS 720 5/4-3(b).
16. *See, e.g.*, Mo. Rev. Stat. §562.011.
17. *Kuntz v. Montana*, 298 Mont. 146 (2000).
18. *Palmer v. State*, 223 Md. 341 (1960).
19. *Queen v. Brown*, 1 Terr. L. Rep. 475 (Can. 1893).
20. *United States v. Knowles*, 26 Fed. Cas. 800 (N.D. Cal. 1864).
21. *Territory v. Manton*, 8 Mont. 95 (1888).
22. *People v. Chapman*, 62 Mich. 280 (1886).
23. *Cheek v. United States*, 498 U.S. 192 (1991).
24. *People v. Wendt*, 183 Ill. App. 3d 389 (2d Dist. 1989).
25. *People v. Cervantes*, 26 Cal. 4th 860 (2001).
26. *See, e.g.,* South Carolina Criminal Code §16-3-5
27. To find the elements of a common law offense, it is necessary to look at the decisional law of the jurisdiction to see how that jurisdiction's courts have defined it.
28. 18 U.S.C. §1341.
29. *United States v. Neder*, 527 U.S. 1 (1999).
30. The seriousness of the offense of theft is determined by the value of the property taken. The value of the property is not an element of the offense. Value is, however, a matter that is submitted to the trier of fact.

Chapter 12
Affirmative Defenses — Excuse

Chapter Objectives

After reading this chapter, you should be able to

- Understand what an affirmative defense is
- Name the different categories of affirmative defenses
- Understand what an excuse defense is
- Explain the basic premises of the insanity defense together with the different standards of that defense
- Understand the defenses of intoxication and infancy
- Explain the elements of the defenses of entrapment and duress

All the several pleas and excuses, which protect the committer of a forbidden act from the punishment which is otherwise annexed thereto, can be reduced to this single consideration, the want or defect of will. An involuntary act, as it has no claim to merit, so neither can it induce guilt: the concurrence of the will, when it has its choice either to do or to avoid the [act] in question, being the only thing that renders human actions either praiseworthy or culpable. —Blackstone, *Commentaries on the Laws of England*, Book IV

In criminal law there are two types of defenses: simple defenses and affirmative defenses.[1] A simple defense is one in which the defendant denies that he committed the crime with which he has been charged or denies one or more of its elements. A simple defense does no more than put the prosecution to the test to prove its case beyond a reasonable doubt and does not require the defendant to put on any evidence. Affirmative defenses require defendants to do more.

A. Introduction to Affirmative Defenses

Burden of production is the obligation to come forward with evidence on a litigant's necessary propositions of fact. *El v. Southeastern Pennsylvania Transp. Authority,* 479 F.3d 232 (3d Cir. 2007).

Burden of persuasion is the obligation to convince the fact finder at trial that a litigant's necessary propositions of fact are true. *El v. Southeastern Pennsylvania Transp. Authority,* 479 F.3d 232 (3d Cir. 2007).

In contrast to simple defenses, with an affirmative defense the defendant must assert it and has the **burden of production,** which requires him to produce some quantum of evidence that shows the defense is applicable.[2] States differ on what that quantum of evidence needs to be. If a defendant fails to assert an affirmative defense or having asserted it fails to produce the required quantum of evidence in support of it, the defense is lost and will not be considered by the judge or a jury at trial.

In many states, for certain affirmative defenses, the defendant also has the **burden of persuasion**. It is difficult to make a general statement about who has the burden of persuasion for a particular affirmative defense because the state laws differ widely. With respect to federal prosecutions, however, the U.S. Supreme Court has made it clear that with affirmative defenses that do not negate an element of the offense the burden of persuasion is on the defendant.[3]

Generally, with affirmative defenses, whether the charges against the defendant are true is irrelevant[4] because affirmative defenses go beyond the elements of the offense charged to prove facts that somehow remove the defendant from criminal liability for his acts.[5] In many states, the defendant is required to advise the prosecutor that he intends to assert an affirmative defense and to identify the affirmative defense he intends to assert.

Affirmative defenses can be classified in a number of different ways. One generally accepted classification scheme and the one used in this book divides affirmative defenses into five categories: (A) excuse defenses, (B) justification defenses, (C) failure of proof defenses, (D) offense modification defenses, and (E) non-exculpatory public policy defenses.[6] In this chapter and the next three chapters, we will examine each of those categories of affirmative defenses and examine the more important defenses contained in them.

The student should be aware that the affirmative defenses discussed in this and the following chapters represent only the most important of the affirmative defenses in each category and that those categories each contain other defenses that are not examined here. It is also important to be aware that while affirmative defenses are generally called by the same name, they are frequently defined differently in different states. For that reason, with respect to the defenses discussed here, the textbook examines only the broad contours of those defenses and some of the major variations in those contours. The paralegal student is urged to look at the criminal code for his jurisdiction so that he can familiarize himself with the affirmative defenses his jurisdiction statutorily recognizes and how his jurisdiction defines them.

Keeping Confidences, Protecting Privileges, and Protecting Lives

A paralegal who is employed in a criminal defense attorney's office will necessarily come into contact with client secrets and confidences. This is particularly true if the defense attorney has a significant white collar defense practice that involves cases with multiple defendants where there are joint defense agreements with attorneys for other defendants and there is information sharing between them. The Rules of Professional Responsibility impose a duty on attorneys not to reveal a confidence or secret of a client.[7] The duty to maintain the confidence or secret continues after the termination of the attorney-client relationship and even after the death of the client himself. Though there are variations of the rule in the different states, in relevant part one common formulation is:

Rule 1.6. Confidentiality of Information

(a) Except when required under Rule 1.6(b) or permitted under Rule 1.6(c), a lawyer shall not, during or after termination of the professional relationship with the client, use or reveal a confidence or secret of the client known to the lawyer unless the client consents to the disclosure.

(b) A lawyer shall reveal information about a client to the extent it appears necessary to prevent the client from committing an act that would result in death or serious bodily harm.

(c) A lawyer may use or reveal:

(1) confidences or secrets when permitted under these Rules or required by law or court order;

(2) the intention of a client to commit a crime in circumstances other than those enumerated in Rule 1.6(b) . . . *Illinois Supreme Court Rules of Professional Conduct*, Rule 1.6.

By its terms the rule is not absolute and its breadth is significantly limited by the required by law and court order exceptions. In the setting of criminal law the most important limitation required by law is the power of a grand jury to gather evidence. The grand jury has the power to require the production of evidence and that power overrides the confidentiality obligations imposed by the ethical rule.[8] As a result, notwithstanding that the Rule states, "A lawyer *may* use or reveal . . . ," an attorney who is served with a grand jury subpoena for client information not only cannot assert the confidentiality rule as a ground for refusing to produce the evidence sought by the grand jury but he *must* produce that evidence.[9]

The attorney-client privilege imposes a limit on the power of the grand jury to obtain evidence about a client from an attorney. If a court determines that the attorney-client privilege is applicable, the attorney is excused from producing the evidence. The attorney-client privilege, however, is not absolute. Everything a client says to an attorney and everything an attorney says to a client is not protected by the privilege. The attorney-client privilege applies only to communications made for the purpose of obtaining or giving legal advice and not to communications made about other matters.[10] Even if the communication may be privileged, the privilege may be destroyed if the client's secrets are revealed by the attorney or client, even if done so inadvertently.[11]

It is critical that the paralegal working in a defense attorney's office neither intentionally nor negligently disclose confidential client information. Such a disclosure could strip the protection of the attorney-client privilege from such information thereby making what would not otherwise be obtainable by the government obtainable, with perhaps disastrous consequences for the client. Unauthorized disclosure of client secrets either by the defense attorney or his employee could subject the defense attorney to professional discipline and a lawsuit and could subject the paralegal to a lawsuit as well.

A prosecutor does not have the same concern with Rule 1.6 because unlike defense attorneys, prosecutors do not have clients. Nonetheless, prosecutor's offices have secrets that must be guarded and that are also protected by privileges that can be lost through disclosure. For example, prosecutors' offices have custody of grand jury material, which by law is to be kept secret. Prosecutors' offices also: (1) are frequently involved in planning or guiding covert law enforcement activity, (2) may know the identity of informants, and (3) know when law enforcement activities such as large-scale arrests or execution of search warrants will take place. Such information is protected from disclosure by the law enforcement investigatory privilege,[12] the informant's privilege,[13] and other related privileges.[14] A paralegal who works in a prosecutor's office will come into contact with such information, and it is important for her to ensure that information is not disclosed inadvertently or otherwise. Disclosure not only will strip the information of any privilege, but can jeopardize the lives of law enforcement agents and informants and can derail covert investigations in which hundreds or thousands of investigative hours have been invested.

B. Excuse Defenses

A fundamental premise of Anglo-American law is that people are responsible for their actions. In criminal law a person is held responsible for the criminal conduct in which he engages. Some defenses rest on the conclusion that because of some condition that exists in the defendant it is inappropriate to hold him criminally responsible for his conduct.[15] Defenses based on the existence of such conditions are called excuse defenses. It is important to note that excuse defenses do not turn legally proscribed conduct into legally permissible conduct;[16] instead, they simply excuse the defendant from punishment for violating a penal statute. This chapter examines seven different excuse defenses: (1) insanity; (2) intoxication; (3) infancy; (4) entrapment; (5) duress; (6) public authority; and (7) entrapment by estoppel.

1. Insanity

Recognition of insanity by the criminal law as a basis for relieving a defendant of responsibility for his criminal acts predates the establishment of psychiatry as a science by hundreds of years. The concept of insanity was first recognized by the criminal law in the thirteenth century when English courts began to allow a special verdict that the defendant committed an offense when mad.[17] That special verdict did not result in the defendant's acquittal but did give him a right to a pardon from the king.[18] By the sixteenth century, the law had evolved and recognized insanity as a defense.[19] Today, despite its long history in the criminal law and the development of modern psychiatry, the insanity defense is rarely used in the United States[20] and in some states it has been abolished.[21]

EYE ON ETHICS

Horse-shedding, Lecturing, and Ethics

It is the rare witness who testifies without having been prepared to testify by the lawyer calling him. Normally a substantial amount of time passes (usually at least a year if not several years) between the event about which a witness will testify and the date of his testimony and because of that if the witness testifies "cold" (that is, without preparation), he often will not have thought about the event about which he will testify since it occurred, and as a result he may have difficulty both remembering the details of the events and describing them coherently. Putting an unprepared witness on the witness stand can also lead to exchanges such as the following:

Attorney: "Please don't shake your head. All your answers must be oral. Did you travel to London?"
Witness: "Oral."[22]

Sometimes referred to as horse-shedding (a term coined by James Fenimore Cooper in the era when horse sheds were close to every rural courthouse and attorneys who rode circuit used them as a place to talk to witnesses before trial), witness preparation is not only ethical when properly done, but is part of what every diligent

lawyer must do to prepare for trial. Paralegals frequently help the prosecutor or defense attorney for whom they work by preparing some or all witnesses for trial. For that reason it is critically important for paralegals to understand the ethics of witness preparation.

When preparing a witness for trial a paralegal can meet with her to discuss her role in the trial as well as what constitutes effective courtroom demeanor. During the meeting with the witness, the paralegal can also discuss what she remembers, reveal the expected testimony of other witnesses, and review with her the questions that will be asked. The witness can also be shown any physical evidence such as documents that will be introduced and about which she will be questioned and the witness can be told about the expected lines of cross-examination. As part of the process of witness preparation the paralegal can also rehearse the witness's actual testimony and suggest a choice of words.[23] If the witness had previously made a statement and a memorandum of that statement was made, for the purpose of refreshing the witness's recollection the paralegal can show the memorandum to her.

There are a number of witness preparation practices that are controversial and in some cases that violate the law or the rules of professional responsibility, or both. Some of those practices are discussed below.

1. The Lecture

One of the oldest witness preparation practices is called the lecture. While frequently used in connection with the initial interview of a defendant-client, it is also sometimes used when interviewing witnesses. As practiced, the lawyer, before hearing the client or witness's version of what occurred, explains the applicable law or the law relating to a possible defense and then asks the client or witness to tell him her version of the events. The lecture is frequently criticized by legal academics as violating Model Rule of Professional Conduct 3.4(b), which prohibits a lawyer from falsifying evidence or counseling or assisting a witness to testify falsely[24] or at least as bordering on such a violation[25] because, it is argued, it encourages a defendant or witness to falsely tailor her testimony to the applicable law. Despite those criticisms, the practice of explaining the law before hearing the client or witness's version of the events has been approved by courts[26] and ethics committees of bar associations.[27]

2. Simultaneous Interviews

Simultaneous interviews of potential witnesses do not violate any rule of professional responsibility, but as a practical matter they should be avoided. A simultaneous interview of witnesses may be an efficient use of time, but if opposing counsel brings it out, such an interview can give the appearance of collusion, can weaken the strength of the witness's testimony in the eyes of the trier of fact, and sometimes so weaken the witness's testimony as to render it worthless. Simultaneous witness interviews also can make it difficult to learn exactly what happened because the witnesses may try to align their testimony instead of openly relating what they believe they saw or heard.

3. Exclusion Orders and Revealing Testimony

At the start of any criminal trial the prosecutor and the defense attorney almost always make a joint motion to exclude witnesses from the courtroom. Courts routinely grant these motions. It is a violation of the exclusion order to provide a witness who has not yet testified with a transcript of another witness's testimony or to relate a summary of the witness's testimony to a witness who has not yet testified.

4. Obstructing Access to a Witness

The law recognizes that in a criminal case both the prosecution and the defense have an equal right to interview witnesses,[28] and Model Rule of Professional Conduct 3.4(a) prohibits an attorney from obstructing another party's access to a witness. A witness has a right to refuse to talk to an attorney who is seeking to interview her and she may choose not to talk to the prosecutor or the defense attorney or both. It is improper for a lawyer who does not represent the witness and for a paralegal who works for that lawyer to tell the witness not to speak to the attorney for the other side, and it is improper for either an attorney or paralegal to insist that he or the attorney be present when the witness meets with the opposing side.[29]

As important as it is to prepare witnesses for trial, as the following colloquy illustrates, the attorney or paralegal preparing a witness must not lose sight of the fact that she, too, must be both prepared for and attuned to what is happening:

Lawyer: "So, your baby was conceived on July 12?"

Witness: "Yes."

Lawyer: "And what were you doing at that time?"[30]

Under the law all persons are presumed to be sane.[31] As a result, the prosecution does not have the burden of proving a defendant was sane at the time she committed a crime. If the defendant believes she was insane at the time she committed the crime with which she is charged, she must assert the defense of insanity and she has the burden of presenting some evidence of her insanity.[32] Once the defendant puts on evidence of her insanity, the court determines whether that evidence is sufficient to place her sanity at issue.

There is a wide difference in practice in different states as to what occurs once the court determines the defendant has introduced sufficient evidence to put her sanity in question. In some states once the court determines that a sufficient quantum of evidence of the defendant's possible insanity has been introduced, the burden shifts to the prosecution to prove beyond a reasonable doubt that the defendant was sane at the time he committed the crime. In many other states, however, the practice is radically different. In those states the law places the burden on the defendant to prove by a preponderance of evidence that he was insane when he committed the crime.[33] At one time, at least one state required the defendant to establish her insanity beyond a reasonable doubt.[34]

It is important to keep in mind that where the insanity defense has been abolished the question of the defendant's mental health at the time she committed the crime is still important. In those states, the fact that a defendant has a mental illness may still result in the defendant's acquittal if the mental illness is such that it prevents him from being able to form the mental state that is an element of the offense with which he is charged.

The question of the defendant's sanity is determined by the trier of fact, which is the judge in a bench trial and the jury in a jury trial. Lay witnesses who have observed the defendant as well as physicians or mental health professionals such as psychiatrists and psychologists who have examined him are competent to testify about the defendant's sanity. The law gives no more weight to the testimony of physicians or mental health professionals than to lay witnesses. As a result it is possible for a trier of fact to find a defendant to have been sane or insane based solely on the testimony of a lay witness, even when there is contrary testimony from mental health professionals.

State v. Corley

Supreme Court of Arizona (1972) 108 Ariz. 240

LOCKWOOD, J. Dr. Sterling C. Corley was formally charged with first degree murder. He pled guilty to second degree murder and raised the issue of insanity. [The] issue was tried to a jury. The jury was unable to reach a verdict, and a mistrial was declared. A second trial was had * * *. The defendant * * * pled not guilty * * * by reason of insanity to an amended information charging second degree murder. The jury returned a verdict of guilty of murder in the second degree. He was sentenced to 20 to 40 years imprisonment.

On June 24, 1969, defendant purchased a full box of .38 caliber special ammunition from Melvin Kiddie, an employee of the Western Auto Store in Bullhead City. On that same day he went to the Holiday Shores Inn to find James Stahlman, Vice-President and General Manager of Holiday Shores Development Company. Not finding him there, defendant proceeded to Stahlman's office. Tom Ryan, real estate salesman, testified that defendant entered Stahlman's office and said "God damn it, Jim you took a hundred feet of my property." He insisted that Stahlman accompany him to the property. Stahlman acquiesced and told Ryan that he would return in fifteen minutes. Ryan "never saw [Stahlman] after that time," and on June 25, 1969 Stahlman's body was found on the shore of the Colorado River. * * *

In this appeal defendant raises six questions. First, he argues that there was insufficient evidence presented at trial to prove that he was sane beyond a reasonable doubt.

Although a defendant is presumed sane, if he raises the issue of insanity, it becomes the state's burden to prove sanity beyond a reasonable doubt. State v. Ganster, 102 Ariz. 490, 433 P.2d 620 (1967). We are of the opinion, however, that the record reveals that the state has met its burden of proof.

The witnesses, Officer Pinner, Officer Moore, Rose Moore, Lillie Callahan, Melvin Kiddie and Officer Vinson, all of whom had seen and observed defendant shortly before or after the homicide, testified that "he was able to organize his thinking", that "he appeared normal", and that he answered questions "clearly and very coherently." * * * Clyde McCune, [the Justice of the Peace before whom the defendant was arraigned] stated that in his opinion when he arraigned defendant, * * * [he] was sane. Lillie Callahan, who observed defendant a few hours before the homicide, said she thought he was sane at that time. Officer Moore, who was present when defendant was interrogated in Winterhaven, likewise testified the defendant appeared to be sane at that time.

The evidence presented at trial consisted of the testimony of both expert and lay witnesses. The rule is that a witness may testify to a defendant's sanity if his opinion is based upon personal observation or knowledge of the past conduct and history of the defendant. State v. Coey, 82 Ariz. 133, 309 P.2d 260 (1957).

Notwithstanding the fact that there was evidence of defendant's insanity consisting primarily of expert testimony, it is well settled that:

> "[t]he issue of criminal responsibility in Arizona [is] a fact question for the jury. In addition, the credibility of expert witnesses and the weight to be given expert testimony has been a jury question in this state * * * [and] a numerical advantage in a head count of witnesses and the mere fact that testimony is elicited from competent psychiatrists do not suffice to necessitate the direction of a verdict for one party or the other." State v. Ganster, supra, 102 Ariz. at 493.

In view of all the evidence presented at trial we hold that the jury's finding of guilty was adequately supported by the evidence. *See* Buatte v. United States, 350 F.2d 389 (9th Cir. 1965) * * *.

The second question raised is whether there was an inference arising out of the failure of the state to call expert medical witnesses in rebuttal to the defendant's evidence as to insanity that the defendant's evidence was true because uncontradicted; and, if there was, was defendant entitled to an instruction so stating.

Defendant quotes language from State v. Schantz, 98 Ariz. 200 (1965) * * *, as support for his view that there is an inference and that he is entitled to a jury instruction to that effect. The pertinent language of that opinion is:

"There is an inference arising out of the failure of the State to call expert medical witnesses in rebuttal that the defendant's evidence as to insanity is true because uncontradicted * * *." State v. Schantz, supra, 98 Ariz. at 213, 214.

Defendant has merely lifted out of context a statement from that opinion and ascribed a meaning to it that was never intended by the Court. The Court by the use of this language did not mean that there was an inference as a *matter of law*.

Certainly an inference *may* arise in the minds of the jurors that defendant's expert evidence is true when uncontradicted, and the jury may properly find it true, but to instruct the jury that they are required to find it true as a matter of law would be an invasion of the jury's province. See Reid v. Topper, 32 Ariz. 381, 259 P. 397 (1927). * * *

Judgment affirmed.

Case Focus

- What does the law presume with respect to a defendant's sanity? What happens if the defendant does not raise an insanity defense? Will the defendant's sanity be an issue?
- Is expert testimony required to establish a defendant's insanity or sanity?
- In a jury trial who determines the defendant's sanity?
- Can lay testimony about a defendant's sanity be used to rebut expert testimony?

• • • • • • • •

It is important to keep in mind that the mere fact that a defendant suffers from some mental illness at the time she commits a crime is not, by itself, a defense. For a defendant to be considered insane under the criminal law, the mental illness must result in a defect of reason that satisfies a specific legal standard defining what constitutes insanity under the criminal law.

The test for what constitutes insanity for purposes of the insanity defense has changed over time, but for many years the test used in virtually all American jurisdictions was the M'Naghten test. The test was named after the English case in which it was first articulated.[35] Under the M'Naghten test a person is considered insane and is excused from being punished for a crime when at the time he committed the crime he suffered from a defect of reason that resulted in him either not being able to know the nature and quality of the act he performed or, if he did know the nature and quality of the act, he did not know that the act was wrong.[36] Thus, the M'Naghten test has two elements that need to be proved for the defendant to be considered insane and for that reason be excused from responsibility for his crime.

The first element that needs to be proved is that the defendant was actually suffering from a defect of reason at the time she committed the crime.[37] If the defendant was not suffering from such a defect at the time of the crime she cannot avail herself of the insanity defense. In most American jurisdictions the defect of reason need not have been permanent or even long-standing. It is sufficient if the defect of reason was temporary so long as it existed at the time the defendant committed the crime.[38]

The second element of the M'Naghten test that must be established is that because of the defect of reason the defendant either was not able to understand the nature and quality of her act or was not able to understand that the act was wrong.

A defendant is considered to know the nature of his act if he knows what act he is performing, and he understands the quality of the act if he understands the consequences that flow from it.[39] For example, if a defendant is charged with murdering her infant son by holding his head underwater and drowning him, to be able to establish the defense of insanity the defendant must be able to establish that at the time she drowned her son she suffered from a defect of reason and because of that defect either she did not know she was holding her baby's head under the water or, that if she did know that, she did not understand that by doing so it would result in his drowning.[40]

If the defendant understood the nature and quality of the criminal act when she performed it then the alternate question is whether because of her defect of reason she was unable to understand that her act was wrong. There is no uniformity as to the meaning of the term "wrong." In some states, "wrong" under their version of the M'Naghten test means only that because of her mental defect the defendant did not understand that her act was illegal when she committed it. In other states, "wrong" means that because of her mental defect the defendant was unable to know that her act was both legally and morally wrong. In most cases the difference is not significant, but in cases where a defendant believes he is acting on the command of God or some other supreme being, he may know his act is illegal but believe his act was not morally wrong. With that type of defendant the meaning of the term is crucial to the outcome of the case.

State v. Worlock

Supreme Court of New Jersey (1990) 117 N.J. 596

The primary issue in this case concerns the adequacy of the jury charge on the defense of insanity, which the Appellate Division sustained in an unreported opinion. We granted certification, 113 *N.J.* 343 (1988), and likewise find the charge to be sufficient. Finding no merit in defendant's other contentions, we affirm his convictions for murder and for possession of a weapon for an unlawful purpose.

I

The following summary is substantially consistent with defendant's version of the facts. Defendant, Carlyle Worlock, and his two victims, Guy Abrahamsen and Shawn Marchyshyn, had an unstable friendship in which Abrahamsen would periodically subject defendant to ridicule and physical abuse. On the night before the killing, the three young men went from Jackson Township to Seaside Heights, where, at defendant's expense, they spent the night smoking marijuana, drinking beer, and "partying" with two women "picked up" by Abrahamsen and Marchyshyn. After returning to Marchyshyn's apartment the following morning, Abrahamsen asked defendant for his pants. The ostensible reason for the request was that defendant's pants were dirty and Abrahamsen wanted to launder them. Apparently, however, the request was a ruse to obtain defendant's wallet, which contained, among other things, approximately $130 and a photograph of defendant dressed in a sadomasochistic costume at a gay parade in Hollywood. Defendant viewed the theft of his wallet as an act of betrayal, and feared that Abrahamsen could "destroy" him by disclosing the photograph.

"Burning and angry," defendant retrieved a semi-automatic .22 caliber rifle that he had hidden in a nearby wooded area * * * [and] decided to "let this guy [Abrahamsen] have it." Defendant proceeded to the vicinity of Marchysyn's apartment, where he waited for the victims.

Shortly thereafter, defendant saw Abrahamsen and Marchyshyn exit from a taxi cab. He knew that neither of them had any money, so the sight of the cab confirmed the suspicion that Abrahamsen had taken his money. According to a defense psychiatrist, defendant was "devastated" by the realization that Abrahamsen had stolen his wallet. Concealing the rifle in a cloth, defendant moved to the far side of the building and "wait[ed] in ambush." As they approached, he moved to within fifteen feet of them and quickly fired twelve rounds.

As defendant testified, "I aimed at Guy, and I * * * hit Shawn." The first bullet struck Marchyshyn in the chest and killed him. Three other bullets hit Abrahamsen, one in each arm and one in the back. Defendant fired a second burst of bullets, hitting Abrahamsen with six more shots as he opened the screen door of a ground-floor apartment. According to the occupants of the apartment, Abrahamsen stumbled into the family room and collapsed on the floor.

Defendant stated that he then tried to "divorce [himself] from the act," ran into the woods, changed his clothes, and went to a pizza parlor. While eating pizza, he saw several police officers "scouting" around, and he asked "what's happening?" Defendant testified that he then walked to the home of Abrahamsen's girlfriend, and told her that he had shot Abrahamsen. According to her, however, defendant said only that Abrahamsen had been shot. She left with two of her friends, one of whom called the police.

Defendant next went to his parents' house. They told him that the police were looking for him. On leaving the house, defendant noticed a police car parked nearby, and decided to "give himself in."

On September 21, 1983, an Ocean County Grand Jury indicted defendant for the capital murder of Abrahamsen and Marchyshyn, in violation of *N.J.S.A.* 2C:11-3, and for the unlawful possession of a weapon, in violation of *N.J.S.A.* 2C:39-4a.

At trial, the principal issue was whether defendant was legally insane when he shot Abrahamsen and Marchyshyn. * * *

B

Defendant urges that the trial court committed plain error by failing to charge expressly that "wrong" as used in *N.J.S.A.* 2C:4-1 includes moral wrong. Although other jurisdictions have considered the issue, it is one of first impression in this state.

The issue harks back to an ambiguity in the first question posed by the House of Lords in the *M'Naghten* case:

> What is the law respecting alleged crimes committed by persons afflicted with insane delusion in respect of one or more particular subjects or persons: as, for instance where at the time of the commission of the alleged crime the accused knew he was acting contrary to law, but did the act complained of with a view, under the influence of insane delusion, of redressing or revenging some supposed grievance or injury, or of producing some supposed public benefit?
> [8 *Eng. Rep.* at 722.]

In reply, Chief Justice Tindal stated that

> assuming * * * the inquir[y is] confined to those persons who labour under such partial delusions only, and are not in other respects insane, we are of the opinion that * * * he is nevertheless punishable according to the nature of the crime committed, if he knew at the time of committing such crime that he was acting contrary to law; by which expression we understand your Lordships to mean the law of the land.
> [*Ibid.*]

Without more, that reply would suggest that "wrong" means legal, not moral, wrong.

In addition to his previously-quoted answer to the second and third questions posed by the House of Lords, *supra* at 603, however, the Chief Justice explained that "[i]f the accused was conscious that the act was one which he ought not to do, and if that act was at the same time contrary to the law of the land, he is punishable." *Id*. at 723. This elaboration suggests that "wrong" means both moral and legal wrong, an apparent conflict with the answer to the first question. The confusion is compounded because "wrong" is undefined in the opinion. At trial, moreover, the court charged the jury that M'Naghten was entitled to an acquittal if, at the time he shot Drummond, he did not know "that he was violating the laws both of God and man," *id*. at 719-720, thereby suggesting that "wrong" meant both legal and moral wrong. * * *

Throughout the country, states have divided on the issue. Several states hold that a defendant is sane if he knows that his conduct is unlawful. *See State v. Hamann*, 285 N.W.2d 180, 183 (Iowa 1979); *State v. Boan*, 235 *Kan*. 800, 810, 686 P.2d 160, 168 (1984); *State v. Crenshaw*, 98 Wash. 2d 789, 796, 659 P.2d 488, 493 (1983). The supporting rationale is that a standard based on morality would be too amorphous to be useful and that "[u]ntil a moral standard becomes law it is an unreliable test for sanity." *Hamann, supra*, 285 N.W.2d at 184. Because murder contravenes all legal and moral standards, moreover, "[t]here is no practical distinction between moral and legal right or wrong in a murder case." *Id*. at 183.

Other jurisdictions hold that "wrong" encompasses both legal and moral wrong. In these jurisdictions, defendants must prove that they were incapable of knowing that their acts were both morally and legally wrong. *See State v. Skaggs*, 120 Ariz. 467, 472 (1978) ("wrong" does not mean "moral" wrong only) * * *. The only generally-recognized instance in which a "moral" wrong standard has provided an insanity defense is when the defendant has killed under the delusion that he or she was acting pursuant to a "command from God." *See People v. Schmidt*, 216 N.Y. 324 (1915) * * *.

In *Schmidt*, Judge Cardozo stated that juries generally should be allowed to consider whether a defendant who claimed that he acted on a command from God was capable of perceiving that his act was morally wrong. 216 N.Y. at 339. As Judge Cardozo explained:

> A mother kills her infant child to whom she has been devotedly attached. She knows the nature and quality of her act; she knows that the law condemns it; but she is inspired by an insane delusion that God has appeared to her and ordained the sacrifice. It seems a mockery to say that, within the meaning of the statute, she knows that the act is wrong. * * * We find nothing either in the history of the [*M'Naghten*] rule, or in its reason or purpose, or in judicial exposition of its meaning, to justify a conclusion so abhorrent.
> [*Ibid*.]

Finding that it was not error to leave "wrong" undefined, *id*. at 337, the court stated that "there are times and circumstances in which the word 'wrong,' as used in the statutory test of responsibility, ought not to be limited to legal wrong." *Id*. at 339. A more recent Arizona case, recognizing that "wrong" encompasses both legal and moral wrong, rejected the converse proposition that wrong should encompass "only a moral wrong." *Skaggs, supra*, 120 Ariz. at 472. * * *

It may distort the analysis, however, to focus on whether the wrong was legal or moral. In the vast majority of cases, if the defendant was capable of understanding that he was acting contrary to law, he would also have sufficient capacity to understand that he was acting contrary to the morals of society. Law is largely the crystallization of societal morals. Rarely would an allegedly illegal act not also be wrongful morally. Thus, "wrong" as used in the insanity defense will generally incorporate notions of both legal and moral wrong.

The "right and wrong" test does not focus on the actual knowledge of the defendant, but rather on his ability to perceive the wrongfulness of his conduct. Under the test, a defendant is excused from criminal liability if at the time of the commission of the offense, he or she lacked the capacity to distinguish right from wrong. *Cordasco, supra*, 2 N.J. at 196 (quoting *Molnar, supra*, 133 N.J.L. at 331). Only that defendant whose mind is impaired to the extent that he or she lacks the ability to comprehend that his or her conduct is wrong may successfully invoke the insanity defense.

Because the insanity inquiry focuses on the defendant's ability to comprehend whether his or her actions would ordinarily be disapproved by society, the concept of moral wrong must be judged by societal standards, not the personal standard of the individual defendant. *People v. Stress*, 205 Cal. App. 3d 1259, 1274 (1988) * * *. As a general rule, it will not be sufficient, therefore, that a defendant's personal moral code justified a killing otherwise prohibited by law and societal morals. * * *

Occasionally * * * the distinction between moral and legal wrong may be critical. For example, if the defendant contends that he or she knowingly killed another in obedience to a command from God, a jury could find that the defendant was insane. *Schmidt, supra*, 216 N.Y. at 340, 110 N.E. at 949 * * * ("The experts disagreed upon whether there was evidence of a psychosis to support the alleged delusion, but none suggested that if defendant in fact suffered an insane delusion that God commanded the deed, he nonetheless was legally sane if he simultaneously appreciated that the deed was contrary to law. Nor did the trial court so intimate."). Although a "command from God" is the only generally-recognized exception, other delusion-based exceptions conceivably might arise. For the purposes of this opinion, however, we need not attempt to identify any such other exception. As we explain more fully below, *infra* at 612-614, defendant sought to justify the killings not by recourse to societal morals, but to his personal moral code.

Because an act that is contrary to law will generally contravene societal morals, a defendant who claims that he or she lacked the capacity to comprehend either legal or moral wrong need not receive a charge distinguishing the two kinds of wrong. In the exceptional case, such as the deific exception in which the defendant claims that he or she acted under a command from God, the court should instruct the jury that "wrong" encompasses both legal and moral wrong.

III

The critical question here is whether the trial court should have expressly defined "wrong" to include moral wrong. * * *

Defendant * * * contends that the trial court committed plain error by not telling the jury that "wrong" encompasses both legal and moral wrong. * * *

[T]he record does not support defendant's claim that the trial court should have instructed the jury that "wrong" includes both legal and moral wrong. Such an instruction is necessary only if the distinction is critical to the facts on which a defendant bases the insanity defense. Here, defendant claims not that he killed Abrahamsen and Marchyshyn because the killings comported with societal morals, but because he was "infuriated" that they had stolen his wallet. He did not kill the victims because of his inability to distinguish "right" from "wrong." He killed them because he "hated" Abrahamsen and Marchyshyn "got in the way." Defendant openly admitted at trial that at the time he killed the victims, he knew his acts were illegal and that they were wrong under societal morals. On this record, we cannot fault the trial court for failing to define more specifically the word "wrong."

The most that can be said for defendant is that he believed the killings were justified under his personal code of morality. He viewed society with contempt, stating: "[t]o me, they're the folly-ridden mass, they're controlled by their popular beliefs." As defendant testified, "the law is not for me. The law is for subservient people." His moral code was based on "indulgence instead of abstinence" and "might makes right." Although defendant believed that under his own moral code he was justified in killing Abrahamsen and Marchyshyn, that belief does not nullify his appreciation that the killings were wrong according to law and the morals of society. Belief in an idiosyncratic code of morality does not constitute the defense of criminal insanity. If the insanity defense were so readily available, the life of each member of society would be imperilled by the whims of every other member. * * *

We perceive no error, much less plain error, in that charge. * * *

The judgment of the Appellate Division is affirmed.

Case Focus

- What are the two aspects of "wrong" embodied in the M'Naghten test?
- In the states that use the M'Naghten test, do they all use those two aspects of "wrong" in their versions of the M'Naghten test?
- In those states that use a version of the M'Naghten test that contain both aspects of "wrong," is the distinction between the two aspects always important and if not when is the distinction important?

• • • • • • • •

The M'Naghten test also addresses the problem of insane delusions. In determining whether a person with delusions is insane under the M'Naghten test it is necessary to know what delusions the defendant had at the time of the criminal act. If the delusion was as to a fact that if true would have justified the defendant's act, then the defendant is considered insane. If, however, the delusion was as to a fact that if true would not have justified the defendant's act, then the defendant would not be considered insane. For example, if because of a delusion Victor believed that the cigar lighter Omar was using to light his cigar was a gun and that Omar was about to shoot him, and for that reason Victor pulled out a gun and shot and killed Omar, Victor would be considered insane because had the facts been as he believed them to be, he would have been justified in shooting Omar in self-defense. However, if Victor's delusion was simply that Omar had swindled him out of a large sum of money and he killed Omar in revenge, his delusion would not be a defense because even if the facts were as he believed them to be, he would not have been legally justified in killing Omar.

One criticism of the M'Naghten test is that it does not provide a defense for those suffering from a defect of reason but, who despite that defect, are able to understand both: (1) the nature and quality of their act and (2) that their act was wrong, but because of the defect are unable to control their actions. To meet this criticism the M'Naghten test has been supplemented in many states by what is often called the irresistible impulse test. Under the irresistible impulse test the defendant must have been afflicted with some defect of the mind that makes it impossible for him to control his actions.[41] It is important to keep in mind that the irresistible impulse test does not provide a defense to a defendant whose will is simply overwhelmed by anger, jealousy, or some other passion.[42] To satisfy the requirements of the irresistible impulse test, the inability of a defendant to control his action must be the result of a mental disease and not simply because at some moment in time he was unable to control himself.

In those states that have retained the insanity defense there is no longer much uniformity as to what constitutes insanity. The M'Naghten test is still followed in federal courts[43] and by approximately a third of the states. Some states, however, have statutorily adopted one of the two elements of the M'Naghten test and rejected the other while other states have discarded the M'Naghten test and in its place have adopted the insanity test contained in the Model Penal Code.[44] Under the Model Penal Code a person is not responsible for criminal conduct if at the time of such conduct, because of mental disease or defect, the person lacked substantial capacity to appreciate the criminality or wrongfulness of his conduct or to conform his conduct to the requirements of the law.[45]

Historically, when an insanity defense was presented a trier of fact was faced with one of two verdicts: guilty or not guilty by reason of insanity. Beginning in the later part of the twentieth century, many states added a third possible verdict: guilty but mentally ill. A defendant who is found guilty but mentally ill is sentenced for whatever crime he committed, but is remanded to mental health authorities for treatment or is sent to prison, where he is given treatment for his mental illness. Once it is determined that no further treatment is needed the defendant is given credit against his sentence for the time in treatment, and if there is still time remaining on his sentence, he is transferred to the prison system to serve out the balance of his time. If the defendant's treatment resulted in him being held as long or longer than his sentence, he is released.[46]

Fitness to Stand Trial

The insanity defense should not be confused with a somewhat related, but completely different concept: fitness to stand trial. A defendant's fitness to stand trial looks at the defendant's mental state at the time of trial and not at the time the crime was committed. The defendant's fitness to stand trial is also determined by a completely different test than his sanity. To be fit to stand trial the defendant must be capable of understanding the charges against him and be capable of assisting his attorney in his defense. The issue of a defendant's fitness to stand trial can be raised by either the defense or the prosecution. If the defendant is found unfit but capable of being rendered fit with treatment, the court will order treatment to be given. If the defendant refuses treatment, a court can order him to be forcibly treated.

2. *Intoxication*

Intoxication from alcohol or some other substance can, under certain circumstances, be a defense to a criminal charge. Whether intoxication is a defense depends in large part on whether the intoxication was voluntary or involuntary. The extent to which voluntary intoxication is a defense has expanded and contracted over time. Historically, voluntary intoxication was not a defense to the commission of a crime.[47] Beginning in the nineteenth century, some courts began to carve out an exception that allowed the defendant's intoxication to be considered when the crime with which he was charged contained a *mens rea* element of specific intent. Under the specific intent exception, a defendant charged with a specific intent crime can successfully assert the defense of voluntary intoxication if at the time he committed the crime he was so intoxicated that he could not form that intent.

State v. Walden

Supreme Court of Tennessee (1941) 178 Tenn. 71

McKinney, J. delivered the opinion of the Court.

Plaintiff in error, Roy Walden, aged thirty-six, hereinafter referred to as defendant, was indicted in the Criminal Court of Knox County on September 17, 1940, for the rape of Nancy Ruth Sorrell, a child eight and one-half years of age. He was put to trial on October 22, 1940, at the conclusion of which the jury returned a verdict of guilty and fixed the punishment at death by electrocution. A motion for a new trial was seasonably filed and presented which the trial court overruled and thereupon entered judgment in accordance with the verdict of the jury. An appeal from said judgment was properly prayed, granted and perfected to this court.

Counsel for defendant entered pleas of "not guilty" and "insanity" in his behalf. In the presentation of the case in this court counsel did not insist seriously that defendant did not commit the crime, and could not do for the reason that the uncontroverted proof establishes his guilt beyond any reasonable doubt, the testimony of defendant being that due to the condition of his mind caused by the use of intoxicants and drugs over a long period of time he was unconscious of having committed the offense.

Mr. and Mrs. Wesley Sorrell, father and mother of Nancy Ruth, lived at 4424 Kingston Pike, which is one and one-half miles west of the city limits of Knoxville * * *. Kingston Pike runs east and west. Mr. and Mrs. Sorrell had a place of business about 1000 feet east of their residence * * * [where they] engaged in selling sandwiches, beer and soft drinks. They had a helper by the name of Mrs. Blanche Whaley who resided in their home. Mr. and Mrs. Sorrell had one other child, a daughter eleven years of age, who at the time of this tragedy was on a visit to relatives in Cannon County.

The defendant lived with his father and mother on the Kingston Pike, their dwelling being two blocks west of the Sorrell home. * * * He had known the Sorrells for several years, was a patron of their lunchroom, and, apparently, was familiar with the habits of the family.

On Sunday evening, September 8, 1940, Nancy Ruth was at the lunchroom of her parents until sometime between eight-thirty and nine o'clock when Mrs. Whaley accompanied her to her home preparatory to her retirement for the night. Mrs. Whaley returned to the lunchroom leaving Nancy Ruth alone with the doors unlocked. * * *

The defendant drove up to this lunchroom about one-fifty on the morning of September 9, 1940, parked his automobile, came in and remained until the place was closed at 3:10 A.M. While there the defendant shot craps for small stakes with Mr. and Mrs. Sorrell and Henry Moneymaker, a brother of Mrs. Sorrell. Defendant lost what money he had, most of which was won by Moneymaker. It was agreed, in the presence of defendant, that the Sorrells, Moneymaker and Mrs. Whaley drive to the business section of Knoxville, a distance of four miles, to eat some oysters. Defendant was not invited to go with them. According to the testimony of the four persons just named, the defendant while at the lunchroom purchased and drank three bottles of beer, was perfectly sober when they left, and at the request of Mr. Sorrell cranked his automobile for him on account of his batteries being weak; then cranked and entered his own car, the engine of which was running when they departed for Knoxville. Upon the return of the four parties to the Sorrell home at 4:20 A.M. Nancy Ruth was missing. The officers of Knox County were notified and a search for the child began.

About noon on the day that the crime was committed Nancy Ruth was discovered coming into her yard, as her mother expressed it, "in a very pitiful looking condition." Her body was covered with scratches, her legs were bleeding, dress muddy, and her hair matted and filled with beggar's-lice. She was in a dazed condition but with sufficient mind to relate to her mother what had transpired, giving a description of the man who assaulted her. She was taken immediately to Dr. Allen Webber who made a very careful and painstaking examination of the child's entire body, from which he testified positively that she had been attacked and that a male had unlawfully had carnal knowledge of her.

Nancy Ruth testified in detail as to this atrocious crime, the substance of which was that after retiring about nine o'clock she was awakened some time later by the defendant, who stated that her daddy and mother wanted her to come to Bearden, whereupon she got up and dressed, but did not put on her shoes as they had been left at the lunchroom to be polished[.] * * * There is no insistence that she was not raped. Neither is it seriously contended that the defendant is not the perpetrator of the crime.

The defendant admits spending the latter part of the night in the woods where the crime was committed, and admits changing clothes because they were muddy when he returned to his home between nine and ten o'clock that morning.

Nancy Ruth knew the defendant by sight but did not know his name. Upon her description of him and the clothes he was wearing the officers immediately began a search for the defendant and obtained the clothes he had taken off, and they fit the description given by Nancy Ruth. Thereafter Nancy Ruth identified defendant from photographs placed in her hands, and subsequently, when carried to the jail, out of a number of prisoners, designated defendant as the man who had assaulted her. She likewise pointed him out in the courtroom while she was testifying, and fully identified the clothes which he removed on returning to his home.

The defendant testified * * * that in 1936, while digging a cistern, he sustained an injury to his back which has continuously caused him pain and suffering, and that as a result of this affliction he has contracted the habit of taking veronal and luminal tablets and drinking considerable quantities of whisky and beer; that while employed as a salesman for the Crisp Cream Doughnut Company he sold Mr. Sorrell doughnuts, and on occasions would talk to Nancy Ruth and give her doughnuts; that during the week preceding the day on which this crime was committed he had been drinking heavily and taking a number of these tablets; that on the morning of September ninth before entering the Canary lunchroom he had taken two of these tablets and a drink of whisky; that while in that place he drank seven or eight bottles of beer and was drunk when he left; that he drove his car from this lunchroom to his home where he tried to back it into the garage, but that the motor died on him so that he could not get it into the yard; that he then drove his car down behind the post office where he took another drink of whisky and laid down in the front seat of his car, and from that time on was unconscious until he woke up in the woods several hours later.

The trial court instructed the jury that ordinarily voluntary drunkenness of an accused at the time a crime is committed is no defense, but that "if drunkenness existed to such an extent at the time so that he had not sufficient understanding to know right from wrong, and was in a state of insanity by reason of long continued drunkenness, it would be an excuse," and they should acquit him.

There is no complaint as to this instruction, and defendant could not have asked for a more favorable charge.

Relative to voluntary intoxication as a defense, we quote from the very full text upon the subject appearing in 22 C. J. S., Criminal Law, section 66, as follows:

"It is a well settled general rule of the common law, and also generally followed under the statute, that voluntary drunkenness of an accused at the time a crime was committed is no defense; and that despite his voluntary drunkenness at the time one may, subject to the qualifications hereinafter pointed out, be guilty of any crime, such as assault, burglary, illegal possession of intoxicating liquor, larceny, rape, or assault with intent to rape. If a person voluntarily drinks and becomes intoxicated, and while in that condition commits an act which would be a crime if he were sober, he is fully responsible * * * unless his drunkenness had resulted in settled insanity * * * or unless it rendered him incapable of entertaining a specific intent which is an essential ingredient of the offense * * *. The effect of drunkenness on the mind and on men's actions when under the full influence of liquor are facts known to everyone, and it is as much the duty of men to abstain from placing themselves in a condition from which such danger to others is to be apprehended as it is to abstain from firing into a crowd or doing any other act likely to be attended with dangerous or fatal consequences. It can make no difference, where no specific intent is necessary, that the intoxication was so extreme that accused was unconscious of what he was doing and had no capacity to distinguish between right and wrong, and, although there may be no actual criminal intent, the law will, by construction, supply the same, except in cases where a specific intent is requisite."

In the crime of rape no intent is requisite other than that evidenced by the doing of the acts constituting the offense. 52 C. J., 1014 * * *.

The rule thus announced finds support in the able and exhaustive opinion of Justice Turley, rendered nearly a century ago in *Pirtle* v. *State,* 28 Tenn. 663, in which it was held that voluntary drunkenness works no mitigation of crime except in a case where deliberation and premeditation is an essential element of the offense. In the opinion it is said:

"If the mental status required by law to constitute crime be one of deliberation and premeditation, and drunkenness or other cause excludes the existence of such mental state, then the crime is not excused by drunkenness or such other cause, but has not in fact been committed.

"This reasoning is alone applicable to cases of murder under our act of 1829, chap. 23. . . ."

Applying the foregoing principles to the facts of this case, if defendant was not drunk when he left the lunchroom, as testified to by the four parties present, but shortly thereafter became intoxicated to the extent that he unconsciously committed this horrible crime, then his drunken condition does not mitigate the crime and cannot be invoked as a defense. * * *

The defendant was represented by able and zealous counsel, was accorded a fair trial before an impartial jury; and while, in a sense, his act may have been partly due to his intoxication, he voluntarily brought about that condition and must abide the consequences.

We see no basis for interfering with the judgment of the trial court which will be affirmed, and the date of execution fixed for Thursday, January 15, 1942.

Case Focus

1. The case holds that voluntary drunkenness is not a defense, but notes that for certain types of offenses it is. What are those types of offenses and under what circumstances is voluntary drunkenness a defense to them?
2. In this case why was voluntary drunkenness not a defense even if the defendant was so intoxicated that he unconsciously committed the crime?

• • • • • • • •

The specific intent exception was widely adopted, but it was not adopted by all of the states[48] and in recent times that exception has been reconsidered and rejected by some courts that had previously adopted it.[49] Beginning in the 1980s some state legislatures statutorily abolished the specific intent exception and legislatively reinstated the old common law rule against considering voluntary intoxication as a defense to any crime.[50] Typically, those states that have statutorily abolished the specific intent exception have done so by redefining the mental state element so that it can be established by showing that the defendant acted with knowledge or purpose or acted under circumstances that would otherwise establish knowledge or purpose if the defendant were not voluntarily intoxicated.

Two reasons are usually cited for the return to the stricter common law rule. One reason often given is the apparently large number of violent crimes committed by intoxicated people. Studies estimate that half of all homicides are committed by intoxicated offenders.[51] In 1989, for example, more homicides were committed by intoxicated persons than by firearms.[52] A second reason cited for returning to the common law rule is that consideration of voluntary intoxication as a defense runs counter to the principle of personal accountability that is the foundation of law. Courts have said that people have a duty to abstain from placing themselves in a condition where they become a danger to others and if they do, they should not escape punishment simply because they chose to ingest an intoxicant.

State v. Vaughn

Supreme Court of South Carolina (1977)
268 S.C. 119

RHODES, **J.** The appellant was indicted for burglary and assault with intent to ravish. These charges arose out of his entry into the mobile home of two Charleston residents on or about August 21, 1975. A jury returned a verdict of guilty of the lesser offenses of housebreaking and assault and battery of a high and aggravated nature. The trial judge sentenced the appellant to terms of four (4) years for housebreaking and five (5) years for aggravated assault to run consecutively. The appellant maintains that he is entitled to a reversal because of alleged trial errors. We disagree with his contentions and affirm the conviction.
* * *

The appellant further excepts to the trial judge's charge to the jury with respect to the extent of voluntary intoxication necessary to negate proof of the element of specific intent required for burglary, housebreaking, and assault with intent to ravish. We have held that voluntary intoxication is not a valid defense to a crime involving a general criminal intent. *State v. Bellue*, 260 S.C. 39, 194 S.E. (2d) 193 (1973); *State v. Blassingame*, 221 S.C. 169, 69 S.E. (2d) 601 (1952). However, this issue is not before us. We are asked to hold that voluntary intoxication is a defense to crimes requiring proof by the State of specific intent, since it appears that we have never had occasion to rule definitely on this particular point. It is clear that the majority of American jurisdictions permit voluntary intoxication to be interposed as a defense to specific intent crimes. The general rule is stated as follows:

"Where a particular purpose, motive, or intent is a necessary element to constitute the particular kind or degree of crime, it is proper to consider the mental condition of accused, although produced by voluntary intoxication, and, where he lacked the mental capacity to entertain the requisite purpose, motive, or intent, such incapacity may constitute a valid defense to the particular crime charged. . . .

"The majority rule, holding intoxication to an extent precluding capacity to entertain a specific intent . . . to be a defense, does so not because drunkenness excuses crime, but because, if the mental status required by law to constitute crime be one of specific intent . . . and drunkenness excludes the existence of such mental state, then the particular crime charged has not in fact been committed."

22 C.J.S. Criminal Law §68(a) (1961). However, it is stated that there are authorities which hold that voluntary intoxication is not a defense to a crime involving a specific intent. *Id.* We adopt the rule that voluntary intoxication, where it has not produced permanent insanity, is never an excuse for or a defense to crime, regardless of whether the intent involved be general or specific. Reason requires that a man who voluntarily renders himself intoxicated be no less responsible for his acts while in such condition. To grant immunity for crimes committed while the perpetrator is in such a voluntary state would not only mean that many offenders would go unpunished but would also transgress the principle of personal accountability which is the bedrock of all law. "The effect of drunkenness on the mind and on men's actions . . . is a fact known to everyone, and it is as much the duty of men to abstain from placing themselves in a condition from which such danger to others is to be apprehended as it is to abstain from firing into a crowd or doing any other act likely to be attended with dangerous or fatal consequences." 22 C.J.S. Criminal Law §66 (1961).

The trial judge based his charge to the jury on the assumption that the rule in this State is, or would be declared to be, that voluntary intoxication may negate the specific intent requisite for the crimes charged. The court erred in this regard. However, such a mistaken assumption does not require us to reverse the judgment below since the appellant received the benefit of a charge which was highly in his favor. The charge on specific intent and voluntary intoxication was in no way prejudicial to the rights of the appellant.

The appellant's contention that the trial judge committed reversible error when he charged the jury that the appellant's intoxication "should be considered in determining the degree of the crime" is likewise without merit. While the choice of language used here was unfortunate and, in isolation, could conceivably have misled a jury, we are satisfied that no prejudice to the appellant resulted. In deciding whether the jury was misled or the appellant prejudiced by allegedly erroneous instructions, the charge must be considered as a whole. *State v. Hoffman*, 257 S.C. 461(1972) * * *. When viewed in context, the language employed clearly did not have a confusing or misleading effect.

Three remaining exceptions concerning the court's refusal to grant the appellant's motion for a directed verdict of not guilty were neither argued nor briefed and are, accordingly, deemed abandoned for purposes of this appeal.

Affirmed.

Case Focus

1. What rule does this court adopt for when the defense of voluntary intoxication applies to specific intent crimes?
2. How does the rule adopted by the court in this case differ from the rule adopted in most states and what reason does the court give for adopting its rule instead of the rule followed in most states?

• • • • • • • •

For the paralegal it is important to keep in mind that like the insanity defense, the defense of voluntary intoxication can vary greatly from state to state, and when confronted with a question relating to voluntary intoxication it is critical that the paralegal review the law of her jurisdiction or speak to the attorney for whom she works about how her jurisdiction defines the defense.

In contrast to voluntary intoxication, involuntary intoxication has long been a defense to a criminal charge if at the time the defendant committed the crime, he was so intoxicated that he reached such a level of mental dysfunction that he would be excused from criminal responsibility under his jurisdiction's insanity test.[53] For example, a defendant who committed a crime in a state that used the M'Naghten test and who was involuntarily intoxicated at the time he committed it would be excused from responsibility for the crime if he were so intoxicated that he was not able to understand the nature or quality of his act or he was not able to determine whether his act was wrong. Some jurisdictions actually treat involuntary intoxication as a species of their insanity defense.[54]

The law recognizes four different types of involuntary intoxication.[55] The first type is coerced intoxication, which occurs when a person is compelled to ingest an intoxicant against his will. The second type of involuntary intoxication is called pathological intoxication, which occurs when the intoxication is grossly excessive in degree relative to the quantity of intoxicant ingested. This type of involuntary intoxication can occur, for example, if a person drinks a single shot of vodka and it affects her the same as if she had ingested a full bottle of vodka. A third type of involuntary intoxication occurs when a person mistakenly ingests the intoxicant. This can occur either when a person is deceived into taking the intoxicant (such as when he is given a spiked drink) or misled into believing that a particular substance is a benign substance (such as a breath mint), when it is in fact an intoxicant. The fourth example of involuntary intoxication is unexpected intoxication by a prescribed drug. This form of intoxication is a defense when the defendant does not know that the prescribed drug is likely to have an intoxicating effect, and the prescribed drug and not some other intoxicant is in fact the cause of the intoxication.

Sluyter v. State

Court of Appeal of Florida, Second District (2006)
941 So. 2d 1178

DAVIS, J. Patrick Sluyter appeals his judgment and sentence for two counts of sexual battery. Because the trial court improperly prevented Sluyter from presenting an insanity defense, we reverse and remand for a new trial.

Sluyter was charged by information with two counts of sexual battery on a child less than twelve years of age. After examination by court-appointed experts, Sluyter filed his notice of intent to rely on an insanity defense based on a steroid psychosis. In response, the State filed a motion in limine, seeking to exclude the doctors' testimony related to such a defense. The trial court granted the State's motion. Following a jury trial at which he was convicted of both charges, Sluyter was sentenced to two life sentences.

The insanity test in Florida is the modified version of the M'Naghten rule [In Florida, the test for insanity as a defense to a criminal charge is whether at the time of the offense the defendant had a mental infirmity, disease, or defect and, as a result, did not know what he was doing or did not know what he was doing was wrong]. *Fisher v. State*, 506 So. 2d 1052, 1054 (Fla. 2d DCA 1987) (citation omitted). The burden is on the defendant to present evidence that shows his insanity. *Milburn v. State*, 742 So. 2d 362, 363 (Fla. 2d DCA 1999) * * *.

Sluyter presented evidence that, due to diminished sexual libido, he had been prescribed Halotestin by his treating physician. Sluyter also proffered the testimony of Dr. Frederick Schaerf, a practicing psychiatrist who was appointed by the court to examine Sluyter. Dr. Schaerf testified that, in his opinion, Sluyter met the test for insanity:

> Well, I strongly believe that he meets the Florida definition of insanity. That, No. 1, he is suffering from a mental infirmity or defect or disease, and that is the Halotestin intoxication.
>
> . . . And so I also believe because of that Halotestin intoxication, he did not know what he was doing at that moment because it was such a driven sexual

behavior. And although afterwards he'll say that it was wrong, at that specific moment he could not tell right from wrong.

However, despite this specific testimony, the trial court denied Sluyter the opportunity to present an insanity defense to the jury.

We begin with the proposition that "[a] party is entitled to present evidence upon the facts that are relevant to his theory of the case, so long as that theory has support in the law." *Zamora v. State*, 361 So. 2d 776, 779 (Fla. 3d DCA 1978).

In the instant case, Sluyter's theory, that he was legally insane at the time of the offenses due to involuntary Halotestin intoxication, finds support in the law. In *Brancaccio v. State*, 698 So. 2d 597 (Fla. 4th DCA 1997), the Fourth District quoted approvingly from an article collecting cases on the defense of involuntary intoxication: "'Generally speaking, an accused may be completely relieved of criminal responsibility if, because of involuntary intoxication, he was temporarily rendered legally insane at the time he committed the offense.'" *Id.* at 599 (quoting Phillip E. Hassman, Annotation, *When Intoxication Deemed Involuntary so as to Constitute a Defense to Criminal Charge*, 73 A.L.R. 3d 195 (1976)). In *Miller v. State*, 805 So. 2d 885, 887 (Fla. 2d DCA 2001), this court followed *Brancaccio*, stating:

> [W]here the intoxication is involuntary, it typically has been raised in an attempt to prove an insanity defense rather than an intoxication defense. The definition of insanity has been expanded to include those situations in which a person could not distinguish right from wrong as the result of an involuntarily-induced intoxicated state.

The State argues, however, that Sluyter's proffered evidence was properly excluded because it would not have demonstrated that Sluyter met this test for insanity. It is the State's position that Sluyter's intoxication was voluntary and that his actions indicated that he knew the difference between right and wrong. However, the record reveals testimony from which the jury could have reached the opposite conclusion.

The State's argument that Sluyter's intoxication was voluntary, not involuntary, finds no support in the law. Where the intoxicating dose of medication has been prescribed or administered by a physician, any resulting intoxication is considered to be involuntary. Hassman, *supra*, §7(a); *see also Boswell v. State*, 610 So. 2d 670 (Fla. 4th DCA 1992) (concluding that a defendant who was under the influence of Prozac and Xanax as prescribed by a doctor was entitled to an instruction on involuntary intoxication). In the instant case, Sluyter was prescribed Halotestin for a medical condition. There was no indication that he took the wrong dose or that he took the drug improperly. Thus, *Gray v. State*, 731 So. 2d 816 (Fla. 5th DCA 1999), which is cited by the State, has no application to this case since the defendant there ingested illegal nonprescription drugs.

The State also argues that Sluyter's intoxication was voluntary because he voluntarily ingested alcohol while taking the Halotestin, resulting in intoxication. However, Dr. Schaerf's testimony provides evidence from which the jury could have found otherwise. He opined: "And were it not for the Halotestin, it would have never happened, in my opinion. That it never happened before, would never happen again." The doctor's use of the term "Halotestin intoxication" does not invalidate the doctor's opinion regarding Sluyter's sanity. The doctor went on to say that it was the Halotestin that "put him in the mental state where he ended up not being able to appreciate what he was doing." Accordingly, because the drugs ingested here were prescription drugs prescribed by a physician and because Halotestin, not alcohol, caused the intoxication, Sluyter's resulting intoxication must be considered involuntary.

Furthermore, although the State argues that Sluyter's actions indicate that he knew the difference between right and wrong, the record offers evidence contrary to that contention. The portion of the record cited by the State as demonstrating that Sluyter knew the difference between right and wrong is a quote taken from Dr. Schaerf's report in which Dr. Schaerf gave Sluyter's explanation of the offense: "He woke up with a recollection of his daughter touching him and the patient touching his daughter." Also, "[h]e told his daughter it was wrong and told her it cannot be discussed." These comments clearly referred to Sluyter's reactions afterwards, not his awareness of the wrongfulness of the events at the time they were occurring. Moreover, Dr. Schaerf specifically testified that he believed that Sluyter met the Florida test for insanity because he did not know what he was doing at the moment of the offense: "[A]t that specific moment he could not tell right from wrong." Accordingly, the record does not support the State's argument that the evidence was properly excluded on this basis.

Although the State presented evidence that may have contradicted Dr. Schaerf's opinion regarding Sluyter's sanity, the trial court erred in not allowing Sluyter to present his evidence and argue his theory of defense to the jury. *See Boswell*, 610 So. 2d 670. When a defendant has competent evidence to support his theory of defense, the trial court denies the defendant his due process rights guaranteed by the constitution when he is prohibited from presenting that defense to the jury. *Washington v. State*, 737 So. 2d 1208, 1221 (Fla. 1st DCA 1999). Because Dr. Schaerf's testimony specifically provided Sluyter with a basis to present an insanity defense, the trial court erred in precluding the doctor from testifying and in denying Sluyter the opportunity to argue his only defense.

Reversed and remanded for a new trial.

CASANUEVA and WALLACE, JJ., Concur.

Case Focus

1. The defendant in this case contended he was intoxicated at the time he committed the crime and sought to assert an insanity defense. What was the basis of that defense?

2. The trial court rejected the insanity defense because the defendant voluntarily ingested the intoxicating substance. The voluntary ingestion notwithstanding, the appellate court held that the defendant should have been allowed to assert the insanity defense. What was the reason the court gave for saying that the defendant should have been allowed to put on evidence of his intoxication?

• • • • • • • •

3. Infancy

At common law, children less than seven years old were deemed incapable of forming the *mens rea* element of an offense and as such were considered incapable of committing a crime. As a result, it was a complete defense if a defendant was less than seven years old when he committed a crime. The common law rebutably presumed that children at least 7 years old but 14 years old or younger were capable of forming the *mens rea* element of offenses. As such, they were rebutably presumed to be capable of committing a crime. As a result, under the common law a child in that age range who was charged with committing a crime could assert the defense of infancy and the trier of fact determined whether the child was sufficiently mature to be able to form the mental state that was an element of the crime. The common law considered children over age 14 to be capable of committing a crime and as such were treated and sentenced as adults.

The common law presumptions have been changed by statute in many states. For the most part these changes have resulted in raising the age of incompetence to commit a crime above the age of seven. Today the age at which a child may be convicted of an offense is different in different states. The Illinois statute, which provides that no person may be convicted of an offense unless he has attained the age of 13 at the time the offense was committed,[56] is typical of that presently found in many states.

The defense of infancy is based on actual chronological age. As a result, the defendant's mental age is irrelevant. For example, if a defendant is 25 years old when he commits a crime, but has a mental age of a 10-year-old, that mental age is no defense to the crime. To the extent that the defendant's mental age may bear on his ability to distinguish right from wrong or to form the *mens rea* element of the offense with which he is charged, that may be defense.[57]

At the beginning of the twentieth century the state of Illinois was the first state to create juvenile courts to deal with, among other things, youthful criminals. Following the Illinois example, juvenile courts for youthful offenders were eventually created in all the states. Under the juvenile court statutes minors who commit crimes generally are to be tried in juvenile courts instead of as adults in criminal courts.

The juvenile court statutes usually have a provision that allows youthful offenders to be tried as adults. Under these statutes the prosecutor must petition the juvenile court to allow the minor to be prosecuted as an adult. The juvenile court statutes usually allow the juvenile court judge to transfer the case from juvenile court to adult criminal court if the judge finds that a juvenile court trial is not in the best interests of the minor or of the public. In making that decision the court is expected to balance the interests of the juvenile offender against society's legitimate interest in being protected from criminal victimization by minors.[58]

4. Entrapment

There are two different forms of the entrapment defense: the subjective form and the objective form. With few exceptions all American states use one of those two forms of the defense. The subjective form of the defense was developed by the courts and has since been codified in many states. That form of the defense focuses on the defendant when determining if entrapment has occurred. The objective form of the defense is a product of the Model Penal Code[59] and its applicability is determined by the action of law enforcement and the effect of that action on a reasonable person.

The entrapment defense is a defense, which, because of how it is defined, can fit into either of two different categories of affirmative defenses. The subjective form, because of its focus on the defendant's state of mind, is usually placed on the excuse category. The objective form, because of its focus on protecting the public from misconduct by law enforcement[60] and not on protecting defendants,[61] is actually a non-exculpating defense. It is important to keep in mind that under either form of the entrapment defense merely offering a target the opportunity to commit a crime is not entrapment.

United States v. Gustin

United States Court of Appeals for the Seventh Circuit (2011) 642 F.3d 573

EASTERBROOK , Chief Judge.

A jury concluded that, while confined at a federal prison, Scott Gustin and a confederate stabbed and wounded another inmate. Gustin was convicted of attempted murder, 18 U.S.C. §113(a)(1), and sentenced to life imprisonment. His defense at trial was that he did not attack the victim, who deliberately mis-identified him as the aggressor in order to settle a score among gangs and protect the true perpetrator. The attack occurred in a common area, so other inmates could have been responsible, but the jury believed the victim, and other evidence also supports the conviction.

* * * Gustin's * * * lawyers make a single argument: That the district judge should have disallowed Gustin's actual defense and insisted that he raise a different one: entrapment. Technically Gustin could have argued entrapment while denying that he attacked the victim, see *Mathews v. United States,* 485 U.S. 58 (1988), but inconsistent defenses usually are the functional equivalent of

a guilty plea. In *Mathews* itself, the defendant admitted that he had committed the charged acts but contended that he lacked criminal intent, in part because of entrapment. Since *Mathews* we have never seen any defendant argue: "I didn't do it, but if I did I was entrapped." So appellate counsel is effectively contending that the trial judge was obliged to override the defense strategy of denying that Gustin stabbed the victim. Appellate counsel suggests "outrageous governmental conduct" as a separate defense, but it is not one this circuit recognizes, see *United States v. Van Engel,* 15 F.3d 623, 631 (7th Cir. 1993) * * *, and in the circumstances would have come to the same thing as entrapment. Failure to remake the defense as one based on entrapment was plain error by the court, appellate counsel insist.

A proposal that a district judge must force counsel to present an entrapment defense is defective at the level of both theory and practice. We start with theory.

Every criminal defendant has a right, in consultation with counsel, to choose a line of defense. See *United States v. Gonzalez—Lopez,* 548 U.S. 140 (2006). Judges must not interfere. As a rule, judges should not even inquire why the defense follows a particular approach. Inquiry might breed distrust between lawyer and client, while providing the prosecutor with valuable information that he could not obtain via discovery. See *Taylor v. United States,* 287 F.3d 658, 662 (7th Cir. 2002). After all, an accused's trial strategy, and the reasons for it, are covered by the attorney-client privilege and the work-product privilege. Perhaps a judge would not err by reminding defense counsel that exploring the possibility of an entrapment defense could help. But the judge would rarely know enough before trial to advise defense counsel about the best lines of argument—and it is not a judge's job to assist one advocate at another's expense.

Gustin's appellate counsel do not contend that the judge should have made a suggestion before trial; they think that the judge should have intervened *at* trial. By then, however, defense strategy is set, and the risk of disruption (and inciting distrust) is substantial. More than that: introducing entrapment as a defense at trial not only undermines the defense plan but also hands a weapon to the prosecutor. For, when entrapment is at issue, the prosecutor must establish that the accused was predisposed to commit the unlawful acts. See *Jacobson v. United States,* 503 U.S. 540, 112 S. Ct. 1535, 118 L. Ed. 2d 174 (1992). To demonstrate predisposition, the prosecutor can introduce evidence about the accused's character and criminal history, subjects that otherwise would be off limits. See, e.g., *United States v. Bastanipour,* 41 F.3d 1178, 1183 (7th Cir. 1994). Few defendants willingly open this door, and no defendant would want a judge to invite evidence of predisposition by injecting entrapment into a case spontaneously.

These considerations lead us to conclude that it can never be error, let alone plain error, for a district judge to permit defense counsel to omit an entrapment defense. If an entrapment defense offers the best chance of acquittal, its omission could reflect ineffective assistance of counsel, but it could not demonstrate *judicial* error. Gustin does not contend that his trial lawyer furnished substandard assistance [.] * * * We have not found any appellate decision, in the history of this nation's jurisprudence, holding that a trial court committed plain error by neglecting to instruct the jury on an entrapment defense never raised by the defendant or his lawyer. Our case will not be the first. So much for theory. Practice is equally dispositive against Gustin's current argument. He is a member of Nuestra Familia, a gang based in northern California. The victim was a member of the Sureños, a gang from southern California. The Sureños are enemies of the Norteños, a gang that has an alliance with Nuestra Familia. Gustin contends, and the prosecutor does not deny, that the constitution and democratically elected leadership of Nuestra Familia require its members to kill members of the Sureños on sight—or be killed themselves. (That a criminal gang has a constitution and practices internal democracy would not be a surprise to a reader of Peter T. Leeson, *The Invisible Hook: The Hidden Economics of Pirates* 23–44 (2009).) Gustin's appellate lawyers contend that putting a member of the Sureños in the same cell as Gustin compelled him to attack and thus should be equated to governmental inducement to do so.

The federal prison in Pekin, Illinois, where this crime occurred, has experienced conflict among members of different gangs. Assigning each gang to its own cellblock could reduce inter-gang violence, but at the expense of allowing one gang to dominate each cellblock. That not only would undercut the authority of the warden and guards but also would imperil non-members of gangs, for they would be in hostile territory without allies. * * *

Pekin's warden decided to scatter gangs' members throughout the general population, so that any given gang was a minority in each cellblock. The warden's policy dealt with the risk of inter-gang violence by trying to identify the most likely aggressors and victims, then assigning the aggressors to segregation while keeping the potential victims in protective custody. The warden and guards also tried to negotiate truces between gangs.

Gustin's insistence that every guard must have known that he was bound to attack his cellmate confesses predisposition, which defeats any entrapment defense. Gustin's trial lawyer omitted this defense because it had no prospect of success, yet would have opened the door to damning evidence that would have painted Gustin as a predator with a history of violence and no qualm beforehand or repentance afterward. And it would not have done trial counsel any good to argue self-defense, duress, or any of the * * * justification defenses. If Gustin feared that his cellmate would attack him, he should have raised the subject with the guards. The law does not permit a preemptive strike when other options are available. See *United States v. Bailey,* 444 U.S. 394 (1980).

A contention that the guards' conduct was "outrageous" because they know how members of gangs behave, and that the guards compelled Gustin to attack by placing him near a member of a rival gang, is the sort of thing that kidnappers and terrorists put in demand notes. It is not a legal argument; it is the opposite of one. A kidnapper may write: "Pay me $5 million or I will kill the victim. The fault will be yours for refusal to pay. If the victim dies, you bring it on yourselves." Terrorists make similar statements when they insist that a nation that fails to withdraw from disputed territory is "responsible" for the deaths from the terrorists' action. * * *

The idea in any of these situations is that a person who makes a sufficiently grave and credible threat shifts to someone else the responsibility if that threat is carried out.

This is not how the criminal law works. A kidnapper who kills his victim when the ransom is not paid is guilty of premeditated murder; he cannot contend that failure to pay is entrapment or "outrageous government conduct" that excuses the killing. Someone who commits a crime willingly, when the opportunity is extended on a silver platter, must pay the penalty. See *United States v. Murphy,* 768 F.2d 1518, 1524 (7th Cir. 1985). Gustin cannot shift the blame to the guards. Placement of the victim in Gustin's cell (or perhaps even his cellblock) played a causal role, to be sure; had Gustin and his victim always been physically separated, the attack could not have occurred. One could equally say that a bank's placement of money in tellers' drawers, rather than a locked vault, is responsible for bank robbery and excuses the robber, who could not turn down the opportunity. So too with people who walk on deserted streets at night: making oneself an easy target does not excuse a mugging. We are nonplussed that Gustin's appellate lawyers could think otherwise.

AFFIRMED

Case Focus

1. Why did the Court say it would have been wrong for the trial judge to intervene during trial and require the defense attorney to assert an entrapment defense for the defendant?
2. What would assertion of the entrapment defense have allowed the prosecutor to do and why would the entrapment defense not have been successful even if it had been asserted?
3. Why was it not outrageous government conduct to place the defendant in a cell with a member of a rival gang?

• • • • • • • •

a. The Subjective Form of Entrapment

The subjective form of the entrapment defense is used in federal courts and in most states and requires that the defendant establish by some quantum of evidence that: (a) the government induced him to commit the crime with which he is charged and (b) he was not predisposed to commit it.[62] If the defendant was predisposed to commit the offense with which he is charged, it is irrelevant that the government induced him to commit it.

To be able to establish that the government induced the defendant to commit the crime, the defendant must establish that an agent of the government induced him to commit it.[63] The agent can be an employee of the government, he can be a private citizen working at the direction of a government agency, or he can be informant, but he must have been acting in that capacity when he induced the defendant to commit the crime. The entrapment defense is not available if the defendant was induced to commit the crime by a person who was not working for or at the direction of the government.[64] The reason there is no defense of private entrapment is because inducement of another by a private party to commit a crime is nothing more than soliciting the commission of a crime, which is itself a criminal offense.[65]

In determining whether the defendant was predisposed to commit the offense with which he is charged, the entrapment defense focuses on the defendant's state of mind before exposure to government agents and asks whether the defendant was an unwary innocent or an unwary criminal who readily seized the opportunity to commit the crime. When determining whether the defendant was predisposed to commit the crime, courts look at whether he manifested that predisposition in some way before, during, and after the commission of the crime. Evidence of predisposition can include having a prior history of engaging in the same type of criminal conduct in which the defendant now claims to have been entrapped or having actively and enthusiastically participated in the crime.[66]

In determining predisposition, the court will also consider the size of the financial gain the defendant derived or stood to derive from the crime. In looking at the gain, a court will consider whether the profits the defendant stood to make from the crime were ordinary profits for the type of crime with which he is charged or whether the profits were disproportionately large in relation to the crime. The size or anticipated size of the gain from the crime is considered significant because if a person is willing to commit a crime for the ordinary amount of gain that can be expected from it he is considered to be predisposed to commit the crime and to be merely waiting for the opportunity to do so.[67] If the anticipated or actual gain is disproportionately large in relation to the crime, that is considered to be the sort of inducement that would entice a person with no predisposition to engage in the crime.[68]

Where over a long period of time the defendant consistently declined multiple offers by the government to commit a criminal act before finally performing it, the defendant will generally be able to establish a lack of predisposition.

United States v. Millet

United States Court of Appeals for the Seventh Circuit (2007) 510 F.3d 668

WILLIAMS , *Circuit Judge.* In August 2004, Harvey Gooden, a police informant, invited an attorney, Christopher Millet, to participate in a robbery of a drug dealer. Millet, who claimed to be well versed in the art of robbing drug dealers, readily accepted Gooden's offer. After the robbery, Gooden asked Millet for a gun, purportedly to protect himself from the dealer they had robbed, and after some prodding, Millet obliged. For his actions, Millet was charged with conspiracy to distribute cocaine, attempting to distribute a controlled substance, and knowingly disposing of a firearm to a known felon. The jury returned a conviction on the drug distribution counts, finding that the offenses involved over 500 grams of cocaine; however, Millet was acquitted on the firearm charge.

Millet appeals the district court's refusal to provide an entrapment instruction on the drug distribution counts, contending that there was insufficient evidence to show that he intended to join a conspiracy to steal drugs (in addition to cash) or that he conspired with anyone other than Gooden. Millet has failed, however, to demonstrate a lack of predisposition to commit the charged crimes, so he was not entitled to an entrapment instruction, and the evidence was sufficient to show that Millet and his co-conspirators expected to recover drugs during the robbery and to give those drugs to a known dealer. * * *

Finally, the government cross-appeals, claiming the court erred in failing to sentence Millet based on the total quantity of fake drugs stolen from the fictitious dealer. This argument has merit because the district court did not make an independent factual determination as to the amount of drugs Millet conspired to steal. Thus, we affirm in part and reverse in part the judgment of the district court, and remand for re-sentencing.

I. BACKGROUND

After more than a decade of sobriety during which he obtained a law degree, Christopher Millet relapsed in 2003 and again became addicted to heroin. That year, Millet met and began purchasing heroin and cocaine from Harvey Gooden. In August 2003, Gooden was arrested by Chicago Police. After that arrest led to federal firearms and drug distribution charges, Gooden agreed to cooperate with investigations by the Bureau of Alcohol, Tobacco, Firearms and Explosives ("ATF") and the Federal Bureau of Investigation ("FBI") to obtain a reduced sentence. In his role as informant, Gooden told federal authorities of Millet's illegal activities. * * *

When the FBI decided to launch an operation centered on Millet, Gooden agreed to be the inside man. On August 3, 2004, Gooden, while wearing an audio recording device, told Millet that a Mexican drug dealer would be coming to Chicago to sell twenty kilograms of cocaine and two hundred pounds of marijuana. Gooden said he intended to buy two kilograms of cocaine, which he called "birds," for $13,000 a piece. Gooden remarked that a kilogram of cocaine would sell for $18,000 to $20,000 in Chicago. Millet agreed, "Right, 20 at least." Gooden again mentioned the amount of drugs the dealer would have and said "I wanna take it." He then invited Millet to participate, saying "we can go in up there . . . ," but vowed to "sting 'em regardless," meaning with or without Millet's help. At that point, Millet interjected the idea of using police in the rip off, affirming that the "Harvey Police [could] do it." Several minutes later, Gooden brought the heist up again, emphasizing that he needed a gun, not Millet's participation in the robbery. * * *

Millet proceeded to explain how he wished to carry out the robbery. He said, he wanted to "go in proper," meaning with police, and he agreed to contact his "people" before his next conversation with Gooden. So, by the end of that first conversation, Millet had unequivocally agreed to participate in the robbery but not to provide Gooden a gun.

The next day, Gooden informed Millet that the dealer had arrived in Chicago and would be in town for four days. Millet said he had just gotten off the phone with his contact and that his folks were on "standby." Gooden said they would do the robbery the next day unless Millet needed more time. Millet said his guys were ready, "on standby," but then suggested that it would be better to wait. * * *

Although Gooden agreed that it would be best to wait for the dealer to convert his drugs to cash, Gooden asked Millet about the obvious possibility that the dealer might still have drugs at the time of the robbery. * * *

With that, Millet agreed to include drugs in the take, and moments later, he recognized that the drugs would translate to cash. * * *

On Thursday, August 5, Gooden called Millet to say that the second half of the dealer's shipment would arrive the next day, and that the dealer would not be leaving Chicago until the following Wednesday. Millet commented that the dealer would be a "cash cow." Gooden agreed, and he added that the dealer probably would not have "many" leftover kilograms of cocaine at the time of the robbery. Gooden said, "remember I want, I want, the uh, the uh, the girl," meaning cocaine. The callers were disconnected before Millet could respond. When Gooden and Millet spoke later that day at Millet's law office, they discussed the benefits of partnering with police in a robbery of dealers. Millet said, "It's always better to go with this lick man." He said, "I done did this both ways man," with and without police, "and [was] willing to do it both ways. . . ." But he and Gooden agreed, working with police minimized resistance. Millet then called his police contact, in Gooden's presence, to confirm that the robbery would take place Sunday or Monday because they were waiting on the second shipment. After the call, Millet told Gooden there would be a total of four conspirators (for a four-way split) and that Millet and the other two conspirators would complete the robbery.

The next recordings occurred on Monday, August 9, 2004, the day of the robbery. That morning, the government parked a gray Cadillac STS in the parking lot of the Chicago Park Hotel in Harvey, Illinois. Before parking the car, federal agents placed a duffel bag containing $20,000 in cash and two fake kilograms of cocaine in the trunk of the car. Gooden made four calls to Millet between 10:41 a.m. and 11:00 a.m. During those calls, Gooden conveyed that he had met the dealer in a Cadillac parked at the Chicago Park Hotel and that he saw the dealer throw a duffel bag into the trunk of the car and remove the cocaine that Gooden purchased from the trunk. He also said, "I saw, I saw, I saw a couple a birds in there, I saw at least 2, 3 of 'em but I saw plenty of money though." At trial, Millet admitted that "bird" was slang for cocaine * * *.

Gooden and Millet exchanged additional calls between 11 a.m. and 2 p.m. Often during the calls, Gooden warned that they might miss the chance to complete the robbery if they did not hurry. * * * Just after noon, Gooden told Millet he was going to drive to get his cousin and brother so they could help him complete the theft. Before Gooden could take this ruse any further, Millet notified him that the conspirators had struck and that the drugs they recovered were fake. Gooden said that he had been sold real cocaine, to which Millet replied, ". . . I'm glad yours is cool. I'm saying that other shit wasn't nothing but fake move." Gooden asked "how many of 'em was it?" Millet replied, "[t]hree," and confirmed "[t]here was three birds[.]"

The observations of federal agents conducting surveillance on August 9 correspond with the recorded conversations. Throughout the morning and early afternoon, agents saw two vehicles pull into the parking lot and park next to or near the target vehicle. At about 1:25 p.m., three men in a car pulled up next to the target automobile. One man exited the car, popped the trunk of the Cadillac, removed the duffel bag, and returned to the car, which quickly drove off. * * *

Millet and Jones were named in a superseding indictment. The indictment charged Millet with: (1) conspiring to possess with intent to distribute more than 500 grams of cocaine in violation of 21 U.S.C. §841(a)(1) and 18 U.S.C. §2; (2) attempting to possess with intent to distribute a controlled substance in violation of 21 U.S.C. §846; and (3) knowingly disposing of a firearm to a known felon in violation of 18 U.S.C. §922(d). During a five-day trial, the jury heard the recordings detailed above, Agent Twohig testified to Millet's confession, and Millet offered his version of events. * * *

During the jury instructions conference, Millet proposed an entrapment instruction on all three counts, but the district court only gave the instruction as to the third, saying the evidence did not justify giving the instruction on the drug distribution counts. The jury convicted Millet on Counts One and Two, and acquitted him on Count Three. He moved for a new trial, and that request was denied. * * *

II. ANALYSIS

A. The District Court Did Not Err in Refusing to Provide an Entrapment Instruction on Counts One and Two

Millet contends the district court erred in refusing to give an entrapment instruction on Counts One and Two. We review the district court's decision de novo. * * * The defendant was not entitled to an entrapment instruction on Counts One and Two because he failed to show that his defense theory was supported by the evidence.

When claiming entrapment, a defendant must proffer evidence in support of both of the elements of entrapment: lack of predisposition on the part of the defendant to engage in criminal conduct and government inducement of the crime. *See United States v. Haddad,* 462 F.3d 783, 789-790 (7th Cir. 2006). If the evidence shows predisposition, we may reject the entrapment defense without considering whether the defendant was induced. *United States v. Bek,* 493 F.3d 790, 800 (7th Cir. 2007).

1. Millet Was Predisposed to Commit the Acts Charged in Counts One and Two

In assessing whether a defendant was predisposed to commit the charged offense, we consider the following factors:

> (1) the defendant's character or reputation; (2) whether the government initially suggested the criminal activity; (3) whether the defendant engaged in the criminal activity for profit; (4) whether the defendant evidenced a reluctance to commit the offense that was overcome by government persuasion; and (5) the nature of the inducement or persuasion by the government.

United States v. Blassingame, 197 F.3d 271, 281 (7th Cir. 1999). We begin with the fourth factor, which we have declared to be the most important in our assessment. *See id.*

Millet contends he was reluctant to include the theft of drugs in the robbery scheme, but the record suggests otherwise. From day one, Millet showed a willingness to join a conspiracy that might include the stealing of drugs. During Gooden and Millet's first conversation about the robbery, Gooden said the dealer would have "20 [kilograms of cocaine] and 200 pounds [of] weed" and stated, "I wanna take it." Gooden did not specify whether "it" referred to drugs or money. But "it" was most likely a reference to the dealer's inventory, which had been the topic of conversation up to that point. Without elaborating on his intentions, Gooden invited, but did not pressure, Millet to participate. In fact, Gooden said he would "sting 'em regardless," and told Millet "if you don't want no parts of it only thing I probably need from you . . . is a sword, a gat." Millet jumped at the opportunity, despite the possibility that the heist would target drugs, saying "Yeah, I want some parts of it."

In subsequent conversations, Millet expressed a preference for money over drugs. He wanted to wait to commit the robbery until the dealer had an opportunity to "money up" and disclaimed any personal interest in the drugs, saying "That's yours, that's yours. No that's yours," "we ain't finna fuck with that like that man," and "all that other shit, you know . . . that's your expertise." So Millet had no personal interest in selling drugs, but was undisturbed by the notion that Gooden might include drugs in his take. * * * Millet has failed to show a reluctance to commit the offense that was overcome only by government persuasion.

The record also belies Millet's argument that the government offered some extraordinary benefit sufficient to overcome an innocent person's resistance to committing the crime. Millet suggests that we find inducement based on the fact that the government introduced drugs into the scheme, applied constant pressure on him to complete the crime, and dangled huge profits in front of him. But, on these facts, the government's actions did not constitute extraordinary inducement.

The mere fact that the government crafted a scheme, which included drugs, is not sufficient. *See United States v. Higham,* 98 F.3d 285, 290-291 (7th Cir. 1996) * * *. The government did not place any exceptional amount of pressure on Millet. Rather, from the outset, Gooden communicated that Millet was welcome to participate but that he did not have to do so. It was Millet who willingly joined the conspiracy when he said, "Yeah, I want some parts of it." * * *.

Finally, Millet contends that the government's inducement was extraordinary because the government suggested that he could make huge profits from the robbery. Given the large quantity of drugs the fictitious dealer was said to possess, the heist could conceivably net several hundred thousand dollars. Still, this case stands in stark contrast to the classic example of extraordinary inducement, i.e., where "the police offered a derelict $100,000 to commit a minor crime that he wouldn't have dreamed of committing for the usual gain that such a crime could be expected to yield, and he accepted the offer and committed the crime. . . ." *United States v. Evans,* 924 F.2d 714, 717 (7th Cir. 1991). Millet was a lawyer (albeit one struggling with a serious addiction), not a derelict, and his offense was no minor offense that any law abiding citizen would commit if only given the right financial incentive. * * *

The remaining factors do little, if anything, to help Millet carry his burden.

Millet next contends that he did not have the character to commit the crimes charged in Counts One and Two. We cannot be so sure. Millet readily admitted a willingness to profit from drug sales, if not to sell drugs himself. He had stolen drug money in the past, at times with the assistance of corrupt officers. * * *

Millet's criminal predisposition is further supported by the fact that he is the one who introduced the idea of robbing drug dealers. While Gooden was the first to suggest robbing a specific dealer (one who did not exist), Millet had previously introduced the broad idea of stealing from dealers, had robbed dealers in the past, and asked Gooden's assistance in doing so. * * *

Finally, Millet expected to profit from the conspiracy * * * he certainly joined the overall conspiracy with the expectation of making a profit.

In sum, because Millet has failed to show that he lacked the predisposition to commit the crimes charged in Counts One and Two, the district court did not err in refusing to give an entrapment instruction on those counts. * * *

For the reasons detailed above, the judgment of the district court is affirmed in part and reversed in part. This case is REMANDED for re-sentencing.

Case Focus

1. Evidence relating to what two propositions of law must a defendant provide to the prosecutor?
2. Does the expectation of large profits from a crime always constitute an extraordinary inducement to commit that crime?

• • • • • • • •

b. Objective Form of Entrapment

The Model Penal Code[69] defines an entrapment defense that is different from that developed by the courts, which is usually referred to as an objective entrapment defense. Under the Model Penal Code a person is entrapped when the government agent induces that person to commit conduct constituting an offense by either: (a) knowingly making false representations designed to induce a belief in the person that the conduct is not illegal or (b) employing methods of persuasion or inducements that create a substantial risk that the offense will be committed by persons other than those predisposed to commit it. The Model Penal Code approach to entrapment has only been adopted in a few states.[70]

c. Necessity of Admitting the Offense

In many states, before a defendant is able to use the defense of entrapment he must admit that he committed the offense with which he is charged. As a result, in those states a defendant who maintains he did not commit the crime or who denies committing some element of the crime cannot assert a defense of entrapment.[71] The rationale for that requirement is that the underlying theory of the entrapment defense is that the defendant committed the crime so it is inconsistent to allow him to deny committing it while at the same time saying that he was entrapped into committing it.[72]

People v. Eaglin

Appellate Court of Illinois (1992)
224 Ill. App. 3d 668 (3d Dist.)

JUSTICE GORMAN delivered the opinion of the court:

Kenneth L. Eaglin was charged by information with one count of solicitation of murder for hire. (Ill. Rev. Stat. 1989, ch. 38, par. 8-1.2.) He was convicted by a jury and sentenced to 34 years imprisonment.

The State alleged that Eaglin solicited an undercover officer to commit first degree murder. The victim was to be Joan C. Scott, the Fulton County State's Attorney. Eaglin's purported animosity arose from an attempt by Scott to remove Eaglin's children from his household under charges of neglect. These custody battles, which ran from 1987 until March of 1990, included the filing by Scott of perjury charges against the defendant's wife and his parents. Defendant's wife was also briefly imprisoned on a contempt charge.

At trial, much of the State's evidence came from the testimony of an informant named Joseph Roberts. Roberts began working at Eaglin's construction company in April of 1990. During this time, Roberts and Eaglin had several conversations about Eaglin's custody problems.

On or about June 27, 1990, Roberts allegedly told Eaglin that State's Attorney Scott had hired a man named Paul Long to kill Eaglin's wife. Long was a former cell mate of Roberts, but there is no evidence that he was actually aware of any of the circumstances described here. Eaglin claims, that out of fear for his family's safety, he wanted to pay off Long.

Defendant and Roberts met several times over the next few days. According to Eaglin, Roberts told him that Roberts had made contact with the hit man and persuaded him to kill State's Attorney Scott for payment instead of killing Mrs. Eaglin. Roberts also allegedly told Eaglin that if he attempted to back out of the deal, his family would be killed.

On July 12, 1990, Roberts telephoned Officer Daniel Daly of the Fulton County Sheriff's Department. He told Daly that Eaglin was planning to have State's Attorney Scott killed. He further stated that Eaglin had inquired whether Roberts knew of anyone who could commit the crime. When Roberts volunteered Long's name, Eaglin reportedly discussed payment and inquired about the length of time Long would need to prepare.

On July 26, 1990, at the request of law enforcement officials, Roberts went to Eaglin's house and told Eaglin that the hit man was ready to proceed. Eaglin provided Roberts with a photo of State's Attorney Scott which had been clipped from a newspaper. This conversation was recorded via an eavesdropping device which was hidden on Roberts.

The next day, again at the request of the police, Roberts telephoned Eaglin. He told Eaglin that Long wanted to talk to Eaglin. Roberts then handed the phone to Gerald Kempf, an undercover officer who was portraying Long. The defendant never affirmatively stated that he wanted Scott dead, but agreed to pay Kempf $2,000 to carry out the scheme. This conversation, which was also recorded, was the basis for the solicitation charge.

Kempf and the defendant then arranged to meet at a parking lot. After a short conversation there, Eaglin was arrested. * * *

At trial, defendant tendered jury instructions on the defense of entrapment. The trial judge refused these instructions on the basis that defendant had denied committing the crime, relying on *People v. Gillespie* (1990), 136 Ill. 2d 496.

The jury found the defendant guilty of solicitation of murder for hire, he was sentenced and this appeal followed.

The defendant's first contention is that the trial court erred in refusing to instruct the jury on entrapment. The defendant does not contend that the evidence established entrapment as a matter of law. Instead, he merely argues that he had presented evidence of the defense and thus was entitled to a jury instruction on the issue.

Traditionally, the rule has been that it is a precondition to raising the entrapment defense that the defendant admit that the crime was committed and that he committed it. *People v. Fleming* (1971), 50 Ill. 2d 141. * * *

The Illinois Supreme Court recently reexamined the issue [and]* * * the court reaffirmed the long-standing rule that in Illinois, a defendant who denies committing the offense charged is not entitled to have the jury instructed on the entrapment defense.

The record here reveals that Eaglin did not admit to the commission of the crime. He also repeatedly denied having the intent to kill, which is a necessary element of the crime. At trial, he testified "I didn't want her killed . . . I didn't want to say 'kill' when I didn't want her killed." At a later point during direct examination by his attorney, Eaglin's denials are even more explicit:

Q. Was it ever your intention to hire anyone to kill Joan Scott?

A. No, sir.

Q. On July 27, 1990, at any time did you hire Paul Long or Gerald Kempf or anyone—

A. No, I did not.

Q.—to kill Joan Scott?

Having denied the crime, the defendant was not entitled to an entrapment instruction. The trial court was correct in finding that *Gillespie* is dispositive and in denying the instruction. * * *

Accordingly, for the foregoing reasons, we affirm the defendant's conviction.

AFFIRMED.

Case Focus

1. What was the reason the court gave for refusing to give the entrapment instruction?

• • • • • • • •

5. *Duress*

The defense of duress had its origins in the common law and excuses a defendant from being held responsible for his criminal act when he performed the act under compulsion. Duress does not render a defendant's act involuntary, nor, except in certain types of specific intent offenses, does it negate the defendant's *mens rea*; instead the defense of duress recognizes that the defendant acted under coercive conditions and for that reason it excuses him from criminal liability.[73]

The Model Penal Code defines a modern form of the duress defense[74] that in varying degrees has been adopted by statute in a majority of states. Despite the influence of the Model Penal Code, there is little uniformity among the states on the actual elements of the defense.[75]

In general, the defense of duress is available when, because of a threat received from another person, the defendant had a reasonable fear of imminent death or of suffering great bodily harm if he did not engage in the criminal conduct with which he has been charged.[76] Because the defense is limited to threats of imminent death or great bodily harm, an economic threat is not sufficient to constitute duress even if the threat is of imminent economic ruin.

To be able to use the defense the defendant must have actually received a direct threat of imminent death or great bodily harm. The defendant cannot rely on a generalized fear of death or great bodily harm at the hands of another, and she must refuse to perform the criminal act until the threat of imminent death or great bodily harm is communicated to her.[77] The defense is not available if the threat is simply of death or great bodily harm at some unspecified time in the future. Under the common law (and still in many states) only threats of death or great bodily harm to the defendant himself could excuse the defendant's criminal acts. A threat to a defendant to inflict imminent death or great bodily harm on some unrelated third person or even on a member of the defendant's family did not excuse the defendant from being held criminally liable for his acts.[78]

D'Aquino v. United States

Unites States Court of Appeals for the Ninth Circuit (1951) 192 F.2d 338

Pope, J. Appellant was convicted of treason against the United States. The indictment charged that she adhered to the enemies of the United States giving them aid and comfort by working as a radio speaker, announcer, script writer and broadcaster for the Imperial Japanese Government and the Broadcasting Corporation of Japan, between November 1, 1943, and August 13, 1945; that such activities were in connection with the broadcasting of programs specially beamed and directed to the American Armed Forces in the Pacific Ocean area; and, that appellant's activities were intended to destroy the confidence of the members of the Armed Forces of the United States and their allies in the war effort, to undermine and lower American and Allied military morale, to create nostalgia in their minds, to create war weariness among the members of such armed forces, to discourage them, and to impair the capacity of the United States to wage war against its enemies. The indictment alleged the commission of eight overt acts. Appellant was found guilty of the commission of overt act No. 6 only, which in the language of the indictment, was: 'That on a day during October, 1944, the exact date being to the Grand Jurors unknown, said defendant, at Tokyo, Japan, in a broadcasting studio of the Broadcasting Corporation of Japan, did speak into a microphone concerning the loss of ships.'

Upon this appeal counsel for appellant have filed briefs asserting the commission of numerous errors on the part of the trial court. * * *

9. QUESTIONS RELATING TO DURESS

Appellant asserts that the trial court committed numerous errors relating to the claimed defense of duress or coercion. She argues that some of the instructions given upon this subject were erroneous; that other instructions requested by her should have been given, and that the court erred in excluding numerous items of evidence which were offered in support of this defense. The court instructed the jury at length upon the defense that the criminal act was not committed, voluntarily but was the result of coercion, compulsion or necessity. The instruction included the statement that 'in order to excuse a criminal act on the ground of coercion, compulsion or necessity, one must have acted under the apprehension of immediate and impending death or of serious and immediate bodily harm. Fear of injury to one's property or remote bodily harm do not excuse an offense.' It will be noted that the court's instruction was almost identical to that approved in Gillars v. United States, supra, 182 F.2d at page 976, note 14. The charge was a correct statement of the law upon this subject. United States v. Vigol, 2 U.S. 346; Respublica v. McCarty, 2 U.S. 86; Shannon v. United States, 10 Cir., 76 F.2d 490; R.I. Recreation Center v. Aetna Casualty & Surety Co., 1 Cir., 117 F.2d 603.

Appellant seriously contends that however correct the instruction might be in an ordinary case where a person accused of crime committed in his own country claims to have been coerced by an individual, the instruction of the court was in error particularly in its requirement of apprehension of immediate and impending death, or of immediate bodily harm, in a case where the accused person was in an enemy country, unable to get protection from the United States and where the compulsion is on the part of the enemy government itself. The contention is that under these circumstances the requirement of 'immediacy' in the court's instructions was error. * * *

[W]e think that under the circumstances here there was no occasion for departing from the ordinary rules applicable to the defense of duress and coercion. We know of no rule that would permit one who is under the protection of an enemy to claim immunity from prosecution for treason merely by setting up a claim of mental fear of possible future action on the part of the enemy. We think that the citizen owing allegiance to the United States must manifest a determination to resist commands and orders until such time as he is faced with the alternative of immediate injury or death. Were any other rule to be applied, traitors in the enemy country would by that fact alone be shielded from any requirement of resistance. The person claiming the defense of coercion and duress must be a person whose resistance has brought him to the last ditch. * * *

In support of this defense of coercion, appellant testified that one Takano, her civilian superior, informed her that she was 'to take army orders * * * you know what the consequences are * * *.' She undertook to give this statement significance by testimony as to atrocities inflicted by the Japanese upon certain internees and prisoners of war who disobeyed military orders. The testimony relating to the statement of Takano is the only evidence in the record which would appear to support the giving of an instruction with respect to duress or coercion. Appellant testified that she was not forced to take her position at Radio Tokyo and said that she did not broadcast because of any actual physical coercion or threats thereof. The only qualification of this testimony was the statement of Takano which she testified was made to her before she began her broadcasting activities. She testified that she was not mistreated by the Japanese police. She performed her duties as script writer and announcer for the Zero Hour from November, 1943, until August, 1945. During this period she had pay raises; she was allowed the usual American holidays, and occasionally she absented herself from the broadcasting for considerable periods of time. These absences did not result in any immediate or drastic measures from her employers. On those occasions she ignored verbal and written demands to return to work and did so with impunity and only returned to work when a Japanese official called upon her. There is no evidence of any determined refusal on her part which might have provoked coercion or brought about immediate and actual danger to her. In other words, there is no evidence that the appellant ever so conducted herself as to bring about a demonstration that death or serious and immediate bodily harm was to be apprehended for a refusal.

Appellant was permitted to introduce a vast amount of testimony which she says was in support of her claim that she operated in fear and under apprehension of harm to herself. Thus, she testified that during her stay in Japan after war began, she was interrogated by the police and was kept under constant surveillance by them. Her living quarters were searched by the police and she was required to obtain permission to move from place to place. She asked to be interned but this was denied her. She also testified that her neighbors, other civilians, were suspicious of her; that she was under fear of mob violence from the Japanese populace. In addition there was received evidence of atrocities practiced on the prisoners of war by the Japanese and evidence that for refusal by prisoners of war to obey orders the penalty of death was inflicted. Other witnesses called by appellant testified to instances in which guards killed prisoners in cold blood and tortured and beat others. Some prisoners of war had been compelled by threats of death or other violence to participate in the operation of the Zero Hour broadcast. In general these experiences relating to such prisoners and to other victims of atrocities were communicated to the appellant.

Appellant says that the court erred in giving the last three paragraphs of the instruction quoted in note 11, supra, to the effect that the fact that she was required to report to the Japanese police was not sufficient; that surveillance of the police was not sufficient; that threats made to other persons were not sufficient, etc. Appellant asserts that by this portion of the court's instruction it emasculated all of this background testimony which was designed to disclose that appellant was operating in an atmosphere of terror.

In order to consider the propriety of the instruction here complained of it is necessary to understand the very wide scope which the court permitted appellant's testimony to take. Although a strict following of the rule laid down in Gillars v. United States, supra, would have excluded evidence of threats or duress against others who participated in the Radio Tokyo broadcast, the trial court here allowed great latitude to appellant's counsel in placing in the record evidence of sundry atrocities committed by the Japanese against persons other than the appellant. * * *

Since we find no prejudicial error in the record the judgment is affirmed.

Case Focus

1. In order to be able to take advantage of the defense of duress, what, through evidence, must a defendant show about the purported duress under which he claims to have acted?

• • • • • • • •

There are a number of important limitations on the duress defense. One important limitation is that the defense is not available to one who, when acting under duress, intentionally kills another. The defense may, however, be used by one who, when under duress, merely assists in such a killing so long as he does not perform the lethal act. For example, Jermaine has bound William and points a gun at Tyrone and tells Tyrone that he will shoot him if he does not stab William through the heart. If Tyrone stabs William and kills him, Tyrone cannot assert the defense of duress. If, however, Jermaine points a gun at Tyrone and tells him to hold William still so that he, Jermaine, can shoot William through the heart and Tyrone then holds William while Jermaine shoots and kills William, Tyrone will be able to assert the defense of duress. The defense of duress is also unavailable if the defendant had the opportunity to escape without exposing himself unduly to the risk of death or great bodily harm and he failed to escape.[79]

6. *Public Authority*

The public authority defense excuses a defendant from being responsible for a crime when at the request of a government official he engages in conduct he, the defendant, knows to be otherwise illegal.[80] This defense usually arises when a defendant is charged with committing a crime such as selling controlled substances and he alleges that he acted at the request of an agent of the government to engage in the illegal conduct. If the defendant can establish that he indeed was recruited by a government agent to engage in the criminal act, it is a defense.[81]

7. Entrapment by Estoppel

The entrapment by estoppel defense is similar to but distinct from the public authority defense. The entrapment by estoppel defense applies when, in reliance on statements of a government agent, the defendant engages in conduct that he believes is legal, but which in fact is a crime.[82] In such cases, entrapment by estoppel is a defense that excuses the defendant's criminal conduct. For example, if a person goes to a public official who works in the office of a state agency that regulates and licenses persons who sell securities to the public and asks if he needs a license to sell securities and the official incorrectly tells him he does not, and the person is later prosecuted for selling securities without a license, he can assert the defense of entrapment by estoppel.

It is important to keep in mind the distinction between the defense of entrapment by estoppel and the objective form of the defense of entrapment. In the former the defendant is receiving information about the legality of his conduct from a person who he knows to be a government agent while in the later the defendant is receiving the information about legality of his conduct from a person who, unknown to the defendant, is a government agent.

CHAPTER TERMS

Burden of persuasion   Burden of production

REVIEW QUESTIONS

1. What is an affirmative defense and how does it differ from a simple defense?
2. What is an excuse defense and does such a defense make illegal conduct permissible?
3. For purposes of the insanity defense, at what point in time must the defendant be suffering from insanity to be able to assert the defense?
4. Assuming a person is suffering from a mental illness at the time he commits an offense, will that always constitute a defense? If so, why, and if not, why not?
5. What are the elements of the M'Naghten test?
6. Under the M'Naghten test what must a defendant be able to understand to be able to know the nature and quality of his act?
7. Under the M'Naghten test what must a defendant be able to understand to be able to know that his act was wrong?
8. How do the concepts of insanity and fitness to stand trial differ?
9. What is the irresistible impulse test?
10. In addition to the verdicts of "guilty" and "not guilty," what other verdict is possible in many states for defendants who are mentally ill at the time they commit a crime, and what are the consequences for a defendant of such a verdict?
11. Can voluntary intoxication of a defendant be a defense to crime?
12. What are the different forms of involuntary intoxication?
13. What is the defense of infancy?
14. What are the two different forms of the entrapment defense and how do they differ?
15. Is it always a defense under the subject form of the entrapment defense when the government agent induces the defendant to commit a crime? If not, when is it not a defense?
16. What role, if any, do the profits derived from a crime play in determining the applicability of the entrapment defense?
17. What type of threat must be made to a defendant to be able to allow him to successfully assert a defense of duress?
18. Under the traditional definition of duress to whom must the threat have been directed to enable a defendant to assert the defense?
19. Can a defense of duress be asserted if a defendant was threatened with imminent death but was able to escape?
20. Is the defense of duress available for all crimes? If not, for what crimes is the defense not available?

ADDITIONAL READING

William Booth, *Kaczynski Resists the Insanity Defense* (February 27, 1998). *http://www.washingtonpost.com/ wp-srv/local/longterm/aron/kaczynski122697.htm*. Site last visited April 18, 2008.

Kimberly Collins, Gabe Hinkebein & Staci Schorgl, *The John Hinckley Trial & Its Effect on the Insanity Defense*. *http://www.law2.umkc.edu/faculty/projects/ftrials/hinck-ley/hinckleyinsanity.htm*. Site last visited June 9, 2011.

Mitchell Keiter, *Just Say No Excuse: The Rise and Fall of the Intoxication Defense*, 87 J. Crim. L. & Criminology 482 (1997).

Prosecuting Kids as Adults (December 1, 2007). *http://www.msnbc.msn.com/id/22055708/fromET/*. Site last visited April 6, 2008.

ENDNOTES

1. *United States v. Petty*, 132 F.3d 373 (7th Cir. 1997).
2. It is frequently said that with affirmative defenses defendants have the burden of proof. Saying that defendants bear the burden of proof with respect to affirmative defenses causes confusion and is frequently incorrect. The term "burden of proof" includes both the concept of burden of production and the concept of burden of persuasion. Depending upon the jurisdiction and the type of affirmative defense asserted, a defendant may bear both burdens or, as with the insanity defense, in many jurisdictions he bears only one, the burden of production.
3. *United States v. Jumah*, 493 F.3d 868 (7th Cir. 2007).
4. *Catlet v. State*, 321 Ark. 1 (1995).
5. *United States v. Petty*, 132 F.3d at 373.
6. Paul H. Robinson, *Criminal Law Defenses: A Systematic Analysis*, 82 Colum. L. Rev. 199 (1982).
7. *See, e.g., Supreme Court Rule of Prof. Conduct*, Rule 1.6 (Illinois Supreme Court 2006).
8. *In re Grand Jury Subpoena*, 533 F. Supp. 2d 602 (D.C.W.D.N.C. 2007).
9. *Id.*
10. *Olender v. United States*, 210 F.2d 795 (8th Cir. 1953).
11. *See, e.g., In re Grand Jury Investigation of Ocean Transportation*, 604 F.2d 672 (D.C. Cir. 1979).
12. *In re Sealed Case*, 856 F.2d 268 (D.C. Cir. 1988).
13. *United States v. Abuhamra*, 389 F.3d 309 (2d Cir. 2004).
14. *United States v. Aref*, 533 F.3d 72 (2d Cir. 2008) (State secrets privilege); *Jade Trading, LLC v. United States*, 65 Fed. Cl. 487 (Fed. Ct. Cl. 2005) (Deliberative process privilege).
15. *United States v. Jumah*, n.3.
16. *People v. Allegri*, 109 Ill. 2d 309 (1985).
17. *State v. Korrell*, 213 Mont. 316 (1984).
18. *Id.*
19. *State v. Watson*, 211 Mont. 401 (1984).
20. Rita Buitendorp, *A Statutory Lesson from "Big Sky Country" on Abolishing the Insanity Defense*, 30 Val. U. L. Rev. 365 (1996).
21. *See, e.g.,* Idaho Code §18-207; Kan. Stat. Ann. §22-3220; Mont. Code Ann. §§46-14-102, 46-14-311; Utah Code Ann. §76-2-305.
22. Gary Slapper. *The Law Explored: Preparing Witnesses* (April 25, 2007). *http://business.timesonline.co.uk/tol/business/law/columnists/gary slapper/article1700573*. Site last visited March 30, 2008.
23. *Restatement of the Law Third*, The Law Governing Lawyers, §116, cmt. (b).
24. J. Alexander Tanford, *The Ethics of Evidence*, 25 Am. J. Trial Advoc. 487 (Spring 2002).
25. Lisa Salmi, *Don't Walk the Line: Ethical Considerations in Preparing Witnesses for Depositions and Trial*, 18 Rev. Litig. 135 (1999).
26. *State v. McCormick*, 298 N.C. 788 (1979).
27. *Nassau County Bar*, Op. No. 94-6 (1994).
28. *Kines v. Butterworth*, 669 F.2d 6 (1st Cir. 1981).
29. *See International Business Machines Corp. v. Edelstein*, 526 F.2d 37 (2d Cir. 1975).
30. Gary Slapper at Note 22.
31. *Hixon v. State*, 165 So. 2d 436 (Fla. App. 1964).
32. *People v. Dwight*, 368 Ill. App. 3d 873 (1st Dist. 2006).
33. *Patterson v. New York*, 432 U.S. 197 (1977).
34. *Leland v. Oregon*, 343 U.S. 790 (1952).
35. *Queen v. M'Naghten*, 8 Eng. Rep. 718 (1843).
36. *Id.*
37. *Commonwealth v. Riley*, 519 Pa. 550 (1988).
38. *Drewry v. State*, 208 Ga. 239 (1951).
39. *State v. Brosie*, 113 Ariz. 329 (1976).
40. *People v. Sherwood*, 271 N.Y. 427 (1936).
41. *State v. Hartley*, 90 N.M. 488 (1977).
42. *Watson v. State*, 177 Ark. 708 (1928).
43. 18 U.S.C. §7.
44. *Clark v. Arizona*, 126 S. Ct. 2709 (2006).
45. Model Penal Code §4.01.
46. *E.g.,* 730 ILCS 5/5-2-6.
47. *Montana v. Egelhoff*, 518 U.S. 37 (1996).
48. *Id.*
49. *McDaniel v. State*, 356 So. 2d 1151 (1978).
50. *Id.*

51. *Id.*
52. Bureau of Justice Statistics, U.S. Department of Justice, *Sourcebook of Criminal Justice Statistics*, 381 tbl. 3.133, 603 tbl. 6.54 (1993).
53. *Torres v. State*, 585 S.W.2d 746 (Texas Ct. of Crim. App. 1979).
54. *Miller v. State*, 805 So. 2d 885 (Fla. 2d DCA 2001).
55. *City of Minneapolis v. Altimus*, 306 Minn. 462 (1976).
56. 720 ILCS 5/6-1.
57. *Commonwealth v. Trippi*, 268 Mass. 227 (1929).
58. *People v. Fuller*, 292 Ill. App. 3d 651 (1st Dist. 1997).
59. Model Penal Code §2.13.
60. *United States v. Steinberg*, 551 F.2d 510 (5th Cir. 1977).
61. *State v. Brown*, 107 Wis. 2d 44 (1982).
62. *United States v. Millet*, 510 F.3d 668 (7th Cir. 2007).
63. *United States v. Jones*, 950 F.2d 1309 (7th Cir. 1981).
64. *Id.*
65. *Id.*
66. *United States v. Rodriguez*, 43 F.3d 117 (5th Cir. 1995).
67. *United States v. Santiago-Godinez*, 12 F.3d 722 (7th Cir. 1993).
68. *Id.*
69. Model Penal Code §2.13.
70. *E.g.*, Haw. Rev. Stat. §702-237.
71. *People v. Eaglin*, 224 Ill. App. 3d 668 (3d Dist. 1992).
72. *State v. Amodei*, 222 Kan. 140 (1977).
73. *United States v. Dixon*, 548 U.S. (2006).
74. The Model Penal Code formulates the defense of duress as follows: (1) It is an affirmative defense that the actor engaged in the conduct charged to constitute an offense because he was coerced to do so by the use of, or a threat to use, unlawful force against his person or the person of another, that a person of reasonable firmness in his situation would have been unable to resist; (2) The defense provided by this Section is unavailable if the actor recklessly placed himself in a situation in which it was probable that he would be subjected to duress. The defense is also unavailable if he was negligent in placing himself in such a situation, whenever negligence suffices to establish culpability for the offense charged; (3) It is not a defense that a woman acted on the command of her husband, unless she acted under coercion as would establish a defense under this Section [the presumption that a woman acting in the presence of her husband is coerced is abolished]; (4) When the conduct of the actor would otherwise be justifiable under Section 3.02, this Section does not preclude such defense. Model Penal Code §2.09.
75. 2 LaFave & Scott, *Substantive Criminal Law*, §9.7 (2d ed. 2007).
76. *D'Aquino v. United States*, 192 F.2d 338 (9th Cir. 1951).
77. *Id.*
78. *People v. Spears*, 727 P.2d 96 (Okl. Cr. 1996).
79. *United States v. Alicea*, 837 F.2d 103 (2d Cir. 1988).
80. *United States v. Jumah*, n.3.
81. *Id.*
82. *Id.*

Chapter 13
Affirmative Defenses — Justification

Chapter Objectives

After reading this chapter, you should be able to

- Understand what justification defenses are and how they differ from excuse defenses
- Name four important justification defenses
- Understand the definitions of those defenses
- Name and understand the elements common to all justification defenses

There is a third species of necessity, which may be distinguished from the actual compulsion of external force or fear; being the result of reason and reflection, which act upon and constrain a man's will, and oblige him to do an action, which without such obligation would be criminal. And that is, when a man has his choice of two evils set before him, and, being under a necessity of choosing one, he chooses the least. —Blackstone, *Commentaries on the Laws of England*, Book IV

In this chapter we will examine the category of defenses called justification defenses. Justification defenses are different from the excuse defenses (examined in the last chapter) because unlike excuse defenses, which focus on the existence of a condition in the defendant and because of that condition excuse the defendant from responsibility for his conduct, justification defenses focus on special circumstances in which harm caused by the defendant's actions is outweighed by the risk of greater harm.[1] Thus, while excuse defenses excuse a defendant from responsibility for his conduct, justification defenses transform what is ordinarily legally proscribed conduct into legally acceptable conduct.[2]

Justification defenses focus on three things: (1) the defendant's act, (2) the circumstances that necessitated the defendant's act, and (3) the possible alternatives to that act and ask whether the defendant's act was the least evil of any of the other possible acts. If, under the circumstances that necessitated the defendant's act, his act was the lesser evil, the justification defenses not only allow, but encourage that act. For example, shooting a person is ordinarily a legally proscribed act. If, however, the conditions of the defense of self-defense are satisfied, then the shooting is legally acceptable.

All justification defenses have the same general elements: (1) a triggering condition and (2) response requirements.[3] The triggering condition is that circumstance or set of facts that the law recognizes as allowing a defendant to act with justification. For example, a triggering condition that will allow Janice, a defendant, to use deadly force against Yuri in self-defense is an action by Yuri that puts Janice in apprehension of imminent death. The existence of the triggering condition does not by itself justify a defendant's response to that condition or those facts. To be justified in acting, the defendant's act must have been engaged in to protect some interest and the defendant's response must be proportional to the threat.

This chapter examines four of the most important justification defenses: (A) self-defense; (B) defense of others; (C) defense of property; and (D) necessity.

A. Self-Defense

Like the insanity defense, at early common law self-defense was not a defense. In that early period, if a defendant was convicted of a crime and the facts revealed that he engaged in the act that constituted the crime in self-defense, the judges reported that to the king, who could issue a pardon. Self-defense did not become recognized as a defense until 1531.[4] Self-defense was long recognized as a defense by American common law and today it is a statutorily defined defense throughout the United States. The details of the defense vary from state to state, and one form of the defense has been codified in the Model Penal Code.[5]

Broadly speaking, the defense of self-defense is available when: (1) the defendant reasonably believes he is in imminent danger of unlawful bodily harm; (2) he reasonably believes force is necessary to avoid the danger; (3) he was not the aggressor; and (4) the amount of force he uses against the aggressor is reasonable.[6]

There are two different types of force a person can use to defend himself: non-deadly force and deadly force. Deadly force is force that will cause death or great bodily harm. Non-deadly force is all other types of force. In determining the amount of force that a defendant can use to defend himself the law looks at the type of force with which he was threatened or reasonably believed he was threatened.

If the defendant is threatened by another with non-deadly force the defendant is entitled to respond only with non-deadly force. For example, if Sonny and Burt are two men of approximately equal size and have approximately equal pugilistic skills and Sonny threatens to use his fists to beat up Burt, Burt would be allowed to defend himself with his fists, but could not defend himself by shooting Sonny. In those circumstances Burt could, however, point a gun at Sonny if he had no intention to use it because merely threatening the use of deadly force does not constitute the use of deadly force.[7] If a person is threatened with imminent death or serious bodily injury the defense of self-defense allows a threatened person to respond with deadly force. Under the law of self-defense, serious bodily injury includes rape.[8] As a result, a person is entitled to use deadly force to defend herself or himself from rape.

To be able to take advantage of the defense of self-defense the defendant's belief in the imminence of harm and the necessity to use force to avoid danger must be reasonable. The perspective from which that reasonableness is determined represents one of the most significant variations in the law of self-defense. In many states reasonableness is determined by what is called an objective test, which asks what a reasonable person of ordinary firmness would have done under the circumstances.[9] In other states reasonableness is determined by a subjective test, which asks whether viewed from the standpoint of the defendant the circumstances were sufficient to induce in him an honest and reasonable belief that he was in danger.[10]

By whichever test of reasonableness is used, if the defendant's belief under it is considered reasonable, the defense of self-defense can be used even if the defendant's belief turns out to be erroneous. For example, if Maury reasonably, but incorrectly, believed he was in imminent danger of death or great bodily harm at the hands of Joshua and as a result Maury pulled out a gun and shot Joshua, that error will not prevent Maury from using the defense of self-defense.[11]

In order to use the defense of self-defense the defendant must have reasonably believed (whether under the objective or subjective standard) that the danger of unlawful bodily harm to him was imminent. For the danger of unlawful bodily harm to be imminent it must be immediate and not a danger that will arise hours or weeks in the future nor can it be a danger that occurred hours or days earlier. If a defendant is defending his home against an intruder, under some formulations of the law of self-defense he may use deadly force even if he is not in apprehension of death or great bodily harm from the hands of the perpetrator as long as he reasonably believes the intruder will commit a felony in the home or injure an occupant of the home.[12]

State v. W.J.B.

Supreme Court of West Virginia (1981) 166 W. Va. 602

MILLER, J. W.J.B. was adjudicated as a juvenile delinquent by the Circuit Court of Wood County on its finding that he had committed voluntary manslaughter. He appeals the adjudication, challenging the sufficiency of the evidence on the grounds that the State has not met its burden of rebutting his evidence of self-defense. In reviewing the evidence in light of our prior decisions regarding self-defense, we agree.

The juvenile was arrested on February 19, 1979, following the shooting death of Michael Watson. The State filed a juvenile delinquency petition, charging him with murder. Subsequently, the State petitioned for transfer to the criminal jurisdiction of the court so that the juvenile could be prosecuted and sentenced as an adult. Following a hearing on this issue, the court denied the motion to transfer. * * *

The testimony at the adjudicatory hearing was substantially undisputed. Nine neighbors and * * * the juvenile himself testified regarding the events surrounding the February 19, 1979, death of Michael Watson, [age 21]. The juvenile admitted the shooting and testified regarding self-defense.

The combined, undisputed testimony established a pattern of violence on the part of Watson, directed toward the family of W.J.B. over the course of the preceding year. * * *

Watson's association with W.J.B.'s family began in the spring of 1978 when he began a courtship of the juvenile's 15-year-old sister. * * * It appears that the 15-year-old attempted to break off the relationship after she had suffered a number of beatings at Watson's hands. * * * On at least one occasion in the summer of 1978, Watson pursued the girl at knifepoint as she fled into her home. Watson continued the pursuit throughout the house. When the juvenile and others attempted to intervene on his sister's behalf, Watson turned with the knife and threatened W.J.B.

On a subsequent occasion, the 15-year-old and her older sister awoke when they heard Watson, in the early morning darkness, climbing on the rooftop beside their bedroom window. As the girls pushed the window closed, Watson broke through the window and chased them as they fled for protection into W.J.B.'s bedroom. Watson forced his way into the bedroom and forcibly dragged the 15-year-old from the bedroom into the family bathroom. When W.J.B. entered the bathroom behind them, Watson attacked the youth, striking him with his fists. This diversion allowed the girl to flee downstairs, where the family concealed her behind the kitchen refrigerator. Unable to locate her, Watson returned outside to the ladder he had used to climb to the roof and drove the ladder through the living-room door. * * *

On the evening of Watson's death, several friends and family of the juvenile were present in the living room of the home watching television. Shortly after midnight, the juvenile's younger sister noticed Watson looking in the living-room window. As she stated, "It's Mike Watson," Watson broke in the living-room door, announcing, "You're damn right it's Mike Watson." It appeared that Watson had been drinking. The girl fled from the room screaming, and, chased by Watson, ran into W.J.B.'s bedroom where she locked herself in and barricaded the door with furniture. Several persons ran to a neighbor's house to call the police * * *. Upon learning that the police had been called, Watson fled out an upstairs window.

Two Parkersburg police officers responded to the call, but departed shortly thereafter, unable to locate Watson. Soon after their departure, Watson reappeared outside the house, shouting threats and challenges and throwing snowballs and other objects against the house. A passerby testified to a brief conversation that he had with Watson at this time, during which Watson appeared intoxicated and "clanked" a butcher knife and beer mug together in his hands while speaking of forthcoming "trouble."

While Watson was outside he challenged W.J.B. to come outside and fight him, but W.J.B. declined and requested that Watson leave the family in peace. During this time, the family had again concealed the 15-year-old behind a barricaded bedroom door. The juvenile took a shotgun from his room and positioned himself on a living-room chair with the shotgun placed across his legs. Two family friends remained seated elsewhere in the living room.

When Watson kicked open the living-room door a second time and confronted W.J.B., he again asked Watson to leave. Watson continued to challenge W.J.B. to fight and dared him to shoot. One of the witnesses testified that Watson held a butcher knife and tapped it against the door frame. At the trial, the juvenile testified that he did not recall seeing the knife, but that Watson's hand was obstructed from his view. Amid continued threats and profanity, Watson advanced upon W.J.B., whereupon the juvenile, without raising the shotgun from his lap, pulled the trigger, shooting Watson in the chest. He died immediately. * * *

The issue before this Court on appeal is whether the facts of this case are sufficient to support a finding of voluntary manslaughter in light of the testimony regarding self-defense.

The law regarding self-defense is often deceptively and simply stated: that a defendant who is not the aggressor and has reasonable grounds to believe, and actually does believe, that he is in imminent danger of death or serious bodily harm from which he could save himself only by using deadly force against his assailant has the right to employ deadly force in order to defend himself. *See State v. Kirtley*, 162 W. Va. 249 (1978) * * *; *State v. Preece*, 116 W. Va. 176 (1935) * * *.

The generality of the foregoing rule does not address in any detail the question of the "retreat" rule, an aspect of which is involved in this case where a person is assaulted in his own home. In this situation, we have recognized that a person in his own home who is subject to an unlawful intrusion and placed in immediate danger of serious bodily harm or death has no duty to retreat but may remain in place and employ deadly force to defend himself. *State v. Preece*, 116 W. Va. 176 (1935) * * *. This principle is sometimes called defense of habitation and springs from the English common law concept that a man's home is his castle. Syllabus Point 4 of *Preece* tersely states this no-retreat rule:

"A man attacked in his own home by an intruder may invoke the law of self-defense without retreating."

The West Virginia cases discussing self-defense in the home are not without some confusion. While it is quite clear that we do not require the defendant to retreat before utilizing deadly force, we have been rather vague on the question of whether the occupant can use deadly force even though the intruder has not threatened the occupant with serious bodily harm or death. In *State v. Bowman*, 155 W. Va. 562, 184 S.E.2d 314 (1971), we upheld a murder conviction where the homeowner had shot his neighbor who had run onto his porch and was at the front screen door when killed. There had been no threats exchanged and the only indicia of ill will was that earlier in the day the defendant and his wife had an argument with the deceased's wife. * * *

In those cases cited in *Bowman*, we have basically stated that "a person has the right to repel force by force in the defense of his person, his family or his habitation, and if in so doing he uses only so much force as the necessity, or apparent necessity, of the case requires, he is not guilty of any offense, though he kill his adversary in so doing." *State v. Laura*, 93 W. Va. 250, 256-257 (1923) * * *.

The foregoing rule on the use of force, however, is merely a bland statement of the general rule that "the amount of force which [a defendant] may justifiably use must be reasonably related to the threatened harm which he seeks to avoid." W. LaFave & A. Scott, *Criminal Law* 392 (1972). The more particular statement as to the amount of force that can be used in self-defense is that normally one can return deadly force only if he reasonably believes that the assailant is about to inflict death or serious bodily harm; otherwise, where he is threatened only with non-deadly force, he may use only non-deadly force in return. *Rose v. Commonwealth*, 422 S.W.2d 130 (Ky. 1967) * * *.

A number of courts with the approval of commentators have taken the position that the occupant of a dwelling is not limited in using deadly force against an unlawful intruder to the situation where the occupant is threatened with serious bodily injury or death, but he may use deadly force if the unlawful intruder threatens imminent physical violence or the commission of a felony and the occupant reasonably believes deadly force is necessary. *Thomas v. State*, 255 Ala. 632 (1951); *People v. Givens*, 26 Ill. 2d 371 (1962) * * *.

We do not find any clear discussion in our cases of whether the occupant in his home may use deadly force to repel an intruder even though the intruder has not placed the occupant in fear of imminent danger of serious bodily harm or death. * * *

The taking of life to prevent the commission of a felony, however, is not limited to self-defense in the home, but is part of a more general rule relating to crime prevention. W. LaFave & A. Scott, *Criminal Law* 406 (1972). Moreover, even though we recognize the rule that an occupant of a dwelling may justifiably kill an intruder who intends to commit a felony, where no other means to prevent it are available, this still does not answer the limited inquiry of whether the occupant may kill to prevent personal violence not amounting to a felony or a threat of death or serious bodily injury.

Despite the lack of a clear statement in our past decisions, when our cases of self-defense in the home are analyzed, it appears that we have not required the occupant to be under a reasonable apprehension of imminent danger of serious bodily harm or death in order to use deadly force on the intruder.

In *Preece*, the defendant, armed with a pistol, shot the victim as he was ascending the apartment steps unarmed and intending to assault the defendant. In *State v. Hurst*, 93 W. Va. 222, 116 S.E. 248 (1923), the victim had been drinking and intruded into the defendant's home. He knew the defendant's family since he was engaged to marry one of its members. After initially pushing the defendant on the porch, he proceeded to go into the house, slam the lid on the sewing machine and engage in some cursing before returning to the porch. He approached the defendant with an upraised arm and when the defendant pushed him away, the victim reached into his pocket at which point he was stabbed by the defendant.

State v. Laura is much like *Preece* except that the victim had used abusive language and threatened to kill the defendant at a restaurant in a hotel operated by the defendant. The defendant, who lived in the hotel, went to his room and obtained a pistol. The deceased was killed as he started up the steps to the defendant's room. * * *

In the foregoing cases, we found that self-defense was available even though the facts did not necessarily show that the defendant home-occupant was in fear of imminent danger of serious bodily harm or death. We recognize that there are some jurisdictions which restrict the use of deadly force in the home to those situations where the intruder imminently threatens death or serious bodily harm. *E.g., Harris v. State*, 104 So. 2d 739 (Fla. App. 1958) * * *.

We believe that there are sound policy reasons for permitting the home-owner to repel with deadly force a violent intrusion into his home where he has reasonable grounds to believe the intruder will commit a felony or personal injury on the occupant and that deadly force is the only means available to prevent it. First, there is still basic vitality to the ancient English rule that a man's home is his castle, and he has the right to expect some privacy and security within its confines. This rule arises from a societal recognition that the home shelters and is a physical refuge for the basic unit of society—the family. In the criminal law there is a marked recognition of this fact, as shown by the difference in the right to arrest a criminal without a warrant as between his home and a public place. *Payton v. New York*, 445 U.S. 573 (1980) * * *.

Second, we believe that from the standpoint of the intruder the violent and unlawful entry into a dwelling with intent to injure the occupants or commit a felony carries a common sense conclusion that he may be met with deadly force, and that his culpability matches the risk of danger. We also recognize that there is often a certain vulnerability to the occupant of a dwelling who is forced to confront the unlawful intruder in the privacy of his home, without any expectation of a public response or help.

Finally, while it can be acknowledged that one element of a mature criminal justice system is to narrow the areas where individuals may resort to self-help in the infliction of punishment or the taking of life, no court has seen fit to abolish the concept of self-defense. * * *

We recognize that the reasonableness of the occupant's belief and actions in using deadly force must be judged "in the light of the circumstances in which he acted at the time and is not measured by subsequently developed facts." *State v. Reppert*, 132 W. Va. 675, 691 (1949). The reasonableness of the defendant's belief and conduct may depend on the past actions of the deceased, and for this reason the victim's history of threats, brandishing of arms, and violence toward the defendant and his family and his general reputation for violence are admissible evidence on the issue of self-defense. *See State v. Bowyer,* 143 W. Va. 302 (1957) * * *.

In the present case, the fact that the juvenile took the precaution of arming and positioning himself in the living room of his home after the first assault on the house and his younger sister by the victim Watson does not diminish his claim of self-defense. Those acts are consistent with the established right to arm and defend himself and his family within the confines of his own home. *State v. Preece*, 116 W. Va. 176 (1935) * * *. We have recognized the accepted rule that the defendant may interpose the defense of self-defense in protecting a member of his family as well as in protecting himself. *State v. Wilson*, 145 W. Va. 261 (1960) * * *.

Consequently, the adjudication of delinquency is vacated and the case is remanded for an entry of a judgment of acquittal.

Case Focus

1. When a person acts in self-defense, what type of force is he generally allowed to use?
2. When a person is in his home and acts in self-defense, is he subject to the same limitations on his use of force as he would be if he were not in his home?
3. When a person is in his home, is he under any duty to retreat before engaging in self-defense? Would it be different if he were not in his home?
4. When a person is in his home, is he allowed to use deadly force when he is not faced with an imminent threat of death or great bodily harm? If so, when can he use deadly force in self-defense in his home?

• • • • • • • •

An important issue with respect to the defense of self-defense is whether the defendant must retreat before using force to defend himself. When a defendant decides to use non-deadly force to defend himself, he need not retreat. When the defendant uses deadly force, the issue is more complicated. If the defendant is in his home or in his business, he does not need to retreat before using deadly force. If the defendant is at a place other than his home or business, in some states he is required to retreat if he can safely do so before resorting to the use of deadly force; in other states he need not retreat.

Self-Defense and the Battered Woman's Syndrome

In recent years there has been widespread advocacy for courts to recognize what has been called battered woman's syndrome (BWS). One aspect of that advocacy has included efforts to eliminate the imminence of physical harm requirement from the defense of self-defense in those cases where female defendants claim to have been suffering from BWS when they killed their husband or domestic partner or had him killed. That effort is driven by the fact that in virtually all of the so-called BWS cases the allegedly abused woman either killed her husband or domestic partner or had him killed at a time when she was not being threatened, such as when the husband or domestic partner was sleeping or eating, thus making the defense of self-defense unavailable.[13]

BWS advocates assert that syndrome sufferers become hypervigilant to cues of impending danger and accurately perceive danger from the abuser before others would perceive it. Such hypervigilance, BWS advocates say, accounts for what amounts to a preemptive strike by the battered woman when she kills her abuser during a period of apparent quiescence.[14] For that reason, they argue the use of deadly force is justified even though physical danger is not imminent.[15]

BWS advocates have faced two hurdles, which have proven formidable. The first hurdle is to convince courts that BWS exists. That has been difficult because there is a serious question about whether the syndrome actually exists, and there has been serious criticism of the research that purports to prove its existence.[16] "That criticism is generally centered upon a lack of scientific rigor in the research methodology."[17]

The second hurdle is the view that if the imminency requirement is eliminated from the defense of self-defense in cases involving defendants allegedly suffering from BWS, it would be akin to allowing a woman to summarily impose capital punishment on her husband or domestic partner for past or future conduct.[18] One court observed that while many people and the media appear to espouse the notion that a victim of an abuser is entitled to kill him, to allow that based on the subjective conclusion of the victim as to the abuser's past or future conduct would amount to a leap into anarchy.[19] As a result, a vast majority of courts have refused to eliminate the imminency requirement in alleged BWS cases.

What do you think about this?

B. Defense of Others

A person is allowed to use reasonable force to defend another person when he reasonably believes that other person is in danger of imminent unlawful bodily harm from an adversary and he reasonably believes the use of force is necessary to avoid that danger. As with the defense of self-defense, the defender's use of force must be proportional to the force being directed at the person being attacked. In most states the defense of others defense is applicable without regard to the nature of the relationship between the defender and the person being defended. In a few states deadly force can be used in defense of others only if the defender has a certain familial or other preexisting relationship with the person he is defending. In those states, for example, if the defender uses deadly force to defend another, the defense of others defense is only applicable if the person being defended is the defender's spouse, parent, child, mistress, employer, or employee, but not if the person being defended is one's neighbor or lifelong friend.[20]

One of the significant problems that arises in some defense of others cases occurs when the defender is mistaken about whether the person to whose rescue he comes is in actual danger of illegal bodily harm. In such cases the defendant's mistake is usually as to the unlawfulness of the force being directed toward the person he is defending. For example, David is walking down a street and he sees Thomas (who is in street clothes) push Edmund against a building and draw a gun. David, thinking that Edmund is being robbed, runs up behind Thomas and strikes him with a rock. Edmund thanks David and runs away, after which David sees a police badge on Thomas's person. It turns out that Thomas was a detective trying to arrest Edmund for a violent crime.

The law has taken two different approaches to determining the applicability of the defense in that situation. In an approach taken in some states the defender has no more privilege to use force to defend a person than the person who he is defending.[21] Under that approach

David in the above example would not be able to assert the defense of others defense in a prosecution for criminal battery to Thomas. An approach taken in other states is that, notwithstanding the actual facts, if the defendant reasonably believed that the person who he was defending was being unlawfully attacked, he can assert the defense of another.[22] Under this approach, notwithstanding that Edmund was not legally allowed to resist the arrest, in a prosecution of David for battery to Thomas, David would be able to assert the defense of others defense.

With modifications to take into account the different circumstances, generally the duty to retreat rules applicable to the defense of self-defense are applicable to the defense of others defense. Under those modified duty to retreat rules, if the person being defended can retreat safely, the person coming to his aid must attempt to convince him to retreat. Consistent with the non-retreat rules of self-defense in one's home or business, a person coming to the aid of another in defending that person's home or business has no duty to convince the victim to retreat and can assist the victim in defending those locations without retreating.

The Debate Over Establishing a Cultural Background Defense

The rise of the multiculturalism movement has given support to attempts to assert a defendant's cultural background as a defense to his criminal conduct.[23] The theory underlying what is called the cultural background defense is that the criminal justice system should recognize that persons of different cultures are entitled to express their cultural identities through practices that may embody values diverging from the values of mainstream society.[24] The cultural background defense has been deployed in a number of cases, including one where a Japanese woman, upon hearing of her husband's infidelity, carried her two young children into the sea and drowned them and tried to drown herself, but survived. When charged with the murder of her children she asserted she was practicing *oyako-shinju*, an accepted and honored custom in Japan.[25] The defense was also deployed in a case where a member of the Hmong tribe living in California abducted a coed at Fresno State University in a ritual of "marriage capture" practiced in his culture, took the woman to his home, and "consummated the marriage." The woman pressed charges for rape.[26] Despite the importuning of defense lawyers and many in legal academia to establish a formal cultural background defense, no American court has recognized it.[27]

An alternate argument deployed in an effort to establish a cultural background defense is that such a defense is required under Article 27 of the International Convention on Civil and Political Rights (the ICCPR), which the United States ratified in 1992. That argument has been rejected because when the U.S. Senate ratified the Convention it did so with the express reservation that certain articles of the ICCPR were not self-executing.[28] As such, Article 27 of the ICCPR does not create enforceable obligations.[29]

Assertion of the cultural background defense as an absolute defense is rare as it is most commonly used as a way of rebutting the *mens rea* element of the crime the defendant is charged with committing.[30] The essential position of advocates of this type of defense is that a defendant's cultural background will negate or mitigate criminal responsibility where acts are committed under a reasonable, good faith belief in their propriety, based upon the defendant's cultural heritage or tradition.[31]

The debate over whether cultural background should be recognized as a formal defense or whether it should be recognized by the criminal justice system in some lesser way, whether such as by possibly negating the *mens rea* element of an offense or at sentencing, raises very serious questions both for society and the criminal law. Those questions include whether a society has the right to prohibit certain conduct by all persons within its borders and make those prohibitions effective by imposing criminal sanctions against all violators, whether or not such a defense is unfair to the majority to whom it is unavailable; and the effect such special cultural defenses have on support for the criminal justice system by the general public and on the cohesiveness of society itself.

What do you think about these issues? How, if at all, does the maxim, "Ignorance of the law is no excuse" apply to this issue, or should it not be applied?

C. Defense of Property

A person is allowed to use reasonable force to protect his property from trespass or theft if he reasonably believes both that his property is in immediate danger of being trespassed upon or stolen and such force is necessary to avoid that danger. Deadly force can never be used to defend property unless the possessor of the property is faced with the danger of immediate death or great bodily harm. In that situation, whether the possessor of the property would be entitled to use deadly force would be determined by the principles of self-defense.

D. Necessity

The defense of necessity is available when a person is faced with a choice of evils: obeying the law (which will result in one evil) or disobeying the law (which will result in a different but lesser evil). For example, there is a forest fire raging out of control that is moving toward and will destroy a town. The only way to stop the fire from consuming the town is to create a firebreak, and to create the firebreak eight homes must be blown up. The law will allow a person to blow up the homes because their destruction is a lesser evil than the destruction of a whole town.

Like the other affirmative defenses, the defense of necessity has been codified in a number of different statutory variations in different states. Broadly speaking the defense of necessity has three elements: (1) the defendant is faced with a clear and imminent danger; (2) the defendant can reasonably expect his action will be effective in abating the danger; and (3) there is no legally permissible alternative action that will be effective.[32]

At common law there was an important distinction between the defense of duress and the defense of necessity: The defense of duress was only available when the imminent danger in response to which the defendant acted emanated from a human source while the defense of necessity was available only when that danger emanated from the forces of nature. For example, if Horatio throws valuable cargo off of a ship because Carlos is holding a gun to him and threatens to kill him if he does not, and Horatio is prosecuted for destroying the cargo, he cannot assert the defense of necessity because the source of danger emanated from human action. (Under those circumstances Horatio may be able to assert the defense of duress, which was discussed in Chapter 12.) But if there is a raging storm and the ship is in danger of sinking if the cargo is not thrown off and Horatio throws it off, then, if the other conditions of the defense are satisfied, should Horatio be charged with a crime based on his action destroying the cargo, he can assert the defense of necessity.

In some statutory formulations of the defense the distinction between the sources of danger has been abolished; in others the forces of nature limitation has been retained; while in others the statutes are silent, leaving it to courts to decide whether the legislature intended to keep or jettison the common law distinction.

Whether or not the defense of necessity is limited to necessity arising from the forces of nature, the defense is not available if the defendant himself had any role in creating the conditions that gave rise to the necessity. For example, a convicted felon, who under the law could not possess a firearm, would be precluded from asserting the defense of necessity when his asserted reason for needing to carry a firearm is that his girlfriend's husband has threatened to kill him and once attempted to run him down with a car. The defense of necessity would be unavailable in that case because by participating in the romantic relationship with the married woman the defendant's action had some role in creating the conditions that gave rise to the necessity of carrying a firearm.[33] The defense of necessity is also unavailable if the legislature has decided to abrogate it as to a particular crime. For example, the legislature may provide that the defense of necessity is not available as a defense to a charge of drunken driving.

Long v. Commonwealth

Court of Appeals of Virginia 23 Va. App. 537 (1996)

ANNUNZIATA, J. Following a jury trial, appellant, Patrick Raymond Long, was convicted of driving after having been adjudicated an habitual offender and after having been previously convicted of the same offense. Appellant contends that the trial court erred in refusing to allow him to present a necessity defense * * *. We disagree and affirm.

I.

At approximately 10:15 a.m. on November 18, 1994, Officer Sherrie Bishop of the Alexandria Police Department stopped a vehicle which appellant was driving and in which appellant's sister, Mary Jacobs, was a passenger. The propriety of the stop is not at issue. Appellant was unable to produce a driver's license in response to Bishop's request, but he identified himself as Jack Keville and provided a date of birth and social security number. Bishop ran a check on the information appellant provided and determined appellant was not Jack Keville. Bishop asked appellant to exit the vehicle and take a seat in her cruiser. Appellant eventually provided Bishop with his true name and social security number. Upon running a check based on that information, Bishop determined that appellant had been adjudicated an habitual offender. Bishop arrested appellant, and appellant was later indicted for driving after having been adjudicated an habitual offender, having been previously convicted of a like offense in violation of Code §46.2-357, which, for all purposes relevant to this appeal, read the same in 1994 as it does today.

Appellant sought to establish the defense of necessity. The Commonwealth filed a motion *in limine* seeking to preclude appellant from offering evidence related to the defense. The trial court ruled that because the statute addressed necessity in the context of mitigation of punishment, the legislature intended to preclude the defense of necessity on the merits. On that ground, the court refused to admit evidence relating to the defense. However, the court nonetheless permitted appellant to relate the facts and circumstances of the offense during the guilt phase of the trial. The court also allowed appellant to elicit limited testimony from three witnesses to corroborate his recitation of the events.

Appellant's motion to dismiss the indictment, in which he challenged the validity of the order declaring him an habitual offender, was denied. The trial court found that the order was clear and unambiguous. The order, entered February 20, 1986, states, in part, that:

> Patrick Rammond [sic] Long is hereby DECLARED to be a Habitual Offender and this [sic] his/her privilege to operate a motor vehicle in the Commonwealth of Virginia, BE and is HEREBY REVOKED. . . . * * *

Appellant testified that he knew he had been adjudicated an habitual offender. He testified that he disregarded that fact, drove the vehicle, and lied about his identity when stopped, because he believed his sister's health was endangered and she needed to get to the hospital.

II.

The trial court ruled that the habitual offender statute abrogates the defense of necessity in such cases and refused to allow appellant to present a necessity defense. The propriety of this ruling is a question of law. [Because we find that the defense of necessity is unavailable, we need not decide whether the evidence is sufficient to support an instruction on that issue.]

The common law defense of necessity is premised on a resolution of conflicting public policy issues.

> [It] traditionally addresses the dilemma created when physical forces beyond the actor's control renders "illegal conduct the lesser of two evils." If one who is starving eats another's food to save his own life, the defense of necessity may bar a conviction for the larceny of the other's food. The essential elements of this defense include: (1) a reasonable belief that the action was necessary to avoid an imminent threatened harm; (2) a lack of other adequate means to avoid the threatened harm; and (3) a direct causal relationship that may be reasonably anticipated between the action taken and the avoidance of the harm.

Buckley v. City of Falls Church, 7 Va. App. 32, 33, 371 S.E.2d 827, 827-828 (1988) (citations omitted).

> The rationale of the necessity defense is not that a person, when faced with the pressure of circumstances of nature, lacks the mental element which the crime in question requires. Rather, it is this reason of public policy: the law ought to promote the achievement of higher values at the expense of lesser values, and sometimes the greater good for society will be accomplished by violating the literal language of the criminal law.

1 W. LaFave & A. Scott, *Substantive Criminal Law* §5.4(a), at 629 (1986).

> In some sense, the necessity defense allows us to act as individual legislatures, amending a particular criminal provision or crafting a one-time exception to it,

subject to court review, when a real legislature would formally do the same under those circumstances.

United States v. Schoon, 971 F.2d 193, 196-197 (9th Cir. 1991), *cert. denied*, 504 U.S. 940 (1992).

However, the legislature may abrogate the common law rule by choosing to resolve the conflicting public policy matters by the enactment of law. It follows, therefore, that

> the defense of necessity is available only in situations wherein the legislature has not itself, in its criminal statute, made a determination of values. If it has done so, its decision governs.

1 LaFave & Scott, *supra*, at 629. In other words, where the legislature has resolved the balance of the harms to be avoided, an individual is preempted from relying on the defense of necessity as a means of re-weighing those harms.

This legislative choice-of-values analysis, while specific to the defense of necessity, comports with general principles of Virginia law relating to the construction of statutes in derogation of the common law. * * *

We find that the plain meaning of Code §46.2-357 clearly "encompasses the entire subject covered by the common law" defense of necessity. The legislature chose to relegate the factual circumstances which would give rise to the common law defense of necessity to the punishment phase of the habitual offender proceedings. This decision was, in effect, a determination of values—that there could be no guilt-nullifying justification for an habitual offender, twice convicted of driving after having been adjudicated an habitual offender, to drive. Accordingly, we find that the legislature intended to abrogate the common law defense of necessity as a justification for the commission of the criminal act by a twice-convicted offender. The trial court's refusal to permit evidence related to this defense was, therefore, not erroneous. * * *

For the foregoing reasons, appellant's conviction is affirmed.

Case Focus

1. What are the elements of the necessity defense?
2. What did the court say is the rationale for the necessity defense?
3. Can the legislature eliminate the necessity defense as a defense to a crime?

• • • • • • • •

In one important way the defense of necessity is broader than the closely related defense of duress: At common law and still in most states today the defense of necessity is available for the crime of murder, a crime for which the defense of duress is not available.[34] Some of the most famous cases involving the defense of necessity for the crime of murder have historically arisen in situations where the death of one or more people was necessary to allow some greater number of people to survive. One such case involved an overcrowded lifeboat that was in imminent danger of sinking unless some of its occupants were thrown overboard and left to drown. In that case the defense of necessity excused throwing some small number of people overboard to save the lives of a larger number of remaining occupants,[35] but an important legal issue was the method by which those who were sacrificed were selected.[36]

Torture and the Defense of Necessity

The propriety of using torture to obtain information from prisoners has been the subject of much debate in the media and in academia. While there is no specific federal statute that makes torture committed in the United States by an agent of the federal government a crime, such conduct clearly constitutes a violation of a number of more general federal statutes and, if committed by an agent of a state, would violate such state criminal statutes as battery or aggravated battery. There are two views on the propriety of using torture: the absolutist view, which is that torture is never acceptable, and the non-absolutist view, a leading proponent of which is Judge Richard Posner of the U.S. Court of Appeals for the Seventh Circuit. Judge Posner has written that no one who doubts that if the stakes are high enough, torture is permissible, should be in a position of responsibility.[37]

The debate about the propriety of torture notwithstanding, from a legal standpoint, if the conditions under which an agent of the government resorts to torture to extract information meet the conditions of the necessity defense, he may be able to assert that defense in any subsequent prosecution of him for that conduct.

The most common situation where many argue torture may be acceptable is the ticking bomb scenario. As postulated in that scenario, a bomb has been planted in a place where, if it is not found and disarmed, a large number of people will be killed, and one of the persons who planted or assisted in planting it is in police custody. The question in that scenario is whether torture can be used to extract information about the location of the bomb. While the ticking bomb scenario is frequently discussed in journals, at legal and academic conferences and often is the subject of movies and novels, it is seldom likely to be encountered by law enforcement, and its element of immediacy is often criticized as lacking reality.[38]

A situation much more likely to be seen by law enforcement, and one drawn on an actual case, would be one where someone, perhaps a young child, has been kidnapped, and the kidnapper is caught but refuses to disclose the location of the child. Can torture be used against the kidnapper to extract information about the location of the child if the life of the child is at stake? In the actual case from which this example is drawn, a police official gave a written directive to his subordinates to use torture to obtain information about the location of the kidnapped child.[39] If a government official uses torture to extract information, and the government agent employing the torture is prosecuted under the applicable criminal statute, is the defense of necessity available to him?

Clearly, in both of these examples the defense of necessity would appear to be applicable because in both, death will likely ensue if the information is not extracted,[40] and the method of extraction, while perhaps considered distasteful at best and barbaric at worst, is not calculated to result in death. What do you think about this?

REVIEW QUESTIONS

1. What are the elements of the defense of self-defense?

2. What are the two different types of force that a person can use in self-defense, and under what circumstances can each of those types of force be used?

3. Is a person always required to retreat before using force to defend himself; if not, under what circumstances is he not required to retreat?

4. When a person comes to the defense of another, what type of force may he use to defend that other person?

5. Is the defense of another available to a person who comes to the aid of a total stranger, or must the defender and the person attacked have some preexisting relationship in order to allow the defender to take advantage of the defense?

6. When can a person assert a defense of property defense, and what type of force can be used to defend property?

7. Historically, what was the difference, if any, between the defense of duress and the defense of necessity?

8. What difference, if any, is there between the type of crimes to which the defense of necessity is applicable and the type of crimes to which the defense of duress is available?

9. What are the characteristics of defenses that fall into the category called justification defenses?

10. How do justification defenses differ from excuse defenses?

ADDITIONAL READING

Alan M. Dershowitz, *Want to Torture? Get a Warrant* (January 22, 2002). *http://articles.sfgate.com/2002=01=22/opinion/17527284_1_physical= pressure=torture=terrorist.* Site last visited May 23, 2008.

R.A. Posner, "Torture, Terrorism, and Interrogation," in S. Levinson (ed.), *Torture: A Collection* (2004).

Eric Posner & Adriane Vermeule, *Should Coercive Interrogation Be Legal?* 104 Mich. L. Rev. 671 (February 2006).

ENDNOTES

1. *United States v. Jumah*, 493 F.3d 868 (7th Cir. 2007).
2. *People v. Allegri*, 109 Ill. 2d 309 (1985).
3. Paul H. Robinson, Myron Moskovitz, & Jane Grall, *Criminal Law Defenses* §121 (2007).
4. *State v. Goldberg*, 12 N.J. Super. 293 (1951).
5. Model Penal Code §3.04.
6. Wayne R. LaFave, *Substantive Criminal Law* §10.4 (2007).
7. *State v. Moore*, 158 N.J. 292 (1999).
8. *People v. Landrum*, 160 Mich. App. 159 (1987).
9. *People v. Goetz*, 68 N.Y.2d 96 (1986).
10. *State v. Hazlett*, 16 N.D. 426 (1907).
11. *Commonwealth v. Glass*, 401 Mass. 799 (1988).
12. *State v. W.J.B.*, 166 W. Va. 602 (1981).
13. In those cases where physical harm to the woman is imminent or actually occurring, BWS is seldom an issue because the victim is usually able to assert self-defense and satisfy the imminence requirement.
14. Milhizer, *Group Status and Criminal Defenses: Logical Relationship or Marriage of Convenience?* 71 Mo. L. Rev. 547 (Summer 2006).
15. *Id.*
16. *Daniels v. Henry*, 2007 WL 424441 (N.D. Cal. 2007).
17. *Id.*
18. *See State v. Stewart*, 243 Kan. 639 (1988).
19. *Jahnke v. State*, 682 P.2d 996 (Wyo. 1984).
20. *E.g.*, S.D. Cod. Laws §22-16-35.
21. *People v. Young*, 11 N.Y.2d 274 (1962).
22. *State v. Fair*, 45 N.J. 77 (1965).
23. Eugene Milhizer, *Group Status and Criminal Defenses: Logical Relationship or Marriage of Convenience?* 71 Mo. L. Rev. 547 (2006).
24. Sharon M. Tomao, *The Cultural Defense: Traditional or Formal?* 10 Geo. Immigr. L.J. 241 (Winter 1996).
25. Taryn F. Goldstein, *Cultural Conflicts in Court: Should the American Criminal Justice System Formally Recognize a Cultural Defense?* 99 Dick. L. Rev. 141 (Fall 1994).
26. *Id.*
27. Tomao, *supra* n.24.
28. *United States v. Rafle*, 2012 WL 1424438 (S.D. Ind. 2012).
29. *Id.*
30. *United States v. Rafle*, 2012 WL at 1424438, n.3.
31. John C. Lyman, Note, *Cultural Defense: Viable Doctrine or Wishful Thinking?* 9 Crim. Just. J. 87 (1986).
32. *United States v. Seward*, 687 F.2d 1270 (10th Cir. 1982).
33. *United States v. Luker*, 395 F.3d 830 (8th Cir. 2005).
34. *Hunt v. State*, 753 So. 2d 609 (Fla. DCA 5th Dist. 2000).
35. *United States v. Holmes*, 26 F. Cas. 360, No. 15383 (C.C.E.D. Pa. 1842).
36. *Id.*
37. Richard A. Posner, *Torture, Terrorism, and Interrogation*, in S. Levinson (ed.), Torture: A Collection (2004), 291.
38. David Luban, *Liberalism, Torture, and the Ticking Bomb*, 91 Va. L. Rev. 1425 (October 2005).
39. Alon Harel & Assaf Sharon, *What Is Really Wrong with Torture?* 6 Intl. Crim. Just. 241 (May 2008).
40. One objection to torture is that information obtained from people subjected to it is not reliable. The problem with this objection is that sometimes the information obtained is reliable. One such example involves a 1995 Al Qaeda plot to bomb 11 U.S. airliners and assassinate the Pope. The plot was

thwarted when Philippine police captured one of the bomb makers and tortured him for weeks until he revealed information about the plot that allowed law enforcement to thwart it. Charles Krauthammer, *The Truth About Torture*, The Weekly Standard, December 12, 2005. *http://weeklystandard.com/Utilities/printer_preview.asp?idArticle=6400&R=13A8B29BA9*. Site last visited May 23, 2008. In another example, following the kidnapping of Israeli soldier Nachshon Waxman by Palestinian terrorists, the Israelis captured the driver of the car used to spirit Waxman away. The Israelis tortured the driver until he revealed where Waxman was being held. *Id.*

Chapter 14
Affirmative Defenses—Failure of Proof and Offense Modification Defenses

Chapter Objectives

After reading this chapter, you should be able to

- Understand what failure of proof defenses are
- Explain the difference between mistakes of law and mistakes of fact
- Understand what offense modification defenses are
- Understand what type of impossibility is a defense to a crime
- Explain the victim-accomplice defense
- Understand the inevitably incident conduct defense and Wharton's Rule

> The want of means to know the Law, totally Excuseth: For the Law whereof a man has no means to enforme himself, is not obligatory. But the want of diligence to enquire, shall not be considered as a want of means.
> —Thomas Hobbes, *Leviathan*, Chapter 27

In this chapter we will examine two categories of affirmative defenses: (A) failure of proof defenses and (B) offense modification defenses. This is the last of the chapters dealing with affirmative defenses where the defenses are culpability based; that is, where the defense is focused on the responsibility of the defendant for criminal conduct.

A. Failure of Proof Defenses

The category of defenses called failure of proof defenses consists of those defenses in which the defense attacks a particular element of an offense. With failure of proof defenses, some condition or circumstance exists that negates an element of the offense with which the defendant is charged. As with all of the affirmative defenses, the defendant must assert the defense; that is, he must claim that a condition or circumstance existed at the time the charged offense was committed that negates an element of that charge, and he must produce some evidence that the asserted condition or circumstance actually existed. In this section we will examine two of the most important failure of proof defenses: (1) mistake and (2) alibi.[1]

1. Mistake

There are two basic types of mistakes that are defenses in criminal law: mistakes of fact and mistakes of law. Mistakes of fact are usually defenses to a criminal charge whereas, depending upon the nature of the mistake, a mistake of law may or may not be a defense.

A mistake of fact or ignorance with respect to a fact (for simplicity, hereinafter referred to simply as "mistake" or "mistake of fact, respectively") is a defense if, because of the mistake, a defendant did not have the mental state that is an essential element of the offense with which he is charged. For example, if a person takes a hog from a neighbor's yard and slaughters it, honestly believing that it is his hog when, in fact, the hog actually belongs to someone else and had wandered into the neighbor's yard, he does not commit the crime of theft because he has not knowingly taken property owned by another.[2]

To be able to use the mistake of fact defense, the defendant's mistake of fact must be an erroneous perception of an existing fact and not a mistaken belief about something that might take place in the future.[3] For example, Stephanie shoots a gun in the direction of Roger to scare him but not to hit him; at the moment Stephanie shoots, Roger steps into the line of fire and is shot and killed. If Stephanie asserts that when she shot she did not know that Roger would step into the line of fire, she did not act under a mistake of fact because her mistake was not about a present fact, but was instead about a future fact.[4]

Whether a mistake of law is a defense is a more complicated question. If the defendant engages in conduct that violates a criminal law and does not know that the conduct is a crime, his mistake as to the existence or meaning of the criminal statute is not a defense.[5] When, however, the ignorance or mistake relates to the understanding of a non-penal statute and that mistaken understanding results in the defendant engaging in conduct that is a crime, that ignorance or mistake may, depending on the *mens rea* element of the offense, be a defense.

If the *mens rea* element of the offense is knowledge or general intent, then the mistake of law is not a defense. For example, if a statute defines the term "security" and makes it a crime to knowingly sell securities that have not been registered with the state securities agency, and Stuart mistakenly believes that the instruments he is selling are not securities, his mistake is no defense to a charge of knowingly selling unregistered securities.[6] If, however, the *mens rea* requires a knowledge of the law, as does the term "willful" in the criminal provisions of the Internal Revenue Code,[7] then the mistake of law is a defense. For example, if Stuart believed that wages were not included within the definition of income in the Internal Revenue Code and as a result did not file income tax returns because he did not believe he had income, his mistake of law as to the meaning of "income" is a defense if he is charged with the crime of failing to file an income tax return.[8]

If the defendant's mistake is as to the unconstitutionality of a statute, that mistake, no matter what the *mens rea* element of an offense, is not a defense because such a mistake necessarily shows a knowledge by the defendant of the statute she violated.[9]

Cheek v. United States

Supreme Court of the United States (1991) 498 U.S. 192

JUSTICE WHITE delivered the opinion of the Court.

Title 26, §7201 of the United States Code provides that any person "who willfully attempts in any manner to evade or defeat any tax imposed by this title or the payment thereof" shall be guilty of a felony. Under 26 USC. §7203, "any person required under this title . . . or by regulations made under authority thereof to make a return . . . who willfully fails to . . . make such return" shall be guilty of a misdemeanor. This case turns on the meaning of the word "willfully" as used in §§7201 and 7203.

I

Petitioner John L. Cheek has been a pilot for American Airlines since 1973. He filed federal income tax returns through 1979 but thereafter ceased to file returns. He also claimed an increasing number of withholding allowances—eventually claiming 60 allowances by mid-1980—and for the years 1981 to 1984 indicated on his W-4 forms that he was exempt from federal income taxes. In 1983, petitioner unsuccessfully sought a refund of all tax withheld by his employer in 1982. Petitioner's income during this period at all times far exceeded the minimum necessary to trigger the statutory filing requirement.

As a result of his activities, petitioner was indicted for 10 violations of federal law. He was charged with six counts of willfully failing to file a federal income tax return for the years 1980, 1981, and 1983 through 1986, in violation of 26 USC. §7203. He was further charged with three counts of willfully attempting to evade his income taxes for the years 1980, 1981, and 1983 in violation of §7201. In those years, American Airlines withheld substantially less than the amount of tax petitioner owed because of the numerous allowances and exempt status he claimed on his W-4 forms. The tax offenses with which petitioner was charged are specific intent crimes that require the defendant to have acted willfully.

At trial, the evidence established that between 1982 and 1986, petitioner was involved in at least four civil cases that challenged various aspects of the federal income tax system. In all four of those cases, the plaintiffs were informed by the courts that many of their arguments, including that they were not taxpayers within the meaning of the tax laws, that wages are not income, that the Sixteenth Amendment does not authorize the imposition of an income tax on individuals, and that the Sixteenth Amendment is unenforceable, were frivolous or had been repeatedly rejected by the courts. During this time period, petitioner also attended at least two criminal trials of persons charged with tax offenses. In addition, there was evidence that in 1980 or 1981 an attorney had advised Cheek that the courts had rejected as frivolous the claim that wages are not income.

Cheek represented himself at trial and testified in his defense. He admitted that he had not filed personal income tax returns during the years in question. He testified that as early as 1978, he had begun attending seminars sponsored by, and following the advice of, a group that believes, among other things, that the federal tax system is unconstitutional. Some of the speakers at these meetings were lawyers who purported to give professional opinions about the invalidity of the federal income tax laws. Cheek produced a letter from an attorney stating that the Sixteenth Amendment did not authorize a tax on wages and salaries but only on gain or profit. Petitioner's defense was that, based on the indoctrination he received from this group and from his own study, he sincerely believed that the tax laws were being unconstitutionally enforced and that his actions during the 1980-1986 period were lawful. He therefore argued that he had acted without the willfulness required for conviction of the various offenses with which he was charged.

In the course of its instructions, the trial court advised the jury that to prove "willfulness" the Government must prove the voluntary and intentional violation of a known legal duty * * *. The court further advised the jury that an objectively reasonable good-faith misunderstanding of the law would negate willfulness, but mere disagreement with the law would not. The court described Cheek's beliefs about the income tax system [Those beliefs included, among other things, that his wages from a private employer, American Airlines, do not constitute income under the Internal Revenue Service laws] and instructed the jury that if it found that Cheek "honestly and reasonably believed that he was not required to pay income taxes or to file tax returns," App. 81, a not guilty verdict should be returned.

After several hours of deliberation, the jury sent a note to the judge that stated in part:

> "We have a basic disagreement between some of us as to if Mr. Cheek honestly & reasonably believed that he was not required to pay income taxes.
>
> . . . .
>
> "Page 32 [the relevant jury instruction] discusses good faith misunderstanding & disagreement. Is there any additional clarification you can give us on this point?" *Id.*, at 85.

The District Judge responded with a supplemental instruction containing the following statements:

> "[A] person's opinion that the tax laws violate his constitutional rights does not constitute a good faith misunderstanding of the law. Furthermore, a person's disagreement with the government's tax collection systems and policies does not constitute a good faith misunderstanding of the law." *Id.*, at 86.

At the end of the first day of deliberation, the jury sent out another note saying that it still could not reach a verdict because "we are divided on the issue as to if Mr. Cheek honestly & reasonably believed that he was not required to pay income tax." *Id.*, at 87. When the jury resumed its deliberations, the District Judge gave the jury an additional instruction. This instruction stated in part that "an honest but unreasonable belief is not a defense and does not negate willfulness," *id.*, at 88 * * *. The court also instructed the jury that "persistent refusal to acknowledge the law does not constitute a good faith misunderstanding of the law." *Ibid.* Approximately two hours later, the jury returned a verdict finding petitioner guilty on all counts.

Petitioner appealed his convictions, arguing that the District Court erred by instructing the jury that only an objectively reasonable misunderstanding of the law negates the statutory willfulness requirement. The United States Court of Appeals for the Seventh Circuit rejected that contention and affirmed the convictions. 882 F.2d 1263 (1989). * * * Because the Seventh Circuit's interpretation of "willfully" as used in these statutes conflicts with the decisions of several other Courts of Appeals, see, *e.g., United States v. Whiteside*, 810 F.2d 1306, 1310-1311 (CA5 1987) * * *.

II

The general rule that ignorance of the law or a mistake of law is no defense to criminal prosecution is deeply rooted in the American legal system. See, *e.g., United States v. Smith*, 18 U.S. 153, 5 Wheat. 153, 182, 5 L. Ed. 57 (1820) (Livingston, J., dissenting) * * *. Based on the notion that the law is definite and knowable, the common law presumed that every person knew the law. This common-law rule has been applied by the Court in numerous cases construing criminal statutes. See, *e.g., United States v. International Minerals & Chemical Corp.*, 402 U.S. 558 (1971). * * *

III

Cheek accepts the * * * definition of willfulness, * * * but asserts that the District Court's instructions and the Court of Appeals' opinion departed from that definition. In particular, he challenges the ruling that a good-faith misunderstanding of the law or a good-faith belief that one is not violating the law, if it is to negate willfulness, must be objectively reasonable. We agree that the Court of Appeals and the District Court erred in this respect.

A

Willfulness, as construed by our prior decisions in criminal tax cases, requires the Government to prove that the law imposed a duty on the defendant, that the defendant knew of this duty, and that he voluntarily and intentionally violated that duty. We deal first with the case where the issue is whether the defendant knew of the duty purportedly imposed by the provision of the statute or regulation he is accused of violating, a case in which there is no claim that the provision at issue is invalid. In such a case, if the Government proves actual knowledge of the pertinent legal duty, the prosecution, without more, has satisfied the knowledge component of the willfulness requirement. But carrying this burden requires negating a defendant's claim of ignorance of the law or a claim that because of a misunderstanding of the law, he had a good-faith belief that he was not violating any of the provisions of the tax laws. This is so because one cannot be aware that the law imposes a duty upon him and yet be ignorant of it, misunderstand the law, or believe that the duty does not exist. In the end, the issue is whether, based on all the evidence, the Government has proved that the defendant was aware of the duty at issue, which cannot be true if the jury credits a good-faith misunderstanding and belief submission, whether or not the claimed belief or misunderstanding is objectively reasonable.

In this case, if Cheek asserted that he truly believed that the Internal Revenue Code did not purport to treat wages as income, and the jury believed him, the Government would not have carried its burden to prove willfulness, however unreasonable a court might deem such a belief. Of course, in deciding whether to credit Cheek's good-faith belief claim, the jury would be free to consider any admissible evidence from any source showing that Cheek was aware of his duty to file a return and to treat wages as income, including evidence showing his awareness of the relevant provisions of the Code or regulations, of court decisions rejecting his interpretation of the tax law, of authoritative rulings of the Internal Revenue Service, or of any contents of the personal income tax return forms and accompanying instructions that made it plain that wages should be returned as income[.]* * *

It was therefore error to instruct the jury to disregard evidence of Cheek's understanding that, within the meaning of the tax laws, he was not a person required to file a return or to pay income taxes and that wages are not taxable income, as incredible as such misunderstandings of and beliefs about the law might be. Of course, the more unreasonable the asserted beliefs or misunderstandings are, the more likely the jury will consider them to be nothing more than simple disagreement with known legal duties imposed by the tax laws and will find that the Government has carried its burden of proving knowledge.

B

Cheek asserted in the trial court that he should be acquitted because he believed in good faith that the income tax law is unconstitutional as applied to him and thus could not legally impose any duty upon him of which he should have been aware. Such a submission is unsound, not because Cheek's constitutional arguments are not objectively reasonable or frivolous, which they surely are, but because * * * *Murdock* [and its progeny do] * * * not support such a position. Those cases construed the willfulness requirement in the criminal provisions of the Internal Revenue Code to require proof of knowledge of the law. This was because in "our complex tax system, uncertainty often arises even among taxpayers who earnestly wish to follow the law," and "it is not the purpose of the law to penalize frank difference of opinion or innocent errors made despite the exercise of reasonable care." *United States v. Bishop*, 412 U.S. 346 (1973) * * *.

Claims that some of the provisions of the tax code are unconstitutional are submissions of a different order. They do not arise from innocent mistakes caused by the complexity of the Internal Revenue Code. Rather, they reveal full knowledge of the provisions at issue and a studied conclusion, however wrong, that those provisions are invalid and unenforceable. Thus in this case, Cheek paid his taxes for years, but after attending various seminars and based on his own study, he concluded that the income tax laws could not constitutionally require him to pay a tax.

We do not believe that Congress contemplated that such a taxpayer, without risking criminal prosecution, could ignore the duties imposed upon him by the Internal Revenue Code and refuse to utilize the mechanisms provided by Congress to present his claims of invalidity to the courts and to abide by their decisions.* * *

We thus hold that in a case like this, a defendant's views about the validity of the tax statutes are irrelevant to the issue of willfulness and need not be heard by the jury, and, if they are, an instruction to disregard them would be proper. For this purpose, it makes no difference whether the claims of invalidity are frivolous or have substance. It was therefore not error in this case for the District Judge to instruct the jury not to consider Cheek's claims that the tax laws were unconstitutional. However, it was error for the court to instruct the jury that petitioner's asserted beliefs that wages are not income and that he was not a taxpayer within the meaning of the Internal Revenue Code should not be considered by the jury in determining whether Cheek had acted willfully.

IV

For the reasons set forth in the opinion above, the judgment of the Court of Appeals is vacated, and the case is remanded for further proceedings consistent with this opinion.

It is so ordered.

Case Focus

1. Was Cheek's mistake a mistake as to the meaning of a criminal statute or some other statute?
2. According to the Court, why is a mistake about the constitutionality of a statute not a defense?

• • • • • • • •

2. Alibi

An alibi defense is a classic example of a failure of proof defense. A defendant who raises an alibi defense asserts that he was somewhere else at the time the crime with which he is charged was committed, and he must produce some evidence to prove that assertion. The significance of an alibi defense is that by raising it and putting on some evidence of an alibi the defendant shifts the burden back to the prosecution to prove beyond a reasonable doubt that the defendant was the person who committed the offense. As a result, it is possible by merely asserting the defense and putting on some evidence to support it that the defendant can be acquitted if the prosecution is not able to rebut that evidence beyond a reasonable doubt.

B. Offense Modification Defenses

Offense modification defenses are defenses that are exceptions to certain types or certain groups of criminal offenses. With these defenses the defendant has engaged in conduct that satisfies all of the elements of the offense, but having done so, he still has not caused the harm or evil at which the offense is aimed and for that reason he is not held criminally responsible for his conduct. In this section we will examine four important offense modification defenses: (1) impossibility, (2) the victim-accomplice rule, (3) the inevitably incident conduct rule, and (4) Wharton's Rule.

1. *Impossibility*

Inchoate offenses are those offenses that make it a crime to take a step toward completing some crime. The three generally recognized inchoate offenses are attempt, solicitation, and conspiracy. For example, if *X*, *Y*, and *Z* agree to rob a bank and in furtherance of the agreement *X* purchases hoods and guns for each of them, at that point the three have engaged in the crime of conspiracy, because while they have not committed the crime of bank robbery, they have agreed with each other to do so and took a substantial step toward committing it.

The defense of impossibility is usually only available for those types of offenses that are referred to as **inchoate offenses**. The law recognizes two different forms of impossibility: (1) factual impossibility and (2) legal impossibility. When a person engages in a course of conduct for the purpose of committing a crime and fails to commit it because it is factually impossible to do so, that factual impossibility is not a defense. For example, Miguel, with the intent to murder Jose, points a gun at him. Believing the gun to be loaded when unknown to him it is not, Miguel pulls the trigger. Miguel has committed attempted murder and notwithstanding that it was impossible to fire the gun, that factual impossibility is not a defense to that crime.[10] Where, however, the conduct in which the defendant was attempting to engage is not a crime, that constitutes a legal impossibility, which is a defense.

People v. Teal

Court of Appeals of New York (1909) 196 N.Y. 372 (1909)

WERNER, J. This appeal presents a question which is both interesting and important. Can a person be convicted of attempted subornation of perjury, upon evidence which would not support a conviction upon the charge of perjury, if the attempt had been successful? As applied to the concrete facts of record the question is whether the defendant was properly convicted of an attempt at subornation of perjury even though the person sought to be suborned could not have been convicted of perjury, if the false testimony attempted to have been procured had been actually given under oath. As appears from the foregoing statement of facts, the defendant was charged with having attempted to procure false testimony from one MacCauslan, in an action for a divorce brought by one Helen K. Gould against Frank J. Gould. At the time when this attempt was made the complaint had been served, and the only issuable charge it contained was that the said Frank J. Gould had been guilty of an act of adultery committed with a woman unknown to the plaintiff, in a house of prostitution in the town of North

Sydney, Cape Breton, Dominion of Canada, on the 25th day of July, 1905. That was the precise and definite issue tendered by the complaint. What was the false testimony which the defendant herein is charged with attempting to procure? That in the month of March, 1908, Mabel MacCauslan saw Frank J. Gould, the defendant charged with the above-mentioned specific act of adultery, come out of a bedroom in the apartment of one Bessie Van Doren (alias De Voe) in the city of New York, under circumstances which might tend to support a charge of adultery between the man Gould and the woman Van Doren at that time and place. Thus we see that the traversable issue of record was whether Gould had committed adultery in a Canadian brothel in 1905, and that the false testimony solicited from MacCauslan was designed to show a separate and distinct act of adultery not referred to in the complaint, committed by Gould in the city of New York in the year 1908. The bare statement of these facts, unrelated both in pleading and in circumstance, is sufficient to draw attention sharply to the utter irrelevancy, incompetency and *immateriality* of the false testimony solicited, to the issue tendered by the complaint in *Gould v. Gould*. (*Stevens v. Stevens*, 54 Hun, 490; *Germond v. Germond*, 6 Johns. Ch. 347; *Reg. v. Southwood*, 1 Fost. & Fin. 356.)

From time immemorial the common law has made the materiality of false testimony an essential ingredient of the crime of perjury. From their earliest beginnings our statutes have always embodied that rule. Our penal laws, but recently recodified, have continued it. That, in short, is the unquestioned law of this state. (Penal Code, sec. 96; Penal Law, sec. 1620.) The language of the statute is that a person who willfully and knowingly testifies falsely, *in any material matter*, is guilty of perjury.

What, then, is subornation of perjury? The answer is that a person who willfully procures or induces another to commit perjury is guilty of subornation of perjury. (Penal Code, sec. 105; Penal Law, sec. 1632.) This plain language of the statute needs no elucidation. Subornation of perjury can only be predicated upon perjury committed. If the person alleged to have been suborned has not committed perjury, the alleged suborner cannot be held guilty of subornation of perjury. (Wharton Cr. Law, vol. 2 [10th ed.], sec. 1330; *Com. v. Smith*, 11 Allen, 243.)

What is attempted subornation of perjury? Turning again to the statutes we read that "an act, done with intent to commit a crime, and tending but failing to effect its commission, is an attempt to commit *that* crime." (Penal Code, sec. 34; Penal Law, sec. 2.) "That" crime, in the case at bar, is subornation of perjury, and could only have been committed if the false testimony, if given, had constituted perjury. It seems to follow, therefore, that if there could have been no subornation of perjury, there was in fact no attempted subornation of perjury within the meaning of the statute. If the person actually giving false testimony is not guilty of perjury, the person through whose procuration the testimony is given cannot be guilty of subornation of perjury and, by the same rule, an unsuccessful attempt to do that which is not a crime when effectuated, cannot be held to be an attempt to commit the crime specified.

If this reasoning is sound, it is clear that the question before us resolves itself into the inquiry whether the actual giving of the false testimony set forth in the indictment would have constituted the crime of perjury. We have already said that the false testimony which the defendant attempted to procure was irrelevant, incompetent and immaterial to the only issue presented by the complaint in *Gould v. Gould*. We may pass without discussion the elements of irrelevancy and incompetency. These could have been waived. They are, moreover, not essential to the commission of perjury as defined in the statute. It is different, however, as to materiality. If false testimony is not material it cannot support an indictment for perjury. The testimony upon which such a charge is predicated must be false "in any material matter." The testimony solicited of MacCauslan was not false in any matter material to the issue in *Gould v. Gould*, and we do not see how the conviction in the case at bar can be sustained unless we adopt the suggestion that if the false testimony, although not material when solicited, might have become so by a subsequent amendment of the complaint, then the facts proved upon the trial support the charge laid in the indictment and sustain the judgment of conviction. We cannot entertain this view. If the charge of perjury could not have been sustained in case the false testimony had actually been given under the complaint as it then stood, no subsequent change in the pleading or issue could relate back to the time when the act was committed. It would be highly dangerous to make the charge of perjury dependent upon issues or events arising after testimony has been given. If that were the rule it would be unsafe to testify with the utmost truthfulness upon any issue which might, by any possibility, be changed by subsequent events. No such shifting rule ought ever to be engrafted upon a system of jurisprudence in which the protection of individual rights is a cardinal principle. * * *

The judgment of conviction herein should be reversed and a new trial ordered.

Case Focus

1. What was the reason the court gave for reversing the defendant's conviction, notwithstanding that the defendant had solicited someone to give false testimony in a court proceeding?
2. What type of impossibility, if any, was present in this case?

• • • • • • • •

2. *Victim-Accomplice Rule*

The victim-accomplice defense is quite simple. The defense provides that an accomplice to a crime can assert as a defense the fact that he is also the victim of the crime to which he was an accomplice. For example, if

Lawrence's son has been kidnapped and, contrary to the advice of law enforcement agents, Lawrence pays the kidnappers $100,000 in ransom, Lawrence can be charged with kidnapping because by paying the ransom he has aided the kidnapper. If Lawrence is charged with kidnapping on the ground that he aided the kidnapper, he can assert as a defense that he was a victim of the crime.

3. *Inevitably Incident Conduct Rule*

The inevitably incident conduct rule provides that a person is not accountable as an aider and abettor for the commission of an offense when the offense is so defined that the aider's conduct is inevitably incident to the commission of the offense.[11] For example, if there is a statute that makes bigamy a crime, and Lilly (who already has a husband) marries Horace (who is single but knows of Lilly's marital status) and Horace is charged with bigamy because he aided Lilly in committing that offense, Horace can assert the inevitably incident conduct rule as a defense because bigamy is defined such that it requires the action of two people to be committed.

It is important to keep in mind that to be able to use the inevitably incident conduct defense it is necessary that the offense be *defined* in such a way that it requires two or more persons to commit and not that as it was *committed* it needed two or more people to commit. For example, a statute makes it a crime for a person to devise a scheme to use the mail to defraud purchasers of securities. The ABC Corporation is engaged in the business of selling securities, and Kimba is a saleswoman at ABC, who devises the scheme and who causes the corporation to defraud customers. Kimba cannot assert the inevitably incident conduct rule as a defense because even though the corporation can only act through agents and thus, as committed, the offense required the action of more than one person (under the law, corporations are considered persons), the offense itself is defined in such a way that it may be committed by a single person.

One definition of the offense of bigamy is as follows: Any person having a husband or wife who subsequently marries another or cohabits in this State after such marriage commits bigamy. 720 ILCS 5/ 11-12(a).

State v. Duffy

Missouri Court of Appeals, Western District (1999) 8 S.W.3d 197

BRECKINRIDGE, **J**. Charles Patrick Duffy appeals his conviction as an accessory to misdemeanor workers' compensation fraud, pursuant to §§287.128.1(8) and 562.041, RSMo 1994. The court sentenced him to pay a $1000.00 fine. On appeal, Mr. Duffy argues * * * his motion for [judgment of acquittal was improperly denied] because (1) §562.041.2(2), the exception to accessory liability for persons necessarily incident to the principal crime, exempted him from liability; * * * This court finds that * * * the necessarily incident exception of §562.041.2(2) does not exempt Mr. Duffy from accessory liability for workers' compensation fraud * * *. The judgment of the trial court is affirmed.

Factual and Procedural Background

* * * Mr. Duffy is a partner in Duffy Construction Company. In the latter part of 1995, Mr. Duffy hired his friend, Shawn Patrick Pannell, to work for Duffy Construction Company as a dump truck driver and general laborer. On July 17, 1996, Mr. Pannell injured his foot in a work-related accident. A physician advised Mr. Pannell to refrain from working until August 26, 1996. Mr. Pannell submitted a claim for reimbursement of his medical expenses and for temporary total disability benefits to Missouri Employers Mutual Insurance Company, Duffy Construction Company's workers' compensation insurance carrier. Mr. Pannell was advised that he was eligible for benefits only so long as he was unable to work. The insurance company approved Mr. Pannell's claim for benefits.

On August 14, 1996, Mr. Duffy came to Mr. Pannell's home. Mr. Duffy told Mr. Pannell that his company was short-handed, and he needed Mr. Pannell to return to work. Mr. Duffy offered to pay Mr. Pannell one-third of his normal salary in cash, and he assured Mr. Pannell that, because they were friends, he would not tell the insurance company Mr. Pannell was working while collecting workers' compensation benefits. Mr. Duffy told Mr. Pannell that if he did not return to work immediately, he would lose his job. Mr. Pannell returned to work for Duffy Construction Company the next day and was paid, in cash, by Mr. Duffy as promised. Mr. Pannell continued to work until August 26, 1996, when he suffered an injury to his finger while working at one of Duffy Construction Company's job sites.

On September 4, 1996, Mr. Pannell told a claims representative for Missouri Employers Mutual Insurance Company that he did not return to work after his July 17, 1996 injury to his foot until August 26, 1996. The insurance company had paid Mr. Pannell temporary total disability benefits for this injury from July 18, 1996 through August 25, 1996. The total amount of temporary total disability benefits the insurance company paid Mr. Pannell for this time period was $1114.28.

Because it was discovered that Mr. Pannell had been working while collecting temporary total disability benefits, the State charged Mr. Pannell with committing workers' compensation fraud. Mr. Pannell pled guilty. The State also charged Mr. Duffy with violating §§287.128.1(8) and 562.041 by knowingly causing a false representation to be made for the purpose of obtaining workers' compensation benefits. The State alleged that Mr. Duffy encouraged Mr. Pannell to return to work before August 26, 1996, by telling him that he could continue to collect temporary total disability benefits while working and receiving pay for working. Following a trial, the jury found Mr. Duffy guilty and the court sentenced him to pay a $1000.00 fine. Mr. Duffy filed this appeal.

The Exception to §562.041.1 Does Not Exempt
Mr. Duffy From Accessory Liability

In his first point on appeal, Mr. Duffy argues that because his conduct was necessarily incident to the commission of Mr. Pannell's crime and there is another statute under which he could have been charged, he is exempted from accessory liability by §562.041.2. The State charged Mr. Duffy as an accessory with violating §§287.128.1(8) and 562.041.1. Section 287.128.1(8) makes it a crime to "knowingly make or cause to be made any false or fraudulent material statement or material representation for the purpose of obtaining or denying any benefit." Section 562.041.1(2) makes a person criminally responsible for the conduct of another when the person aids the principal in the commission of a crime. Aiding is "any form of affirmative advancement of the enterprise." State v. Brown, 924 S.W.2d 3, 5 (Mo. App. 1996). "The law of aiding and abetting has long been deemed to include acts of encouragement." State v. Richardson, 923 S.W.2d 301, 317 (Mo. banc 1996). The State alleged in the information that Mr. Duffy caused Mr. Pannell to make a false representation to obtain benefits in that he encouraged Mr. Pannell to work and accept pay for working while receiving benefits.

Mr. Duffy argues that he is exempted from liability because he falls under one of the exceptions to accessory liability listed in §562.041.2. Section 562.041.2 states that a person is *not* criminally responsible for the conduct of another in the following situations:

(1)   He is the victim of the offense committed or attempted;

(2)   The offense is so defined that his conduct was necessarily incident to the commission or attempt to commit the offense. If his conduct constitutes a related but separate offense, he is criminally responsible for that offense but not for the conduct or offense committed or attempted by the other person; * * *

Mr. Duffy alleges that he falls under §562.041.2(2), the "necessarily incident" exception, because the crime as charged could not have been committed without his participation. Mr. Duffy claims that his alleged criminal conduct of telling Mr. Pannell to return to work before August 26, 1996, paying Mr. Pannell for working while receiving benefits, and telling Mr. Pannell that he could collect benefits while working and receiving pay for working, were necessarily incident to Mr. Pannell's commission of the crime of workers' compensation fraud.

Section 562.041 does not define the term "necessarily incident." This court must therefore "ascertain and give effect to the legislative intent by considering the language used in its plain and ordinary meaning." State v. Lyles, 695 S.W.2d 945, 946 (Mo. App. 1985). * * *

The dictionary describes the definition of "necessary" as [either absolutely physically necessary or merely convenient, useful, or conducive to the end sought.]

This word must be considered in the connection in which it is used, as it is a word susceptible of various meanings. It may import absolute physical necessity or inevitability, or it may import that which is only convenient, useful, appropriate, suitable, proper, or conducive to the end sought . . . . Its force and meaning must be determined with relation to the particular object sought.

BLACK'S LAW DICTIONARY 1029 (6th ed. 1990). The definition of "incident" is:

Something dependent upon, appertaining or subordinate to, or accompanying something else of greater or principal importance, something arising or resulting from something else of greater or principal importance . . . . It denotes anything which inseparably belongs to, or is connected with, or inherent in, another thing called the "principal". Also, less strictly, it denotes anything which is usually connected with another, or connected for some purposes, though not inseparably.

Id. at 782. Thus, pursuant to the dictionary, the meaning of "necessary" is either absolutely physically necessary or merely convenient, useful or conducive to the end sought. Likewise, "incident" has two possible meanings. It means either inseparably connected to something of greater importance or usually connected, but not inseparably.

This court interpreted the "necessarily incident" exception to accessory liability in a manner consistent with these dictionary definitions in Bass v. State, 950 S.W.2d 940 (Mo. App. 1997). The defendant in *Bass* had physically forced her daughter to have sexual intercourse with the defendant's boyfriend. Id. at 941. The jury convicted the defendant of rape as an accessory to the crime. Id. at 942. In determining whether the necessarily incident exception applied to exempt the defendant from accessory liability, this court found that although the defendant clearly had been instrumental in perpetrating the rape, rape was a crime that could be committed without the participation of a third party. Id. at 944. To be exempt under the necessarily incident exception, this court held that the defendant must show that the crime could not have been committed without his or her participation. Id. "Thus, if the conduct is not a necessary part of the crime . . . the exception does not apply." Id. Because the defendant was not necessarily incident to the commission of rape, the exception did not apply to her. Id.

When this court found in *Bass* that the "necessarily incident" exception exempts from accessory liability only those persons whose participation is essential to the commission of the defined offense it considered the purpose for the exceptions to accessory liability. When interpreting statutory language, courts must consider the language in the context of the whole statute and in light of the statute's object and purpose. State v. Haskins, 950 S.W.2d 613, 615 (Mo. App. 1997). The Model Penal Code's exceptions to accessory liability are similar to those found in §562.041.2. MODEL PENAL CODE §2.06(6) (1985). The Comment to 1973 Proposed Code §562.041 and the Explanatory Note following §2.06 of the Model Penal Code set forth the purpose for and the policy behind the necessarily incident exception to accessory liability. * * *

In this case, Mr. Duffy argues that his conduct was necessarily incident to Mr. Pannell's committing the crime of workers' compensation fraud by making a false material representation for the purpose of obtaining workers' compensation benefits. Mr. Duffy maintains that the crime *as charged* could not have been committed without his involvement. Mr. Duffy misapplies the necessarily incident exception. The question is not whether Mr. Duffy's conduct was useful or conducive to Mr. Pannell's crime under the facts of this case; it is whether the crime of workers' compensation fraud "is so defined" that the crime could not have been committed without a third party's involvement. Section 562.041.2(2). See also *Bass*, 950 S.W.2d at 944. While Mr. Duffy's conduct of encouraging Mr. Pannell to return to work by telling him that he could collect benefits while receiving pay for working certainly was conducive to Mr. Pannell making false representations to the insurance company, a violation of §287.128.1(8) can certainly occur without a third party's aid or encouragement. Because Mr. Duffy's conduct was not necessarily incident to Mr. Pannell's commission of the crime of workers' compensation fraud, the exception to §562.041.1 does not apply to Mr. Duffy.

Point I is denied.

Case Focus

1. Is the applicability of necessarily incident exception to accomplice liability dependent on the manner in which a crime is committed, or how it is defined? Based on this case, why is that distinction important to understand?

• • • • • • • •

4. *Wharton's Rule*

An **object offense** is the offense that conspirators conspire to commit. For example, if *X* and *Y* agree to murder *Z*, the object offense of their conspiracy is murder.

Wharton's Rule applies only to the crime of conspiracy and is similar to the inevitably incident conduct rule. Wharton's Rule is a defense to the crime of conspiracy when the **object offense** is defined in such a way that it requires the participation of two or more persons to commit.[12] For example, if Hussein, a public official, agrees to accept a bribe from Rod not to arrest him for running a gambling house, and both men are charged with the offense of conspiracy to commit bribery, they can assert Wharton's Rule as a defense to the conspiracy charge because the offense of bribery can only be committed with the action of two people, the person paying the bribe and the person accepting the bribe.[13]

CHAPTER TERMS

Inchoate offense   Object offense

REVIEW QUESTIONS

1. What is a failure of proof defense?
2. What are the two types of mistakes that are defenses in criminal law?
3. What type of mistake of fact is a defense to a criminal charge, and what type of mistake of fact is not a defense to a criminal charge?
4. When is a mistake of law a defense to a criminal charge, and what type of mistake of law is not a defense to a criminal charge?
5. What is an offense modification defense in criminal law?
6. What are the two forms of impossibility recognized by the law, and which of those forms is a defense?

7. To what category of crimes is impossibility a defense?
8. What is the victim-accomplice defense?
9. What is the inevitably incident conduct defense, and to what type of crimes does it apply?
10. To what type of crimes is Wharton's Rule a defense?
11. How does Wharton's Rule differ from the inevitably incident conduct defense?

ENDNOTES

1. It should be noted that some of the defenses examined in previous chapters are, in their broader form, classified as failure of proof defenses. For example, the defense of intoxication, which was examined in the chapter on excuse defenses, may be a defense either where the defendant is so intoxicated that he reaches a level of mental dysfunction that satisfies the insanity test or, if he does not reach that level of intoxication, where he is merely so intoxicated that he cannot form the *mens rea* element of offense with which he has been charged. The latter form of the intoxication defense is a failure of proof defense.
2. *Stanley v. State*, 61 Okla. Crim. 382 (1937).
3. *State v. Silveira*, 198 Conn. 454 (1980).
4. *Id.*

5. *E.g.*, Utah Code Ann. §76-2-304(2) ("Ignorance or mistake concerning the existence or meaning of a penal law is no defense to a crime.").
6. *People v. McCalla*, 63 Cal. App. 783 (1st Dist. 1923).
7. *United States v. Bishop*, 412 U.S. 346 (1973).
8. *Cheek v. United States*, 498 U.S. 192 (1991).
9. *Id.*
10. *State v. Damms*, 9 Wis. 2d 183 (1960).
11. *See, e.g.*, 720 ILCS 5/5-2(C), which provides that a person is not accountable as an aider unless the statute defining the offense so provides, if, "(2) The offense is so defined that his conduct is inevitably incident to its commission."
12. *Ianelli v. United States*, 420 U.S. 770 (1975).
13. *People v. Wettengel*, 98 Colo. 193 (1935).

Chapter 15
Affirmative Defenses— Non-Exculpatory Defenses

Chapter Objectives

After reading this chapter, you should be able to

- Explain what non-exculpatory affirmative defenses are
- Understand the defense of double jeopardy and how it is applied
- Explain the statute of limitations defense and how it differs from the pre-indictment delay defense
- Explain what a speedy trial defense is
- Understand the elements of the defense of selective prosecution
- Understand and explain the limits of the legislative immunity defense

"Outrageousness" as a defense does more than stretch the bounds of due process. It also creates serious problems of consistency. The circuits that recognize a "due process defense" can't agree on what it means. How much is "too much"? The nature of the question exposes it as (a) unanswerable, and (b) political. —*United States v. Miller*, 891 F.2d 1265 (7th Cir. 1985) (Easterbrook, J., concurring)

In this chapter we will examine the category of defenses called non-exculpatory defenses and some of the more important defenses included in that category. Non-exculpatory defenses differ from the affirmative defenses that were examined in the previous chapters because, without regard to the defendant's actual culpability for committing an offense, non-exculpatory defenses allow a defendant to escape criminal responsibility for his conduct because some policy reflected in constitutional or statutory law or a common law rule determines that for reasons unrelated to the defendant's guilt or innocence he should not be punished. In fact, defendants who assert one of the defenses in the non-exculpatory defense category by all measures deserve condemnation and punishment if they engaged in the criminal conduct with which they are charged.[1]

The defenses in this chapter also differ from the affirmative defenses previously examined in several other important ways. To the extent the defenses in this chapter involve issues of fact, those issues are not resolved by a jury in a jury trial. Instead they are heard and decided by the judge outside of (and in many cases prior to) trial. In addition, most of the defenses in this category are raised by pre-trial motions to dismiss instead of as defenses at trial. As a result the successful assertion of a non-exculpatory defense usually will have the effect of precluding a trial on the merits of the case.

In this chapter we will examine the following non-exculpatory defenses: (A) double jeopardy, (B) statute of limitations, (C) pre-indictment delay, (D) speedy trial, (E) ex-post facto laws and bills of attainder, (F) selective prosecution, (G) legislative immunity, and (H) outrageous government conduct.

A. Double Jeopardy

The double jeopardy defense is based on the double jeopardy clause found in the U.S. Constitution's Fifth Amendment and on similarly worded double jeopardy clauses found in the constitution of every state. The Fifth Amendment's double jeopardy clause provides that no person shall be twice put in jeopardy of life or limb for the same offense.[2] The prohibition on twice placing persons in jeopardy for the same offense was long recognized by the common law. Despite the reference to life and limb in the Fifth Amendment double jeopardy clause, the courts have construed the clause as applying to all criminal offenses without regard to the form of punishment attached to them.[3]

The federal constitution's double jeopardy clause has been construed as applying when a defendant is placed in jeopardy by the same sovereign for the same offense through successive trials. The defense of double jeopardy applies without regard to whether the first trial ended in an acquittal or conviction. The **double jeopardy** clause also prohibits successive punishment for the same offense.

1. Jeopardy

Jeopardy is said to attach (i.e., a defendant is considered to have been placed in jeopardy) when a defendant is placed on trial. In a bench trial, this generally means when the first trial witness is sworn, and in a jury trial this means when the jury is empaneled and sworn.[4] Dismissals and rulings before jeopardy attaches do not bar a reprosecution of a defendant for the same offense by the same sovereign. For example, if immediately before the first witness in a bench trial is sworn the prosecutor dismisses a case or charge or a court dismisses a criminal case or charge, the double jeopardy clause does not bar the prosecutor from charging the defendant a second time with the dismissed offenses.

Even if jeopardy has attached, that does not necessarily mean that a second prosecution for the same offense is barred. If a criminal trial is aborted after jeopardy attaches because of a mistrial caused by the defendant, the government is not barred from trying the defendant a second time for that offense. If the trial is aborted after jeopardy attaches because of a mistrial caused by the prosecution, then the double jeopardy clause bars a retrial.

If the defendant is convicted and he successfully appeals his conviction, depending on how the appellate court ruled, he may or may not be subject to being retried. If the appellate court reverses the defendant's conviction on the ground that the evidence did not prove him guilty, the double jeopardy clause bars a retrial. If, however, the appellate court reverses because of some other error by the trial court, such as allowing admission of evidence that should not have been admitted, the defendant may be re-tried.

In order for the double jeopardy clause to bar a second prosecution by the same sovereign for the same offense, the defendant must have actually been put in jeopardy. A defendant is not put in jeopardy and for that reason the double jeopardy clause will not bar a second prosecution for the same offense if the reason the defendant was acquitted was because he bribed the trier of fact. The reason jeopardy does not attach in such a situation is that if the trier of fact is bribed, the defendant is never at risk of conviction.

Aleman v. The Honorable Judges of The Circuit Court of Cook County

United States Court of Appeals for the Seventh Circuit (1998)
138 F.3d 302

Flaum, J. Harry Aleman successfully bribed a Cook County Circuit Judge to acquit him of a murder charge in a 1977 bench trial. A grand jury returned a second indictment against Aleman on this murder charge in 1993 after evidence of the bribery surfaced. In addition, Aleman was indicted for the first time on a different murder charge. Aleman moved to dismiss both indictments, but the

Illinois state courts rejected his arguments. In a last-ditch effort to avoid (re)trial, Aleman requested a stay of state court proceedings while a federal district court considered his challenge to the indictments in a petition for a writ of habeas corpus. The case proceeded to trial after the district court denied this petition and motion to stay, and a Cook County jury convicted him of both murders; the trial judge thereafter sentenced Aleman to 100-300 years in prison. Aleman appeals the district court's denial of the petition challenging his indictments[.] * * * These convictions will stand, though, because we affirm the district court's denial of Aleman's petition.

I. BACKGROUND

While walking to work on the morning of September 27, 1972, William Logan was shot and killed by Harry Aleman. Three years later, in October 1975, Aleman also shot and killed Anthony Reitinger, allegedly because Reitinger neglected to pay a "street tax" [Street taxes are monies paid to criminal organizations in exchange for protection of the "taxpayer's" illegal operations from either law enforcement interference or mob takeover.] on his bookmaking operation to local organized crime figures. A grand jury indicted Aleman for the Logan murder in December 1976, but he was not charged at this time with the Reitinger murder. After numerous substitutions of counsel and judges, the Logan case proceeded to a bench trial before Cook County Circuit Court Judge Frank Wilson, who acquitted Aleman of the Logan murder in May 1977.

Nearly twenty years after the trial, however, two witnesses from the Federal Witness Protection Program were made available to testify that Aleman had murdered both Logan and Reitinger and that he had purchased the Logan acquittal with a $10,000 bribe to Judge Wilson. The first witness, Vincent Rizza, was a former Chicago police officer who ran an illegal bookmaking operation in order to supplement his government salary]* * *.

Rizza also supplied corroboration of Aleman's bribe of Judge Wilson in the Logan murder trial. In the early winter of 1977, after Aleman's indictment but before the trial, Aleman told Rizza that the trial was "all taken care of." Aleman said that he requested a bench trial "because the case was all taken care of" and that this way he was not going to jail. Later, when newspaper accounts began to paint a bleak picture of Aleman's chances of gaining an acquittal, he again told Rizza calmly that the case was "taken care of."

The second federal government informant was Robert Cooley, a former lawyer steeped in corruption who admitted that he frequently bribed judges, prosecutors, clerks, and sheriffs before entering the Federal Witness Protection Program. Cooley was a close friend of Judge Wilson and, at the request of some local organized crime figures, pitched the idea of a "fix" to Wilson. Cooley told Wilson that the case against Aleman was weak, that it could be handled very easily, and that an acquittal would be worth $10,000. Wilson agreed to fix the case if Aleman's counsel, Thomas Maloney, a good friend of Wilson's, would withdraw from the case in order to reduce the appearance of impropriety. Cooley thereupon paid Wilson $2,500, and the two men agreed that Wilson would receive the remaining $7,500 after the acquittal. Unbeknownst to Wilson, Cooley had also arranged a $10,000 payment to secure the favorable testimony of an eyewitness to the murder. Cooley then met with Aleman and assured him that an acquittal was guaranteed.

The evidence against Aleman, however, was not as flimsy as Cooley had indicated to Judge Wilson. After the second day of trial, Cooley met with Wilson, who was upset at Cooley's misrepresentations and at the prosecutor's allegations that a witness had received $10,000 in exchange for offering false testimony. Amazingly, the issue for Wilson was not *whether* he would still acquit Aleman, but for *how much.* Wilson expressed annoyance that a witness was getting the same amount of money as a "full circuit judge"; he said to Cooley that he would "receive all kinds of heat" for the acquittal and requested more bribe money: "That's all I get is ten thousand dollars? I think I deserve more."

Throughout these meetings, the acquittal itself was never in question. Judge Wilson fulfilled his end of the bargain on May 24, 1977, when he acquitted Aleman in a brisk oral ruling and quickly exited the courtroom.] * * *

In addition to this extraordinary informant testimony, other evidence confirmed the bribery. An F.B.I. agent interviewed Judge Wilson at his retirement home in Arizona in November 1989. The agent informed Wilson that Cooley had become a government informant, that Cooley had secretly taped a recent conversation with Wilson in which the two men discussed the $10,000 Aleman bribe, and that the Government was currently investigating allegations that Wilson accepted a bribe to acquit Aleman. Wilson denied the accusations, but he failed to appear in Chicago for a grand jury subpoena concerning the matter on December 6, 1989. A few months later, Judge Wilson walked into the backyard of his home and shot himself to death.

Finally, Monte Katz, a friend of Aleman's in federal prison [At the time this prosecution was initiated Aleman was serving a 12 year federal sentence on a conviction for racketeering.], claimed that Aleman admitted that he murdered William Logan. Katz and Aleman became friends in prison, and, apparently, Aleman often discussed his criminal exploits. Specifically, Aleman told Katz that he "fixed" the Logan trial by paying money to "reach" the judge. Aleman stated that he was not worried about being tried again for the murder because it "was a double jeopardy situation."] * * *

Based on this body of evidence, in December 1993, the Cook County State's Attorney again charged Aleman for the Logan murder and for the first time charged Aleman with the murder of Reitinger. A grand jury returned indictments on both counts. Aleman claimed to the Circuit Court, as he claims to us on appeal, that the Logan indictment violated the Double Jeopardy Clause] * * *. After an evidentiary hearing concerning the alleged bribe, the Circuit Court rejected the double jeopardy argument based on the overwhelming factual evidence that Aleman's first trial was a sham. * * *

[That ruling was] * * * upheld on appeal. *See People v. Aleman,* 281 Ill. App. 3d 991 (Ill. App. Ct.), *review denied,* 168 Ill. 2d 600 (Ill. 1996).

II. DISCUSSION

Aleman raises three claims on appeal. First, he takes issue with the Circuit Court's factual findings that he bribed Judge Wilson in the Logan trial [and] * * * he challenges the effect of those factual findings upon his double jeopardy claim. *See Benton v. Maryland,* 395 U.S. 784, 23 L. Ed. 2d 707, 89 S. Ct. 2056 (1969) (holding that the protections of the Double Jeopardy Clause apply to the states). * * * Our collateral review, however, is quite limited. Under 28 U.S.C. §2254(d)(1), we can only grant Aleman's petition if one of the Circuit Court's legal rulings was either "contrary to, or involved an unreasonable application of clearly established Federal law, as determined by the Supreme Court of the United States." Aleman's factual challenge can succeed only if he can show by "clear and convincing evidence" that the Circuit Court's findings are erroneous. *See id.* §2254(d)(2). He meets neither of these stringent standards

A. Double Jeopardy Claims

Aleman's challenge to the Circuit Court's factual findings can be dismissed in short order. He rightly points out that the common law has always presumed the neutrality of judges. *See, e.g.,* 3 W. Blackstone, Commentaries *361 ("The law will not suppose a possibility of bias or favour in a judge, who is already sworn to administer impartial justice, and whose authority greatly depends upon that presumption and idea.") * * *. Aleman seems to think that reciting this principle alone can somehow overcome the great weight of evidence showing that he bribed Judge Wilson. However, we have always recognized that the presumption of a judge's neutrality is a rebuttable one. *See Bracy v. Gramley,* 520 U.S. 899 (1997). As in Bracy, the Circuit Court found that the ordinary presumption had been soundly rebutted in this case. * * *

Aleman's legal challenge presents a unique and interesting question, but it ultimately fares no better than his factual one. The Fifth Amendment's Double Jeopardy Clause guarantees that no one shall "be subject for the same offence to be twice put in jeopardy of life or limb." Aleman argues that the Double Jeopardy Clause unambiguously bars his re-indictment on the Logan murder charge because he faced trial on that murder charge in 1977 and was acquitted by Judge Wilson. In support of his position, he points to a long line of Supreme Court cases reiterating that an acquittal on a charge absolutely bars retrial on that charge. *See, e.g., Arizona v. Washington,* 434 U.S. 497 (1978) * * * Aleman argues that it is irrelevant how he obtained his acquittal and that there is no room for courts to question those circumstances and lift the double jeopardy bar to re-prosecution. *See, e.g., Burks v. United States,* 437 U.S. 1, 11 n.6, 57 L. Ed. 2d 1, 98 S. Ct. 2141 (1978) ("Where the Double Jeopardy Clause is applicable, its sweep is absolute. There are no 'equities' to be balanced, for the Clause has declared a constitutional policy, based on grounds which are not open to judicial examination.") * * *. Aleman contends that the Circuit Court's decision is contrary to, or an unreasonable application, of this body of the Supreme Court's interpretations of federal law.

The legal conclusion urged by Aleman might not be an unreasonable application of Supreme Court precedent, but the highly deferential standard of collateral review leads us to hold that the contrary interpretation—the one adopted by the Illinois courts in this case—is also not unreasonable. The Illinois courts viewed the authority cited by Aleman as begging the question; the Double Jeopardy Clause may well be absolute when it applies, *see Burks,* 437 U.S. at 11 n.6, but determining if it applies is the real issue in this case. Similarly, the State argues that the protections of the Double Jeopardy Clause only extend to a defendant who was once before in jeopardy of conviction on a particular criminal charge; the State contends that, by bribing Judge Wilson, Aleman created a situation in which he was never in jeopardy at his first trial. The first trial, therefore, was a sham and the acquittal there rendered has no effect for double jeopardy purposes. Under this theory, the State was free to re-indict him because he has never been in jeopardy of conviction on the Logan murder charge.

The Circuit Court concluded that Aleman's first trial was a nullity because he was never truly at risk of conviction. The Supreme Court has emphasized that "jeopardy denotes risk. In the constitutional sense, jeopardy describes the risk that is traditionally associated with criminal prosecution." *Breed v. Jones,* 421 U.S. 519, 528 (1975); *Serfass v. United States,* 420 U.S. 377, 391-392, 43 L. Ed. 2d 265, 95 S. Ct. 1055 (1975) ("Without risk of a determination of guilt, jeopardy does not attach, and neither an appeal nor further prosecution constitutes double jeopardy. . . .") * * * Indeed, the Court has stated that preventing the hazards associated with risking conviction is the *raison d'etre* of the Double Jeopardy Clause:

> The underlying idea, one that is deeply ingrained in at least the Anglo-American system of jurisprudence, is that the State with all its resources and power should not be allowed to make repeated attempts to convict an individual for an alleged offense, thereby subjecting him to embarrassment, expense and ordeal and compelling him to live in a continuing state of anxiety and insecurity, as well as enhancing the possibility that even though innocent he may be found guilty.

Green v. United States, 355 U.S. 184, 187-188 (1957).

Aleman had to endure none of these risks because he "fixed" his case; the Circuit Court found that Aleman was so sanguine about the certainty of his acquittal that he went so far as to tell Vincent Rizza before the trial that jail was "not an option." Aleman may be correct that some risk of conviction still existed after Judge Wilson agreed to fix the case, but it cannot be said that the risk was the sort "traditionally associated" with an impartial criminal justice system. *See Breed,* 421 U.S. at 528. It seems only appropriate that a defendant should not be allowed to escape punishment for murder because he bribed the judge. To allow Aleman to profit from his bribery and escape all punishment for the Logan murder would be a perversion of justice, as well as establish an unseemly and dangerous incentive for criminal defendants. The Illinois courts' holdings, therefore, were not contrary to, or unreasonable applications of, federal law as interpreted by the Supreme Court.

For these reasons, we affirm the district court's rejection of the double jeopardy claims contained in Aleman's petition.

Case Focus

1. The defendant in this case was charged with and acquitted of murder and 20 years later was again charged with murdering the same individual. Why did the double jeopardy clause not bar the second prosecution?

2. In its decision the court acknowledged the defendant's argument that he had the same risk of conviction in his first trial. What was the reason the court gave for rejecting that argument? What was the risk to which the court and defendant referred and on what basis did the court determine that risk should not be considered?

• • • • • • • •

2. Same Offense

The double jeopardy defense is offense based. That means the defense prohibits successive prosecutions or successive punishments for the same offense, but it does not prohibit successive prosecutions or punishments for different offenses that are based on the same conduct. For example, if Heather's conduct constitutes both the crime of forgery and the crime of theft by deception and Heather is prosecuted first for forgery and acquitted, the double jeopardy defense will not prohibit the subsequent prosecution of Heather for theft merely because that prosecution is based on the same conduct that was the basis of the prior prosecution.

Courts use what is called the same-elements test to determine whether an offense in a successive prosecution or upon which a successive punishment is imposed is the "same" offense that was the basis of an earlier prosecution or punishment.

Under the same-elements test, the question that is asked is whether each of the offenses contains an element not found in the other offense. If

Double Jeopardy Analysis

If *A* forges a check and gives it to a car dealer to purchase a car and as a result is charged with the crime of forgery and is placed on trial and acquitted or convicted, and his conduct also constituted the crime of theft by deception, whether he can now be placed on trial for that crime is determined by an analysis of the elements that constitute the definition of each offense.

FORGERY	THEFT BY DECEPTION
720 ILCS 5/17-3(a)(2)	720 ILCS 5/16-1(a)
A person commits forgery when he:	A person commits theft when he:
1. With intent to defraud	1. Knowingly
2. He knowingly	2. Obtains
3. Delivers a document	3. By deception
4. The document is capable of defrauding another	4. Control over property
	5. Of the owner
	6. With the intent to permanently deprive the owner of the use or benefit of the property

By looking at the elements of each of the above statutory offenses it can be seen that each offense contains at least one element not contained in the other. The offense of forgery contains as an element the delivery of a document (Element #3), an element not found in the offense of theft by deception, while the offense of theft by deception contains as an element the intent to permanently deprive the owner of the use or benefit of property (Element #6), an element not found in the offense of forgery. Under the same-elements test, the crimes of forgery and theft by deception are not the same offenses for double jeopardy purposes and therefore the double jeopardy clause does not bar the prosecution of *A* for theft by deception following his conviction or acquittal on the charge of forgery.

Collateral estoppel means that once a fact has been determined by a valid and final judgment, that issue cannot again be litigated between the same parties. *United States* v. *Wells*, 347 F.3d 280 (8th Cir. 2004). The doctrine of collateral estoppel was first developed in civil litigation but was applied in criminal litigation early in the last century and today is an established rule of federal criminal law. *Ashe v. Swenson*, 397 U.S. 436 (1970).

not, the double jeopardy clause bars the second prosecution.[5] Stated in a different way, if each offense contains an element that is not contained in the other offense, the double jeopardy clause does not prohibit a subsequent prosecution.

The term "same offense" generally does not include the prosecution of a defendant who is placed on trial successively for the same crime committed at the same time but against different victims. The double jeopardy clause does, however, incorporate the doctrine of **collateral estoppel**. Under that aspect of the double jeopardy clause, when the prosecution of the first offense results in an acquittal and the acquittal

An **ultimate fact** in a criminal case is a fact that pertains to an issue the prosecution must prove beyond a reasonable doubt. *People v. Smith,* 154 Cal. App. 4th 547 (6th Dist. 2007). For example, if a defendant is charged with possession of a controlled substance on April 13, an ultimate fact in that prosecution is that the defendant possessed the controlled substance on that date. If the defendant is acquitted and later charged with possession of a controlled substance on April 20, an ultimate fact in that prosecution is proving possession on April 20 and the defendant's acquittal on the first charge does not bar the second prosecution because the ultimate fact determined in the first has no bearing on the issue of possession in the second. *United States v. Wells,* 347 F.3d 280 (8th Cir. 2004).

necessarily adjudicated an **ultimate fact** in favor of the defendant that is common to each of the other offenses he is charged with committing against different victims at the same time, prosecution of the defendant for the crimes committed against those other victims is prohibited.[6]

For example, someone with a gun enters a room where Heather, Boris, and Pavel are playing poker and that person aims the gun at them, telling each of them to place their money in a bag. Heather, Boris, and Pavel comply and the gunman flees with the bag of money. Later Luis is charged with committing the robberies and can be separately prosecuted for the robbery of Heather, the robbery of Boris, and the robbery of Pavel without violating the double jeopardy clause. If, however, in the first prosecution, where Luis is charged with robbing Heather, Luis defends by asserting an alibi defense, saying that he was somewhere else when the crime occurred and at trial the only serious question is whether Luis was the perpetrator, and Luis is acquitted, that verdict necessarily includes a finding that Luis was not the robber. Under the doctrine of collateral estoppel as it is incorporated into the double jeopardy clause, Luis cannot subsequently be prosecuted for the robberies of Boris or Pavel.

3. *Multiple Prosecutions and Punishments*

The double jeopardy clause not only prohibits multiple prosecutions for the same offense, it also prohibits multiple criminal punishments for the same offense when those multiple punishments occur in successive proceedings.[7] The question of multiple punishments arises either when the government imposes some civil punishment on the defendant before he is prosecuted for the underlying crime or when he has previously been prosecuted for a crime and the government now seeks to impose a civil sanction, such as a civil fine or license revocation, that is based on the defendant's criminal act. For example, if Sulieman files fraudulent income tax returns for the years 2005-2008, the Internal Revenue Service may initially choose to impose a civil fraud penalty on him equal to 50% of the tax due. Sometime thereafter, the U.S. Attorney in the federal district where Sulieman filed the fraudulent returns decides to charge Sulieman with the crime of filing fraudulent income tax returns for the same years. Clearly, if Sulieman is convicted, he will be punished successively for filing the same fraudulent income tax returns. In this example, the double jeopardy clause would only prohibit the prosecution of Sulieman if the civil fraud penalty that was imposed first were considered a criminal punishment.

In determining whether a punishment is civil or criminal, the courts look at a number of factors, no one of which is dispositive. One factor is whether the intent of the legislature was to create a criminal or civil punishment. In determining that, courts take a formalistic approach

Scienter is the unlawful intent or design necessary to any criminal act that is not a strict liability offense. *Morrison v. Commonwealth,* 37 Va. App. 273 (2003). The term is interchangeable with *mens rea. State v. Schaefer,* 266 Wis. 2d 719 (Wis. App. 2003).

and look at whether the statutory provision is labeled criminal or civil. Other factors include whether the statute imposes a disability or restraint, something that is usually only shown if the statute provides for some type of incarceration,[8] and whether the statute requires **scienter** before the sanction can be imposed. If the statute does not require scienter, that is a factor in favor of construing the penalty as civil. If it does require scienter, that indicates that the penalty is criminal in nature. In addition to the above, courts consider numerous other factors.

4. *Same Sovereign*

The double jeopardy defense only applies when the second prosecution or punishment is being pursued by the same sovereign who pursued the first. If the second prosecution is done by a different sovereign, the double jeopardy defense does not apply. For purposes of the double jeopardy defense, with respect to each other the federal government and the states are separate sovereigns, the states are separate sovereigns as to each other, and Indian tribes are separate sovereigns as to the federal government and as to the states. For example, if Clyde is prosecuted by the U.S. Attorney in Chicago, Illinois for violating the federal bank robbery statute by robbing a federally chartered bank and he is acquitted, that acquittal does not prevent the Cook County State's Attorney in Chicago from prosecuting him for bank robbery under Illinois law. The only limitation on the separate sovereign doctrine is when there is coordination between the two sovereigns to the extent that the prosecutor for one sovereign is acting as an arm of the other sovereign's prosecutor.

Heath v. Alabama

Supreme Court of the United States (1985)
474 U.S. 82

JUSTICE O'CONNOR delivered the opinion of the Court.

The question before the Court is whether the Double Jeopardy Clause of the Fifth Amendment bars Alabama from trying petitioner for the capital offense of murder during a kidnaping after Georgia has convicted him of murder based on the same homicide. In particular, this case presents the issue of the applicability of the dual sovereignty doctrine to successive prosecutions by two States.

I

In August 1981, petitioner, Larry Gene Heath, hired Charles Owens and Gregory Lumpkin to kill his wife, Rebecca Heath, who was then nine months pregnant, for a sum of $2,000. On the morning of August 31, 1981, petitioner left the Heath residence in Russell County, Alabama, to meet with Owens and Lumpkin in Georgia, just over the Alabama border from the Heath home. Petitioner led them back to the Heath residence, gave them the keys to the Heaths' car and house, and left the premises in his girlfriend's truck. Owens and Lumpkin then kidnaped Rebecca Heath from her home. The Heath car, with Rebecca Heath's body inside, was later found on the side of a road in Troup County, Georgia. The cause of death was a gunshot wound in the head. The estimated time of death and the distance from the Heath residence to the spot where Rebecca Heath's body was found are consistent with the theory that the murder took place in Georgia, and respondent does not contend otherwise.

Georgia and Alabama authorities pursued dual investigations in which they cooperated to some extent. On September 4, 1981, petitioner was arrested by Georgia authorities. Petitioner waived his *Miranda* rights and gave a full confession admitting that he had arranged his wife's kidnaping and murder. In November 1981, the grand jury of Troup County, Georgia, indicted petitioner for the offense of "malice" murder under Ga. Code Ann. §16-5-1 (1984). Georgia then served petitioner with notice of its intention to seek the death penalty * * *. On February 10, 1982, petitioner pleaded guilty to the Georgia murder charge in exchange for a sentence of life imprisonment, which he understood could involve his serving as few as seven years in prison. See Record 495.

On May 5, 1982, the grand jury of Russell County, Alabama, returned an indictment against petitioner for the capital offense of murder during a kidnaping. See Ala. Code §13A-5-40(a)(1) (1982). Before trial on this indictment, petitioner entered pleas of *autrefois convict* and former jeopardy under the Alabama and United States Constitutions, arguing that his conviction and sentence in Georgia barred his prosecution in Alabama for the same conduct. * * *

After a hearing, the trial court rejected petitioner's double jeopardy claims. It assumed, *arguendo*, that the two prosecutions could not have been brought in succession by one State but held that double jeopardy did not bar successive prosecutions by two different States for the same act. * * *

On January 12, 1983, the Alabama jury convicted petitioner of murder during a kidnaping in the first degree. After a sentencing hearing, the jury recommended the death penalty. Pursuant to Alabama law, a second sentencing hearing was held before the trial judge. The judge accepted the jury's recommendation, finding that the sole aggravating factor, that the capital offense was "committed while the defendant was engaged in the commission of a kidnapping," outweighed the sole mitigating factor, that the "defendant was convicted of the murder of Rebecca Heath in the Superior Court of Troup County, Georgia, . . . and received a sentence of life imprisonment in that court." *Id.*, at 718-720. See Ala. Code §§13A-5-49(4), 13A-5-50 (1982). * * *

On appeal, the Alabama Court of Criminal Appeals rejected petitioner's pleas of *autrefois convict* and former jeopardy under the Alabama and United States Constitutions and affirmed his conviction. 455 So. 2d 898 (1983). Petitioner then filed a petition for writ of certiorari with the Alabama Supreme Court, stating the sole issue to be "whether or not the prosecution in the State of Alabama constituted double jeopardy in violation of the 5th Amendment of the United States Constitution." App. 92. The court granted his petition, and unanimously affirmed his conviction. *Ex parte Heath*, 455 So. 2d 905 (1984). * * *

Petitioner sought a writ of certiorari from this Court, raising double jeopardy claims[.] * * * For the reasons explained below, we affirm the judgment of the Alabama Supreme Court. * * *

II

Successive prosecutions are barred by the Fifth Amendment only if the two offenses for which the defendant is prosecuted are the "same" for double jeopardy purposes. Respondent does not contravene petitioner's contention that the offenses of "murder during a kidnaping" and "malice murder," as construed by the courts of Alabama and Georgia respectively, may be considered greater and lesser offenses and, thus, the "same" offense under *Brown v. Ohio*, [432 U.S. 161 (1977)], absent operation of the dual sovereignty principle. See *id.*, at 169 * * *. We therefore assume, *arguendo*, that, had these offenses arisen under the laws of one State and had petitioner been separately prosecuted for both offenses in that State, the second conviction would have been barred by the Double Jeopardy Clause.

The sole remaining question upon which we granted certiorari is whether the dual sovereignty doctrine permits successive prosecutions under the laws of different States which otherwise would be held to "subject [the defendant] for the same offence to be twice put in jeopardy." U.S. Const., Amdt. 5. Although we have not previously so held, we believe the answer to this query is inescapable. The dual sovereignty doctrine, as originally articulated and consistently applied by this Court, compels the conclusion that successive prosecutions by two States for the same conduct are not barred by the Double Jeopardy Clause.

The dual sovereignty doctrine is founded on the common-law conception of crime as an offense against the sovereignty of the government. When a defendant in a single act violates the "peace and dignity" of two sovereigns by breaking the laws of each, he has committed two distinct "offences." *United States v. Lanza*, 260 U.S. 377, 382 (1922). As the Court explained in *Moore v. Illinois*, 14 How. 13, 19 (1852), "[an] offence, in its legal signification, means the transgression of a law." Consequently, when the same act transgresses the laws of two sovereigns, "it cannot be truly averred that the offender has been twice punished for the same offence; but only that by one act he has committed two offences, for each of which he is justly punishable." *Id.*, at 20.

In applying the dual sovereignty doctrine, then, the crucial determination is whether the two entities that seek successively to prosecute a defendant for the same course of conduct can be termed separate sovereigns. This determination turns on whether the two entities draw their authority to punish the offender from distinct sources of power. See, *e.g., United States v. Wheeler*, 435 U.S. 313, 320 (1978)[.] Thus, the Court has uniformly held that the States are separate sovereigns with respect to the Federal Government because each State's power to prosecute is derived from its own "inherent sovereignty," not from the Federal Government. *Wheeler, supra*, at 320, n.14. See *Abbate v. United States*, 359 U.S. 187, 193-194 (1959) (collecting cases); *Lanza, supra*. As stated in *Lanza, supra*, at 382:

"Each government in determining what shall be an offense against its peace and dignity is exercising its own sovereignty, not that of the other.

"It follows that an act denounced as a crime by both national and state sovereignties is an offense against the peace and dignity of both and may be punished by each." * * *

The States are no less sovereign with respect to each other than they are with respect to the Federal Government. Their powers to undertake criminal prosecutions derive from separate and independent sources of power and authority originally belonging to them before admission to the Union and preserved to them by the Tenth Amendment. See *Lanza, supra*, at 382. The States are equal to each other "in power, dignity and authority, each competent to exert that residuum of sovereignty not delegated to the United States by the Constitution itself." *Coyle v. Oklahoma*, 221 U.S. 559, 567 (1911). See *Skiriotes v. Florida*, 313 U.S. 69, 77 (1941). Thus, "[each] has the power, inherent in any sovereign, independently to determine what shall be an offense against its authority and to punish such offenses, and in doing so each 'is exercising its own sovereignty, not that of the other.'" *Wheeler, supra*, at 320 (quoting *Lanza, supra*, at 382). * * *

In those instances where the Court has found the dual sovereignty doctrine inapplicable, it has done so because the two prosecuting entities did not derive their powers to prosecute from independent sources of authority. Thus, the Court has held that successive prosecutions by federal and territorial courts are barred because such courts are "creations emanating from the same sovereignty." *Puerto Rico* [*v. Shell Co.*, 302 U.S. 253, 264 (1937).] * * * See also *Grafton* [*v. United States*] (the Philippine Islands). Similarly, municipalities that derive their power to try a defendant from the same organic law that empowers the State to prosecute are not separate sovereigns with respect to the State. See, *e.g., Waller* [*v. Florida,* 397 U.S 3987 (1970)]. These cases confirm that [HN7] it is the presence of independent sovereign authority to prosecute, not the relation between States and the Federal Government in our federalist system, that constitutes the basis for the dual sovereignty doctrine.

III

Petitioner invites us to restrict the applicability of the dual sovereignty principle to cases in which two governmental entities, having concurrent jurisdiction and pursuing quite different interests, can demonstrate that allowing only one entity to exercise jurisdiction over the defendant will interfere with the unvindicated interests of the second entity and that multiple prosecutions therefore are necessary for the satisfaction of the legitimate interests of both entities. This balancing of interests approach, however, cannot be reconciled with the dual sovereignty principle. This Court has plainly and repeatedly stated that two identical offenses are *not* the "same offence" within the meaning of the Double Jeopardy Clause if they are prosecuted by different sovereigns. See, *e.g., United States v. Lanza*, 260 U.S. 377 (1922) (same conduct, indistinguishable statutes, same "interests"). If the States are separate sovereigns, as they must be under the definition of sovereignty which the Court consistently has employed, the circumstances of the case are irrelevant. * * *

It is axiomatic that "[in] America, the powers of sovereignty are divided between the government of the Union, and those of the States. They are each sovereign, with respect to the objects committed to it, and neither sovereign with respect to the objects committed to the other." *McCulloch v. Maryland*, 4 Wheat. 316, 410 (1819). It is as well established that the States, "as political communities, [are] distinct and sovereign, and consequently foreign to each other." *Bank of United States v. Daniel*, 12 Pet. 32, 54 (1838). See also *Skiriotes v. Florida*, 313 U.S., at 77; *Coyle v. Oklahoma*, 221 U.S., at 567. The Constitution leaves in the possession of each State "certain exclusive and very important portions of sovereign power." The Federalist No. 9, p.55 (J. Cooke ed. 1961). Foremost among the prerogatives of sovereignty is the power to create and enforce a criminal code. See, *e.g., Alfred L. Snapp & Son, Inc. v. Puerto Rico ex rel. Barez*, 458 U.S. 592, 601 (1982); *McCulloch, supra*, at 418. To deny a State its power to enforce its criminal laws because another State has won the race to the courthouse "would be a shocking and untoward deprivation of the historic right and obligation of the States to maintain peace and order within their confines." *Bartkus*, 359 U.S., at 137. * * *

A State's interest in vindicating its sovereign authority through enforcement of its laws by definition can never be satisfied by another State's enforcement of *its* own laws. Just as the Federal Government has the right to decide that a state prosecution has not vindicated a violation of the "peace and dignity" of the Federal Government, a State must be entitled to decide that a prosecution by another State has not satisfied its legitimate sovereign interest. In recognition of this fact, the Court consistently has endorsed the principle that a single act constitutes an "offence" against each sovereign whose laws are violated by that act. The Court has always understood the words of the Double Jeopardy Clause to reflect this fundamental principle, and we see no reason why we should reconsider that understanding today.

The judgment of the Supreme Court of Alabama is affirmed.

It is so ordered.

Case Focus

1. The defendant in this case was charged and convicted of murder in the state of Georgia and later in Alabama was charged with and convicted of murdering the same person. On what basis did the Court hold that the Alabama prosecution was not barred by the double jeopardy clause?

• • • • • • • •

B. Statute of Limitations

Every jurisdiction in the United States has a statute of limitations that applies to most offenses and that bars prosecution after some specific period of time. In some jurisdictions, including under federal law, the statute of limitations is a defense that the defendant must raise,[9] while in others, when a charging instrument alleges as the date of the offense a date that is beyond the statute of limitations, the charging instrument must allege facts that invoke an exception to the statute of limitations and must cite the applicable exception.[10] In those states, facts that invoke an exception to the statute of limitations become an element of the offense that the prosecution must prove beyond a reasonable doubt.

While different states have different limitations periods for different offenses and differ to some extent about which offenses are subject to their statute of limitations, common to all of the states are questions about the point in time from which the limitations period is calculated. With offenses that consist of a single act (e.g., counterfeiting a credit card) or which make it a crime to bring about a particular result (e.g., murder), the limitations period begins to run, respectively, from the date the act is performed and from the date the result is brought about.

Where, however, the crime consists of a series of acts, the period of limitations is computed from the date of the last act in the series. For example, Rafik, Walid, and Hanif are engaged in a conspiracy to overthrow the United States government by force. In furtherance of the conspiracy, on January 5, 2004 Rafik purchases firearms; on May 8, 2004 Rafik, Walid, and Hanif obtain driver's licenses in fictitious names; on December 1, 2004 Rafik and Walid purchase precursor chemicals to formulate an explosive; and on February 2, 2005 all three travel to San

Francisco where they receive training in bomb building. The statute of limitations for the offense is calculated from February 2, 2005.

Certain events can either stop the running of the statute of limitations or extend it. For example, under some statutes of limitations the limitations period does not run while the person is not a resident of the state in which he committed the crime, and in the case of public officials it may not begin to run until after they leave office.

C. Pre-indictment Delay

Somewhat related to the concept embodied in the statute of limitations is the non-exculpatory defense of pre-indictment delay. This particular defense is based upon the due process clause of the U.S. Constitution and prohibits a prosecution where, because of the time that has elapsed between the date of the crime and the initiation of prosecution, the defendant suffered prejudice to his ability to defend against the criminal charge. The defense of pre-indictment delay supplements the statute of limitations and is not precluded merely because the prosecution was initiated within the applicable statute of limitations.

In order to be able to successfully assert the defense of pre-indictment delay, unlike with the statute of limitations where the mere passage of some specified period time is sufficient to give rise to a defense, the defendant must be able to establish that the delay actually and substantially prejudiced him in his ability to defend against the charges.[11] The prejudice to which this defense refers is usually the loss of evidence. The inability of the defendant to remember where he was or who he was with at the time he is alleged to have committed the crime with which he is charged is usually insufficient to establish the actual and substantial prejudice that the pre-indictment delay defense requires.[12]

Once the defendant establishes actual and substantial prejudice, the prosecution has the opportunity to show that the delay was reasonable. If the prosecution can establish that the delay was reasonable, the defense will fail. When the crime charged involves multiple complex financial transactions or business transactions across state lines and national borders, the courts will usually find even lengthy delays to be reasonable. The delay will also be considered reasonable when, despite investigation, key evidence identifying the defendant was not found, but years later becomes available either because a witness who previously had not been known comes forward or the development of a new scientific technique such as DNA testing allows forensic analysis that was previously unknown.

D. Speedy Trial

Once a defendant is charged with an offense he is entitled to a speedy trial. If he does not receive a speedy trial the court will dismiss the charges against him, and any further prosecution of the defendant on those charges will be barred. The rules relating to the calculation of the speedy trial term are technical, but critical for a paralegal to understand because often paralegals who assist prosecutors and defense attorneys will be responsible for keeping track of the days elapsed in the speedy trial term.

The right to a speedy trial grows out of the Sixth Amendment right to trial and is usually defined by statutes that set dates by which defendants charged with crimes must be brought to trial. Under these statutes, whether a defendant is in custody or out on bond is usually a critical fact that determines the period within which he must be brought to trial. In most states, a defendant who is on bond must affirmatively invoke his right to a speedy trial by demanding trial. If an on-bond defendant does not invoke his right to a speedy trial, he does not need to be brought to trial within the speedy trial period. When a defendant makes a demand for trial, that demand starts the speedy trial clock running. Under many statutes the demand is not effective unless it is made in writing. Once a defendant who is on bond demands trial he must, under most statutes, be brought to trial within 160 days. If he is not brought to trial within that time he is released and the prosecutor is barred from charging him again with the same offense.

If a defendant is in custody, under many statutes he does not need to demand trial to receive the benefit of the right to a speedy trial. When a defendant is arrested and unable to post bond or held without bond, under most statutes he must be brought to trial within 120 days. If he is not brought to trial within that period he will be released and the prosecutor will be prohibited from recharging him with the same offense.

For a paralegal who is charged with keeping track of speedy trial terms, it is critically important that the record accurately reflect the date of arrest, whether the defendant is in custody or on bond, and the date on which the defendant demands trial. The record must also accurately reflect each subsequent court date and to whom a continuance or delay is attributed. Generally, motions other than discovery motions filed by the defense (such as a motion to suppress evidence, a motion for a psychological examination, or a motion for scientific tests) will stop the running of the speedy trial term until the motions are decided or, in the case of tests, the results are obtained. If the defendant asks for or agrees to a continuance, that will also stop the running of the speedy

NAME _____ ARREST DATE _____ BOND _____ CUSTODY_____ CONTINUATION SUSPEND

DEMAND DATE _____

| 1 | 2 | 3 | 4 | 5 | 6 | 7 | 8 | 9 | 10 | 11 | 12 | 13 | 14 | 15 | 16 | 17 | 18 | 19 | 20 | _____ |

| 21 | 22 | 23 | 24 | 25 | 26 | 27 | 28 | 29 | 30 | 31 | 32 | 33 | 34 | 35 | 36 | 37 | 38 | 39 | 40 | _____ |

| 41 | 42 | 43 | 44 | 45 | 46 | 47 | 48 | 49 | 50 | 51 | 52 | 53 | 54 | 55 | 56 | 57 | 58 | 59 | 60 | _____ |

| 61 | 62 | 63 | 64 | 65 | 66 | 67 | 68 | 69 | 70 | 71 | 72 | 73 | 74 | 75 | 76 | 77 | 78 | 79 | 80 | _____ |

| 81 | 82 | 83 | 84 | 85 | 86 | 87 | 88 | 89 | 90 | 91 | 92 | 93 | 94 | 95 | 96 | 97 | 98 | 99 | 100 | _____ |

| 101 | 102 | 103 | 104 | 105 | 106 | 107 | 108 | 109 | 110 | 111 | 112 | 113 | 114 | 115 | 116 | 117 | 118 | 119 | 120 | _____ |

| 121 | 122 | 123 | 124 | 125 | 126 | 127 | 128 | 129 | 130 | 131 | 132 | 133 | 134 | 135 | 136 | 137 | 138 | 139 | 140 | _____ |

| 141 | 142 | 143 | 144 | 145 | 146 | 147 | 148 | 149 | 150 | 151 | 152 | 153 | 154 | 155 | 156 | 157 | 158 | 159 | 160 | _____ |

EXTENSION

| 21 | 20 | 19 | 18 | 17 | 16 | 15 | 14 | 13 | 12 | 11 | 10 | 9 | 8 | 7 | 6 | 5 | 4 | 3 | 2 | 1 | _____ |

trial term. Under the law of speedy trial, when a court must continue a case on its own motion because of a heavy trial call or for some other reason, that continuance will not stop the running of the speedy trial term.

Many defense attorney and prosecutor's offices use a form called a term counter to keep track of the time that has elapsed and that is remaining on a speedy trial term. It is critical for a paralegal who is charged with maintaining that record that she keep it accurately and that she familiarize herself with her jurisdiction's speedy trial rules. A sample of one commonly used form of a term counter appears above.

E. Ex Post Facto Laws and Bills of Attainder

Ex post facto laws were discussed in Chapter 7. As discussed in that chapter, the U.S. Constitution bars the adoption of such laws. Should a defendant be prosecuted for violating an ex-post facto law, he may assert the unconstitutionality of the statute as a defense to the prosecution. The Constitution also bars enactment of bills of attainder. As discussed in Chapter 7, a bill of attainder is a legislative act that punishes a person for violating a statute. Should a legislative body enact a bill of attainder, the person punished by the bill would be able to assert the unconstitutionality of the bill as a defense or to overturn the legislative act.

Jones v. Slick

Supreme Court of Florida (1952) 56 So. 2d 459

THOMAS, J. The appellants as members of the City Council of North Miami Beach instituted a suit against the appellee as mayor of that city seeking an injunction against his suspension of the city manager and city attorney, a declaration of the legality of an ordinance creating the office of manager, and a definition of this officer's duties. * * *

The very day the manager was selected it appears that a feud was started between the council and the mayor by the latter's removal of the manager on the grounds that the "appointment [was] a waste of the tax payers money," the majority of the voters in the municipality was opposed to such form of government and the ordinance was "contrary to the charter," hence illegal. Three days later the council voted not to sustain the suspension of Hansell so Hansell was reinstated. The following day the mayor again suspended the manager, giving but one new ground this time, namely, the usurpation by the manager of "the office of the Mayor." Three days passed and the council again voted not to approve this action by the mayor, therefore Hansell was again reinstated. The very next day the mayor suspended Hansell for the third time on the ground that the ordinance was invalid.

Meanwhile the mayor had also turned his guns on the attorney, removing him May 1 by verbal order for causes that do not appear in the record. The council, three days thereafter, disapproved this action and the following day the mayor again suspended the attorney because he was "unqualified" and so biased and prejudiced that he could not "fairly represent the City impartially." The council refused to confirm and the attorney was consequently reinstated, whereupon the mayor, the same day, removed the attorney on the same grounds and added one more—that he was "inexperienced." But these unusual goings on as they were detailed in the bill did not stop here. From an amendment it appears that both manager and attorney were continued in office by vote of the council and immediately suspended by the mayor, all since the bill was filed. * * *

This brings us to ordinance No. 233, enacted 8 May 1951 while the suspensions and reinstatements were in full career. Passed as an emergency measure it contained the provision that all ordinances, resolutions and orders of the council should be obeyed by all city officials and that any official who should be found guilty of disobedience "*by a two thirds vote of the City Council*" should be fined or imprisoned, or both, and removed from office. (Italics ours.) We will forego any

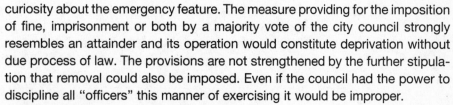

curiosity about the emergency feature. The measure providing for the imposition of fine, imprisonment or both by a majority vote of the city council strongly resembles an attainder and its operation would constitute deprivation without due process of law. The provisions are not strengthened by the further stipulation that removal could also be imposed. Even if the council had the power to discipline all "officers" this manner of exercising it would be improper.

Reversed in part and affirmed in part.

Case Focus

1. What about ordinance No. 233 makes it "strongly" resemble a bill of attainder?

• • • • • • • •

F. Selective Prosecution

The equal protection clause of the Fourteenth Amendment is the basis for the defense of selective prosecution. To successfully assert the defense of selective prosecution the defendant must establish (1) that others similarly situated to him have not been proceeded against for engaging in the type of conduct that forms the basis of the charge against him and (2) the government's selection of him for prosecution was based upon impermissible considerations such as race, religion, or the desire to prevent or punish him for the exercise of a constitutionally protected right.[13]

It is important to note that this defense does not prohibit the government from selecting persons for prosecution because they exercise a constitutional right who also break the law so long as the government prosecutes others who break the same law. For example, the government may, without engaging in prohibited selective prosecution, decide to prosecute a vocal and public opponent for failing to register for the draft if it also prosecutes others who fail to register.

G. Legislative Immunity

The United States Constitution contains what is commonly referred to as the "speech and debate" clause. The constitutions of virtually all of the states contain similar clauses. Generally, these provisions provide that legislators are immune from prosecution for criminal acts arising from the performance of their legislative duties. Legislative duties include voting, debating, and expressing opinions. The immunity conferred by these clauses is not confined to performance of duties in the legislative chamber and, in fact, applies wherever the legislator performs his official duties. For example, if the legislator is holding hearings in an office building 200 miles from the capitol, the immunity afforded by the speech and debate clause is applicable.[14] The immunity conferred by these clauses does not extend to the acceptance of bribes to take certain legislative action.[15] As a result, a legislator who accepts a bribe to introduce legislation or to vote for a specific bill cannot assert the immunity conferred by the speech and debate clause as a defense.

For any speech or debate in either house, they shall not be questioned in any other place. *U.S. Const.*, Art. I, Sec. 6, cl. 1.

H. Outrageous Government Conduct

The defense of outrageous government conduct had its genesis in a 1973 Supreme Court decision[16] and is based on the due process clause of the Fifth Amendment to the U.S. Constitution.[17] The defense is different than entrapment and provides that a court must dismiss a prosecution when the government's conduct is "shocking to the universal sense of justice" embodied in the due process clause.[18] The defense has been asserted in numerous cases and attacks the methods by which the government conducted its investigation.

Invariably the defense is used to attack some aspect of a government sting operation that the defendant argues meets the standard of outrageousness set by the Supreme Court. For example, defendants have claimed it was outrageous for government agents to create false criminal cases and use them as vehicles to bribe judges,[19] for law enforcement to hire men to pay for and engage in sex with prostitutes and then arrest the prostitutes,[20] and for government agents to recruit a female drug user and direct her to develop a sexual relationship with a target and use that relationship as a way to obtain evidence against him.[21] In none of these cases was the conduct found to be outrageous.

The outrageous government conduct defense has been criticized as being standardless because of its highly subjective nature and the fact that what shocks one judge may not shock another. The defense is seldom successful when it is raised.

United States v. Miller

United States Court of Appeals for the Seventh Circuit (1985) 891 F.2d 1265

CUDAHY, Circuit Judge. Curtis Miller was charged and convicted in a bench trial on one count of conspiracy to possess and distribute cocaine in violation of 21 U.S.C. section 841(a)(1) and two counts of distributing cocaine in violation of 21 U.S.C. section 841(a)(1) and 18 U.S.C. section 2. He now challenges his conviction and sentence on three grounds. First, Miller argues that the government engaged in "outrageous conduct" by employing a drug addict with whom Miller was romantically involved to induce him to sell drugs. * * * We affirm the judgment of the district court * * *.

I.

Miller was arrested in August 1988 in Knox County, Illinois, after making two sales of cocaine to Agent Randy Squire of the Multi-County Narcotic Enforcement Group ("MEG"). The first sale occurred on March 18, 1988, when Squire purchased 3.5 grams of cocaine from Miller for $275. On April 4, 1988, Miller sold Squire another 6.9 grams for $500. * * *

Squire was introduced to Miller by Linda Zefo (a.k.a. "Lin Ford"), who was also present at the March 18 and April 4 transactions. Zefo first met Miller on New Year's Eve of 1987 and became intimate with him soon after. They had dated for one and a half to two weeks in January 1988 before their relationship ended. In February 1988, Zefo became a confidential informant for MEG. MEG paid her living expenses while they employed her, and she also received $60 for each drug transaction that she arranged for MEG. At trial, Zefo admitted to being a cocaine addict both before and during her employment with MEG. Agent Squire and Special Agent Dan Bates knew of Zefo's drug habit, discouraged her from using cocaine, placed her in a drug treatment program and ultimately discontinued her employment when she failed to abandon her drug habit. Both agents testified that they had never personally witnessed her using drugs. * * * In addition to testifying about the two MEG buys, Zefo also told the court that Miller supplied her with small amounts of cocaine (quarter, half and single grams) and that he would sometimes visit her apartment late at night, saying he had been selling similar amounts in local bars. While Miller occasionally spent the night at Zefo's apartment during the MEG investigation, both he and she testified that they did not resume a sexual relationship. * * *

Having heard all the evidence, the district judge found Miller guilty on all three counts. Miller filed a post-trial motion for a new trial, claiming that the government's use of Zefo, Miller's former girlfriend and a known drug abuser, as an informant against him constituted "outrageous conduct." The district court denied the motion and imposed concurrent prison terms of 32 months for each of the counts. Miller appeals from these rulings.

II.

Miller urges us to conclude that the government's employment of Linda Zefo as a paid informant constituted "outrageous conduct" in violation of the due process clause. The Supreme Court introduced the concept of outrageous governmental conduct and distinguished it from the defense of entrapment in *United States v. Russell*, 411 U.S. 423 (1973). In that case, the Court found neither entrapment nor outrageous governmental conduct, but it left open the possibility that "we may some day be presented with a situation in which the conduct of law enforcement agents is so outrageous that due process principles would absolutely bar the government from invoking judicial processes to obtain a conviction. . . ." *Id.* at 431-432.

In order to preclude prosecution, the government's conduct must "violate that fundamental fairness, shocking to the universal sense of justice, mandated by the Due Process Clause of the Fifth Amendment." *Id.* at 432 (citing *Kinsella v. United States ex rel. Singleton*, 361 U.S. 234, 246 (1960)). Following *Russell*, this circuit has declared that "government conduct must be truly outrageous before due process will prevent conviction of the defendant." *United States v. Kaminski*, 703 F.2d 1004, 1009 (7th Cir. 1983). While several criminal appellants have charged the government with outrageous conduct in their cases, this court has yet to overturn a conviction on that basis. *See United States v. Valona*, 834 F.2d 1334 (7th Cir. 1987); *United States v. Shoffner*, 826 F.2d 619 (7th Cir.), *cert. denied sub nom. Stange v. United States*, 484 U.S. 958 (1987); *United States v. Swiatek*, 819 F.2d 721 (7th Cir.), *cert. denied*, 484 U.S. 903 (1987); *United States v. Bruun*, 809 F.2d 397 (7th Cir. 1987); *United States v. Podolsky*, 798 F.2d 177 (7th Cir. 1986); *United States v. Belzer*, 743 F.2d 1213 (7th Cir. 1984), *cert. denied sub nom. Clements v. United States*, 469 U.S. 1110 (1985); *United States v. Thoma*, 726 F.2d 1191 (7th Cir.), *cert. denied*, 467 U.S. 1228 (1984). Like those before him, Miller has failed to demonstrate that the government's conduct leading to his arrest and indictment was sufficiently outrageous to preclude his prosecution and conviction. * * *

EASTERBROOK, Circuit Judge, concurring.

I join the court's opinion, which observes that Miller loses no matter the state of the "outrageous governmental conduct" defense. Our court has never reversed a conviction on the basis of this defense and has questioned language looking favorably on it. E.g., *United States v. Bontkowski*, 865 F.2d 129, 131-132 (7th Cir. 1989); *United States v. Podolsky*, 798 F.2d 177, 181 (7th Cir. 1986). When push comes to shove, we should reject the contention that the criminal must go free because the constable was too zealous. Why raise false hopes? Why waste litigants' and judges' time searching for and rejecting on the facts defenses that ought not exist as a matter of law? Everyone has better things to do. Cf. *United States v. Wesson*, 889 F.2d 134 (7th Cir. 1989), slip op. 3.

Justice Rehnquist's opinion in *Hampton v. United States*, 425 U.S. 484, 490 (1976), supplies adequate reasons not to recognize a "due process" defense. Any claim to reversal of the conviction must rest on the proposition that the government's "outrageous" conduct violated a right *of the* defendant—a personal right secured by the Constitution rather than invented for the occasion. The entrapment defense reflects a conclusion that the statute does not punish conduct that the government has induced the defendant to commit by breaking down his resistance. *Sorrells v. United States*, 287 U.S. 435 (1932); *Sherman v. United States*, 356 U.S. 369 (1958). The "due process defense" does not rest on a claim that the prosecutor seeks to exceed the reach of the statute; it supposes that the defendant committed the crime defined by law. It is more like a claim that the government is violating the community's moral standards.

Defendants who think that the government went "too far" may make an entrapment defense or say that they lack the *mens rea* required of the offense. Miller had the necessary *mens rea*, however, and predisposition was established by earlier sales. So the traditional defenses were unavailable. As he committed the crime, he should stand convicted. If the investigators were too creative or squandered their limited resources, this is a political problem. Congress can hold oversight hearings or pass a law; we shouldn't apply a chancellor's foot veto. Dissipating law enforcement resources injures persons who become victims of crime when the deterrent force of the law declines. Reversing convictions of the guilty cannot apply balm to these wounds. Those who protest that social interests would have been served by prosecuting someone else (or some additional, similarly situated persons) routinely lose. E.g., *Wayte v. United States*, 470 U.S. 598 (1985) * * *. We deem it enough to support punishment that this person committed this offense, leaving to other institutions the redirection of investigative or prosecutorial resources. * * * Cf. *McCleskey v. Kemp*, 481 U.S. 279, 306-312 (1987); *Falls v. Town of Dyer*, 875 F.2d 146 (7th Cir. 1989). So it should be here.

Justice Rehnquist's opinion in *Hampton* did not speak for a majority of the Court, and some have read Justice Powell's concurring opinion, 425 U.S. at 492-495, as adopting an "outrageousness" defense. Put this together with the dissenting Justices in *Hampton* and you have five. If Justice Powell opened that door in *Hampton*, he shut it in *United States v. Payner*, 447 U.S. 727 (1980), writing for a majority of six. Investigators hired a women to cultivate "friendship" with a bank's courier. The courier paid a visit to the woman's apartment; after a time they went to dinner. While they were gone, the agents rifled his briefcase and found documents incriminating the bank's customers, who were prosecuted. They could not challenge the search under the fourth amendment because they did not have privacy interests in the briefcase. So they contended that the use of the evidence, gathered by "wilfully lawless activities", 447 U.S. at 734, should be suppressed under the Due Process Clause and the court's supervisory power. The Court declined the invitation, reasoning that the rules developed under the fourth amendment fully reflected the interests of society and suspects, and that replacing these rules with ill-defined supervisory or due process standards would undermine a balance properly struck. 447 U.S. at 733-737. And there was another problem:

> Even if we assume that the unlawful briefcase search was so outrageous as to offend fundamental "canons of decency and fairness," the fact remains that "the limitations of the Due Process Clause . . . come into play only when the Government activity in question violates some protected right of the *defendant*," *Hampton v. United States, supra*, at 490 (plurality opinion).

447 U.S. at 737 n.9 (emphasis and ellipsis by the Court; citations and internal quotes omitted). This footnote quotes from and adopts the core of Justice Rehnquist's assessment in *Hampton*. * * *

"Outrageousness" as a defense does more than stretch the bounds of due process. It also creates serious problems of consistency. The circuits that recognize a "due process defense" can't agree on what it means. How much is "too much"? The nature of the question exposes it as (a) unanswerable, and (b) political. What, if anything, could separate stirring up of crime in unpalatable ways here from the Operation Greylord methods sustained in *United States v. Murphy*, 768 F.2d 1518, 1528-1529 (7th Cir. 1985)? From the "creative" endeavors in Abscam? *United States v. Jannotti*, 673 F.2d 578 (3d Cir. 1982) (en banc). From any of the "sting" operations? From the rest of the sordid drug business, so dependent on caitiff assistants? Any line we draw would be unprincipled and therefore not judicial in nature. More likely there would be no line; judges would vote their lower intestines. Such a meandering, personal approach is the antithesis of justice under law, and we ought not indulge it. Inability to describe in general terms just what makes tactics too outrageous to tolerate suggests that there is no definition—and "I know it when I see it" is not a rule of any kind, let alone a command of the Due Process Clause.

The kinds of prosecutions that trouble me most are not those like Operation Greylord or offers of sex in exchange for cocaine, but those that impose costs on the innocent. Take for example a sting in which the FBI sets up a fence and buys stolen goods. The money the government pumps into the business must lead people to steal things to sell to the FBI—with misery for the victims of the burglary and potential violence in the process. Stings have been upheld consistently, however, and we have concluded that the innocent victims cannot recover damages from the government. *Powers v. Lightner*, 820 F.2d 818 (7th Cir. 1987). Methods such as those used to ensnare Miller do not injure bystanders and so do not trouble me. Other judges are offended by immorality (such as sponsoring an informant's use of sexual favors as currency) or by acts that endanger informants (such as supplying them with drugs for personal use) but not by a traditional sting. This shows the subjective basis of the concern—all the more reason not to have such a doctrine in our law.

Case Focus

1. What is the outrageous government conduct defense and what reason does Judge Easterbrook give for rejecting it as a rule of law?
2. How does the outrageous government conduct defense differ from the entrapment defense?

• • • • • • • •

CHAPTER TERMS

Collateral estoppel   Scienter   Ultimate fact

REVIEW QUESTIONS

1. How, if at all, does a defendant's culpability for committing a crime affect his ability to successfully assert a non-exculpatory defense?
2. When a defendant asserts a non-exculpatory defense that involves an issue of fact, who resolves that issue?
3. For purposes of the double jeopardy defense, when does jeopardy attach?
4. What does the double jeopardy clause prohibit?
5. What test is used to determine whether, for double jeopardy purposes, two offenses are the same or different?
6. When is a second prosecution for the same offense not barred by the double jeopardy clause?
7. What is the statute of limitations?
8. When an offense consists of a series of acts, how is the statute of limitations computed?
9. What is the defense of pre-indictment delay, and how does that defense differ from the statute of limitations?
10. What is the right to a speedy trial?
11. When does a defendant need to assert the right to a speedy trial to take advantage of it, and when is he automatically given the benefit of that right without the need of invoking it?
12. What must a defendant prove to be able to successfully assert the defense of selective prosecution?

ENDNOTES

1. Paul H. Robinson, Myron Moskovitz & Jane Grall, *Criminal Law Defenses* §201 (2007-2008).
2. The specific language of the double jeopardy clause reads as follows: ". . . nor shall any person be subject to the same offense to be twice put in jeopardy of life or limb . . ." *U.S. Const.* Amend. V.
3. *Ex parte Lange*, 85 U.S. 163 (1874).
4. *Crist v. Bretz*, 437 U.S. 28 (1978).
5. *United States v. Dixon*, 509 U.S. 688 (1993).
6. *Ashe v. Swenson*, 397 U.S. 436 (1970).
7. *Hudson v. United States*, 522 U.S. 93 (1997).
8. *Brewer v. Kimel*, 256 F.3d 222 (4th Cir. 2001).
9. *People v. Kohut*, 30 N.Y.2d 183 (1972); *United States v. Cook*, 84 U.S. 168 (1872).
10. *People v. Thingvold*, 145 Ill. 2d 441 (1991).
11. *People v. Lawson*, 67 Ill. 2d 449 (1977).
12. *Id.*
13. *United States v. Berrios*, 501 F.2d 1207 (2d Cir. 1974).
14. *Coffin v. Coffin*, 4 Mass. 1 (1808).
15. *United States v. Brewster*, 408 U.S. 501 (1972).
16. *United States v. Russell*, 411 U.S. 423 (1973).
17. *Id.*
18. *United States v. Simpson*, 891 F.2d 1265 (7th Cir. 1989).
19. *United States v. Murphy*, 768 F.2d 1518 (7th Cir. 1985).
20. *Hawaii v. Tookes*, 67 Haw. 608 (1985).
21. *United States v. Simpson*, 813 F.2d 1462 (9th Cir. 1987).

Criminal Procedure

Criminal procedure refers to the rules that govern: (1) how the government investigates crime, (2) how a person is charged with the commission of a crime, (3) what occurs in a case between the time a defendant is charged with a crime and the time of trial, (4) how a trial is conducted, and (5) what occurs following trial if a conviction is obtained. The chapters in this section examine those subjects in chronological order in the context of the stage of the criminal justice process in which they arise: investigation, arrest, charging, pre-trial, trial, and post-trial.

Today most American criminal procedure at both the federal and state level is determined by the United States Constitution and by four constitutional amendments. The nationalization of criminal procedure is a relatively recent development in American constitutional law and is the result of a series of U.S. Supreme Court decisions. Prior to the 1950s, the U.S. Constitution and the four amendments to it that regulate criminal procedure were understood as applying only to federal criminal investigations and prosecutions.

At that time state constitutions and state laws determined the procedures that were followed in state criminal investigations and prosecutions.

While the U.S. Supreme Court has nationalized criminal procedure, in doing so it has not completely supplanted procedural rights granted by state constitutions and state law. States remain free to adopt procedural laws that provide broader protections than those found in the federal constitution.

While most criminal procedure today is determined by the U.S. Constitution, important aspects of it continue to be determined by common law doctrines, statutes, and court rules. For example, common law doctrines determine when a court has *in personam* jurisdiction over a defendant, statutes regulate procedures for obtaining search warrants and eavesdropping orders, and court rules establish and regulate discovery in criminal cases.

Chapter 16
Criminal Procedure During the Investigative Stage — Search and Seizure

Chapter Objectives

After reading this chapter, you should be able to

- Explain when the Fourth Amendment requires a search warrant to conduct a search
- Understand when the Fourth Amendment does not require use of a search warrant to conduct a search
- Understand when the Fourth Amendment does not apply to a search
- Explain what must be established to obtain a search warrant
- Explain when law enforcement agents can make an arrest
- Understand the exclusionary rule
- Understand the fruit of the poisonous tree doctrine and when it applies
- Explain the three different levels of citizen-law enforcement agent encounters

> "... the house of everyone is to him as his castle and fortress, as well as for his defense against injury and violence, as for his repose; ..." —Semayne's Case, 77 Eng. Rep. 194, 195 (1620)

During the investigative stage of the criminal justice process law enforcement agents attempt to do three things: (1) determine whether a crime is being committed or has been committed; (2) identify who is committing or who has committed that crime; and (3) arrest the person they have identified as the perpetrator of the crime. In the Unites States, provisions of the Fourth and Fifth Amendments to the U.S. Constitution, and in some cases treaties, confer rights on individuals that have application during the investigative stage of the criminal justice process and that also regulate or affect how law enforcement agents conduct their investigations.

In this chapter we will examine the nature and scope of the rights conferred on individuals by the Fourth Amendment and see how those rights operate and regulate actions of law enforcement agents during the investigative stage of the criminal justice process. In the next chapter we will examine the nature and scope of the rights conferred on individuals by the Fifth Amendment and by certain treaties entered into by the United States and see how those rights operate and regulate actions of law enforcement agents during the investigative stage of the criminal justice process. In both chapters we will also examine the work paralegals perform during the investigative stage of the criminal justice process.

The Fourth Amendment to the United States Constitution prohibits unreasonable searches and seizures and regulates both when and how searches and seizures may be conducted. Under the Fourth Amendment the term "seizure" includes both seizures of property as well as seizures of persons. Thus, the Amendment protects against both unreasonable arrests and against unreasonable searches[1] and is violated when an unreasonable search or seizure is accomplished.[2] In this chapter we will examine: (A) when the Fourth Amendment applies to searches and seizures; (B) how the Fourth Amendment applies to searches; and (C) how the Fourth Amendment applies to arrests and other police-citizen encounters.

The Fourth Amendment reads as follows: "The right of the people to be secure in their persons, houses, papers, and effects, against unreasonable searches and seizures, shall not be violated, and no Warrants shall issue, but upon probable cause, supported by Oath or affirmation, and particularly describing the place to be searched, and the persons or things to be seized."

A. When the Fourth Amendment Applies to Searches and Seizures

Whether the Fourth Amendment applies to a particular search or seizure is determined by where the search or seizure is conducted and who is conducting it. When a search or seizure is conducted by government agents within American territory, the Fourth Amendment always applies. The Fourth Amendment, however, has no application to a search or seizure conducted by a private person who is acting without inducement by the government even if the reason that the private person conducts the search or seizure is to assist the government in its law enforcement function.[3]

For example, Adam is a security guard at a shopping mall that employs security guards for the purpose of apprehending and turning over to police persons who commit crimes on mall property. One day Adam stops Jorge, a convicted felon, on mall property and conducts a search of Jorge, which, if done by the police, would violate Jorge's rights under the Fourth Amendment. During that search Adam discovers that Jorge is carrying a concealed weapon that, because Jorge is a convicted felon, is a violation of the law for him to possess. Adam also discovers that Jorge has some goods that were stolen from a store in the mall. The Fourth Amendment does not apply to that search, and no Fourth Amendment right of Jorge has been violated by it, even though the sole purpose for conducting it is to assist the government by apprehending law breakers and turning them over to the police.[4]

When a search is conducted outside of American territory by American government agents, the Fourth Amendment only applies when the search is directed against American citizens. The Amendment has no application to searches conducted by American government agents outside of American territory when those searches are directed against foreign nationals.[5] That limitation is of particular importance when American law enforcement agents search foreign flagged vessels. Ships are considered to be part of the territory of the nation whose flag the ship flies. As a result, without regard to whether a foreign flagged ship is in international waters[6] or is docked in American territorial waters, because a vessel is considered to be part of the territory of the nation under which it is flagged, the Fourth Amendment does not apply to searches of it except to the extent the search may be directed against an American citizen.[7] To the extent the search is not directed against an American citizen, the Fourth Amendment has no application to that search.[8]

United States v. Vilches-Navarette

United States District Court for the District of Puerto Rico 413 F. Supp. 2d 60 (2006)

PEREZ-GIMENEZ, **Judge**. Before the Court is defendant Pedro Valladares-Benitez's "Motion to * * * Suppress Evidence and Statements" (Docket No. 95). For the reasons set forth below, defendant Valladares-Benitez's motion is DENIED with regards to * * * suppression of evidence * * *.

On January 31, 2005, a United States Coast Guard Cutter was instructed to intercept and board the 165-foot coastal freighter *M/V Babouth*, which was located on the high seas approximately 70 nautical miles off the coast of Trinidad and Tobago. The government has proffered that the initial decision to approach the *Babouth* was based on "specific and reliable intelligence" regarding the vessel's transportation of "a large quantity of cocaine" (Docket No. 131 at 14), and on the fact that the Coast Guard had monitored the ship throughout the previous night and observed smaller vessels traveling at high speeds towards it. Upon approaching the vessel * * *. The Coast Guard officers determined that the ship bore the flag of Honduras and, after obtaining a verbal statement of no objection to board the vessel and exercise jurisdiction over it from that nation, boarded the *Babouth.* Coast Guardsman Michael Azevedo first had a two-man team perform an Initial Safety Inspection of the vessel to guarantee its integrity and seaworthiness, while another two-man team secured the crew at the front of the ship's superstructure. After asking the master of the vessel routine questions, officer Azevedo requested that he produce the ship's registration documentation. Though the ship's master handed officer Azevedo a Trinidadian affidavit stating that the original documentation had been lost, the boarding crew later found it on board the vessel. Officer Azevedo also noticed that, while the ship carried 560 pallets of concrete, only 350 were slated for delivery, a fact the master could not explain. Additionally, the ship's global positioning system and navigation charts had been erased of all their data making it impossible to trace the *Babouth's* travels.

The Coast Guard boarding team continued searching the vessel throughout the night and into the morning of February 1, 2005. Officer Azevedo requested that he be given more personnel to continue the boarding of the mammoth vessel, and told his officer in charge that a dockside boarding would be safer and more productive. On February 2, 2005, officer Azevedo was informed that the USCG vessel *Shamal* would be on scene to assist and augment the boarding team. * * *

On February 3, 2005, Officer Azevedo found 17 grams of what appeared to be amphetamines and 58 grams of what appeared to be heroin in common spaces throughout the vessel. * * * On February 4, 2005, while the boarding and search of the *Babouth* continued at 29 nautical miles west of St. Croix, USVI, officer Azevedo was directed to take the vessel to San Juan. * * * At 7:25 a.m. of February 5, 2005, the *M/V Babouth* docked at the Coast Guard pier in San Juan.

Once the vessel was moored, the boarding continued, now aided by a multi-agency team. * * *

Armed with information [obtained surreptitiously from a crewman, Azevedo discovered a secret tank in the ship.] * * * Lieutenant Junior Grade Nicholas Friedman removed the bolts [from] * * * the tank to ensure that the space was gas-free and safe for entry [and upon doing so] * * * observed the tank to be almost completely full of bags * * *. The [search] team subsequently removed a total of 35 bales from inside the tank, all of which contained cocaine for a total of approximately 918 kilograms (2,030 lbs.) of the substance. Upon discovering the contraband, the boarding team transferred it to the custody of Customs and Border Patrol. Defendants were arrested and advised of their *Miranda* rights the same day. * * *

III. Valladares-Benitez's Motion to Suppress (Docket No. 95)

Defendants argue that the cocaine discovered in, and seized from, the *M/V Babouth* should be suppressed as fruit of an illegal search, raising the protections afforded by the Fourth Amendment. (Docket No. 95 at 17-26). * * *

B. Applicability of the Fourth Amendment

The Fourth Amendment to the U.S. Constitution guarantees "the right of the people to be secure in their persons, houses, papers, and effects, against unreasonable searches and seizures . . ." U.S. CONST. amend. IV. However, it is axiomatic that the Fourth Amendment was not "understood by contemporaries of the Framers to apply to activities of the United States directed against aliens in foreign territory or in international waters." *United States v. Verdugo-Urquidez*, 494 U.S. 259, 267 (1990). Though neither party has raised or briefed the *Verdugo-Urquidez* issue, the Court thinks it essential to the case. In light of the Supreme Court's holding in *Verdugo-Urquidez*, it is pellucid that the Fourth Amendment does not apply to the search of non-resident aliens on a ship in international waters. All defendants in the instant case are aliens to whom the guarantees of the Fourth Amendment do not apply, at least while the ship was in the high seas. Thus, that portion of defendants' motion that challenges the Coast Guard's search while the ship was on the high seas is **DENIED** without need to go any further.

However, this holding does not dispose of defendants' challenge of the dockside search in Puerto Rico. At first glance, it would appear that the Court's holding in *Verdugo-Urquidez* would not extend to that portion of the Coast Guard's search that took place while the *M/V Babouth* was moored in San Juan. See *Verdugo-Urquidez*, 494 U.S. at 274-275 (holding that the Fourth Amendment did not apply in part because the place searched was located in Mexico). * * * However, for at least two reasons, the Court is persuaded that the analysis and language adopted by the *Verdugo Urquidez* majority extends to the case at hand and makes inescapable the conclusion that the Fourth Amendment does not protect these defendants.

First, it is a fundamental rule of maritime law that "ships shall sail under the flag of one State only and, save in exceptional cases . . . shall be subject to its *exclusive jurisdiction* on the high seas." Convention on the High Seas art. 6(1), *opened for signature* April 29, 1958, 13 U.S.T. 2312 (entered into force Sept. 30, 1962) (emphasis added); see also United States v. Hensel, 699 F.2d 18, 27 (1st Cir. 1983) (citing the Convention on the High Seas). Given flag nations' *exclusive* jurisdiction over their vessels, it would logically follow that, like embassies, ships are the functional equivalent of their flag nations. If this is so, then a search of a foreign-flagged vessel is the equivalent of a search in foreign territory where the Fourth Amendment does not apply. *Verdugo-Urquidez*, 494 U.S. at 267. In this case, the *M/V Babouth* was a Honduran-flagged vessel. Thus, the search of the *Babouth* by the Coast Guard and other federal law enforcement agencies was the equivalent of a search conducted within the territory of Honduras. Consequently, in light of *Verdugo-Urquidez*, defendants, as aliens, find no protection in the Fourth Amendment, as the search they complain of for all practical purposes was conducted in foreign territory. Id.

Second, even if the vessel is not deemed to be the functional equivalent of foreign territory, the Court's conclusion still stands. The lynchpin of the Supreme Court's holding in *Verdugo-Urquidez* was the fact that the defendant in that case was "an alien who had no previous significant voluntary connection with the United States . . ." Verdugo-Urquidez, 494 U.S. at 271. In fact, the Court expressly rejected the defendant's argument that his presence within the U.S. at the time of the search (he was incarcerated in California awaiting trial) granted him shelter under the Fourth Amendment. Id. (holding that "this sort of presence—lawful but involuntary—is not of the sort to indicate any substantial connection with our country."). * * * Just as the applicability of the Fourth Amendment to the search of property located in Mexico should not "turn on the fortuitous circumstance of whether the custodian of its nonresident alien owner had or had not transported him to the United States at the time the search was made," we do not believe that it should turn on the equally fortuitous circumstance that the search of a foreign-flagged inter-coastal shipping vessel manned completely by aliens was completed within U.S. territory.

Consequently, defendants' motion to suppress is **DENIED**, as they cannot claim any rights under the Fourth Amendment. * * *

So ordered.

Case Focus

1. The court in this case held the Fourth Amendment did not apply to the portion of the search conducted on the high seas. On what basis did the court reach that conclusion?
2. What were the reasons the court gave for holding that the Fourth Amendment did not apply to the portion of the search that was conducted in American territorial waters?

• • • • • • • •

B. How the Fourth Amendment Applies to Searches

As it applies to searches, the courts have held the Fourth Amendment determines: (1) what areas are subject to its protection and what in those areas may be seized; (2) what must be established to obtain a search warrant; (3) how descriptive the warrant and the complaint which supports it must be; (4) how the search warrant must be executed; (5) the exceptions to its warrant requirements; and (6) how rights under it are enforced. This section examines each of those subjects.

1. Protection Afforded by the Fourth Amendment

By its terms the Fourth Amendment protects against unreasonable seizures and searches of a person, his home, his papers, and his effects. Historically, the Fourth Amendment was understood to apply only to the physical property enumerated in it and not to what could be heard or observed.[9] Under the historic understanding of the Fourth Amendment, a seizure occurs when there is some meaningful interference with an individual's possessory interest in his home, papers, or effects by agents of the government.[10] So, for example, the Amendment's protection applies where police make a trespassory entrance into Fiona's home to seize a CD (an effect) which contains images of her carrying packages of controlled substances into her home, but it does not extend to a trespassory entry by police onto an open field owned by Fiona that is across the road from her home from which they observe Fiona carrying controlled substances into her home.[11]

The driving force behind the adoption of the Fourth Amendment was the widespread hostility of American colonists to writs of assistance, which empowered royal tax collectors to search for smuggled goods, and to general warrants,[12] which permitted agents of the Crown to search and seize whatever and whomever they pleased while investigating crimes or affronts to the Crown.[13] Consistent with that history and the terms of the Amendment itself, Fourth Amendment jurisprudence was long tied to the common law of trespass.[14] A trespass occurs when a person makes an unauthorized entry on the property of another.[15] Even a minor unauthorized physical intrusion is sufficient to constitute a trespass.[16] For example, the placement of a self-powered tracking device on a car while the car is parked in a public parking lot is a sufficient unauthorized intrusion to constitute a trespass.[17]

Thus, the Fourth Amendment was seen as protecting the items enumerated in it (persons, their homes, papers, and effects) from trespassory searches.[18] Accordingly, a Fourth Amendment search was seen as occurring when there was a trespass to a person's home, papers, or effects by an agent of the government to find something or to obtain information.[19]

For example, Juan is suspected of being a drug dealer. Police officers enter Juan's home without a search warrant and without Juan's consent for the purpose of searching for heroin. In that case the police have trespassed a place specifically enumerated in the Fourth Amendment (a home) to find something (heroin). A Fourth Amendment search has occurred. If instead, the police enter an open field owned by Juan, again without a warrant and without Juan's consent, looking for a container they believe holds heroin belonging to Juan, a Fourth Amendment search has not occurred because an open field is not one of the protected areas enumerated in the Fourth Amendment.[20]

More recently the courts have given the Fourth Amendment a broader sweep than either history or the language of the Amendment would suggest it has. In 1967, in *Katz v. United States,* [21] the U.S. Supreme Court appeared to cut the Fourth Amendment from the moorings of its language, holding that the Amendment protects privacy without regard to whether there was a physical intrusion, and that it protects against the unreasonable seizure of both physical objects and intangible things, such as conversations overheard through a wiretap.[22]

The *Katz* decision created some confusion about whether its invasion of privacy analysis of when a search occurred supplanted or supplemented the older enumerated items/trespass analysis. In *United States v. Jones,*[23] the Supreme Court made clear that instead of supplanting the enumerated items/trespass analysis that predated *Katz*, the *Katz* decision merely added to it[24] and that the property specifically enumerated in the Fourth Amendment is protected from trespassory searches and seizures by government agents even if there was not an invasion of privacy under *Katz*.[25] Thus, the *Jones* decision makes it clear that a Fourth Amendment search occurs when: 1) there is a trespass by government agents to the items specifically enumerated in the Fourth Amendment, or 2) there is an invasion of privacy under *Katz*, and 3) that trespass or invasion of privacy is conjoined with an attempt to find something or obtain information.[26]

The *Katz* decision was somewhat vague about how to determine what areas are protected by the privacy it found the Fourth Amendment protects, but it is now understood as holding that the Amendment protects any area in which (1) a person has an actual expectation of privacy and (2) that person's expectation of privacy in that area is one that society is prepared to accept as objectively reasonable.[27]

A person has an actual expectation of privacy in certain places such as his home and, when he demonstrates such an expectation by conduct or otherwise in other places, he can be found to have an actual expectation of privacy in those other places as well. Conduct that demonstrates an expectation of privacy can include keeping items in closed containers or otherwise shielded from public view or by fencing one's property and placing a locked gate across a private access road into it.

Under *Katz*, demonstrating an expectation of privacy is not, by itself, sufficient to create Fourth Amendment protection in a particular place or thing. In addition to that expectation, *Katz* requires that a person's expectation of privacy be one that society is prepared to accept as objectively reasonable. If a court determines that the person's expectation of privacy in some place or thing is not one that society is prepared to accept as objectively reasonable, then notwithstanding the person's expectation of privacy in that place or thing, it will be outside the protection of the Fourth Amendment.[28]

Since *Katz* courts have generally held that a person has an expectation of privacy that society will recognize as reasonable in things such as certain parts of his body, his home, his office, his desk, his locked briefcase, a hotel room, and a rented storage room. In contrast, the courts have held that absent a special relationship, such as a physician-patient or attorney-client relationship, persons generally do not have an expectation of privacy in things they reveal to another because by revealing something to another person, any expectation of privacy is destroyed.

For example, if James is a covert government agent the Fourth Amendment does not prohibit him from engaging Tyrone in conversations about Tyrone's drug-dealing business nor does it prohibit James from recording that conversation, because if Tyrone reveals information about that business to James, he no longer has an expectation of privacy in that information.[29]

United States v. Hoffa

Supreme Court of the United States (1966) 385 U.S. 293

MR. JUSTICE STEWART delivered the opinion of the Court.

Over a period of several weeks in the late autumn of 1962 there took place in a federal court in Nashville, Tennessee, a trial by jury in which James Hoffa was charged with violating a provision of the Taft-Hartley Act. That trial, known in the present record as the Test Fleet trial, ended with a hung jury. The petitioners now before us—James Hoffa, Thomas Parks, Larry Campbell, and Ewing King—were tried and convicted in 1964 for endeavoring to bribe members of that jury. The convictions were affirmed by the Court of Appeals. A substantial element in the Government's proof that led to the convictions of these four petitioners was contributed by a witness named Edward Partin, who testified to several incriminating statements which he said petitioners Hoffa and King had made in his presence during the course of the Test Fleet trial. Our grant of certiorari was limited to the single issue of whether the Government's use in this case of evidence supplied by Partin operated to invalidate these convictions. 382 U.S. 1024.

The specific question before us, as framed by counsel for the petitioners, is this:

"Whether evidence obtained by the Government by means of deceptively placing a secret informer in the quarters and councils of a defendant during one criminal trial so violates the defendant's Fourth Amendment rights that suppression of such evidence is required in a subsequent trial of the same defendant on a different charge."

At the threshold the Government takes issue with the way this question is worded, refusing to concede that it "'placed' the informer anywhere, much less that it did so 'deceptively.'" In the view we take of the matter, however, a resolution of this verbal controversy is unnecessary to a decision of the constitutional issues before us. * * *

The controlling facts can be briefly stated. The Test Fleet trial, in which James Hoffa was the sole individual defendant, was in progress between October 22 and December 23, 1962, in Nashville, Tennessee. James Hoffa was president of the International Brotherhood of Teamsters. During the course of the trial he occupied a three-room suite in the Andrew Jackson Hotel in Nashville. One of his constant companions throughout the trial was the petitioner King, president of the Nashville local of the Teamsters Union. Edward Partin, a resident of Baton Rouge, Louisiana, and a local Teamsters Union official there, made repeated visits to Nashville during the period of the trial. On these visits he frequented the Hoffa hotel suite, and was continually in the company of Hoffa and his associates, including King * * *. During this period Partin made frequent reports to a federal agent named Sheridan concerning conversations he said Hoffa and King had had with him and with each other, disclosing endeavors to bribe members of the Test Fleet jury. Partin's reports and his subsequent testimony at the petitioners' trial unquestionably contributed, directly or indirectly, to the convictions of all four of the petitioners. * * *

I.

It is contended that only by violating the petitioner's rights under the Fourth Amendment was Partin able to hear the petitioner's incriminating statements in the hotel suite, and that Partin's testimony was therefore inadmissible under the exclusionary rule of *Weeks v. United States*, 232 U.S. 383. The argument is that Partin's failure to disclose his role as a government informer vitiated the consent that the petitioner gave to Partin's repeated entries into the suite, and that by listening to the petitioner's statements Partin conducted an illegal "search" for verbal evidence.

The preliminary steps of this argument are on solid ground. A hotel room can clearly be the object of Fourth Amendment protection as much as a home or an office. *United States v. Jeffers*, 342 U.S. 48. The Fourth Amendment can certainly be violated by guileful as well as by forcible intrusions into a constitutionally protected area. *Gouled v. United States*, 255 U.S. 298. And the protections of the Fourth Amendment are surely not limited to tangibles, but can extend as well to oral statements. *Silverman v. United States*, 365 U.S. 505. Where the argument falls is in its misapprehension of the fundamental nature and scope of Fourth Amendment protection. What the Fourth Amendment protects is the security a man relies upon when he places himself or his property within a constitutionally protected area, be it his home or his office, his hotel room or his automobile [We do not deal here with law of arrest under the Fourth Amendment.]. There he is protected from unwarranted governmental intrusion. And when he puts something in his filing cabinet, in his desk drawer, or in his pocket, he has the right to know it will be secure from an unreasonable search or an unreasonable seizure. * * *

In the present case, however, it is evident that no interest legitimately protected by the Fourth Amendment is involved. It is obvious that the petitioner was not relying on the security of his hotel suite when he made the incriminating statements to Partin or in Partin's presence. Partin did not enter the suite by force or by stealth. He was not a surreptitious eavesdropper. Partin was in the suite by invitation, and every conversation which he heard was either directed to him or knowingly carried on in his presence. The petitioner, in a word, was not relying on the security of the hotel room; he was relying upon his misplaced confidence that Partin would not reveal his wrongdoing. As counsel for the petitioner himself points out, some of the communications with Partin did not take place in the suite at all, but in the "hall of the hotel," in the "Andrew Jackson Hotel lobby," and "at the courthouse."

Neither this Court nor any member of it has ever expressed the view that the Fourth Amendment protects a wrongdoer's misplaced belief that a person to whom he voluntarily confides his wrongdoing will not reveal it. Indeed, the Court unanimously rejected that very contention less than four years ago in *Lopez v. United States*, 373 U.S. 427. In that case the petitioner had been convicted of attempted bribery of an internal revenue agent named Davis. The Court was divided with regard to the admissibility in evidence of a surreptitious electronic recording of an incriminating conversation Lopez had had in his private office with Davis. But there was no dissent from the view that testimony about the conversation by Davis himself was clearly admissible.

As the Court put it, "Davis was not guilty of an unlawful invasion of petitioner's office simply because his apparent willingness to accept a bribe was not real. Compare *Wong Sun v. United States*, 371 U.S. 471. He was in the office with petitioner's consent, and while there he did not violate the privacy of the office by seizing something surreptitiously without petitioner's knowledge. * * * The only evidence obtained consisted of statements made by Lopez to Davis, statements which Lopez knew full well could be used against him by Davis if he wished. . . ." 373 U.S., at 438. In the words of the dissenting opinion in *Lopez*, "The risk of being overheard by an eavesdropper or betrayed by an informer or deceived as to the identity of one with whom one deals is probably inherent in the conditions of human society. It is the kind of risk we necessarily assume whenever we speak." *Id.*, at 465. See also *Lewis v. United States, ante*, p. 206.

Adhering to these views, we hold that no right protected by the Fourth Amendment was violated in the present case.

• • • • • • • •

Courts have also held that a person has no expectation of privacy in something that can be seen with the naked eye from a place any member of the public can be. For example, if Phillip, a government agent, hires a helicopter and flies it through public airspace, and with his naked eye, can see marijuana plants growing in a backyard greenhouse owned by Walid, the Fourth Amendment does not prohibit Phillip's conduct, because he saw the plants growing when he was in a location any member of the public had a right to be.[30]

Courts have also said that a person has no expectation of privacy in things that any member of the public can access. For example, if Ronald places his garbage in a garbage can located on the curb of a public street, the Fourth Amendment does not apply to a search of the garbage, because any member of the public could look through it.[31]

2. What Must Be Established to Obtain a Search Warrant

The fact that the Fourth Amendment applies to protect certain areas from government intrusion does not mean those areas are beyond the reach of law enforcement. Instead, it simply means that before law enforcement agents can search a protected area and seize something from it they must first obtain a search warrant from a magistrate, usually a judge, which authorizes a search of that area and the seizure of the things described in it.[32]

In order to obtain a search warrant law enforcement agents usually must present a magistrate with a document that in many jurisdictions is called a complaint for search warrant or a petition for a search warrant. The complaint for search warrant must be executed under oath or be supported by a separate statement made under oath by the person seeking issuance of the search warrant. In some jurisdictions the complaint for search warrant and the search warrant itself may be prepared by law enforcement agents and presented by them to a magistrate; in other jurisdictions those documents are prepared in the prosecutor's office. Paralegals working in prosecutors' offices frequently will assist in the preparation and drafting of both the complaint for search warrant and the search warrant itself.

Historical Perspective

The Warrant Requirement: A Creation of the Fourth Amendment or a Later Creation of the Judiciary?

As discussed in the text the Supreme Court has held that unless an exception is applicable a search warrant must be obtained before law enforcement agents can search a location in which a person has a reasonable expectation of privacy that society will recognize. The relevant language of the Fourth Amendment, however, neither by its express terms nor by necessary implication imposes a warrant requirement and in the context of arrests the same clause of the Amendment has been read as not imposing a requirement that law enforcement agents obtain a warrant before taking a person into custody.[33] On its face the Amendment would appear to merely prohibit unreasonable searches and seizures and to create a standard that must be satisfied before a judge can issue a warrant. The relevant language of the Fourth Amendment reads:

> The right of the people to be secure in their persons, houses, papers and effects, against unreasonable searches and seizures shall not be violated; and no warrant shall issue but upon probable cause, supported by Oath or affirmation, and particularly describing the places to be searched, and the persons or things to be seized.[34]

As at least one judge when called upon to construe a virtually identical provision of his state's constitution[35] rhetorically asked, how can that guaranty be "distorted" to require that a warrant be obtained before all searches and in effect read:

> No person or his house or effects shall be searched, or himself or things in his possession seized, except by virtue of a search warrant issued after a showing of probable cause supported by affidavit particularly describing the place to be searched and the person or things to be seized?[36]

As the judge who wrote those words observed: "If the writers of the state and federal Constitutions had intended that there could be no lawful search and seizure without a warrant, they would have said so." [37]

While the Fourth Amendment can certainly be read as imposing a warrant requirement, a look at the historical backdrop against which the Amendment was adopted raises a significant question about whether that is what the Amendment was intended to do.

During the colonial period and at the time the Fourth Amendment was adopted, the common law allowed agents of the government to perform searches without a warrant if they had probable cause.[38] The Fourth Amendment was drafted by James Madison who had studied law and who undoubtedly knew the common law allowed such searches if government agents had probable cause. If the Amendment was directed at changing what had long been the practice under the common law, it would seem reasonable, as dissenting Judge Thompson in the *Castree* case said, that the Amendment would have explicitly stated that a warrant must be obtained before government agents conduct any search.

During the colonial period, if the person whose property was searched by government agents believed the agents did not have probable cause when they searched, he could sue the agents who conducted the search for trespass and if he prevailed (i.e., if it was found that the government agents did not have probable cause when they searched his property), he would obtain not only the return of his property, if any was seized, but also an award of money damages.[39] As a result, in case they were mistaken about the existence of probable cause, during the colonial period government agents obtained search warrants, not because warrants were required before conducting a search, but instead to insulate themselves against personal liability for trespass assessed by colonial juries.[40]

As discussed in the main text, the Fourth Amendment was adopted in response to writs of assistance and general warrants issued by royal judges, which among other things authorized searches of private homes.[41] General warrants were warrants that were issued without probable cause, which described neither the place to be searched nor the things or person to be seized.[42] Thus, many legal scholars believe that the Fourth Amendment was adopted in response to what the colonists saw as an abuse by judges and as a limit on the power of judges to issue search and arrest warrants.[43] That view is supported by early state court decisions interpreting similar provisions of state constitutions, which construed those provisions as limiting the power of judges to issue search warrants and not as imposing a requirement that government agents obtain search warrants before performing a search.[44]

In some jurisdictions a judge can issue a search warrant based on a telephonic or other electronic communication.[45] In those jurisdictions, when a judge determines that it is reasonable to dispense with a written complaint he can issue a search warrant based on information communicated to him by telephone or by some other reliable electronic means.[46] In such a situation the judge must place the applicant under oath and make a verbatim record of the conversation with a recording device, by using a court reporter, or in a writing he makes himself.

Historically, search warrants were only issued to search for the fruits, instrumentalities, and evidence of crimes that had already been committed and for which there was evidence to show that those items were located at the place to be searched. In order to obtain a search warrant relating to a completed crime, the complaint for search warrant must contain information that is sufficient to show **probable cause** to believe that: (1) a crime has been committed, (2) the items to be searched for and seized are the fruits, instrumentalities, or evidence of that crime, and (3) the items to be searched for and seized will be found at the

Probable cause exists when there is a rational basis for official action. *Avila v. Pappas,* 591 F.3d 552 (7th Cir. 2010).

location to be searched. In most states the crime that forms the basis for issuing a search warrant can be either a misdemeanor or a felony.

More recently, particularly in cases involving possession of contraband such as controlled substances and child pornography, law enforcement agents have sought and courts have approved the issuance of what are called anticipatory search warrants. Anticipatory search warrants differ from ordinary search warrants because they authorize searches for items relating to crimes that have not yet been committed and of locations where those items are not yet located. Anticipatory search warrants contain what is usually called a triggering condition and do not become effective until that triggering condition is satisfied.[47] Triggering conditions are usually the occurrence of some future event, such as the delivery of a contraband-containing package to the place described in the search warrant. A triggering condition must be something other than the mere passage of time.[48]

To obtain an anticipatory search warrant, the search warrant complaint must show probable cause to believe that the triggering condition will occur.[49] For example, Maurice in Michigan purchases several pounds of marijuana from Yolanda in Florida and has it shipped to his home by UPS. In a UPS sorting facility the package bursts when a heavier package falls on it. UPS employees recognize the contents of the burst package to be marijuana and notify the DEA. The DEA obtains agreement from UPS to have a DEA agent pose as a UPS deliveryman to deliver the package to Maurice. Prior to delivery, DEA agents obtain a warrant to search Maurice's home for marijuana when he takes the marijuana-filled package inside the house. In that example, the triggering condition is Maurice taking the package inside the home and the fact that the package is addressed to Maurice and will be delivered there by an undercover DEA agent constitutes the probable cause to believe that the triggering condition will occur.

In the law of search and seizure the concept of probable cause is a fluid one. Probable cause is determined on a case-by-case basis and involves an assessment by the judge of probabilities in the particular factual context of each case.[50] The determination of probable cause is made from an examination of what is referred to as the "totality of the circumstances" and involves a practical and nontechnical analysis of the facts[51] that includes considering whether the information set out in the complaint is reliable. The fact that there is an innocent explanation for certain occurrences does not foreclose a finding of probable cause.[52]

Probable cause may be established in a number of ways. One way in which probable cause can be established is from the direct observation of a law enforcement agent. Another way in which probable cause can be established is from the direct observation of a private citizen who is either the victim of or a witness to a crime and who relates information about what he observed to a law enforcement agent. For example, Carl, the owner of a jewelry store, flags down a passing police car, points to Raphael who is running down the street with a bag in his hand and tells the police officer that Raphael just robbed his store of both money and jewelry. The police officer gives chase and sees Raphael run into a warehouse. If the police officer were to seek a search warrant to search the warehouse, in the search warrant complaint the police officer would be able to establish probable cause that a crime had been committed through the statements made to him by Carl and, through his own visual observations, establish probable cause to believe that fruits of the crime would be found in the warehouse. Information provided to law enforcement by victims and private-citizen witnesses is usually considered reliable without corroboration.

Probable cause can also be and frequently is established using information from informants. When information from informants is used as the basis for establishing probable cause there must be some evidence to show that the information is reliable. Reliability can be established in a number of ways, including by showing that the informant has provided information in the past that has proven to be accurate,[53] by corroborating in some way some of the information provided by the informant,[54] or by showing that the informant had some basis for knowing the information upon which the finding of probable cause is to be based.[55]

The experience and expertise of a law enforcement agent in investigating particular types of crimes can also be used to help establish probable cause[56] as can the expertise of third parties such as accountants, forensics experts, and computer experts as long as that expertise is reflected in the search warrant complaint. For example, a U.S. postal inspector who has investigated numerous cases involving mortgage fraud schemes that attorneys as co-conspirators have facilitated is now seeking a search warrant for records located in attorney Proust's office that are related to a suspected mortgage fraud scheme in which Proust handled the real estate transactions. For the purpose of trying to establish probable cause that certain documents exist and are located in Proust's office, he might state the following in the search warrant complaint:

> I have conducted more than fifty mortgage fraud investigations. Based on my experience in those investigations I have learned that the following documents are usually brought to or generated at the closing of real estate transactions and that attorneys representing buyers in real estate transactions customarily retain copies of those documents in a file identified to the parcel of property being transferred or the name of the purported client: sales contracts, copies of the HUD-1 closing statements, copies of the title insurance commitment, copies of surveys of the property being purchased, copies of correspondence with the client's lender, copies of mortgage applications, copies of an appraisal of the property, and copies of checks brought to the closing or issued by the agency closing the transaction.

3. Descriptiveness Required for Complaint and Warrant

In addition to facts to establish probable cause, the Fourth Amendment also requires particularity and forbids overbreadth.[57] The two concepts are similar yet they are distinct.[58] A warrant is overbroad when there is lack of probable cause to seize some or all of the items listed on it as "to be seized." A warrant is sufficiently particularized when it: 1) identifies the offenses for which law enforcement has established probable cause; 2) describes the place to be searched; and 3) specifies the items to be seized in relation to the designated crimes.[59]

The description of the items to be seized must be sufficiently specific that it permits law enforcement agents to look at it and exercise rational judgment in selecting the items to seize.[60] The description requirement can be particularly challenging in complex white collar crime investigations, which frequently require the assembly of a "paper puzzle" from a large number of seemingly innocuous pieces of individual evidence.[61]

When the seizure of documents is sought the search warrant complaint must describe the documents or categories of documents to be seized and identify the crime to which they relate.[62] For example:

"documents containing fraudulent statements in relation to political asylum applications, fraudulent birth certificates, 'boiler-plate' political asylum applications, fictitious stories outlining political persecution, and receipts and financial records relating to fraudulent asylum applications."[63]

When the seizure of property is sought the search warrant complaint must describe the property to be seized so definitely that the law enforcement officer performing the search will not seize the wrong property.[64] When the search is for contraband property it is usually sufficient to describe the contraband to be seized by its nature rather than to particularly describe the property itself.[65] For example:

methamphetamine, records of drug transactions, and drug paraphernalia.[66]

Where the place to be searched contains similar items, some of which are contraband subject to seizure and some of which are not, the search warrant complaint must contain an explanation of how to distinguish the contraband items from the similar noncontraband items. That explanation must also be contained in the search warrant itself. For example, if law enforcement agents are seeking a search warrant to search for and seize pirated CDs and the search will be executed at a retail store that has in its inventory both pirated and nonpirated CDs, both the search warrant complaint and the search warrant itself must contain some explanation of how to distinguish between the two.

In such cases the complaint must also contain some explanation of how the **affiant** knows that the method described in the complaint and warrant to distinguish between the contraband and noncontraband items

Affiant is one who has made an affidavit. *People ex rel. Livington v. Wyett,* 186 N.Y. 383 (1906). An affidavit is a written statement sworn to before some officer authorized to administer Oaths, *Id.,* such as judge or a notary.

is a reliable one.[67] One way the affiant can establish that knowledge is by relating in the complaint that the information was provided to him by an expert who he interviewed and who explained to him how to distinguish the contraband from the noncontraband items. If an expert is consulted the complaint should also contain facts that show the person's expertise. Those facts can be experience, education, or both. Often in such situations the search warrant will specifically require[68] or will authorize law enforcement to have an expert present[69] during its execution to assist in distinguishing between or to actually identify the contraband and noncontraband items.

The search warrant complaint must also describe the place to be searched. Generally the description must be such that it will allow a person who reads the warrant to find the location to be searched. The description will usually include the street address (if the number appears on the building to be searched), a description of the building, and if it contains more than one unit (e.g., multiple apartments or places of business), a way of identifying the particular unit or place of business to be searched. That might be done by referencing a number or name on a door.

Once a search warrant complaint is completed it is presented to a judge. The complaint may be presented by the prosecutor and the law enforcement agent executing it or by the law enforcement agent without the prosecutor. If the judge determines that the complaint contains sufficient facts to establish probable cause, an adequate description of the place to be searched, and a sufficient description of the things to be seized, the judge will sign the search warrant and will note on the warrant the date and time he signed it. A search warrant must be executed within a certain period of time after being issued. In many jurisdictions the time period is 96 hours. If the warrant is not executed within that period of time it automatically becomes void.

The Fourth Amendment and Grand Jury Subpoenas

Despite the fact that the terms of the Fourth Amendment specifically refer to unreasonable searches and seizures, courts have held that the Amendment provides protection against enforcement of grand jury and other subpoenas that are overly broad. Overly broad subpoenas are considered to be unreasonable and hence to violate the Fourth Amendment.[70] Critical in determining whether a subpoena is reasonable are three factors: (1) whether it commands production of relevant material; (2) whether it specifies with particularity the materials to be produced; and (3) whether the period of time to which the material relates is reasonable.[71] The witness who challenges a subpoena has the burden of showing that the subpoena is unreasonable.[72]

If the witness challenges a grand jury subpoena on the ground that it seeks irrelevant material the prosecutor frequently must at least identify to the court the offenses that the grand jury is investigating. To establish that the

STATE OF ILLINOIS   )
COUNTY OF ████████████   ) SS   THE PEOPLE OF THE STATE OF ILLINOIS

IN RE:

)
)
A MATTER BEFORE THE   )   NO.
GRAND JURY OF ████████ COUNTY,   )
ILLINOIS   )

TO: First National Bank of ██████
       Keeper of Records
       201 N. ████████ St.
       ██████ Illinois ████████

GRAND JURY SUBPOENA

   YOU ARE HEREBY COMMANDED to personally be and appear before the ██████████ County Grand Jury at the ██████████ County Courthouse, ██████████████ Illinois on the _19th_ day of _JUNE_ , 200 _2_ at 1:30 p.m. and testify and produce the documents and things described in **Schedule A** and **Schedule B** attached, and this you will in no wise omit.

   YOUR FAILURE TO APPEAR IN RESPONSE TO THIS SUBPOENA WILL SUBJECT YOU TO PUNISHMENT FOR CONTEMPT OF THIS COURT.

                              WITNESS this 16th day of May, 2002

                              [signature]   ████████████
                              CLERK OF THE CIRCUIT COURT
                              (SEAL OF COURT)

Direct Inquiries To:
████████████
Assistant Attorney General
100 W. ████████████
████████ Illinois ████████

I served this subpoena by handing a copy to _____ on
_____, 2002.

Fees: $_____   _____

Subscribed and sworn (or affirmed) to before me December _____ by _____ .

                              _____
                              Notary Public

SCHEDULE A

This schedule is attached to and made a part of certain grand jury subpoena dated May 16, 2002 issued by the Grand Jury of ███████ County, Illinois. You are hereby commanded to produce the following instruments, articles, and things relating to all accounts identifiable to Mary L.███████ Box ██ C███ Illinois for the period from June 10, 1985 through May 16, 2002:

1. Applications, signature cards and statements for any and all checking accounts.
2. Applications, signature cards and statements for any and all savings accounts.
3. Front and back copies of any and all items deposited to and/or drawn on any and all checking accounts.
4. Front and back copies of any and all items deposited to any and all saving accounts.
5. Copies and deposit slips for any and all checking and/or savings accounts.
6. All loan and/or line of credit records, including applications, record of amounts borrowed, payments, collateral agreements and ledger sheets.
7. Financial statements and credit reports.
8. Safe deposit box records, including applications and records of access.
9. Copies of all promissory notes.
10. Mortgage records and applications.
11. Copies of Certificates of Deposit and related deposits and disbursements of funds.
12. Records of purchase of bearer bonds.
13. Receipts of delivery of all securities.
14. Investment and/or custodian accounts.
15. Records of transfer or collection of funds by wire.
16. Copies of all applications for purchase of counter checks, manager's checks, cashier's checks, treasurer's checks and/or money orders, together with the checks and/or money orders that were purchased and related documents showing the manner in which these checks or money orders were purchased.
17. Credit card applications, monthly statements and records of purchases, cash advances and payments.
18. Retained copies of all Currency Transaction Reports relating to the above transactions and records documenting each transaction.
19. Copies of the institution's Currency Transaction Report "Exempt List" and any documentation received or internally generated justifying the exemption.
20. Records of any and all "Cash station" or other Automated Teller Machine transactions.

SCHEDULE B

This schedule is attached to and made a part of certain grand jury subpoena dated May 16, 2002 issued by the Grand Jury of ███████ County, Illinois. You are hereby commanded to produce the following instruments, articles, and things relating to Robert ███████:

1. All applications for made for mortgage loans during the year 2002;

2. All income tax returns provided to the bank by Robert ███████ in connection with any mortgage loan application made by him to the bank during the year 2002;

3. All profit and loss statements, income statements, and balance sheets provided to the bank by Robert ███████ in connection with any mortgage loan application made by him to the bank during the year 2002

subpoena seeks irrelevant material the witness must then prove that there is no reasonable possibility that the material sought by the grand jury will produce evidence relevant to the general subject of the investigation.[73]

As with a search warrant, a grand jury subpoena must also specify with some particularity the materials being sought or it will be considered overly broad. A subpoena is sufficiently particular when it specifies the production of documents that relate to specific subjects.[74] For example, a subpoena that requires the production of books and records of an entity that:

reflect sales of tangible personal property at retail, purchase orders and other documents relating to the purchase of goods for resale, and journals and other documents reflecting accounts payable and accounts receivable

satisfies the particularity requirement.

A subpoena that is unlimited as to time and description (i.e., a subpoena that seeks production of "all records") will, if challenged, be found to be unreasonable.[75] In contrast, a subpoena that is limited as to time and as to the type of documents being sought will, if not overly broad in other respects, usually be found to be reasonable notwithstanding that it seeks "all records." For example, if the grand jury is investigating corruption in the awarding of public works contracts by a government agency during the years 2002 through 2006, a subpoena to that agency that demands "all bid specifications, all bids received, and all correspondence relating to all public works contracts awarded from December 31, 2001 through December 31, 2006" will, notwithstanding that it demands production of all records, be considered reasonable.

The search warrant is usually prepared at the same time the search warrant complaint is prepared, and both it and the search warrant complaint are presented to the judge at the same time. Like the complaint for search warrant, the search warrant itself must contain a description of the location to be searched and a description of the things to be searched for and seized. Those descriptions should be identical to the descriptions contained in the search warrant complaint. The search warrant must also contain a finding by the judge that probable cause has been established.

Checklist for Search Warrant Complaint

Information Needed for a Search Warrant Complaint

✓ Facts that will establish probable cause
✓ Name of offenses believed to have been committed and statutory citations of those offenses
✓ Description of the place to be searched
✓ Description of the things to be seized

Considerations When Preparing a Search Warrant Complaint

✓ If the complaint will contain information from an informant to establish probable cause, will the informant be identified by name or by some other designation such as "Jane Doe" or "Informant #602?"
✓ Will individuals be named in the complaint? If so, should they be referred to by name or by some other designation such as "Public Official A?"
✓ Should a "no-knock" warrant be issued? If so what facts support its issuance?
✓ Should the complaint for search warrant be sealed?

If the application for a search warrant was presented telephonically or by some other electronic means, the applicant for the warrant must read or otherwise transmit the contents of the proposed warrant to the judge, who must enter its contents into an original warrant that he prepares.[76]

4. Execution of a Search Warrant

The Fourth Amendment requires that before law enforcement agents force entry to execute a search warrant, they knock on the door of the premises to be searched, identify themselves and the fact that they have a search warrant, and allow a reasonable time for an occupant to open the door.[77] In drug cases the Supreme Court has held that a reasonable time to wait before forcing entry is 15-20 seconds after knocking and announcing.

The law allows law enforcement agents to ignore the knock-and-announce requirement if they have a reasonable suspicion that knocking and announcing could create a risk of violence, could result in the destruction of evidence,[78] or would be futile.[79] In many jurisdictions at the time a warrant is being requested law enforcement agents can ask

F I L E D

JUL 1 5 1997

AURELIA PUCINSKI
CLERK OF CIRCUIT COURT

STATE OF ILLINOIS   )
)
COUNTY OF COOK   )

IN THE CIRCUIT COURT OF COOK COUNTY, ILLINOIS

COMPLAINT FOR SEARCH WARRANT

Now comes, G███████████, Complainant, and requests the issuance of a search warrant to search the units commonly known as units 1513 and 1515 █████ Drive, ████████ Village, Illinois, of the single story, multi-unit, red brick building located on the east side of █████ Drive, in █████████████, Illinois; the building having multiple entrance doors on its south side with the number "1513" being on the second most eastern door located on the south side of the building and the number "1515" along with the words "█████Express" being on the most eastern door located on the south side of the building; the north side of the building having at least 3 loading docks; the east side having an overhead type garage door.

Complainant requests a search warrant for the purpose of seizing the following described instruments, articles and things of █████Express, Inc. (hereinafter "V███"):

a) All daily ledger type records which contain the names of drivers, miles driven, shipment origin and destination, routes taken and the billing amount;

b) All documents of approximately 4-1/2 inches by 9-1/2 inches in size with printed lines on their face which contain information including driver name, miles driven, shipment origin and destination and routes taken and the billing amount;

c) All records contained in black three ring binder type books that contain the names of drivers and records of all trips made by drivers for V███;

d) All other fruits, instrumentalities and evidence of the offenses of Failure to File Motor

Fuel Use Tax Returns and Failing to Pay Motor Fuel Use Tax, violations of <u>Illinois</u>

<u>Compiled Statutes</u>, Chapter 35, Section 505/15(2).

e) All checks, ledger sheets, spreadsheets which show payment of wages or salary to

employees of V███;

f) All other fruits, instrumentalities and evidence of the offenses of failure to file

Withholding Tax Returns and failure to remit Withholding Tax, violations of <u>Illinois</u>

<u>Compiled Statutes</u>, Chapter 35, Sections 5/1301 and 5/1302, respectively.

Complainant has probable cause to believe, based upon the following facts, that the above

offenses have been committed and that the things to be seized are now located at the premises

described above.

Your affiant states that he is a special agent with the Illinois Department of Revenue,

Bureau of Criminal Investigations, who is assigned to the Motor Fuel Enforcement group of the

Bureau and that he is conducting an investigation of a business known as V███ Your affiant

further states that V███ obtained a Motor Fuel Use Tax license from the Illinois Department of

Revenue on August 16, 1996, that V███ renewed its license in February of 1997 and continues to

be so licensed as of this date. Under <u>Illinois Compiled Statutes</u>, Chapter 35, Section 505/13a.3

persons holding Motor Fuel Use Tax licenses issued by the Department of Revenue are required

to file Motor Fuel Use Tax Returns by the last day of the month following each calendar quarter.

That since renewing its Motor Fuel Use Tax license in February 1997 V███ has obtained 85

license decal sets from the Department of Revenue. Each truck operated by V███ or under

V███'s authority is required to display a license decal on the doors of the truck cab.

Your affiant further states that on June 12, 1997 he spoke to ███ Bl███████. On that date Bl████ advised your affiant that he had worked for V███ and that he knew from personal knowledge that V███ had not filed Motor Fuel Use Tax Returns. On June 13, 1997 your affiant spoke to ███████ M██████ of the Motor Fuel Use Tax Section of the Department of Revenue and at that time she advised your affiant that the Department's computerized records showed that since V███ registered with the Department no Motor Fuel Use Tax Returns have been received from V███.

On June 16, 1997 your affiant again spoke to ███████ Bl█████████. At this time Bl█████ told your affiant that he started to work at V███ in October 1996 and severed his employment there the last week of May, 1997. Bl███████ informed your affiant that V███ maintained two types of records that memorialize the mileage driven by its drivers and the routes taken by them. These records are: 1) a ledger type of record that lists the driver's name, the mileage driven, the origin and destination, and the routes taken and 2) driver files that are kept in black three ring binder books and contain the names of the each driver and a record of all trips made by the driver. According to Bl████████ these records are kept at the above described premises in ████████████, Illinois.

On July 3, 1997 your affiant spoke to ████████K██████. K██████ advised your affiant that he has been a dispatcher for V███ for the last five months. K██████ said his duties include maintaining the spreadsheets described to your affiant by ████████ Bl█████████. According to K██████ these sheets contain shipment destination and origin, mileage driven, routes taken, and billing amounts. K██████ also said that he has seen the black three ring binder books, that the books contain the drivers' names and a record of the all trips of the drivers, but that he does not work with these books. K██████ further advised your affiant that the ledger records and the black three ring binder books are kept at the above described premises in ████████ Village, Illinois and he last saw them there late in the morning of July 3, 1997.

On July 3, 1997, K████ also advised your affiant that as part of his job at V██ he maintains "load cards". According to K█████, load cards are documents approximately 4-1/2" by 9-1/2" in size with lines printed on them. The "load cards" contain the same information as contained on the spreadsheets. K█████ advised your affiant that these cards are kept at the above described premises in ████████████, Illinois and he saw them there late in the morning of July 3, 1997.

Your affiant spoke to K█████ on July 7, 1997 and at that time K█████ told your affiant that he has quit working at V██ because he has not been paid.

Both B█████████ and K█████ also have advised your affiant that V██ has at least three female employees, their names being Jenny, Monica, and Sonia. On July 8, 1997 your affiant reviewed the computer records of the Illinois Department of Revenue and that review indicated that V███. was not registered with the Department of Revenue for withholding tax, that no withholding tax returns had been received by the Department of Revenue from V███ and that no withholding tax payments had been received by the Department of Revenue from V███.

On July 8, 1997 your affiant spoke to K█████ and at that time K█████ informed your affiant that V███ has only one location, the above described premises in ██████████████, Illinois and that to K█████s knowledge all business records of V██ are kept at that location. K█████ also told your affiant that V██ paid him by cash and by check. Your affiant further states that he has been a special agent of the Department of Revenue since 1990 and that based on his experience businesses with employees keep records of the amounts paid to their employees.

Wherefore, your affiant, special agent G███████████, respectfully requests that a search warrant be issued for the ██████████, Illinois location described.

██████████████████████

G████████████, Special
Agent, Illinois Department of
Revenue

STATE OF ILLINOIS   )
COUNTY OF COOK   )

Your affiant, G█████████, being first duly sworn on oath deposes and says that he has read the above and foregoing Complaint for Search Warrant by him subscribed and that the same is true in substance and fact to the best of his knowledge.

████████████████████

G███████████

Subscribed and sworn to before me this
8th day of July, 1997

Judge of the Circuit Court

██████████
Assistant Attorney General
████████ St. ████████
██ Illinois ██ ██████
████████████

STATE OF ILLINOIS   )
)
COUNTY OF COOK   )

IN THE CIRCUIT COURT OF COOK COUNTY, ILLINOIS

SEARCH WARRANT

THE PEOPLE OF THE STATE OF ILLINOIS, to any Peace Officer of the State of

Illinois, GREETINGS:

On this day appeared G███████████, complainant in person and made complaint in

writing on oath subscribed and sworn to before the undersigned Judge of the Circuit Court of

Cook County, Illinois. Upon examination of the Complaint, I find that it states facts sufficient to

show probable cause.

I therefore command you search the units commonly known as units 1513 and 1515

████████ Drive, ███████ Village, Illinois, of the single story, multi-unit, red brick building

located on the east side of ██████ Drive, in ██████████, Illinois; the building having

multiple entrance doors on its south side with the number "1513" being on the second most

eastern door located on the south side of the building and the number "1515" along with the

words "█████ Express" being on the most eastern door located on the south side of the building;

the north side of the building having at least 3 loading docks; the east side having an overhead

type garage door; and seize the following described instruments, articles and things:

a) All daily ledger type records which contain the names of drivers, miles driven,

shipment origin and destination, routes taken and the billing amount;

b) All documents of approximately 4-1/2 inches by 9-1/2 inches in size with printed lines

on their face which contain information including driver name, miles driven, shipment

1 of 2

origin and destination and routes taken and the billing amount;

c) All records contained in black three ring binder type books that contain the names of drivers and records of all trips made by drivers for V███;

d) All other fruits, instrumentalities and evidence of the offenses of Failing to File Motor Fuel Use Tax Returns and Failing to Pay Motor Fuel Use Tax, violations of <u>Illinois Compiled Statutes</u>, Chapter 35, Section 505/15(2).

e) All checks, ledger sheets, spreadsheets which show payment of wages or salary to employees of V█████████, Inc.;

f) All other fruits, instrumentalities and evidence of the offenses of failure to file Withholding Tax Returns and failure to remit Withholding Taxes, violations of <u>Illinois Compiled Statutes</u>, Chapter 35, Sections 5/1301 and 5/1302, respectively.

I further command that a return of anything so seized shall be made without unnecessary delay before me or before any other Judge or Court of competent jurisdiction.

Judge

5:10 P.M.
8 July 1997

Time and Date of Issuance

Assistant Attorney General
███ St. ██████
IL █████
████████

2 of 2

the judge to issue what is called a "no-knock" warrant. If a court issues a no-knock warrant, law enforcement agents can force entry to the premises to be searched without first knocking and announcing.

When law enforcement agents execute a search warrant the warrant allows them to search anywhere in the specified premises where the items described in the warrant could be found. For example, if a search warrant ordered law enforcement agents to search for packets of cocaine, law enforcement agents could open drawers, cabinets, and closets to look for them because such packets could be kept in any of those places. If instead a search warrant authorized a search for and the seizure of stolen desktop computer towers, law enforcement agents could open closets and perhaps certain large cabinets because the towers could be hidden within them, but because the towers could not be hidden inside drawers, law enforcement agents could not open drawers while executing the warrant.

Once a search warrant has been executed law enforcement agents leave a copy of the search warrant at the place they searched. After execution of the warrant law enforcement agents must make what is called a "return" of the warrant to a judge. In many states the return does not need to be made to the issuing judge and can instead be made to any judge with jurisdiction over those matters. The return is made in writing, is signed by a law enforcement agent who executed the search warrant, and contains an inventory of the items seized and a statement that relates the date and time of execution. The return is accompanied by the original search warrant complaint and the original search warrant. In many jurisdictions paralegals in the prosecutor's office prepare an order for the judge to sign in which the judge accepts the return and inventory and directs a specific law enforcement agency to hold the seized items at a specific location.

5. Exceptions to the Warrant Requirement

A search warrant is not always needed to search an area protected by the Fourth Amendment. The courts have created more than 20 exceptions to the warrant requirement.[80] Seven of the more important exceptions are discussed below.

One of the most important exceptions to the warrant requirement is consent. If a person gives his consent to law enforcement agents to search an area that would otherwise be considered protected by the Fourth Amendment, the agents do not need to obtain a search warrant before searching it. The consent to search must be given voluntarily, but it does not need to be a knowing consent.[81] As a result, law enforcement agents do not need to inform a person that she has a right to refuse to give consent nor does the prosecution need to prove that the person giving consent knew she had the right to refuse.[82] The fact that law enforcement agents informed a person of the right to refuse to consent to a search may be considered in determining whether the consent to search was voluntarily given, but failure to inform does not, by itself, render consent involuntary.

In determining whether consent is voluntary the courts look at the totality of the circumstances surrounding the consent. The existence of certain facts can, however, be seen as rendering the consent involuntary. One fact that will result in a finding that the consent was given involuntarily is if when consent was requested the individual was faced with a show of force by law enforcement agents. The show of force can range from simply being confronted by a large number of law enforcement agents to a law enforcement agent brandishing a gun. Another fact that courts consider in assessing the voluntariness of a person's consent is the maturity and education of the person giving consent. If the person consenting is young and poorly educated, a court is more likely to find the consent to be involuntary. If, however, the consenting person is well educated, older, or has experience in business matters, courts are more likely to find that person's consent to have been voluntarily given.

In determining the voluntariness of a person's consent, courts will also consider whether at the time a person consenting to a search was under the influence of an intoxicating substance. The mere fact that a person was intoxicated,[83] so intoxicated that she could not legally drive, or even that her blood alcohol level was twice the legal limit to drive is not by itself sufficient to render her incapable of giving voluntary consent.[84] Generally, as long as the person giving consent is able, despite being intoxicated, to understand the nature of her acts, she will be considered capable of giving voluntary consent.[85]

United States v. Willie

United States Court of Appeals for the Eighth Circuit (2006) 462 F.3d 892

MELLOY, J. David Lee Willie appeals the judgment * * * of the district court following his conviction for possessing pseudoephedrine while knowing or having reasonable cause to believe that it would be used to manufacture a controlled substance under 21 U.S.C. §841(c)(2). * * *

Willie makes three arguments on appeal: (1) the search of the motel room where the pseudoephedrine was found was unlawful under the Fourth Amendment * * *. We affirm.

I. BACKGROUND

Around 4:00 on the morning of June 10, 2003, Eureka, Missouri, Police Department Officer William Knittel stopped to investigate an illegally-parked vehicle in the fire lane of the local Super 8 Motel. The owner of the car, David Lee Willie, was loading boxes into the vehicle when Knittel first observed him. Knittel quickly recognized Willie as a local resident and asked why he was loading boxes at a motel at such an early hour, particularly because Willie had a home in the area. Willie claimed that he and his wife were separating, and he was loading boxes to return to her. When Knittel asked where his wife was located, Willie claimed he did not know where to find her. During this exchange, Knittel also observed symptoms of methamphetamine use or production, including sores on Willie's face, the smell of anhydrous ammonia, and Willie's inability to stand still.

As Knittel was writing Willie a citation for illegal parking, Officer Michael Smith arrived as backup. Smith noticed a knife in Willie's pocket and, upon receiving Willie's consent, removed the knife. Smith also noticed and removed a cut straw from the pocket. The straw had a white residue on it that field-tested positive for methamphetamine. Smith arrested, handcuffed, and placed Willie in the back of Knittel's squad car. * * *

Upon questioning, Willie said he was staying with two other people in room 124 of the motel. Knittel knocked at the door to room 124, met briefly with the two occupants, and then re-joined Smith to conduct an inventory search of Willie's car. That search uncovered significant evidence of drug use and trafficking. * * *

Sergeant Jason Randall arrived on the scene during the inventory search and asked for Willie's consent to search the motel room. Willie gave his consent to the search, and Randall and Smith proceeded to search room 124. In it, they saw numerous boxes stacked along the walls of the room, several rifles that Smith believed he recognized from an unrelated visit to Willie's home a few weeks before, and two duffel bags on the floor. The two remaining occupants of the room disclaimed ownership of any of the items other than a small pile of clothing.

The officers seized the duffel bags but left the rifles, which Smith assumed to be unloaded. One duffel bag contained more than 13,000 pseudoephedrine pills, a chemical used in the production of methamphetamine. The other bag contained equipment that could be used to manufacture methamphetamine. Later that day, Knittel received confirmation from the motel that room 124 was registered to Willie.

A grand jury indicted Willie for possession of pseudoephedrine with knowledge or reasonable cause to believe that it would be used to manufacture a controlled substance under 21 U.S.C. §841(c)(2). The district court denied Willie's motion to suppress the evidence gathered from the motel room. Willie proceeded to trial and a jury found him guilty. * * *

II. DISCUSSION

A. Willie's Consent to Search the Motel Room

First, Willie contends that the search of his motel room was unlawful under the Fourth Amendment because his consent to the search was given involuntarily. In particular, he points out that he was under arrest when Officer Randall asked for his consent, he had not received any *Miranda* warnings at that time, and he was visibly intoxicated from methamphetamine use, all of which served to vitiate his purported consent to the search.

The government bears the burden of proving voluntary consent to a search by a preponderance of the evidence, *United States v. Czeck*, 105 F.3d 1235, 1239 (8th Cir. 1997), and we review a district court's finding of voluntary consent under a clear error standard. *United States v. Siwek*, 453 F.3d 1079, 1083 (8th Cir. 2006). The question of voluntariness requires a broad factual inquiry; there is no bright-line rule to determine when an "essentially free and unconstrained choice," *Schneckloth v. Bustamonte*, 412 U.S. 218, 225 (1973) (quotation omitted), becomes one that is "the result of duress or coercion." *Id.* at 248. Instead, we consider the "totality of all the circumstances." *Id.* at 227.

Our case law offers a catalogue of factors to consider in judging the voluntariness of a defendant's consent to search. Some relate to the characteristics and behavior of the defendant, such as the defendant's age, intelligence and education, knowledge of his constitutional rights (whether from *Miranda* warnings in the encounter at issue or from previous interactions with police), whether he was under the influence of drugs or alcohol, and whether he objected to the search or stood by silently as it was occurring. *United States v. Chaidez*, 906 F.2d 377, 381 (8th Cir. 1990). Others relate to the environment surrounding the defendant at the time he gave his consent, such as whether he was in custody or under arrest and whether he was in a public or secluded place. *Id.* Still others relate to the interaction between police and the defendant in the encounter, such as whether police officers detained and questioned the defendant for a long time before obtaining his consent, whether they threatened, physically intimidated, or punished him, and whether they made promises or misrepresentations upon which the defendant relied in giving his consent. *Id.* No one factor is dispositive; they are merely tools for analyzing the "totality of all the circumstances." *Bustamonte*, 412 U.S. at 227.

While some of these factors weigh against voluntariness in this case, we cannot say that the district court clearly erred in its determination of the ultimate question: whether Willie's "will ha[d] been overborne and his capacity for self-determination critically impaired" such that his consent to the search of his motel room was involuntary. *United States v. Watson*, 423 U.S. 411 (1976) (alteration in original) (quoting *Bustamonte*, 412 U.S. at 225). Willie was forty-eight years old at the time of his arrest. He was a high school dropout, but he possessed the aptitude to operate his own extermination business from 1989 to 2002. He may have been under the influence of methamphetamine at the time of his arrest, but the evidence does not suggest that he was so intoxicated that he was not "competent to understand the nature of his acts." *United States v. Rambo*, 789 F.2d 1289, 1297 (8th Cir. 1986). He generally cooperated with police, responded to their questioning, and knew the number of the motel room where he was registered. We cannot presume (as Willie would have us do) that his inability to offer the police a convincing explanation of his activities that morning is proof positive that he lacked the mental capacity to consent to the search. * * *

Willie also offers no evidence of police intimidation or misrepresentation, nor of an environment that would give rise to a presumption of involuntary choice.

Willie was under arrest and handcuffed at the time he gave his consent, but he had not been subjected to extended questioning and had only been under arrest for, at most, the time that it took officers to meet briefly with the fellow occupants of room 124 and complete an inventory search of his vehicle. In addition, he was in a public place (the motel parking lot) at all times leading up to his grant of consent. *See Watson*, 423 U.S. at 424 (finding valid consent despite a defendant's arrest when the consent was given in a public setting and there was no evidence of coercive police tactics). In short, the totality of the circumstances does not suggest that Willie's consent was anything other than a free choice, and the district court did not err in so finding. * * *

For the foregoing reasons, we affirm the judgment and sentence of the district court.

Case Focus

1. At the time Willie consented to the search he was under the influence of meth. On what basis did the court conclude that his intoxication did not prevent him from giving a valid consent?
2. What does the court look at when determining whether a consent to search is voluntary?

• • • • • • • •

Another factor that can affect the determination of voluntariness is whether law enforcement agents tell the individual that if he does not consent they can search anyway. If law enforcement agents tell an individual that, the individual's consent will be considered involuntarily given. Sometimes law enforcement agents will tell an individual if he does not consent they will obtain a search warrant. Depending on the circumstances, that can render consent involuntary. If the statement is a pretext to obtain consent, the consent will be considered involuntarily given. If at the time the statement was made the law enforcement agent knew sufficient facts to constitute probable cause, the consent is considered voluntary. If, however, the law enforcement agents simply tell the individual that if she does not consent to a search they will seek a search warrant that usually will not be seen as rendering her consent involuntary.

Assuming the individual voluntarily consents to a search, the law enforcement agent is limited to searching the area that the individual agreed to let him search. For example, if a person consents to allowing a law enforcement agent to search the living room of his home, that consent does not allow the law enforcement agent to search any other room in the home.[86] Also, an individual who has consented to a search is free at any time to revoke his consent to search.[87]

A second exception to the warrant requirement is for motor vehicles. While a mere traffic stop is not sufficient to allow a warrantless search of a vehicle, if law enforcement agents have probable cause to believe that a motor vehicle contains contraband or the fruits, instrumentalities, or evidence of a crime, they can search the motor vehicle without first obtaining a search warrant. The primary limitation on the scope of a motor vehicle search is the items or things for which the law enforcement agents are searching. For example, if a policeman is searching a vehicle trying to determine whether the vehicle is stolen, that will not by itself allow him to open closed containers in the vehicle. However, if the police have probable cause to believe the vehicle contains stolen gemstones, then because of their small size, the police could conduct a much more thorough search, which could include opening closed compartments and cutting open seat cushions.

The courts have struggled with whether the motor vehicle exception allows the warrantless search in a vehicle of closed containers such as luggage or a briefcase. Generally, if the items for which there is probable cause to search the vehicle will fit in the closed container, law enforcement agents can search that container without first obtaining a warrant. For example, if law enforcement agents have probable cause to search a vehicle for stolen gems, not only can they search the vehicle, but they can also search luggage or a briefcase inside the vehicle. If law enforcement agents have probable cause to believe the vehicle is transporting illegal aliens, they could search the trunk of the vehicle, but would not be able to search luggage or a briefcase found in the passenger compartment or trunk.

One important limitation on the vehicle-container exception is when law enforcement agents know that a container belongs to a passenger who they have no reason to believe is connected with the criminal activity they are investigating. In that case, law enforcement agents cannot search the container that belongs to the passenger.

Another important exception to the warrant requirement is a search incident to an arrest. When law enforcement agents make an arrest they are allowed to search the person being arrested together with areas within that person's reach. For example, law enforcement agents are allowed to open drawers, cabinets, and containers within the radius of an arrestee's reach. That exception is driven by a concern for officer safety, and the purpose is to allow the law enforcement agents to locate any weapons that the person being arrested might be able to grab and use against them.

A fourth exception to the warrant requirement arises when police are executing an arrest warrant for a defendant at his home. In that situation the police are allowed to search anywhere in the home where a person would be able to hide. As with the search incident to arrest exception, this exception is driven by a concern for officer safety. The purpose for allowing such searches is to allow law enforcement agents to locate both the person for whom they have an arrest warrant and anyone else in the home who might give assistance to that person. For example, if the police have an arrest warrant for Roxie and go to Roxie's home to arrest her, they are allowed to look in all of the rooms and closets of the home and under beds. The arrest warrant would not, however, allow them to open drawers and small cabinets that are not within the Roxie's reach that would be too small to conceal a person.

A fifth exception to the warrant requirement is called the plain view exception. Law enforcement agents do not need a search warrant to seize contraband or the fruits, instrumentalities, or evidence of a crime that are in plain view from a place that the agents have a legal right to be. For example, law enforcement agents go to Rafik's home to execute a search warrant for stolen guns and while executing the warrant they open a closet in the home and find packages of cocaine laying on the floor of the closet. The law enforcement agents can seize the drugs because the warrant authorized them to be in the home and to look in closets because closets might contain the guns they were authorized to search for and seize.

A sixth exception to the warrant requirement is the so-called exigent circumstances exception. In cases involving exigent circumstances, law enforcement or other government agents enter an area protected by the Fourth Amendment for a purpose other than making an arrest or searching for and seizing evidence or other items.

In exigent circumstances cases the government agents frequently enter the protected area because they believe or have reason to believe a person's life or property may be at risk. In such situations any search conducted by law enforcement is limited by what is necessary to address the particular emergency. For example, the police receive a call telling them that a man has been shot in a particular apartment and in response to that call they proceed to the apartment and knock on the door. If no one answers the police can enter the apartment without a warrant and search it for the purpose of finding the possible victim.[88] In that situation the exigent circumstances exception would allow a search of all of those places where a body might be found and any place in the apartment where a perpetrator might be hiding, but it would not justify a search of other areas such as drawers and desks.[89]

A seventh exception to the warrant requirement is the foreign intelligence exception. Under this exception the government does not need a warrant to conduct surveillance to gather intelligence for national security purposes when the surveillance is directed against agents of a foreign power reasonably believed to be outside the United States.[90] Under this exception the government does not need a warrant to monitor phone conversations of foreign agents and suspected terrorists who are reasonably believed to be located outside the United States even if the monitoring is done from within the country.

6. *Enforcing the Fourth Amendment Requirements for Searches*

When a defendant believes that there has been a search in violation of the Fourth Amendment the defendant must file what is called a motion to suppress. It is through a hearing on a motion to suppress that a court determines whether or not law enforcement agents actually violated the Fourth Amendment. A court will not consider the legality of a search and seizure unless a motion is filed, and a court has no authority to suppress evidence without a hearing on the motion in which the prosecution has an opportunity to present evidence.[91] In most states the motion to suppress is required to be in writing, must state facts that show that the search was unlawful,[92] and should also list or describe the evidence that the defendant seeks to suppress. In most states the defendant has the burden of producing evidence that shows that an illegal search was performed.[93]

Historical Perspective

The Exclusionary Rule: The Continuing Debate

The rule requiring exclusion of unconstitutionally obtained evidence from trial, usually referred to as the exclusionary rule, represents a relatively recent and controversial development in Anglo-American criminal procedure. Prior to its adoption in *Weeks v. United States*,[94] American courts, including the U.S. Supreme Court itself, had ruled that illegally seized evidence was admissible against the person from whom it was seized.[95] Instead of excluding such evidence, both federal and state courts had held that a person aggrieved by an illegal search could sue the offending law enforcement agents for trespass and also noted that law enforcement agents who conducted illegal searches were subject to prosecution for criminal trespass and disciplinary action by the agency that employed them.

The *Weeks* decision only applied to federal prosecutions and left the states free to adopt the exclusionary rule or continue to follow the common law and allow illegally seized evidence to be used. Nearly 45 years later, in *Mapp v. Ohio*,[96] the Supreme Court mandated that the states use the exclusionary rule as the remedy for illegal searches and seizures by law enforcement agents. Interestingly, other major common law nations, such as the United Kingdom and Canada, have not adopted the exclusionary rule.[97]

From the time it was first adopted in the *Weeks* case, the exclusionary rule has been controversial and its merits the subject of vigorous debate among both judges and legal commentators.[98] That controversy and debate continues today.[99] In the ten years following the *Weeks* decision, 46 state courts heard cases in which they considered whether to continue to follow the traditional common law rule of allowing unconstitutionally seized evidence to be used as evidence in court or to adopt the exclusionary rule for such cases.[100] The vast majority of the state courts that considered the issue refused to adopt the exclusionary rule and chose instead to continue to follow the common law.[101]

Of the post-*Weeks* state cases to consider and reject adoption of the exclusionary rule, one of the most famous was the decision of the New York Court of Appeals in a case called *People v. Defore*.[102] In that decision, written by Judge Benjamin Cardozo, who would later be named to the U.S. Supreme Court, the court discussed many of the issues surrounding the rule that continue to be debated today. In the *Defore* case the court refused to adopt the exclusionary rule, saying that in terms of the valuable and probative evidence that would be lost to criminal prosecutions through its application and the corresponding loss of protection for society, the cost would be too high when compared to what would be gained by its adoption.

One of the arguments frequently made in favor of the exclusionary rule is that if illegally seized evidence is not excluded, the right to be free from unreasonable searches and seizures becomes an illusion. Judge Cardozo acknowledged that argument, but rejected it noting the criminal, civil, and administrative sanctions to which offending law enforcement agents are subject if they conduct an illegal search and holding those sanctions were sufficient to protect the right to be free from unreasonable searches and seizures.

Another frequently made argument in favor of the exclusionary rule is that jurors are reluctant to give verdicts against law enforcement agents for illegal searches because the plaintiffs in such suits are criminals.[103] While some studies suggest that to be true, the fact remains that colonial juries did render trespass verdicts against government agents who illegally searched the homes of private citizens,[104] and one of the reasons government agents obtained search warrants in that era was to insulate themselves from such suits.[105] Judge Cardozo addressed this argument in the *Defore* case asking whether juries in his day were more indifferent to civil liberties than colonial juries were.

In some respects this is a curious argument. If a society enshrines juries in its constitution and trusts juries to render verdicts in complex civil cases involving millions of dollars, determine the guilt or innocence of criminal defendants, and in some cases to determine whether to impose the death penalty, how can juries not be trusted to render a proper verdict in a simple trespass action, and what does this argument say about the jury system itself?

A third frequently made argument in favor of the exclusionary rule is that it deters illegal searches by law enforcement agents. While some studies suggest that to be true in some instances, it has not been clearly established that the exclusionary rule does or does not deter law enforcement agents from conducting illegal searches.[106]

A fourth argument that is often made in favor of the exclusionary rule is that the courts should not sully their hands with illegally obtained evidence. Judge Cardozo rejected that argument, noting that if evidence is obtained by a private person through an illegal search, that illegally obtained evidence is admissible. In Judge Cardozo's view the object of the trespass rather than the official character of the trespasser should determine the admissibility of evidence.

A violation of the Fourth Amendment does not necessarily give a defendant the right to have evidence suppressed in his trial. In order to be able to obtain suppression of evidence based on a violation of the Fourth Amendment a defendant must establish that: (1) he has an adversary interest in the outcome of the case in which the allegedly illegally seized evidence will be used and (2) the search was conducted in violation of his rights and not in violation of the rights of some third party.[107]

A defendant has an adversary interest in the outcome of a case when the prosecution seeks to use illegally seized evidence against him.[108] For example, if the police illegally seize evidence from Michael and the prosecution seeks to use that evidence against him, he has an adversary interest in the outcome of the case. If, instead, the prosecution seeks to use that evidence against Maurice, Michael has no adversary interest in the outcome and thus cannot obtain suppression of the evidence.[109]

A search is conducted in violation of the rights of a defendant when the search is of a place or of things which the Fourth Amendment specifically protects[110] or in which the defendant has an expectation of privacy and his expectation of privacy is reasonable.[111] For example, Brittany lives in an apartment and invites an acquaintance named Rolanda to the apartment to help her cut and package heroin. The police, without a search warrant and when no exception to the warrant requirement is applicable, enter and search the apartment for drugs. Brittany's Fourth Amendment rights have been violated because the apartment is her home and the Fourth Amendment specifically protects dwellings, but Rolanda's Fourth Amendment rights have not been violated because she is neither living nor staying in Brittany's apartment and as a result as to her the apartment is not a specifically protected place under the Fourth Amendment and she has no expectation of privacy there.[112]

As discussed above, the courts have developed the exclusionary rule to deter and punish violations of the Fourth Amendment by law enforcement agents. Under that rule and its corollary, the "fruit of the poisonous tree doctrine," when a court determines that law enforcement agents have violated the Fourth Amendment rights of a person against whom the prosecutor is seeking to use that evidence, the prosecutor is generally barred from using at trial both the illegally seized evidence and any evidence obtained or derived from it.

One very important exception to the exclusionary rule and the fruit of the poisonous tree doctrine is that illegally obtained evidence can be used by the prosecution for impeachment.[113] For example, the police illegally search Pedro's apartment and find packages of cocaine. Pedro is subsequently charged with possession of a controlled substance and, prior to trial, he files a motion to suppress the cocaine, which the court grants. If during Pedro's trial he testifies that he has never possessed cocaine, the prosecution can introduce the suppressed cocaine for the purpose of attacking the credibility of Pedro's denial of ever possessing the drug.[114]

The exclusionary rule and the fruit of the poisonous tree doctrine are designed to deter law enforcement agents from conducting illegal warrantless searches. As a result, under what is called the good faith exception to the exclusionary rule, if law enforcement agents have presented a complaint for search warrant to a judge and the judge erroneously concludes that it states probable cause when, in fact, it does not, and based on that erroneous conclusion issues a search warrant which the police properly execute, the evidence seized pursuant to that warrant and anything derived from that evidence will not be suppressed and can be used by the prosecution as evidence at trial.[115]

C. How the Fourth Amendment Applies to Seizures of Persons

The Fourth Amendment also confers a right on individuals to be free from unreasonable seizures. Under the Fourth Amendment a seizure occurs when either by means of physical force or show of authority a law enforcement agent in some way restrains the liberty of a citizen.[116] To effectuate the Fourth Amendment right to be free from unreasonable seizures courts have construed it (1) as regulating certain police-citizen encounters; (2) as regulating the issuance and content of arrest warrants; and (3) as requiring certain remedies for its violation. This section examines each of those subjects.

1. Police-Citizen Encounters

The Fourth Amendment does not proscribe all contact between the police and citizens, but instead is designed to prevent arbitrary and oppressive interference by law enforcement agents with the personal security of individuals.[117] Consequently, the Fourth Amendment is not violated by every police-citizen encounter. For analytical purposes courts have divided police-citizen encounters into three different categories: (1) consensual encounters; (2) investigative stops; and (3) arrests.[118]

A consensual encounter occurs between law enforcement agents and an individual when, under circumstances that would lead a person to feel free to terminate the encounter, such agents approach an individual on the street or in some other public place and pose questions to her.[119] A person is not seized and the Fourth Amendment is not violated simply because a law enforcement agent approaches a person and asks her questions,[120] even if the questions he asks are incriminating.[121] A law enforcement agent can initiate a consensual encounter with any individual at any time, even if he has no basis for suspecting that individual of being involved in any crime.

The second type of police-citizen encounter is called an investigative stop. An investigative stop, sometimes called a Terry stop after *Terry v. Ohio*,[122] the Supreme Court case that first authorized them, is a seizure for Fourth Amendment purposes and occurs when law enforcement agents use their authority to detain a citizen for some limited period of time and for a limited purpose such as questioning. When a law enforcement agent makes an investigative stop of an individual, he can question that individual and he can "pat down" or frisk the individual, but he cannot transport that individual to some other location.[123] For example, if police officer Johnson has a basis for making an investigatory stop of Steve, he can stop Steve on the street, frisk him there, and question him there, but he cannot take Steve for questioning to some other location (unless Steve consents to go there), such as a station house. The Fourth Amendment allows law enforcement agents to make an investigative stop of an individual when they have a reasonable and articulable suspicion that the individual may be involved in criminal activity.

The most intrusive police-citizen encounter is an arrest. An arrest occurs when law enforcement agents use their authority to seize a citizen and take him to a detention facility, police station, or some other location, even if the purpose is to question him or obtain physical evidence, but not to charge him with a crime. Law enforcement agents must have probable cause before they can make an arrest. If law enforcement agents believe they have probable cause, they can make an arrest without first obtaining a warrant,[124] unlike with searches where law enforcement agents must obtain a warrant before searching.

Law enforcement agents can base their belief that probable cause to make an arrest exists on what they observe or on information they receive from third parties. In most states the rule is the same for both felony and misdemeanor arrests. Some states, however, require law enforcement agents to obtain an arrest warrant before making a misdemeanor arrest based on third-party information.

Law enforcement agents sometimes make what is called a pretextual arrest. A pretextual arrest occurs when law enforcement agents arrest someone for some, usually minor, criminal violation in the hope that it will yield evidence of a much more serious criminal offense. For example, police officer Fuller believes that Felicia is carrying drugs in a car, but lacks probable cause to stop her and search the car for drugs. Officer Fuller observes that Felicia is driving five miles per hour over the speed limit and stops her for the traffic violation, hoping that he will find evidence of the drug crime. Fuller has made a pretextual arrest. A pretextual arrest does not violate the Fourth Amendment as long as there was probable cause to support the initial arrest. So, in the above example, as long as Felicia was speeding when officer Fuller stopped her, under the Fourth Amendment it makes no difference if the reason Fuller stopped Felicia was for some purpose other than enforcing the traffic laws and issuing a speeding ticket.

Whren v. United States

Supreme Court of the United States (1996) 517 U.S. 806

JUSTICE SCALIA delivered the opinion of the Court.

In this case we decide whether the temporary detention of a motorist who the police have probable cause to believe has committed a civil traffic violation is inconsistent with the Fourth Amendment's prohibition against unreasonable seizures unless a reasonable officer would have been motivated to stop the car by a desire to enforce the traffic laws.

I

On the evening of June 10, 1993, plainclothes vice-squad officers of the District of Columbia Metropolitan Police Department were patrolling a "high drug area" of the city in an unmarked car. Their suspicions were aroused when they passed a dark Pathfinder truck with temporary license plates and youthful occupants waiting at a stop sign, the driver looking down into the lap of the passenger at his right. The truck remained stopped at the intersection for what seemed an unusually long time—more than 20 seconds. When the police car executed a U-turn in order to head back toward the truck, the Pathfinder turned suddenly to its right, without signaling, and sped off at an "unreasonable" speed. The policemen followed, and in a short while overtook the Pathfinder when it stopped behind other traffic at a red light. They pulled up alongside, and Officer Ephraim Soto stepped out and approached the driver's door, identifying himself as a police officer and directing the driver, petitioner Brown, to put the vehicle in park. When Soto drew up to the driver's window, he immediately observed two large plastic bags of what appeared to be crack cocaine in petitioner Whren's hands. Petitioners were arrested, and quantities of several types of illegal drugs were retrieved from the vehicle.

Petitioners were charged in a four-count indictment with violating various federal drug laws, including 21 U.S.C. §§844(a) and 860(a). At a pretrial suppression hearing, they challenged the legality of the stop and the resulting seizure of the drugs. They argued that the stop had not been justified by probable cause to believe, or even reasonable suspicion, that petitioners were engaged in illegal drug-dealing activity; and that Officer Soto's asserted ground for approaching the vehicle—to give the driver a warning concerning traffic violations—was pretextual. The District Court denied the suppression motion, concluding that "the facts of the stop were not controverted," and "there was nothing to really demonstrate that the actions of the officers were contrary to a normal traffic stop." App. 5.

Petitioners were convicted of the counts at issue here [and t]he Court of Appeals affirmed[.] * * * We granted certiorari. 516 U.S. 1036 (1996).

II

The Fourth Amendment guarantees "the right of the people to be secure in their persons, houses, papers, and effects, against unreasonable searches and seizures." Temporary detention of individuals during the stop of an automobile by the police, even if only for a brief period and for a limited purpose, constitutes a "seizure" of "persons" within the meaning of this provision. See *Delaware v. Prouse*, 440 U.S. 648, 653 (1979). * * * As a general matter, the decision to stop an automobile is reasonable where the police have probable cause to believe that a traffic violation has occurred. See *Prouse, supra*, at 659.

Petitioners accept that Officer Soto had probable cause to believe that various provisions of the District of Columbia traffic code had been violated. * * * They argue, however, that "in the unique context of civil traffic regulations" probable cause is not enough. Since, they contend, the use of automobiles is so heavily and minutely regulated that total compliance with traffic and safety rules is nearly impossible, a police officer will almost invariably be able to catch any given motorist in a technical violation. This creates the temptation to use traffic stops as a means of investigating other law violations, as to which no probable cause or even articulable suspicion exists. Petitioners, who are both black, further contend that police officers might decide which motorists to stop based on decidedly impermissible factors, such as the race of the car's occupants. To avoid this danger, they say, the Fourth Amendment test for traffic stops should be, not the normal one (applied by the Court of Appeals) of whether probable cause existed to justify the stop; but rather, whether a police officer, acting reasonably, would have made the stop for the reason given.

A

Petitioners contend that the standard they propose is consistent with our past cases' disapproval of police attempts to use valid bases of action against citizens as pretexts for pursuing other investigatory agendas. * * *

Petitioners' difficulty is not simply a lack of affirmative support for their position. Not only have we never held, outside the context of inventory search or administrative inspection that an officer's motive invalidates objectively justifiable behavior under the Fourth Amendment; but we have repeatedly held and asserted the contrary. In *United States v. Villamonte-Marquez*, 462 U.S. 579,

584, n.3 (1983), we held that an otherwise valid warrantless boarding of a vessel by customs officials was not rendered invalid "because the customs officers were accompanied by a Louisiana state policeman, and were following an informant's tip that a vessel in the ship channel was thought to be carrying marihuana." We flatly dismissed the idea that an ulterior motive might serve to strip the agents of their legal justification. In *United States v. Robinson*, 414 U.S. 218 (1973), we held that a traffic-violation arrest (of the sort here) would not be rendered invalid by the fact that it was "a mere pretext for a narcotics search," *id.*, at 221, n.1 * * *. And in *Scott v. United States*, 436 U.S. 128, 138 (1978), in rejecting the contention that wiretap evidence was subject to exclusion because the agents conducting the tap had failed to make any effort to comply with the statutory requirement that unauthorized acquisitions be minimized, we said that "subjective intent alone . . . does not make otherwise lawful conduct illegal or unconstitutional." We described *Robinson* as having established that "the fact that the officer does not have the state of mind which is hypothecated by the reasons which provide the legal justification for the officer's action does not invalidate the action taken as long as the circumstances, viewed objectively, justify that action." 436 U.S. at 136, 138.

We think these cases foreclose any argument that the constitutional reasonableness of traffic stops depends on the actual motivations of the individual officers involved. We of course agree with petitioners that the Constitution prohibits selective enforcement of the law based on considerations such as race. But the constitutional basis for objecting to intentionally discriminatory application of laws is the Equal Protection Clause, not the Fourth Amendment. Subjective intentions play no role in ordinary, probable-cause Fourth Amendment analysis. * * *

Here the District Court found that the officers had probable cause to believe that petitioners had violated the traffic code. That rendered the stop reasonable under the Fourth Amendment, the evidence thereby discovered admissible, and the upholding of the convictions by the Court of Appeals for the District of Columbia Circuit correct. The judgment is
Affirmed.

Case Focus

1. What must exist for a police officer to make a traffic stop that does not violate the Fourth Amendment?
2. Is it a violation of the Fourth Amendment for a police officer who observes a driver go through a red light to stop the car if the police officer making the stop is doing so because he suspects there might be drugs in the car and wants the opportunity to look into the passenger compartment of the car?

• • • • • • • •

When a person is arrested without a warrant the Fourth Amendment requires that he be given a prompt judicial hearing to determine if there is probable cause to hold him for the crime for which he was arrested.[125] Generally that means that a defendant must be given a hearing within 48 hours of his arrest.[126] If a defendant is not given a hearing within that period of time, that failure will not result in the voiding of any subsequent conviction.[127] Thus, as practical matter only those in pre-trial custody can benefit from the 48-hour rule.

2. Arrest Warrants

The Fourth Amendment requires that in order to obtain an arrest warrant there must be probable cause to believe that a crime has been committed and probable cause to believe that the person whose arrest is being sought committed the crime.[128] The determination of probable cause must be made by a neutral and detached magistrate. While the Fourth Amendment does not require that the person issuing an arrest warrant be a lawyer or judge, it does require that he be capable of determining whether probable cause exists.[129]

In most cases, when a criminal prosecution of a defendant is initiated prior to his arrest, the prosecutor will obtain an arrest warrant for the defendant and give it to law enforcement agents to execute. Paralegals in prosecutors' offices frequently prepare arrest warrants. Most jurisdictions require that arrest warrants be in writing, state the nature of the offense, state the date when it is issued, identify the jurisdiction that issued it, be signed by a judge, and specify an amount of bail.[130] In many jurisdictions the warrant may also state geographical limits (e.g., Carbon County only, or the State of South Dakota only, or state that it has no geographical limits).

As with search warrants, the Fourth Amendment also imposes a particularity requirement on arrest warrants. To satisfy the particularity requirements of the Fourth Amendment arrest warrants must name the person to be arrested and provide a description of that person that includes the person's age and sex.[131] Most arrest warrants also contain other identifying information such as height, weight, eye color, and hair color.

In some instances the name of the defendant is unknown, but his description is known. In such cases so-called "John Doe" warrants can be issued. Such warrants identify the defendant by the name "John Doe" but contain a physical description of the person for whom the warrant has been issued. More recently, when a perpetrator's name and physical description are unknown, but DNA of the suspected perpetrator has been recovered, John Doe arrest warrants have been issued using the perpetrator's DNA profile to describe him. Such descriptions have been held to satisfy the particularity requirements of the Fourth Amendment.[132]

People v. Robinson

Court of Appeal of California, Third Dist. (2007) 156 Cal. App. 4th 508

BLEASE, Acting P.J.—* * * Defendant Paul Eugene Robinson was convicted by a jury of one count of forcible oral copulation * * * and two counts of rape * * *. * * *

[FACTS]

In the early morning hours of August 25, 1994, 24-year-old Deborah L., the victim in this case, awoke to find defendant, a man she had never seen before, standing in her bedroom. He told her to be quiet and that he was there "to get some pussy." He was wearing garden gloves and holding a kitchen knife. When she started to scream, he called her a "white bitch" and threatened to kill her if she did not shut up.

He climbed on top of the victim and held a knife to her chest, cutting her finger when she attempted to grab it. Defendant then directed the victim to cover her face with a pillow and fondled her breasts, placed his mouth on her vagina, inserted his fingers in her vagina and rectum, and raped her. After losing and then regaining an erection, he raped her a second time, then withdrew his penis, ejaculated on her legs, and rubbed his semen all over her stomach.

When he was finished assaulting the victim, he put the gloves back on, dressed himself, and told her not to look at him or call the police or he would kill her. After he left, she called 911 and reported the attack. The police arrived shortly thereafter and the victim was transported to a medical facility where she was examined and a rape kit prepared. A vaginal swab tested positive for the presence of semen.

A few days later, Detective Willover of the Sacramento City Police Department interviewed the victim. At that time, she described her assailant as a Black male adult who "sounded black," was about 25 pounds overweight with a round face, and approximately five feet eight inches tall. * * *

In August 2000, Jill Spriggs, assistant director of the DOJ crime laboratory in Sacramento, developed a DNA profile of the assailant from the vaginal swab of the victim. Spriggs then requested Henry Tom, a DOJ DNA criminalist, to search the DOJ convicted offender databank to determine whether the DNA profile of the assailant matched the DNA profile of any convicted offender in the databank. He entered the DNA profile of the evidentiary sample into the computer, ran a search that compared the profile to the DNA profile of all other entrants in the databank, and obtained a "cold hit," which is a match between the assailant's profile and the profile of a person previously entered into the databank. DOJ records disclosed the matching profile belonged to defendant and Tom sent the information to Spriggs.

After receiving that information, Spriggs conducted an independent DNA analysis using a blood sample obtained from defendant upon his arrest.

Spriggs developed his DNA profile, compared it with the DNA profile of the evidentiary sample from the vaginal swab, found the two profiles matched along all 13 loci, and concluded they belonged to the same person.

Spriggs testified that once a profile is developed, a statistical calculation is performed to determine the frequency of that particular genetic profile in a random unrelated population. The probability of a 13-loci match as in this case is one in 650 quadrillion in the African-American population, one in six sextillion in the Caucasian population, and one in 33 sextillion in the Hispanic population. There are no reported cases of two people matching at all 13 loci other than identical twins.

Defendant did not take the stand but contested the reliability of the statistical probability evidence. We shall discuss that evidence in more detail as pertinent in the discussion portion of our decision.

DISCUSSION

I. John Doe/DNA Arrest Warrant

Defendant contends that issuance of a John Doe/DNA arrest warrant failed to toll the statute of limitations * * *.

We set forth the pertinent procedural background before addressing * * * [that] claim.

A. Procedural Background

The governing period of limitations for the sexual offenses charged in this case is six years. (§800.) Since the offenses were committed on August 25, 1994, the period of limitations was set to expire on August 25, 2000.

On August 21, 2000, four days before that expiration date, the Sacramento County District Attorney filed a felony complaint against "John Doe, unknown male," described by a 13-loci DNA profile. The next day, Detective Willover prepared and presented an arrest warrant which incorporated the DNA profile, and a statement of probable cause to Magistrate Jane Ure, who signed it.

Three weeks later, on September 15, 2000, Detective Willover received a message from the DOJ DNA laboratory (DOJ Lab) that there was a cold hit match between the DNA profile obtained from the vaginal swab of the victim and the DNA profile of Paul Eugene Robinson, whose genetic profile had been entered in the state's DNA data bank program. * * * The DNA arrest warrant apparently was amended to insert defendant's name. It was executed by the arrest of defendant on September 15, 2000. A first amended complaint was filed four days later on September 19, 2000, naming Paul Eugene Robinson as the defendant.

Defendant moved to dismiss the first amended complaint for lack of jurisdiction. The trial court held an evidentiary hearing and denied the motion * * *.

B. Statute of Limitations

Defendant contends the trial court lacked personal jurisdiction over him because the six-year statute of limitations had expired by the time the amended complaint was filed. In his view, issuance of a John Doe arrest warrant with a DNA profile does not validly commence the prosecution because a genetic profile does not particularly describe the person to be arrested and therefore fails to satisfy the statutory and constitutional particularity requirement.

Respondent contends this claim has no merit because a DNA profile is a generally accepted forensic identification tool that satisfies the particularity requirement. We agree with respondent and hold that an arrest warrant, which identifies the person to be arrested for a sexual offense by incorporation of the DNA profile of the assailant, satisfies the * * * pertinent constitutional provisions. * * *

Defendant appears to argue that the [statutory] particularity requirement * * * must be read in light of the federal and state Constitutions. With this we agree. * * *

With respect to the particularity required for naming the person to be arrested, an arrest warrant may describe the person to be arrested by a fictitious name and * * * must name the defendant with the same degree of particularity required for an indictment, information, or complaint which may be filed using a fictitious name. *Ernst v. Municipal Court* (1980) 104 Cal. App. 3d 710, 718.

However, the Constitution and statutory scheme require that "a 'John Doe' warrant . . . describe the person to be seized with reasonable particularity." (*People v. Montoya, supra*, 255 Cal. App. 2d at p. 142.) A fictitious name is the same as a John Doe name and is insufficient to identify anyone let alone with particularity. Thus, the California Constitution, article I, section 13, provides that "a warrant may not issue, except on probable cause . . . particularly describing the . . . persons and things to be seized." The Fourth Amendment to the United States Constitution contains a similar particularity requirement. (*West v. Cabell, supra*, 153 U.S. 78; *Powe v. City of Chicago* (7th Cir. 1981) 664 F.2d 639.) * * *

The purpose of the constitutional particularity requirement is to avoid general warrants by which anyone may be arrested in order to ensure "nothing is left to the discretion of the officer executing the warrant." (*United States v. Hillyard* (9th Cir. 1982) 677 F.2d 1336, 1339.)

It is therefore well established that an arrest warrant, which merely identifies a defendant *solely* by use of a fictitious name is void. * * * The test is whether the warrant provides sufficient information to identify the defendant with "reasonable certainty. [Citations.] This may be done by stating his occupation, his personal appearance, peculiarities, place of residence or other means of identification [citation]." (*People v. Montoya, supra*, 255 Cal. App. 2d at p.142.) The particularity requirement does not however, demand complete precision. (*People v. Amador* (2000) 24 Cal. 4th 387, 392.)

Applying these principles, we find an arrest warrant, which describes the person to be arrested by his or her DNA profile, more than satisfies the reasonable certainty standard because DNA is the most accurate and reliable means of identifying an individual presently available to law enforcement. * * *

Defendant argues however, that a DNA profile is merely "information about the genetic makeup of a human being; [and] is not an identification of that person" that would enable an officer in the field to execute the warrant based solely on the DNA profile stated in the warrant. We see no legal merit in this argument.

Neither section 804, subdivision (d), section 813, nor the state and federal Constitutions specify or limit the *manner* or *criteria* for particularly describing a person. All that is required is "reasonable certainty" that the person may be identified. Indeed, defendant concedes that while a DNA profile "may be probative of identity," it is not infallible. But infallibility is not required for issuance of a warrant (*People v. Amador, supra*, 24 Cal. 4th at p.392) or a charging document. * * *

Nevertheless, in light of the astronomical rarity of an individual's DNA profile in the general population (*People v. Johnson* (2006) 139 Cal. App. 4th 1135, 1153) and of defendant's particular 13-loci profile, it cannot be disputed that DNA analysis is as close to an infallible measure of identity as science can presently obtain. Given the mobility of our society, the availability of plastic surgery and other medical procedures and devices that may alter physical characteristics, and the growing problem of identity theft, unlike a person's DNA profile, all other identifying criteria are subject to theft, change, or alteration.

Defendant also contends that for Fourth Amendment purposes, extrinsic evidence cannot be used to make up the deficiencies of an insufficient arrest warrant. This argument is based on the fact an officer in the field cannot execute the warrant by visually identifying a suspect with his DNA profile in hand and must resort to information outside of the warrant.

We disagree. Defendant confuses the requirements for issuance of a warrant with those necessary to execute one. Extrinsic evidence is always necessary to locate the suspect and confirm his identity in order to execute an arrest warrant. (*United States v. Doe* (3d Cir. 1983) 703 F.2d 745, 748 ["No matter how detailed the written description on a warrant is, extrinsic information will be necessary to execute it"].) * * *

For these reasons, we hold that an arrest warrant, which describes the person to be arrested by his DNA profile, satisfies the statute of limitations. * * *

[T]he judgment of conviction is affirmed.

Case Focus

1. Must an arrest warrant carry a physical description of the person for whose arrest it is issued?
2. What are the problems with a physical description?
3. Can the perpetrator of a crime whose identity is unknown be charged with committing the crime? If so, under what circumstances can a charge be brought?

• • • • • • • •

3. Enforcement of Fourth Amendment Requirements for Arrests

In the event a citizen is arrested without probable cause or otherwise in violation of the Fourth Amendment, his remedies for the violation are limited. The remedy for a violation of the Fourth Amendment is suppression of evidence and not dismissal of charges.[133] As a result, if a citizen is seized in violation of his Fourth Amendment rights, any evidence seized pursuant to that arrest together with any fruits thereof will be suppressed, but the court will not dismiss the criminal charges pending against him.

CHAPTER TERMS

Affiant   Probable cause

REVIEW QUESTIONS

1. To what extent, if any, does the Fourth Amendment apply to searches conducted by private security guards? Does it make any difference to the application of the Fourth Amendment if the private security guards are simply trying to recover stolen property or if they are searching for evidence for the purpose of turning it and the person they detain over to law enforcement agents?

2. Does the Fourth Amendment apply to all searches conducted by American law enforcement agents? If not, when does the

Fourth Amendment not apply to such a search?

3. If the Fourth Amendment is applicable, what area or areas does the Fourth Amendment protect?

4. Does the Fourth Amendment only protect against the search and seizure of tangible things such as documents, stolen goods, and contraband such as drugs or does it protect against searches and seizures of intangible things as well?

5. In order to obtain a search warrant, what does the law require that law enforcement agents establish?

6. Historically, for what things were search warrants issued?

7. Must a crime have already been committed to obtain a search warrant, or can law enforcement agents obtain a search warrant if they believe a crime is going to be committed in the future?

8. The existence of what is determined by an analysis of the "totality of the circumstances?"

9. Generally, whose observations are sufficient to establish probable cause?

10. If information is provided by an informant, what usually must be shown to make the informant's information sufficient to establish probable cause, and what are some ways by which that can be done?

11. When is a subpoena considered so broad that it violates the Fourth Amendment?

12. What are "no-knock" search warrants, and what must be established to obtain them?

13. When law enforcement agents execute a search warrant on specific premises, where are they allowed to search on those premises to find the items they have been authorized to search for and seize?

14. What are some of the situations or times when law enforcement agents do not need to obtain a search warrant before conducting a search?

15. What are the three different types of police-citizen encounters and how do they differ?

16. Must law enforcement agents always obtain an arrest warrant before arresting a person suspected of committing a crime? If not, when can law enforcement agents make arrests without having a warrant?

17. What is the fruit of the poisonous tree rule and how does it operate?

ENDNOTES

1. *Wrightson v. United States*, 222 F.2d 556 (D.C. Cir. 1955).
2. *United States v. Calendra*, 414 U.S. 338 (1974).
3. *United States v. Shahid*, 117 F.3d 322 (7th Cir. 1997).
4. *Id.*
5. *United States v. Verdugo-Urquidez*, 494 U.S. 259 (1990).
6. *United States v. Bravo*, 489 F.3d 1 (1st Cir. 2007).
7. *United States v. Vilches-Navarette*, 413 F. Supp. 2d 60 (2006).
8. *Id.*
9. *Olmstead v. United States*, 277 U.S. 438 (1928).
10. *United States v. Jones*, 565 U.S. ___, 132 S. Ct. 945 (2012), n.5.
11. *Hester v. United States*, 265 U.S. 57 (1924).
12. *United States v. Verdugo-Urquidez*, 494 U.S. at 266.
13. *Ashcroft v. al-Kidd*, 563 U.S. ___, 131 S.Ct. 2074 (2011).
14. *United States v. Jones*, 565 U.S. at ___, 132 S. Ct. at 949.
15. *Heller v. New York N.H. & H.R. Co.*, 265 F 192 (2d Cir. 1920).

16. *See, United States v. Jones*, 565 U.S. at ___, 132 S. Ct. at 945.
17. *Id.*
18. *Id.* at n.8.
19. *Id.* at n.5.
20. *Id.* at ___, 953.
21. 389 U.S. 347 (1967).
22. In a dissenting opinion in *Katz* Justice Hugo Black criticized extension of the Fourth Amendment beyond physical intrusions and seizures of material objects to eavesdropping through use of wiretaps. Justice Black conceded that wiretapping was unknown to the founders, but noted that eavesdropping certainly was known to them because in the founding-era people listened outside windows under the eaves of homes, to overhear conversations on the inside. Justice Black pointed out that despite that knowledge, the founders did not specifically include eavesdropping within the prohibition of the Fourth Amendment, which they easily could have done if they had intended to prohibit such activity by government agents. *Katz v. United States*, 389 U.S. 347 (1967), Black, J., dissenting.
23. 565 U.S. ___, 132 S. Ct. 945 (2012).
24. *United States v. Jones*, 565 U.S. at ___, 132 S. Ct. at 945.
25. *El-Nahal v. Yassky*, 993 F. Supp. 2d 460 (S.D.N.Y. 2014).
26. *United States v. Jones*, 565 U.S. at ___, 132 S. Ct. at 945, n.5.
27. *United States v. Oliver*, 657 F.2d 85 (6th Cir. 1981).
28. *California v. Greenwood*, 486 U.S. 35 (1988).
29. *United States v. White*, 401 U.S. 35 (1988).
30. *Florida v. Riley*, 488 U.S. 445 (1989).
31. *California v. Greenwood*, 486 U.S. at 35.
32. It is interesting to note that despite the fact that by its terms the operative language of the Fourth Amendment makes no distinction between how it operates as to searches and how it operates as to arrests, courts have held that the Amendment operates differently as to each. With respect to searches courts have said that if the Fourth Amendment is applicable, law enforcement agents must always obtain a search warrant before searching, unless an exception to the warrant requirement applies. In contrast, with respect to arrests, courts have said that law enforcement agents can make warrantless arrests if they determine that sufficient evidence exists to justify the arrest. Thus, with searches, unless an exception to warrant requirement exists, law enforcement agents cannot search and seize without a warrant even if they correctly conclude that they have sufficient evidence of probable cause to justify a search; but with respect to arrests, if law enforcement agents believe they have sufficient evidence to justify it, they can make an arrest without a warrant.
33. *United States v. Watson*, 423 U.S. 411 (1976). As discussed later in this chapter the term "seizure" includes arrests of persons. As a result the Fourth Amendment regulates searches as well as arrests.
34. *U.S. Const.*, Amend. 4.
35. The state constitutional clause referred to reads as follows: *The right of the people to be secure in their persons, houses, papers and effects, against unreasonable searches and seizures, shall not be violated; and no warrant shall issue without probable cause, supported by affidavit, particularly describing the place to be searched, and the persons or things to be seized.* Ill. Const. 1870, Art. 2, Sec. 6.
36. *People v. Castree*, 311 Ill. 392 (1924), Thompson, J., dissenting.
37. *Id.*
38. *Id.*
39. Akhil Amar, *The Bill of Rights as a Constitution*, 100 Yale L.J. 1131 (1991).
40. *Id.*
41. *United States v. Verdugo-Urquidez*, 494 U.S. 259 (1990).
42. *People v. Castree*, 311 Ill. at 392, Thompson, J. dissenting
43. Akhil Amar, *The Bill of Rights as a Constitution*, 100 Yale L.J. 1131.
44. *See e.g., Wakely v. Hart*, 6 Binn. 316 (Pa. 1814).
45. *Federal Rules of Criminal Procedure*, 41(d)(2)(B).
46. *Fed. Rules Crim. Proc.*, 41(2)(B).
47. *United States v. Loy*, 191 F.3d 360 (3d Cir. 1999).
48. *People v. Bui*, 381 Ill. App. 3d 397 (1st Dist. 2008).
49. *Id.*
50. *Illinois v. Gates*, 462 U.S. 213 (1983).
51. *Id.*
52. *United States v. Funches*, 327 F.3d 582 (7th Cir. 2003).
53. *Jones v. United States*, 362 U.S. 257 (1960).
54. *Illionois v. Gates*, 462 U.S. at 213.
55. *Id.*
56. *United States v. Mueller*, 902 F.2d 336 (5th Cir. 1990).
57. *United States v. Jacobson*, 4 F. Supp. 3d 515 (E.D.N.Y. 2014).
58. *Id.*
59. *United States v. Galpin*, 720 F.3d 436 (2d Cir. 2013).
60. *United States v. Shi Yan Liu*, 239 F.3d 138 (2nd Cir. 2000).
61. *Andresen v. Maryland*, 427 U.S. 463 (1976).

62. *United States v. Shi Yan Liu*, 239 F.3d at 138.
63. *Id.*
64. *People v. McCarty*, 223 Ill. 2d 109 (2006).
65. *Id.*
66. *Id.*
67. *United States v. Klein*, 565 F.2d 183 (1st Cir. 1977).
68. *State v. Sweatt*, 427 A.2d 940 (Me. 1981).
69. *United States v. Noushfar*, 78 F.3d 1442 (9th Cir. 1996).
70. *In re Grand Jury Investigation (Local 542-International Union of Operating Engineers)*, 381 F. Supp. 1295 (E.D. Pa. 1974).
71. *Id.*
72. *United States v. R. Enterprises, Inc.*, 498 U.S. 292 (1991).
73. *Id.*
74. *In re Grand Jury Investigation*, 381 F. Supp. at 1295.
75. *See People ex rel. Legislative Commission on Low Income Housing*, 36 Ill. 2d 460 (1967).
76. *Fed. Rules Crim. Proc.*, 41(3)(A), (B).
77. *Wilson v. Arkansas*, 514 U.S. 927 (1995).
78. *Id.*
79. *Richards v. Wisconsin*, 520 U.S. 385 (1997).
80. *California v. Acevedo*, 500 U.S. 565 (1991), Scalia, J., dissenting.
81. *Schneckloth v. Bustamonte*, 412 U.S. 218 (1973).
82. *United States v. Luton*, 486 F.2d 1021 (5th Cir. 1974).
83. *United States v. Scheets*, 188 F.3d 829 (7th Cir. 1999).
84. *State v. Edwards*, 434 So. 2d 395 (La. 1983).
85. *United States v. Rambo*, 789 F.2d 1289 (8th Cir. 1986).
86. *People v. Sanders*, 44 Ill. App. 3d 510 (5th Dist. 1976).
87. *United States v. Buckingham*, 433 F.3d 508 (6th Cir. 2006).
88. *See People v. Thompson*, 770 P.2d 1282 (Colo. 1989).
89. *Id.*
90. *In re Directives Pursuant to the Foreign Intelligence Surveillance Act*, 551 F.3d 1004 (Foreign Intel. Surv. Ct. Rev. 2008).
91. *People v. Wells*, 273 Ill. App. 3d 349 (5th Dist. 1995).
92. *Id.*
93. *See, e.g.*, 720 ILCS 5/114-12(b).
94. 232 U.S. 383 (1915).
95. *Adams v. New York*, 192 U.S. 585 (1904).
96. 367 U.S. 643 (1961).
97. *Bivens v. Six Unknown Named Agents of the Federal Narcotics Bureau*, 403 U.S. 388 (1971), Burger, J., dissenting.
98. *See People v. Defore*, 242 N.Y. 13 (1926).
99. *See, e.g.*, Guido Calabresi, *Law and Truth Debate: Exclusionary Rules*, 26 Harv. J.L. & Pub. Pol'y 111 (Winter 2003).
100. *People v. Defore*, 242 N.Y. at 13.
101. *Id.*
102. *Id.*
103. *See, e.g.*, Calabresi, *Law and Truth Debate*.
104. *United States v. Acevedo*, 500 U.S. 565 (1991), Scalia, J., dissenting.
105. Akhil Amar, *The Bill of Rights as a Constitution*, 100 Yale L.J. 1131 (1991).
106. 1 Wayne LaFave, *Searches and Seizures* §1.2 (4th ed. 2008).
107. *State v. Wilson*, 594 N.W.2d 268 (Ct. of App. Minn. 1999).
108. *State v. Carter*, 569 N.W.2d 169 (Minn. 1997); *reversed on other grounds, sub nom. Minnesota v. Carter*, 525 U.S. 83 (1998).
109. *United States v. Kember*, 648 F.2d 1354 (D.C. Cir. 1980).
110. *United States v. Jones*, 565 U.S. at ___.
111. *Minnesota v. Carter*, 525 U.S. 83 (1998).
112. *Id.*
113. *United States v. Tweed*, 503 F.2d 1127 (7th Cir. 1974).
114. *Id.*
115. *United States v. Leon*, 468 U.S. 897 (1984).
116. *Florida v. Bostick*, 501 U.S. 429 (1991).
117. *Immigration and Naturalization Service v. Delgado*, 466 U.S. 210 (1984).
118. *People v. Luedemann*, 222 Ill. 2d 530 (2006).
119. *United States v. Hendricks*, 319 F.3d 993 (7th Cir. 2003).
120. *People v. Luedemann*, 222 Ill. 2d 429.
121. *United States v. Ringold*, 335 F.3d 1168 (2003).
122. 392 U.S. 1 (1968).
123. *Dunaway v. New York*, 422 U.S. 200 (1979).
124. *United States v. Watson*, 423 U.S. 411 (1976).
125. *Gerstein v. Pugh*, 420 U.S. 103 (1975).
126. *County of Riverside v. McLaughlin*, 500 U.S. 44 (1991).
127. *Montoya v. Scott*, 65 F.3d 405 (5th Cir. 1995).
128. *Giordenello v. United States*, 357 U.S. 480 (1958).
129. *Shadwick v. City of Tampa*, 407 U.S. 345 (1972).
130. *See, e.g.*, 725 ILCS 5/107-9(d).
131. *Id.*
132. *State v. Dabney*, 264 Wis. 2d 843 (2003).
133. *United States v. Rodriguez*, 948 F.2d 914 (5th Cir. 1991).

Chapter 17
Criminal Procedure During the Investigative Stage — Privilege Against Self-Incrimination and Other Rights

Chapter Objectives

After reading this chapter, you should be able to

- Explain what the privilege against self-incrimination is
- Explain who can assert the privilege against self-incrimination
- Explain when the Fifth Amendment privilege against self-incrimination is applicable
- Understand how the privilege against self-incrimination operates
- Explain what Miranda rights are and when they must be administered
- Understand how the fruit of the poisonous tree rule applies to violations of the requirement to administer Miranda rights
- Understand when the Vienna Convention applies and what it requires

[E]xcept in the context of custodial interrogation, * * * the responsibility for keeping a citizen informed of his constitutional rights [is] with the preeminent guardian of those rights: the citizen himself. —Judge Alex Kozinski *United States v. Kilgroe*, 959 F.2d 802 (9th Cir. 1992)

The Fifth Amendment to the U.S. Constitution and the Vienna Convention on Consular Relations (a treaty entered into by the United States with certain foreign countries), each confer certain rights on individuals that have application during the investigative stage of the criminal justice process. In this chapter we will examine what those rights are, see how they operate, and see how they regulate actions of law enforcement agents during that stage of the criminal justice process.

A. Rights Conferred by the Fifth Amendment

Generally, a citizen is under no duty to answer questions of a government agent or to provide information to the government. The government, however, is entitled to everyone's evidence.[1] To compel production of that evidence government bodies issue subpoenas to citizens and adopt statutes and regulations that mandate the reporting of certain information. When a citizen is subpoenaed to appear before an official body (such as a grand jury) or a government agency (such as the Securities & Exchange Commission), he is required to make disclosures to the government by answering questions he is asked and by producing any **Physical evidence** that body demands. When a citizen is subject to a statute such as the Internal Revenue Code or a regulation that mandates that he provide certain information, the citizen usually makes the required disclosures to the government in reports (such as income tax returns) that he must file by a certain time.

Physical evidence includes fingerprints, handwriting, vocal characteristics, stance, stride, gestures, and blood characteristics. *United States v. Verlarde-Gomez*, 263 F.3d 1023 (9th Cir. 2001).

The Fifth Amendment to the U.S. Constitution contains what is called the privilege against self-incrimination. When a citizen has a duty to disclose, if the Fifth Amendment privilege is applicable to that disclosure, the privilege excuses a citizen from making it. The privilege against self-incrimination, like other privileges, provides an exception to the general rule that all evidence must be revealed.[2] The Fifth Amendment privilege states:

Other privileges recognized by law include the attorney client privilege, the doctor patient privilege, and executive privilege.

> No person . . . shall be compelled in any criminal case to be a witness against himself. *U.S. Const.* Amend V.

The privilege against self-incrimination operates differently during the investigative stage of the criminal justice process than it does during the trial stage of the process. Here we will examine how the privilege operates during the investigative stage, and in a later chapter we will examine how it operates during the trial stage. In this section we will explore: (1) the nature of the privilege against self-incrimination; (2) when the privilege is applicable; (3) how a person's privilege against self-incrimination can be eliminated; (4) when there is a duty to inform a person of the privilege; and (5) the exception to the privilege for required records.

Before proceeding further the student should note the special sense in which the term "witness" is used in this chapter. In this chapter the term "witness" refers to anyone from whom the government seeks disclosures who is not also a defendant in a criminal proceeding. Thus, as used in this chapter the term "witness" includes not only persons usually thought of as witnesses (such as persons required to appear and testify at a trial, grand jury proceeding, or legislative hearing) but also persons not usually thought of as being witnesses but who are nonetheless required by law to provide some type of information to the government (such as those who must file some type of government-mandated report).

1. *Nature of the Privilege Against Self-Incrimination*

The privilege against self-incrimination was a creation of English common law that was incorporated into the U.S. Constitution as part of the original Bill of Rights[3] and that has also been incorporated into the constitution of almost every state.[4] The Fifth Amendment privilege is considered to be one of the foundation stones of our adversary system of justice[5]; in 1964 the U.S. Supreme Court made it applicable to the states.[6] In some states the state constitutional privilege against self-incrimination has been interpreted as providing broader protection than the Fifth Amendment privilege. For that reason a paralegal who receives any research assignment that involves a question relating to the privilege against self-incrimination should always ascertain whether the question relates to the federal privilege, her state's own privilege, or both.

It is important to understand the precise nature of the right the privilege against self-incrimination confers on witnesses. The privilege does not confer on a witness a right to be free from being asked incriminating questions. Instead, the privilege simply confers on a witness the right to refuse to answer such questions.[7] As a result, whether it is a prosecutor in a grand jury proceeding, a defense attorney questioning a witness at trial, or a senator questioning a witness in a legislative hearing, an inquisitor is free to ask a witness questions whose answers are or might be incriminating and it is up to the witness to decide whether to answer those questions or to refuse to answer them and assert the privilege in response. For example, Agnes shot and killed Cornelius and she is being questioned before a grand jury that is investigating Cornelius's murder. The privilege does not prohibit the prosecutor from asking Agnes, "Did you shoot Cornelius?" Instead, the privilege permits Agnes to choose either to answer that question or to assert the privilege and refuse to answer it. If a witness chooses to answer an incriminating question she must answer it truthfully because the privilege does not excuse perjury.[8]

The Fifth Amendment privilege is a personal privilege,[9] which means that only the witness can assert it. Third parties such as the witness's spouse and agents of the witness (such as his attorney) are not allowed to assert it for him.[10] If a witness fails to assert the privilege and instead answers the question posed or otherwise discloses the information being sought from him, the privilege is lost as to that answer or disclosure and the answer or disclosure may be used against him.[11]

Asserting the Privilege

When a witness decides not to answer a question because she believes the answer will incriminate her, the witness must actually invoke the privilege as the reason for her refusal. There are no talismanic words that must be spoken to invoke the privilege against self-incrimination, but the words must at least be such that a judge is able to understand that the witness is invoking it.[12] Merely stating, "I refuse to answer," is insufficient to invoke the privilege. Words such as, "I plead the 'Fifth'" or "I decline to answer because my answer may incriminate me" are sufficient. When invoking the privilege the witness cannot simply make a blanket assertion of it that she says applies to all questions that will be asked. Instead, the witness must invoke the privilege on a question-by-question basis or, if documents are sought, on a document-by-document basis.

When a witness has been subpoenaed to produce documents, in response to which the witness will be asserting the Fifth Amendment or some other privilege, the witness's attorney will often have a paralegal prepare what is called a privilege log. A privilege log usually contains, at a minimum, the following information as to each document for which a privilege is being asserted: a description of the document, the number of pages of the document, the specific privilege being asserted as to it, and information from which it can be determined whether that privilege is applicable.

The privilege generally does not excuse the filing of a government-mandated report when the report is due.[13] As a result, when a witness who is required to make a report of information to the government (e.g., report the information required to be reported on an income tax return) believes that he will incriminate himself by disclosing some of the information that he is required to disclose in that report, he cannot refuse to make the report. Instead, the witness must assert the privilege as to the particular item of information he believes to be incriminating. To the extent disclosure of the other information required to be provided will not incriminate him, he must disclose that in the report and file it.[14] For example, if a taxpayer believes he will incriminate himself if he discloses his occupation on an income tax return, he cannot refuse to file the return; instead, he must assert the privilege as to that item, provide the other information required to be disclosed, and file the return when it is due. As with blanket assertions of privilege to all questions to be asked, a person required to make a report to the government cannot validly assert the privilege by making a blanket assertion on the mandated report, such as by writing "Fifth Amendment" across the face of the form on which the report is to be made.

When invoking the privilege in a state proceeding or as to a state-mandated disclosure it is important that the witness be clear about whether she is invoking the Fifth Amendment privilege, her state's own privilege against self-incrimination, or both. If she invokes only one privilege (e.g., the Fifth Amendment privilege) at the time of being questioned or at the time disclosure to the government is required and the applicability of the privilege to the disclosure being sought is challenged, the judge will decide only whether the privilege actually invoked (e.g., the Fifth Amendment privilege) is applicable and will not consider whether the other privilege (e.g., the state's constitutional privilege against self-incrimination) is also applicable. In a state where the state privilege against self-incrimination is broader than the Fifth Amendment privilege, a witness's assertion of only the Fifth Amendment privilege could result in her being required to make a disclosure that under state law she would not be required to make.

It is also important to understand that the federal constitutional privilege does not excuse a witness from appearing before whatever body or agency has subpoenaed him, even if he correctly believes either that the questions he will be asked will call for answers that incriminate him or that he is the target of a criminal investigation.[15] Also, a witness cannot avoid appearing before the body that subpoenaed him by informing the issuer of the subpoena or the prosecutor that he will assert the privilege in response to all questions.[16] As a result, a witness who has been subpoenaed must appear before the body that subpoenaed him, allow questions to be posed to him, and then either answer the questions asked or refuse to answer them and assert the privilege.[17]

United States v. Pilnick

267 F. Supp. 791 (1967)
United States District Court for the Southern District of New York

WEINFELD, District Judge.

The indictment charges Pilnick, five other individuals and one corporation with offenses arising out of the sale of undeveloped land in Florida to the public in 1965 and 1966. Count 1 charges all the defendants, and others not named as defendants, with conspiring to violate the mail and wire fraud statutes, and counts 2 through 57 charge five of the individual defendants and the corporation with a scheme to defraud through the use of the mails. Pilnick is named in all 57 counts. * * *

The defendant makes a further contention that his privilege against self-incrimination was violated when he was subpoenaed to testify before the grand jury after a complaint had been filed and he had been arrested, and after the Assistant United States Attorney had been advised, in advance of his scheduled appearance, that he would assert his privilege before the grand jury.

The argument is two-pronged: (1) that as a prime target of the investigation and a potential defendant he was not subject to grand jury questioning, and (2) that since the United States Attorney had been advised the defendant would assert the privilege, to require him to do so before the grand jury constituted compelled demeanor evidence which prejudices him before the grand jury and necessarily influenced it in voting a true bill.

These contentions are without validity. The fact that a witness is a potential defendant does not immunize him from being called upon to testify before a grand jury. Neither does the fact that the witness has been arrested in a matter which is the subject of the grand jury inquiry gain for him automatic immunity from grand jury process. As to the further contention that because his lawyer gave advance notice that he intended to assert his privilege against self-incrimination, he was excused from appearing before the grand jury, sufficient answer is this court's observation on a related issue:

> "To uphold the defendant's plea in advance of the taking of his testimony upon the mere filing of his affidavit asserting the privilege would take from the Court the determination of the basic issue of whether or not an answer in response to specific questions would incriminate the defendant or subject him to real danger and leave its determination entirely to the defendant. This is not the law."

The doctrine asserted by the defendant would serve as a handy vehicle automatically to render sterile grand jury subpoenaes and to deprive the government of its right to the testimony of witnesses—a right subject only to constitutional limitations and not to the unilateral judgment of the witness.

Finally, the claim of the defendant that he was prejudiced in the eyes of the grand jury, which in consequence was influenced to return an indictment because of the assertion of his constitutional right, equally is without foundation. No implication of guilt was permissible because he invoked his Fifth Amendment privilege before the grand jury. * * *

[The motion is denied.]

Case Focus

1. Does the privilege against self-incrimination excuse the chief suspect in a crime from being subpoenaed to testify before a grand jury?
2. Can a witness who has been subpoenaed to appear before a grand jury avoid appearing by having his attorney inform the prosecutor that he will assert his privilege against self-incrimination?

Whether the disclosures being sought are answers to questions, physical evidence (such as business records), or information mandated by statute to be disclosed to the government, neither the witness nor his attorney is the sole judge of whether the privilege applies.[18] When a witness asserts the privilege the inquisitor can challenge that assertion by filing a motion in court in which he asks a judge to decide whether the privilege permits the witness to refuse to make the disclosures being sought from him.

At the hearing on that motion, unless the disclosure is obviously incriminatory (e.g., the answer to the question, "Did you shoot X?"), the witness has the burden of establishing that the privilege is applicable. If the witness meets his burden, the inquisitor has an opportunity to rebut the witness's arguments and to explain to the judge why he believes the privilege does not apply. After hearing both sides the

EYE ON ETHICS

The American Bar Association vs. The Law

The American Bar Association (ABA) has developed what it calls the *ABA Standards for Criminal Justice,* which in part purports to set standards for American prosecutors to follow. As the ABA is a private professional organization similar to any number of private trade associations (such as the National Manufacturers Association) that purport to represent various industries, such purported standards do not have the force of law and prosecutors are free to ignore them if they choose. At least two of the ABA's purported standards would impose restrictions on prosecutors that courts have held the law does not and that most legislative bodies have not imposed by statute.

In Standard 3-3.6(d) the ABA asserts that a prosecutor should not call and question a person before a grand jury who the prosecutor believes to be a potential defendant without informing him that he may be charged and advising him to seek legal advice.[19] As a matter of law the courts have very clearly held that the grand jury has the right to subpoena a person who is a potential defendant,[20] that there is no constitutional requirement to advise a witness that he is a potential defendant or target,[21] and there is no legal requirement to advise a witness about seeking legal advice.[22]

In Standard 3-3.6(e) the ABA asserts that a prosecutor should not seek to compel the appearance of a witness before the grand jury if the witness states in advance that he intends to assert the privilege against self-incrimination unless the prosecutor intends to challenge the assertion of privilege or grant the witness immunity.[23] Again, the ABA's position has been rejected by the courts, which have held that a witness cannot foreclose his appearance before a grand jury by stating in advance that he will assert the privilege against self-incrimination and that subpoenaed witnesses must appear and assert the privilege on a question-by-question basis.[24]

judge then decides whether the witness must make the disclosure being sought.[25] If the judge determines that the privilege does not excuse the witness from making the disclosures and the witness persists in his refusal to make them, the judge can hold the witness in civil contempt and, in most states, order the witness jailed until he does. In that situation the prisoner is said to hold the key to her jail cell.

As with Fourth Amendment violations, when a witness's privilege is violated the fruit of the poisonous tree rule applies. With violations of the privilege against self-incrimination, that means that neither the extracted evidence nor evidence derived from it can be used against the person whose privilege was violated.

The fact that evidence is obtained in violation of a witness's privilege against self-incrimination does not, however, foreclose the use of that evidence in all criminal proceedings. Illegally compelled evidence or its fruits can be used against persons other than the witness whose privilege was violated.[26] For example, Mahmoud, who has not been charged with a crime but who was an agent of Rafik, is testifying at the Rafik's trial. During questioning by the prosecutor Mahmoud asserts his Fifth Amendment privilege in response to certain questions. The judge incorrectly determines that the answers will not incriminate Mahmoud, when in fact they will incriminate both Mahmoud and Rafik, and orders Mahmoud to answer those questions. Mahmoud complies with the judge's order and answers. Notwithstanding that Mahmoud was illegally compelled to answer, his answers can be used as evidence against Rafik.[27]

It is important to understand the point in time at which the privilege against self-incrimination is violated. As you may recall, a violation of the Fourth Amendment's bar on unreasonable search and seizures occurs when the illegal search is accomplished. The point in time when a violation of the Fifth Amendment privilege occurs is different. The Fifth Amendment privilege is not violated when a disclosure is illegally extracted from a witness; instead the violation occurs when the illegally extracted disclosure or evidence derived from it is used against that witness at trial.[28]

2. *When the Fifth Amendment Privilege Against Self-Incrimination Is Applicable*

The Fifth Amendment privilege against self-incrimination applies when: (1) a person; (2) is compelled; (3) by his testimony; (4) to incriminate himself.[29] For the privilege to apply to a disclosure sought from a witness all four of those elements must exist. In this section we will examine those four elements.

a. Persons

The privilege against self-incrimination only protects natural persons and, as a result, only natural persons can assert it. The privilege does not apply to corporations and other collective entities such as labor unions and business partnerships.[30] As a consequence collective entities cannot assert the privilege to avoid making disclosures of records or information that will incriminate them.[31]

Collective entities can only act through human agents and human agents have physical custody of the entity's records. What happens when a collective entity's records are subpoenaed from the agent who has custody of them and the subpoenaed records contain evidence or information that will incriminate that agent? Will the privilege against self-incrimination excuse the agent from producing the records? In such situations the privilege does not excuse the agent or employee of the entity from producing the subpoenaed records.[32] For example, Phineas is an employee of a labor union and has custody of union records that show that he assisted the union's president in a scheme in which they obtained secret kickbacks from a financial manager who managed the union's pension fund. A grand jury issues a subpoena to Phineas for those records. The privilege does not permit Phineas to refuse to produce them even though they will provide evidence that Phineas committed the offense of wire fraud while participating in the kickback scheme.

b. Compulsion

A necessary element of compulsory self-incrimination is that there be some kind of compulsion.[33] In the absence of compulsion, the privilege has no application.

The privilege was originally understood as applying only to judicial compulsion (i.e., compulsion that had its source in a judicial order), and it was viewed as having no application to extra-legal police station confessions.[34] Over time the U.S. Supreme Court has expanded the privilege so that today it is understood to apply to both extra-legal compulsion that has its source in government, such as torture by the police, and to judicial compulsion, such as a judge's order to a witness to answer certain questions or be held in contempt.[35] Assuming there is compulsion the privilege is only applicable when that compulsion is directed at the witness himself.[36]

As it is used in the Fifth Amendment privilege against self-incrimination the term "compulsion" has a special meaning. For Fifth Amendment privilege purposes, unless physical coercion has been used, a witness is only considered compelled if he has asserted the privilege where it is applicable and a court has incorrectly ordered the witness to make the disclosure sought or be held in contempt.[37] As a result, if instead of asserting the privilege a witness either answers questions posed to him or otherwise makes the disclosures demanded from him by the government, his answers and his disclosures are considered voluntary.[38]

The fact that a person was subpoenaed to testify at a proceeding (such as a trial) or is required by law to disclose certain information to the government (such as the information required to be disclosed on an income tax return) is not considered compulsion under the Fifth Amendment privilege.[39] For example, Wadislaw receives a grand jury subpoena that requires him to appear before the DuPage County, Illinois Grand Jury. In compliance with that subpoena Wadislaw appears before the Grand Jury and is asked by a prosecutor whether on February 22 he, Wadislaw, drove a getaway car for Simeon after Simeon committed a bank robbery during which Simeon killed a bank guard. If Wadislaw does not assert his Fifth Amendment privilege and admits that he drove the car for Simeon, his answer has not been compelled. But if instead of answering Wadislaw asserts the privilege and is ordered by a judge to answer the question, on threat of being held in contempt, then Wadislaw has been compelled.

The compulsion to which the privilege applies is compulsion that has its source in the government. The privilege has no application when the compulsion comes from some source other than the government.[40] For example, Roland has murdered Arthur and hidden Arthur's body. Roland is arrested for the murder. After his arrest Roland has a vision in which he believes that God has told him that he will receive divine punishment if he does not tell the police where the victim's body is hidden and why he killed the victim. Roland, now believing that he will be punished by God if he does not provide that information to law enforcement agents, calls a jail guard to his cell, confesses to the murder, and tells the guard where Arthur's body is hidden. In that situation there is no compulsion for purposes of the Fifth Amendment privilege because the compulsion on Roland to talk to the jail guard did not have its source in the government.

Because the Fifth Amendment privilege only applies to compelled self-incrimination, the privilege has no application to and is not violated when evidence is obtained from the witness through a ruse.[41] As a result it is not a violation of the privilege to obtain statements or other evidence from the target of a criminal investigation or a witness through the use of a ruse such as a covert law enforcement activity because such activities neither use nor involve the use of compulsion.

c. Testimonial

The Fifth Amendment privilege applies only when the compelled self-incrimination is testimonial.[42] For purposes of the Fifth Amendment privilege a witness's communication is considered to be testimonial when the content of the communication explicitly or implicitly relates a factual assertion or information.[43] Generally, that means the privilege applies when a witness's words or conduct will convey the contents of his mind. For example, a witness can be required to read a passage from *King Lear* so that a victim can hear and possibly identify the witness's voice because the words read by the witness do not convey the contents of the witness's mind.

Under what is called the acts of production doctrine certain physical acts of a witness are considered to be testimonial even if the witness does not speak. The doctrine recognizes that when a witness produces records in response to a subpoena for his records the witness is implicitly admitting that the records produced are his, are genuine, and are the records being sought.[44] As a result a witness can assert the Fifth Amendment privilege in response to a subpoena issued to him for his personal records.[45] The act of production doctrine does not excuse agents of a collective entity from producing entity records that will incriminate them.[46]

The privilege does not apply to non-testimonial evidence that is self-incriminating.[47] As a result a witness can be required to provide physical evidence such as blood,[48] a voice exemplar,[49] a handwriting exemplar,[50] or a name signed in a particular way,[51] and he can be required to put on an article of clothing.[52]

d. Self-Incrimination

For the Fifth Amendment privilege to be applicable the witness's testimonial communication must incriminate him in a criminal case. While the term "criminal case" might suggest that the privilege applies only in a criminal trial, that term has long been given a much broader meaning by the courts. Federal courts have held that as long as the witness's testimonial communication will incriminate him under the criminal law, the witness can assert the privilege against self-incrimination in either a civil or criminal proceeding[53] as well as in response to disclosures mandated by regulatory statutes such as the income tax laws.[54]

For the privilege to be applicable the criminal law under which the witness will incriminate himself through self-disclosure must be a criminal law established in the American political system.[55] The privilege does not apply if the answers of the witness will only incriminate him under the criminal law of some foreign country.[56]

The privilege only applies when the witness himself will be incriminated by his disclosure and does not apply merely because some other person will be incriminated by it, even if that other person is a close family member.[57] Finally, the self-incrimination must be under the criminal law. The privilege does not apply if the compelled disclosure will be degrading to the witness[58] or will only provide evidence against the witness in a civil suit.

3. *Immunity and Elimination of the Privilege*

A witness's privilege against self-incrimination can be eliminated and he can be compelled to answer questions that would otherwise be self-incriminating when he is given a formal grant of immunity. Only formally granted immunity can eliminate a witness's privilege, but not all types of immunity, even if formally granted, are legally sufficient to do so. Two types of immunity, either of which if formally granted are constitutionally sufficient to eliminate a witness's privilege against self-incrimination, are (1) transactional immunity and (2) use and derivative use immunity.[59]

Transactional immunity and use and derivative use immunity differ significantly from each other and it is important to understand the difference between the two. A witness who receives transactional immunity cannot be prosecuted for any crimes about which he testifies. In contrast, a witness who receives use and derivative use immunity can still be prosecuted for any crimes about which he testifies, but neither his testimony nor any evidence derived from his testimony can be used against him in any criminal prosecution.

The power to grant immunity, the type of immunity that can be granted, and the procedure for granting it are determined by statute. At the federal level U.S. Attorneys with the approval of the Justice Department are allowed to give use and derivative use immunity when certain statutory conditions are satisfied.[60] All of the states have their own immunity statutes. Those statutes differ greatly as to the form of immunity that can be conferred[61] and as to the conditions under which it can be given. A paralegal who works in the field of criminal law should familiarize herself with her state's immunity statute.

On the federal level the power to grant immunity is a discretionary executive branch power that has been given to it by Congress.[62] While under federal law a judge must sign the immunity order to make it effective, a federal judge cannot refuse the executive branch's application to give immunity.[63] Under federal law the judiciary has no power on its own to grant immunity[64] and judges can only issue an immunity order upon the request of the executive branch.[65] The judiciary has no power to order the executive branch to grant immunity.[66]

On the state level there is an alternate source of immunity. Some state regulatory statutes contain provisions that, without judicial action, automatically provide immunity to witnesses who receive and comply with administrative subpoenas issued by certain administrative agencies. Under the provisions of many of these statutes a witness who receives an administrative subpoena issued by such an agency, who in compliance with that subpoena appears before an official of that agency, and who under oath answers questions posed to him or produces records sought by the agency automatically receives transactional immunity.[67]

Paralegals who work for regulatory agencies that have subpoena power often prepare administrative subpoenas and arrange for them to be served. Because such agencies also enforce criminal statutes that relate to the programs they administer and because an erroneously issued subpoena can result in foreclosing a criminal prosecution, it is very important that a paralegal employed by a regulatory agency learn whether the statute that gives her agency subpoena power contains an automatic immunity provision and that she only issue such subpoenas when properly authorized.

Regulatory agencies that operate under statutes that have such automatic immunity provisions frequently have a statutory alternative to administrative subpoenas. In many states that alternative is called a "demand letter." While demand letters operate similarly to administrative subpoenas they do not carry the power to confer immunity by virtue of a witness's compliance with it.[68] Demand letters usually require that a witness make records in his custody available at his place of business so that agents of the issuing agency can inspect and copy them. It is very important for a paralegal employed at an administrative agency to learn whether her agency issues demand letters or their equivalent and be able to identify and distinguish between them and the agency's administrative subpoena.

In addition to formal grants of immunity there are also informal grants of immunity that prosecutors frequently confer on witnesses. Prosecutors give informal immunity by promising a witness that if he testifies or otherwise cooperates he will not be prosecuted. This form of immunity can be given verbally, but is usually made in writing in the form of a letter from the prosecutor. For that reason this type of immunity is often referred to as "letter" immunity.

Letter immunity is not sufficient to eliminate a witness's privilege against self-incrimination, but defense attorneys frequently will advise their clients to accept it if that is all the prosecutor is willing to offer. If, in reliance on a prosecutor's promise not to prosecute, a witness provides information that is self-incriminating and the prosecutor breaches her promise and charges that witness, the courts will enforce the prosecutor's promise and dismiss the charge or charges to which the promise not to prosecute relates.

Paralegals who work in prosecutors' offices usually prepare motions and orders for grants of immunity as well as letters conferring informal immunity. A paralegal who prepares such letters as well as one who prepares the motions and orders for formal grants of immunity should be sure to keep a copy of those documents as well as a record in the case file that lists which witnesses have been given which form of immunity. If any of those witnesses will be called to testify at a defendant's trial, the prosecutor will need to identify those witnesses to the defense who received some form of immunity and will need to provide the defense with copies of the immunity-granting documents.

Proffer Letters, Evidence, and Prosecution

Often a person who has some involvement in a crime will have information that would be valuable to an investigation and later during trial. In an effort to induce such a person to disclose information about that crime and as a way to obtain and evaluate the usefulness and quality of that information without giving such a person immunity, prosecutors often offer such a person a proffer agreement. The terms of the proffer agreement are usually contained in a document called a proffer letter that is addressed to the person possessing the information or to her attorney. In a typical proffer letter the prosecutor agrees that if that person provides him with evidence and the prosecutor later charges the person with a crime, he will not use that evidence against the person in the **prosecution's case in chief** or at sentencing unless at trial the person testifies in a manner inconsistent with or "presents a position" that is different from what she discloses to law enforcement. A person is generally considered to have presented a different position at trial if she introduces evidence that is inconsistent with the evidence she disclosed to law enforcement or if her lawyer cross-examines a prosecution witness in such a way as to elicit such evidence.[69]

A person with some involvement in a crime will frequently accept a proffer agreement instead of demanding immunity or remaining silent because the person expects the prosecutor to charge her if she does not provide evidence or cooperation and because she hopes that the information and cooperation she provides will be of such value to the prosecutor that in return for it the prosecutor will agree not to charge her, to charge her with a lesser offense, or to recommend a lenient sentence to the sentencing judge and advise the judge of her assistance and of its value to the government.

If a person accepts the terms of a proffer agreement the person will attend what is usually called a proffer session (sometimes it is simply referred to as a proffer) where she will meet with law enforcement agents and usually the prosecutor. During the proffer session law enforcement agents and the prosecutor will ask the person questions, show her documents, and ask her to explain the documents and their significance to the crime under investigation. Law enforcement agents will prepare written reports that summarize the witness's statements during each proffer session. Sometimes the witness will be placed in the grand jury to repeat those statements under oath and thereby make her subject to a charge of perjury if she knows her statements are false. In complex white collar crime and public corruption investigations, the person will usually attend numerous proffer sessions over a period of many months and will review large quantities of documents.

Paralegals frequently will prepare proffer letters for the prosecutors for whom they work and may assist prosecutors and law enforcement agents with proffers by organizing and copying documents for the proffer session.

The prosecution's case in chief is the evidence presented by the prosecutor between the time the prosecutor calls his first witness and the time that the prosecutor rests his case. With respect to proffer agreements, that means that during the trial stage of a criminal case the prosecutor is promising not to use the witness's disclosures as evidence against her between the time he calls his first witness and when he rests his case.

September 19, 20XX

Mr. T G
Attorney at Law
210 Main Street
City, State 99999

Re: Mary Smith   BY FAX TO: 111-222-3333

Dear Mr. G:

As you are aware, the STATE Attorney General is conducting an investigation of a matter about which we believe your client, Mary Smith, may have information. The Attorney General seeks a proffer of the testimony of your client regarding her knowledge of the facts underlying that matter. The Attorney General requires a completely truthful statement of your client in the proffer.

In the event your client is charged in relation to the matters about which your client provides information pursuant to this proffer agreement, anything related by you or your client to the Attorney General pursuant to this proffer agreement will not be used against your client, Mary Smith, in the Attorney General's case in chief or in aggravation at any sentencing hearing involving your client. You and your client agree that the Attorney General remains free to use in any manner he may determine and in any type of proceeding any information, statements, or evidence known to the Attorney General, or any other law enforcement agency prior to entering into this proffer agreement.

You and your client also agree that: 1) the Attorney General is completely free to pursue any and all investigative leads derived in any way from the proffer which could result in the acquisition of evidence admissible against your client and 2) if your client should subsequently testify contrary to the substance of the proffer or if you or your client in any manner otherwise present a position inconsistent with the proffer, the Attorney General may use statements made by you or your client during any meeting with the Attorney General and all evidence obtained directly or indirectly from those statements for any purpose, including, but not limited to: impeachment of your client, if she testifies; to rebut any evidence, argument, or representation offered by or on behalf of your client in connection with or at any trial; at any sentencing hearing; or in a prosecution for perjury or obstructing justice.

Page Two
Mr. T G
September 19, 20XX

This letter embodies the entire agreement with the Attorney General to make a proffer. No other promises or agreements exist between you or your client and the Attorney General regarding the proffer and no representations, other than those contained in this letter, have been made to you by the Attorney General.

You and your client should sign one copy of this letter and return that copy to me.

Sincerely,

_____

John Doe,
Assistant Attorney General
1 Capitol Street
Capital City, State 99999

I, Mary Smith, have read the above letter, discussed its provisions with my attorney, and voluntarily agree to its terms. I also acknowledge receipt of a copy of this letter on or before the date next to my signature.

Date:_____   _____
                                  Mary Smith

Date:_____   _____
                                  Attorney for Mary Smith

4. Right to Be Informed of the Privilege

Generally a witness has no right to be informed of his privilege against self-incrimination[70] because, as in all other matters, witnesses (like all persons) are considered to know the law.[71] The most important exception to that general rule was created by the U.S. Supreme Court in the case known as *Miranda v. Arizona*.[72] In that case the Court held that under certain circumstances, before government agents question a person they must advise him of what have come to be called the Miranda rights: that he has a right to remain silent (the Fifth Amendment privilege), that anything he says may be used against him, that he has a right to an attorney, and if he cannot afford an attorney one will be provided to him.

It is important to keep in mind that the Miranda decision does not require that law enforcement agents administer Miranda rights every time they question a person. The *Miranda* decision requires that Miranda rights be given only when law enforcement agents subject a person to custodial interrogation.[73]

United States v. Kilgroe

959 F.2d 802 (1992)
United States Court of Appeals for the Ninth Circuit

KOZINSKI, Circuit Judge.

Appellant Kilgroe was subpoenaed to testify for the defense in a criminal trial. During the course of cross-examination he made several self-incriminating statements that were later used by the government to convict Kilgroe of fraud. The question presented is whether Kilgroe was entitled to have the court or the prosecutor read him *Miranda* warnings before he took the stand for the defense.

Facts

Kilgroe, in-house counsel for National Business Printers, was subpoenaed to testify for the defense in the criminal mail fraud prosecution of Albert Clark, another employee of National. * * * On cross-examination, the Assistant United States Attorney sought to impeach Kilgroe by getting him to admit that he was a participant in the mail fraud scheme, not just a disinterested attorney giving legal advice to Clark. Sure enough, Kilgroe made several incriminating statements disclosing his in-depth involvement in the mail fraud scheme. Defendant Clark was convicted.

Not long thereafter, events turned from bad to worse: Relying on Kilgroe's incriminating testimony in the Clark trial, the United States Attorney charged him with mail fraud. At trial, the district court admitted, over defense objection, a redacted version of Kilgroe's testimony in the Clark case. The jury convicted Kilgroe for mail fraud and he was sentenced to thirty months' imprisonment.

Kilgroe's only contention is that before he testified in the Clark trial, either the prosecutor or the court was required, in accordance with *Miranda v. Arizona*, 384 U.S. 436 (1966), to inform him of his right against compelled self-incrimination

A **putative defendant** is one against whom the government already possesses incriminating evidence at the time of his appearance before a tribunal, or upon whom the government has focused as having committed a crime. *United States v. Anfield,* 539 F.2d 674, 676 n.2 (9th Cir. 1976).

and warn him that anything he said could be used to convict him. He relies heavily on the fact that he was forced to testify under the weight of a subpoena and on his surmise that the prosecutor considered him a **putative defendant** at the time of the Clark trial.

Discussion

"Fidelity to the doctrine announced in *Miranda* requires that it be enforced strictly, but only in those types of situations in which the concerns that powered the decision are implicated." *Berkemer v. McCarty,* 468 U.S. 420, 437 (1984). Although "those types of situations" may vary, they all share two essential elements: "custody *and* official interrogation." *Illinois v. Perkins,* 496 U.S. 292, 296-297 (1990). Thus, the scope of *Miranda* is not, and never has been, coextensive with the scope of the right against compelled self-incrimination. *See Murphy,* 465 U.S. at 429-434. *Miranda* only comes into play when government-generated coercion risks "undermin[ing] the individual's will to resist," thereby leading him to disclose information he would otherwise not voluntarily reveal.

Although the courtroom is the paradigmatic setting for invoking the right against compelled self-incrimination, it is not the type of setting that would justify invoking *Miranda*'s prophylactic rule. The *Miranda* Court itself recognized that "the compulsion to speak in the isolated setting of the police station may well be greater than in courts or other official investigations, where there are often impartial observers to guard against intimidation or trickery." *Miranda,* 384 U.S. at 461. Nor does the "obligation to appear and testify truthfully" created by a subpoena "constitute compulsion to give incriminating testimony" of the sort that implicates *Miranda*'s policies. *United States v. Jenkins,* 785 F.2d 1387, 1393 (9th Cir. 1986). Unlike custodial interrogation—which usually takes place without warning and, therefore, without the chance for reflection or legal advice—the subpoena gives the witness the opportunity in advance to obtain whatever counsel he deems appropriate and carefully contemplate his testimony. He remains free, of course, to refuse to answer questions that would incriminate him.

Kilgroe's claim that he required special protection because he was a putative defendant subjected to high pressure cross-examination is without merit. Cross-examination by a prosecutor, conducted in public and in the presence of both judge and jury, is hardly tantamount to custodial questioning by the police. While it is no doubt a powerful tool, cross-examination lacks the elements of isolation and intimidation associated with custodial police interrogation. That Kilgroe may have been a putative defendant when he testified is beside the point: The *internal* knowledge of a government agent that a witness may have been involved in criminal activity generates no *external* coercion on the witness.

It is easy to think of *Miranda* as an expansive shelter against a citizen's ignorance of his constitutional rights—especially because for the past 25 years the *Miranda* warning "has been ingrained in the American public," Ceol, '*Right to Remain Silent,*' Wash. Times, June 13, 1991, at A3, and "become part of our common awareness." Caplan, *Questioning* Miranda, 38 Vand. L. Rev. 1417,

Indeed, the clearest roots of the right against compelled self-incrimination stem from assertions of that right by witnesses in court, including Sir Edward Coke's argument that his client had a right against self-incrimination on the charge of unlawful carnal knowledge in the 1589 matrimonial case of *Collier v. Collier* and John Lilburne's refusal to incriminate himself before the Star Chamber during his 1637 sedition trial in England. L. Levy, *Origins of the Fifth Amendment* 221, 271-276 (1986). The philosophical foundations for the right probably originated in ancient Rome, J. Story, *Commentaries on the Constitution of the United States* 663 (Rotunda & Nowak eds. 1987), and were best developed by John Lambert, Sir Thomas More, and Christopher St. Germain. L. Levy at 3-5, 64-70.

1418 (1985). But the *Miranda* litany is a palliative only against the unique pressures inherent in custodial interrogation. It is not a judicially crafted civics lesson, to be recited whenever someone might find it useful to hear. Thus, except in the context of custodial interrogation, *Miranda* leaves the responsibility for keeping a citizen informed of his constitutional rights with the preeminent guardian of those rights: the citizen himself.

Conclusion

The district court's judgment is AFFIRMED.

Case Focus

1. When must agents of the government inform an individual of his Miranda rights?

• • • • • • • •

Custodial interrogation occurs when law enforcement agents initiate questioning after a person is taken into custody.[74] If a person is not in custody, the fact that law enforcement agents have focused their investigation on him or have probable cause to arrest him do not separately or in combination give rise to a duty to give Miranda rights before questioning him.[75]

In this section we will examine: (i) what constitutes custody under *Miranda*; (ii) what constitutes interrogation under *Miranda*; and (iii) how the Miranda rights operate.

a. Custody Under Miranda

A person is considered to be in custody for purposes of Miranda when he has been formally arrested or his freedom of movement has been restrained to the degree associated with formal arrest.[76] In the absence of a formal arrest the determination of whether interrogation is custodial is determined by such things as the location, length, and mode of questioning and whether law enforcement agents have imposed any restrictions on the movements of the person being questioned.[77] A person who has been sentenced to and is serving time in prison is not in custody for purposes of Miranda unless some restriction on his movement beyond that he experiences as a prisoner is imposed.[78]

The rationale that underlies the Miranda decision is that custodial interrogation is inherently coercive and advising a person of the rights mandated by that decision serves to dissipate the coerciveness of that type of questioning.[79] A consequence that flows from that rationale is that only persons who know they are in custody must be advised of their Miranda rights before questioning. A person who does not know he is in custody can be questioned by law enforcement agents without first being given Miranda rights.[80] For example, law enforcement agents have an arrest warrant for Igor for the crime of burglary and with the intent to arrest him they go to his home where, without disclosing to him that they have the warrant, they question him about the burglary without first giving him Miranda warnings. They have not violated Igor's rights under Miranda because Igor did not realize he was effectively in custody when he was questioned.

People v. Bury

199 Ill. App. 3d 207 (1990)
Appellate Court of Illinois (Fourth District)

JUSTICE LUND delivered the opinion of the court:

On September 2, 1988, defendant Donald Bury was charged by information in the circuit court of Vermilion County with committing the offense of computer fraud. (Ill. Rev. Stat. 1987, ch. 38, par. 16D-5(a)(3).) On April 18, 1989, defendant filed a motion to suppress, seeking to exclude as evidence all oral and written statements of defendant [made] * * * on September 2. The court granted defendant's motion. The State now appeals.

* * * The State's evidence establishes that on September 2, 1988, two State police officers, Sergeant Abigail Abraham and agent Mark Maton, and two security agents for the U.S. Sprint phone company proceeded to defendant's home around 9 p.m. At the time, they had an arrest warrant for defendant for the instant offense in their possession. Defendant, after being told who they were, invited them inside. The warrant was not served at this point.

Defendant, his wife, and the four investigators proceeded to defendant's kitchen. The officers indicated they wished to speak about defendant's dealings with U.S. Sprint and Call Indiana. Defendant agreed and did so. * * *

During [the conversation] * * * [the] defendant discussed his involvement in the charged offense. Defendant was asked if he would give a written statement, and he agreed. The statement was given around 9:30 p.m. and placed on a preprinted form entitled "Voluntary Statement." Defendant read the form and statement, and then signed it. Defendant had not yet been placed under arrest and never asked if he was or would be.

[After completing the written statement the] * * * [d]efendant * * * asked if something was going to happen or if he should consult an attorney. Defendant was then told of the arrest warrant [which the police then executed]. * * * Upon the close of the State's evidence [in the motion to suppress hearing], the court stated:

"[I] [b]elieve even in the 80's which we're presently in, that there are certain modes of conduct which go to an extreme. It is shocking in my opinion that the State Police went out there with their arrest warrant, they knew about the constitutional provisions. They were playing games with the constitution if you have an arrest warrant and they know, as she said at the very end, that she knew that when she saw this man that she had to arrest him, because she went as far as to call Chicago to get advi[c]e as to how not [to] arrest him.

Motion will be allowed to suppress and the fruits thereof." * * *

Now, turning to the statements defendant gave, the State acknowledges that the warnings required by *Miranda v. Arizona* (1966), 384 U.S. 436, were not given. However, the State maintains they are not required in this case.

The rules of *Miranda* apply to admissions made by a defendant while he is in custody or otherwise deprived of his freedom in any significant way. (*Brown,* 136 Ill. 2d at 124.) As the *Brown* court explained:

"The ultimate inquiry is whether there is a formal arrest or restraint on freedom of movement of the degree associated with a formal arrest." (*California v. Beheler* (1983), 463 U.S. 1121, 1125.) Although what constitutes police custody is not always self-evident, the Court in *Miranda* was concerned with interrogations that take place in a police-dominated environment containing "inherently compelling pressures which work to undermine the individual's will to resist and to compel him to speak where he would not otherwise do so freely." *Miranda,* 384 U.S. at 467.

The determination of whether an interrogation is custodial should focus on all of the circumstances surrounding the questioning, such as location, time, length, mood and mode of interrogation, the number of police present, the presence or absence of family and friends of the accused, any indicia of formal arrest or evidence of restraint, the intentions of the officers, the extent of knowledge of the officers and focus of their investigation, and the age, intelligence, and mental makeup of the accused. (*Brown,* 136 Ill. 2d at 124.) After reviewing these factors, the court must make an objective determination as to what a reasonable man, innocent of any crime, would have thought had he been in defendant's shoes. (*Brown,* 136 Ill. 2d at 124.) Again, a reviewing court should not disturb a trial court's motion to suppress ruling unless it is against the manifest weight of the evidence. *People v. Garcia* (1983), 97 Ill. 2d 58.

After reviewing the record in the present case and considering the relevant factors, we conclude that the statements were not given in a custodial setting. Defendant is a middle-aged man and there is no indication of any mental abnormality. The interview occurred in defendant's own kitchen, with his wife present. The mood was nonthreatening. Defendant gave the questioned statements within 30 minutes of the police arriving. Admittedly, there were a number of people present and there is a certain coercive factor when police officers ask an individual questions. But, this is true of any interview by the police and is not controlling. See *Oregon v. Mathiason* (1977), 429 U.S. 492.

We are aware that at the time the police arrived they had an arrest warrant for defendant, about which they did not immediately advise defendant. Thus, it is clear he was the focus of their investigation, and it was their intention to arrest him. However, an interrogation is custodial only when a reasonable person in the position of the defendant, innocent of any wrongdoing, would believe that he was under arrest, given all the circumstances with which he was then confronted.

The focus of the inquiry must always be on what the defendant thought and believed, not the officers. "Coercion is determined from the perspective of the suspect." (*Illinois v. Perkins* (1990), 496 U.S. 292.) In weighing all of these circumstances, the subjective intent of the police officers is relevant only to the extent that it might color their outward behavior. These intentions become probative when there is a conflict in the evidence between the defendant and the officers over how the officers behaved. If the officers intended all along to arrest the defendant, then the court might reasonably resolve such a conflict by doubting the ability of the officers to hide their intentions. But, the fact that the officers might have intended to arrest the defendant when their interrogation ceased is of no significance if their behavior was such that this intent was never revealed to the defendant. In other words, that the investigation had focused upon the defendant, even to the extent, as here, that the officers possessed an arrest warrant as the interrogation was taking place, does not matter as long as the defendant was not aware of the officers' intentions.

Here, in considering the short duration of the interview, its setting and the presence of defendant's wife, we conclude that the presence of the unarticulated intent to arrest defendant does not, by itself, transform the setting into the type with which *Miranda* is concerned. A reasonable, innocent person would not believe he was in custody at the time of the interview.

Accordingly, for the foregoing reasons, we find the trial court's order against the manifest weight of the evidence.

Reversed and remanded.

Case Focus

1. Why did the fact that the defendant was the focus of the investigation not require the law enforcement agents in this case to advise the defendant of his Miranda rights?
2. Why did the fact the law enforcement agents in this case had an arrest warrant for the defendant not require them to advise the defendant of his Miranda rights?
3. Given the facts in this case, at what point would the law enforcement agents have been required to give the defendant his Miranda rights?

• • • • • • • •

b. Interrogation

The Miranda warnings need only be given when law enforcement agents question a person in custody. If law enforcement agents do not engage in questioning there is no requirement to give Miranda warnings.[81] If law enforcement agents take a person into custody and do not give that person his Miranda rights and, without questioning or prompting by the agents the person in custody makes incriminating statements to them, there has been no violation of that person's rights under Miranda, and the statements will be able to be used against him.

If a person in custody does not know that the person to whom he is speaking is a law enforcement agent, such as if he believes he is speaking to a fellow prisoner when the purported fellow prisoner is in fact a law enforcement agent working in a covert capacity, Miranda rights need not be given before the undercover agent begins to pose questions to the prisoner.[82] For example, if James is a law enforcement agent posing as a prisoner in a penitentiary and he approaches Juan who is a prisoner, James does not need to advise Juan of his Miranda rights before he asks Juan about a murder Juan is suspected of committing.

Perkins v. Illinois
496 U.S. 292 (1990)
Supreme Court of the United States

JUSTICE KENNEDY delivered the opinion of the Court.

An undercover government agent was placed in the cell of respondent Perkins, who was incarcerated on charges unrelated to the subject of the agent's investigation. Respondent made statements that implicated him in the crime that the agent sought to solve. Respondent claims that the statements should be inadmissible because he had not been given *Miranda* warnings by the agent. We hold that the statements are admissible. *Miranda* warnings are not required when the suspect is unaware that he is speaking to a law enforcement officer and gives a voluntary statement.

I

In November 1984, Richard Stephenson was murdered in a suburb of East St. Louis, Illinois. The murder remained unsolved until March 1986, when one Donald Charlton told police that he had learned about a homicide from a fellow inmate at the Graham Correctional Facility, where Charlton had been serving a sentence for burglary. The fellow inmate was Lloyd Perkins, who is the respondent here. Charlton told police that, while at Graham, he had befriended respondent, who told him in detail about a murder that respondent had committed in East St. Louis. * * *

By the time the police heard Charlton's account, respondent had been released from Graham, but police traced him to a jail in Montgomery County, Illinois, where he was being held pending trial on a charge of aggravated battery, unrelated to the Stephenson murder. The police wanted to investigate further respondent's connection to the Stephenson murder, but feared that the use of an eavesdropping device would prove impracticable and unsafe. They decided instead to place an undercover agent in the cellblock with respondent and Charlton. The plan was for Charlton and undercover agent John Parisi to pose as escapees from a work release program who had been arrested in the course of a burglary. Parisi and Charlton were instructed to engage respondent in casual conversation and report anything he said about the Stephenson murder.

Parisi, using the alias "Vito Bianco," and Charlton, both clothed in jail garb, were placed in the cellblock with respondent at the Montgomery County jail. * * * Respondent greeted Charlton who, after a brief conversation with respondent, introduced Parisi by his alias. Parisi told respondent that he "wasn't going to do any more time" and suggested that the three of them escape. * * * The trio met in respondent's cell later that evening, after the other inmates were asleep, to refine their plan. Respondent said that his girlfriend could smuggle in a pistol. Charlton said: "Hey, I'm not a murderer, I'm a burglar. That's your guys' profession." After telling Charlton that he would be responsible for any murder that occurred, Parisi asked respondent if he had ever "done" anybody. Respondent said that he had and proceeded to describe at length the events of the Stephenson murder. Parisi and respondent then engaged in some casual conversation before respondent went to sleep. Parisi did not give respondent *Miranda* warnings before the conversations.

Respondent was charged with the Stephenson murder. Before trial, he moved to suppress the statements made to Parisi in the jail. The trial court granted the motion to suppress, and the State appealed. The Appellate Court of Illinois affirmed, 176 Ill. App. 3d 443 (1988), holding that *Miranda v. Arizona*, 384 U.S. 436 (1966), prohibits all undercover contacts with incarcerated suspects that are reasonably likely to elicit an incriminating response.

We granted certiorari, 493 U.S. 808 (1989), to decide whether an undercover law enforcement officer must give *Miranda* warnings to an incarcerated suspect before asking him questions that may elicit an incriminating response. We now reverse.

II

In *Miranda v. Arizona, supra,* the Court held that the Fifth Amendment privilege against self-incrimination prohibits admitting statements given by a suspect during "custodial interrogation" without a prior warning. Custodial interrogation means "questioning initiated by law enforcement officers after a person has been taken into custody. . . ." *Id.* 384 U.S., at 444. The warning mandated by

Miranda was meant to preserve the privilege during "incommunicado interrogation of individuals in a police-dominated atmosphere." *Id.,* at 445. That atmosphere is said to generate "inherently compelling pressures which work to undermine the individual's will to resist and to compel him to speak where he would not otherwise do so freely." *Id.,* at 467. * * *

Conversations between suspects and undercover agents do not implicate the concerns underlying *Miranda.* The essential ingredients of a "police-dominated atmosphere" and compulsion are not present when an incarcerated person speaks freely to someone whom he believes to be a fellow inmate. Coercion is determined from the perspective of the suspect. *Rhode Island v. Innis,* 446 U.S. 291 (1980). When a suspect considers himself in the company of cellmates and not officers, the coercive atmosphere is lacking. *Miranda,* 384 U.S., at 449 ("[T]he 'principal psychological factor contributing to a successful interrogation is *privacy*—being alone with the person under interrogation'"); *id.,* at 445. There is no empirical basis for the assumption that a suspect speaking to those whom he assumes are not officers will feel compelled to speak by the fear of reprisal for remaining silent or in the hope of more lenient treatment should he confess.

It is the premise of *Miranda* that the danger of coercion results from the interaction of custody and official interrogation. We reject the argument that *Miranda* warnings are required whenever a suspect is in custody in a technical sense and converses with someone who happens to be a government agent. Questioning by captors, who appear to control the suspect's fate, may create mutually reinforcing pressures that the Court has assumed will weaken the suspect's will, but where a suspect does not know that he is conversing with a government agent, these pressures do not exist. The state court here mistakenly assumed that because the suspect was in custody, no undercover questioning could take place. When the suspect has no reason to think that the listeners have official power over him, it should not be assumed that his words are motivated by the reaction he expects from his listeners. "[W]hen the agent carries neither badge nor gun and wears not 'police blue,' but the same prison gray" as the suspect, there is no "*interplay* between police interrogation and police custody." Kamisar, *Brewer v. Williams, Massiah* and *Miranda:* What is "Interrogation"? When Does it Matter?, 67 Geo. L.J. 1, 67, 63 (1978).

Miranda forbids coercion, not mere strategic deception by taking advantage of a suspect's misplaced trust in one he supposes to be a fellow prisoner. As we recognized in *Miranda:* "[C]onfessions remain a proper element in law enforcement. Any statement given freely and voluntarily without any compelling influences is, of course, admissible in evidence." 384 U.S., at 478, 86 S. Ct., at 1629. Ploys to mislead a suspect or lull him into a false sense of security that do not rise to the level of compulsion or coercion to speak are not within *Miranda*'s concerns. * * *

The tactic employed here to elicit a voluntary confession from a suspect does not violate the Self-Incrimination Clause. We held in *Hoffa v. United States,* 385 U.S. 293 (1966), that placing an undercover agent near a suspect in order to gather incriminating information was permissible under the Fifth Amendment. [There we approved using Hoffa's statements against him at trial because no claim had been or could have been made that the statements were the product of coercion.] * * * The only difference between this case and *Hoffa* is that the suspect here was incarcerated, but detention, whether or not for the crime in question, does not warrant a presumption that the use of an undercover agent to speak with an incarcerated suspect makes any confession thus obtained involuntary. * * *

We hold that an undercover law enforcement officer posing as a fellow inmate need not give *Miranda* warnings to an incarcerated suspect before asking questions that may elicit an incriminating response. The statements at issue in this case were voluntary, and there is no federal obstacle to their admissibility at trial. We now reverse and remand for proceedings not inconsistent with our opinion.

It is so ordered.

Case Focus

1. The defendant in this case was in jail and questioned by a law enforcement agent. Why was the agent not required to advise the defendant of his Miranda rights?

2. Why does the tactic used in this case not violate the defendant's privilege against self-incrimination?

• • • • • • • •

c. Operation of Miranda

The Miranda decision delineates two rights about which law enforcement agents must advise persons who will be subjected to custodial interrogation: a right to silence and a right to an attorney. The latter is frequently referred to as the Miranda right to counsel because the right to counsel at the investigatory stage of the criminal justice process arises solely from the Miranda decision itself. The Fifth Amendment privilege does not itself contain a right to counsel and as discussed in a later chapter, the Sixth Amendment right to counsel does not apply before the prosecutor initiates prosecution. Invocation of one of those rights has significantly different legal consequences than invocation of the other.

When a person in custody invokes his right to silence, law enforcement agents must stop questioning him, but after a reasonable period of time they are allowed to ask him if he might have changed his mind and would now be willing to speak to them.[83] For a person in custody to be able to take advantage of the Miranda right to silence he must actually invoke it by saying something like, "I don't want to talk to the police" or "I want to remain silent."[84] If a person simply remains silent, his silence is not considered an invocation of the Miranda right to silence and law enforcement agents can continue to question that person.[85] A person who has invoked his right to silence can, without being reapproached by law enforcement agents, also change his mind at any time and ask to reinitiate discussions with them.

As with the Miranda right to silence, a person who is in custody must actually invoke his Miranda right to counsel if he wishes to take advantage of that right. When a person in custody invokes his Miranda right to counsel, unlike with the Miranda right to silence, while he remains in custody he cannot be approached by law enforcement agents about reinitiating discussions with them until he has had an opportunity to meet with an attorney.[86] Before meeting with an attorney the person in custody is, however, free to change his mind about talking to an attorney and can, on his own, reinitiate discussions with law enforcement agents.[87] Once a person has invoked his Miranda right to counsel, law enforcement agents are prohibited from questioning him about any crime unless his attorney is present.[88] If, however, a person is released from custody, after a period of two weeks from his release law enforcement agents may approach him and again question him without violating the Miranda right to counsel.[89]

Only the person in custody can invoke the Miranda right to counsel.[90] That means that if the person in custody does not ask for an attorney, law enforcement agents are not required either to advise him that an attorney has been retained for him or to allow him to consult with an attorney who has been retained for him by some third person[91] such as a family member or unarrested coconspirator. Also, the Miranda right to counsel can only be invoked by a person when he is in custody.[92] That means that when a person being questioned is not in custody Miranda does not apply and the person has no right to an attorney even if he asks for one.[93] Thus, if a person is not in custody and is being questioned by law enforcement agents and advises them that he wants an attorney, the law enforcement agents are allowed to continue to question him.[94]

The purpose of the Miranda right to counsel is to allow a person's attorney to be present during custodial interrogation to ensure that his client is not compelled to speak.[95] As a result, the quality of legal advice a person receives from his attorney during custodial interrogation plays no role in determining whether his Miranda right to counsel has been satisfied. For example, Andrew has been arrested for the murder of Penelope, but has not yet been charged. When Andrew is taken into custody he invokes his Miranda right to counsel. Andrew's attorney arrives at the police station shortly thereafter where, for the next hour, in the presence of his attorney, and without any compulsion being directed to him, Andrew is questioned by law enforcement agents and the prosecutor about the murder. An hour into the interrogation, without having reached any type of plea or sentencing agreement with the prosecutor, Andrew's attorney advises Andrew to make a confession. Andrew follows that advice, admits to killing Penelope, and is subsequently charged with Penelope's murder. Despite that clearly questionable legal advice from Andrew's attorney, Andrew's Miranda right to counsel was satisfied because Andrew's attorney was present to ensure that Andrew was not illegally compelled by law enforcement officers to make incriminating statements and no such compulsion was used on Andrew.[96]

Claudio v. Scully

791 F. Supp. 985 (1992)
United States District Court (E.D.N.Y)

KORMAN, District Judge.

In the early morning hours of May 15, 1980, Steven Zweikert was returning home from a high school prom. As he emerged from the subway in Queens at about 4:00 a.m., he was followed and accosted by four youths. Among them was the petitioner, Angel Claudio, who brandished a gun. When one of the boys demanded money, Steven tried to wrest the gun from Claudio and in the struggle was fatally shot. Claudio and his cohorts fled the scene.

On May 21, 1980, the police were advised that an individual named Andrew Boyle had information about the murder. * * * In response to police questioning, Boyle told the police that on May 14, 1980, between 6:00 and 8:00 p.m., he was in a "green mustang" with some other boys, one of whom had a gun. Boyle was then shown several photos. He identified Angel Claudio as the one with the gun. Claudio had previously been picked up for questioning * * * [and] released.

As a result of this encounter with the police, Claudio consulted the yellow pages and called attorney Mark Heller on May 21, 1990. Claudio met with Heller the next day and retained him as his attorney. After a discussion with Heller, Claudio agreed to turn himself in to the Queens District Attorney, John J. Santucci. Although some conflict existed as to the advice Heller gave to Claudio, the trial court found that Heller did not advise him of the seriousness of the charges he faced or his available defenses. Rather, he urged Claudio to surrender, explaining that Claudio might be able to obtain probation if he did so. When they arrived at the District Attorney's Office later that afternoon, however, Santucci informed Heller that there would be no plea bargain. Heller did not relay this information to his client. Instead, he advised Claudio to make a statement.

In the presence of his attorney, and after *Miranda* warnings were given, Claudio indicated that he wanted to confess because he was so troubled by what had happened that he was unable to eat or sleep. Claudio gave the following account of the events of May 15, 1980. He and his friends were in a car when they saw Steven Zweikert exiting the subway. One of Claudio's friends asked him to retrieve a gun that had been placed under the seat. The group then got out of the car and followed Steven down the street. Claudio pointed the gun at Steven while another demanded money. When Steven tried to grab the gun from Claudio, it accidentally discharged, fatally striking Steven in the chest. Claudio and his friends fled empty-handed. * * *

Claudio was tried and convicted of the crimes of murder, attempted robbery and possession of a weapon. The Appellate Division affirmed the conviction, although it held that the trial court erred in imposing consecutive rather than concurrent sentences. Accordingly, it modified petitioner's sentence to 25 years to life. *People v. Claudio,* 130 A.D.2d 759 (2d Dep't 1987). Judge Hancock denied Claudio's application for leave to appeal to the Court of Appeals. *People v. Claudio,* 70 N.Y.2d 873. * * *

After exhausting his post-conviction appeals, Claudio filed this petition for a writ of habeas corpus. * * * The petition, which raises four separate issues, is denied for the reasons that follow.

Petitioner argues that his confession should have been suppressed because it was the result of his attorney's ineffective advice. * * *

Commonwealth v. Moreau, 30 Mass. App. Ct. 677 (1991), *cert. denied,* 502 U.S. 1049 (1992), upon which petitioner relies, does not provide a sound basis for a contrary holding. * * * The Appeals Court * * * held that the defendant was "entitled to the aid of counsel to protect his Fifth Amendment privilege against self-incrimination under *Miranda v. Arizona,* 384 U.S. 436 (1966); *United States v. Gouveia,* 467 U.S. 180 n. 5, (1984)." Accordingly, it concluded that the defendant was entitled to a hearing on his claim that his lawyer was ineffective because he advised him to make a post-arrest confession.

Unlike the defendant in *Moreau,* it is hardly clear that petitioner was subject to the kind of custodial interrogation that would entitle him to the assistance of counsel under *Miranda v. Arizona. See Oregon v. Mathiason,* 429 U.S. 492 (1977); *California v. Beheler,* 463 U.S. 1121(1983). There is a more compelling reason, however, for rejecting petitioner's argument that he was denied the effective assistance of counsel to which he claims he was entitled. While *Miranda v. Arizona* holds that a suspect who is subject to custodial interrogation is entitled to counsel "to protect the Fifth Amendment privilege against self-incrimination * * * [t]he sole concern of the Fifth Amendment, on which *Miranda* was based, is governmental coercion." *Colorado v. Connelly,* 479 U.S. 157, 170 (1986). Accordingly, an attorney who ensures that his client has not been compelled to speak effectively performs the role that the Supreme Court envisioned for him in *Miranda.*

Particularly apposite here is the discussion in *Miranda* concerning the advice an attorney would give a suspect and the role he would play during an ensuing interrogation. Chief Justice Warren observed that, if a suspect asked to speak to an attorney before submitting to a custodial interrogation, the "attorney may advise [him] not to talk to police until he has had an opportunity to investigate the case, or [the attorney] may wish to be present during any police questioning." *Miranda,* 384 U.S. at 480.

> If the accused decides to talk to his interrogators, the assistance of counsel can mitigate the dangers of untrustworthiness. With a lawyer present the likelihood that the police will practice coercion is reduced, and if coercion is nevertheless exercised the lawyer can testify to it in court. The presence of a lawyer can also help to guarantee that the accused gives a fully accurate statement to the police and that the statement is rightly reported by the prosecution at trial.

Id. at 470.

"The Court's vision of a lawyer mitigating the dangers of 'untrustworthiness' by witnessing coercion and assisting accuracy is largely a fancy; for if counsel arrives there is rarely going to be a police station confession." *Miranda v. Arizona,* 384 U.S. at 516 n.12, (Harlan, J., dissenting). Nevertheless, Chief Justice Warren's "vision" of the role of counsel is fundamentally consistent with the premise of the *Miranda* majority that a suspect is entitled to counsel to prevent law enforcement officers from coercing a confession and not to prevent a defendant from confessing voluntarily. Indeed, the Chief Justice emphasized that "[c]onfessions remain a proper element in law enforcement. Any statement given freely and voluntarily without any compelling influences is, of course, admissible in evidence." 384 U.S. at 478.

The situation would be otherwise if petitioner had been advised foolishly to take the stand at his trial and confess. While he could not have alleged that he was compelled to be a witness against himself, he could have argued that he was deprived of the effective assistance of counsel. Unlike a defendant at a trial, who is entitled to the effective assistance of counsel, "to ensure that the prosecutor's case encounters 'the crucible of meaningful adversarial testing,'" *Moran v. Burbine,* 475 U.S. 412, 430 (1986) (quoting *United States v. Cronic,* 466 U.S. 648, 656 (1984)), petitioner was entitled to the presence of counsel when he was interrogated only "in order to protect the Fifth Amendment privilege" against self-incrimination. *Miranda,* 384 U.S. at 470. Accordingly, his voluntary confession was not subject to suppression merely because his attorney gave him bad advice. *See Colorado v. Connelly,* 479 U.S. at 170; *Oregon v. Elstad,* 470 U.S. 298, 305 (1985).

There is a suggestion here that it is somehow unjust that petitioner should suffer because of the incompetent advice of his attorney. The answer, to quote the words of Judge Keating in a related context, is that while petitioner may not have been fortunate enough to have chosen competent counsel, "[t]his is a wholly different thing from talking about justice." *People v. McQueen,* 18 N.Y.2d 337, 350 (1966) (Keating, J. concurring). Petitioner, it should be recalled, murdered Steven Zweikert, a young man at the threshold of his adult life. Petitioner's guilt was established by a confession that was freely and voluntarily given. If his attorney had given petitioner the sound advice to which he claims he was entitled, he would have gotten away with murder.

The Supreme Court recently observed in *McNeil v. Wisconsin,* that "the ready ability to obtain uncoerced confessions is not an evil but an unmitigated good, [without which] society would be the loser. Admissions of guilt resulting from valid *Miranda* warnings 'are more than merely "desirable" they are essential to society's compelling interest in finding, convicting and punishing those who violate the law.'" 501 U.S. 171 (1991) (quoting *Moran v. Burbine,* 475 U.S. at 426). This language applies with equal force here. * * *

Conclusion

Accordingly, for the foregoing reasons, the petition for a writ of habeas corpus is denied. * * *

SO ORDERED.

Case Focus

1. What is the role of an attorney under the Miranda right to counsel?
2. How, if at all, is a person's Miranda right to counsel violated when, as a result of ineffective legal advice, the person makes self-incriminating statements to law enforcement agents?

• • • • • • • •

When a person's Miranda rights have been violated, the statements so obtained will be suppressed at his trial, but unlike with violations of the Fourth Amendment and violations of the Fifth Amendment privilege itself, the fruits of those statements (such as physical evidence) will not be suppressed.[97] For example, the police arrest Raul for murdering Sandra and without giving Raul Miranda rights begin questioning him. During that questioning Raul admits to shooting Sandra and tells the police where he hid the gun. Raul's admission about shooting Sandra will be suppressed as will his statement telling the police where the gun was hidden, but the gun and any ballistics evidence that can be derived from it will not be suppressed.

5. *Required Records Exception*

In modern society government frequently mandates either by statute or regulation that businesses, individuals who operate businesses, or persons who participate in certain government programs create and maintain certain records. For example, retailers are required by many state sales or retailer's occupation tax statutes to keep inventory records, bills of lading, purchase orders, and invoices for goods. Such records are called required records. Required records would be of little value to the government if individuals subject to such recordkeeping requirements could assert the privilege against self-incrimination to shield them from disclosure to the government.

To ensure that required records are made available to the government the Supreme Court has carved out an exception to the Fifth Amendment privilege. That exception, called the required records doctrine, requires persons who are subject to mandatory records-keeping laws to make them available to the government, notwithstanding that they may contain information or evidence that is incriminating to their owner or custodian.[98] The required records doctrine applies when: (1) the recordkeeping requirement is primarily regulatory; (2) the records contain the type of information the regulated party normally would keep; and (3) the records have assumed public aspects.[99]

The recordkeeping requirement is considered to be primarily regulatory when the activity about which the records are kept is a legal one, notwithstanding that the records can be used as evidence in a criminal prosecution. The records are considered to take on public aspects if they are subject to inspection by the government and some type of report is made to the public or government from the information contained in them.[100] For example, a person in the retail furniture business can be required to keep and upon subpoena produce certain records relating to his purchases, inventory, and sales, notwithstanding that the records could be used to prosecute him for tax evasion because the business (selling furniture at retail) is a legal one, because such records contain information he would normally keep (information about purchases, inventory, and sales), and because the retailer uses such information to prepare sales and income tax returns he files with the government.

B. Vienna Convention on Consular Relations

The Vienna Convention on Consular Relations is a treaty that was ratified by the U.S. Senate in 1969. That treaty imposes duties on American law enforcement agencies that detain or arrest aliens in the United States and also grants certain rights to such aliens. The Vienna Convention is supplemented by a number of bilateral agreements between the United States and specific nations. Taken together the Vienna Convention and the bilateral agreements create two types of nations: mandatory notice nations and nonmandatory notice nations.

If the detained or arrested alien is a national of a mandatory notice country (see inset) two notices must be given: (1) the nearest consular official of the alien's nation must be informed of the alien's detention or arrest, even if the alien does not want such notice to be given; and (2) the detained or arrested alien must be advised that the notification is being made. If the detained or arrested alien is a national of a nonmandatory notice country he must be advised that if he wishes, the nearest consulate of his nation will be notified of his detention or arrest. A national of either type of country must also be informed that he has a right to meet with a consular officer of his nation. Under the terms of the treaty the law enforcement agency that detains or arrests an alien is required to advise the alien of his rights under the treaty and is required to give the required notices to the consular offices.

While the Convention imposes a duty to advise the alien of his right to meet with an official of his home nation's consulate's office, the Convention does not require that law enforcement agents allow the alien to contact a consular officer before they begin interrogation.[101] Nor does the Convention require that law enforcement agents delay interrogation until contact with consular officers is made.[102]

In some prosecutor's offices paralegals who handle the intake of new cases from law enforcement agencies are expected to determine whether the arresting law enforcement agency has complied with the Vienna Convention and related bilateral treaties and, if not, to take the appropriate action to comply with them. Notices required by the treaty can be given by fax, phone call, or other means, but whatever means is used, the paralegal should maintain some record to prove that notice was given.

The U.S. State Department warns against simply notifying the consulates of all detained or arrested aliens because the privacy wishes of aliens from nonmandatory notice countries who do not want their government told of their detention or arrest should be respected and because in some cases aliens from a nonmandatory notice country may be afraid of their home-nation's government.[103] As a result, a paralegal who is responsible for ensuring compliance with the Convention and bilateral treaties should not simply notify the home-nation consulates of all arrested or detained aliens.

In many instances the detained or arrested alien will not speak English or will assert that he speaks very little English. Either assertion will make effectively communicating Vienna Convention rights difficult. The U.S. State Department has established an area on its website[104] that includes written notification of Vienna Convention rights in many different languages. Those notices can be printed out and shown to the detained or arrested alien as a means of advising him of his rights under the Convention and bilateral treaties.

Mandatory Notification Countries

Antigua and Barbuda
Armenia
Azerbaijan
Bahamas
Barbados
Belarus
Belize
Brunei
Bulgaria
China[1]
Costa Rica
Cyprus
Czech Republic
Dominica
Fiji
Gambia
Ghana
Grenada
Guyana
Hong Kong[2]
Hungary
Jamaica
Kazakhstan
Kiribati
Kuwait
Kyrgyzstan
Malaysia
Malta

Mauritius
Mongolia
Moldova
Nigeria
Philippines
Poland (non-permanent residents only)
Romania
Russia
Saint Kitts and Nevis
Saint Lucia
Saint Vincent and the Grenadines
Seychelles
Sierra Leone
Singapore
Slovakia
Tajikistan
Tanzania
Tonga
Trinidad and Tobago
Turkmenistan
Tuvalu
Ukraine
United Kingdom[3]
U.S.S.R.[4]
Uzbekistan
Zambia
Zimbabwe

Source: U.S. State Department. *Consular Notification and Access*

---

[1] Does not include persons who carry passports of the Republic of China. Such persons should be informed that the nearest office of the Taipei Economic and Cultural Representative Office can be notified at their request.

[2] Must notify nearest Chinese consulate.

[3] Also covered are residents of Anguilla, British Virgin Islands, Bermuda, Montserrat, and the Turks and Caicos Islands. Their residents carry British passports.

[4] Although the U.S.S.R. no longer exists, some nationals of its successor states may still be traveling on its passports. Mandatory notification should be given to consular officers for all nationals of such states, including those traveling on old U.S.S.R. passports. The successor states are listed above.

In addition to the consular notification rights, the Vienna Convention provides other rights. Under the Convention a consular officer of the detained or arrested alien's home country is entitled to visit and communicate with the alien. The arresting law enforcement agency is, however, allowed to establish reasonable visitation regulations for consular officers. Consular officers who visit one of their detained or arrested nationals at a jail are subject to jail security rules and, like all other jail visitors, are subject to search.

The means of enforcing Vienna Convention rights has been the source of much litigation and controversy in the United States. One of the most basic issues raised by the Vienna Convention is whether the rights it establishes are personal rights that the detained or arrested alien may personally assert in a judicial proceeding or whether they are only rights that the alien's nation can raise through diplomatic avenues. Most American courts sidestep the issue of whether the Convention creates personally enforceable rights and, without deciding that question, hold that even if the Convention creates personal rights and those rights are violated, a court cannot, as a remedy for that violation, suppress the defendant's statement[105] or dismiss the indictment against him.[106]

The American courts that have considered the matter have split with some holding that the Convention creates rights that are personally enforceable by the arrested or detained alien while others have held that it does not create personally enforceable rights.[107] The U.S. Supreme Court has avoided deciding the issue.[108]

The U.S. State Department, however, takes the position that the Convention only creates state-to-state rights that are not judicially enforceable.[109] As a result virtually all American violations of the Vienna Convention are remedied at the diplomatic level by negotiations between the United States government and the government whose national's Convention rights were violated. The U.S. Supreme Court has noted that diplomatic avenues constitute the primary means of enforcing the Convention[110] and that no other signatory nation remedies treaty violations through its criminal justice system.[111]

CHAPTER TERMS

Physical evidence   Prosecution's case in chief   Putative defendant

REVIEW QUESTIONS

1. Does the Fifth Amendment privilege against self-incrimination protect witnesses from being asked questions that will incriminate them? If not, what protection does the privilege provide to witnesses?
2. Does the Fifth Amendment privilege excuse witnesses who know they will be asked incriminating questions from the necessity of appearing before the tribunal or entity that subpoenaed them? If not, what must such witnesses do?
3. When does the Fifth Amendment privilege against self-incrimination apply?
4. What is a search warrant complaint and what must it contain?
5. Is a person considered compelled for purposes of the Fifth Amendment privilege against self-incrimination when he is required to appear before a body such as a grand jury and be questioned? If not, when would such a person be considered to have been compelled to answer questions?
6. Is a person considered compelled for purposes of the Fifth Amendment privilege when he is required by law to file a report with the government and to disclose certain information to the government in that report?
7. To what type of persons does the Fifth Amendment privilege against self-incrimination apply?
8. Does the Fifth Amendment privilege against self-incrimination apply to the disclosure by a witness of any type of evidence, or is the privilege limited to certain types of disclosures and, if so, to what type of disclosures is it limited?
9. What are the two forms of immunity that will eliminate a witness's Fifth Amendment privilege against self-incrimination and how do those two forms of immunity differ?
10. Under federal law when can a court confer immunity on a witness?
11. What is a proffer letter and who issues it?
12. What is the difference between formal immunity and informal immunity?
13. What are the Miranda rights?
14. When is a person required to be informed of his rights under Miranda?
15. How is a violation of a person's Miranda rights treated differently from a violation of a person's Fifth Amendment privilege against self-incrimination?
16. What is the required records exception to the Fifth Amendment privilege against self-incrimination?
17. What are the two classes of nations that are created by the Vienna Convention on Consular Relations, and in terms of rights, how are nationals from nations in either of those categories treated differently?
18. Who is required to advise a detained alien of his rights under the Vienna Convention?
19. Must Miranda rights be given when law enforcement agents meet with and question a person on whom they have focused their investigation?

ADDITIONAL READING

Peter Brooks, *The Truth About Confessions* (September 1, 2002). *http://www.nytimes.com/2002/09/01/opinion/the-truth-about-confessions.html*. Site last visited June 9, 2011.

Amir Efrati, *Madoff Aide Allegedly Got Fake 'Tickets' of Trading* (March 9, 2009). *http://forexdaily.org.ru/Dow_Jones/page.htm?id=483597*. Site last visited June 9, 2011.

Ron Chapman, *Proffer Agreements in Federal Criminal Cases* (September 16, 2008). *http://www.justiceflorida. com/2008/09/articles/federal-crimes1/proffer-agreements-in-federal-criminal-cases/*. Site last visited June 9, 2011.

Laurel Calkins, *Stanford, Invoking Constitutional Rights, Won't Testify in Case* (March 12, 2009). *http://www.bloomberg.com/apps/news? pid=20670001&refer=home&sid=aSBXbsrhUILM*. Site last visited June 9, 2011.

ENDNOTES

1. *Garner v. United States*, 424 U.S. 648 (1976).
2. *Ex parte McClelland*, 521 S.W.2d 481 (Mo. App. 1975).
3. *Michigan v. Tucker*, 417 U.S. 433 (1974).
4. *Id.*
5. *See Id.*
6. *See Malloy v. Hogan*, 378 U.S. 1 (1964).
7. *Minnesota v. Murphy*, 465 U.S. 420 (1984).
8. *United States v. Wong*, 431 U.S. 174 (1977).
9. *Couch v. United States*, 409 U.S. 322 (1973)
10. *United States v. Schmidt*, 816 F.2d 1477 (10th Cir. 1987), n.3.
11. *Garner v. United States*, 424 U.S. at 648.
12. *Mills v. United States*, 281 F.2d 736 (4th Cir. 1960).
13. *United States v. Sullivan*, 274 U.S. 259 (1927).
14. *Garner v. United States*, 424 U.S. 648 (1976).
15. *United States v. Picketts*, 655 F.2d 837 (7th Cir. 1981). In some states where the state constitutional privilege against self-incrimination is interpreted more broadly than the Fifth Amendment privilege, the state constitutional privilege prohibits issuance of subpoenas to witnesses who are targets of a criminal investigation. *See, e.g., People v. Steuding*, 6 N.Y.2d 214 (1959).
16. *United States v. Pilnick*, 267 F. Supp. 791 (S.D.N.Y 1967).
17. *Condon v. Inter-Religious Foundation for Community Organization, Inc.*, 18 Misc. 3d 874 (2008).
18. *Hoffman v. United States*, 341 U.S. 479 (1951).
19. *ABA Standards for Criminal Justice*, Prosecution Function, Standard 3-3.6(d).
20. *United States v. Picketts*, 655 F.2d 837 (7th Cir. 1981).
21. *United States v. Washington*, 431 U.S. 181 (1977).
22. *United States v. Kilgroe*, 959 F.2d 802 (9th Cir. 1992).
23. *ABA Standards* at 3-3.6(e).
24. *United States v. Pilnick*, 267 F. Supp. 791 (S.D.N.Y. 1967).
25. *Id.*
26. *People v. Portelli*, 15 N.Y.2d 235 (1965).
27. Should Mahmoud later be charged with a crime, he could obtain suppression of his answers to the questions he was ordered to answer and would also be able to obtain suppression of any evidence derived from those answers.
28. *In re Terrorist Bombings of U.S. Embassy in East Africa*, 548 F.3d 237 (2d Cir. 2008).
29. *Doe v. United States*, 487 U.S. 201 (1988).
30. *United States v. Braswell*, 487 U.S. 99 (1999).
31. *Id.*
32. *Id.*
33. *Hoffa v. United States*, 385 U.S. at 293.
34. *Owens v. Commonwealth*, 186 Va. 689 (1947); 8 *Wigmore on Evidence* §2266 (McNaughton rev. 1961). The rationale for not applying the privilege to police station interrogation was that because the police have no legal right to compel answers there is no legal obligation to which the privilege can apply. 8 *Wigmore on Evidence* at §2252, n.27. Put more simply, it makes no sense to say that a person is excused from making a disclosure when he is under no obligation to disclose. *Id.* The use of extra-legal methods to obtain confessions was viewed as prohibited by the due process clauses of the Fifth and Fourteenth Amendments.
35. *Colorado v. Connelly*, 479 U.S. 157 (1986).
36. *Couch v. United States*, 409 U.S. at 322.
37. *Garner v. United States*, 424 U.S. at 648. In the case of filers of government-mandated reports, the filer of the report must assert the privilege on the report at the time the report is filed. If he fails to assert the privilege on the report the privilege is lost as to those entries. If the filer asserts the privilege on the report he may later be prosecuted for not filing an adequate report or for not providing the information required to be disclosed. That prosecution does not violate the privilege because if the privilege permitted him to refuse to provide the information called for in the report, the privilege is a defense to the prosecution. *Id.*
38. *Id.*
39. *Id.*

40. *Beaty v. Schiriro*, 509 F.3d 994 (9th Cir. 2007).
41. *United States v. Reynolds*, 762 F.2d 489 (6th Cir. 1985).
42. *Doe v. United States*, 487 U.S. 201 (1988).
43. *Id.*
44. *United States v. Hubbell*, 530 U.S. 27 (2000).
45. *Id.*
46. *See United States v. Braswell*, 487 U.S. at 99.
47. *United States v. Holloway*, 906 F. Supp. 1437 (D. Kan. 1995).
48. *Schmerber v. California*, 384 U.S. 757 (1966).
49. *United States v. Wade*, 388 U.S. 218 (1967).
50. *Gilbert v. California*, 388 U.S. 263 (1967).
51. *Id.*
52. *Holt v. United States*, 218 U.S. 245 (1910).
53. *In re Daley*, 549 F.2d 469 (7th Cir. 1977).
54. *Garner v. United States*, 424 U.S. at 648.
55. *United States v. Balsys*, 524 U.S. 666 (1998).
56. *Id.*
57. *Young v. Knight*, 329 S.W.2d 195 (Ky. App. Ct. 1959).
58. *United States v. Calandra*, 414 U.S. 338 (1974).
59. *Kastigar v. United States*, 406 U.S. 441 (1972). A third form of immunity, use immunity, is constitutionally insufficient to eliminate a witness's privilege. Use immunity prohibits using the witness's disclosures against him in a criminal case, but does not prohibit the use against him of evidence derived from those disclosures.
60. *See* 18 U.S.C. §6003.
61. Sara Beal et al., *Grand Jury Law and Practice* §7:8 (2d ed. 2008).
62. *United States v. Lenz*, 616 F.2d 960 (6th Cir. 1980).
63. *United States v. Leyva*, 513 F.2d 774 (5th Cir. 1975).
64. *United States v. Lenz*, 616 F.2d at 960.
65. *United States v. Serrano*, 406 F.3d 1208 (10th Cir. 2004).
66. *United States v. De La Cruz*, 996 F.2d 1307 (1st Cir. 1993).
67. *See, e.g.,* ILCS 120/9, which is contained in the Retailers' Occupation Tax Act (sales tax) and which provides as follows: *No person shall be excused from testifying or from producing any books, papers, records, or memoranda in any investigation or upon any hearing, when ordered to do so by the department (Illinois Department of Revenue) or any officers or employee thereof, upon the ground that the testimony or evidence, documentary or otherwise, may tend to incriminate him or subject him to a criminal penalty, but no person shall be prosecuted or subject to any criminal penalty for, or on account of, any transaction made or thing concerning which he may testify or produce evidence, documentary or otherwise before the department or an officer or employee thereof; provided that such immunity shall extend only to natural persons who, in obedience to a*

subpoena, gives testimony under oath or produces evidence, documentary or otherwise, under oath. No person so testifying shall be exempt from prosecution and punishment for perjury committed in so testifying.
68. *See People v. Witvoet*, 212 Ill. App. 3d 48 (3d Dist. 1991). Demand letters also differ from administrative subpoenas in that unlike administrative subpoenas, which can be enforced using a court's contempt power, demand letters cannot be enforced that way. Under some statutes the failure to produce records in response to a demand letter is a misdemeanor offense.
69. *United States v. Krilich*, 159 F.3d 1020 (7th Cir. 1998).
70. *See United States v. Kilgroe*, 959 F.2d 802 (9th Cir. 1992).
71. *Burke v. State*, 104 Ohio St. 220 (1922).
72. 384 U.S. 436 (1966).
73. *Id.*
74. *Illinois v. Perkins*, 496 U.S. 292 (1990).
75. *United States v. Reynolds*, 762 F.2d 489 (6th Cir. 1985).
76. *Stansbury v. California*, 511 U.S. 318 (1994).
77. *People v. Bury*, 199 Ill. App. 3d 207 (4th Dist. 1990).
78. *Maryland v. Shatzer*, 559 U.S. 98 (2010).
79. *Id.*
80. *People v. Bury*, 199 Ill. App. 3d at 207.
81. *United States v. Willis*, 397 F. Supp. 1078 (D.C. Pa. 1975).
82. *Illinois v. Perkins*, 496 U.S. at 292.
83. *Michigan v. Mosley*, 423 U.S. 96 (1975).
84. *Berghuis v. Thompkins*, 560 U.S. 370 (2010).
85. *Id.*
86. *Edwards v. Arizona*, 451 U.S. 477 (1981).
87. *United States v. Wyatt*, 179 F.3d 532 (7th Cir. 1999).
88. *Minnick v. Mississippi*, 498 U.S. 146 (1990).
89. *Maryland v. Shatzer*, 559 U.S. at 98.
90. *Moran v. Burbine*, 475 U.S. 412 (1986).
91. *Id.*
92. *United States v. Wyatt*, 179 F.3d at 532..
93. *United States v. Conrad*, 2014 WL 1165860 (N.D. Ia. 2014).
94. *United States v. Wyatt*, 179 F.3d at 532.
95. *United States v. Conrad* 2014 WL at 1165860.
96. *Claudio v. Scully*, 791 F. Supp. 985 (E.D.N.Y. 1992)..
97. *United States v. Sterling*, 283 F.3d 216 (2002).
98. *See Shapiro v. United States*, 335 U.S. 1 (1948).
99. *In re Underhill*, 781 F.2d 64 (6th Cir. 1986).
100. *Id.*
101. *People v. Villagomez*, 313 Ill. App. 3d 799 (1st Dist. 2000).
102. *Id.*
103. U.S. State Department, *Consular Notification and Access, FAQs, http://travel.state.gov/pdf/cna/CNA_Manual_3d_Edition.pdf.* Site last visited June 9, 2011.

104. *http://travel.state.gov/law/consular/consular_5126.html.* Site last visited June 9, 2011.

105. *Sanchez-Llamas v. Oregon,* 548 U.S. 331 (2006). The United States is not unique in refusing to suppress evidence obtained in violation of the Convention. No other signatory to the Vienna Convention requires that evidence obtained through its violation be suppressed. *See Id.,* n.3.

106. *United States v. De La Pava,* 268 F.3d 157 (2d Cir. 2001).

107. *Ledezma v. State,* 626 N.W.2d 134 (Lowa. 2001).

108. *Medellin v. Texas,* 552 U.S. 491 (2008), n.4.

109. *See United States v. Nai Fook Li,* 206 F.3d 56 (1st Cir. 2000).

110. *Sanchez-Llamas v. Oregon,* 548 U.S. at 331.

111. *Id.*

Chapter 18
Criminal Procedure at the Charging Stage

Chapter Objectives

After reading this chapter, you should be able to

- Explain the different methods by which criminal prosecutions are initiated
- Understand what informations and indictments are and how they differ
- Discuss the rights that arise when a criminal prosecution is initiated
- Describe the different events that constitute the initiation of a criminal prosecution
- Explain what venue is and how it is determined in a criminal prosecution
- Understand what the Sixth Amendment right to counsel is and when it is applicable
- Explain what critical stages are in a criminal prosecution and name several different such stages
- Explain the different forms of ineffective assistance of counsel

"I would rather have my fate in the hands of 23 representative citizens of the county [the grand jury] than in the hands of a politically appointed judge." —Robert Morganthau District Attorney, New York County, quoted in *Time Magazine*, April 8, 1985

A criminal prosecution can be started in a number of different ways and, depending upon how the prosecution is initiated, the event that marks its actual commencement differs. It is important to know both what event commences a criminal prosecution and when that event occurs, because the commencement of a criminal prosecution gives rise to important constitutional rights and the date on which the commencing event occurs determines whether a prosecution was brought within the applicable statute of limitations. In this chapter we will examine: (A) the different methods by which a criminal prosecution is commenced and (B) the important constitutional rights that arise when that occurs.

A. Commencement of Prosecutions

How a criminal prosecution is started depends upon the jurisdiction in which the prosecution will be initiated and whether the offense being prosecuted is a felony or misdemeanor. In this section we will examine the different methods by which both felony and misdemeanor prosecutions can be initiated and when, depending upon the method used, a prosecution is considered to have been commenced. The student should keep in mind that American jurisdictions differ significantly in how criminal prosecutions may be initiated as well as in what constitutes the commencement of such prosecutions. For that reason the student should be sure to familiarize herself both with the ways in which her jurisdiction allows criminal prosecutions to be initiated and what in her jurisdiction constitutes their commencement.

1. Felony Prosecutions

On the federal level the initiation of felony prosecutions is governed by the grand jury clause of the Fifth Amendment, which, in relevant part, provides as follows:

A **presentment** is an accusation of a crime made by a grand jury on its own and not at the request of the prosecutor. *Wood v. Hughes*, 9 N.Y.2d 141 (1961), n.1. Today, presentments are rarely voted. *Id.*

> No person shall be held to answer for a capital, or otherwise infamous crime, unless on a presentment or indictment of a Grand Jury, except in cases arising in the land or naval forces, or in the Militia, when in actual service in time of War or public danger. *U.S. Const.* Amend V.

Over time that provision of the Fifth Amendment has come to be understood as meaning that in non-military federal prosecutions the prosecution of a person for a capital or felony offense[1] must be initiated by a grand jury and that a grand jury can initiate such prosecutions either by a **presentment** or an **indictment**. This process is sometimes referred to as grand jury review.

An **indictment** is an accusation of a crime made by a grand jury at the request of the prosecutor. *Wood v. Hughes*, 9 N.Y.2d 141 (1961), n.1.

When the person against whom a capital or felony prosecution is being initiated is a natural person, the Supreme Court has held that the grand jury clause applies without regard to whether that person is a citizen or a legal or illegal alien.[2] When the person against whom a felony prosecution is being initiated is an artificial person such as a corporation, it is not clear if the grand jury clause requires that the prosecution be initiated by indictment. The U.S. Supreme Court has never addressed the question[3] and the lower federal courts that have faced it have not given a clear answer.[4] History offers no guidance in the matter because the concept of entity responsibility for committing serious crimes did not develop until more than 100 years after the Fifth Amendment was adopted.[5] On the federal level the question seldom arises because federal prosecutors commonly use grand jury indictments to initiate felony prosecutions of artificial entities.[6]

By its terms the grand jury clause of the Fifth Amendment does not apply to cases arising in the military. As a result, capital and felony prosecutions by the military of military personnel do not need to be initiated by a grand jury indictment and instead are initiated as provided for in the Uniform Code of Military Justice. Also, the Supreme Court has held that the grand jury clause does not apply to cases involving violations of the law of war.[7] As a result, the prosecution of illegal combatants can also be initiated under military law and without a grand jury indictment.[8]

In the charging process the function of the grand jury is to stand between the prosecutor and the citizen[9] and, without regard to the wishes of the prosecutor, determine whether criminal charges should be brought.[10] In performing that function the grand jury is considered to be the primary security of the innocent against hasty, malicious, or oppressive prosecutions[11] and against oppressive actions of courts.[12]

Historical Perspective

Grand Jury Independence and Charging Persons with Crimes

There is much contemporary criticism of the grand jury on the grounds that it does not safeguard individuals from unfounded criminal prosecutions and that it is little more than a tool of the prosecutor. Those criticisms notwithstanding, the institution of the grand jury has a long history of acting on its own and of refusing to charge defendants despite pressure from the government.

In 1681 English officials sought the indictment of an individual named Stephen College for treason. College was a Protestant who was targeted for prosecution by the Stuart regime. After being forced to hear evidence against College in open court the grand jury demanded that the witnesses be heard before it in private, a demand to which the Crown prosecutors acceded.[13] Following the secret session the grand jury returned and told the Lord Chief Justice that it would ignore the recommendation to indict College. Later that same year the British Crown sought the indictment of the Earl of Shaftsbury for treason. After hearing the witnesses, the grand refused to indict, returning the bill of indictment to the prosecutor with the word "ignoramus" written upon it.[14]

American colonial grand juries showed similar independence. In 1735 the Colonial Governor of New York demanded that a New York City grand jury indict John Zenger for libel. Zenger was the editor and publisher of the *Weekly Journal* who wrote an article critical of the governor.[15] Despite the governor's demand, the grand jury refused to indict. In the aftermath of the Boston Tea Party, when the Crown prosecutor sought the indictment of some of the Party's perpetrators, the grand jury hearing the evidence refused to indict. The incidents of such exercises of independence by grand juries are not isolated in American history.[16] It is not clear why the grand jurors of today should be thought to be or why they would be any less independent and any less resistant to official pressures than their predecessors.

When deciding whether to initiate a criminal prosecution the grand jury determines whether there is sufficient evidence to establish probable cause to believe that a crime has been committed and that a specific individual committed that crime.[17] In making that decision the grand jury's role is not limited solely to determining the existence of probable cause. The grand jury can also act as the conscience of the community[18] and has the power to refuse to indict even when there is sufficient evidence to obtain a conviction.[19]

The power of a federal grand jury to indict or refuse to indict is almost unfettered.[20] Federal courts have no power to review whether the grand jury based its decision to charge on legally sufficient evidence[21] nor do federal courts have the power to review a grand jury's decision not to charge.[22] If a grand jury decides not to charge, the prosecutor may present the case to a new grand jury, but in most jurisdictions the prosecutor is required to advise the new grand jury that a previous grand jury considered the matter and did not indict.

When deciding whether to charge, the grand jury is expected to determine whether the evidence the prosecutor presents to it is sufficient to accuse a person of committing a crime.[23] It is not the function of the grand jury to determine guilt or innocence or to consider possible defenses a suspect may have to the charges being considered.[24] As a result, when presenting evidence to the grand jury the prosecutor is under no obligation to present exculpatory evidence[25] and the person against whom charges are being sought does not have a right to appear before the grand jury, a right to cross-examine any of the witnesses who testify before it, or to present rebuttal evidence.[26]

When deciding whether or not to charge a person with a criminal offense the grand jury is expected to base its decision on evidence. That evidence comes to the grand jury in the form of testimony and exhibits and can include **hearsay** evidence. The prosecutor is allowed to outline for the grand jury the evidence it can expect to hear, he can explain in advance of a witness's testimony what the witness is expected to say, and he can explain how that testimony fits into the case.[27] In most jurisdictions the prosecutor is also considered to be an advisor to the grand jury and in that role he is allowed to provide the grand jury with advice about the law applicable to the matter it is considering.[28]

The prosecutor usually selects the witnesses who will be called to testify and decides what questions to ask them. By selecting the witnesses and deciding what to ask them the prosecutor has a great deal of control over the evidence the grand jury will hear. If the grand jury has any doubt about the sufficiency of the evidence to charge a person with a crime, the grand jury has the power to subpoena additional witnesses as well as physical evidence before making a decision. In many jurisdictions, before the grand jury considers a matter, it must be informed of those rights by the prosecutor.[29] The grand jurors themselves are also free to pose their own questions to any witnesses.

Hearsay is an out-of-court statement made by a person other than the testifying witness, which, through the testifying witness, is offered to prove the truth of the matter asserted in it and which depends for its value on the credibility of the out-of-court declarant. *People v. Rodriguez*, 312 Ill. App. 3d 920 (1st Dist. 2000).

State v. Childs

Superior Court of New Jersey (1990) 242 N.J. Super. 121

BRODY, J. The State appeals from an order in which the trial judge dismissed this three-count State grand jury indictment charging thefts, on the ground that a deputy attorney general infringed upon the grand jury's independent judgment. * * * We reverse because in our view the deputy attorney general's conduct did not infringe upon the grand jury's independent judgment.

The indictment charges defendant Richard Childs (defendant) with deceptive fund-raising activities for Supreme Newark, Inc. (corporation), a corporation he owned and controlled. Our recitation of the facts assumes, solely for the purpose of this appeal, that the testimony given before the grand jury is true.

The corporation operated several stores that sold furniture on credit to poor people. The typical mark-up was 300%. The corporation factored the credit paper, with recourse, to two commercial factors at substantial discounts.

Although the total amount of furniture sales was high and the stores were busy, the corporation always operated at a loss because the uncertain long-term credit payments of its customers did not enable it to meet the insistent short-term credit demands of the factors.

In order to raise cash for his corporation, defendant borrowed money by continually issuing short-term unsecured notes of his corporation, bearing high interest, to an ever widening circle of friends and friends' relatives and friends. Noteholders could, and many did, allow the notes to "roll over" as they matured. Defendant made the notes more attractive by assuring prospective holders that they could demand repayment of all or part of their loans at any time without penalty. Holders frequently took advantage of this feature thereby increasing the drain on the corporation's meager cash reserves. Defendant further induced prospective noteholders to lend the corporation cash by making false representations that the notes were rated AAA, that the corporation was profitable, that its debts were no greater than its liquid assets, that Seton Hall University was a major investor and that the noteholders would somehow be protected by insurance.

Count One of the indictment charges that "between on or about January 1, 1982 and on or about August 31, 1984" defendant used these misrepresentations to commit thefts by deception from twenty named noteholders, totalling an aggregate of $319,605, a second-degree crime. *N.J.S.A.* 2C:20-4; *N.J.S.A.* 2C:20-b(1)(a). * * *

Charles Provini, defendant's former associate in an investment business, and his wife, Susan, were another source of cash for the corporation. Defendant persuaded the Provinis to factor what he represented to be the corporation's better credit paper. He assured the Provinis that the corporation would segregate the paper for them and collect customers' payments. The Provinis formed a corporation, Chalis, Inc., which conducted these factoring transactions for over a year and a half. As he had with the noteholders, defendant assured the Provinis that they could withdraw their cash at any time, and Chalis made withdrawals from time to time. Contrary to his representations to the Provinis, defendant was factoring all the corporation's credit paper of value to the commercial factors, leaving none for Chalis.[3] * * *

We first consider whether the trial judge correctly dismissed the indictment because the deputy attorney general allegedly pressured the grand jury to return it. An indictment may not be dismissed except on the clearest and plainest grounds. *State v. Murphy*, 110 *N.J.* 20, 35 (1988). Unless the deputy's conduct before the grand jury infringed upon its decision-making function, it may not be the basis for dismissing the indictment. *State v. Vasky*, 218 *N.J.* Super. 487, 491 (App. Div. 1987). * * *

This was not a simple case to present to the grand jury. As defendant correctly notes in the introduction to the arguments in his brief:

> The grand jury which returned this indictment heard evidence from a total of 23 witnesses over seven separate sessions. The transcript of grand jury proceedings runs approximately 530 pages. Hundreds of documents were moved into evidence.

Most of this evidence was presented to enable the jury to understand the complexities of the financing arrangements pertinent to the web of deceit that defendant is charged with having spun. In the usual criminal case, evidence presented to a grand jury is easy to follow and speaks for itself. Here, however, the grand jury needed guidance if it was to follow defendant's financial machinations, be able to distinguish fraud from breaches of contract and be able to see the manner in which individual thefts were part of a single criminal venture.

In order to help the jury follow the evidence, the deputy began the first session with a statement that was similar to a prosecuting attorney's opening statement at trial. He outlined the evidence he expected to produce. As witnesses were called, the deputy sometimes explained to the jurors in advance what he expected the witness to say and how that testimony fit into the total picture. He sometimes commented after a witness's testimony about how it was significant to the total picture.

Recognizing that jurors might mistakenly treat his explanations as evidence, the deputy forcefully and repeatedly impressed upon them throughout the proceedings that his statements were not evidence and that the jurors had the responsibility of deciding for themselves what the evidence meant and whether it was sufficient to return an indictment.

We have said that in presenting a case to a grand jury, a prosecutor may not "express his views on questions of fact." *State v. Hart,* 139 *N.J.* Super. 565, 567-568 (App. Div. 1976). However, without expressing his personal views on questions of fact, a prosecutor may fairly explain the significance of evidence placed before the grand jury to aid its understanding of a complex or unfamiliar course of events. Here the deputy's statements and the perceptive questions and comments of grand jurors demonstrate that he did not cross the line that separates proper explanations of the evidence from improper expressions of defendant's guilt that would cause the jurors to abdicate or lose sight of their responsibilities.

The trial judge also concluded that the deputy infringed on the grand jury's independence when he made it clear that he did not want the jury to indict certain of defendant's alleged cohorts who had been granted immunity, and certain noteholders who may have received cash preferences when they tried to recoup a small part of their losses. Although the deputy discouraged the grand jury from indicting these people, his decision not to seek an indictment against them is not an infringement of the grand jury's independence.

A prosecutor has broad discretion, which "includes both the decision to prosecute an individual whom he has probable cause to believe has violated the law, and the converse decision to refrain from prosecuting any such offender." *State v. Hermann,* 80 *N.J.* 122, 127 (1979). Although that discretion is not boundless, it may only "be reviewed for arbitrariness or abuse." *In re Investigation Regarding Ringwood Fact Finding Comm.,* 65 *N.J.* 512, 516 (1974).

It appears that the attorney general did not seek an indictment against certain of defendant's alleged criminal partners in order to obtain from them evidence against defendant that may be used in this prosecution. As to the noteholders who may have received preferences, he could have believed that they had not committed a crime and, even if they had, that it would not be just to prosecute them for their desperate efforts to recoup a small portion of their losses. We find no abuse of prosecutorial discretion in making these judgments, and we would be overstepping our authority to dismiss this indictment in order to pressure the attorney general to exercise his discretion differently.

Even if there were a basis for considering that the deputy improperly infringed on the grand jury's independence when he discouraged it from investigating whether others may have committed crimes, defendant would not thereby be entitled to a dismissal of the indictment against him. An important function of the grand jury is "to protect individuals against arbitrary, oppressive and unwarranted criminal accusations." *State v. Porro*, 152 *N.J. Super.* 179, 184 (App. Div. 1977). Here the grand jury unquestionably performed that function in weighing the evidence respecting defendant's guilt. There is therefore no reason why the indictment of defendant should be dismissed even if the prosecutor improperly discouraged the grand jury from investigating whether to indict others. Defendant does not claim that by seeking an indictment against him, the attorney general engaged in unconstitutional invidious and arbitrary law enforcement. "The mere fact that a law has not been fully enforced against others does not give a defendant the right to violate it." *State v. Boncelet*, 107 *N.J. Super.* 444, 453 (App. Div. 1969). * * *

Reversed and remanded for trial.

Case Focus

1. Is it proper for the prosecutor to express his opinions to the grand jury on questions of fact and is it proper for the prosecutor to explain to the grand jury the significance of evidence it will hear or has heard?
2. According to the court, why is it not an infringement on the role of the grand jury for a prosecutor to ask it not to indict a certain person who, based on evidence presented to it, there is probable cause to believe may have committed or been involved in committing a crime?

• • • • • • • •

In simple cases, the grand jury usually hears the evidence on which it will base its charging decision through the summary testimony of a law enforcement agent. In complex white collar crime cases, if there is summary testimony by a law enforcement agent, that testimony will usually have been preceded by the testimony of numerous witnesses over a period of many months. Some of the witnesses the grand jury hears may be testifying under a grant of immunity, others may be experts who have examined voluminous documents and testify about the results of their examination, while others may be forensics experts who testify about the results of some scientific analysis they performed.

In long grand jury investigations, paralegals working in a prosecutor's office frequently will be responsible for numbering the grand jury exhibits and for creating and maintaining an exhibit log that identifies each exhibit by number, briefly describes what each exhibit is, and may contain notes that identify the witness or witnesses who testified about each exhibit and what that testimony was.

While the testimony of grand jury witnesses is secret, in most jurisdictions a court reporter is present in the grand jury room when witnesses are examined. The court reporter takes down the questions posed to and the answers given by the witnesses and in some jurisdictions will also take down statements made to the grand jury by the prosecutor. In long grand jury investigations, transcripts of the witnesses's testimony will be made available to the grand jury.

Before asking the grand jury to deliberate on a charge, the prosecutor usually prepares the indictment that contains the charges he will be asking the grand jury to bring and provides it to the grand jury's foreperson. In many jurisdictions, before asking the grand jury to deliberate the prosecutor will read the proposed charges to it, and in some cases he may also read to it the applicable criminal statute or explain the applicable law.

The grand jury's deliberations are secret. Neither the prosecutor nor the court reporter is allowed in the grand jury room during deliberations. No record is kept of the grand jurors' discussions during deliberations and no record is kept of how any individual grand juror voted. The only record that is kept is of the number of votes cast in favor of charging and the number of votes cast against charging. Once the grand jury reaches a decision one of its members will step out of the grand jury room and inform the prosecutor or bailiff that it has reached a decision. At that time the prosecutor and court reporter are allowed to re-enter the grand jury room where the foreperson will inform the prosecutor of the grand jury's decision. In most jurisdictions the court reporter will take down the decision announced by the foreperson.

If the grand jury voted not to charge, it is said to have returned a "no bill." If the grand jury voted to charge, it is said to have voted a "true bill" or a "true bill of indictment." At the conclusion of a day's grand jury session any presentments or indictments the grand jury has voted are, at that time, usually returned in open court. In some instances the return is done at some later date. In most jurisdictions the return is done by the foreperson who, accompanied by the prosecutor, takes the indictments to a judge and advises the judge which indictments the grand jury has voted and whether it has voted any no bills. If any no bills were voted the court will order them sealed.

After the indictments have been returned the court clerk assigns them case numbers and files them in her office. Once returned the indictments are public record and open to inspection by both the public and the news media. In some cases the prosecutor may ask the judge to seal an indictment. The prosecutor usually asks to seal an indictment either when the defendant has not yet been arrested and law enforcement agents believe the defendant is a flight risk or may violently resist arrest or when the indictment or indictments charge a large number of individuals who will be arrested in an organized sweep.

When the indictment is returned, if the defendant has not already been arrested, the prosecutor will usually ask the judge before whom it is returned to issue an arrest warrant and set a bond. Paralegals who work in prosecutors' offices usually prepare arrest warrants in advance of the return so that the prosecutor can present them to the judge when he asks the judge to issue them. At the time the paralegal prepares the warrant she also usually obtains a current copy of the defendant's criminal history or what is commonly referred to as a "rap sheet." The prosecutor will use that information in determining the amount of bond he asks the judge to set.

The return of an indictment in open court is an important point in the criminal justice process. In most of the jurisdictions that still use grand juries, the return marks the actual commencement of a criminal prosecution. As a result, in most jurisdictions that still use grand juries, the date upon which an indictment is returned in open court and not the date on which it was voted determines whether the prosecution has been brought within the applicable statute of limitations period.

The Fifth Amendment's grand jury clause is not applicable to the states.[30] Consequently, some states have abolished the grand jury and allow prosecutors to initiate a felony prosecution by filing a document called an **information**. Many states, however, allow prosecutors the option of commencing felony prosecutions by information or indictment.[31] In most jurisdictions that allow felony prosecutions to be started by the filing of an information, it is the filing of the information by the prosecutor that formally commences the criminal prosecution, and the date on which the information is filed determines whether the prosecution has been brought within the applicable statute of limitations period. Usually at the time the prosecutor files an information he

An **information** is a document filed by the prosecutor in which the prosecutor instead of the grand jury formally accuses a person of having committed a crime. In most jurisdictions the filing of an information commences a criminal prosecution.

Historical Perspective

The History of Charging by Information

The charging instrument known as a criminal information is almost as old as the indictment and traces its history back to the Middle Ages. The filing of criminal informations was the method by which the medieval criminal justice system was put in motion.[32] If a crime occurred, the king would "inform" his courts and ask them to act. At some point during the medieval period, the exact time of which is unknown, the use of informations to initiate felony prosecutions came to be viewed as improper, and the use of informations to initiate criminal proceedings was limited to misdemeanor prosecutions.[33]

By the 1500s English judges determined that there was no clear precedent that prohibited the use of informations to initiate felony prosecutions and despite abuses of them about which English legal commentators of the era complained, judges approved the use of criminal informations to initiate felony prosecutions.

will ask the judge to issue an arrest warrant for the defendant and to set a bond.

In most states when a criminal prosecution is initiated by the filing of an information a defendant is entitled to a **preliminary hearing**, which must be held within a certain number of days after the information is filed.[34] At the preliminary hearing a judge determines whether there is sufficient evidence to require placing the defendant on trial.[35] In making that determination the judge must decide if there is probable cause to believe that the defendant committed the crime with which he has been charged in the information.

A preliminary hearing is significantly different from a grand jury proceeding. Preliminary hearings are held in open court, the witnesses who the prosecutor uses to establish probable cause are subject to cross-examination by the defense, the defendant can call his own witnesses to rebut the prosecutor's evidence, and the defendant can testify. Defendants, however, rarely testify at their preliminary hearing and seldom call witnesses because their statements can be used against them at any subsequent hearing or trial, and if the defendant or any of the witnesses testify at trial and their trial testimony differs from their preliminary

A **preliminary hearing** is a court proceeding in which a judge determines whether there is sufficient evidence to require that a defendant be placed on trial for committing a crime. *See, e.g.,* 720 ILCS 5/109-3(a).

Impeachment is an attack on the credibility of a witness that is accomplished by various methods, including by use of a witness's prior inconsistent statements. *State v. Wood,* 194 W. Va. 525 (1995).

hearing testimony, their preliminary hearing testimony can be used to **impeach** them.

At a preliminary hearing, as in a grand jury proceeding, the prosecution's evidence is usually put in through the summary testimony of a law enforcement agent. Hearsay evidence is allowed at preliminary hearings, so instead of calling numerous witnesses the prosecution will usually call one law enforcement agent who will relate what witnesses and others have told him during the investigation. Paralegals working in a prosecutor's office often are responsible for notifying law enforcement agents and other witnesses of the preliminary hearing date.

There is no due process right to a preliminary hearing[36] and, as a result, some states do not use them. In those states the prosecutor is allowed to file an information and the defendant is required to stand trial without either judicial or grand jury review of the prosecutor's assessment of probable cause.

If at the close of a preliminary hearing the judge determines there was probable cause, he will usually set dates by which the prosecutor and the defense must complete discovery, he may set a deadline by which all pre-trial motions must be filed, and he may set a trial date. If the judge finds no probable cause he will enter that finding and order the defendant released. In such cases, in jurisdictions that give the prosecutor the option of initiating felony prosecutions through the grand jury, the prosecutor may decide to present the case to a grand jury and ask it to return an indictment. In most such states the prosecutor is required to advise the grand jury that the case was previously presented to a judge who found no probable cause.

In states that allow a felony prosecution to be initiated by an information or an indictment, prosecutors sometimes file an information and prior to the date of the preliminary hearing obtain an indictment. When that happens the information is said to have been superseded by indictment, the prosecutor dismisses the information, and there is no preliminary hearing.

Without regard to the jurisdiction in which a prosecution is initiated, a defendant may waive indictment by a grand jury, or if the defendant is in a jurisdiction where a preliminary hearing is required before he can be placed on trial, he may waive a preliminary hearing. On the federal level defendants frequently waive indictment by a grand jury when they have worked out some type of pre-indictment plea agreement with the prosecutor. Under federal law, when a defendant waives indictment by a grand jury a federal felony prosecution can be initiated by the filing of an information.

2. Misdemeanor Prosecutions

In most American jurisdictions a prosecution for a misdemeanor can be commenced either by the filing of a criminal complaint or by the filing of an information.[37] Some of the states that have kept the grand jury also allow misdemeanor prosecutions to be started by indictment.[38] A defendant who is charged with a misdemeanor is not entitled to a probable cause hearing.

Unlike an information, which can only be executed and filed by the prosecutor, in most jurisdictions a criminal complaint can be executed and filed in court by a law enforcement agent or by a private citizen. Like an information, a criminal complaint names a specific defendant, alleges the commission of a crime on a specific date, and contains a statement that sets out the elements of the crime the defendant is alleged to have committed. A criminal complaint may be prepared in the prosecutor's office or by a law enforcement agency. Before a criminal complaint is filed the complainant must (under oath, by affirmation, or under penalty of perjury) state that the allegations in the complaint are true.

The Role of the Criminal Complaint in Federal Prosecutions

In federal criminal practice the criminal complaint is used in several different ways. As in the states, a criminal complaint can be used to initiate a misdemeanor prosecution. In federal practice, however, the primary role of criminal complaints is to serve as a basis for obtaining an arrest warrant for a defendant[39] prior to the initiation of a criminal case. If a federal law enforcement agent believes a person has committed an offense, he can prepare and file a complaint that states the facts supporting that belief and take it to a judge and ask him to issue an arrest warrant for the defendant.[40]

Law enforcement agents usually consult with the United States Attorney's Office before filing such a complaint and paralegals often assist in drafting them. The complaint is executed under oath and frequently includes some type of supporting attachment or schedule that explains in detail the basis on which the law enforcement agent concluded that a crime was committed and the person for whom he is requesting an arrest warrant committed it. If the judge to whom the complaint is presented determines that it states probable cause, he will issue an arrest warrant.

When federal agents make an arrest without a warrant the criminal complaint serves yet another function. Persons who are arrested by federal agents without a warrant are entitled to a probable cause hearing within 48 hours of their arrest. The filing of a criminal complaint satisfies that requirement and eliminates the need for a hearing.[41]

UNITED STATES DISTRICT COURT
DISTRICT OF NEW JERSEY

UNITED STATES OF AMERICA	:	**CRIMINAL COMPLAINT**
	:	
v.	:	
	:	
LAVERN WEBB-WASHINGTON	:	Mag. No. 09-8142 (MCA)

I, Robert J. Cooke, being duly sworn, state the following is true and correct to the best of my knowledge and belief.

From in or about March 2009 to in or about May 2009, in Hudson County, in the District of New Jersey and elsewhere, defendant

LAVERN WEBB-WASHINGTON

and others, to include JC Official 1 and the Consultant, did knowingly and willfully conspire to obstruct, delay, and affect interstate commerce by extortion under color of official right, by accepting and agreeing to accept corrupt payments that were paid and to be paid by another, with that person's consent, in exchange for defendant Lavern Webb-Washington's future official assistance in Jersey City Government matters.

In violation of Title 18, United States Code, Sections 1951(a) and 2.

I further state that I am a Special Agent with the Federal Bureau of Investigation, and that this complaint is based on the following facts:

SEE ATTACHMENT A

continued on the attached page and made a part hereof.

_____

Robert J. Cooke, Special Agent
Federal Bureau of Investigation

Sworn to before me and subscribed in my presence,
July ___, 2009, at Newark, New Jersey

HONORABLE MADELINE COX ARLEO   _____
UNITED STATES MAGISTRATE JUDGE   Signature of Judicial Officer

<u>ATTACHMENT A</u>

I, Robert J. Cooke, am a Special Agent with the Federal Bureau of Investigation ("FBI"). I have personally participated in this investigation and am aware of the facts contained herein, based upon my own investigation, as well as information provided to me by other law enforcement officers. Because this Attachment A is submitted for the limited purpose of establishing probable cause, I have not included herein the details of every aspect of the investigation. Statements attributable to individuals contained in this Attachment are related in substance and in part, except where otherwise indicated. All contacts discussed herein were recorded, except where otherwise indicated.

1.   At all times relevant to this complaint, defendant LaVern Webb-Washington (hereinafter, "Webb-Washington") was a candidate for the Jersey City Ward F City Council seat with the election to be held on or about May 12, 2009. Her candidacy was unsuccessful. In addition, Webb-Washington, also a self-described housing activist, served as the head of the Webb-Washington Community Development Corporation ("WWCDC").

2.   At all times relevant to this Complaint:

a.   There was an individual who served as the Vice President of the Jersey City Board of Education (until on or about May 2009), and a commissioner of the Jersey City Housing Authority ("JC Official 1");

b.   There was an individual who represented himself to be the owner of a consulting firm based in New Jersey (the "Consultant");

c.   There was a cooperating witness (the "CW") who had been charged with bank fraud in a federal criminal complaint in May 2006. Thereafter, for the purposes of this investigation conducted by the FBI, the CW posed as a real estate developer interested in development in the greater Jersey City area. The CW represented that the CW did business in numerous states, including New York and New Jersey, and that the CW paid for goods and services in interstate commerce.

3.   On or about March 20, 2009, at approximately 10:50 a.m., FBI agents intercepted an incoming call from defendant Webb-Washington to the Consultant over the Consultant's cell phone. During this call, the Consultant invited Webb-Washington to a meeting the following Tuesday to receive some

"contributions" from a "developer" — a reference to the CW — who would give the Consultant the money and the Consultant would give it to Webb-Washington, according to the Consultant.

   4.   On or about March 21, 2009, at approximately 10:55 a.m., FBI agents intercepted an outgoing phone call from the Consultant to JC Official 1 over the Consultant's cell phone. The Consultant and JC Official 1 confirmed the existence of upcoming, separate meetings between two Jersey City council candidates (one of whom was defendant Webb-Washington) and the CW. They also agreed that the CW has been "planting a lot of seeds" with various government officials in New Jersey.

   5.   On or about the afternoon of March 24, 2009, defendant Webb-Washington, along with her campaign manager, met the Consultant, JC Official 1 and the CW at a diner in Bayonne, New Jersey. Prior to meeting with defendant Webb-Washington and her campaign manager, the CW confirmed with the Consultant and JC Official 1 that the CW could make a cash payment to defendant Webb-Washington through JC Official 1 and the Consultant, prompting JC Official 1 to reply "[t]hat's right." After the CW was introduced to defendant Webb-Washington, the CW explained that the CW was a real estate developer with projects in Florida, New York City and the Carolinas. The CW also discussed the CW's purported development plans for Garfield Avenue in Jersey City and the impediment created by the restriction on the number of stories that could be built at the location. Defendant Webb-Washington also was informed by the CW that the CW would be seeking a zoning change from the Jersey City Council, and the Consultant added that "[d]ensity is the key to making money." Defendant Webb-Washington further was informed by the CW that the CW would be looking for defendant Webb-Washington's support for "zone change[s], resolution[s], approvals, stuff like that," prompting defendant Webb-Washington to reply, "Oh definitely, definitely. I get that done." Subsequently, the CW added that "what I'll do is, I'll give, uh, [the Consultant], uh, to start five thousand, as we get closer to the election, you know, we'll meet again . . ." As defendant Webb-Washington departed, the CW reiterated that the CW would "give [the Consultant] the envelope" for defendant Webb-Washington and added that it would not be done by check "'cause I don't wanna have any conflicts." In response, defendant Webb-Washington asked, "Can you do it as soon as possible?" The CW replied that "I'll give him [referring to the Consultant] the cash."

   6.   On or about March 24, 2009, at approximately 5:01 p.m., FBI agents intercepted an incoming call from JC Official 1 to the Consultant over the Consultant's cell phone. During the

call, among other things, JC Official 1 and the Consultant agreed that things had gone well at the meeting that day. The Consultant and JC Official 1 discussed plans for the CW and agreed, per the Consultant, "Let's get him to give . . . three candidates [including defendant Webb-Washington] money. . . ."

7.   On or about March 25, 2009, at approximately 8:44 p.m., FBI agents intercepted an incoming call from JC Official 1 to the Consultant over the Consultant's cell phone. During this call, JC Official 1 told the Consultant that there would be no meeting the next day [Thursday], and they instead agreed to meet on Friday. JC Official 1 told the Consultant that Friday they would "do the two" – likely a reference to cash payments to be made to defendant Webb-Washington and another council candidate.

8.   On or about March 26, 2009, at approximately 11:30 a.m., FBI agents intercepted an outgoing call from the Consultant over the Consultant's cell phone to JC Official 1. During this call, the Consultant asked JC Official 1 how their "buddy" [a reference to the CW] was doing, and JC Official 1 responded that JC Official 1 was postponing the meetings, a reference to meetings with defendant Webb-Washington, among others, until Monday at twelve o'clock at a diner in Hudson County, New Jersey. JC Official 1 stated that he would not "have them come in" the restaurant, but rather the CW would "have to go outside to them." JC Official 1 thus was indicating that the corrupt cash payments would be made to defendant Webb-Washington, among others, outside of the restaurant. JC Official 1 asked the Consultant if he "thought that was the best way to do it," and the Consultant said that he thought that it was.

9.   On or about March 27, 2009, at approximately 11:36 a.m., FBI agents intercepted an incoming call from defendant Webb-Washington to the Consultant over the Consultant's cell phone. During the call, defendant Webb-Washington asked the Consultant if there "was any good news yet," to which the Consultant responded, "Yes," and told defendant Webb-Washington that she was to meet him "and [the CW] on Monday at twelve o'clock" at a particular restaurant in Hudson County where the CW would "give her the contribution." Defendant Webb-Washington said that she would just have to "try and make some other moves in the meantime [meaning take action to acquire money]."

10.   On or about March 30, 2009, at approximately 10:54 a.m., FBI agents intercepted an incoming call from JC Official 1 to the Consultant over the Consultant's cell phone. During this call, JC Official 1 asked the Consultant to confirm that they were still planning to meet at the diner at noon. The Consultant

told JC Official 1 that the Consultant had called others, including defendant Webb-Washington, who would arrive at the diner at 12:30 p.m. Regarding defendant Webb-Washington and others who were scheduled to meet them at various times that day, JC Official 1 said, "Let's spread them out fifteen minutes difference, okay?" The Consultant agreed and asked JC Official 1: "How are we operating this? [They] are coming into the restaurant to see [the CW]?" JC Official 1 responded, "Yes they are coming in to see [the CW] and then whatever conversation you want and then they'll leave." The Consultant agreed and then asked JC Official 1, "And then how are we dealing with the money?" JC Official 1 responded to the Consultant that they would "talk to [the CW] about the money." JC Official 1 [laughing] then stated that, like he had said before, "they don't get any money" [meaning that JC Official 1 did not want to discuss the passing of payments to these individuals, including defendant Webb-Washington, over the telephone].

11. On or about March 30, 2009, at approximately 11:45 a.m., FBI agents intercepted an incoming call from defendant Webb-Washington to the Consultant over the Consultant's cell phone. During the call, the Consultant told defendant Webb-Washington to "be there at 12:30" and defendant Webb-Washington agreed.

12. Thereafter, that same day, defendant Webb-Washington met the Consultant, JC Official 1 and the CW at a diner in Bayonne. Defendant Webb-Washington and the CW discussed the location of the CW's proposed development on Garfield Avenue. A short time later, the CW asked defendant Webb-Washington if she wanted to "go for a little walk," and, as the two walked toward the diner's parking lot, defendant Webb-Washington was informed by the CW that "like we spoke about before. I'm gonna give you the 5,000 now," prompting defendant Webb-Washington to reply "[o]kay, no problem." After the CW explained that the $5,000 was in the trunk of the CW's car, the CW told Washington that "[t]hen I'll give you another five before the election. And . . . after you get in, and I know you're on my team, I'll give you another 5,000." Defendant Webb-Washington replied "[n]o problem." The CW then removed an envelope from the trunk of the CW's vehicle and handed it to defendant Webb-Washington, stating "[t]hat's, uh, 5,000. That's cash. This way there's no, you know, no conflicts or anything." Defendant Webb-Washington accepted the envelope containing the $5,000 in cash, stating "good, you don't need none." The CW then asked defendant Webb-Washington to "just make sure you expedite my stuff, and I know you'll . . ." Defendant Webb-Washington interjected, "Oh, no, you don't need to worry about me." The CW then asked "[a]nd you'll vote for me on

that zone change," prompting defendant Webb-Washington to reiterate, "You don't have to worry." Defendant Webb-Washington and the CW then exchanged contact information before defendant Webb-Washington drove away.

13. On or about April 21, 2009, the Consultant and JC Official 1 met the CW at a diner in Jersey City. The Consultant and JC Official 1 set forth the schedule and the identities of individuals with whom they would be meeting as well as the amounts of money to be paid to certain public officials and candidates. In particular, the Consultant informed the CW that they would then meet with defendant Webb-Washington at a diner in Bayonne around mid-day on April 23rd, at which time the CW would provide defendant Webb-Washington with an additional $5,000.

14. On or about April 23, 2009, defendant Webb-Washington met JC Official 1, the Consultant and the CW at a diner in Bayonne. During the meeting, defendant Webb-Washington continued to promise to support a proposed zone change for CW's purported Garfield Avenue project once she was elected to the Jersey City Council. Defendant Webb-Washington told the CW that the CW was on the "top" of her list. In the diner's parking lot, while inside of her vehicle, defendant Webb-Washington accepted $5,000 in cash from the CW in an envelope. Defendant Webb-Washington further indicated that to conceal the CW as the source of the contributions, she would indicate that the money was from her and then transfer it to her election fund. She agreed that she did not want the CW name on "nothing" so that down the line when she supported the CW's initiative regarding the Garfield Avenue project, no one could say that she was officially supporting the CW because the CW provided financial support to her.

15. On or about May 7, 2009, defendant Webb-Washington met with the CW in defendant Webb-Washington's vehicle in a parking lot of a diner in North Bergen, New Jersey. Defendant Webb-Washington indicated that another person had told her that she was ahead in the polls. Defendant Webb-Washington indicated to the CW that she needed money for her campaign. She further told the CW that she had the CW's "back" and was the main one to support the CW's purported Garfield Avenue development project. She responded "definitely," when the CW asked if the CW had her vote on this project. Defendant Webb-Washington also promised to obtain the vote of another Jersey City Council member for the CW. Defendant Webb-Washington then accepted $5,000 in cash from the CW. Agreeing with the CW, defendant Washington indicated that she would not report the CW's name in connection with this cash payment because when she went to assist the CW after the election, she did not want anyone to connect the two of them.

Defendant Webb-Washington further remarked to the CW that she had "common sense" and it did not take "nine degrees" to make her do the "right thing." Responding to the CW's request not to forget the CW in July, defendant Webb-Washington said that the CW did not have to say this anymore and that she "got" the CW. As the conversation concluded, defendant Webb-Washington further remarked that the CW had her "back," and she had the CW's back.

16. On or about May 13, 2009, at approximately 4:52 p.m., FBI agents intercepted an incoming call from defendant Webb-Washington to the Consultant's cell phone. During this conversation, defendant Webb-Washington complained to the Consultant about the procedures surrounding the Jersey City election the previous day, which culminated in defendant Webb-Washington being behind in the vote count to her main opposition for a city council seat. The discussion turned to the run-off election, which defendant Webb-Washington said that she believed she was a part of, and the Consultant said: "They're going to try to pull every trick in the book." Defendant Webb-Washington said, "This isn't helping our friend [meaning the CW]. . . . [I]t don't help [the CW]. It don't help nobody, it don't help anybody to play with her [meaning the current Council member, whom defendant Webb-Washington hoped to unseat]." Defendant Webb-Washington and the CW then discussed, among other things, using the legal process to challenge the results of the election. Defendant Webb-Washington told the Consultant to tell the CW, among other things, that she was "not playing you know, because [the CW] will really get screwed over with [the incumbent Council member]. For real now. We have her in there and [the CW] stands to lose a lot of money."

B. Rights at Charging

The due process clauses of the Fifth Amendment and the Fourteenth Amendment guarantee a fair trial and through its provisions the Sixth Amendment defines what a fair trial is.[42] The Sixth Amendment contains a number of rights, some of which are applicable upon charging and some of which are applicable at trial. The relevant part of the Sixth Amendment provides as follows:

> In all criminal prosecutions, the accused shall enjoy the right to a speedy and public trial, by an impartial jury of the State and district wherein the crime shall have been committed . . . , and to be informed of the nature and

cause of the accusation; to be confronted with the witnesses against him; to have compulsory process for obtaining witnesses in his favor, and to have the Assistance of Counsel for his defense. *U.S. Const.,* Amend. VI.

In this section we will examine four Sixth Amendment rights that arise upon charging. In a later chapter we will examine the trial rights that the Sixth Amendment confers.

1. *Venue*

Venue is the place where a criminal case may be tried. *Skillern v. State,* 890 S.W.2d 849 (Ct. of App. of Tex. 1994).

In criminal procedure **venue** means the place where a case may be tried.[43] On the federal level the Constitution provides that the trial of a criminal must be conducted in the state where the crime was committed.[44] The Sixth Amendment restates that requirement and then further specifies that criminal cases must be tried in the federal district[45] in which the crime was committed.[46] Basing the place of trial on the location where the crime was committed is often referred to as the "crime committed" venue formula.

Distinguishing Jurisdiction and Venue

While similar, the concepts of jurisdiction and venue are distinct and should not be confused. Jurisdiction concerns the power of a court to hear and determine a case[47] and cannot be waived. Challenges to jurisdiction can be raised at any time, including for the first time on appeal. In contrast, venue in its procedural aspect refers to the place where a case may be tried[48] and can be waived by the defendant.

If a court does not have jurisdiction it has no power to hear and determine a case.[49] If, however, a case is brought before a court that has jurisdiction but in which venue is improper, the court has the power to hear and determine that case.[50] For example, if a prosecutor brings a criminal prosecution in an improper venue, the court in which that case is brought still has the power to hear and determine the defendant's guilt or innocence, whereas if the prosecutor brings a case in a court that has no jurisdiction, the court must dismiss the case and if it does not, any judgment it enters is void.

State constitutions and statutes have venue provisions similar to those contained in the U.S. Constitution, but which set the place of trial in the county or parish in which the crime was committed.[51] If a charge is brought in an improper venue and the defendant objects to being placed on trial there, the case may be dismissed or simply transferred to the proper venue. If the defendant proceeds to trial without objecting to improper venue, he is considered to have waived his right to be tried where venue was proper.

In most cases there is little trouble in determining where a crime was committed. For example, if Aaron goes to a liquor store in Chicago, puts a loaded gun in the store clerk's face and fatally shoots the clerk, the crime of murder was committed in Cook County (the county in which Chicago is located), Illinois and consequently the proper place to try Aaron for murdering the liquor store clerk is in Cook County, Illinois. Certain types of offenses, however, may be committed in more than one place and as a result venue for those crimes may be in more than one county, parish, or district.

Historical Perspective

The Historical Significance of Venue in the United States

The constitutional venue provisions are deeply rooted in our nation's colonial experience.[52] During the colonial period, officials of the Crown became concerned that American colonial courts would not adequately protect royal interests.[53] To address that problem Parliament adopted a statute under which American colonists could be charged with committing a crime on colonial soil and then moved to England or another British colony for trial.[54] That practice angered the American colonists and was one of the reasons listed in the Declaration of Independence as justifying independence. It was that historical experience that led to the inclusion of the explicit venue provision contained in Article III of the Constitution.[55]

The policy concerns behind the venue provisions of the Constitution and the Sixth Amendment are the protection of a defendant from being prosecuted in a place far from his home and far from the support system necessary to mount an adequate defense.[56] Other concerns at which the constitutional venue provisions are directed are that a trial in a distant location will result in a trial before jurors who may feel no sympathy for the defendant and who may even have prejudices against him and the cost and expense to the defense of procuring witnesses to help establish the defendant's innocence.[57]

A **continuing offense** is an offense committed over a period of time instead of at a single point in time. 4 Wayne LaFave et al. *Criminal Procedure* §16.1(d) (3d ed. 2008).

One category of offenses that can be committed in more than one place consists of offenses that are called **continuing offenses**. Continuing offenses are offenses that are considered to be committed over a period of time instead of at a single point in time.[58] An example of a continuing offense is the crime of kidnapping. In most jurisdictions the offense of kidnapping is considered to begin when the victim is kidnapped and continue until the victim is no longer under the control of his kidnappers.[59] In the case of continuing offenses, venue is proper in any county in which the crime is committed. For example, Bart and Anton kidnap Tina in Chicago, Cook County, and take Tina to Sycamore in DeKalb County, and while transporting Tina to Sycamore they pass through DuPage County and Kane County. Venue to try Bart and Anton for kidnapping would be proper in any of those four counties because the crime is considered to have occurred in all of them.

A second category of offenses that can be committed in more than one place consists of those offenses that contain two or more distinct parts.[60] An example of such an offense is the crime of conspiracy.[61] As it is usually defined, the offense of conspiracy includes among its elements an agreement to commit a crime and an overt act in furtherance of the agreement. In many cases the agreement may be entered into in one county or district and some act in furtherance of it may be committed in another.

When one part of a multipart offense is committed in one county and another part is committed in another county, the offense is considered to have been committed in both and venue is proper in either.[62] For example, Walid and Patti are in White County and they agree to rob a bank while posing as police officers. In furtherance of that agreement Walid travels to a store in adjacent Jersey County where he purchases the police uniforms that he and Patti will use in the planned robbery. In that example the crime of conspiracy is considered to have occurred in White County where the agreement between Walid and Patti to commit the bank robbery was made, and in Jersey County where an overt act in furtherance of the conspiracy, purchasing the uniforms, was committed.

The venue provisions of the U.S. Constitution and those found in state constitutions and statutes treat venue as a procedural matter (i.e., as a set of rules that determine where a defendant can be placed on trial for a crime). Under the common law[63] and still under federal law and the law of most states, venue also has a substantive aspect. The substantive aspect of venue treats venue as a material allegation and requires that the location of the crime be alleged in the charging instrument and proved at trial.[64] A few states have eliminated the common law rule and in those states venue is treated solely as a procedural right that need not be alleged and proved.[65]

The jurisdictions that have retained the substantive aspect of venue all require that venue be alleged in the charging instrument, but differ as to the degree of proof necessary to establish that fact. In some of those jurisdictions venue is not considered to be an element of the offense and in those jurisdictions venue can be proved by a preponderance of evidence.[66] In other substantive venue jurisdictions, venue is considered to be a material allegation that must be proved beyond a reasonable doubt.[67]

In a procedure only jurisdiction, proof at trial that the crime occurred in a venue other than as alleged in the charging instrument is of no consequence. In either type of substantive venue jurisdiction, the consequence of failing to allege in the charging instrument the county or district in which the crime occurred[68] or to prove at trial that the crime occurred in the venue where the charging instrument alleges that it occurred is fatal to the prosecution and will result in the defendant's acquittal, notwithstanding that all the elements that define the offense have been proven.[69] For example, Luis commits an armed robbery in Lake County, which is adjacent to Prairie County. Both the Lake County and Prairie County prosecutors mistakenly believe the robbery occurred in Prairie County and as a result the Prairie County prosecutor files an information charging Luis with the robbery and alleging that the robbery occurred within Prairie County. In a procedure only jurisdiction, if Luis does not object to venue in Prairie County before trial, any error as to venue is considered waived, and if at trial the evidence establishes that Luis committed the robbery, but establishes that he committed it in Lake County instead of Prairie County, that variance between the proof and the charging instrument has no effect on the proceeding or the verdict against Luis. If that were to occur in a substantive venue jurisdiction, Luis would have to be acquitted because the state failed to prove the venue element (i.e., that as alleged in the information the robbery occurred in Prairie County).

Many paralegals who work in prosecutors' offices and those who work for law enforcement agencies are responsible for handling victim intake, which includes obtaining basic information about the crime, including where the crime occurred. For paralegals whose duties include an intake function it is critically important that they obtain information about where the crime was committed and accurately record that information on the intake form. If there is any doubt about where the crime was committed or about the district or county in which the site of the alleged crime is located, the paralegal should be sure to note that uncertainty and draw that to the attention of the prosecutor or investigator to whom she transfers the intake file or information.

People v. Gallegos

Appellate Court of Illinois (3d Dist. 1998)
293 Ill. App. 3d 873

HOMER, J. After a bench trial, the defendant was convicted of driving under the influence of alcohol. On appeal, he contends that the 1995 amendment to section 5/1-6 of the Criminal Code of 1961 (720 ILCS 5/1-6 (West Supp. 1995)), which provides that the State is no longer required to prove venue at trial, is unconstitutional. He argues, therefore, that his conviction must be reversed because the State failed to prove venue beyond a reasonable doubt. We affirm.

FACTS

On December 17, 1995, Elk Grove Village Police Officer Frank Vrchota came upon the disabled vehicle of the defendant, Vince Gallegos, near the county line dividing Du Page and Cook Counties. The defendant was charged in Du Page County with driving too fast for conditions, improper lane usage, leaving the scene of an accident involving property damage, and driving under the influence of alcohol.

The case proceeded to a bench trial. After completion of the State's case, the defendant moved for a directed verdict contending that the State failed to prove venue. In response, the State asserted that the 1995 amendment of section 5/1-6 of the Criminal Code of 1961 (the Criminal Code) removed venue as an element of a criminal offense and that all objections to place of trial are waived unless raised prior to trial. * * *

[The defendant] . . . was found guilty of driving under the influence of alcohol and not guilty of the other charged offenses. He was sentenced to one year of court supervision, ordered to attend alcohol counseling, and assessed a fine of $300 plus costs. The instant appeal followed.

The defendant contends that the State's obligation to prove venue beyond a reasonable doubt is a "penumbra" of a defendant's constitutional right to trial by jury (Ill. Const. 1970, art. I, §8). He also argues that this obligation flows from judicial interpretation of our constitution and that it cannot be revoked by the legislature absent a constitutional amendment. He asserts, therefore, that the legislature's attempt do so by its amendment of section 5/1-6 of the Criminal Code constituted a violation of the separation of powers doctrine (Ill. Const. 1970, art. II, §1). We disagree.

At common law, venue was defined as that particular county, or geographical area, in which a court with jurisdiction may hear and determine a case. See Black's Law Dictionary 1557 (6th ed. 1990). In Illinois, venue in criminal cases has emerged as having two separate elements, one procedural and the other substantive. *People v. Carroll,* 260 Ill. App. 3d 319, 327 (1992). The distinction between these two elements is dispositive of the issue at hand.

The procedural aspect of venue is rooted in the Illinois Constitution of 1970 which provides that a person accused of a crime in this state is entitled "to have a speedy public trial by an impartial jury of the county in which the offense is alleged to have been committed." Ill. Const. 1970, art. I, §8. This provision has been interpreted to mean that the accused has a right to be tried in the county where the charging instrument alleges that the offense took place. *Carroll,* 260 Ill. App. 3d at 327. Although the constitution conferred this right upon all defendants, its judicial interpretation reveals that this right was never intended to be unequivocal. See *Carroll,* 260 Ill. App. 3d at 327. Rather, the right is a "privilege" of the accused that may be waived. Therefore, it has long been held that all objections of improper place of trial are waived unless raised prior to trial. *People v. McClellan,* 46 Ill. App. 3d 584, 587 (1977).

Consistent with this longstanding interpretation of the procedural aspect of venue, the legislature enacted section 5/1-6 of the Criminal Code which defines the place of trial in particular circumstances. Prior to its amendment in 1995, section 5/1-6 provided, in pertinent part:

"(a) Generally.

Criminal actions shall be tried in the county where the offense was committed, except as otherwise provided by law. All objections of improper place of trial are waived by a defendant unless made before trial." 720 ILCS 5/1-6(a) (West 1994).

In contrast, the substantive aspect of venue at common law placed an obligation upon the State to prove that the offense took place in the county in which the State alleged it took place. Therefore, it was through the development of the common law that venue became a material allegation of every criminal offense, an allegation which the State was obligated to prove beyond a reasonable doubt with the other elements of an offense. See *People v. Hagan,* 145 Ill. 2d 287, 300 (1991). Unlike the procedural element, the substantive element of venue could give rise to a "failure of proof," an issue which may be raised for the first time on appeal because the State's failure to prove a necessary element is fatal to a conviction. *Carroll,* 260 Ill. App. 3d at 327. * * *

We have found no authority supporting the defendant's argument that the State's obligation to prove venue at trial is a constitutionally guaranteed extension of the right to trial by jury. Instead, our research reveals that proof of venue as a material element of an offense was an independent obligation placed upon the State by the common law. See *Rice v. People,* 38 Ill. 435 (1865) * * *.

In 1995, the legislature eliminated this common law element of venue by amending section 5/1-6(a) as follows:

"(a) Generally.

Criminal actions shall be tried in the county where the offense was committed, except as otherwise provided by law. *The State is not required to prove during trial that the alleged offense occurred in any particular county in this State.* When a defendant contests the place of trial under this Section, all proceedings regarding this issue shall be conducted under Section 114-1 of the Code of Criminal Procedure of 1963. All objections of improper place of trial are waived by a defendant unless made before trial." (Emphasis added.) 720 ILCS 5/1-6(a) (West Supp. 1995).

In considering the constitutionality of a statute, this court is not at liberty to inquire into the motives of the legislature, but may only examine the legislature's powers under the constitution. The Illinois General Assembly has broad discretion in defining the elements that constitute a crime. See *People v. Arna,* 168 Ill. 2d 107, 114 (1995). The legislature also has the inherent power to repeal or change the common law, or do away with all or part of it. *People v. Gersch,* 135 Ill. 2d 384, 395 (1990). Contrary to the defendant's assertions, we determine that the substantive element of venue is neither a derivative right of the constitutional right to a jury trial nor an obligation that flows from judicial interpretation of the constitution. Therefore, its extinguishment by the legislature does not constitute a violation of the separation of powers doctrine.

CONCLUSION

For the foregoing reasons, the judgment of the circuit court of Du Page County is affirmed.

Case Focus

1. Why is the difference between venue as a matter of procedure and venue as a matter of substantive law important and how do the two differ?
2. Why can one aspect of venue be eliminated by statute but the other aspect of venue cannot?

• • • • • • • •

Under federal law and in all of the states there are laws or court rules that permit a trial court to order that a prosecution be moved from the geographic area where venue is proper to a different geographic area.[70] American jurisdictions differ as to who can ask for a change of venue and as to the grounds upon which a court can grant such a request.[71] Some states only allow defendants to ask for a change of venue while others allow either the defense or the prosecution to ask for a venue change.[72] The most commonly recognized ground on which venue can be changed is to ensure a fair trial.[73] Many states also allow venue to be changed in the interest of witness convenience.[74]

2. *Sufficiency of the Charge*

The Sixth Amendment requires that a charging instrument inform the defendant of the nature and cause of the charge against him. That requirement is satisfied when a charging instrument alleges a crime with sufficient specificity that the defendant can prepare a defense and can establish a record sufficient to allow a defendant to use it to plead double jeopardy should he later be charged with the same offense.[75] A charging instrument satisfies those requirements either when it states the nature of the offense and sets out the elements of the offense[76] or, if the statute contains all the elements of the offense, when the charging instrument alleges the crime in the words of the statute.[77] The date of the offense usually is not considered to be an element of the offense.[78] As a result, instead of alleging that a crime occurred on a specific date, charging instruments may allege that the offense was committed "on or about" a certain date or between certain dates.

3. *Right to Counsel*

By its terms the Sixth Amendment guarantees defendants a right to the assistance of an attorney. The right to counsel guaranteed by the Sixth Amendment was long understood as only guaranteeing a defendant that he had the right to be represented by retained counsel and not as creating a right to be represented by appointed counsel.[79] It was not until 1938 that the Supreme Court held that the Amendment guaranteed federal defendants representation by an attorney if they could not afford one.[80] Four years later the Court held that the Sixth Amendment right to counsel did not apply to the states and that whether a state extended a right to appointed representation to state defendants was a matter of state policy.[81] In 1963 the Supreme Court reversed itself and held that the Sixth Amendment right to counsel was applicable to the states.[82]

Historical Perspective

The Right to Counsel: A Right to Hire an Attorney or a Right to an Appointed Attorney?

The common law allowed defendants in misdemeanor prosecutions to be represented by an attorney, but on the theory that in felony cases and cases involving treason it was the judge himself who was the attorney for the defendant,[83] the common law prohibited defendants in such cases from being represented by a lawyer.[84] Thus, under the common law even if a defendant charged with treason or a felony could afford to hire an attorney the defendant could not be represented by him in court. The American colonial legislatures rejected the common law rule and by the time the Sixth Amendment was written, all of the states gave defendants the right to be represented by an attorney in both misdemeanor and felony cases.[85]

The focus of those state level rights to counsel was, however, on the right of the defendant to use his own assets to hire an attorney and not on a right to have free representation.[86] That understanding of the state level rights to counsel is underscored by how the states of that era addressed the issue of appointed counsel. To the extent the states had a policy regarding the appointment of counsel, they dealt with that specifically[87] and to the extent the states provided for appointment of counsel, they varied with some states providing for appointment in all cases tried on an indictment[88] and others limiting appointed counsel to capital cases.[89]

Given the historical backdrop against which the state level rights to counsel came into existence and the right they were understood to confer, it is reasonable to conclude that the purpose of the Sixth Amendment right to counsel was to guarantee a similar right: to be represented by retained counsel and not to create a right to have appointed counsel. Adding support to that conclusion is the fact that during the period when the Sixth Amendment was being ratified, Congress passed a statute that specifically provided for the appointment of counsel for indigent defendants, but limited its application to capital prosecutions.[90] If Congress understood the Sixth Amendment to require the appointment of counsel and not simply as guaranteeing the right to representation by retained counsel, Congress would have had no reason to adopt that statute, particularly since it would have been in violation of the constitutional amendment it had recently sent to the states for ratification.

The Sixth Amendment right to counsel is broader for defendants with retained counsel than it is for defendants with appointed counsel. In the case of defendants who hire their own attorney, subject to certain limitations, the Sixth Amendment creates a right to counsel of choice.[91] That right is violated if a court improperly denies a defendant representation by the attorney he has hired. If a court violates a defendant's right to counsel of choice and as a consequence the defendant had to obtain or accept the services of a different attorney and the defendant is subsequently convicted, the defendant's conviction will be reversed, even if the substitute attorney's representation was not deficient and the defendant cannot show that his case was adversely affected (i.e., that he was prejudiced by the substitution).[92] The Sixth Amendment does not create a right to representation by counsel of choice for defendants whose attorneys are appointed for them.[93]

The Sixth Amendment right to counsel does not arise until the initiation of an adversary judicial proceeding.[94] Prior to the initiation of adversary judicial proceedings, the Sixth Amendment right to counsel has no application, even if the prosecutor has already decided to charge a target or contacts a target for the purpose of negotiating a pre-indictment plea agreement.[95]

Adversary judicial proceedings that will trigger attachment of the Sixth Amendment right to counsel are initiated by a preliminary hearing, an indictment, an information, a formal charge, or arraignment.[96] For purposes of the Sixth Amendment right to counsel, an arraignment occurs when a defendant makes his initial appearance before a judicial officer where he is informed of the charges and his liberty is subject to restriction.[97]

The Supreme Court has never elaborated on what instruments beyond an indictment or information would constitute a formal charge for Sixth Amendment purposes.[98] The filing of a federal criminal complaint does not qualify as a "formal proceeding" because unlike securing an indictment or an information, both of which require prosecutor participation, no statute or rule requires prosecutor participation in filing a federal criminal complaint.[99] In the absence of a formal charge and prior to an initial appearance before a judge, neither an arrest warrant issued pursuant to a federal criminal complaint sworn out by a prosecutor[100] nor the defendant's actual arrest on such a warrant triggers attachment of the Sixth Amendment right to counsel.[101] So for example, if an Assistant United States Attorney swears to and files a criminal complaint charging Rafael with Wire Fraud and obtains a warrant for Rafael's arrest, neither that filing nor Rafael's later arrest on that warrant by FBI agents will trigger attachment of the Sixth Amendment right to counsel for Rafael.

United States v. Hayes

United States Court of Appeals for the Ninth Circuit (2000) 231 F.3d 663

RYMER, Circuit Judge:

Darnell Hayes was one of several targets of an investigation into a complicated, multi-party scheme to sell grades for classes that foreign students did not attend, perform course work for, or take exams in. The government asked for (and got) court approval to take material witness depositions of several of the foreign students so that they could go home. Hayes was notified and was represented by counsel. Meanwhile, the government wired a co-conspirator who agreed to cooperate and to allow the government to tape a conversation with Hayes. Hayes was indicted nearly a year later, and sought to exclude the tape on *Massiah* grounds. *See Massiah v. United States*, 377 U.S. 201, 12 L. Ed. 2d 246, 84 S. Ct. 1199 (1964). The district court found no *Massiah* violation because the depositions and the non-custodial taped conversation occurred before formal criminal proceedings were initiated against Hayes. * * *

Having reheard the matter en banc, we recognize that we are not writing on a clean slate. In *Kirby v. Illinois*, 406 U.S. 682 (1972), *United States v. Gouveia*, 467 U.S. 180 (1984), and on numerous other occasions, the Supreme Court has clearly articulated the rule: "The Sixth Amendment right to counsel does not attach until after the initiation of formal charges." *Moran v. Burbine*, 475 U.S. 412, 431 (1986). Because no formal charges were pending against Hayes at the time of the surreptitious taping, it follows that the district court correctly determined that *Massiah* was not implicated and Hayes's Sixth Amendment rights were not violated.

As the remaining issues raised on appeal do not require reversal, we affirm.

I

Beginning in 1989, Sam Koutchesfahani solicited and accepted money from Middle Eastern foreign students to gain their admission to San Diego City College (SDCC) even though they did not meet SDCC's admissions criteria. He gave counterfeit documents to Richard Maldonado, an admissions officer, and paid him to issue fraudulent INS Form I-20s that falsely certified that the foreign students had met SDCC's admissions requirements. Then Koutchesfahani paid instructors at SDCC, Mesa College, and Palomar College to give passing grades to students who never attended classes or took any exams.

One of these instructors was Hayes, an adjunct professor at Mesa who taught classes in marketing and business. * * * Beginning in 1992, Hayes sold approximately sixty-five passing grades in his Mesa classes to approximately thirty-one foreign students who never attended class or completed class work and examinations. Although he never dealt with the students himself, Hayes was paid $150 per grade by Koutchesfahani for the Mesa classes, and $50 per course for thirty-four foreign students in eighty-seven correspondence courses for which he fraudulently certified the examinations as properly administered. * * * As a result of Hayes's participation in the conspiracy, these foreign students were able to maintain their non-immigrant F-1 student status and to obtain college credits and degrees.

Hayes received between $11,513 and $14,150 in bribes from Koutchesfahani, but failed to report any of this income to the IRS or to State Unemployment officials. * * *

At some point a criminal investigation was begun into the grade selling scheme, which stopped when Koutchesfahani and the foreign students found out about the investigation in the fall of 1994. However, Hayes and Koutchesfahani continued to talk. On November 30, 1995, Hayes received a target letter and consented to an interview by federal agents at his home, but told them a number of things that were untrue (for example, that Middle-Eastern students attended class and he did not give passing grades to students who did not go to class; that no Middle-Eastern students were enrolled in Mesa classes in 1994; that money he received from Koutchesfahani was for marketing work on "pharmaceuticals" for Koutchesfahani's company; and that he personally supervised the students' correspondence exams at Mesa).

Later, when Hayes learned in March 1996 that Koutchesfahani was thinking about cooperating with the government, Hayes asked him not to cooperate against him. Nevertheless, Koutchesfahani did enter into a cooperation agreement and on May 5, 1996, allowed agents to monitor and record a conversation he had with Hayes at a coffee house. During the conversation, Hayes said that he planned to lie at trial.

Meanwhile, on November 15, 1995, material witness complaints were filed under seal charging Abdulla K. Al-Rumaithi, Khallfan J. Al-Romaithi, Khalfan S. Al-Romaithi and Ghanem J. Al-Romaithi as material witnesses under 18 U.S.C. §3144, which allows for the arrest and detention of material witnesses but also provides that they may not be detained if their testimony can be secured by deposition. * * * The witnesses were arraigned November 16 and the conditions of release that were imposed included appearing to testify if subpoenaed and not leaving the United States without permission of the United States Attorney or the court. They were scheduled to graduate during the middle of May 1996 and to return to the United Arab Emirates. On April 19, 1996, the government filed a motion to take pre-indictment videotaped depositions of these four student witnesses, and to modify the conditions of release to allow them to return to their country after the depositions had been taken. * * * A few days before May 6, 1996, when the depositions were to begin, Hayes's privately-retained counsel substituted out and counsel was appointed for him. The depositions took place thereafter.

On April 17, 1997, a federal grand jury indicted Hayes for conspiracy to defraud the United States in violation of 18 U.S.C. §371, and to commit mail fraud in violation of 18 U.S.C. §§1341, 1346 (Count 1); aiding and abetting mail fraud—*i.e.*, fraudulent mailings of grade reports, transcripts, and correspondence examination certifications—in violation of 18 U.S.C. §§2, 1341, 1346 (Counts 2—54); filing false tax returns in violation of 26 U.S.C. §7206(1) (Counts 55-56); and failing to file a tax return in violation of 26 U.S.C. §7203 (Count 57). * * *. After a jury trial, Hayes was convicted on all counts.

II

Hayes argues that the tape recording of his conversation with Koutchesfahani was obtained in violation of *Massiah* because he had been served with a target letter on November 30, 1995, the government knew at least as of February 7, 1996 (when he was subpoenaed to appear before the grand jury) that Hayes was represented by counsel, and in May 1996 the government conducted depositions of material witnesses based on a court order. He submits that the government's invoking Rule 15 of the Federal Rules of Criminal Procedure was the functional equivalent of an indictment, and that the trial process effectively began when the government sought to take the depositions. Thus, as he puts it, the government chose to create a "trial type situation," which, in his view, *Massiah* forbade it from doing.

The government counters that, although Hayes was a target, he was not accused of anything when Koutchesfahani was wired. It points out that it merely indicated in its motion to take the depositions that it *might* seek indictments against the targets, and that telling a person that he is a target (which Hayes had known since November 1996) and may be prosecuted does not trigger the Sixth Amendment's right to counsel. * * *

The Sixth Amendment provides that "in all criminal *prosecutions*, the *accused* shall enjoy the right . . . to have the Assistance of Counsel for his defence." U.S. Const. amend. VI (emphasis added). Literally, these prerequisites are not met here, as there was neither a "prosecution" nor was Hayes an "accused" at the time Koutchesfahani was wound up and wired to talk to him.

Right to counsel cases in general, and the *Massiah* line of cases in particular, involve incidents that occurred *after* the initiation of adversary criminal proceedings and that arose during a critical, *post*-indictment proceeding. As the Court explained in *Gouveia*, "our cases have long recognized that the right to counsel attaches only at or after the initiation of adversary judicial proceedings against the defendant." 467 U.S. at 187. Then-Justice Rehnquist embraced for the majority the plurality's description of the right to counsel in *Kirby v. Illinois*:

> "In a line of constitutional cases in this Court stemming back to the Court's landmark opinion in *Powell v. Alabama*, it has been firmly established that a person's Sixth and Fourteenth Amendment right to counsel attaches only at or after the time that adversary judicial proceedings have been initiated against him.

> ". . . While members of the Court have differed as to the existence of the right to counsel in the contexts of some of the above cases, *all* of those cases have involved points of time at or after the initiation of adversary judicial criminal proceedings—whether by way of formal charge, preliminary hearing, indictment, information, or arraignment."

Gouveia, 467 U.S. at 187-188. * * *

The Court has consistently held that the right to counsel attaches only after the initiation of formal charges, reiterating this rule in different, but analogous, contexts. For example, in *Burbine*, where the defendant sought to exclude inculpatory statements made to the police after his family had retained an attorney but before formal charges had been brought, the Court made it clear that "the possibility that the encounter may have important consequences at trial, standing alone, is insufficient to trigger the Sixth Amendment right to counsel." *Burbine*, 475 U.S. at 432. Instead, "the suggestion that the existence of an attorney-client relationship itself triggers the protections of the Sixth Amendment misconceives the underlying purposes of the right to counsel. The Sixth Amendment's intended function is not to wrap a protective cloak around the attorney-client relationship for its own sake any more than it is to protect a suspect from the consequences of his own candor." *Id.* at 430. The Court continued:

> Its purpose, rather, is to assure that in any "criminal prosecution," U.S. Const., Amdt. 6, the accused shall not be left to his own devices in facing the "'prosecutorial forces of organized society.'" By its very terms, it becomes applicable only when the government's role shifts from investigation to accusation. For it is only then that the assistance of one versed in the "intricacies . . . of law," is needed to assure that the prosecution's case encounters "the crucible of meaningful adversarial testing." * * *

Id. at 430-431 (citations omitted). Likewise in *McNeil v. Wisconsin*, 501 U.S. 171 (1991), the Court considered whether statements provided to the police after McNeil's Sixth Amendment right to counsel had attached and had been invoked with respect to one armed robbery protected statements with respect to other offenses, and concluded that it did not "because petitioner provided the statements at issue here before his Sixth Amendment right to counsel with respect to the [other] offenses had been (or even could have been) invoked." *Id.* at 176. The reason is that the Sixth Amendment right to counsel is "offense specific" and "cannot be invoked once for all future prosecutions, for it does not attach until a prosecution is commenced, that is, 'at or after the initiation of adversary judicial criminal proceedings—whether by way of formal charge, preliminary hearing, indictment, information, or arraignment.'" *Id.* at 175 (quoting *Gouveia*, 467 U.S. at 188). * * *

The law in this circuit is equally clear. In *United States v. Kenny*, 645 F.2d 1323 (9th Cir. 1981), we explicitly rejected a *Massiah* challenge to a tape recording made by an informant of a conversation with a defendant (who was represented by counsel) before his indictment. As we noted, Kenny had not been charged, arrested or indicted at the time of the recording:

The short answer to Kenny's contention that his right to counsel was breached is that the right to counsel is not viewed to attach prior to the initiation of adversary judicial proceedings against an accused. Where a case is still in the investigative stage, or in the absence of a person's being charged, arrested, or indicted, such adversary proceedings have not yet commenced, and thus no right to counsel has attached.

Id. at 1338. * * *

Here, there is no dispute that no formal charge, preliminary hearing, indictment, information, or arraignment had occurred when Hayes met Koutchesfahani at the coffee shop. The only question is whether asking for an order to take the depositions (thus to free the witnesses from detention), which included notice to the targets so that they could appear (thus to make the deposition potentially useable at trial, if there were one), is the "functional equivalent" of the initiation of formal charges. We think not, under the Supreme Court's test. Asking for and taking the depositions did not formally initiate any criminal proceeding against Hayes. He was not thereby charged, indicted, or arraigned—and may never have been. Instead, the government remained an investigator rather than a prosecutor and Hayes was a target, not "the accused." * * *

We simply hold that the Sixth Amendment right upon which Hayes seeks reversal did not attach before criminal proceedings were formally instituted against him, in his case when an indictment was returned.

Case Focus

1. When does the Sixth Amendment right to counsel attach?
2. In this case why did the Sixth Amendment right to counsel not attach when the government initiated proceedings to detain and obtain deposition testimony from witnesses?

• • • • • • • •

Once an adversary judicial proceeding has begun, the right to counsel attaches even if the defendant does not ask for a lawyer.[102] As a consequence, at the defendant's first appearance in court on a criminal charge, judges usually appoint a public defender for an indigent defendant even if he does not ask for one.

Once the Sixth Amendment right to counsel attaches, it is very important for law enforcement agents to know whether a defendant has requested a lawyer or one was simply appointed for him without request. If the defendant asked for a lawyer, then law enforcement agents are prohibited from asking the defendant outside the presence of his lawyer if he is willing to talk to them about the offense with which he is charged.[103] If law enforcement agents violate that prohibition and obtain statements from the defendant, those statements will, on motion of the defendant, be suppressed.

If, however, the defendant did not ask for a lawyer and a court simply appointed one to represent him, law enforcement agents may approach the defendant outside the presence of the lawyer and ask the defendant if he would be willing to talk to them about the charged offense.[104] If such a defendant is willing to talk to the law enforcement agents without a lawyer he may elect to do so, and any statements he makes to them may be used against him.[105] For that reason, if a paralegal is assisting an attorney in court by making notes on the attorney's file about what occurred at a particular hearing, and at a hearing a court appoints an attorney to represent the defendant, it is very important that the paralegal accurately record whether the appointment was made at the request of the defendant or without the defendant's request.

EYE ON ETHICS

The No-Contact Rule, Paralegals, and Law Enforcement Agents

The American Bar Association's Model Rules of Professional Conduct, which nearly all of the states have adopted in whole or part, includes what is sometimes called the "no-contact rule." That rule, Rule 4.2, mandates that "a lawyer shall not communicate about the subject of a representation with a party the lawyer knows to be represented by another lawyer in the matter, unless the lawyer has the consent of the other lawyer or is authorized to do so by law or a court order."[106] The no-contact rule is different from the Sixth Amendment right to counsel and depending on where a paralegal is employed, she may or may not be bound by that rule[107] or by the Sixth Amendment.

For a paralegal who works in an attorney's office, including the prosecutor's office, the no-contact rule applies to her and as a consequence it is important that she not have any discussion with a represented defendant about the criminal charges for which the defendant has representation. The no-contact rule is only applicable to lawyers.[108] As a consequence, the rule has no application to a paralegal that works with a law enforcement agency and as long as she is not acting as the alter ego of the prosecutor, she can contact and speak to a represented defendant[109] who did not ask for counsel.

As the Supreme Court has observed, ". . . the Constitution does not codify the ABA's Model Rules, and does not make investigating police officers lawyers."[110]

A **critical stage** of a criminal prosecution is any stage when a substantial right of a defendant may be affected. *Mempa v. Ray*, 389 U.S. 128 (1967).

The Sixth Amendment right to counsel is not limited to trial representation.[111] Once the Sixth Amendment right to counsel attaches, a defendant is entitled to have counsel present at all **critical stages** of the prosecution.[112] Every post-attachment proceeding, however, is not a critical stage.[113] For example, a post-attachment extradition proceeding is not a critical stage.[114]

A critical stage is generally any stage of the prosecution where substantial rights of a defendant may be affected.[115] Critical stages have been held to include matters that occur outside court such as post-indictment police lineups,[116] and both overt[117] and covert[118] questioning of the defendant by law enforcement agents about the crime with which he has been charged, and matters that occur in court such as preliminary hearings, arraignment, and trial.[119] Critical stages, also include sentencing and appeal, if the jurisdiction gives defendants an **appeal of right**.[120] The right to counsel does not apply to **discretionary appeals**.[121]

An **appeal of right** is an appeal where the court to which it is taken does not have the power to refuse to hear it.

A **discretionary appeal** is an appeal where the court to which it is taken has the power to refuse to hear it.

The Sixth Amendment right to counsel is offense specific, which means it only applies to offenses with which the defendant has been charged.[122] As a result, while law enforcement agents are in some circumstances prohibited by the Sixth Amendment from interviewing a defendant without his attorney's consent about any crimes for which he has been charged, the Sixth Amendment right to counsel does not require that law enforcement agents obtain the consent of a defendant's attorney before interviewing the defendant about crimes with which he has not been charged.[123] For example, Jorge has been charged by information with the murder of Andrea and at his preliminary hearing Jorge asked for and was given an appointed attorney. Without the prior consent of his attorney, the Sixth Amendment prohibits law enforcement agents from interviewing Jorge about Andrea's murder, but law enforcement agents do not need that attorney's prior consent to interview Jorge about the murder of Barbara.

Without regard to whether the defendant's attorney is retained or appointed, the due process clauses of the Fifth and Fourteenth Amendments in combination with the Sixth Amendment right to counsel require that the defendant's attorney provide him with effective assistance.[124] If a convicted defendant's attorney rendered ineffective assistance, the defendant is entitled to have his conviction reversed and given a new trial. There are two different categories of ineffective assistance that can result in the reversal of a defendant's conviction: (1) per se ineffectiveness and (2) actual ineffectiveness.

Per se ineffectiveness occurs when a defendant: (1) is completely denied representation by counsel, (2) when the defendant has an attorney and the attorney entirely fails to subject the prosecution's case to meaningful adversarial testing, or (3) when an attorney is called upon to render assistance under circumstances where competent counsel's assistance very likely could not be effective.[125] In such cases, if the defendant is convicted he is entitled to have his conviction reversed without showing that the attorney's action or inaction adversely affected the outcome of his case (i.e., without the need of showing prejudice).[126]

The actual ineffectiveness category relates to how competently the attorney performed in representing his client.[127] A defendant's right to effective assistance of counsel is violated when his attorney's performance is deficient and the defendant can show that the deficient performance adversely affected the outcome of the his case (i.e., prejudiced the defendant).[128] In determining whether the attorney's performance was deficient the court must look at the reasonableness of the attorney's conduct at the time he engaged in it.[129] If the attorney's deficient performance did not affect the outcome of the case, her deficient performance does not require reversal of the defendant's conviction.[130]

The Sixth Amendment right to counsel also includes the right of a defendant to represent himself.[131] A court cannot force a defendant to have representation.[132] When a defendant represents himself he is said to be a **pro se defendant**.

Before allowing a defendant to proceed pro se, the judge must ensure that the defendant knowingly and intelligently waives his right to counsel.[133] For the defendant's waiver to be valid the judge must: (1) ascertain the age and degree of the defendant's education, (2) inform the defendant of the crimes with which he has been charged and the maximum possible sentence, and (3) determine whether the defendant understands the charges.[134] In addition, the judge must also inform the defendant that he will be expected to conduct himself in accordance with the rules of criminal procedure and the rules of evidence.[135] Judges also usually inform such a defendant that they will not assist him in questioning or cross-examining witnesses or by making objections where they might properly or should be made.

> Pro se defendant is a defendant who represents himself.

4. Right to a Speedy Trial

The Sixth Amendment also provides that upon being charged a defendant is entitled to a speedy trial. Because the violation of that right will result in the dismissal of a criminal charge and bars re-charging, the right to speedy trial is usually treated as a non-exculpatory defense. The right to speedy trial is discussed more fully with other non-exculpatory defenses in Chapter 15.

CHAPTER TERMS

Appeal of right	Hearsay	Presentment
Continuing offense	Impeachment	Pro se defendant
Critical stage	Indictment	Venue
Discretionary appeal	Information	

REVIEW QUESTIONS

1. What are the different methods by which felony prosecutions are usually initiated?
2. With any of the methods used to initiate felony prosecutions what event or events constitute commence of the prosecution?
3. Why is it important to know when a criminal prosecution has been initiated?
4. What is a preliminary hearing and how does it differ from a grand jury proceeding?
5. What do the provisions of the Sixth Amendment define?
6. Under the Sixth Amendment where must the trial of crimes be held?
7. What are continuing offenses?
8. What are multipart offenses?
9. Under the Sixth Amendment, where may trials of continuing and multipart offenses be held?
10. On what ground, if any, can a judge order a trial to be held other than in the place where the Sixth Amendment requires it to be held?
11. Why is it important to know the location where a crime was committed and the county, parish, or district of that location?
12. When does the Sixth Amendment right to counsel arise?
13. How do the right to appointed counsel and the right to retained counsel differ?
14. At what point or points in a criminal prosecution is a defendant entitled to the assistance of lawyer?
15. What are the two categories of ineffective assistance of counsel?
16. Under the Fifth Amendment, when must a federal prosecution be brought by a grand jury?
17. When determining whether a person should be charged with a felony offense, what must a grand jury determine is shown by the evidence it hears?
18. If there is sufficient evidence to convict a person of committing a crime and the prosecutor presents that evidence to a grand jury and asks the grand jury to charge that person with the crime, is the grand jury required to do so?
19. In deciding whether to charge a defendant with committing a crime, is the grand jury limited to considering only evidence presented to it by the prosecutor?
20. What power, if any, does a court have to review whether the grand jury's decision to charge a person with a crime is based on legally sufficient evidence?

ENDNOTES

1. *Mackin v. United States*, 117 U.S. 348 (1886).
2. *Wong Wing v. United States*, 163 U.S. 228 (1896).
3. *Id.*
4. *See Id.*
5. 4 Wayne LaFave et al. *Criminal Procedure* §15.1(b) (3d ed. 2008).
6. *Id.*
7. *Ex parte Quirin*, 317 U.S. 1 (1942).
8. *Id.*
9. *Hoffman v. United States*, 341 U.S. 79 (1951).
10. John R. Fletcher, *Charge to the Grand Jury*, 18 F.R.D. 211 (Calvert Cty., Md. 1955).
11. *United States v. Leverage Funding Systems, Inc.*, 637 F.2d 645 (9th Cir. 1980).

12. *Gaither v. United States*, 413 F.2d 1061 (D.C. Cir. 1969).
13. Irving R. Kaufman, *The Grand Jury—Its Role and Its Powers*, 17 F.R.D. 331 (1955).
14. *Id.*
15. *Id.*
16. *Id.*
17. *United States v. Leverage Funding Systems, Inc.*, 637 F.2d at 645.
18. *Gaither v. United States*, 413 F.2d at 1061.
19. *Vasquez v. Hillery*, 474 U.S. 254 (1986).
20. Fletcher, *Charge to a Grand Jury*, 18 F.R.D. at 211.
21. *United States v. Leverage Funding Systems, Inc.*, 637 F.2d at 645.
22. Fletcher, *Charge to a Grand Jury*, 18 F.R.D. at 211.
23. *United States v. Williams*, 504 U.S. 36 (1992).
24. *Id.*
25. *Id.*
26. *United States v. Salsedo*, 607 F.2d 318 (9th Cir. 1979).
27. *State v. Childs*, 242 N.J. Super. 121 (1990).
28. *People v. Linzy*, 78 Ill. 2d 106 (1979). In some states the prosecutor is required to provide legal guidance to the grand jury. *See People v. Calbud, Inc.*, 49 N.Y.2d 389 (1980).
29. *See, e.g.*, 725 ILCS 5/112-4(b).
30. *Hurtado v. California*, 110 U.S. 516 (1884).
31. *See, e.g.*, 725 ILCS 5/111-2(a).
32. IX W.S. Holdsworth, *A History of English Law* 236 (3d ed. 1944).
33. *Id.* at 238.
34. *Id.*
35. *See, e.g.*, 725 ILCS 5/109-3(a).
36. *Lem Woon v. Oregon*, 229 U.S. 586 (1913), *cited with approval, Gerstein v. Pugh*, 420 U.S. 103 (1975).
37. 725 ILCS 5/111-2(b).
38. *Id.*
39. *United States v. Alvarado*, 440 F. 3d 191 (4th Cir. 2006).
40. 1 Charles Wright et al., *Federal Practice and Procedure Criminal* §41 (3d ed. 2009).
41. *Id.*
42. *United States v. Gonzalez-Lopez*, 548 U.S. 140 (2006).
43. *Skillern v. State*, 890 S.W.2d 849 (Ct. of App. Tex. 1994).
44. *U.S. Const.*, Art. III, Sec. 2, cl. 3.
45. Chapter 2 discusses how Congress divides many states into two or more federal districts and how some sparsely populated and geographically small states, constitute a single federal district.
46. *U.S. Const.*, Amend. VI.
47. *Skillern v. State*, 890 S.W. 2d 849 (Ct. of App. Tex. 1994).

48. *People v. Gallegos*, 293 Ill. App. 3d 873 (3d Dist. 1998).
49. *Skillern v. State*, 890 S.W.2d at 849.
50. *Id.*
51. *See, e.g.*, 720 ILCS 5/1-6.
52. *United States v. Muhammad*, 502 F. 3d 646 (7th Cir. 2007).
53. Drew L. Kershen, *Vicinage*, 29 Okla. L. Rev. 803 (1976).
54. *Id.*
55. *United States v. Muhammad*, 502 F.3d at 646.
56. *Id.*
57. *Id.*
58. 4 Wayne LaFave et al., *Criminal Procedure* at §16.1(d).
59. *Cozzaglio v. State*, 289 Ark. 33 (1986).
60. 4 Wayne LaFave et al., *Criminal Procedure* at §16.1(d).
61. *Reass v. United States*, 99 F.2d 752 (4th Cir. 1938).
62. 4 Wayne LaFave et al., *Criminal Procedure* at §16.1(d).
63. *People v. Gallegos*, 293 Ill. App. 3d 873 (3d Dist. 1998).
64. *Id.*
65. *See, e.g.*, 720 ILCS 5/1-6.
66. *United States v. Muhammad*, 502 F.3d 646 (7th Cir. 2007).
67. *Jones v. State*, 272 Ga. 900 (2000).
68. *People v. Hill*, 68 Ill. App. 3d 369 (1st Dist. 1966)
69. *People v. Carroll*, 260 Ill. App. 3d 319 (2d Dist. 1992).
70. 4 Wayne LaFave et al., *Criminal Procedure* at §16.3(a).
71. *Id.*
72. *Id.*
73. *Id.*
74. *Id.*
75. *United States v. Hinkle*, 637 F.2d 1154 (7th Cir. 1981).
76. *People v. Rhoden*, 253 Ill. App. 3d 805 (4th Dist. 1993).
77. *United States v. Hinkle*, 637 F.2d at 1154.
78. *People v. Rhoden*, 253 Ill. App. 3d at 805.
79. *Hernandez v. State*, 726 S.W.2d 53 (Tex. Ct. Cr. App. 1986) (en banc)
80. *See Johnson v. Zerbst*, 304 U.S. 458 (1938).
81. *Betts v. Brady*, 316 U.S. 455 (1942).
82. *See Gideon v. Wainwright*, 372 U.S. 335 (1963).
83. *Powell v. Alabama*, 287 U.S. 45 (1932).
84. *Betts v. Brady*, 316 U.S. 455 (1942).
85. *Powell v. Alabama*, 287 U.S. at 45.
86. 3 LaFave et al., *Criminal Procedure* §11.1(a) (3d Ed. 2008).
87. *Betts*, 316 U.S. at 455.

88. New Jersey. *See Act of New Jersey of Mch. 6, 1795,* §2.
89. New Hampshire. *See Act of February 8, 1791, Metcalf's Laws of New Hampshire, 1916,* Vol. 5, pp.596-599.
90. 3 LaFave et al., *Criminal Procedure* at §11.1(a).
91. *United States v. Gonzalez-Lopez,* 548 U.S. at 140.
92. *Id.*
93. *Id.*
94. *United States v. Hayes,* 231 F.3d 663 (9th Cir. 2000).
95. *Id.*
96. *Rothgery v. Gillespie County, Texas,* 554 U.S. 191 (2008).
97. *Id.*
98. *United States v. Boskic,* 545 F.3d 69 (1st Cir. 2008).
99. *Id.* The same may not be true in the case of a state criminal complaint. State law determines the manner in which criminal proceedings are commenced and in some states the filing of a criminal complaint commences a prosecution, *See, e.g. State v. Nelson,* 390 N.W.2d 589 (Iowa 1986), while in other states it does not. *See, e.g. People v. Thompkins,* 121 Ill. 2d 401 (1988).
100. *United States v. Moore,* 670 F.3d 222 (2d Cir. 2012).
101. *United States v. Reynolds,* 762 F.2d 489 (6th Cir. 1985).
102. *Carnley v. Cochran,* 396 U.S. 506 (1962).
103. *Michigan v. Jackson,* 475 U.S. 625 (1986).
104. *Montejo v. Louisiana,* 556 U.S. 778 (2009).
105. *Id.*
106. American Bar Association, *Model Rules of Professional Conduct,* Rule 4.2.
107. *United States v. Lemonakis,* 485 F.2d 941 (D.C. Cir. 1973).
108. *People v. White,* 209 Ill. App. 3d 844 (5th Dist. 1991).
109. *Id.*
110. *Montejo v. Louisiana,* 556 U.S. at 778.
111. *Maine v. Moulton,* 474 U.S. 159 (1985).
112. *Montejo v. Louisiana,* 556 U.S. at 778.
113. *Rothgery v. Gillespie County Texas,* 554 U.S. at 191.
114. *State v. Jeleniewski,* 147 N.H. 462 (2002).
115. *Mempa v. Ray,* 389 U.S. 128 (1967).
116. *United States v. Wade,* 388 U.S. 218 (1967).
117. *Montejo v. Louisiana,* 556 U.S. at 778.
118. *Massiah v. United States,* 377 U.S. 201 (1964).
119. *United States v. Hayes,* 231 F.3d at 663.
120. *See, Evitts v. Lucey,* 469 U.S. 387 (1985). An appeal is an appeal of right when the court to which the appeal is made cannot refuse to hear it.
121. *Ross v. Moffitt,* 417 U.S. 600 (1974). An appeal is discretionary if the court to which the appeal is made has the power to refuse to hear it.
122. *McNeil v. Wisconsin,* 501 U.S. 171 (1991).
123. *Kight v. Singletary,* 50 F.3d 1539 (11th Cir. 1995).
124. *See United States v. Gonzalez-Lopez,* 548 U.S. at 140.
125. *Bell v. Cone,* 535 U.S. 685 (2002).
126. *Id.*
127. *United States v. Gonzalez-Lopez,* 548 U.S. at 140.
128. *Strickland v. Washington,* 466 U.S. 668 (1984).
129. *Id.*
130. *Id.*
131. *Faretta v. California,* 422 U.S. 806 (1975).
132. *Id.*
133. *United States v. Moya-Gomez,* 860 F.2d 706 (7th Cir. 1988).
134. *Id.*
135. *Id.*

Chapter 19
Criminal Procedure During the Pre-Trial Stage

Chapter Objectives

After reading this chapter, you should be able to

- Explain what *in personam* jurisdiction is and how a court acquires it
- Explain what a bond hearing is and what factors a court considers when setting bond
- Understand what *Brady* material is and explain when it must be disclosed
- Explain what discovery is and how it is performed in criminal cases
- Understand what plea bargaining is and explain what can be the subjects of a plea bargain
- Explain what a blind plea is
- Explain how courts can control extra-judicial comments that can affect the fairness of a trial

> This Court has never departed from the rule announced in *Ker* that the power of a court to try a person for a crime is not impaired by the fact that he had been brought into the court's jurisdiction by forcible abduction. No persuasive reasons are now presented to overrule this line of cases. —*United States v. Alvarez-Machain*, 504 U.S. 655 (1992)

The pre-trial stage of the criminal justice process begins when a charged defendant first appears before the court and continues until the case is disposed of in some manner before trial or trial of the case is commenced. In criminal cases a number of important things occur and are done during the pre-trial period. These include: (a) acquisition of *in personam* jurisdiction over the defendant, (b) a bond hearing, (c) arraignment, (d) disclosure of evidence, (e) filing of various motions, and (f) plea bargaining. In this chapter we will examine each of those subjects. In cases of high public interest, media coverage and the extra-judicial conduct of government officials and the defense during the pre-trial period can affect the fairness of any subsequent trial. In this chapter we will also examine the subject of pre-trial publicity.

A. Acquisition of *In Personam* Jurisdiction

In personam jurisdiction in a criminal case is the power to proceed against a particular defendant. *People v. Posey,* 32 Cal. 4th 193 (2004).

Assuming a sovereign has legislative jurisdiction to apply its law to a defendant (Chapter 6), before a defendant in a criminal case can be subject to a sovereign's judicial process the sovereign's court must have adjudicative jurisdiction over him. A sovereign's court may exercise jurisdiction over a defendant if the relationship of the sovereign to the defendant is such as to make the exercise reasonable.[1] In a criminal case a court obtains adjudicative jurisdiction over a defendant when it acquires *in personam* jurisdiction over him. A court has no power to hear and no power to adjudicate a criminal charge against a defendant until it has acquired *in personam* jurisdiction over him.[2] For example, if Beth is charged with murder, until a court acquires *in personam* jurisdiction over her, other than to issue a warrant for her arrest, a court has no power to place her on trial for the crime or enter a discovery order against her.

A court acquires *in personam* jurisdiction over a defendant through the defendant's first appearance before it.[3] Once a court acquires *in personam* jurisdiction over a defendant, the defendant's subsequent acts cannot abrogate that jurisdiction.[4] For example, Jasmine is charged with murder and the court acquires *in personam* jurisdiction over her. If Jasmine subsequently flees the country, her flight does not strip the court of jurisdiction over her; the court retains the power to place her on trial and enter a valid judgment of conviction against her even though she is not present.

How a defendant's first appearance in court is obtained generally has no effect on the court's power to hear and decide the case against him. As a result, a court acquires *in personam* jurisdiction over a defendant without regard to whether his first appearance before it is voluntary because he surrendered to the court[5] or was involuntary because he was arrested.

Extradition: Obtaining Fugitives from Justice

When a person wanted in a state or nation flees to another state or nation he is usually returned to the jurisdiction from which he fled through a process called extradition. Extradition is the surrender by one state or nation (the "asylum state") of an individual accused or convicted of a crime outside of its own territory and within the territorial jurisdiction of the state or nation that demands (the "demanding state") the surrender.[6] Thus, extradition involves a demand by one sovereign upon another sovereign for the surrender of a fugitive to the demanding sovereign.[7]

In the United States extradition between the states is governed by the extradition clause of the U.S. Constitution[8] and by a combination of federal statutes enacted pursuant to that clause and state statutes designed to supplement federal extradition law.[9] Under federal and state law the authority to demand the extradition of a fugitive and the duty to surrender that person is vested in the executive authority of each state,[10] which means the governor.

When all the constitutional and statutory requirements have been satisfied, without regard to the nature of the crime or the laws of the demanding state,[11] the governor of the state to whom an extradition demand is made must surrender the fugitive. The Constitution allows a governor no discretion to refuse extradition because of the anticipated unfairness of the judicial proceedings in the demanding state[12] or because of the fugitive's poor health.[13]

The only grounds for a state to refuse to extradite a fugitive to another state are that the extradition documents are defective on their face, the person has not been charged with a crime in the demanding state, the person is not the person named in the extradition documents, or the person being sought is not a fugitive.[14] By statute some states have adopted the doctrine of duality under which the asylum state will not surrender the fugitive to the demanding state unless the crime charged in the demanding state is also a crime in the asylum state.[15]

When a fugitive is arrested in another state she is taken before a court in that state where a judge will decide whether or not to release her on bond and where the fugitive will be given the option of waiving extradition. If the fugitive waives extradition she will have no further court appearances in that state and law enforcement agents of the demanding state will transport her back to their state.

If extradition is not waived there is a series of steps that must be followed before the fugitive will be returned to the demanding state. First, the demanding state must issue a formal request for extradition. That request comes from the governor, but is usually based on information and documents supplied by the local prosecutor of the jurisdiction where the crime was committed. Paralegals who work in prosecutors' offices are often tasked with assembling that information and completing the necessary documents.

Typically the necessary documents include: a copy of the arrest warrant, a copy of the charging instrument, copies of the statutes the fugitive is charged with violating, and information for identification of the fugitive, such as fingerprints or photos. In many states these documents are sent to the governor's office where they are reviewed for legal sufficiency and if determined to be complete are forwarded to the governor of the state where the fugitive is located.

Once the governor of the asylum state is satisfied that the demanding state has met the necessary requirements for extradition, the governor of the asylum state issues a Governor's Warrant that serves as an authorization for taking the fugitive into custody if he is not already in custody, and for turning the fugitive over to the demanding state. Once extradition is granted, law enforcement agents designated by the prosecutor of the demanding state are sent to retrieve the fugitive.

International extradition is significantly different from interstate extradition. The right of one nation to demand the extradition of a fugitive from another nation and the duty of the other nation to surrender that fugitive only exists when there is a treaty between the two nations.[16] Thus, in the absence of a treaty a nation is under no obligation to surrender a person within its borders to foreign authorities for prosecution.[17]

The United States has extradition treaties with most foreign governments.[18] Most of the treaties contain provisions that exempt the parties from any requirement to extradite their own nationals,[19] but which permit them to do so at their discretion.[20] Extradition treaties specify the offenses for which extradition is allowed, and extradition is limited to only those specified offenses.[21] Generally, political offenses are offenses for which a person cannot be extradited[22] and what constitutes a political offense is defined in the treaty. In the United States the Secretary of State has discretion to refuse extradition on humanitarian grounds, but the judiciary has no similar power and cannot refuse extradition on those grounds.[23]

Unless an extradition treaty provides otherwise, the doctrine of duality is applicable to all international extraditions. As a result, an asylum nation will not surrender a fugitive to a demanding nation unless the crime with which the fugitive is charged in the demanding nation is also a crime in the asylum nation. In international extraditions, once a fugitive is extradited a principle called the doctrine of speciality becomes applicable. Under that doctrine a fugitive who is extradited to a demanding state can only be placed on trial for the offenses specified in the extradition proceeding.[24]

The extradition process for international fugitives can differ significantly depending on the nation in which the fugitive is found. The U.S. Department of Justice's Office of International Affairs provides federal and state prosecutors with advice and information about the procedures for obtaining extradition from abroad.

A court acquires *in personam* jurisdiction over a defendant even when his first appearance before it is obtained through illegal acts.[25] For example, Walid is wanted for murder in Grand Rapids, Michigan. The Grand Rapids police learn that Walid is living at a certain location in Chicago, Illinois. Two Grand Rapids police officers travel to Chicago, arrest Walid there (even though they have no arrest powers in Illinois), and, ignoring the extradition laws, drive Walid back to Grand Rapids where he appears in court. The Michigan court acquired *in personam* jurisdiction over Walid when he appeared before it, notwithstanding that the Grand Rapids police had no power to make an arrest in Illinois and that Walid was brought to Michigan illegally.

Kasi v. Commonwealth

Supreme Court of Virginia (1998) 256 Va. 407

COMPTON, J. On Monday, January 25, 1993, near 8:00 a.m., a number of automobiles were stopped in two north-bound, left-turn lanes on Route 123 in Fairfax County at the main entrance to the headquarters of the Central Intelligence Agency (CIA). The vehicle operators had stopped for a red traffic light and were waiting to turn into the entrance.

At the same time, a lone gunman emerged from another vehicle, which he had stopped behind the automobiles. The gunman, armed with an AK-47 assault rifle, proceeded to move among the automobiles firing the weapon into them. Within a few seconds, Frank Darling and Lansing Bennett were killed and Nicholas Starr, Calvin Morgan, and Stephen Williams were wounded by the gunshots. All the victims were CIA employees and were operators of separate automobiles. The gunman, later identified as defendant Mir Aimal Kasi, also known as Mir Aimal Kansi, fled the scene.

At this time, defendant, a native of Pakistan, was residing in an apartment in Reston with a friend, Zahed Mir. Defendant was employed as a driver for a local courier service and was familiar with the area surrounding the CIA entrance.

The day after the shootings, defendant returned to Pakistan. Two days later, Mir reported to the police that defendant was a "missing person." * * *

On February 16, 1993, defendant was indicted for the following offenses arising from the events of January 25th: Capital murder of Darling as part of the same act that killed Bennett; murder of Bennett; malicious woundings of Starr, Morgan, and Williams; and five charges of using a firearm in commission of the foregoing felonies.

Nearly four and one-half years later, on June 15, 1997, agents of the Federal Bureau of Investigation (FBI) apprehended defendant in a hotel room in Pakistan. Defendant had been traveling in Afghanistan during the entire period, except for brief visits to Pakistan.

On June 17, 1997, defendant was flown from Pakistan to Fairfax County in the custody of FBI agents. During the flight, after signing a written rights waiver form, defendant gave an oral and written confession of the crimes to FBI agent Bradley J. Garrett.

Following 15 pretrial hearings, defendant was tried by a single jury during ten days in November 1997 upon his plea of not guilty to the indictments. The jury found defendant guilty of all charges and, during the second phase of the bifurcated capital proceeding, fixed defendant's punishment at death based upon the vileness predicate of the capital murder sentencing statute. * * *

There is no conflict in the evidence relating to any of the facts presented during the guilt phase of this trial; the defendant presented no evidence.

Near 4:00 A.M. on June 15, 1997, Agent Garrett and three other armed FBI agents, dressed in "native clothing," apprehended defendant in a hotel room in

Pakistan. Defendant responded to a knock on the room's door and the agents rushed inside. Defendant, who has "a master's degree in English," immediately began screaming in a foreign language and refused to identify himself. After a few minutes, defendant was subdued, handcuffed, and gagged. Garrett identified him through the use of fingerprints. During the scuffle, defendant sustained "minor lacerations" to his arm and back.

When the agents left the hotel with defendant in custody, he was handcuffed and shackled, and a hood had been placed over his head. He was transported in a vehicle for about an hour to board an airplane. During the trip, Garrett told defendant he was an FBI agent.

The ensuing flight lasted "a little over an hour." After the plane landed, defendant was transferred to a vehicle and driven for about 40 minutes to a "holding facility" where he was turned over to Pakistani authorities. The FBI agents removed defendant's handcuffs, shackles, and hood when the group arrived at the holding facility, but the persons in charge of the facility put other handcuffs on him. Defendant was placed in one of the eight cells in the facility, where he remained until the morning of June 17.

During defendant's stay in the facility, the FBI agents never left his presence or allowed him to be interrogated or "harassed." He was allowed to eat, drink, and sleep. On two occasions, the agents removed defendant from his cell to "look at his back and look at his arm" and to take his blood pressure and pulse. The agents did not interrogate defendant in the holding facility and made certain he was treated "fairly and humanely."

On June 16, "late in the day," Garrett was advised by an official at the U.S. Embassy in Pakistan that defendant would be "released" the next morning. On June 17 near 7:00 a.m., defendant "was allowed to be released" from the facility in the custody of the FBI agents. He was handcuffed, shackled, and hooded during a 15-minute ride to an airplane. Once on the plane, the hood was removed. Shortly after boarding the aircraft, a physician checked defendant's "well being." * * *

Next, defendant, attacking the jurisdiction of the trial court, contends that "* * * the Extradition Treaty between the United States and Pakistan * * * [was] violated" requiring "sanctions" to be imposed for these alleged violations. He argues the "abduction/seizure of Kasi was conducted outside and in express violation of the Extradition Treaty between the United States and Pakistan and without invoking the procedures set out by the laws of each country" and was contrary to law. He says the "sanction" for violation of the treaty should be reversal of the capital murder conviction and "repatriation to Pakistan without prejudice for a new trial." * * *

The defendant relies upon an Extradition Treaty between the United States and the United Kingdom. 47 Stat. 2122 (1931). Apparently, there is no extradition treaty directly between the United States and Pakistan. But the Attorney General is willing to assume, as represented by the defendant, that the "Islamic Republic of Pakistan has continued in force the treaty promulgated between its former colonial sovereign, the United Kingdom, and the United States," and that it applies to this case.

The defendant focuses on Article 8 of the treaty, which provides:

"The extradition of fugitive criminals under the provisions of this Treaty shall be carried out in the United States and in the territory of His Britannic Majesty respectively, in conformity with the laws regulating extradition for the time being in force in the territory from which the surrender of the fugitive criminal is claimed."

Contrary to defendant's contention, nothing in this treaty can be construed to affirmatively prohibit the forcible abduction of defendant in this case so as to divest the trial court of jurisdiction or to require that "sanctions" be imposed for an alleged violation of the treaty. The decision on this issue is controlled by *United States v. Alvarez-Machain*, 504 U.S. 655 (1992).

There, the respondent, a citizen and resident of Mexico, was forcibly kidnapped from his home and flown by private plane to Texas, where he was arrested for his participation in the kidnapping and murder of a federal Drug Enforcement Administration (DEA) agent and his Mexican pilot. DEA agents were "responsible" for the abduction, although they were not personally involved in it. *Id.* at 657. The United States has an extradition treaty with Mexico. The issue in the case was "whether a criminal defendant, abducted to the United States from a nation with which it has an extradition treaty, thereby acquires a defense to the jurisdiction of this country's courts." *Id.*

The Supreme Court, answering that query in the negative, said: "Extradition treaties exist so as to impose mutual obligations to surrender individuals in certain defined sets of circumstances, following established procedures." *Id.* at 664. The Court held that the treaty's language, "in the context of its history," failed to support the proposition that the treaty expressly prohibited abductions outside its terms. *Id.* at 666. The Court went on to hold that the treaty should not be interpreted to include an implied term prohibiting prosecution where a defendant's presence is obtained by means other than those established by the treaty. *Id.* at 666, 668-669. *See Ker v. Illinois*, 119 U.S. 436 (1886) (criminal defendant forcibly abducted from Peru to United States had no right to be returned to this country only in accordance with terms of extradition treaty between United States and Peru).

In the present case, as in *Alvarez-Machain* and *Ker*, defendant's seizure in a foreign country and his return to this country were not accomplished pursuant to an extradition treaty. The treaty language here does not expressly or impliedly prohibit prosecution in the United States where the defendant's presence was obtained by forcible abduction. Like the treaty in *Alvarez-Machain*, this treaty "does not purport to specify the only way in which one country may gain custody of a national of the other country for the purposes of prosecution." 504 U.S. at 664. In sum, defendant was not "extradited" under the provisions of this treaty.

As a corollary to the treaty argument, defendant contends his seizure was "illegal and unreasonable" in violation of the Fourth Amendment to the U.S. Constitution and the equivalent Article I, §10 of the Constitution of Virginia. We do not agree.

In *United States v. Verdugo-Urquidez*, 494 U.S. 259, 266 (1990), the Supreme Court held: "The available historical data show . . . that the purpose of the Fourth Amendment was to protect the people of the United States against arbitrary action by their own Government; it was never suggested that the provision was intended to restrain the actions of the Federal Government against aliens outside of the United States territory." The Court also said, "There is like-wise no indication that the Fourth Amendment was understood . . . to apply to activities of the United States directed against aliens in foreign territory or in international waters." *Id.* at 267. * * *

Consequently, we hold the trial court committed no reversible error, and we have independently determined from a review of the entire record that the sentence of death was properly assessed. Thus, we will affirm the trial court's judgment.

Affirmed.

Case Focus

1. In this case federal agents forcibly abducted Kasi from Pakistan and brought him to Virginia for trial in state court. How, if at all, did the conduct of the federal agents affect the Virginia court's jurisdiction to place Kasi on trial?

2. The U.S. government did not follow the terms of the applicable extradition treaty in this case. Why did that failure not affect the Virginia court's power to place Kasi on trial?

• • • • • • • •

B. Bond Hearing

In our society liberty is the norm and detention prior to trial is a carefully limited exception to that norm.[26] The liberty norm is reflected in the Eighth Amendment, which provides that "Excessive bail shall not be required," [27] and in the constitutions of almost all the states, which contain similar provisions. The terms of many of those state constitutional bail provisions differ significantly from the Eighth Amendment, because unlike the Eighth Amendment, which simply prohibits excessive bail, they expressly state that, except for defendants charged with a capital offense, all offenses are bailable.

When a defendant is arrested, without regard to whether the arrest was made with or without a warrant, the defendant is entitled to have what in most states is called a bond hearing and what in the federal system is called a detention hearing. At the bond hearing a judge will either consider the appropriateness of a previously set bond or, in the case of those who were arrested without a warrant, will set a bond.

Under the Eighth Amendment the primary purpose of bail is to ensure that a defendant will not flee the jurisdiction and will appear for trial.[28] When setting bail a judge can consider the defendant's ties to the community and the seriousness of the offense. In determining the defendant's ties to the community the judge will consider such things as whether the defendant has a job and how long he has had it, how long the defendant has lived in the community, whether the defendant owns a home or other real estate and the amount of equity he has in it, whether the defendant is married and has children, and whether he lives with his wife and children. In setting the amount of bond the court will also consider the defendant's ability to raise money to post for bond.

By statute, Congress has directed federal courts to consider certain additional factors and to deny bail if those factors are satisfied. In the Bail Reform Act of 1984 Congress directed that when setting bond for a defendant a federal court must consider whether allowing a defendant out on bond poses a danger to any person or the community. In making that determination the judge must consider the defendant's background and characteristics, the nature and seriousness of the danger he poses, and the nature and seriousness of the charges.[29] If the court determines that the defendant poses a danger to either, the court is to deny him bail.[30] Many states have similar provisions.

Most bond hearings are short, informal, and frequently include little more than brief testimony by the defendant, representations by the prosecutor and the defense attorney about the defendant's background and criminal history, and an inquiry by the judge about how much money the defendant can raise. In cases involving defendants who are alleged to be major drug dealers, terrorists, or perpetrators of high-dollar white collar crimes where there is a high risk of flight, bond hearings are formal and can be lengthy. During bond hearings for defendants in those types of cases the prosecutor will often introduce detailed testimony and other evidence about the extent and location of the defendant's assets and will disclose some of his trial evidence so that the court can judge not only the seriousness but also the strength of the case against the defendant.

Typically, bond is set in terms of a sum of money, which the judge orders that a defendant must post before being released from jail. Sometimes, a judge will set what in many jurisdictions is called an individual recognizance bond or simply an "I" bond. If a defendant is given an individual **recognizance bond**, the judge sets the bond in a specified amount of money (e.g., $10,000), but instead of having to post that amount the defendant simply signs a form in which he promises to appear in court and agrees that if he does not appear a judgment in the bond amount will be entered against him.

When setting bond, judges can and often do impose other conditions that must be satisfied before a defendant can be released. One frequently imposed condition requires that in addition to posting a cash bond the defendant surrender his passport. Another frequently imposed condition is that before being released the defendant must execute a waiver of extradition. Paralegals who work in prosecutors' offices frequently are asked to prepare such waivers in anticipation of a bond hearing.

Recognizance bond is a type of bail bond that does not require a defendant to post cash or property as a condition of being released from custody.

When setting bond, courts also frequently impose conditions that the defendant must follow while he is out on bond. Those conditions can include not leaving the jurisdiction without the court's approval, not leaving the jurisdiction except for work-related purposes, not having any contact with the victims of the crime the defendant is alleged to have committed, submitting to random drug testing, refraining from the use of alcoholic beverages, and home monitoring with the use of an electronic ankle bracelet.

IN THE CIRCUIT COURT OF THE FIFTEENTH JUDICIAL CIRCUIT, STEPHENSON COUNTY, ILLINOIS

PEOPLE OF THE STATE OF ILLINOIS,	)	
	)	
Plaintiff	)	
	)	
v.	)	**No.**
	)	
	)	
	)	
Defendant	)	

WAIVER OF RIGHT TO CONTEST EXTRADITION

As a condition of my release on bond, I hereby waive my right to resist extradition to the State of Illinois from any state or territory of the United States and from any other country and agree that I will not contest any effort to return me to the United States or the State of Illinois.

This waiver shall be of no force or effect after _____.

I fully understand that I have the right under the Constitution of the United States and under law to contest an effort to extradite me from another state and return me to Illinois and may have such a right under treaties to which the United States is a party. I freely and knowingly waive those rights as a condition of my release on bond.

In witness whereof, I have executed this waiver at Stephenson County, Illinois this _____ day of _____, 20____.

_____
,Defendant

I certify that _____ personally appeared before me and executed this waiver in my presence this _____ day of _____, 20____.

_____
Judge of Circuit Court of Stephenson County

Page 1 of 1

Trial *in absentia* is a trial conducted when the defendant is not present.

When a judge sets bond he will also usually advise the defendant that he must appear at every court date and that if he fails to appear he could be placed on trial even if he is not present.[31] Such a trail is called a **trial *in absentia***. A defendant can only be tried *in absentia* when he has been advised that if he fails to appear, a trial *in absentia* is a possibility.

If a defendant is admitted to bond and violates a condition of the bond or commits a new crime while on bond, the prosecutor can file a motion to revoke or modify the defendant's bond. If after a hearing the court finds that the defendant violated a condition of his bond, the judge can increase the amount of the defendant's bond, add new conditions, or revoke the bond and order the defendant held in custody until trial. A defendant who has been admitted to bail can ask a court to modify the conditions of his bond.

If a defendant fails to appear in court for a hearing or fails to appear for trial the judge can order the defendant's bond revoked and issue a warrant for the defendant's arrest. In addition, the judge will order the money or property posted as bail forfeited and, in jurisdictions that allow a defendant to post less than the full amount of bail, enter a judgment against the defendant for the balance.

Posting Bond

If a defendant is financially able he can always post bond in cash or by pledging property such as real estate. Many states continue to employ the bail bondsmen system. In those states if the defendant is not able to post the entire amount of his bond he can call a bail bondsmen, who for a fee will post the bond set by the Court. If a defendant is unable to find a bail bondsman who will post the bond for him, he will remain in custody.

Some states have abolished commercial bail bondsmen and instead allow a defendant to post with the Sheriff or Clerk of the Court a statutorily predetermined percentage of the bond set by the court. That percentage is usually 10% of the bond amount and can be posted in cash or property. In such states courts frequently have the power to order the defendant to post the entire amount of bond instead of the statutorily set percentage of it.

Today many jurisdictions also allow defendants to post bond by charging the required amount on a credit card.

C. Arraignment

From a constitutional standpoint one of the more important proceedings during the pre-trial stage is **arraignment**. Arraignment is a critical stage of the prosecution that requires the presence of the defendant and at which the defendant has a right to be represented counsel.[32] The purpose of arraignment is to inform the defendant of the charge against him and to obtain an answer to the charge from him.[33]

At arraignment the defendant appears before a judge, who reads the charge to him or informs him of its substance. The judge then asks the defendant whether he pleads guilty or not guilty to the charge and enters the defendant's plea in the court record.[34] If a defendant refuses to answer the charge by pleading guilty or not guilty, under the procedural rules of most jurisdictions the court is required to enter a plea of not guilty.[35] At the arraignment the court also provides the defendant with a copy of the indictment or information in which the charge against him is contained.[36]

While the procedure is different in federal practice, in many jurisdictions today, if the defendant is in custody, he is not physically taken before a judge for arraignment. Instead, the arraignment is conducted by closed circuit television or video conferencing, with the judge and lawyers in a courtroom and the defendant at some location in a jail.[37]

D. Disclosure

During the pre-trial period the defense and prosecution disclose to each other certain information and evidence. In criminal cases disclosure by the defense is governed by discovery rules and disclosure by the prosecution is governed both by those rules and the constitution. In this section we will examine both constitutionally and non-constitutionally required disclosure.

1. Constitutionally Mandated Disclosures

In *Brady v. Maryland*[38] the U.S. Supreme Court held that the due process clause imposes a duty on prosecutors to disclose to the defense evidence that is favorable to the defendant that the prosecutor knows or reasonably should know exists and that is not available to the defendant through the exercise of due diligence.[39] Evidence favorable to the

Brady material is admissible evidence, *United States v. Kennedy*, 890 F.2d 1056 (9th Cir. 1989), that is exculpatory or that can be used by the defendant for impeachment. *United States v. Knight*, 342 F.3d 697 (7th Cir. 2003).

defendant, often referred to as *Brady* **material**, consists of admissible[40] exculpatory evidence or evidence that could be used for impeachment.[41] *Brady* does not require the disclosure of inadmissible evidence that is favorable to the defendant because that evidence will not be heard by the trier of fact.[42] While *Brady* does not specifically require that disclosure be made during the pre-trial period, it is during that period that *Brady* material is usually disclosed.

The principle of *Brady* is violated and a convicted defendant will receive a new trial if the prosecution either willfully or inadvertently withholds *Brady* material until it is too late for the defendant to make use of it and if there is a reasonable probability that the outcome of the case might have been different had that evidence been disclosed.[43] Because a new trial will be granted even if there was only an inadvertent failure by the prosecutor to disclose *Brady* material, it is important that paralegals employed in prosecutors' offices always advise the prosecutor if they become aware of such evidence. For the same reason, if a paralegal is employed in an investigative agency and learns of the existence of *Brady* material in a case under investigation or that has been referred for prosecution, she should inform her supervisor.

As discussed above, under *Brady* the prosecution's duty to disclose evidence favorable to the defendant extends to evidence the prosecution knows or reasonably should have known exists.[44] The prosecution's knowledge of evidence is considered to include what is contained in its files as well as what is contained in the files of the law enforcement and non-law enforcement agencies that worked on the case.[45] If the files are of an agency whose files the prosecutor is charged with having knowledge of and they contain *Brady* material and that material is not disclosed to the defendant when required, a defendant's conviction will be reversed even if the prosecutor did not have actual knowledge that the material existed. For a paralegal working in a prosecutor's office who is tasked with finding out whether *Brady* material exists and obtaining it for the prosecutor, this means that she must not only review her office's file for such material, but must also ask the law enforcement and other agencies involved in the investigation whether they have any such evidence or information.

The prosecutor's knowledge of the existence of *Brady* material is not considered to include what is contained in the file of an agency in another jurisdiction[46] or an agency that did not work on the investigation.[47]

Discovery is the formal exchange of evidentiary information and material between parties in a pending action, *Arnett v. Dal Cielo*, 14 Cal. 4th 4 (1996); in a criminal case the exchange is between the prosecutor and the defense.

2. Discovery

Discovery is the formal exchange of evidentiary information and materials between parties to a pending action.[48] In criminal cases then,

The Duty to Disclose Evidence Favorable to the Defense

The duty of a prosecutor to disclose evidence favorable to the defendant is also found in the Rules of Professional Conduct adopted by many states. The following is a version of one such rule:

3.8: SPECIAL RESPONSIBILITIES OF A PROSECUTOR

1. The duty of a public prosecutor is to seek justice, not merely to convict. The prosecutor in a criminal case shall: . . .

   (d) make timely disclosure to the defense of all evidence or information known to the prosecutor that tends to negate the guilt of the accused or mitigates the offense, and, in connection with sentencing, disclose to the defense and to the tribunal all unprivileged mitigating information known to the prosecutor, except when the prosecutor is relieved of this responsibility by a protective order of the tribunal

Thus, the prosecutor is not only constitutionally obligated to disclose information favorable to the defense, but he is also ethically required to do so. As a consequence failure to disclose such information not only can result in the reversal of a defendant's conviction, but can also subject the prosecutor to professional discipline, which can include suspension of his law license or disbarment.

---

discovery is the process by which the defendant and the prosecutor formally exchange such information and materials. The purpose of discovery in criminal cases is to foster the search for truth based on all relevant evidence.[49] Discovery is not intended to open the government's files to all persons charged with crimes.[50]

Pre-trial discovery is a relatively recent development in American criminal procedure[51] and did not become widespread until the 1950s. At common law, beyond the right in some jurisdictions to pre-trial inspection of a thing that would be admissible in evidence, there was no general right to pre-trial discovery[52] and neither the Constitution nor the *Brady* decision create such a right.[53]

Because of the danger of witness intimidation and the heightened danger of perjury and subornation of perjury, discovery in criminal cases cannot really be compared with discovery in civil cases.[54] Discovery in criminal cases is narrower than discovery in civil cases,[55] and typical discovery tools used in civil cases (such as interrogatories and motions for the production of documents), are not available in criminal prosecutions in most states. Depositions, which are a major discovery device in civil cases, are only available in a few states as a basic discovery procedure in criminal cases.[56] In most states and in federal courts, depositions in criminal cases are only allowed upon a court order and then only for the purpose of preserving the testimony of a witness at trial.[57]

Discovery in criminal cases is governed by rules and statutes that differ significantly from jurisdiction to jurisdiction. For example, in some jurisdictions the prosecutor is required to make discovery materials available to the defendant within a certain period of time after arraignment[58] while in other jurisdictions to obtain discovery materials the defendant must file a written motion for discovery and the court must enter an order on the prosecution to produce the material sought.[59] In those jurisdictions that require the entry of a court order for discovery, if the defendant does not file a motion for discovery, the prosecution is not required to provide discovery to him, and at some point the defendant will be deemed to have waived his right to obtain discovery.[60]

While there are variations between the states, the discovery rules in most states either require (or on the defendant's motion give a court the power to order) the prosecution to disclose to the defense: (1) the names and addresses of the persons the prosecution intends to call as witnesses at trial or at a hearing; (2) copies of those witness's written or recorded statements, if any, and memoranda summarizing their oral statements; (3) written or recorded statements of the defendant and the substance of any oral statements made by the defendant together with the names and addresses of any witnesses to those statements; (4) any documents the prosecution intends to use at trial or which were obtained from the defendant; (5) reports or statements by experts; and (6) the qualifications of all experts.[61]

Such memoranda are usually contained in reports made by law enforcement agents in which they memorialized the substance of statements made to them by witnesses during interviews.

The substance of a defendant's oral statement is usually contained in the reports made by law enforcement agents in which they memorialized the substance of statements made to them by the defendant during an interview or during custodial interrogation.

Discovery Rule Example Used by the Defense: Illinois Supreme Court Rule 412. Disclosure to Accused

(a) Except as is otherwise provided in these rules as to matters not subject to disclosure and protective orders, the State shall, upon written motion of defense counsel, disclose to defense counsel the following material and information within its possession or control:

(i) the names and last known addresses of persons whom the State intends to call as witnesses, together with their relevant written or recorded statements, memoranda containing substantially verbatim reports of their oral statements, and a list of memoranda reporting or summarizing their oral statements. Upon written motion of defense counsel memoranda reporting or summarizing oral statements shall be examined by the court in camera and if found to be substantially verbatim reports of oral statements shall be disclosed to defense counsel;

(ii) any written or recorded statements and the substance of any oral statements made by the accused or by a codefendant, and a list of witnesses to the making and acknowledgment of such statements;

(iii) a transcript of those portions of grand jury minutes containing testimony of the accused and relevant testimony of persons whom the prosecuting attorney intends to call as witnesses at the hearing or trial;

(iv) any reports or statements of experts, made in connection with the particular case, including results of physical or mental examinations and of scientific tests, experiments, or comparisons, and a statement of qualifications of the expert;

(v) any books, papers, documents, photographs or tangible objects which the prosecuting attorney intends to use in the hearing or trial or which were obtained from or belong to the accused; and

(vi) any record of prior criminal convictions, which may be used for impeachment, of persons whom the State intends to call as witnesses at the hearing or trial.

If the State has obtained from the defendant, pursuant to Rule 413(d), information regarding defenses the defendant intends to make, it shall provide to defendant not less than 7 days before the date set for the hearing or trial, or at such other time as the court may direct, the names and addresses of witnesses the State intends to call in rebuttal, together with the information required to be disclosed in connection with other witnesses by subdivisions (i), (iii), and (vi), above, and a specific statement as to the substance of the testimony such witnesses will give at the trial of the cause.

(b) The State shall inform defense counsel if there has been any electronic surveillance (including wiretapping) of conversations to which the accused was a party, or of his premises.

(c) Except as is otherwise provided in these rules as to protective orders, the State shall disclose to defense counsel any material or information within its possession or control which tends to negate the guilt of the accused as to the offense charged or which would tend to reduce his punishment therefor. The State shall make a good-faith effort to specifically identify by description or otherwise any material disclosed pursuant to this section based upon the information available to the State at the time the material is disclosed to the defense. At trial, the defendant may not offer evidence or otherwise communicate to the trier of fact the State's identification of any material or information as tending to negate the guilt of the accused or reduce his punishment.

(d) The State shall perform its obligations under this rule as soon as practicable following the filing of a motion by defense counsel.

(e) The State may perform these obligations in any manner mutually agreeable to itself and defense counsel or by:

(i) notifying defense counsel that material and information, described in general terms, may be inspected, obtained, tested, copied, or photographed, during specified reasonable times; and

(ii) making available to defense counsel at the time specified such material and information, and suitable facilities or other arrangements for inspection, testing, copying and photographing of such material and information.

(f) The State should ensure that a flow of information is maintained between the various investigative personnel and its office sufficient to place within its possession or control all material and information relevant to the accused and the offense charged.

(g) Upon defense counsel's request and designation of material or information which would be discoverable if in the possession or control of the State, and which is in the possession or control of other governmental personnel, the State shall use diligent good-faith efforts to cause such material to be made available to defense counsel; and if the State's efforts are unsuccessful and such material or other governmental personnel are subject to the jurisdiction of the court, the court shall issue suitable subpoenas or orders to cause such material to be made available to defense counsel.

(h) Discretionary Disclosures. Upon a showing of materiality to the preparation of the defense, and if the request is reasonable, the court, in its discretion, may require disclosure to defense counsel of relevant material and information not covered by this rule.

(i) Denial of Disclosure. The court may deny disclosure authorized by this rule and Rule 413 if it finds that there is substantial risk to any person of physical harm, intimidation, bribery, economic reprisals, or unnecessary annoyance or embarrassment resulting from such disclosure which outweighs any usefulness of the disclosure to counsel.

(j) Matters Not Subject to Disclosure.

(i) Work Product. Disclosure under this rule and Rule 413 shall not be required of legal research or of records, correspondence, reports or memoranda to the extent that they contain the opinions, theories or conclusions of the State or members of its legal or investigative staffs, or of defense counsel or his staff.

(ii) Informants. Disclosure of an informant's identity shall not be required where his identity is a prosecution secret and a failure to disclose will not infringe the constitutional rights of the accused. Disclosure shall not be denied hereunder of the identity of witnesses to be produced at a hearing or trial.

(iii) National Security. Disclosure shall not be required where it involves a substantial risk of grave prejudice to national security and where a failure to disclose will not infringe the constitutional rights of the accused. Disclosure shall not thus be denied hereunder regarding witnesses or material to be produced at a hearing or trial.

Effective October 1, 1971; amended October 1, 1976, effective November 15, 1976; amended June 15, 1982, effective July 1, 1982; amended March 1, 2001, effective immediately, except when in the opinion of the trial, Appellate, or Supreme Court the application of the amended provisions in a particular case pending at the time the amendment becomes effective would not be feasible or would work an injustice, in which case former procedures would apply.

How the prosecution makes documents available to the defense usually depends on the quantity of documents. If the quantity is not large the prosecution may provide the defendant with copies of the documents it intends to use. In major white collar crime prosecutions where there are literally thousands of documents the prosecution may scan them and provide them to the defense on a disk or simply make them available for inspection by the defense at the prosecutor's office. In such instances a paralegal working in the prosecutor's office may be assigned to supervise the inspection of documents by the defense team.

The defendant is also subject to discovery rules. As is the case with discovery by the defense, in many jurisdictions the defense is not required to provide discovery to the prosecution until the prosecutor files a motion for discovery and a court enters an order requiring the defense to provide it.

The discovery rules of most states either mandate that the defense disclose to the prosecutor or on motion of the prosecutor authorize a court to order the defense to disclose: (1) any defense the defendant intends to assert; (2) the names and addresses of any witnesses it intends to call; (3) copies of all memoranda summarizing statements of the those witnesses; (4) all books, papers, and documents it intends to use as evidence or for impeachment; and (5) if the defendant intends to assert an alibi, the location where the defendant maintains he was at the time the offense was committed. Under the discovery rules of many jurisdictions, on motion of the prosecution the court can also order the defendant to appear in a lineup and to provide blood or tissue samples, handwriting exemplars, and fingerprints.

Example of Discovery Rule Used by the Prosecution: Illinois Supreme Court Rule 413 Disclosure to the Prosecution

(a) The person of the accused. Notwithstanding the initiation of judicial proceedings, and subject to constitutional limitations, a judicial officer may require the accused, among other things, to:

(i)   appear in a line-up;

(ii)   speak for identification by witnesses to an offense;

(iii)   be fingerprinted;

(iv)   pose for photographs not involving reenactment of a scene;

(v)   try on articles of clothing;

(vi)   permit the taking of specimens of material under his fingernails;

(vii)   permit the taking of samples of his blood, hair and other materials of his body which involve no unreasonable intrusion thereof;

(viii) provide a sample of his handwriting; and

(ix)   submit to a reasonable physical or medical inspection of his body.

(b) Whenever the personal appearance of the accused is required for the foregoing purposes, reasonable notice of the time and place of such appearance shall be given by the State to the accused and his counsel, who shall have the right to be present. Provision may be made for appearances for such purposes in an order admitting the accused to bail or providing for his release.

(c) Medical and scientific reports. Subject to constitutional limitations, the trial court shall, on written motion, require that the State be informed of, and permitted to inspect and copy or photograph, any reports or results, or testimony relative thereto, of physical or mental examinations or of scientific tests, experiments or comparisons, or any other reports or statements of experts which defense counsel has in his possession or control, including a statement of the qualifications of such experts, except that those portions of reports containing statements made by the defendant may be withheld if defense counsel does not intend to use any of the material contained in the report at a hearing or trial.

(d) Defenses. Subject to constitutional limitations and within a reasonable time after the filing of a written motion by the State, defense counsel shall inform the State of any defenses which he intends to make at a hearing or trial and shall furnish the State with the following material and information within his possession or control:

(i) The names and last known addresses of persons he intends to call as witnesses, together with their relevant written or recorded statements, including memoranda reporting or summarizing their oral statements, any record of prior criminal convictions known to him; and

(ii) any books, papers, documents, photographs, or tangible objects he intends to use as evidence or for impeachment at a hearing or trial;

(iii) and if the defendant intends to prove an alibi, specific information as to the place where he maintains he was at the time of the alleged offense.

(e) Additional disclosure. Upon a showing of materiality, and if the request is reasonable, the court in its discretion may require disclosure to the State of relevant material and information not covered by this rule.

Paralegals who work in prosecutors' offices and defense attorneys' offices are frequently tasked with preparing motions for discovery and answers to discovery and with assembling the materials the discovery rules require to be disclosed. Because there can be significant differences between jurisdictions, the paralegal is urged to familiarize herself with the discovery rules used in her jurisdiction and with what those rules require to be disclosed or authorize a court to order to be disclosed.

Many jurisdictions limit the application of their discovery rules to felony cases and have much more limited discovery in misdemeanor cases. For example, in misdemeanor prosecutions in some jurisdictions, prior to trial the prosecution is only required to provide a defendant with a list of witnesses, a copy of any confession made by the defendant, any *Brady* material, and the results of any scientific tests; and at trial the prosecution is required to provide the defense with copies of all reports made by law enforcement agents.[62]

Some prosecutors' offices follow what is called an **open file policy**. With an open file policy the prosecutor makes his entire case file available for inspection by the defense. Such policies, however, do not necessarily satisfy the prosecutor's obligations under the discovery rules[63] and defense attorneys seldom will rely solely on such policies. As a result, despite the existence of a prosecutor's open file policy, in jurisdictions where discovery is not automatic, a defense attorney will still file a motion for discovery.

Open file policy is a policy of a prosecutor's office under which he makes his entire file on a case available for inspection by the defense.

E. Motions

During the pre-trial period the defense may often file several other types of motions. These motions can include motions to dismiss the charge because the prosecution is barred for some legal reason, such as by double jeopardy or by a grant of transactional immunity, and motions to suppress because of alleged misconduct by law enforcement agents in gathering evidence during the investigation. The subjects of those motions have been examined in previous chapters.

F. Plea Bargaining

A **plea bargain** is an agreement between the defendant and the prosecutor, *Elmore v. State*, 258 Ark. 42 (1985), pursuant to which the defendant will plead guilty in the reasonable expectation that he will receive some type of consideration from the state. 5 LaFave et al., *Criminal Procedure* §21.1(a) (3d ed. 2007-2008).

Plea bargaining is ubiquitous in the American criminal justice system. In most jurisdictions, 70-90 percent of criminal cases are disposed of by plea agreement[64] and the vast majority of those agreements are struck during the pre-trial period. There is no constitutional right to plea bargain[65] and a prosecutor has discretion about whether or not to plea bargain.[66] A prosecutor can refuse to plea bargain on certain types of cases and he can offer different plea agreements to different defendants in the same or similar cases. In multiple defendant cases he can offer a plea agreement to one defendant but none to a co-defendant[67] or he can chose to offer only what is called a "package deal" in which he offers a plea agreement to a defendant only if all of the co-defendants also plead guilty.[68]

A plea bargain is an agreement by a defendant to plead guilty to a criminal charge with the reasonable expectation that he will receive some type of consideration from the state.[69] The simplest form of plea agreement is one in which in return for pleading guilty to one or more

Sentencing is the exclusive province of the court, and a prosecutor has no power to bind the court to a particular sentence. For that reason all the prosecutor can promise is to recommend a particular sentence.

pending charges the prosecutor agrees to recommend a specific sentence, such as probation or a specific number of years in prison, and to dismiss the other pending charges. In a variation of that form of plea bargain the prosecutor can agree to charge the defendant with a less serious offense than those pending against the defendant, and in return for the defendant's plea to that less serious offense agree to recommend a specific sentence to the court on that less serious charge and to dismiss the more serious charges.

Pre-Indictment Plea Agreements and Blind Pleas

Most plea bargaining takes place after a defendant has been charged with a crime. Frequently, particularly in white collar crime and public corruption cases, plea bargaining begins during the investigation. The investigation of those kinds of cases usually takes significant amounts of time and the targets not only retain attorneys to represent them during the investigation, but expect to be charged. Defense attorneys in such cases know that the first people to reach an agreement with the prosecutor, particularly if it is early in the investigation and includes cooperation, usually receive better deals than those who wait until late in the investigation or until being charged. As a result, in white collar crime cases many defense attorneys begin plea negotiations during the investigation. If a pre-indictment plea agreement is reached the prosecutor usually files an information to which the defendant will immediately plead guilty. Sentencing on the guilty plea may be immediate or may deferred until other conditions of the plea agreement, such as cooperation, have been satisfied.

Blind plea is a plea of guilty by a defendant when he has no agreement with the prosecutor.

Frequently a defendant would like to dispose of a pending case without the time and expense of a trial, but is unable to reach a plea agreement with the prosecutor. In such situations the defendant may decide to plead guilty without an agreement. Such a plea is called a **blind plea** and because in most jurisdictions a court cannot force the prosecutor to dismiss a charge, it must necessarily be a plea of guilty to all the charges pending against the defendant. In such cases the court will hold a sentencing hearing at which the prosecutor and defense will present evidence and will each recommend a sentence to the judge. Following the hearing the court will impose a sentence it thinks is appropriate, which may be more or less than what either the prosecutor or the defense attorney recommended.

Plea bargains can often require the defendant to do much more than simply plead guilty to a charge. In some cases the defendant's plea deal can require him to cooperate with the prosecutor in the prosecution of others. That cooperation can include providing information to the prosecutor and testifying against either co-defendants or defendants in other cases. Sometimes cooperation includes working in a covert capacity in an ongoing investigation and surreptitiously recording conversations with the targets of that investigation.

As long as the prosecutor has evidence that would support it, a prosecutor is allowed to try to induce a defendant to enter into a plea agreement by threatening to charge the defendant with a more serious offense[70] or by threatening to charge some third person with a crime.[71] That third person is usually the defendant's spouse, someone with whom the defendant is romantically involved, or a defendant's child. As a result, as part of a plea bargain the prosecutor may agree not to file more serious charges against the defendant or not to charge a third party or to charge a third party with a less serious offense.

Initially plea bargaining is a matter solely between the defense and the prosecution. The judiciary has no role in plea negotiations and is prohibited from initiating them.[72] The reason for excluding the judiciary from the negotiating process is because such participation is considered to be inherently coercive.[73]

Once the prosecution and defense have reached an agreement on a plea the terms are usually presented to a judge in open court. At that point the judge will indicate whether the terms of the plea agreement are acceptable to him or he will reject the agreement. If the judge rejects the terms of the plea agreement, the prosecutor and the defense can try to negotiate a plea bargain they think the judge will accept, they can go to trial, or in an extreme case the prosecutor can *nolle prosequi* all or some of the pending charges.

In some cases the terms of the plea agreement may be presented to the judge in chambers and sealed until the sentence is imposed, at which time the terms of the plea agreement are made public. That procedure is usually followed where as a part of his agreement the defendant will perform some type of covert work for the government and the defendant wants to make sure that the terms of the plea agreement will be accepted by the judge.

The terms of simple plea agreements are seldom reduced to writing and are instead simply announced in court where a court reporter takes them down. Complex plea agreements are, however, reduced to writing and signed by the defendant, her attorney, and the prosecutor.

A plea agreement can only be accepted by and only becomes binding when the defendant pleads guilty pursuant to its terms. That means that the prosecutor can withdraw the agreement any time before the defendant pleads guilty, notwithstanding that an agreement was reached and that the defendant partially performed the agreement in some way, such as by providing information or working in a covert capacity.[74]

People v. Navarroli

Supreme Court of Illinois 121 Ill. 2d 516 (1988)

WARD, J. The defendant, Enricho Navarroli, was charged on September 21, 1982, in the circuit court of Peoria County in an indictment of two counts with unlawful possession of cocaine with intent to deliver (a Class X offense) and with unlawful possession of cocaine (a Class 1 offense). There were plea negotiations between the defendant and the State's Attorney, and on August 27, 1984, the defendant moved to compel the State to carry out a claimed plea agreement. He stated that under the terms of the plea agreement, he acted as an informant in various drug investigations in exchange for the State's promise to reduce the charges against him and to agree to his being given probation plus a fine. The defendant alleged that after he assisted law enforcement officials the State's Attorney refused to reduce the charges against him. The State denied both the existence of an agreement and the claimed terms.

At a hearing on the motion, the trial court found that there had been the plea agreement the defendant claimed and it ordered "specific performance" of the agreement. The appellate court reversed (146 Ill. App. 3d 466), and we granted the defendant leave to appeal. * * *

The appellate court, in reversing, held that even if the plea agreement did exist, the defendant was not entitled to specific performance of the agreement, because he was not deprived of his liberty or any other constitutionally protected interest in reliance on the agreement. * * *

The defendant contends too that the appellate court erred in concluding that he was not entitled to specific performance of the proposed plea agreement because he was not deprived of any constitutionally protected interest. He asserts that he surrendered constitutional rights guaranteed by the first, fourth, fifth and sixth amendments in reliance upon the State's agreement to reduce the charge and recommend probation in exchange for his cooperation. * * *

The State argues that even if there was a plea agreement, the defendant was not deprived of any constitutional right by virtue of the State's refusal to comply with the agreement. The defendant is at liberty to proceed to trial. The appellate court, the State says, correctly held that the defendant was not entitled to specific performance of the claimed plea bargain, and the State finally argues that the trial court incorrectly applied a subjective test determining whether there was a plea agreement.

A plea agreement results when the prosecutor and the defendant exchange promises to perform or refrain from performing specified actions. (*People v. Davis* (1981), 94 Ill. App. 3d 809.) The existence of a plea agreement and its terms and conditions are questions of fact which the trier of fact must determine after assessing the credibility of witnesses and the weight to be given their testimony. (*People v. Starks* (1986), 146 Ill. App. 3d 843.) * * * It will not be necessary for us to consider whether, as the State contends, the circuit court's finding that there was a plea agreement, as the defendant claimed, was contrary to the manifest weight of the evidence, nor need we decide whether, in making that finding, the court erroneously employed a subjective, rather than an objective, test. Even assuming, *arguendo*, that the circuit court correctly found that an agreement existed with terms as the defendant alleges, we must conclude that the prosecutor's denial of an agreement and refusal to carry out the claimed bargain did not deprive the defendant of due process, and that therefore, the defendant was not entitled to have the assumed agreement enforced.

The enforceability of plea agreements was recognized in *Santobello v. New York* (1971), 404 U.S. 257, where the Supreme Court held that a defendant who enters a guilty plea in reliance upon the promise of the prosecutor is entitled to a remedy when the prosecutor breaches that promise. The Court cautioned that, "[w]hen a plea rests in any significant degree on a promise or agreement of the prosecutor, so that it can be said to be part of the inducement or consideration, such promise must be fulfilled." 404 U.S. at 262, 30 L. Ed. 2d at 433, 92 S. Ct. at 499.

In *Santobello*, however, the prosecutor breached the plea agreement after the defendant entered a plea of guilty. In *Mabry v. Johnson* (1984), 467 U.S. 504, the Supreme Court determined that the same constitutional concerns are not implicated when the prosecutor takes a course of action inconsistent with an alleged plea agreement before the defendant enters a guilty plea. In *Mabry*, the prosecutor proposed a plea bargain but then withdrew the offer after the defendant's acceptance and proposed a second, less favorable, plea agreement. The Supreme Court rejected the defendant's claim that his acceptance of the first plea bargain created a constitutional right to have that bargain specifically enforced. Relying on due process principles, the *Mabry* Court defined the scope of the constitutional protection afforded a defendant who enters a plea agreement, stating:

> "[A] plea bargain standing alone is without constitutional significance; in itself it is a mere executory agreement which, until embodied in the judgment of a court, does not deprive an accused of liberty or any other constitutionally protected interest. *It is the ensuing guilty plea that implicates the Constitution.* Only after respondent pleaded guilty was he convicted, and it is that conviction which gave rise to the deprivation of respondent's liberty at issue here." (Emphasis added.) (467 U.S. at 507-508.) * * *

The Supreme Court in *Mabry* made it clear that due process principles govern the enforceability of plea agreements. (*United States v. Coon,* (8th Cir. 1986), 805 F.2d 822, 824.) Therefore, the controlling issue here is whether the State's repudiation of the asserted plea agreement constituted a denial of due process, which can be remedied only by allowing the defendant specific enforcement of the agreement. This court recently denied enforcement of a plea agreement in a case involving circumstances resembling those here. (*People v. Boyt* (1985), 109 Ill. 2d 403.) Our holding there governs the disposition of this appeal. In *Boyt*, the defendant agreed to testify against her codefendant in exchange for the State's promise to reduce the charge against her. Before the defendant could testify, however, the codefendant pleaded guilty. When the State thereafter refused to reduce the charges, the defendant sought to enforce the bargain. This court held that, even if there had been an agreement, the defendant did not have a constitutional right under the due process clause to have the agreement enforced. The court reasoned that the State's repudiation of the agreement did not deprive the defendant of liberty or any other constitutionally protected interest because the defendant did not plead guilty in reliance on the agreement.

Here, as in *Boyt*, the defendant has not entered a plea of guilty in reliance on the proposed plea agreement. He cannot say he was deprived of liberty by virtue of the State's refusal to abide by the terms of the claimed plea agreement. The defendant still has the option of pleading not guilty and proceeding to trial. * * *

The defendant states he performed his part of the bargain in reliance on the agreement, making restoration of the pre-plea-agreement status impossible. He urges that specific enforcement is the only remedy which will adequately insure his rights under the due process clause.

Federal decisions have rejected similar arguments in circumstances where, as here, the defendant cooperated with government agents in reliance on an agreement, but did not enter a plea of guilty in reliance on it. In *United States v. Coon* (8th Cir. 1986), 805 F.2d 822, the defendant agreed to plead guilty to a drug offense and to cooperate with Federal authorities in narcotics investigations in exchange for the government's promise not to bring additional charges and to make no recommendation to the court regarding the sentence. The prosecutor, through error, advised the defendant that the crime of which he was accused carried a maximum fine of $25,000. After the defendant fully cooperated with authorities, however, the parties learned that the maximum fine had been increased by statute to $250,000. The defendant pleaded guilty, knowing of the increased fine, and was fined $100,000. The defendant then sought to have his fine reduced to the amount discussed in the plea agreement. The defendant argued that by cooperating with the Federal agents, he had so changed his position in reliance on the erroneous statement in the plea agreement that he could not be restored to the pre-agreement status by pleading not guilty and proceeding to trial. The court rejected the defendant's contention, explaining:

> "The only change in position that can be considered 'detrimental reliance' is the actual entry of an involuntary guilty plea. Not until that point has the defendant been deprived of any constitutionally protected liberty interest. See *Mabry*, 104 S. Ct. at 2546. When, as in this case, the defendant learns of a change in the terms of a plea agreement prior to entering his plea, a detrimental reliance argument is inappropriate. At that stage, the defendant still has the option of pleading not guilty and proceeding to trial." 805 F.2d at 825. * * *

Upon consideration of the circumstances in this case, we have concluded that the prosecutor's stated unwillingness to carry out the alleged bargain did not deprive the defendant of due process and accordingly we reject his claim that specific performance of the bargain is the only adequate remedy. Here, as in *Coon* and *McGovern*, the defendant still has the option of pleading not guilty and going to trial. His right to a fair trial is unimpaired. We agree with one court's observation that "[t]his fundamental right would be belittled if we held it to be an insufficient 'remedy' or result for a defendant who has not been induced to rely on the plea to his detriment." *Government of Virgin Islands v. Scotland* (3d Cir. 1980), 614 F.2d 360, 365. * * *

For the reasons given, the judgment of the appellate court is affirmed and the cause is remanded to the circuit court of Peoria County for further proceedings consistent with this opinion.

Appellate court affirmed; cause remanded.

Case Focus

1. What reason did the court give for rejecting the defendant's claim that due process required the enforcement of the plea agreement?
2. For what reason did the court reject the defendant's argument that, because he did certain undercover work in reliance on the prosecutor's promise of a certain disposition of his case, he was entitled to enforcement of the plea agreement?

• • • • • • • •

G. Pre-Trial Publicity

Reporting by the news media about criminal investigations and criminal prosecutions is protected by the First Amendment.[75] Such reporting can have a positive impact on the criminal justice process. Media reporting at the pre-arrest stage can uncover the existence of certain crimes, warn the public about certain dangers, and aid in the apprehension of suspects.[76] Media reporting, particularly during the pre-trial stage, can also assure the community that law enforcement is doing its job, assuage fears of citizens by reporting that a particularly infamous criminal has been apprehended, and can bring to light evidence that is helpful in exonerating or convicting the defendant.[77]

Media reporting also can have a substantial negative effect, particularly during the pre-trial stage. These effects can include: (1) creating and fanning such a public demand for conviction that a law enforcement agent, prosecutor, or judge will not properly perform his job; (2) poisoning of the jury pool so that any jury that is ultimately chosen will not be impartial and will not base its verdict solely on evidence it hears at trial; and (3) creating an appearance of unfairness where in fact the trier of fact has not been prejudiced.[78]

Courts have the power and the duty to address and try to prevent the negative effects of media reporting. One common way courts do that is by imposing gag orders on both the prosecutor and defense attorney. Such orders prohibit both the prosecutor and the defense attorney from making extra-judicial comments about specific aspects of the case.[79] Such an order can include prohibiting the attorneys for either side from making extra-judicial statements about the character and credibility of a party, the identity or expected testimony of witnesses, the contents of a confession or statement given by a defendant or a defendant's refusal or failure to make a statement, the nature of any physical evidence expected to be presented or the absence of such evidence, the strengths or weaknesses of the case of either party, and any information the lawyer knows or reasonably should know is likely to be inadmissible.[80] The courts also have the power to prohibit witnesses from discussing their proposed testimony with the news media.[81]

EYE ON ETHICS

Limits on Disclosures to the Media

The rules of professional responsibility of every state include a provision that places limits on the content of statements made by the both the defense attorney and the prosecutor.[82] Those rules are enforced through professional discipline and are applicable in all cases.[83] Such rules generally note that certain subjects pose a serious threat to the fairness of a jury trial and then list subjects about which attorneys are forbidden to make extra-judicial statements. The rules also contain a list of subjects about which attorneys are permitted to make extra-judicial statements. An example of one such rule is the following:

RULE 3.6: TRIAL PUBLICITY

1. (a) A lawyer who is participating or has participated in the investigation or litigation of a matter shall not make an extrajudicial statement that the lawyer knows or reasonably should know will be disseminated by means of public communication and would pose a serious and imminent threat to the fairness of an adjudicative proceeding in the matter.

(b) Notwithstanding paragraph (a), a lawyer may state:

(1) the claim, offense or defense involved and, except when prohibited by law, the identity of the persons involved;

(2) information contained in a public record;

(3) that an investigation of a matter is in progress;

(4) the scheduling or result of any step in litigation;

(5) a request for assistance in obtaining evidence and information necessary thereto;

(6) a warning of danger concerning the behavior of a person involved, when there is reason to believe that there exists the likelihood of substantial harm to an individual or to the public interest; and

(7) in a criminal case, in addition to subparagraphs (1) through (6):

(i) the identity, residence, occupation and family status of the accused;

(ii) if the accused has not been apprehended, information necessary to aid in apprehension of that person;

(iii) the fact, time and place of arrest; and

(iv) the identity of investigating and arresting officers or agencies and the length of the investigation.

(c) Notwithstanding paragraph (a), a lawyer may make a statement that a reasonable lawyer would believe is required to protect a client from the substantial undue prejudicial effect of recent publicity not initiated by the lawyer or the lawyer's client. A statement made pursuant to this paragraph shall be limited to such information as is necessary to mitigate the recent adverse publicity.

(d) No lawyer associated in a firm or government agency with a lawyer subject to paragraph (a) shall make a statement prohibited by paragraph (a). *Ill. S. Ct. Rule of Professional Responsibility*, Rule 3.6.

In addition to the generally applicable proscriptions contained in such rules, the Rules of Professional Conduct of many jurisdictions impose additional restrictions that apply only to prosecutors. Those restrictions include a duty to refrain from making extra-judicial comments that would pose an imminent threat of heightening public condemnation of the defendant, except when necessary to inform the public of the nature and extent of the prosecutor's action and that serve a legitimate law enforcement purpose. In addition, such rules often impose a duty on prosecutors to exercise reasonable care that investigators, employees of, or persons assisting prosecutors do not make extra-judicial statements that are forbidden by the rules. An example of one such rule is the following:

3.8: SPECIAL RESPONSIBILITIES OF A PROSECUTOR

1. The duty of a public prosecutor is to seek justice, not merely to convict. The prosecutor in a criminal case shall:

   (f) except for statements that are necessary to inform the public of the nature and extent of the prosecutor's action and that serve a legitimate law enforcement purpose, refrain from making extrajudicial comments that pose a serious and imminent threat of heightening public condemnation of the accused and exercise reasonable care to prevent investigators, law enforcement personnel, employees or other persons assisting or associated with the prosecutor in a criminal case from making an extrajudicial statement that the prosecutor would be prohibited from making under Rule 3.6 or this Rule. *Ill. S. Ct. Rule of Professional Responsibility*, Rule 3.8.

The Duke Rape Case: Prosecutorial Misconduct on Steroids Aided and Abetted by the Media

Christened by the media as the Duke lacrosse team rape case, but ultimately recharacterized as the rape that never happened case,[84] the Duke lacrosse team rape prosecution saw the conjunction of a rogue district attorney with an ideologically driven media that produced a perversion of justice[85] and resulted in the prosecution of three innocent men.[86] Within ten months of initiation the prosecution's case fell apart. The North Carolina Attorney General took over the prosecution from the district attorney, dismissed all of the charges, and in a rare action declared the three defendants innocent. In the aftermath, Michael Nifong, the district attorney who initiated the prosecution and pursued it until the Attorney General stepped in, resigned from office and was disbarred for failing to disclose exculpatory evidence, for making numerous improper statements to the news media, and other actions that violated the state's rules of professional conduct for attorneys.[87]

The facts of the case were simple. The co-captains of the Duke University lacrosse team held a party in their home in Durham, North Carolina and hired two strippers from an escort service to provide entertainment.[88] Both of the strippers were black. One of the strippers was Crystal Magnum, who showed up at midnight and performed for approximately four minutes. By 12:30 a.m. Magnum was passed out in the apartment. The other stripper put Magnum in her car and drove to a grocery store where she asked for help for Magnum. A security guard at the store who called the police assumed that Magnum was drunk and had passed out.

When the police took Magnum into custody she said nothing about being raped. Some time later, apparently in an effort to account for her incoherent condition and to avoid being re-committed to a mental health facility,[89] Magnum claimed to have been gang raped at the party. Early in the morning of March 14, 2006, shortly after the rape allegedly occurred, a rape kit was used to collect evidence from Magnum's body.[90] On March 23, 2006 DNA evidence was secured from all the Caucasian members of the lacrosse team and District Attorney Nifong learned of the alleged gang rape.[91] The next day Nifong personally took charge of the case.[92]

The evidence collected from Magnum's body was sent to the state crime lab, which on March 30, 2006 informed Nifong that it could not find any semen, blood, or saliva in the samples taken.[93] Nifong had that evidence plus the DNA samples collected from the Caucasian lacrosse team members sent to a private lab, DNA Security, Inc. (DSI) for more sophisticated testing.[94] In addition to that material Nifong also had two false fingernails sent to DSI. The fingernails had been found by police when they executed a search warrant for the apartment where the crime was alleged to have occurred.

By April 20, 2006 DSI had identified DNA from four different males in evidence collected from Magnum's body but excluded all the Duke lacrosse team members as possible sources of that DNA.[95] DSI informed Nifong of those findings.[96] The findings were exculpatory not only because they tended to exclude the defendants as persons who had engaged in sex with Magnum, but also because they showed recent sexual activity by her, which could explain swelling found on parts of Magnum's body during her medical examination.[97]

DSI found DNA material on one of the false fingernails recovered during the search of the apartment and was able to match it with the DNA of one of the lacrosse team members. Since the lacrosse team member to whom the DNA matched lived in the apartment where the fingernail was found, the DNA match was not particularly probative. Once DSI's findings became known to Nifong he met with the president of DSI. During that meeting, Nifong and DSI's president agreed that only the results of the DNA matches would be reported.[98]

Early in the investigation Magnum was interviewed several times and told prosecutors different and implausible accounts of the alleged rape.[99] As part of the investigation Magnum viewed three different photo-identification lineups. In two of the lineups Magnum could not identify anyone as her rapist.[100] In a third photo lineup at which Nifong told Magnum all of the photos were lacrosse team players Magnum identified three men as her rapists.[101] None of the men Magnum identified bore any resemblance to the descriptions that she had previously given to police.[102] In fact, one of the three men was able to produce cell phone records, a time stamped photo at an ATM, and taxi records that showed he could not have been at the party when the rape allegedly occurred.[103] Ultimately the three men were charged.

From the time he took over the case and until the filing of ethics complaints forced him to turn the prosecution over to the North Carolina Attorney General, Nifong repeatedly violated professional responsibility rules whose purpose is to try to ensure a fair trial and ignored his duty as a prosecutor to "do justice."

The North Carolina Bar charged Nifong with making 49 different pre-trial statements to the media the contents of which violated either Rule 3.6(a), making statements having a substantial likelihood of materially prejudicing an adjudicative proceeding or Rule 3.8(f), making statements that would heighten the condemnation

of the accused.[104] Among those statements were ten statements relating to the lacrosse team members' failure or refusal to give information to law enforcement and their invocation of their constitutional rights, another ten were alleged to be improper commentary on the guilt of the defendants or expressions of opinion that a crime occurred, and statements that asserted a racial motivation for the alleged attack.[105]

The North Carolina Bar also charged Nifong with failing to disclose potentially exculpatory information regarding the male DNA found in the evidence obtained from Magnum's body, failure to comply with discovery requirements, and making false statements to opposing counsel and the court regarding the DNA.[106]

The North Carolina Bar found that Nifong violated both Rule 3.6(a) and Rule 3.8(f), as well as other rules of professional conduct.[107] Ultimately, Nifong resigned as district attorney and was disbarred.

Nifong's improper extra-judicial statements were magnified by mainstream media coverage of the incident that resembled the yellow journalism of an earlier era and that, in its rush to judgment, largely failed to critically examine the purported facts. Indeed, the print and broadcast media coverage of the incident has been criticized as politically predisposed and non-sceptical if not institutionally reckless in its rush to adopt a race-sex-privilege angle[108] and declare the defendants guilty before any evidence was heard.

Coverage by the *New York Times* has been singled out as being particularly egregious and of largely ignoring the law of defamation.[109] While the *Times*'s internal investigation of its coverage exonerated the newspaper and attributed problems in its reporting to journalistic lapses, other members of the media view that conclusion as at odds with the evidence that they claim shows *Times* reporters made mean-spirited, highly inculpatory quantum leaps of logic based on no evidence other than speculation.[110] As an example they cite a 5,600-word article that appeared in the *Times* on August 20, 2006, which attempted to put to rest alarming inconsistencies in Magnum's story. Within hours of its publication the article became a laughing stock.[111] Blogs tore it to shreds exposing factual errors, the omission of critical evidence, and an overall pro-Nifong bias.[112] Dan Abrams, the general manager of MSNBC characterized the article as a "shameful" editorial on the front page of what is supposed to be the news division of the newspaper.[113]

CHAPTER TERMS

Arraignment

Blind plea

Brady material

Discovery

In personam jurisdiction

Open file policy

Plea bargain

Recognizance bond

Trial *in absentia*

REVIEW QUESTIONS

1. In criminal cases, why is *in personam* jurisdiction important?
2. How is *in personam* jurisdiction established in a criminal case?
3. What is the primary purpose of bail?
4. What does a court consider when setting bond?
5. If a defendant violates a condition of bond, what sanctions can a judge impose on him?
6. What is a defendant asked to do at arraignment?
7. Who is required to disclose *Brady* material and when must the disclosure be made?
8. Will a failure to disclose *Brady* material always result in a defendant being given a new trial? Does it make any difference if the prosecutor was not aware that the *Brady* material existed?
9. In addition to pleading guilty, what other things, if any, can a defendant be required to do as part of a plea bargain?
10. To induce a defendant to plead guilty, is a prosecutor allowed to threaten to charge a defendant with a more serious offense or to threaten to charge some third person with a crime and, if so, under what circumstances can he do so?
11. How can pre-trial publicity related to a specific case have a positive impact on the criminal justice process?
12. What type of negative effects can pre-trial publicity have on a specific case?

ADDITIONAL READING

Stuart Taylor, Jr. & K.C. Johnson, *Until Proven Innocent* (2007).

Dorothy Rabinowitz, *No Crueler Tyrannies* (2005).

ENDNOTES

1. *Restatement (Third) of The Foreign Relations Law of the United States* §421 (1987) (Database updated June 2015).
2. *State v. So*, 71 Idaho 324 (1951).
3. *State v. Haase*, 446 N.W.2d 62 (S.D. 1989).
4. *State v. Arnold*, 379 N.W.2d 322 (S.D. 1986).
5. *State v. Judkins*, 200 Iowa 1234 (1925).
6. *Terlinden v. Ames*, 184 U.S. 270 (1902).
7. *United States v. Godwin*, 97 F. Supp. 252 (W.D. Ark. 1951), *aff'd*, 191 F.2d 932 (8th Cir. 1951).
8. *U.S. Const.*, Art. IV, Sec. 4, cl. 2; *Biddinger v. Commissioner of Police*, 245 U.S. 128 (1917).
9. *Application of Williams*, 76 Idaho 173 (1955).
10. *People ex rel. Stanton v. Meyerling*, 345 Ill. 598 (1931).
11. *Ex parte Hubbard*, 201 N.C. 472 (1931).
12. *Ex parte Gust*, 828 S.W.2d 575 (Tex. App. Houston 1st Dist. 1992).
13. *State v. Miller*, 480 N.W.2d 894 (Iowa 1992).
14. *State of Ala. ex rel. Governor and Atty. Gen. v. Engler*, 85 F.3d 1205 (6th Cir. 1996).
15. *In re Taylor*, 66 Misc. 2d 1006 (Sup. Ct. 1971).
16. *Factor v. Laubenheimer*, 290 U.S. 276 (1933).
17. *United States v. Alvarez-Machain*, 504 U.S. 655 (1992).
18. *Magisano v. Locke*, 545 F.2d 1228 (9th Cir. 1976).
19. *U.S. ex rel. Neidecker v. Valentine*, 81 F.2d 32 (2d Cir. 1936).
20. *Matter of Extradition of Russell*, 805 F.2d 1215 (5th Cir. 1986).
21. *United States v. Medina*, 985 F. Supp. 397 (S.D.N.Y. 1997).
22. *U.S. ex rel. Giletti v. Commissioner of Immigration*, 35 F.2d 687 (2d Cir. 1929).
23. *Matter of Extradition of Mainero*, 990 F. Supp. 1208 (S.D. Cal. 1997).
24. *United States v. Rauscher*, 119 U.S. 407 (1886).
25. *Ker v. Illinois*, 119 U.S. 436 (1888).
26. *United States v. Salerno*, 481 U.S. 739 (1987).
27. *U.S. Const.*, Amend. 8.
28. *United States v. Salerno*, 481 U.S. at 739.
29. 18 U.S.C. §3142(g).
30. *United States v. Salerno*, 481 U.S. at 739.
31. *Taylor v. United States*, 414 U.S. 17 (1973).
32. *People v. Lindsey*, 201 Ill. 2d 45 (2002).
33. *United States v. Gray*, 441 F.2d 164 (9th Cir. 1971).
34. *Caldwell v. United States*, 160 F.2d 371 (8th Cir. 1947).
35. *See, e.g.*, 725 ILCS 5/113-4(b).
36. *See, e.g.*, 725 ILCS 5/113-4(a) and FRCrP 10(a)(1).
37. *See People v. Lindsey*, 201 Ill. 2d at 45. Under Federal Rule of Criminal Procedure 10(c) video conferencing is only allowed with the consent of the defendant.
38. 373 U.S. 83 (1963).
39. *United States v. Knight*, 342 F.3d 697 (7th Cir. 2003).
40. *United States v. Kennedy*, 890 F.2d 1056 (9th Cir. 1989).
41. *United States v. Knight*, 342 F.3d at 697.
42. *United States v. Kennedy*, 890 F.2d at 1056.
43. *United States v. Knight*, 342 F.3d at 697.
44. *Id.*
45. *In re C.J.*, 166 Ill. 2d 264 (1995).
46. *Lovitt v. True*, 403 F.3d 171 (4th Cir. 2005).
47. *United States v. Pelullo*, 399 F.3d 197 (3d Cir. 2005).
48. *Arnett v. Dal Cielo*, 14 Cal. 4th 4 (1996).
49. *See, e.g., United States v. Pollack*, 417 F. Supp. 1332 (D. Mass. 1976).
50. *See, e.g., United States v. Brown*, 179 F. Supp. 893 (E.D.N.Y. 1959).
51. The rule that established pre-trial discovery in federal criminal cases was not proposed until 1944, 2 Wright & Miller, *Federal Practice and Procedure* §251 (4th ed. 2009), and most states did not adopt discovery rules for criminal cases until the 1950s.
52. *People v. Lemon*, 245 N.Y. 24 (1927).

53. *Weatherford v. Bursey*, 429 U.S. 545 (1979).

54. *United States v. Smith*, 209 F. Supp. 907 (E.D. Ill. 1962).

55. *United States v. Hancock*, 441 F.2d 1285 (5th Cir. 1971).

56. 5 LaFave et al., *Criminal Procedure* §20.2(e) (3d ed. 2007-2008).

57. *Id.*

58. *See, e.g.,* 16A *Ariz. Rev. Stat. Rules Crim. Proc.,* Rule 15.1.

59. *See, e.g., Fed. Rules Crim. Proc.,* Rule 16.

60. *United States v. Alexander*, 789 F.2d 1046 (4th Cir. 1986).

61. *Illinois Supreme Court* Rule 412.

62. *See, e.g., People v. Schmidt*, 56 Ill. 2d 572 (1974).

63. *State v. Skakel*, 276 Conn. 633 (2006).

64. 5 LaFave et al., *Criminal Procedure* at §21.1(a), n.1.

65. *Weatherford v. Bursey*, 429 U.S. 545 (1976).

66. *Newman v. United States*, 382 F.2d 479 (D.C. Cir. 1967).

67. *Id.*

68. *United States v. Gonzalez-Vazquez*, 219 F.3d 37 (1st Cir. 2000).

69. 5 LaFave et al., *Criminal Procedure*, §21.1(a).

70. *Bordenkircher v. Hayes*, 434 U.S. 357 (1978).

71. *United States v. Nuckols*, 606 F.2d 566 (5th Cir. 1979).

72. *See, e.g., Ill. Sup. Ct.,* Rule 402(d)(1).

73. *United States v. Barrett*, 982 F.2d 193 (6th Cir. 1996).

74. *People v. Navarroli*, 121 Ill. 2d 516 (1988).

75. *Nebraska Press Association v. Stuart*, 427 U.S. 539 (1976).

76. 6 LaFave et al., *Criminal Procedure* at §23.1(a).

77. *Id.*

78. *Id.*

79. *Levine v. United States District Court*, 764 F.2d 590 (9th Cir. 1985).

80. *Id.*

81. *In re Russell*, 726 F.2d 1007 (4th Cir. 1984).

82. 6 LaFave et al., *Criminal Procedure* at §23.1(b).

83. *Id.*

84. David J. Elder, *A Libel Law Analysis of Media Abuses in Reporting the Duke Lacrosse Fabricated Rape Charges*, 11 Vand. J. Ent. & Tech. L. 99 (Fall 2008).

85. *Id.*

86. Abigail Thernstrom, *The Massacre of Innocence*, The Wall Street Journal, September 6, 2007.

87. Robert Mosteller, *The Duke Lacrosse Case, Innocence, and False Identifications: A Fundamental Failure to "Do Justice,"* 76 Fordham L. Rev. 1337 (December 2007).

88. Thernstrom, *supra.*

89. *Id.*

90. Mosteller, *supra* at 1358.

91. *Id.*

92. *Id.* at 1348.

93. *Id.* at 1358.

94. *Id.* at 1359.

95. *Id.*

96. *Id.*

97. *Id.*

98. *Id.*

99. Thernstrom, *supra.*

100. *Id.*

101. *Id.*

102. *Id.*

103. *Id.*

104. Mosteller, *supra* at 1348-1349.

105. *Id.* at 1349.

106. *Id.* at 1358.

107. *North Carolina State Bar v. Nifong*, 06 DHC 35, *Findings of Fact and Conclusions of Law* (2007).

108. Elder, *supra* at 102.

109. *Id.*

110. *Id.* at 154.

111. *Id.* at 157.

112. *Id.* at n.399.

113. *Id.*

Chapter 20
Criminal Procedure During the Trial Stage

Chapter Objectives

After reading this chapter, you should be able to

- Explain who has the burden of proof in a criminal trial
- Explain what jury instructions are, who drafts them, and how juries are instructed
- Understand what rights are embodied in a defendant's right to confront his accusers
- Explain what rights are included in the defendant's right to compulsory process
- Understand how the Fifth Amendment privilege against self-incrimination operates during a criminal trial
- Name the different stages of a trial and explain what occurs during each of those stages

> Every person accused as a criminal has a right to be tried according to the law of the land, the fixed law of the land; and not by the law as the jury may understand it, or choose, from wantonness or ignorance or accidental mistake to interpret it. —Justice Joseph Story *United States v. Battiste*, 24 F. Cas. 1042, 1043 (C.C.D. Mass. 1835)

The criminal trial is the culmination of months and sometimes years of investigative work and often many months of pre-trial proceedings and litigation. In this chapter we will examine: (a) the burden of proof in a criminal trial; (b) the rights the constitution gives to those defendants who choose to go to trial; and (c) the stages of a criminal trial.

A. Presumption of Innocence and the Burden of Proof in a Criminal Trial

In criminal cases the defendant is presumed innocent until proven guilty.[1] As a result, in all criminal cases the prosecution has the initial burden of producing evidence that establishes the defendant's guilt. In addition to the burden of producing evidence, through the evidence it offers at trial,[2] the prosecution has the burden of proving all of the elements of the offense charged beyond a reasonable doubt.[3] For example, Maurice kills Linda and is charged with intent to kill murder. To convict Maurice the prosecution must introduce evidence that shows that he committed the crime and that evidence must be strong enough to convince the trier of fact beyond a reasonable doubt that Maurice committed the act that caused Linda's death and that Maurice's act was actuated by his intent to kill Linda.

The presumption of innocence is not specifically stated in the Constitution, but it is considered to be a basic component of a fair trial.[4] Like the presumption of innocence, the beyond a reasonable doubt standard also does not appear in the U.S. Constitution, but by looking at the history and traditions of the United States when the Constitution was adopted, the U.S. Supreme Court has determined that standard is constitutionally mandated.[5]

B. Defendant's Rights at Trial

The U.S. Constitution specifically grants defendants in criminal cases certain trial rights. Those rights were long understood as applying only in federal criminal trials. State constitutions and state law were the source of trial rights for defendants prosecuted in state courts.[6] As with other procedural rights, in a series of cases beginning in the 1950s the U.S. Supreme Court made the trial rights guaranteed by the U.S. Constitution applicable in state criminal trials.

In this section we will examine five basic trial rights found in the U.S. Constitution: (1) the right to trial by jury; (2) the right to a public trial; (3) the right to confront witnesses; (4) the right to use court process to compel the attendance of witnesses; and (5) the privilege against self-incrimination.

1. Right to Trial by Jury

The Sixth Amendment to the U.S. Constitution guarantees defendants in criminal cases a right to a trial by jury. In *Duncan v. Louisiana* [7] the U.S. Supreme Court held that the Sixth Amendment right to trial by jury is applicable to the states. As a result, in criminal cases all trials are by jury unless the defendant waives his right to a jury trial.

The jury that hears a criminal or civil trial is called a **petit jury**. Historically, petit juries consisted of 12 persons and were required to reach their verdict unanimously. Despite that history neither the 12-person size of the petit jury[8] nor verdict unanimity[9] is constitutionally required. Today, federal courts and most states continue to use 12-person juries and continue to require verdict unanimity. Some states, however, have reduced the size of petit juries to fewer than 12 persons and other states allow their juries to reach verdicts by less than unanimous agreement. While each action by itself is constitutionally acceptable, the U.S. Supreme Court has held that in combination both reducing the size of the jury and eliminating the unanimity requirement violates the Sixth Amendment right to trial by jury.[10]

In relevant part the Sixth Amendment provides, "In all criminal prosecutions, the accused shall enjoy the right to a . . . trial, by an impartial jury." *U.S. Const.*, Amend. VI.

Petit jury is a jury usually consisting of 12 persons that in a criminal case determines whether a defendant is guilty or not guilty of the crime with which he is charged.

Jury Selection

Jury selection is done through a process called **voir dire**.[11] During voir dire the prospective jurors (usually called venire persons) are asked questions about their background and about whether they have any knowledge of the case, know any of the parties, witnesses, or attorneys, or have any biases or prejudices. In some jurisdictions the voir dire questioning is done by the judge while in others it is done by the attorneys. In either case, the venire persons are questioned in open court and their questions and answers are taken down by a court reporter. In those jurisdictions where voir dire questioning is done by the judge, both the prosecution and the defense often present proposed voir dire questions to the judge who will decide whether or not to ask them.

Depending on the practice of the judge the prospective jurors may be questioned in panels of 12 or in panels consisting of less than 12 persons. Once questioning of a panel is complete each side is given an opportunity to exercise challenges to any of the persons in the panel. There are two types of challenges. One is called a challenge for cause. Each side has an unlimited number of challenges for cause. An attorney can exercise a challenge for cause when, based on the voir dire questioning, he believes the venire person will not decide the case fairly because of bias; some life

Voir dire is the preliminary examination by a judge or lawyers of prospective jurors for the purpose of exposing any bias or prejudice the potential jurors may have.

experience such as having been a victim of a crime similar to that alleged in the case to be tried; or because of some relationship to the victim, a witness, or the attorneys.

A second type of challenge is called a peremptory challenge. By statute or court rule the prosecution and defense are each given a specific number of peremptory challenges. A prosecutor or a defense attorney can exercise a peremptory challenge to excuse a venire person for any reason other than the venire person's race or sex. When a defense attorney or prosecutor decides to exercise a peremptory challenge he must inform the court that he is exercising it, but he does not need to give any reason for doing so. If a paralegal is assisting a defense attorney or prosecutor during jury selection, often one of her tasks is to keep count of the peremptory challenges used by each side.

Once the peremptory challenges have been exercised and challenges for cause have been ruled on, the judge replaces the removed venire persons with new venire persons. The new venire persons are subjected to voir dire questioning and based on their answers may also be subject to peremptory challenges and challenges for cause. In a practice called back striking, after questioning the replacements an attorney may decide to exercise a challenge against a member of the panel he has already accepted. Many judges do not allow back striking.

Depending on the nature of the trial a court will often seat two or more alternate jurors. The alternate jurors are subject to the same voir dire process as the other jurors and once accepted serve with the other jurors until the jury begins its deliberation. Even though alternate jurors are dismissed when deliberations begin they can be recalled during deliberations if for some reason the number of jurors falls below 12.[12] When that occurs the jury must begin its deliberations over again.[13]

In a jury trial the jurors are the judges of the facts (in bench trial the judge is the judge of the facts),[14] which means that from the evidence it hears the jury determines what occurred. For example, Jorge is charged with murdering Yolanda. At trial Zeke testifies that even though it was dark outside when the murder was committed, he recognizes Jorge as the person who shot Yolanda. In his defense Jorge testifies that he was asleep in bed at the time of the shooting. In a jury trial the jury decides whether Jorge was the shooter.

In both a jury trial and a bench trial the judge is the judge of the law,[15] which means the judge decides what law is applicable to the case. Before the jury considers its verdict the judge tells the jury what the applicable law is, and it is the duty of the jurors to follow the law as the judge gives it to them.[16] The judge relates the law to the jury through jury instructions that he reads to them and that, in most jurisdictions, he also gives to them in written form. The instructions given by the judge cover a number of subjects: They explain the role of the court and jury as well as the role of the prosecutor and defense attorney; they explain the burden of proof; and unless the law of the jurisdiction provides otherwise, they explain that the jury's verdict must be unanimous.

The instructions also include what are often referred to as definitions instructions and issues instructions. The definitions instructions define terms used in the instructions and also define the offense with which the defendant is charged. For example, if a defendant were charged with Mail Fraud, the definition instruction relating to the offense would be as follows:

> A person commits the offense of Mail Fraud when he devises a scheme to obtain money by means of false or fraudulent representations and for the purpose of executing the scheme causes mail to be deposited in the mail in Illinois.

The issues instructions set out each element of the offense charged and tell the jurors that to find the defendant guilty of that offense they must determine that the prosecution has proven each of those elements beyond a reasonable doubt. The issues instructions also tell the jurors that if any one of the elements has not been proven beyond a reasonable doubt they should find the defendant not guilty.

Included with the instructions given to the jurors by the judge are what are called verdict forms. There are two verdict forms for each offense with which the defendant is charged. One form is the not guilty verdict form and the other is the guilty verdict form. The judge's instructions to the jury tell the jurors that they are to select the verdict form that reflects the verdict they have reached and they are to sign that verdict form.

Jury nullification is the name for the proposition that a jury may disregard the law as given by the court and decide a case based on other considerations. *People v. Smith*, 296 Ill. App. 3d 435 (4th Dist. 1998), Steigmann, J., concurring.

A subject often discussed in connection with jury trials is **jury nullification**. Jury nullification is the name for the proposition that a jury may disregard the law as given by the court and decide a case based upon other considerations.[17] Jury nullification occurs when a jury decides to ignore the law or the evidence and acquits a defendant because the jury believes the law under which the defendant is being prosecuted is unjust or because of the race, sex, or some other status of the victim or the defendant. From time to time, in certain cases, American juries have exercised their power to nullify and because there is no appeal from a verdict of not guilty their exercise of that power is not subject to review.[18]

While juries have the power to engage in nullification, they do not have the right to do so.[19] As a result, a defendant has no right to have the jury defy the law or ignore undisputed evidence[20] and consequently, the defense is prohibited from arguing to the jury for nullification[21] and juries are not informed about that power.[22]

People v. Smith

296 Ill. App. 3d 435 (1998)
(Appellate Court of Illinois Fourth District)

McCullough , **J**. Following a jury trial in the circuit court of Sangamon County, defendant Dee M. Smith was found guilty of aggravated battery. 720 ILCS 5/ 12-4(b)(8) (West 1994). She was sentenced to 24 months' probation. The issues are whether * * * (2) the trial court committed an abuse of discretion by answering "no" to the jury's question of whether the jury had "the option of downgrading to a charge of battery," even if it had found the elements of aggravated battery had been proved. Only the facts relevant to the issues will be discussed. * * *

The next issue is whether the trial court committed an abuse of discretion by answering "no" to the jury's question of whether it could downgrade to a charge of battery even if it had found the elements of aggravated battery had been proved.

At trial, prior to jury deliberations, the trial court's instructions to the jury included the following instructions:

> "The defendants are charged with the offense of aggravated battery. The defendants have pleaded not guilty. Under the law, a person charged with aggravated battery may be found (1) not guilty; or (2) guilty of aggravated battery; or (3) guilty of battery."

See Illinois Pattern Jury Instructions, Criminal, No. 2.01 (3d ed. 1992) (hereinafter IPI Criminal 3d). * * *

> "To sustain the charge of aggravated battery the State must prove the following propositions:
>
> First proposition: that the defendant or one for whose conduct he is legally responsible knowingly caused bodily harm to Michelle Ray; and
>
> Second proposition: that the defendant did so while on or about a public place of amusement.
>
> Third proposition: that the defendant was not justified in using the force which she used.
>
> If you find from your consideration of all the evidence that each one of these propositions has been proven beyond a reasonable doubt, you should find the defendant guilty.
>
> If you find from your consideration of all the evidence that any one of these propositions has not been proved beyond a reasonable doubt, you should find the defendant not guilty."

See IPI Criminal 3d No. 11.16.

During deliberations, the jury sent an inquiry to the trial judge. The trial judge's discussion with the attorneys concerning the inquiry was as follows:

"THE COURT: The note which I am marking as Court's Exhibit 1 states: [']Your Honor, twelve out of twelve agree to meeting the following propositions: one, defendants knowingly caused harm to Miss Ray; two, did the above in a public place of amusement; three, degree of force was not justified. Realizing this indicates aggravated battery, do we have the option of downgrading to a charge of battery?[']

What would you like me to respond, [defendant's attorney]?

[DEFENDANT'S ATTORNEY]: Well, I mean I think the answer to the question is yes, under—you know, they can do whatever they decide to do unanimously.

THE COURT: But they have already said they found them guilty of aggravated battery in a public place of amusement.

[DEFENDANT'S ATTORNEY]: But also indicated they don't feel that is a just verdict, but that's reading between the lines; and jury nullification is an appropriate—

* * *

[PROSECUTOR]: Your Honor, I think that they've got the verdicts back there. If they want to come back with a battery, they can elect to do that; and I don't think we should advise them one way or other which verdict form they should use.

THE COURT: What they just said to me—[prosecutor], let me read it again. Defendants knowingly caused harm to Miss Ray. They did it in a public place of amusement. It was not justified. They realize this constitutes aggravated battery, and they want to know that even though they find proposition 1, 2, and 3, can they find—can they downgrade to battery. That's against my instructions.

[PROSECUTOR]: That's right.

THE COURT: So I am going to indicate no in response to the question.

[DEFENDANT'S ATTORNEY]: Then that would be a response over our objection.

THE COURT: Yes, over defendant's objection."

* * *

On appeal, defendant argues that the trial court's response negated the jury's power of "nullification" or "lenity."

Although jury nullification is a possibility (see *People v. Ganus,* 148 Ill. 2d 466, 473 (1992)), the defendant has no right to argue or instruct on jury nullification (*People v. Moore,* 171 Ill. 2d 74, 109-110 (1996)). We also agree with the statement in *People v. Montanez,* 281 Ill. App. 3d 558, 565 (1996), "The power of jury nullification exists, but it is not authorized by the law. A defendant has no right to have the jury defy the law or ignore the undisputed evidence." The question indicated all 12 jurors agreed that all the elements of aggravated battery had been proved. The answer given by the trial court to the jury's inquiry in this case was direct and simply paraphrased an instruction already given to it.

"If you find from your consideration of all the evidence that each one of these propositions has been proven beyond a reasonable doubt, you should find the defendant guilty."

See IPI Criminal 3d No. 11.16. Furthermore, the jurors were provided three verdict forms: (1) not guilty, (2) guilty of aggravated battery, and (3) guilty of battery. They were instructed to select the verdict form which reflected their verdict as to defendant. IPI Criminal 3d No. 26.01. In addition, they were advised that the jury instructions contained the law applicable to this case and that it was their duty to follow all the instructions and not to disregard some. IPI Criminal 3d No. 1.01. In this case, the response given by the trial judge to the jury's inquiry was the correct response in light of the objection raised by defendant. * * *

Affirmed and remanded with directions.

JUSTICE STEIGMANN , specially concurring:

Although I agree with the majority opinion, I write specially to express my rejection of the legitimacy of the concept of jury nullification. However much surface appeal that concept may have, careful analysis shows it to be vacuous and intellectually bankrupt.

Jury nullification constitutes the proposition that the jury may disregard the law as provided by the trial court and instead decide a case based upon considerations that have no legal justification, such as the race, character, or status of either the victim or the accused. Supporters of jury nullification cite instances in which juries have supposedly achieved "true justice" by acquitting a defendant when the evidence concededly proved him guilty beyond a reasonable doubt. Leaving aside the many flaws in such examples, the primary difficulty with the concept of jury nullification is that no principled basis exists for claiming that a jury may choose to disregard the court's instructions on the law *only* when such disregard benefits the accused.

In every criminal case, the trial court instructs the jury on principles of law that are designed to protect the accused, such as the following: (1) the defendant is presumed innocent of the charge against him, and the State has the burden of proving the charge beyond a reasonable doubt (Illinois Pattern Jury Instructions, Criminal No. 2.03 (3d ed. 1992) (hereinafter IPI Criminal 3d)); (2) the defendant is not required to prove his innocence (IPI Criminal 3d No. 2.03); (3) if the defendant does not testify, that fact may not be considered against him in any way (IPI Criminal 3d No. 2.04); and (4) neither sympathy nor prejudice should influence the jury (IPI Criminal 3d No. 1.01). * * *

In addition to instructing the jury regarding things it must do or avoid doing to protect the defendant's rights, the trial court also defines the offense with which the defendant is charged and the State's burden of proof regarding the elements of that offense. For instance, the burglary issues instruction, which sets forth the three propositions that the State must prove, concludes with the following two paragraphs (which are the *same concluding paragraphs* in all but a few of the many dozen issues instructions contained in IPI Criminal 3d):

"If you find from your consideration of all the evidence that each one of [the previously stated] propositions has been proved beyond a reasonable doubt, you should find the defendant guilty.

   If you find from your consideration of all the evidence that any one of these propositions has not been proved beyond a reasonable doubt, you should find the defendant not guilty." IPI Criminal 3d No. 14.08.

Supporters of jury nullification think the second of these paragraphs—the one instructing the jury that it must find the defendant not guilty if the State did not prove him guilty beyond a reasonable doubt—is just fine. Somehow, however, those same supporters claim that a jury may disregard the first paragraph of this instruction. But why should this be so? After all, if a jury is free to use its status as "representative of the community" or "the community's conscience" (or whatever else supporters of jury nullification claim gives the jury the prerogative to reject the trial court's instructions of law), then should the jury not be able to question *any* instruction that it finds questionable or archaic?

   For instance, why should a jury accept the trial court's admonition that the defendant's failure to testify should not be held against him? Clearly, this admonition is counterintuitive. Most jurors would expect in their daily lives that someone accused of criminal behavior would provide some defense or explanation. Most jurors would also conclude that a person's failure to provide some explanation would indicate that he was guilty of the charge.

   In fact, this real-world expectation is the law in almost every other jurisdiction in the world; it just so happens that in the United States, our courts have interpreted the fifth amendment to proscribe such an expectation by holding that a defendant cannot be punished for exercising his constitutional right of silence, even at trial. But, if—as the supporters of jury nullification contend—a jury can reject the trial court's instructions of law, what can be wrong with a juror's thinking the following:

"Not holding a defendant's failure to testify against him might have worked just fine 200 years ago when a bunch of rich, white guys wrote that protection into the Constitution to deal with the kinds of crimes and trials that occurred then, but clearly this archaic bit of colonial fluff has no legitimacy in the modern world of urban violence and street gang murders. It is a concept that has outlived its usefulness, and if it weren't for a bunch of bleeding-heart ACLU-types, we would have gotten rid of it a long time ago so that we could really get tough on vicious criminals."

I note in passing that the above argument might be particularly shocking to those who—in other contexts—endorse the concept of a "living constitution"—that is, the meaning of the constitution must "evolve" over time to meet the exigencies of modern society. Adherents of this view typically argue for a more expansive reading of the constitution, claiming that political positions the adherents deem desirable are required or protected by the constitution. However, no principled reason exists to limit the notion of a living constitution to only *expansion* of constitutional rights; if the constitution is as flexible as the adherents of the "living constitution" assert, then it can just as well diminish the protections it provides (if that is what modern society requires). Indeed, many legal scholars argue that such a reduction has already occurred regarding fourth amendment protections.

Another trial court instruction that a juror might question or disregard is the State's burden to prove the defendant guilty beyond a reasonable doubt. After all, this standard does not even appear anywhere in either the federal or state constitution. Instead, the United States Supreme Court has found this standard to be constitutionally mandated by looking to the history and traditions of this nation almost 210 years ago when the constitution was adopted. But so what? Why should a jury, acting as the modern day "conscience of the community," be limited in its real-world assessment of an accused's conduct by an "understanding" among a bunch of Virginia plantation owners and New England merchantmen, who were running around in three-cornered hats, frequently owned slaves, and observed other customs and practices that would be viewed as highly objectionable—or at least very strange—through modern eyes?

It will not suffice for supporters of jury nullification to point out that when a jury disregards the trial court's instructions and acquits, the State cannot appeal, whereas when a jury disregards the trial court's instructions and convicts, the defendant can appeal. First, the defendant's right to appeal on the basis of jury deliberations is extremely restricted. *People v. Towns,* 157 Ill. 2d 90, 112 (1993) (in evaluating a verdict's validity, a reviewing court may not consider evidence showing jury's deliberative process or its motives or methods in reaching the verdict) * * *. Thus, a defendant who presents affidavits or live testimony from a juror about the jury's disregard of the court's instruction not to hold against the defendant his failure to testify will lose on this claim because a jury is not permitted to impeach its own verdict. The same thing would happen to other claims, such as that the jury disregarded the defendant's presumption of innocence or intentionally lessened the State's burden of proving him guilty beyond a reasonable doubt.

Second, a defendant's appeal on this ground is premised upon a juror's willingness to talk about the jury deliberations and to admit that he or some other juror disregarded some of the court's instructions. However, jurors are under no obligation to speak to anyone about jury room discussions, and one could assume they would be particularly unlikely to do so if they had intentionally disregarded some of the court's instructions designed to provide procedural protections to the defendant, resulting in the defendant's conviction.

The historical circumstances that allegedly justified the concept of jury nullification have long since passed. Justice Harlan explained this best, as follows:

> "[The] principal original virtue of the jury trial—the limitations a jury imposes on a tyrannous judiciary—has largely disappeared. We no longer live in a medieval or colonial society. Judges enforce laws enacted by democratic decision, not by regal fiat. They are elected by the people or appointed by the people's elected officials, and are responsible not to a distant monarch alone but to reviewing courts, including this one." *Duncan v. Louisiana,* 391 U.S. 145, 188, 20 L. Ed. 2d 491, 518, 88 S. Ct. 1444, 1469 (1968) (Harlan, J, dissenting, joined by Stewart, J.).

* * *

As Professor Andrew D. Leipold of the University of Illinois pointed out in his thoughtful article, *Rethinking Jury Nullification,* 82 Va. L. Rev. 253, 294 (1996):

"Virtually every federal court that considered the question [of jury nullification] held, often in blunt language, that there was no right to have juries told of their power. The most detailed opinion came in *United States v. Dougherty*[, 154 U.S. App. D.C. 76, 473 F.2d 1113 (D.C. Cir. 1972), quoting *United States v. Moylan,* 417 F.2d 1002, 1009 (4th Cir. 1969),] where the court not only rejected the defendants' arguments, but denounced the whole notion of jury nullification:

'This so-called right of jury nullification is put forward in the name of liberty and democracy, but its explicit avowal risks the ultimate logic of anarchy. . . . "No legal system could long survive if it gave every individual the option of disregarding with impunity any law which by his personal standard was judged morally untenable."

* * *

Last, we should not forget the disgraceful episodes in our criminal justice system in the 1950s and 1960s when southern juries routinely acquitted those accused—including local law enforcement officers—of beating or killing civil rights protesters despite overwhelming evidence of guilt. With good reason, supporters of jury nullification choose not to remind us of those grim times, but those acquittals reflected the concept of jury nullification "in all its glory."

This court should join the other Illinois courts that have rejected this pernicious doctrine and emphasize that it has no place in any system of justice worthy of that name.

Case Focus

1. What is jury nullification and when, if ever, is a defendant allowed to argue for or ask a court to instruct a jury on jury nullification?
2. Supporters of jury nullification assert that when juries exercise the power of jury nullification by acquitting a defendant who is guilty beyond a reasonable doubt when the interests of "true justice" can be served. How does Justice Steigmann answer that argument?
3. When the court said that juries have the power of nullification but not the authority to nullify what does the court mean?

• • • • • • • •

2. Right to Public Trial

For more than a thousand years Anglo-American law has adhered to the principle that trials should be open to the public.[23] The Sixth Amendment, which guarantees defendants in criminal cases the right to a public trial embodies that principle and makes it a constitutional requirement in criminal cases. The Sixth Amendment right to a public trial is satisfied when a trial is held under circumstances that do not inhibit public attendance or freedom of access[24] and extends from jury selection[25] through the return of verdict.[26] The right also includes certain trial-like pre-trial proceedings, such as motions to suppress.[27]

The U.S. Supreme Court has identified three important benefits that flow from a public trial: (1) knowledge that a trial is or may be reported publicly serves as an effective restraint on the possible abuse of judicial power; (2) the presence of spectators increases testimonial trustworthiness by inducing fear in witnesses that false testimony will be detected; and (3) public disclosure of criminal proceedings may call them to the attention of key witnesses who will come forward.[28] An important exception to the public trial requirement are proceedings in juvenile court. Juvenile court proceedings adjudicate most cases involving crimes committed by underage offenders and are closed to the public.

In some cases defendants have, with the consent or agreement of the prosecutor, sought to close their trial to the public. The Supreme Court has rejected attempts to close criminal trials to the public. In rejecting those attempts the Supreme Court has held that the First Amendment guarantees the public and the news media a right to attend criminal trials that is separate from the defendant's Sixth Amendment right to a public trial and that the public and news media's right to attend such trials cannot be abridged or limited by an agreement between the defendant, the prosecutor, and the court.[29] The Court has held that the First Amendment right to attend a criminal trial extends to pre-trial proceedings.[30]

3. Right to Use Court Process to Compel Attendance of Witnesses

The Sixth Amendment specifically gives defendants the right to use the court's subpoena power to compel the attendance of witnesses favorable to them at trial. In *Washington v. Texas*[31] the U.S. Supreme Court held that this provision of the Sixth Amendment is applicable in state criminal trials. The right to compulsory process includes other rights, such as the right of a defendant to call witnesses at trial,[32] the right to question those witnesses, and the right to present a defense.[33] The defendant's right to compulsory process includes the right to interview witnesses before trial.[34] Witnesses, however, are not obligated to speak to the defendant or his attorney[35] and cannot be compelled by a court to do so.[36]

In relevant part the Sixth Amendment provides, "In all criminal prosecutions, the accused shall enjoy the right . . . to have compulsory process for obtaining witnesses in his favor." *U.S. Const., Amend. VI.*

The right to compulsory process applies only to pending criminal prosecutions[37] and can be lost through waiver or failure to exercise it in a timely manner.[38]

4. Right to Confront Witnesses

In what is usually referred to as the confrontation clause the Sixth Amendment provides that an accused has the right to be confronted by the witnesses against him. The rights embodied in the confrontation clause are viewed as serving several important purposes: (a) assisting the fact finder in evaluating a witness's testimony; (b) establishing the identity of witnesses; (c) impressing on witnesses the seriousness of the occasion; and (d) ensuring that witnesses are not coached or influenced during their testimony.[39] In *Pointer v. Texas*[40] the Supreme Court held that the Sixth Amendment right to confront witnesses applies in state as well as federal criminal trials.

In relevant part the Sixth Amendment provides, "In all criminal prosecutions, the accused shall enjoy the right . . . to be confronted by the witnesses against him." *U.S. Const.*, Amend. VI.

Cross-examination is the opportunity to question a witness for the purpose of attacking the credibility of the witness. *Davis v. Alaska,* 415 U.S. 308 (1974).

The Sixth Amendment right to confront witnesses requires the state to place the defendant's accusers on the witness stand so that the defendant can hear their accusations against him in open court and so that he has the opportunity to **cross-examine** them.[41] Consequently, as it relates to witnesses, the confrontation clause accords a defendant two rights: (a) the right to physically face the witnesses against him and (b) the right to cross-examine those witnesses.[42] The Supreme Court has acknowledged that the face-to-face confrontation of a defendant and his accuser can be a traumatic experience for the accuser, but has said such confrontations are important because they enhance the accuracy of fact-finding by reducing the risk that a witness will wrongfully implicate an innocent person.[43] In that regard the Supreme Court has opined:

> That face to face presence may, unfortunately upset the truthful rape victim or the abused child; but by the same token it may confound and undo the false accuser, or reveal the child coached by a malevolent adult.[44]

To satisfy the Sixth Amendment, the opportunity to cross-examine witnesses must be a meaningful opportunity. Generally that means that defense counsel must have an opportunity to question a witness for the purpose of attacking the witness's credibility by eliciting the existence of any prior felony conviction of the witness, by revealing the witness's bias, prejudice, or ulterior motives[45] or by showing that a witness's testimony is exaggerated or otherwise unbelievable.[46]

The Sixth Amendment right to confront witnesses applies only to criminal prosecutions[47] and does not arise until prosecution is initiated.[48] Once a defendant's guilt has been determined his Sixth Amendment right to confront witnesses ends.[49] Consequently, the Sixth Amendment right to confront witnesses does not apply at sentencing[50] and it does not apply at a hearing to revoke a defendant's probation[51] or parole.[52]

The Sixth Amendment right to confront witnesses is not absolute.[53] Recognizing that and the fact that in cases involving child victims the emotional trauma a child may experience from facing the defendant might render her unable to testify in the defendant's presence, particularly if the defendant is her assailant, many states have adopted statutes that allow such child victims to testify via a one-way closed-circuit television connection so that the child does not see the defendant.[54] Noting that with the exception of the witness not being able to see the defendant, such statutes preserve the essential elements of the confrontation right,[55] the Supreme Court has held such statutes to be constitutional when before using the closed-circuit television procedure the statute requires a court to make a finding that the child will suffer trauma caused by seeing the defendant in the courtroom.[56]

Allowing child testimony by one-way closed-circuit television is a narrow exception to the confrontation clause's physical-presence-in-the-courtroom requirement and is only allowed when the trauma caused to the child witness is caused by the defendant's presence; trauma caused to the child by testifying in court is not by itself sufficient to justify such extra-courtroom testimony.[57]

Defendants can lose their Sixth Amendment right to confront witnesses through forfeiture or waiver. A defendant forfeits his right to confront witnesses against him if he procures a witness's silence or absence through threats, actual violence, or murder.[58] If a defendant is found to have wrongfully procured a witness's silence, the witness's out-of-court statements can be admitted into evidence against the defendant at trial.[59] A defendant can waive the right to confront witnesses against him in a number of ways, including by pleading guilty,[60] failing to object to the use of an out-of-court statement,[61] or failing to exercise the right to cross-examine.[62]

Witnesses often make statements prior to trial that for various reasons the prosecutor wants to use at trial. If the witness appears at trial and is subject to cross-examination the confrontation clause does not bar admission against the defendant of the witness's out-of-court statements.[63] Sometimes, however, because of illness, death, or some other reason a witness who previously made statements implicating the defendant becomes unavailable. Depending on whether or not the witness's statement was testimonial and the satisfaction of certain other conditions, use of those statements against the defendant at trial may or may not be barred by the confrontation clause.

The confrontation clause prohibits the introduction of testimonial statements of an unavailable witness against a defendant unless at the time the witness made the statements the defendant had an opportunity to cross-examine him.[64] Testimonial statements include in-court testimony in some proceeding other than the defendant's trial or its functional equivalent; extra-judicial statements contained in formalized testimonial materials such as affidavits, depositions, prior testimony, or confessions; and statements made under circumstances that would lead an objective observer to believe that the statement would be available for use at a later trial.[65] Generally, statements made to a person who the declarant knows to be a police officer are considered testimonial when there is no ongoing emergency and the primary purpose of the police officer's questions is to establish or prove past events potentially relevant to a later criminal prosecution.[66]

As pointed out above, for an unavailable witness's previous testimonial statements to be admitted against the defendant, at the time those statements were made the defendant must have had an opportunity to cross-examine the witness about them. To satisfy that requirement the defendant must not only have had the opportunity to cross-examine the witness, but at the time he had that opportunity he must have had the same or similar motive and focus to cross-examine as he has at the trial in which the statement is offered. If the defendant did not have that same motive and focus, the admission of the unavailable witness's statement violates the confrontation clause, notwithstanding that the defendant had an opportunity to cross-examine the witness.[67]

For example, on February 18 Luis is charged by indictment with robbing Heather. The indictment alleges that Luis robbed Heather on February 3. On February 23 Luis is arrested and placed on bond, a condition of which is that Luis is not to commit any crimes. On March 6 Luis is arrested again, this time for allegedly robbing Heather on that date. On the basis of the March 6 arrest the prosecutor files a motion to revoke Luis's bond. At the hearing to revoke bond the prosecutor calls Heather as a witness and questions her about what occurred during both the February 3 robbery and the March 6 robbery. The defense attorney only cross-examines Heather about what occurred during the March 6 robbery. Heather dies before trial of the February 3 robbery charge. At Luis's trial on the February 3 robbery charge the prosecutor attempts to introduce into evidence Heather's bond revocation hearing testimony about the February 3 robbery.

Admission of Heather's bond revocation hearing testimony about the February 3 robbery would violate the confrontation clause, notwithstanding that at that hearing Luis's attorney had an opportunity to cross-examine Heather about it, because the motive and focus of Luis's cross-examination of Heather at the bond-revocation hearing was different from what it would be at trial. The motive and focus of Luis's cross-examination in the two proceedings would be different because the issues to be decided in them are different. In the hearing on the motion to revoke bond, the issue the court needed to decide was whether the prosecutors proved that the defendant had violated bond by robbing Heather on March 6, whereas in the trial on the February 3 robbery charge, the issue to be decided is whether Luis robbed Heather on February 3.

People v. Brown

374 Ill. App. 3d 726 (2007)
Appellate Court of Illinois, First District

McNULTY, J. This case comes before us for a second time. The first appeal resulted in a remand for a new trial. On retrial a jury found defendant, Henry Brown, guilty of the aggravated kidnaping and aggravated battery of Gaddis Johnson. Defendant now argues that section 115-10.4 of the Code of Criminal Procedure of 1963 (the Code) did not authorize the introduction into evidence of testimony Johnson gave at defendant's bond hearing. We agree with defendant and therefore we reverse the conviction and again remand for a new trial.

BACKGROUND

On March 8, 1995, two persons came to the apartment Johnson shared with his sister and her children. Johnson left with the two persons. Johnson returned home two days later. Burn marks and other wounds covered much of Johnson's body. Following discussions with Johnson, police arrested defendant. The court released defendant on a bond of $125,000, conditioned on an order not to contact Johnson or his family.

Prosecutors petitioned for a hearing on violation of bail bond, alleging that defendant contacted Johnson and that defendant possessed heroin. At the hearing, begun on August 9, 1996, Johnson testified in great detail, over a continuing relevancy objection, about the kidnaping and battery. He also swore that defendant contacted him and offered him cash and cocaine in exchange for testimony favorable to defendant.

The court delayed cross-examination of Johnson until August 13, 1996. Defense counsel limited his cross-examination to the testimony regarding defendant's contact with Johnson after defendant's release on bond. When the court excused Johnson, the prosecutor asked, "Judge, is counsel waiving his right to complete a meaningful cross of Mr. Johnson?" The attorneys discussed with the court the ramifications of the question:

"MR. KUSATZKY [Defense counsel]: * * * I believe the State has a theory if Mr. Johnson does not appear at trial, they will be asking of the Court to use a transcript of that hearing * * *.

THE COURT: Mr. State's Attorney, do you have any information this witness will not be available for purposes of trial?

MR. ANDERSON [Prosecutor]: I don't know whether he'll be available [f]or trial
* * *. I believe he will be available at trial. * * *

* * *

MR. KUSATZKY: Your Honor, I just want to be clear, I did not cross examine
him on the points of the substantive nature of the allegation * * *.

* * *

THE COURT: * * * I won't have this Court have a legal chess game gentlemen,
it's not going to happen. I called the witness. You have an opportunity to
examine the witness * * * as to all his testimony in this cause. I don't know
whether or not this witness will be available * * * and in fact if he isn't, I don't
even know whether or not I would allow the testimony to stand * * *, but I'm
not going to have this legal chess game * * *.

* * *

* * * Let me end it right now, recall the witness.

You may have an opportunity to examine him."

Defense counsel's subsequent cross-examination of Johnson occupied the
next 35 pages of record.

Johnson died in 1997 from causes unrelated to the offense at issue. Defendant's trial began in 1998. The trial court denied defendant's motion to bar use of
Johnson's prior testimony at trial. The jury found defendant guilty and the court
entered judgment on the verdict.

Defendant appealed, arguing that the court erred by admitting Johnson's
testimony into evidence. We analyzed the admissibility of the testimony under
the standards enunciated in Ohio v. Roberts, 448 U.S. 56, 66 (1990). We said:

> "Where there was adequate opportunity to cross-examine the witness at the prior
> hearing and defense counsel took advantage of that opportunity, the transcript
> bears sufficient indicia of reliability and affords the trier of fact a satisfactory basis
> for evaluating the truth of the prior statement. [Citation.] The opportunity to cross-
> examine is considered adequate and effective only when the motive and focus of
> the cross-examination at the time of the initial proceeding were the same or similar
> to that of the subsequent proceeding. People v. Rice, 166 Ill. 2d 35, 41 (1995).
>
> The motive and focus of the cross-examination at Henry's bond rehearing
> differed significantly from that of his trial. The purpose of the bond rehearing was to
> determine whether Henry had violated the conditions of his bond by contacting
> Gaddis. Although the court improperly expanded the scope of this hearing by
> permitting the State to question Gaddis extensively about the crime itself, the motive
> of the defense during cross-examination remained limited to the allegations of
> Henry's bond violations. As such, we find that Henry did not have an adequate
> opportunity to effectively cross-examine Gaddis at the bond rehearing and that the
> admission of the testimony violated the confrontation clause." People v. Brown,
> No. 1-98-1411, slip op. at 9 (2001) (unpublished order under Supreme Court Rule 23).

* * *

On remand prosecutors moved for permission to introduce Johnson's testimony into evidence pursuant to section 115-10.4 of the Code. * * *

The court held:

"There was a cross-examination at the bond hearing. I've reviewed the cross-examination of Mr. Kusatzky of Mr. Johnson. It's within this Court's opinion that it was an adequate cross-examination."

The court allowed the prosecutor to read Johnson's testimony to the jury on retrial. * * *

The jury found defendant guilty of aggravated battery and aggravated kidnaping. The court sentenced defendant, as a habitual criminal, to natural life in prison. Defendant filed a timely appeal.

ANALYSIS

Defendant raises only one issue on appeal. He contends that the trial court erred again by permitting prosecutors to read to the jury the testimony Johnson gave at the bond hearing. We review the trial court's decision for abuse of discretion.

Defendant has a constitutional right to confront the witnesses against him. Crawford v. Washington, 541 U.S. 36 (2004). The constitution permits use of a witness's testimonial statement against a defendant only if (1) the declarant cannot appear at trial and (2) the defendant had an opportunity to cross-examine the witness when the witness made the statement. Crawford, 541 U.S. at 60. Most courts have required that the cross-examiner must have had the same motive at the time of cross-examination as he would have for cross-examination of the witness at trial. See Willingham v. State, 279 Ga. 886, 887 (2005). * * *

* * *

As we held in our order on the initial appeal here, the issues at the bond hearing differed significantly from the issues at trial. Persuasive precedent from other jurisdictions holds that issues at the bond hearings in those cases differed too much from the issues at trial for the admission into evidence of testimony from the bond hearings. Dickson v. State, 281 Ga. App. 539, 540, 636 S.E.2d 721, 723 (2006); People v. Vera, 153 Mich. App. 411, 416 (1986).

Here, at the bond hearing the court needed to decide whether the prosecutors proved that defendant had contacted Johnson in violation of the conditions of the bond and whether defendant possessed heroin while free on bond. At trial the jury needed to decide whether prosecutors proved beyond a reasonable doubt that defendant kidnaped Johnson and committed aggravated battery against him. The issues at the two hearings have little in common.

The prosecution argues that the judge changed the motive for the cross-examination at the bond hearing. The judge told defense counsel that counsel could not reserve for trial the cross-examination of Johnson on testimony about the aggravated battery and aggravated kidnaping. After the ruling counsel questioned Johnson about the offenses. The extended cross-examination uses 35 pages of the trial record.

In effect the trial court sought to change the character of the bond hearing. As defense counsel pointed out at the bond hearing, the prosecutors questioned

Johnson as though they expected him not to appear at trial. The trial court permitted the prosecution to proceed as though the bond hearing became an evidence deposition, which would preserve for trial Johnson's testimony on issues that had no bearing on the allegations that defendant violated the conditions of his bond. See Suffolk v. Chapman, 31 Ill. 2d 551, 559 (1964). * * * [A court can only allow an evidence deposition upon motion of a party with 21 days advance notice and when the party filing the motion shows certain specified grounds for that exceptional procedure. The prosecution failed to provide the required advance notice and did not show the necessary grounds to obtain an evidence deposition.]

The attempt to convert the bond hearing to an evidentiary deposition did not change defense counsel's basic motivation at the hearing. The court needed to decide only whether defendant contacted Johnson in violation of the conditions of the bond. While defense counsel had reason to attack that aspect of Johnson's testimony, he had no reason to reveal his trial strategy for impeaching Johnson's testimony concerning the kidnaping and battery. We hold that defense counsel did not have a similar motive for cross-examining Johnson at the bond hearing as he would have had for cross-examination at trial. * * *

Reversed and remanded.

Case Focus

1. When does the confrontation clause allow the out of court statement of a witness to be used against a defendant at trial?
2. In this case the defendant's lawyer had the opportunity to cross-examine the witness about the bond hearing. Why did the court of appeals hold that it was error to admit the witness's bond hearing testimony at the defendant's trial?

• • • • • • • •

If the statements made by the unavailable witness were non-testimonial, the confrontation clause does not bar their admission if the statements bear particularized guarantees of trustworthiness.[68] Generally, statements elicited by law enforcement agents to secure a volatile scene or to determine the need for medical care[69] and statements made to direct police to a crime in progress[70] are considered to be non-testimonial.

In addition to embodying a right of a defendant to insist that his accusers physically appear in court, the confrontation clause also embodies a right of the defendant to be present at every stage of a criminal proceeding.[71] A defendant can forfeit that right by choosing not to be present at some stage of the proceeding or trial[72] or by being disruptive during court proceedings.[73] If a defendant is disruptive at trial or during some court proceeding, a court has the power to remove him from the courtroom.[74]

5. *Privilege Against Self-Incrimination*

In an earlier chapter we examined the Fifth Amendment privilege against self-incrimination and how that privilege operated in the investigative stage of the criminal justice process. The Fifth Amendment privilege also operates in the trial stage of the criminal justice process, though differently than it operates in the investigative stage. During the trial stage the Fifth Amendment privilege prohibits the prosecutor from calling the defendant as a witness[75] thereby foreclosing the prosecutor from putting the defendant on the witness stand and in the presence of the trier of fact posing questions to the defendant and forcing her either to answer those questions or to assert the Fifth Amendment privilege.

The Fifth Amendment privilege allows a defendant to choose whether or not to testify at his trial. When a defendant chooses not to testify at his trial, it necessarily raises a question of whether the prosecutor can comment on the defendant's failure to testify and whether and how the jury should be instructed about the defendant's silence.

Historically, the states differed. Some states held that under their state privilege against self-incrimination the prosecutor could comment in closing argument on the defendant's failure to testify and had jury instructions through which the court told the jury that it could infer that if the defendant could truthfully deny or explain the evidence against him he would have testified.[76] Others states held that comment by the prosecutor about the defendant's failure to testify and giving an instruction that told the jury it could infer the defendant's guilt from his failure to testify violated the defendant's privilege against self-incrimination.[77]

In *Griffin v. California*[78] the U.S. Supreme Court held that both a comment by the prosecutor on the defendant's failure to testify and an instruction by the court that told the jury it could infer guilt from the defendant's failure to testify violate the defendant's Fifth Amendment privilege against self-incrimination.[79] Today, in many jurisdictions the defendant is given the option of having the court instruct the jury that the fact the defendant did not testify should not be held against her. In those jurisdictions a court can only give that instruction if the defendant requests it.

While the privilege against self-incrimination prohibits a prosecutor from commenting on a defendant's failure to testify, it does not prohibit him from commenting on the state of the evidence.[80] Accordingly, it does not violate the Fifth Amendment privilege of a defendant who did not testify for a prosecutor to point out during closing argument that certain evidence is uncontradicted or is unrebutted.[81]

C. Stages of a Criminal Trial

Opening statement in a criminal case is a statement made by the prosecutor or defense attorney to the trier of fact that acquaints the trier of fact with the facts he expects to prove at trial. *Illinois Pattern Jury Instructions* 1.03.

Direct examination is the initial questioning of a witness by the party who called the witness to testify.

A **leading question** is a question that suggests or puts an answer in the mouth of a witness and is not simply a question that calls for a yes or no answer. *Porter v. State*, 386 So. 2d 1209 (Dist. Ct. of App. of Fla. 3d Dist. 1980). A question that calls for a yes or no answer is leading only if it suggests one of those answers. *Id.* For example, the following question is not leading: "At any time did you intentionally strike anybody with this axe?" *State v. Abbott*, 36 N.J. 63 (1961), but a question phrased as follows would be leading: "At no time did you intentionally strike anybody with this axe, did you?"

All criminal trials consist of several distinct stages. In this section we will learn what those stages are and briefly examine what occurs in each of them.

In the ordinary course of a trial the first stage is the **opening statement**. In that stage the prosecutor and the defense attorney each give the trier of fact an overview of what the case is about, the facts they each expect to prove, and the evidence that will be introduced to prove those facts. In their opening statements the attorneys frequently will tell the trier of fact not only who the witnesses at trial will be but what they expect those witnesses will say when they testify. The prosecutor makes his opening statement first, following which the defense attorney has an opportunity to make an opening statement. In some jurisdictions the defense is allowed to postpone making an opening statement until after the prosecution rests and it is the defense's turn to put on evidence.

When opening statements are completed the evidentiary stage of the trial begins. Paralegals may assist defense attorneys and prosecutors in a number of ways during this stage. That assistance can include giving the attorneys the documents and other exhibits they will use when they question a particular witness and operating computers and other devices that project pictures and documents for the trier of fact to see when the witness is being questioned about them.

The evidentiary stage of the trial starts with what is called the prosecution's case in chief. During the prosecution's case in chief the prosecutor calls witnesses and introduces exhibits for the purpose of proving the elements of the crimes with which the defendant stands charged. The prosecutor's initial questioning of his witnesses is called **direct examination**. On direct examination the questions must call for relevant and material testimony from the witnesses[82] and, except in certain limited situations, **leading questions** are not permitted.[83]

When the prosecutor completes his direct examination of a witness the defense attorney is given an opportunity to cross-examine the witness. Generally, cross-examination is limited to questioning on the subjects covered during direct examination and to developing circumstances within the witness's knowledge that explain, qualify, discredit, or destroy the credibility of his testimony.[84] On cross-examination an attorney is allowed to ask the witness leading questions.

When the defense completes cross-examination of the witness, the prosecution is given an opportunity to question the witness again. That

Re-direct examination is the questioning of a witness after cross-examination.

second round of questioning is called **re-direct**. On re-direct the prosecutor is limited to asking questions about matters covered in cross-examination and, as on direct examination, leading questions are not permitted.[85] When re-direct examination is completed the defense is again given an opportunity to question the witness in what is called re-cross.

When all of the prosecutor's witnesses have testified and all of the prosecutor's exhibits have been offered and their admission ruled on by the court, the prosecution rests its case and at that point the prosecution's case in chief is over. Once the prosecution rests the defense may, if it chooses to do so, make a motion for a directed verdict. If the case is being tried before a jury, that motion is made and argued outside the presence of the jury. In the motion for a directed verdict the defendant argues that, and the court must decide whether the prosecution's evidence was insufficient to prove the elements of the offenses charged.[86] If the judge agrees with the defendant and grants the motion, the defendant is found not guilty and the case is over.

If the judge denies the defendant's motion for a directed verdict, the evidence stage of the trial continues and the defense begins its case in chief. Just as in the prosecution's case in chief, during the defense's case in chief the defense calls its witnesses and attempts to introduce its exhibits. As with the prosecution's witnesses, defense witnesses are subject to direct and re-direct examination by the defense attorney and to cross- and re-cross-examination by the prosecutor.

At some point before the defense concludes its case in chief and, if it is a jury trial, outside the presence of the jury, the judge will inquire whether the defendant is going to testify and usually will ask the defendant if he has discussed that decision with his attorney. The judge will then have a colloquy with the defendant. If the defendant has said he will not be testifying, during the colloquy the judge will advise the defendant that he has a right to testify, will ask the defendant if he understands that right, and will ask him, if knowing that he has that right he is still choosing not to testify. If the defendant has told the judge that he has decided to testify, during the colloquy the judge will advise the defendant that he has a right not to testify and will ask if knowing about that right it is still his decision to testify.

When the defense rests, the prosecution has the opportunity to put on what is called its rebuttal case. In the rebuttal case the prosecution can call witnesses and seek to introduce other evidence that rebuts the evidence that the defendant introduced during his case in chief. If the prosecution puts on a rebuttal case, the defense is also given an opportunity to put on a rebuttal case. In the defense's rebuttal case the defendant can call witnesses and introduce other evidence that answers evidence put on by the prosecution during its rebuttal case. If the prosecution chooses not to put on a rebuttal case, the evidentiary stage of the trial ends.

Instruction conference in a criminal trial is the meeting of the prosecutor, the defense attorney, and the judge outside the presence of the jury during which the prosecutor and defense attorney offer their proposed instructions for the jury to the judge and the judge decides what instructions will be given.

If the trial is a jury trial, at this point the judge will usually hold what in many jurisdictions is called an **instruction conference**. The instruction conference is held outside the presence of the jury. At the instruction conference the prosecution and the defense offer jury instructions that they feel state the law applicable to the case. The judge reviews the proposed instructions with the parties and indicates for the record and to them which instructions he will give and which ones he is refusing. The defense and the prosecution are given an opportunity to object to the

Drafting Jury Instructions

One of the tasks frequently assigned to paralegals who work in the field of criminal law is to prepare jury instructions. Virtually every American jurisdiction has standard jury instructions for criminal cases, which are usually referred to as pattern jury instruction. Those instructions cover all aspects of the trial, including telling the jury its role in a criminal trial and what the prosecution must prove to establish the defendant's guilt. Each instruction is given a unique number by which it is identified. In criminal trials the prosecution prepares and provides to the judge and the defense a complete set of instructions for the case. The defense usually prepares only the specific instructions it is requesting the court to give that differ from or are not covered by the jurisdiction's pattern instructions.

Jury instructions given to the judge and opposing counsel for use in the instruction conference are put in a standard format. The instructions state each proposition of law in a neutral fashion. Each legal proposition is stated on a single page on the lower left-hand side of which the instruction: (1) indicates whether it is a prosecution or defense instruction; (2) states the pattern instruction number that the instruction reproduces or states that it is not a pattern instruction; and (3) if it is not a pattern instruction, it cites the legal authority on which the instruction is based. The cited legal authority can be a statute, a court decision, or an administrative regulation.

When the prosecutor and the defense tender their proposed jury instructions to the judge, they also provide the judge with a duplicate set of instructions. The duplicate set of instructions sometimes referred to as "the clean set" is identical to the other set given to the judge except that the duplicate instructions contain no indication that they are either the prosecution's or defense's instructions and do not contain any citation to the authority upon which the instruction is based. When the judge decides what instructions he will give to the jury, he selects those instructions from the duplicate set and has them physically given to the jury before it begins its deliberations.

giving of any particular instruction and to give argument to the court to support their position.

Following the instruction conference or, in the case of a bench trial, after the close of the evidentiary stage of the trial, is the **closing argument** stage. In the closing argument stage of the trial the prosecution and the defense are given an opportunity to argue to the trier of fact about what facts they believe the evidence established, what can be inferred from the evidence, and why the testimony of certain witnesses may or may not be credible. In his closing argument the prosecutor frequently will read the issues instruction to the jury and then explain how the evidence proves each proposition it contains. Similarly, a defense attorney may use the jury instructions to argue how the evidence establishes the elements of an affirmative defense.

In most jurisdictions the prosecutor makes his closing argument first. In some jurisdictions this is referred to as the prosecutor's "opening-close." After the prosecutor completes his closing argument the defense has an opportunity to make its closing argument. If the defense chooses to make a closing argument, the prosecution has the opportunity to make a rebuttal argument. In the rebuttal argument the prosecutor is limited to responding to arguments made by the defense in its closing argument. In some cases, usually involving bench trials, the prosecutor will waive the opening close but reserve rebuttal.

In some jurisdiction the closing argument order is different. In those jurisdictions, the defense makes its closing argument first after which the prosecution makes its closing argument. In these jurisdictions there is no rebuttal argument.

Once the closing arguments are completed the instruction stage of the trial begins. During the instruction stage the judge instructs the jury as to the law applicable to the case by reading the jury the instructions that, during the instruction conference, the judge decided should be given. When the judge has finished instructing it the jury is taken to a jury room where it deliberates on the verdict. A court official such as a bailiff is assigned to assist the jury. Before deliberations begin, that official brings the jury the exhibits that were admitted during the trial and the instructions that the judge read when he instructed the jury on the law. During deliberations he brings meals to the jury and if the jury has questions he takes notes containing those questions to the judge.

When a verdict is reached the jury notifies a court officer, usually a bailiff assigned to the jury, that it has reached a decision. The bailiff then informs the judge that a verdict has been reached following which the prosecutor and defense attorney are contacted so that they can return to the courtroom.

Once the judge, the attorneys, and defendant are present in court the jurors are brought back into the courtroom. In most jurisdictions the foreperson of the jury gives all of the verdict forms to the bailiff who

Closing argument in a criminal trial is an argument made by the prosecutor or the defense attorney to the trier of fact that discusses the facts and circumstances of the case and is limited to the evidence and reasonable inferences that can be drawn from the evidence. *Illinois Pattern Jury Instruction* 1.03.

hands them to the court clerk or judge. The verdict forms executed by the jurors are then read out loud in open court. Once the verdict is read the defense, and in some jurisdictions, the prosecutor as well, can ask the judge to poll the jury. In that process the judge asks each individual juror in open court if the verdict reached is his or her verdict.

If the jury acquits the defendant the case is over and if the defendant is in custody he is released from jail. If the jury finds the defendant guilty the judge will set the case for a sentencing hearing (sentencing is discussed in the next chapter) and give the defense time to file post-trial motions, such as a motion for a new trial or a motion for judgment notwithstanding the verdict, often referred to as "judgment nov." If the defendant is on bond when the guilty verdict is returned, the prosecutor will frequently make a motion to revoke the defendant's bond or to increase it.

Hung jury is a jury that is not able to reach a verdict.

If the jury is not able to reach a verdict, it is said to be deadlocked. That is commonly referred to as a **hung jury**. When the jury is unable to reach a verdict, the judge will declare a mistrial and will usually give the prosecutor some short period of time to decide whether he will re-try the defendant on the charges on which the jury deadlocked or dismiss them.

CHAPTER TERMS

Closing argument
Cross-examination
Direct examination
Hung jury

Instruction conference
Jury nullification
Leading question
Opening statement

Petit jury
Re-direct examination
Voir dire

REVIEW QUESTIONS

1. In a jury trial who is the judge of the law and who is the judge of the facts?
2. What is jury nullification and does a defendant have a right to have a jury engage in nullification?
3. What are three benefits that the U.S. Supreme Court has identified as flowing from a public trial?

4. When, if at all, can a defendant have a court close his trial to the public?
5. What rights of a defendant, if any, are included in the compulsory process clause of the Sixth Amendment?
6. Are witnesses obligated to speak to defense attorneys about their testimony prior to trial?

7. What does the confrontation clause of the Sixth Amendment require the prosecution to do with a defendant's accusers?

8. As it relates to witnesses, what rights does the Sixth Amendment's confrontation clause give to defendants?

9. When, if ever, may a court allow a child witness to testify via a one-way closed-circuit television connection?

10. How can defendants lose their Sixth Amendment right to confront witnesses against them?

11. When can out-of-court statements of an unavailable witness be used at trial against a defendant?

12. For purposes of the confrontation clause, what are testimonial statements of a witness?

13. Does the Fifth Amendment privilege against self-incrimination prohibit the prosecutor from calling a defendant to the witness stand at the defendant's trial or does it allow the prosecutor to call the defendant and ask him questions about the offense?

14. In closing argument, is the prosecutor allowed to point out to the jury that the defendant did not testify and that ordinarily a person who is accused of a crime would want to testify, if he could do so truthfully, that he did not commit the crime with which he is charged?

15. What occurs during the evidentiary stage of a trial?

16. What is an instruction conference and when does it usually take place?

17. In a criminal trial, what is a motion for a directed verdict and when is it made?

18. What occurs when a jury is polled?

19. Who has the burden of proof in a criminal trial?

20. When a jury is deadlocked, what does the judge do?

ENDNOTES

1. *Clark v. Arizona*, 548 U.S. 735 (2006).
2. *Government of the Virgin Island v. Torres*, 161 F. Supp. 699 (D. V.I. 1958).
3. *Sherrod v. State*, 280 Ga. 275 (2006).
4. *State v. Snell*, 892 A.2d 108 (R.I. 2006).
5. *People v. Smith*, 296 Ill. App. 3d 435 (4th Dist. 1998), Steigmann, J., concurring.
6. State constitutions and state law gave state defendants virtually the same trial rights as federal defendants. Some states, however, interpreted some of their state's trial rights more narrowly than the same federal trial right.
7. 391 U.S. 145 (1968).
8. *Williams v. Florida*, 399 U.S. 78 (1970).
9. *Apodaca v. Oregon*, 406 U.S. 404 (1972).
10. *Burch v. Louisiana*, 441 U.S. 130 (1979).
11. *See United States v. Orenuga*, 430 F.3d 1158 (D.C. Cir. 2005).
12. *See United States v. Warner*, 498 F.3d 666 (7th Cir. 2007). *Warner* includes a discussion about misconduct by prospective jurors during voir dire as well as removal of jurors after deliberations have begun when it is discovered that certain jurors gave false answers during voir dire questioning.
13. *Id.*
14. *Sparf & Hansen v. United States*, 156 U.S. 51 (1895). Early in American history some jurisdictions allowed or provided that a jury in a criminal case determined both the law and the facts. *See, e.g., State v. Wilkinson*, 2 Vt. 480 (1829).
15. *Sparf & Hansen v. United States*, 156 U.S. at 51.
16. *Id.*
17. *People v. Smith*, 296 Ill. App. 3d at 435, Steigmann, J., concurring.
18. *People v. Rollins*, 108 Ill. App. 3d 480 (1st Dist. 1982).
19. *United States v. Kerly*, 838 F.2d 932 (7th Cir. 1988).
20. *People v. Rollins*, 296 Ill. App. 3d at 480.
21. *People v. Moore*, 171 Ill. 2d 74 (1996).
22. *United States v. Anderson*, 716 F.2d 446 (7th Cir. 1983).
23. *Bright v. States*, 875 P.2d 100 (Ct. of App. of Alaska 1994).

24. *Id.*
25. *People v. Harris*, 10 Cal. App. 4th 672 (4th Dist. 1992).
26. *People v. Martinez*, 172 App. Div. 2d 428 (1st Dept. 1991).
27. *Waller v. Georgia*, 467 U.S. 39 (1984).
28. *Richmond Newspapers, Inc. v. Virginia*, 448 U.S. 555 (1980).
29. *Id.*
30. *Press-Enterprise Co. v. Superior Court*, 478 U.S. 1 (1986).
31. 388 U.S. 14 (1967).
32. *Pennsylvania v. Ritchie*, 480 U.S. 39 (1987).
33. *Faretta v. California*, 422 U.S. 806 (1975).
34. *State v. Wilson*, 149 Wash. 2d 1 (2003).
35. *People v. Slabaugh*, 323 Ill. App. 3d 723 (2d Dist. 2001).
36. *Johnson v. State*, 271 Ga. 375 (1999).
37. *United States v. Pizarro*, 717 F.2d 336 (7th Cir. 1983).
38. *Smith v. United States*, 809 A.2d 1216 (D.C. 2002).
39. *State v. Megard*, 320 Mont. 323 (2004).
40. 380 U.S. 400 (1965).
41. *State v. Snowden*, 385 Md. 64 (2005).
42. *Brinson v. Walker*, 407 F. Supp. 2d 456 (W.D.N.Y. 2006).
43. *Craig v. Maryland*, 497 U.S. 836 (1990).
44. *Id.*
45. *Davis v. Alaska*, 415 U.S. 308 (1974).
46. *Pennsylvania v. Ritchie*, 480 U.S. at 39.
47. *Commonwealth v. Wilcox*, 446 Mass. 61 (2006).
48. *SEC v. Jerry T. O'Brien, Inc.*, 467 U.S. 735 (1984).
49. *Commonwealth v. Wilcox*, 446 Mass. at 61.
50. *Commonwealth v. Nunez*, 446 Mass. 54 (2006).
51. *Commonwealth v. Wilcox*, 446 Mass. at 61.
52. *United States v. Hall*, 419 F.3d 980, 985 n.4 (9th Cir. 2005).
53. *United States v. Turning Bear, III*, 357 F.3d 730 (8th Cir. 2004).
54. *See, e.g.,* Maryland Cts. & Jud. Proc. Code §9-102.
55. The elements of the confrontation right are: testimony under oath, contemporaneous cross-examination, and the ability of the judge and jurors to view the demeanor of the witness. *Craig v. Maryland*, 497 U.S. at 836.
56. *Craig v. Maryland*, 497 U.S. at 836.
57. *United States v. Turning Bear, III*, 357 F.3d at 730.
58. *State v. Ivy*, 188 S.W.3d 132 (Tenn. 2006).
59. *Id.*
60. *Florida v. Nixon*, 543 U.S. 175 (2004).
61. *Fowler v. State*, 829 N.E.2d 459 (Ind. 2005).
62. *State v. Fullwood*, 199 Conn. 281 (1986).
63. *California v. Green*, 399 U.S. 149 (1970).
64. *Crawford v. Washington*, 541 U.S. 36 (2004).
65. *Id.*
66. *Davis v. Washington*, 547 U.S. 813 (2006).
67. *People v. Brown*, 374 Ill. App. 3d 726 (1st Dist. 2007).
68. *State v. Pierre*, 277 Conn. 42 (2006).
69. *Commonwealth v. Foley*, 445 Mass. 1001 (2005).
70. *State v. Maclin*, 183 S.W.3d 335 (Tenn. 2006).
71. *Illinois v. Allen*, 397 U.S. 337 (1970).
72. *Taylor v. United States*, 414 U.S. 17 (1973).
73. *Illinois v. Allen*, 397 U.S. at 337.
74. *Id.*
75. *United States v. Housing Foundation of America*, 176 F.2d 665 (3d Cir. 1949).
76. *See, e.g., State v. Baker*, 115 Vt. 94 (1947).
77. *See, e.g., Staples v. State*, 89 Tenn. 231 (1890).
78. 380 U.S. 609 (1965).
79. Because a federal statute barred such argument in federal prosecutions, prior to the *Griffin* decision in 1965 the Supreme Court had never addressed the question of whether the Fifth Amendment barred it. The Supreme Court only faced the issue in *Griffin* because the year before, in *Malloy v. Hogan*, 378 U.S. 1 (1964) the Court decided that the Fifth Amendment privilege against self-incrimination applied to the states.
80. *People v. Turner*, 34 Cal. 4th 406 (2004).
81. *State v. Mason*, 317 N.C. 283 (1986).
82. *People v. Grisset*, 228 Ill. App. 3d 620 (1st Dist. 1997).
83. *People v. Kopcziack*, 312 Ill. App. 3d 843 (3d Dist. 2000).
84. *People v. Piscotti*, 136 Ill. App. 3d 420 (1st Dist. 1985).
85. *People v. Culbreath*, 343 Ill. App. 3d 998 (4th Dist. 2003).
86. *State v. Allen*, 205 Conn. 370 (1987).

Chapter 21

Criminal Procedure During the Post-Trial Stage—Sentencing and Beyond

Chapter Objectives

After reading this chapter, you should be able to

- Understand what collateral consequences of a criminal conviction are
- Explain what a post-trial motion is
- Understand what limits the Eighth Amendment imposes on criminal sentences
- Explain what constitutes cruel and unusual punishment
- Understand the most common types of statutorily authorized sentences for criminal conduct
- Explain who imposes a criminal sentence
- Explain what clemency is and who has the power to grant it

> A punishment, is an evil inflicted by public Authority, on him that hath done, or omitted that which is judged by the same Authority to be a transgression of the law; to the end that the will of men may thereby the better be disposed to obedience. —Thomas Hobbes, *Leviathan*, Chapter XXVIII

The post-trial stage of the criminal justice process begins after a guilty verdict is rendered. A number of different events occur during the post-trial stage of the criminal justice process.

Those events include: the filing of post-trial motions and sentencing and may also include filing of an appeal, filing of post-conviction motions, and filing of a petition for clemency. In this chapter we will examine each of those events.

From a legal standpoint a guilty verdict represents a significant change in a defendant's status. From arrest to charging and throughout trial a defendant is presumed innocent. Once a defendant has been afforded a fair trial and convicted of the offense with which she was charged the presumption of innocence disappears and the defendant is converted to a person found guilty beyond a reasonable doubt.[1]

Being convicted of a crime can often have important **collateral consequences** for a defendant. Frequently, one of the most significant collateral consequences is the loss of certain rights. The states differ widely as to what rights are lost upon conviction of a specific crime.

A **collateral consequence** of a criminal conviction is a consequence that results from an action that may or may not be taken by an agency that the trial court does not control. *People v. Delvillar*, 235 Ill. 2d 507 (2009). For example, for a physician a collateral consequence of being convicted of a felony offense would be the possibility that because of that conviction the state agency that licenses physicians would revoke her license to practice medicine.

In many states a person who is convicted of a felony permanently or temporarily loses his right to vote and also loses his right to possess firearms. In most states a public official who is convicted of committing a felony relating to her official duties, such as being convicted of the felony offense of accepting a bribe, loses her public office, loses her right to hold public office in the future, and loses her government pension. In some states convictions for certain offenses will legally disqualify a person from obtaining certain government-issued licenses. For example, in some states if an individual is convicted of the offense of selling liquor to a minor, that conviction will disqualify him from ever holding a retail liquor license.

Another significant collateral consequence of a criminal conviction is the effect such a conviction can have on an alien. For an alien defendant, depending on the offense, a criminal conviction may bar her from obtaining U.S. citizenship and may also make her subject to deportation.

A. Post-Trial Motions

After a guilty verdict and, in most jurisdictions, before sentencing, a defendant can file a motion that directs the judge to what the defendant believes are erroneous rulings the judge made during trial and based on those alleged errors asks the judge to vacate the guilty finding and grant the defendant a new trial. That motion is called by different names in different jurisdictions, but in many it is referred to as a motion for new trial. Generally, the errors to which that motion is directed must be ones that the defendant preserved during trial through proper objections. If during trial the defendant failed to preserve an error by objecting, the defendant is usually foreclosed from citing that error in a post-trial motion as a basis for a new trial. The post-trial motion is important for defendants because issues not raised in that motion ordinarily cannot be raised on appeal.[2]

B. Sentencing

The sentencing phase of the criminal justice process is the point at which a statutorily authorized punishment is imposed on a defendant for the crimes the defendant was found guilty of committing. The punishment authorized in a sentencing statute and the sentence imposed on a defendant pursuant to that statute are both subject to the limitations of the Eighth Amendment. In this section we will examine three subjects: (1) the limits imposed on criminal sentences by the Eighth Amendment; (2) the most common types of authorized criminal sentences; and (3) who determines which statutorily authorized criminal sentence to impose and how that determination is made.

1. Limitations Imposed by the Eighth Amendment on Criminal Sentences

The Eighth Amendment contains two provisions that impose limits on sentences in criminal cases: the clause that prohibits cruel and unusual punishment and the clause that prohibits excessive fines. Those prohibitions were long understood as applying only to federal criminal sentences. In *Robinson v. California*[3] those prohibitions were made applicable to the states.

The Eighth Amendment provides, "Excessive bail shall not be required, *nor excessive fines imposed, nor cruel and unusual punishments inflicted." U.S. Const.,* Amend. VIII (emphasis added).

a. Cruel and Unusual Punishment

As it relates to sentencing the Eighth Amendment's prohibition on cruel and unusual punishment has two different aspects: it limits the type of punishment that can be imposed and it prohibits punishment that is disproportionate to the crime.[4] In limiting the type of punishment that can be imposed on a defendant the cruel and unusual punishment clause prohibits two types of punishments: those that were considered cruel and unusual at the time the Eighth Amendment was adopted[5] (such as tortuous punishment[6]) and those that are inconsistent with "modern standards of decency."[7]

The Eighth Amendment's cruel and unusual punishment clause does not prohibit capital punishment[8] and, based on practice at the time the Amendment was adopted and the terms of the Constitution itself, it is quite clear that when it was adopted the Eighth Amendment was not intended to prohibit capital punishment.[9] There were, however, certain enhancements to the death penalty at which the Eighth Amendment was clearly directed.[10] Those enhancements were practices that, in an effort to deter certain forms of criminal conduct, were designed to intensify a death sentence by imposing punishments such as execution by burning at the stake and live disembowelment that were worse than death.[11]

As noted above, the cruel and unusual punishment clause also prohibits sentences that are disproportionate to the crime.[12] The method used to determine whether a sentence is disproportionate depends on whether the case involves a non-capital or a capital sentence.

In the case of non-capital sentences the cruel and unusual punishment clause does not require strict proportionality between the crime and the sentence and forbids only extreme sentences that are "grossly disproportionate" to the crime.[13] Within those broad parameters the legislature is free to statutorily prescribe the authorized sentence for a crime,[14] and a sentence imposed within the limits of a statute that conforms to the Eighth Amendment generally will not be regarded as cruel and unusual.[15] Historically, courts have seldom invalidated a non-capital sentence on disproportionality grounds.[16]

In the case of capital sentences the courts engage in a detailed proportionality analysis[17] and apply the proportionality rule much more strictly than in non-capital cases. By applying the proportionality rule in this manner the U.S. Supreme Court has determined that capital sentences can only be imposed for the most serious crimes.[18] Consequently, today the Eighth Amendment's proportionality requirement is understood as limiting application of the death penalty to cases involving intentional murder and crimes that lead to the death of the victim.[19] Judicially excluded from application of the death penalty on proportionality grounds are serious crimes against persons that do not result in death, such as the rape of an adult[20] and the rape of a child.[21] In holding that the death penalty is disproportionate to such crimes the Supreme Court has explained:

> "Rape is without doubt deserving of serious punishment; but in terms of moral depravity and of injury to the person and to the public it does not compare to murder, which does involve the unjustified taking of human life. Although it may be accompanied by another crime, rape by definition does not include the death of . . . another person. The murderer kills; the rapist, if no more than that, does not." *Kennedy v. Louisiana*, 544 U.S. 407 (2008), citing *Coker v. Georgia*, 433 U.S. 584 (1977).

b. Excessive Fines

The Eighth Amendment also prohibits the imposition of excessive fines as punishment for a crime. The prohibition on excessive fines applies to payments made to a sovereign as punishment for a crime[22] and to the forfeiture of a convicted criminal's assets.[23] The prohibition on excessive fines applies without regard to whether the government extracts payment in cash or kind.[24] In determining whether a fine is excessive a court considers whether the fine is disproportionate to the gravity of the offense.[25] For example, a fine of $1 million imposed as punishment on a stockbroker who engaged in insider trading that equals the losses caused by such trading is not excessive,[26] but a $1 million fine imposed on a stockbroker who embezzled $10,000 from his employer would be excessive.

2. *Types of Authorized Sentences*

Legislative bodies have created a broad spectrum of authorized sentences for defendants convicted of crimes. Depending on the crime, a defendant can receive a sentence as severe as death or as slight as a small fine. Authorized sentences can be imposed singly or in combination. For example, a defendant convicted of felony theft could be sentenced to two years in prison and ordered to pay the victim the value of the stolen property. The types of sentences authorized are different for different types of crimes and are often called by different names in different jurisdictions. A paralegal working in the field of criminal law should familiarize herself with the different sentencing alternatives available in her jurisdiction.

A **jail** is a local government's detention center, where persons awaiting trial or those convicted of misdemeanors are confined. *Maryland v. Shatzer*, 559 U.S. 98 (2010), n.2.

The most severe sentenced imposed by some states and the federal government is the death sentence. In jurisdictions with the death penalty, that sentence is limited to certain types of murder cases and to certain other serious offenses.

A **prison** is a state or federal facility of confinement for convicted criminals, usually felons. *Maryland v. Shatzer*, 559 U.S. 98 (2010), n.2.

The punishment most often associated with criminal conduct is a **jail** or **prison** sentence. Legislative bodies usually classify offenses in some manner and for each class of offense authorize imposition of a jail or prison sentence within a specific range of time. For example, a state may classify the crime of forgery as a Class B felony and in its sentencing statutes authorize a sentence of three to five years in prison for Class B felonies. The fact that an offense carries a jail or prison sentence authorizes, but does not require, the court to impose one. Legislative bodies in many jurisdictions have created mandatory minimum prison sentences for certain offenses. When a person is convicted of such an offense the court must sentence the convicted defendant to at least that minimum period of incarceration.

Work release is a sentence in a criminal case in which the defendant is confined to jail for a specified period of time during which he is allowed to leave the jail to go to work and required return to jail at the end of his work day.

Many state sentencing statutes authorize sentences that entail less than full-time incarceration. One such sentence is referred to in many states as **work release**. If a defendant is sentenced to work release he is confined to a jail for a specified period of time (e.g., six months), but during his confinement he is allowed to leave the jail to go to work and at the end of his work day he is required to return to the jail. Work release is often imposed on employed defendants so that they can earn money to pay restitution to the victims of their crimes and to support a family. In most jurisdictions a defendant sentenced to work release is also required to pay the county in which he is incarcerated for the cost of housing him in the jail. An alternative to work release is a sentence of weekends in jail.

Home confinement is a sentence in a criminal case in which except for certain specified reasons a defendant is ordered to remain in his home for some specified period of time.

An alternative to incarceration in a jail or prison that many sentencing statutes authorize is a sentence of **home confinement**. Sentences of home confinement usually allow a defendant to leave his home for certain limited purposes, such as to go to a grocery store, obtain medical treatment, and appear in court. Defendants sentenced to home confinement are required to wear an ankle or wrist bracelet that electronically monitors their movement to ensure that they do not leave their home other than for an authorized purpose.

Probation is a sentence in a criminal case in which instead of confinement the defendant is allowed to remain in or is released back into the community.

Another sentencing alternative commonly authorized by statute is called **probation**. A defendant sentenced to probation is allowed to remain in or is released back into the community instead of being incarcerated. As with a jail or prison sentence a sentence of probation is for some specific period of time (e.g., 30 months).

Statutory conditions of probation are conditions that are imposed by statute on all sentences of probation that the probationer must satisfy.

Special conditions of probation are conditions that are imposed on a sentence of probation by a judge that must be satisfied by the probationer.

Most probation statutes impose certain conditions, usually called **statutory conditions,** with which the probationer must comply. Statutory conditions often include requirements that while on probation the probationer report at certain intervals to a probation officer and that the probationer not violate the criminal law of any jurisdiction. Judges frequently impose additional or what are sometimes called **special conditions of probation** with which the probationer must also comply. Such special conditions may include that the probationer submit to unannounced drug testing, the probationer attend school, or that the probationer have no contact with the victim of his crime. If a probationer violates any condition of probation the court can resentence the probationer to any sentence it could have originally imposed or extend or add conditions to the original probation sentence.

Most sentencing statutes also authorize an order of restitution. An order of restitution is a court order that requires the defendant to pay the victim of his crime a sum of money that represents some or all of the economic loss the defendant's crime caused him. For example, if Gina embezzled $50,000 from her employer, the ABC Company, as part of a sentence a court can order her to repay some or all of that $50,000 to ABC. Restitution is usually made a special condition of probation, but can be ordered to be paid independent of that sentence. Restitution can be ordered to be paid in a lump sum or it can be ordered to be paid in installments at some regular interval. Restitution can be ordered to be paid either in lieu of or in addition to a fine and a jail or prison sentence.

The sentencing statutes of all American jurisdictions authorize imposition of fines as a punishment for crimes. The size of the authorized fine is usually based on the seriousness of the offense. For example, many sentencing statutes authorize higher fines for felonies than they do for misdemeanors. In addition to authorizing fines, most sentencing statutes usually authorize (and in some instances require) courts to order defendants to pay court costs, and certain other costs, such as the costs of administering the defendant's probation and costs of court-ordered drug and alcohol testing.

Another sentence that is frequently authorized in many sentencing statutes is the performance of community service work. A sentence to perform community service work is usually stated in terms of hours (e.g., the defendant is to perform 500 hours of community service work), and as with orders to pay restitution, is frequently made a special condition of probation. The defendant's progress in performing the community service work is often monitored by his probation officer.

All of the sentencing alternatives discussed above result in a criminal conviction for the defendant that may give rise to some or all of the collateral consequences discussed earlier in this chapter. For less serious offenses, such as for misdemeanors and, in some jurisdictions for certain felonies, there is often an authorized disposition (called supervision in some states, deferred sentencing in other states, and by other names in still other states) that does not result in a criminal conviction, notwithstanding that the defendant committed the crime for which the sentence is imposed.

For example, in the state of Prairie a person convicted of gambling is disqualified from holding a liquor license. Frank is charged with gambling, a misdemeanor, and in the state of Prairie supervision is an authorized sentence for misdemeanors. Frank enters into a plea agreement with the prosecutor pursuant to which he pleads guilty to the gambling charge and is sentenced to 12-months supervision. At the end of the 12 months, if Frank has satisfied the conditions of supervision, the gambling charge against him will be dismissed, he will not have a conviction for gambling, and he will not be disqualified from obtaining a liquor license. If, however, Frank were to have been sentenced to probation instead of supervision, he would have a conviction for gambling that would foreclose him from obtaining a liquor license in Prairie.

As with probation, a sentence of supervision or a conceptually similar sentence usually has certain statutory conditions that must be satisfied and can have special conditions added to it by the sentencing court. As with probation, those special conditions can include payment of restitution, the performance of community service work, and the payment of fines and court costs. Finally, as with probation, a sentence of supervision is served for a specified period of time and if during that period the defendant violates a condition of the supervision, a court can resentence the defendant to what ever sentence it could have originally imposed, which could result in the defendant having a conviction for the crime on which the sentence was imposed. In many jurisdictions, when a defendant satisfactorily completes such a sentence, he can have the record of his arrest expunged.

3. *Who Determines What Criminal Sentence Is Imposed and How That Sentence Is Determined*

This section examines who determines what sentence is imposed following a conviction and how that sentence is determined. There is a significant difference between sentencing in capital cases and in non-capital cases, both as to how a sentence is determined and who determines it.

a. Sentencing in Capital Cases

In capital cases there is significant uniformity among the states both in how and in who determines that the death penalty be imposed. All American death penalty statutes require that before a defendant can be eligible for a death sentence one or more specific facts must be found to exist. That determination is made after the verdict of guilty is returned in what is called the sentencing or death phase of the trial and, unless a jury is waived, that fact must be found by a jury,[27] which typically is the trial jury. In most states the facts that will qualify a defendant for a sentence of death are called **aggravating facts** or in some states, aggravating circumstances. The states differ somewhat as to what facts or circumstances constitute aggravating facts or circumstances, but generally include facts such as that the murder victim was a peace officer killed in the course of performing his official duties, the murder involved the infliction of torture, or that the murder was committed pursuant to a contract or for money.[28]

An **aggravating fact (or circumstance)** is a fact (circumstance) whose existence makes a defendant eligible for a sentence of death.

Aggravating Circumstances Which Allow a Sentence of Death to Be Imposed Idaho Statutes §19-2515(9)

(9) The following are statutory aggravating circumstances, at least one (1) of which must be found to exist beyond a reasonable doubt before a sentence of death can be imposed:

(a) The defendant was previously convicted of another murder.

(b) At the time the murder was committed the defendant also committed another murder.

(c) The defendant knowingly created a great risk of death to many persons

(d) The murder was committed for remuneration or the promise of remuneration or the defendant employed another to commit the murder for remuneration or the promise of remuneration.

(e) The murder was especially heinous, atrocious, or cruel, manifesting exceptional depravity.

(f) By the murder, or circumstances surrounding its commission, the defendant exhibited utter disregard for human life.

(g) The murder was committed in the perpetration of or attempt to perpetrate, arson, rape, robbery, burglary, kidnapping or mayhem and the defendant killed, intended a killing, or acted with reckless indifference to human life.

(h) The murder was committed in the perpetration of, or attempt to perpetrate, an infamous crime against nature, lewd and lascivious conduct with a minor, sexual abuse of a child under sixteen (16) or seventeen (17) years of age, or forcible sexual penetration by use of a foreign object, and the defendant killed, intended a killing, or acted with reckless indifference to human life.

(i) The defendant, by his conduct, whether such conduct was before, during, or after the commission of the murder at hand, has exhibited a propensity to commit murder which will probably constitute a continuing threat to society.

(j) The murder was committed against a former or present peace officer, executive officer, officer of the court, judicial officer, or prosecuting attorney because of the exercise of official duty or because of the victim's former or present official status.

(k) The murder was committed against a witness or potential witness in a criminal or civil legal proceeding because of such proceeding.

Under the capital sentencing statutes, if the jury, or the judge if a jury is waived, finds the existence of an aggravating factor beyond a reasonable doubt, the jury then considers whether one or more statutory mitigating factors is sufficiently compelling that imposition of the death penalty would be unjust.[29]

In many states, before a judge can impose the death penalty, the jury must not only have found the existence of an aggravating fact, but it must also recommend that death be imposed. In some states, as long as the jury finds the existence of an aggravating fact, the court is allowed to impose a death sentence even if the jury does not recommend it.

b. Sentencing in Non-Capital Cases

In non-capital cases, the states differ as to who determines the sentence that will be imposed on a convicted defendant. In most states, a judge decides what sentence will be imposed. A few states, however, have jury sentencing.[30]

Except for those states which use jury sentencing, in non-capital cases, unless there is a plea agreement, a sentence is not imposed until after there has been a sentencing hearing before the judge who will be imposing the sentence. That hearing may occur shortly after the defendant is found guilty or as much as six to eight weeks or more after that. The purpose of the sentencing hearing is to bring out any information that might reasonably bear on the proper sentence for the particular defendant given the crime committed.[31] That information includes facts about the crime and characteristics of the defendant.[32]

Prior to the sentencing hearing, in most jurisdictions a probation officer or some other court officer will prepare what is called a pre-sentence report. The pre-sentence report will contain information about the crime and the victim and information about the defendant, such as the extent of his education, whether he has any history of drug or alcohol abuse, whether he has any psychiatric problems, whether he was sexually abused as a child, and whether the defendant has been involved in other criminal activity. The pre-sentence report is provided to the judge, the prosecution, and the defense before the sentencing hearing.

At the sentencing hearing the rules of evidence are relaxed and hearsay testimony is allowed. During the hearing the judge will hear evidence of **aggravating factors** (often referred to as evidence in aggravation) from the prosecution, which the prosecution will use to argue for a harsh sentence. Evidence in aggravation usually includes testimony or a statement from the victim about the impact of the crime on her and may include testimony from victims of other crimes committed by the defendant. In cases involving a defendant who has perpetrated a wide-ranging scheme against many victims or operated a large-scale criminal enterprise, evidence in aggravation often includes testimony from an investigator or analyst who outlines the breadth of the scheme perpetrated by the defendant or the scope of his criminal enterprise and the financial losses or harm it caused to the victims and the economic gain the defendant realized from it.

During a sentencing hearing the defendant is given an opportunity to put on evidence of **mitigating factors** (usually referred to as evidence in mitigation). The defense will use such evidence to argue for a lenient sentence. Evidence in mitigation may include such things as testimony about a defendant's psychiatric or substance abuse problems, her low IQ, her good character, and her lack of prior criminal activity.

Aggravating factors are factors that are accorded weight in favor of imposing a sentence of imprisonment. *See* 730 ILCS 5/5-5-3.2. To be considered when deciding whether to impose a sentence of imprisonment the factor must be above and beyond the elements of the crime for which the defendant is being sentenced. *Hill v. State*, 318 Ark. 408 (1994).

Mitigating factors are factors that must be accorded weight in favor of withholding or minimizing a sentence of imprisonment. *See* 730 ILCS 5/5-5-3.1.

The defendant has a right to testify at his sentencing hearing. If the defendant chooses to testify, the same as all the other witnesses who testify at the sentencing hearing, he is subject to cross-examination. Before sentence is imposed a defendant also has a right to make what is called an **allocution statement**.[33] In an allocution statement the defendant is allowed to address the court for the purpose of presenting information to mitigate his sentence.[34] A court can bar a defendant from making argument during an allocution statement that is not related to mitigation of the sentence to be imposed.[35] A defendant who makes an allocution statement is not subject to cross-examination.

An **allocution statement** is an unsworn statement made by a defendant to a court for the purpose of presenting information to mitigate his sentence. *United States v. Alden,* 527 F.3d 653 (7th Cir. 2008).

In determining the sentence it will impose, the court will consider information contained in the pre-sentence report and the facts and arguments it has heard during the sentencing hearing and apply the jurisdiction's sentencing statute to them. There are two different types of sentencing statutes. One is the traditional sentencing statute, which lists factors that the judge can consider in aggravation and mitigation when determining what sentence to impose.

Factors in Mitigation 730 ILCS 5/5-5-3.1

(a) The following grounds shall be accorded weight in favor of withholding or minimizing a sentence of imprisonment:

(1) The defendant's criminal conduct neither caused nor threatened serious physical harm to another.

(2) The defendant did not contemplate that his criminal conduct would cause or threaten serious physical harm to another.

(3) The defendant acted under a strong provocation.

(4) There were substantial grounds tending to excuse or justify the defendant's criminal conduct, though failing to establish a defense.

(5) The defendant's criminal conduct was induced or facilitated by someone other than the defendant.

(6) The defendant has compensated or will compensate the victim of his criminal conduct for the damage or injury that he sustained.

(7) The defendant has no history of prior delinquency or criminal activity or has led a law-abiding life for a substantial period of time before the commission of the present crime.

(8) The defendant's criminal conduct was the result of circumstances unlikely to recur.

(9) The character and attitudes of the defendant indicate that he is unlikely to commit another crime.

(10) The defendant is particularly likely to comply with the terms of a period of probation.

(11) The imprisonment of the defendant would entail excessive hardship to his dependents.

(12) The imprisonment of the defendant would endanger his or her medical condition.

(13) The defendant was mentally retarded as defined in Section 5-1-13 of this Code.

(b) If the court, having due regard for the character of the offender, the nature and circumstances of the offense and the public interest finds that a sentence of imprisonment is the most appropriate disposition of the offender, or where other provisions of this Code mandate the imprisonment of the offender, the grounds listed in paragraph (a) of this subsection shall be considered as factors in mitigation of the term imposed.

Factors in Aggravation 720 ILCS 5/5-5-3.2

(a) The following factors shall be accorded weight in favor of imposing a term of imprisonment or may be considered by the court as reasons to impose a more severe sentence under Section 5-8-1 or Article 4.5 of Chapter V:

(1) the defendant's conduct caused or threatened serious harm;

(2) the defendant received compensation for committing the offense;

(3) the defendant has a history of prior delinquency or criminal activity;

(4) the defendant, by the duties of his office or by his position, was obliged to prevent the particular offense committed or to bring the offenders committing it to justice;

(5) the defendant held public office at the time of the offense, and the offense related to the conduct of that office;

(6) the defendant utilized his professional reputation or position in the community to commit the offense, or to afford him an easier means of committing it;

(7) the sentence is necessary to deter others from committing the same crime;

(8) the defendant committed the offense against a person 60 years of age or older or such person's property;

(9) the defendant committed the offense against a person who is physically handicapped or such person's property;

(10) by reason of another individual's actual or perceived race, color, creed, religion, ancestry, gender, sexual orientation, physical or mental disability, or national origin, the defendant committed the offense against (i) the person or property of that individual; (ii) the person or property of a person who has an association with, is married to, or has a friendship with the other individual; or (iii)

the person or property of a relative (by blood or marriage) of a person described in clause (i) or (ii). For the purposes of this Section, "sexual orientation" means heterosexuality, homosexuality, or bisexuality;

(11) the offense took place in a place of worship or on the grounds of a place of worship, immediately prior to, during or immediately following worship services. For purposes of this subparagraph, "place of worship" shall mean any church, synagogue or other building, structure or place used primarily for religious worship;

(12) the defendant was convicted of a felony committed while he was released on bail or his own recognizance pending trial for a prior felony and was convicted of such prior felony, or the defendant was convicted of a felony committed while he was serving a period of probation, conditional discharge, or mandatory supervised release under subsection (d) of Section 5-8-1 for a prior felony;

(13) the defendant committed or attempted to commit a felony while he was wearing a bulletproof vest. For the purposes of this paragraph (13), a bulletproof vest is any device which is designed for the purpose of protecting the wearer from bullets, shot or other lethal projectiles;

(14) the defendant held a position of trust or supervision such as, but not limited to, family member as defined in Section 12-12 of the Criminal Code of 1961, teacher, scout leader, baby sitter, or day care worker, in relation to a victim under 18 years of age, and the defendant committed an offense in violation of Section 11-6, 11-11, 11-15.1, 11-19.1, 11-19.2, 11-20.1, 12-13, 12-14, 12-14.1, 12-15 or 12-16 of the Criminal Code of 1961 against that victim;

(15) the defendant committed an offense related to the activities of an organized gang. For the purposes of this factor, "organized gang" has the meaning ascribed to it in Section 10 of the Streetgang Terrorism Omnibus Prevention Act;

(16) the defendant committed an offense in violation of one of the following Sections while in a school, regardless of the time of day or time of year; on any conveyance owned, leased, or contracted by a school to transport students to or from school or a school related activity; on the real property of a school; or on a public way within 1,000 feet of the real property comprising any school: Section 10-1, 10-2, 10-5, 11-15.1, 11-17.1, 11-18.1, 11-19.1, 11-19.2, 12-2, 12-4, 12-4.1, 12-4.2, 12-4.3, 12-6, 12-6.1, 12-13, 12-14, 12-14.1, 12-15, 12-16, 18-2, or 33A-2 of the Criminal Code of 1961;

(16.5) the defendant committed an offense in violation of one of the following Sections while in a day care center, regardless of the time of day or time of year; on the real property of a day care center, regardless of the time of day or time of year; or on a public way within 1,000 feet of the real property comprising any day care center, regardless of the time of day or time of year: Section 10-1, 10-2, 10-5, 11-15.1, 11-17.1, 11-18.1, 11-19.1, 11-19.2, 12-2, 12-4, 12-4.1, 12-4.2, 12-4.3, 12-6, 12-6.1, 12-13, 12-14, 12-14.1, 12-15, 12-16, 18-2, or 33A-2 of the Criminal Code of 1961;

(17) the defendant committed the offense by reason of any person's activity as a community policing volunteer or to prevent any person from engaging in activity as a community policing volunteer. For the purpose of this Section, "community policing volunteer" has the meaning ascribed to it in Section 2-3.5 of the Criminal Code of 1961;

(18) the defendant committed the offense in a nursing home or on the real property comprising a nursing home. For the purposes of this paragraph (18), "nursing home" means a skilled nursing or intermediate long term care facility that is subject to license by the Illinois Department of Public Health under the Nursing Home Care Act;

(19) the defendant was a federally licensed firearm dealer and was previously convicted of a violation of subsection (a) of Section 3 of the Firearm Owners Identification Card Act and has now committed either a felony violation of the Firearm Owners Identification Card Act or an act of armed violence while armed with a firearm;

(20) the defendant (i) committed the offense of reckless homicide under Section 9-3 of the Criminal Code of 1961 or the offense of driving under the influence of alcohol, other drug or drugs, intoxicating compound or compounds or any combination thereof under Section 11-501 of the Illinois Vehicle Code or a similar provision of a local ordinance and (ii) was operating a motor vehicle in excess of 20 miles per hour over the posted speed limit as provided in Article VI of Chapter 11 of the Illinois Vehicle Code;

(21) the defendant (i) committed the offense of reckless driving or aggravated reckless driving under Section 11-503 of the Illinois Vehicle Code and (ii) was operating a motor vehicle in excess of 20 miles per hour over the posted speed limit as provided in Article VI of Chapter 11 of the Illinois Vehicle Code;

(22) the defendant committed the offense against a person that the defendant knew, or reasonably should have known, was a member of the Armed Forces of the United States serving on active duty. For purposes of this clause (22), the term "Armed Forces" means any of the Armed Forces of the United States, including a member of any reserve component thereof or National Guard unit called to active duty;

(23) the defendant committed the offense against a person who was elderly, disabled, or infirm by taking advantage of a family or fiduciary relationship with the elderly, disabled, or infirm person; or

(24) the defendant committed any offense under Section 11-20.1 of the Criminal Code of 1961 and possessed 100 or more images.

For the purposes of this Section:

"School" is defined as a public or private elementary or secondary school, community college, college, or university.

"Day care center" means a public or private State certified and licensed day care center as defined in Section 2.09 of the Child Care Act of 1969 that displays a sign in plain view stating that the property is a day care center.

There are significant differences between state statutes both as to aggravating and mitigating factors, and in most states a judge or jury is not limited to considering only those factors when deciding what sentence to impose. A paralegal who works in the field of criminal law should familiarize herself with the aggravating and mitigating facts contained in the sentencing statute of the jurisdiction in which she works.

In states with a traditional sentencing statute a judge will make a finding on the record as to which factors he has found or not found and based on that announce the sentence. Under most traditional sentencing statutes the judge does not need to do any further analysis to justify the sentence he imposes.

In federal criminal prosecutions and in those states that have adopted them, courts use the Federal Sentencing Guidelines[36] in determining what sentence to impose. The Guidelines, which were developed by the United States Sentencing Commission, create a complex and technical sentencing scheme that is designed to produce some degree of uniformity in the criminal sentences imposed by federal judges. The Guidelines create a system in which the range of time that a defendant can be sentenced to serve in prison is determined by two factors: the nature of the offense committed by the defendant and the defendant's criminal history.

The sentencing ranges contained in the Guidelines are not mandatory, but federal courts must consult the Guidelines when formulating a sentence[37] and must make a correct determination of the Guidelines sentencing range before deciding on what sentence to impose.[38] To determine the sentencing range a court must make two preliminary determinations: the base offense level for the offense the defendant was convicted of committing and the defendant's criminal history category. Those determinations are made by reference to specific provisions of the Guidelines.

The Guidelines assign all federal criminal offenses to one of more than 40 base offense levels and specifies a sentencing range for each level. To determine the base offense level it is necessary to look at the Guidelines to determine to what level the offense is assigned. For example, for the offense of mail fraud the base offense level is 7, a level to which the Guidelines assign a minimum sentence in the range

PARTIAL FEDERAL SENTENCING GUIDELINES TABLE				
(In months of imprisonment)				

| Criminal History → | I | II | III | IV | V-VI |
Offense Level ▽	(0-1 Pts)	(2-3 pts)	(4-6 pts)	(7-9 pts)	(10- ≥ 13 pts)
1	0-6	0-6	0-6	0-6	X
2-6	X	X	X	X	X
7	3-6	2-8	4-10	11-14	X
8-24	X	X	X	X	X
25	57-71	53-75	70-87	94-105	X
26-43	X	X	X	X	X

of 3-6 months in prison. The Guidelines, however, contain a list of factors that can result in the adjustment or enhancement of the base offense level if a sentencing court finds that any of those factors exist. Continuing to use the mail fraud example above, if that offense was perpetrated against ten or more people and was committed through mass marketing, the Guidelines will increase the offense level by two levels[39] and if the loss the perpetrator intended exceeded $1 million but did not exceed $2.5 million, the Guidelines would increase the base offense level by 16 levels.[40] The result is the base offense level for the mail fraud offense would be 25 with a minimum sentencing range of from 57 to 71 months in prison instead of the 3-6 month range.

Once a court has determined the base offense level it must then determine the criminal history category into which the defendant fits. As you can see from looking at the table above, the criminal history category into which a defendant fits can increase the sentencing range to which he is subject for the base level offense he committed. A defendant's criminal history category is determined by a point system that gives points for the different types of crimes the defendant has committed or in which he has been involved. Continuing to use the mail fraud example above, if the perpetrator of the base-level 25 mail fraud offense had no criminal history he would be subject to the minimum sentencing range of 57-71 months, but if instead of having no prior criminal history the perpetrator had a previous conviction for attempted solicitation of murder for hire, under the Guidelines that conviction would result in him receiving 7 Criminal History Points, which would put him in Criminal History Category IV and thereby increase his sentencing range from 57-71 months to 94-105 months.

Once a federal court determines the Guidelines sentencing range it is then required to consider whether a number of other factors exist.

A finding by the sentencing judge that one of those other factors exists will, depending on what factor it is, allow a court, if it chooses to do so, to impose a sentence that is above or below the applicable Guidelines range.[41] The factors that will allow a court to depart from a Guidelines sentencing range include: (1) the history and characteristics of the defendant; (2) the need for the sentence to reflect the seriousness of the offense, deter criminal conduct, protect the public from the defendant, and provide the defendant with needed training or treatment; (3) the kinds of sentences available; (4) the appropriate sentencing range under the applicable Guidelines issued by the federal Sentencing Commission; (5) any pertinent policy statement; (6) the need to avoid unwarranted sentencing disparities among similarly situated defendants; and (7) the need to provide restitution to any victims of the offense.[42]

A federal judge does not need to apply all of the factors in a checklist fashion, but he must at least give an adequate statement of the reasons, consistent with those factors, for why he believes the sentence he selects is appropriate. If the judge does that and the sentence imposed is within the applicable Guidelines range, the sentence is presumed to be reasonable.[43]

C. Appeals

In criminal cases defendants are usually able to obtain at least one level of appellate review of their convictions. Generally, no appeals are allowed until a final judgment has been entered.[44] Because the final judgment in a criminal case is the pronouncement of the defendant's sentence, a criminal case usually is not reviewable by an appellate court until after sentencing.[45]

An **interlocutory appeal** is an appeal taken from a proceeding before entry of a final judgment. *In re R.B.,* 186 S.W.3d 255 (Mo. 2006).

In some limited instances **interlocutory appeals** are allowed. Interlocutory appeals are usually allowed only when the order appealed from conclusively determines a question, the question is unrelated to the merits of the case, and the order will be effectively unreviewable on appeal from a final judgment.

One commonly allowed interlocutory appeal is an appeal from a ruling adverse to the prosecution on a motion to suppress. Without interlocutory review of such rulings, in the vast majority of instances there would be no appellate review of a trial court's decision to suppress evidence because without the suppressed evidence the prosecution often will need to dismiss the case due to insufficient evidence, or, if the prosecution proceeds to trial and the defendant is acquitted, the prosecution cannot obtain review because there is no appeal from a verdict of not guilty.

Once a defendant has been sentenced virtually all American jurisdictions allow him an appeal as a matter of right to an intermediate-level court of review that is usually called an appellate or appeals court. To obtain appellate review the defendant must file his appeal within a certain period of time after sentencing. In most jurisdictions that period of time is within 30 days from the date of sentencing. If a defendant does not file his appeal within that period he will be deemed to have waived appellate review and any right to appellate review will be lost.

The method by which an appeal is filed is different in different states and a paralegal working in the field of criminal law should familiarize herself with how an appeal in her jurisdiction is perfected. In many states to obtain an appeal the defendant must file a document called a notice of appeal with the clerk of the trial court. When a notice of appeal is filed the trial court clerk transmits the trial court file to the appellate court, where the case is docketed by the clerk of that court. Once the appeal is docketed the appellate court will set a schedule for the filing of briefs and, if it decides to hear them, set a time for oral arguments.

Paralegals who work in defense attorneys' offices frequently prepare the notice of appeal or equivalent document required by the jurisdiction in which they work in order to start an appeal. In addition, the paralegal may be tasked with ordering the transcript of the proceedings and with obtaining or ordering the trial court record from the appellate court.

With some exceptions, in almost all the states the highest court (called the "supreme court" in virtually all the states, but called the Court of Appeals in New York) has the power to select which appeals it will hear. In non-capital cases defendants seldom have a right to review by the jurisdiction's highest court.

When an intermediate appeals court decides an appeal, the losing side is allowed to request a review of that ruling by the jurisdiction's highest court. To obtain review of an appellate court decision, the losing party must file a document with the supreme court requesting to be allowed to file an appeal. If the supreme court denies an appeal, in most instances the criminal case is over. A defendant in a state criminal case can ask the U.S. Supreme Court to review rulings by a state appellate or supreme court on matters of federal constitutional law, but as with state supreme courts the U.S. Supreme Court has discretion to accept or reject such appeals. The U.S. Supreme Court will not hear appeals on issues of state law.

Generally, appeals are limited to questions of law that were raised in the trial court and preserved in a written post-trial motion. Reviewing courts seldom examine findings of fact made by the trial court or a jury. With some exceptions, questions not raised in the trial court will not be considered on appeal.[46] Two questions that can be raised for the first time on appeal are questions related to the sufficiency of the charging instrument[47] and jurisdictional challenges.

D. Post-Conviction Remedies and Habeas Corpus

The fact that a defendant loses his appeal does not necessarily end his ability to obtain judicial review of his conviction. Most states provide what are called post-conviction remedies. These remedies are sometimes referred to as collateral proceedings or collateral attacks. Post-conviction remedies are called by different names in different states; in some states they are remedies that were available at common law while in other states they are statutory or rule-based remedies that have replaced the common law remedies. The general purpose of all such post-conviction remedies is to challenge the validity of a defendant's conviction or sentence,[48] not to provide a second appeal.[49] There is no constitutional right to post-conviction remedies[50] and whether they are available and the grounds on which they can be sought are matters within the discretion of the legislature.[51]

In virtually all American jurisdictions motions seeking a post-conviction remedy must be filed within a certain period of time after judgment is entered in the criminal case. If the motion is not filed within that period of time the defendant is barred from obtaining post-conviction review. The period of time within which such motions must be filed is different in different states. Acknowledging the development of DNA technology most states have enacted statutes that allow post-conviction motions based on DNA evidence to be filed long after non-DNA-based post-conviction petitions are barred.

The grounds upon which a post-conviction remedy can be sought and what can be raised in such a proceeding are also different in different states. Generally, however, such proceedings are limited to issues unknown at trial.[52] Consequently the basis of a post-conviction remedy generally cannot be an issue that could have been raised at trial or on appeal, but was not,[53] nor can it be an issue that was raised on appeal and ruled on.[54] One ground upon which a post-conviction remedy can be based is newly discovered evidence that was not reasonably available at the time of the defendant's conviction.

Writ of habeas corpus is a legal device available to individual to raise constitutional challenges to their imprisonment. *Herrera v. Collins*, 506 U.S. 390 (1993).

The **writ of habeas corpus** is an ancient common law writ that is expressly referred to in the U.S. Constitution.[55] The federal writ of habeas corpus is a vehicle that individuals can use to raise constitutional challenges to their imprisonment.[56] The federal writ of habeas corpus is solely concerned with whether the petitioner's constitutional rights have been preserved and does not deal with the question of a petitioner's innocence or guilt.[57]

E. Clemency

Clemency is an umbrella term that refers to pardons, commutations, remission of fines, and reprieves. *Herrera v. Collins*, 506 U.S. 390 (1993), n.12.

Clemency is deeply rooted in Anglo-American law and is the historic remedy for preventing miscarriages of justice where judicial process has been exhausted[58] or is no longer available. For example, James is convicted of murder and five years after the time for filing a post-conviction motion expires and filing such a motion would be barred, new evidence is discovered that exonerates him. Based on that evidence James can apply for executive clemency. Before 1907 when there was no right of appeal in federal criminal cases and when most offenses were still capital offenses, clemency was the primary mode of relief for individuals convicted of federal crimes.[59]

Herrera v. Collins

Supreme Court of the United States (1993) 506 U.S. 390

CHIEF JUSTICE REHNQUIST delivered the opinion of the Court.

Petitioner Leonel Torres Herrera was convicted of capital murder and sentenced to death in January 1982. He unsuccessfully challenged the conviction on direct appeal and state collateral proceedings in the Texas state courts, and in a federal habeas petition. In February 1992—10 years after his conviction—he urged in a second federal habeas petition that he was "actually innocent" of the murder for which he was sentenced to death, and that the Eighth Amendment's prohibition against cruel and unusual punishment and the Fourteenth Amendment's guarantee of due process of law therefore forbid his execution. He supported this claim with affidavits tending to show that his now-dead brother, rather than he, had been the perpetrator of the crime. Petitioner urges us to hold that this showing of innocence entitles him to relief in this federal habeas proceeding. We hold that it does not.

Shortly before 11 p.m. on an evening in late September 1981, the body of Texas Department of Public Safety Officer David Rucker was found by a passerby on a stretch of highway about six miles east of Los Fresnos, Texas, a few miles north of Brownsville in the Rio Grande Valley. Rucker's body was lying beside his patrol car. He had been shot in the head.

At about the same time, Los Fresnos Police Officer Enrique Carrisalez observed a speeding vehicle traveling west towards Los Fresnos, away from the place where Rucker's body had been found, along the same road. Carrisalez, who was accompanied in his patrol car by Enrique Hernandez, turned on his flashing red lights and pursued the speeding vehicle. After the car had stopped briefly at a red light, it signaled that it would pull over and did so. The patrol car pulled up behind it. Carrisalez took a flashlight and walked toward the car of the speeder. The driver opened his door and exchanged a few words with Carrisalez before firing at least one shot at Carrisalez' chest. The officer died nine days later.

Petitioner Herrera was arrested a few days after the shootings and charged with the capital murder of both Carrisalez and Rucker. He was tried and found guilty of the capital murder of Carrisalez in January 1982, and sentenced to death. In July 1982, petitioner pleaded guilty to the murder of Rucker.

At petitioner's trial for the murder of Carrisalez, Hernandez, who had witnessed Carrisalez' slaying from the officer's patrol car, identified petitioner as the person who had wielded the gun. A declaration by Officer Carrisalez to the same effect, made while he was in the hospital, was also admitted. Through a license plate check, it was shown that the speeding car involved in Carrisalez' murder was registered to petitioner's "live-in" girlfriend. Petitioner was known to drive this car, and he had a set of keys to the car in his pants pocket when he was arrested. Hernandez identified the car as the vehicle from which the murderer had emerged to fire the fatal shot. He also testified that there had been only one person in the car that night. * * *

Once a defendant has been afforded a fair trial and convicted of the offense for which he was charged, the presumption of innocence disappears. * * * Here, it is not disputed that the State met its burden of proving at trial that petitioner was guilty of the capital murder of Officer Carrisalez beyond a reasonable doubt. Thus, in the eyes of the law, petitioner does not come before the Court as one who is "innocent," but, on the contrary, as one who has been convicted by due process of law of two brutal murders.

Based on affidavits here filed, petitioner claims that evidence never presented to the trial court proves him innocent notwithstanding the verdict reached at his trial. Such a claim is not cognizable in the state courts of Texas. For to obtain a new trial based on newly discovered evidence, a defendant must file a motion within 30 days after imposition or suspension of sentence. Tex. Rule App. Proc. 31(a)(1) (1992). The Texas courts have construed this 30-day time limit as jurisdictional. See *Beathard v. State*, 767 S.W.2d 423, 433 (Tex. Crim. App. 1989).

Claims of actual innocence based on newly discovered evidence have never been held to state a ground for federal habeas relief absent an independent constitutional violation occurring in the underlying state criminal proceeding. * * *

This rule is grounded in the principle that federal habeas courts sit to ensure that individuals are not imprisoned in violation of the Constitution—not to correct errors of fact. See, *e.g., Moore v. Dempsey*, 261 U.S. 86, 87-88 (1923) (Holmes, J.) ("What we have to deal with [on habeas review] is not the petitioners' innocence or guilt but solely the question whether their constitutional rights have been preserved") * * *.

More recent authority construing federal habeas statutes speaks in a similar vein. * * * "Society's resources have been concentrated at that time and place in order to decide, within the limits of human fallibility, the question of guilt or innocence of one of its citizens." *Wainwright v. Sykes*, 433 U.S. 72, 90 (1977). Few rulings would be more disruptive of our federal system than to provide for federal habeas review of freestanding claims of actual innocence. * * *

This is not to say, however, that petitioner is left without a forum to raise his actual innocence claim. For under Texas law, petitioner may file a request for executive clemency. See Tex. Const., Art. IV, §11; Tex. Code Crim. Proc. Ann., Art. 48.01 (Vernon 1979). Clemency is deeply rooted in our Anglo-American tradition of law, and is the historic remedy for preventing miscarriages of justice where judicial process has been exhausted.

In England, the clemency power was vested in the Crown and can be traced back to the 700's. W. Humbert, The Pardoning Power of the President 9 (1941). Blackstone thought this "one of the great advantages of monarchy in general, above any other form of government; that there is a magistrate, who has it in his power to extend mercy, wherever he thinks it is deserved: holding a court of equity in his own breast, to soften the rigour of the general law, in such criminal cases as merit an exemption from punishment." 4 W. Blackstone, Commentaries *397. Clemency provided the principal avenue of relief for individuals convicted of criminal offenses—most of which were capital—because there was no right of appeal until 1907. 1 L. Radzinowicz, A History of English Criminal Law 122 (1948). It was the only means by which one could challenge his conviction on the ground of innocence. United States Dept. of Justice, 3 Attorney General's Survey of Release Procedures 73 (1939).

Our Constitution adopts the British model and gives to the President the "Power to grant Reprieves and Pardons for Offences against the United States." Art. II, §2, cl. 1. In *United States v. Wilson*, 7 Pet. 150, 160-161 (1833), Chief Justice Marshall expounded on the President's pardon power:

> "As this power had been exercised from time immemorial by the executive of that nation whose language is our language, and to whose judicial institutions ours bear a close resemblance; we adopt their principles respecting the operation and effect of a pardon, and look into their books for the rules prescribing the manner in which it is to be used by the person who would avail himself of it.
>
> "A pardon is an act of grace, proceeding from the power entrusted with the execution of the laws, which exempts the individual, on whom it is bestowed, from the punishment the law inflicts for a crime he has committed. It is the private, though official act of the executive magistrate, delivered to the individual for whose benefit it is intended, and not communicated officially to the court. It is a constituent part of the judicial system, that the judge sees only with judicial eyes, and knows nothing respecting any particular case, of which he is not informed judicially. A private deed, not communicated to him, whatever may be its character, whether a pardon or release, is totally unknown and cannot be acted on. The looseness which would be introduced into judicial proceedings, would prove fatal to the great principles of justice, if the judge might notice and act upon facts not brought regularly into the cause. Such a proceeding, in ordinary cases, would subvert the best established principles, and overturn those rules which have been settled by the wisdom of ages."

* * *

Of course, although the Constitution vests in the President a pardon power, it does not require the States to enact a clemency mechanism. Yet since the British Colonies were founded, clemency has been available in America. C. Jensen, The Pardoning Power in the American States 3-4 (1922). The original States were reluctant to vest the clemency power in the executive. And although this power has gravitated toward the executive over time, several States have split the clemency power between the Governor and an advisory board selected by the legislature. See Survey of Release Procedures, *supra*, at 91-98. Today, all 36 States that authorize capital punishment have constitutional or statutory provisions for clemency.

Executive clemency has provided the "fail safe" in our criminal justice system. K. Moore, Pardons: Justice, Mercy, and the Public Interest 131 (1989). It is an unalterable fact that our judicial system, like the human beings who administer it, is fallible. But history is replete with examples of wrongfully convicted persons who have been pardoned in the wake of after-discovered evidence establishing their innocence. In his classic work, Professor Edwin Borchard compiled 65 cases in which it was later determined that individuals had been wrongfully convicted of crimes. Clemency provided the relief mechanism in 47 of these cases; the remaining cases ended in judgments of acquittals after new trials. E. Borchard, Convicting the Innocent (1932). Recent authority confirms that over the past century clemency has been exercised frequently in capital cases in which demonstrations of "actual innocence" have been made. See M. Radelet, H. Bedau, & C. Putnam, In Spite of Innocence 282-356 (1992).

In Texas, the Governor has the power, upon the recommendation of a majority of the Board of Pardons and Paroles, to grant clemency. Tex. Const., Art. IV, §11; Tex. Code Crim. Proc. Ann., Art. 48.01 (Vernon 1979). The board's consideration is triggered upon request of the individual sentenced to death, his or her representative, or the Governor herself. In capital cases, a request may be made for a full pardon, Tex. Admin. Code, Tit. 37, §143.1 (West Supp. 1992), a commutation of death sentence to life imprisonment or appropriate maximum penalty, §143.57, or a reprieve of execution, §143.43. The Governor has the sole authority to grant one reprieve in any capital case not exceeding 30 days. §143.41(a).

* * * In this case, petitioner has apparently sought a 30-day reprieve from the Governor, but has yet to apply for a pardon, or even a commutation, on the ground of innocence or otherwise. Tr. of Oral Arg. 7, 34.

As the foregoing discussion illustrates, in state criminal proceedings the trial is the paramount event for determining the guilt or innocence of the defendant. Federal habeas review of state convictions has traditionally been limited to claims of constitutional violations occurring in the course of the underlying state criminal proceedings. Our federal habeas cases have treated claims of "actual innocence," not as an independent constitutional claim, but as a basis upon which a habeas petitioner may have an independent constitutional claim considered on the merits, even though his habeas petition would otherwise be regarded as successive or abusive. History shows that the traditional remedy for claims of innocence based on new evidence, discovered too late in the day to file a new trial motion, has been executive clemency.

We may assume, for the sake of argument in deciding this case, that in a capital case a truly persuasive demonstration of "actual innocence" made after trial would render the execution of a defendant unconstitutional, and warrant federal habeas relief if there were no state avenue open to process such a claim. But because of the very disruptive effect that entertaining claims of actual innocence would have on the need for finality in capital cases, and the enormous burden that having to retry cases based on often stale evidence would place on the States, the threshold showing for such an assumed right would necessarily be extraordinarily high. The showing made by petitioner in this case falls far short of any such threshold. * * *

The judgment of the Court of Appeals is

Affirmed.

Case Focus

1. The defendant in this case claimed that evidence not presented during his trial showed him to be innocent of the crime he was convicted of committing and for which he was sentenced to death. For what reason did the Court deny his petition for a writ of habeas corpus?
2. Where did the Court say the defendant was able to raise his claim of actual innocence and what was the remedy the Court said was available there?

● ● ● ● ● ● ● ● ●

In most instances clemency is sought not because of new evidence, but because convicted defendants feel their sentence was unduly harsh or because since committing the crime of which they were convicted they have done or accomplished things that they feel should entitle them to be released from further punishment. In some cases individuals seek clemency even before they are convicted of a crime.

The U.S. Constitution vests the power to grant clemency in the President.[60] At the federal level the clemency power includes not only the power to pardon an individual, but also the power to reduce a sentence[61] and the power to reduce or remit fines.[62] The President's clemency power extends to all federal offenses, but does not extend to either impeachments[63] or non-federal offenses.[64] When the President grants clemency, that grant can be either absolute or with conditions that the individual must satisfy to obtain clemency.[65]

At the state level the clemency power is usually vested in the governor. In some states the clemency power is split between the governor and some type of board or commission; in other states clemency power is vested solely in the governor. In those states where clemency power is vested solely in governor, the governor's exercise of that power cannot be limited by the legislature and is controlled only by governor's conscience and sense of duty.[66] Paralegals who are employed by private attorneys who handle clemency matters may be tasked with obtaining materials needed to support a clemency application and with drafting the application itself.

In states where the clemency power is vested solely in the governor the legislature can regulate the application process and often creates a board or commission to whom applications for clemency must be directed and whose function it is to make clemency recommendations to the governor. The recommendations of such boards are advisory only and do not restrain the governor's exercise of the clemency power.

The most commonly requested act of clemency is a pardon. Pardons are considered an act of grace by the executive branch.[67] In the United States there are two views about the legal effect of a pardon.[68] In many states[69] and under federal law[70] a pardon releases the individual from further punishment, but it does not erase the underlying conviction. In some states a pardon relieves the individual from the punishment for an offense and also erases his guilt.[71] The other clemency request is a request for remission of a sentence. If granted, a sentence remission reduces the sentence imposed by a court, but has no effect on a defendant's conviction.

Petition for Executive Clemency

Before the Illinois Prisoner Review Board

Advising the Honorable _____, **Governor**:

The undersigned petitioner prays for a pardon and expungement and in support thereof states as follows:

1. **Required Information:**

   Full name: _____
                                     First   _Middle_   _Last_

   Address: _____
                               Number   _Street_   _Apt/Unit #_

   _____
              City   _State_   _Zip Code_

   Telephone Number _(include area code)_: _____

   Date of Birth: _____   Place of Birth: _____

   Social Security Number: _____

   State Prisoner Number _(if applicable)_: _____

   Name Convicted Under and any Aliases: _____

   _____

   Have you ever served in the military?   ☐ Yes ☐ No
   If yes, please state your discharge status and date of discharge, and attach a copy of your DD-214.

   Have you ever petitioned for clemency before? ☐ Yes   ☐ No
   If yes, please state the month and year your petition was considered.

2. **Conviction(s) for Which Pardon is Sought**
    For each conviction please provide the following information:

    Offense: _____

    Case Number: _____

    Date of Arrest: _____

    County of Conviction: _____

    ☐ Plea ☐ Bench Trial ☐ Jury Trial

    Sentencing Judge: _____

    Date Sentenced: _____

    Sentence: _____
    (Includes probation, any time served, and conditional discharge)

    Time served: _____

    Date of Discharge: _____

    If you appealed your conviction or sentence, provide the status of any pending appeals, including the date of decision(s) by the Court:

    _____

    Provide a complete and detailed account of the offense(s) for which you seek pardon. Provide your own version of the factual circumstances of the offense(s), including the date and location. *Add additional pages if necessary:*

    _____

    _____

    _____

    _____

    _____

    _____

    _____

    _____

3. **Non-Conviction(s)**
   For each incident for which you were arrested, taken into custody, or charged by any law enforcement agency, except for traffic violations, provide the following information:

   Case Number: _____

   Offense Charged: _____

   Date of Arrest: _____

   County of Arrest: _____

   Disposition: _____
   (Includes SOL, nolle pros, nonsuit, section 10 or 410 probation, FNPC, supervision)

   Date probation or supervision terminated *(if applicable):* _____

   Attach a copy of your police record (rap sheet)

4. **Personal Life History**:
   Write a detailed narrative biography that includes date and place of birth, educational and employment history, marital status, names and ages of children, substance abuse and mental health information, military record, charitable and community activities. You may also include information on degrees or diplomas earned or anticipated, awards of commendations at school or work, counseling or rehabilitation programs you have attended or completed, military awards, civil or occupational licenses or certifications, and life changing events. You may attach any documents that demonstrate or reflect your achievements.

5. **Reason(s) for Seeking Clemency:**
   State your reasons for seeking a pardon. Include opportunities that have been denied because of your criminal record.

6. **Type of Clemency Desired:**
   ☐ Commutation of Sentence
   ☐ Reprieve
   ☐ Pardon
   ☐ Expungement (authorization to file in circuit court)

7. **Supporting Documentation**
   Attach materials that support the claims made in this petition. These may include DD 214, rap sheet, resume, letters of recommendation, diplomas, certifications, etc...

8. **Certification and Personal Oath**
   The following statement must be signed and sworn before a Notary Public:

   I declare under perjury that all of the assertions made in this petition are complete, truthful, and accurate.

   Respectfully Submitted this _____ day of _____, _____
                                         (Month)   *(Year)*

   _____
   (Signature of Petitioner)

   Signed and sworn before me this _____ day of _____, _____
                                           (Month)   *(Year)*

   _____
   (Notary Public)

9. **Hearing Information:**
   Petitioners may request a public hearing before the Prisoner Review Board. Personal presentations at the hearing are limited to 20 minutes. Petitioners may appear with their supporters, but no more than four people may speak during a presentation.

   Representatives of incarcerated petitioners my request to speak to the Board at a public hearing, but a personal appearance is not required for the processing of a petition for executive clemency. The Board will make a confidential recommendation for the Governor. Board recommendations to the Governor are confidential.

   Would you, the petitioner, like to request a public hearing? ☐ Yes   ☐ No

10. Filing and Mailing the Petition:

1. *Deliver or mail the original petition __and__ three copies to:*

   Illinois Prisoner Review Board
   3█ East M█████, Suite █
   Springfield, IL

   Within the completed petition to the Prisoner Review Board, include proof that the parties in numbers 2 and 3 listed below were sent copies of the petition. You may do this by affidavit __or__ by including a registered or certified mail receipt.

2. *Deliver or mail a copy of the petition to the sentencing judge for each conviction. If the sentencing judge is no longer on the bench, send a copy to the chief judge of the circuit in the county of conviction.*

   Cook County: The Honorable ████████████
             Chief Judge, Criminal Division
             2600 South California Avenue
             Chicago, IL 60608

3. *Deliver or mail a copy of the petition to the current state's attorney in the county of conviction.*

   Cook County: Cook County State's Attorney
             Room 11D38
             2650 South California Avenue
             Chicago, IL 60608

This form must be typewritten. The Prisoner Review Board needs original signatures and they need to be notarized.   No faxes will be accepted.

CHAPTER TERMS

Aggravating fact	Interlocutory appeal	Statutory conditions
Aggravating factors	Jail	of probation
Allocution statement	Mitigating factors	Writ of habeas corpus
Clemency	Prison	Work release
Collateral consequence	Probation	
Home confinement	Special conditions of probation	

REVIEW QUESTIONS

1. When does the post-trial stage of the criminal justice process begin?

2. How does a guilty verdict in a trial change a defendant's status in the eyes of the law?

3. What types of collateral consequences can flow from a criminal conviction?

4. What is one purpose of a post-trial motion?

5. What two types of limits does the cruel and unusual punishment clause place on criminal sentences?

6. What two types of punishment does the cruel and unusual punishment clause prohibit?

7. To what types of crimes does the cruel and unusual punishment clause limit application of the death sentence?

8. In the United States who determines what statutorily authorized sentence to impose on a defendant convicted of a crime?

9. In a capital case who determines whether an aggravating fact exists?

10. What is the purpose of a sentencing hearing?

11. When is a defendant allowed to file an appeal in his case?

12. What is the purpose of a post-conviction remedy?

13. What is the writ of habeas corpus and with what is it concerned?

14. Under the U.S. Constitution by what branch of government is the clemency exercised?

15. Can federal clemency power be exercised to give clemency to persons convicted of state offenses?

16. At the state level who exercises clemency power?

17. What are the two views about the legal effect of a pardon?

ENDNOTES

1. *Herrera v. Collins*, 506 U.S. 390 (1993).
2. *People v. Nelson*, 235 Ill. 2d 386 (2009).
3. 370 U.S. 660 (1962).
4. *Ingraham v. Wright*, 430 U.S. 651 (1977). Unrelated to sentencing, the clause also imposes limits on what the legislative branch of government can make a crime. *Id.* Generally that limitation prohibits the creation of status crimes. For example, the cruel and unusual punishment clause forbid the legislature from making it a crime to be a heroin addict, but does not prohibit the legislature from making it a crime to purchase or possess heroin.
5. *Penry v. Lynaugh*, 492 U.S. 302 (1987).
6. *Estelle v. Gamble*, 429 U.S. 97 (1976).
7. *Id.*
8. *Baze v. Rees*, 553 U.S. 35 (2008).
9. *Id.*, Thomas, J., concurring. At the time the Eighth Amendment was adopted capital punishment was the standard penalty for all serious crimes, *Id.*, and remained so well into the early twentieth century. *See Herrera v. Collins*, 506 U.S. at 390. The Constitution itself clearly contemplates imposition of the death penalty. Both the Fifth and Eighth Amendment were written by James Madison, both were proposed at the same time, and both were adopted at the same time. Within its express terms the Fifth Amendment twice recognizes use of the death penalty: once in its grand jury clause, which requires a grand jury indictment for all capital cases, and once in its due process clause, which provides that life, liberty, and property shall not be taken without due process of law. *U.S. Const.* Amend. 5.
10. *Baze v. Rees*, 553 U.S. at 35, Thomas, J., concurring.
11. *Id.* Burning at the stake was considered so horrible a punishment that before the sentence could be carried out, merciful sheriffs sometimes hanged the offender as an act of charity. *Id.*
12. *United States v. Gillespie*, 452 F.3d 1183 (10th Cir. 2006).
13. *Id.*
14. *United States v. Hughes*, 901 F.2d 830 (10th Cir. 1990).
15. *Id.*
16. *United States v. Gillespie*, 452 F.3d at 1183. The Supreme Court has invalidated a non-capital sentence on Eighth Amendment grounds on only two occasions: in 1910 a defendant was sentenced to 15 years in chains and hard labor for falsifying a public document, and in 1983 a defendant was sentenced to life without parole after committing six

nonviolent felonies, one of which was writing a bad $100 check. *Id.* Illustrative of how narrow the application of the cruel and unusual punishment is in non-capital cases, the Supreme Court has sustained sentences such as two consecutive 25-year-to-life sentences under a recidivist statute for a defendant convicted of two counts of petty theft. *Id.*

17. *Rickman v. State,* 343 Mont. 120 (2008).
18. *Kennedy v. Louisiana,* 544 U.S. 407 (2008).
19. *Cross v. Commonwealth,* 2009 WL 4251649 (Ky. 2009).
20. *Coker v. Georgia,* 433 U.S. 584 (1977).
21. *Kennedy v. Louisiana,* 544 U.S. at 407.
22. *Browning-Ferris Industries of Vermont, Inc. v. Kelco Disposal, Inc.,* 492 U.S. 257 (1989).
23. *Alexander v. United States,* 509 U.S. 544 (1993).
24. *United States v. Bajakajian,* 84 F.3d 334 (9th Cir. 1996).
25. *Alexander v. United States,* 509 U.S. at 544.
26. *United States v. Blackwell,* 459 F.3d 739 (6th Cir. 2006).
27. *Hurst v. Florida,* 577 U.S. ___ (2016).
28. *See, e.g., Idaho Statutes,* §19-2515(9).
29. *Idaho Statutes,* §19-2515(3)(b).
30. Wayne LaFave et. al., *Criminal Procedure* §26.2(b) (3d ed. 2007-2008).
31. *Wasman v. United States,* 468 U.S. 559 (1984).
32. *State v. George,* 323 S.C. 496 (1996).
33. *United States v. Eibler,* 991 F.2d 1350 (7th Cir. 1993).
34. *United States v. Alden,* 527 F.3d 653 (7th Cir. 2008).
35. *Id.*
36. 18 U.S.C. §3553.
37. *United States v. Lawrence,* 405 F.3d 888 (10th Cir. 2005).
38. *United States v. Vrdolyak,* 593 F.3d 676 (7th Cir. 2010).
39. *Guidelines* §2B1.1(b)(2)(A).
40. *Guidelines* §2B1.1(b)(1)(J).
41. *See Rita v. United States,* 551 U.S. 338 (2007).
42. *United States v. Rogers,* 400 F.3d 640 (8th Cir. 2005).
43. *Id.*
44. *Flanagan v. United States,* 465 U.S. 259 (1984).
45. *United States v. Lewis,* 368 F.3d 1102 (9th Cir. 2004).
46. *State v. Doss,* 754 N.W.2d 150 (Wis. 2008).
47. *People v. Butler,* 192 A.D.2d 543 (2d Dept. 1993).
48. *State v. Evans,* 669 S.W.3d 708 (Tenn. Crim. App. 1984).
49. *Drope v. Missouri,* 420 U.S. 162 (1975).
50. *Commonwealth v. Alcorn,* 703 A.2d 1054 (Pa. Super. Ct. 1997).
51. *Pike v. State,* 164 S.W.3d 257 (Tenn. 2005).
52. *Tope v. State,* 477 N.E.2d 873 (Ind. 1985).
53. *Darling v. State,* 966 So. 2d 366 (Fla. 2007); *Ritchie v. State,* 875 N.E.2d 706 (Ind. 2007).
54. *Pooler v. State,* 980 So. 2d 460 (Fla. 2008), *cert. denied* 129 S. Ct. 255 (2008).
55. U.S. Const., Art. I, Sec. 9, cl. 3.
56. *Herrera v. Collins,* 506 U.S. at 390 (1993).
57. *Id.*
58. *Herrera v. Collins,* 506 U.S. at 390.
59. *Id.*
60. U.S. Const., Art. II, Sec. 2, cl. 1.
61. *Biddle v. Perovich,* 274 U.S. 480 (1927).
62. *United States v. Harris,* 26 F. Cas. 174 (D. Ky. 1866).
63. *Ex parte Wells,* 59 U.S. 307 (1855).
64. *In re Bocchaioro,* 49 F. Supp. 37 (W.D N.Y. 1943).
65. *United States v. Klein,* 80 U.S. 128 (1871).
66. *Hobley v. Chicago Police Commander,* 445 F. Supp. 2d 990 (N.D. Ill. 2006).
67. *Herrera v. Collins,* 506 U.S. at 390.
68. *People v. Thon,* 319 Ill. App. 3d. 855 (2d Dist. 2001).
69. *Talarico v. Dunlap,* 177 Ill. 2d 185 (1997).
70. *Bjerkan v. United States,* 529 F.2d 1255 (7th Cir. 1975).
71. *See, e.g., Doe v. State,* 595 So. 2d 212 (Fla. App. 1992).

Glossary

Accessory after the fact: one who, knowing that a person has committed a felony, gives aid to that person for the purpose of hindering that person's apprehension, conviction, or punishment.

Accessory before the fact: a person who aids, counsels, commands, or encourages a person to commit a crime, but was not actually or constructively present at the time the crime was committed.

Accomplice: a person who, intending to promote the commission of a crime encourages or requests another to commit it or agrees or provides aid to another in its commission.

Adjudicative jurisdiction: the power of a court to subject a particular person or thing to the judicial process.

Affiant: one who has made an affidavit. An affidavit is a written statement sworn to before some officer authorized to administer oaths such as a judge or notary.

Agent: one who acts on behalf of another person with that other person's consent and subject to that other person's control.

Aggravating fact (circumstance): a fact (circumstance) whose existence makes a defendant eligible for a sentence of death.

Aggravating factors: factors above and beyond the elements of the crime for which the defendant has been convicted that are accorded weight in favor of imposing a sentence of imprisonment.

Allocution statement: an unsworn statement made by a defendant to a court for the purpose of presenting information to mitigate his sentence.

Appeal of right: an appeal where the court to which it is taken does not have the power to refuse to hear it.

Arraignment: the stage of a criminal prosecution in which the defendant is informed by a court of the charge against him and enters his plea to that charge.

Attorney general: the chief legal officer of a state. The attorney general represents state officials and state agencies in court and provides them with advice. In states that do not have county prosecutors the Attorney General also handles state criminal prosecutions.

Bench trial: in a criminal case, a trial in which a judge and not a jury determines whether a defendant is guilty or not guilty.

Bill of attainder: a legislative act that inflicts punishment on a person or an easily identifiable group of persons without a judicial trial.

Bill of Rights: the first ten amendments to the United States Constitution.

Blind plea: a plea of guilty by a defendant when he has no agreement with the prosecutor.

***Brady* material:** admissible evidence that is exculpatory or that can be used by the defendant for impeachment.

Burden of persuasion: the obligation to convince the fact finder at trial that a litigant's necessary propositions of fact are true.

Burden of production: the obligation to come forward with evidence on a litigant's necessary propositions of fact.

Clemency: an umbrella term that refers to pardons, commutations, remission of fines, and reprieves.

Closing argument: in a criminal trial, an argument made by the prosecutor or the defense attorney to the trier of fact, which discusses the facts and circumstances of the case and is limited to the evidence and reasonable inferences that can be drawn from the evidence.

Collateral consequence: a consequence of a criminal conviction that results from an action that may or may not be taken by an agency that the trial court does not control.

Collateral estoppel: a rule that states that once a fact has been determined by a valid and final judgment, that issue cannot again be litigated between the same parties.

Constitutional privilege: a privilege created by the United States Constitution or the constitution of a state; e.g., the Fifth Amendment privilege against self-incrimination.

Constructive presence: occurs when, without regard to his physical proximity to the place where a crime will be committed, a person places himself where he can render assistance to the perpetrator of the crime if needed.

Continuing offense: an offense committed over a period of time instead of at a single point in time.

Criminal procedure: the body of legal rules that governs the course of the proceedings that bring defendants into court and the course of the proceedings thereafter.

Critical stage: any stage of a criminal prosecution when a substantial right of a defendant may be affected.

Cross-examination: the opportunity to question a witness for the purpose of attacking the credibility of the witness.

Direct examination: the initial questioning of a witness by the party who called the witness to testify.

Discovery: the formal exchange of evidentiary information and material between parties in a pending action; in a criminal case, the exchange is between the prosecutor and the defense.

Discretionary appeal: an appeal where the court to which it is taken has the power to refuse to hear it.

Discretionary power: the power to do or refrain from doing a certain thing.

Evidentiary privilege: a privilege created by the law of evidence; e.g., the attorney-client privilege.

Ex post facto law: a law that (1) punishes conduct that was innocent when performed; (2) makes more burdensome the punishment for a crime, after its commission; (3) deprives one charged with a crime of any defense available at the time the act was committed; or (4) alters the legal rules of evidence to require less or different evidence to convict that the law required at the time the act was committed.

Felony: an offense for which a sentence of death or a term of imprisonment for one or more years may be imposed.

Hearsay: an out-of-court statement made by a person other than the testifying witness that, through the testifying witness, is offered to prove the truth of the matter asserted in it and that depends for its value on the credibility of the out-of-court declarant.

Home confinement: a sentence in a criminal case in which, except for certain specified reasons, a defendant is ordered to remain in his home for some specified period of time.

Honest services fraud: when a public official or public or private employee receives a bribe to perform his official duty or receives a kickback for performing his official duty.

Hung jury: a jury that is not able to reach a verdict.

Impeachment: an attack on the credibility of a witness that is accomplished by various methods, including by use of a witness's prior inconsistent statements.

Inchoate offenses: those offenses that make it a crime to take a step toward completing some crime. The three generally recognized inchoate offenses are attempt, solicitation, and conspiracy.

Indictment: an accusation of a crime made by a grand jury at the request of the prosecutor.

Information: a document filed by the prosecutor in which the prosecutor instead of the grand jury formally accuses a person of having committed a crime. In most jurisdictions the filing of an information commences a criminal prosecution.

In personam jurisdiction: in a criminal case the power of a court to proceed against a particular defendant.

Instruction conference: in a criminal trial, the meeting of the prosecutor, the defense attorney, and the judge outside the presence of the jury during which the prosecutor and defense attorney offer their proposed instructions for the jury to the judge, and the judge decides what instructions will be given.

Intangible personal property: property that has no physical existence that is generally defined as a right. Intangible rights may be evidenced by or represented in physical objects, such as a stock certificate or promissory note or they can be in electronically stored data.

Intellectual property: property that is derived from the work of the mind, such as trademarks, formulas, data, and patents.

Interlocutory appeal: an appeal taken from a proceeding before entry of a final judgment.

Jail: a local government's detention center where persons awaiting trial or those convicted of misdemeanors are confined.

Judicial review: the power of the judiciary to determine whether acts of the other two branches of government are void because those acts violate the Constitution.

Jurisdiction: the power to act. As to agencies of government, it is the power to administer and enforce the law and as to courts, it is the power to hear and decide a case.

Jury nullification: the name for the proposition that a jury may disregard the law as given by the court and decide a case based on other considerations.

Leading question: a question that suggests or puts an answer in the mouth of a witness; not simply a question that calls for a yes-or-no answer.

Legislative jurisdiction: the power of a sovereign to apply its law to prescribe or regulate conduct.

***Malum in se* offense:** an offense that involves conduct that without regard to the existence of a statute is inherently wrong.

***Malum prohibitum* offense:** an offense that involves conduct that is not inherently wrong, but that is made so because it is prohibited by statute.

Mens rea: guilty mind. *Mens rea* refers to the mental state element of a criminal offense that the perpetrator of the offense must have when he commits the offense. Common forms of *mens rea* are intent, knowledge, and recklessness.

Misdemeanor: an offense for which a term of imprisonment for less than one year may be imposed.

Mitigating factors: factors that must be accorded weight in favor of withholding or minimizing a sentence of imprisonment.

Nolle prosequi: a formal statement by the prosecutor that he will not proceed with the prosecution of either all charges or some charges. The effect of a prosecutor's *nolle prosequi* motion is to terminate the proceedings on the charges to which the action relates, and if it is to all charges, it releases the defendant.

Object offense: the offense that conspirators conspire to commit.

Open file policy: a policy of a prosecutor's office under which the prosecutor makes his entire file on a case available for inspection by the defense.

Opening statement: in a criminal case, a statement made by the prosecutor or defense attorney to the trier of fact that acquaints the trier of fact with the facts he expects to prove at trial.

Personal property: all property that is not real property.

Petit jury: a jury usually consisting of 12 persons that in a criminal case determines whether a defendant is guilty or not guilty of the crime with which he is charged.

Physical evidence: evidence such as fingerprints, handwriting, vocal characteristics, stance, stride, gestures, and blood characteristic.

Plea bargain: an agreement between the defendant and the prosecutor, pursuant to which the defendant will plead guilty in the reasonable expectation that he will receive some type of consideration from the state.

Police power: the power inherent in government to enact laws to protect the order, safety, health, morals, and general welfare of society.

Preliminary hearing: a court proceeding in which a judge determines whether there is sufficient evidence to require that a defendant be placed on trial for committing a crime.

Presentment: an accusation of a crime made by a grand jury on its own and not at the request of the prosecutor.

Principal in the first degree: the person who either actually performs a criminal act or causes an innocent person to perform it.

Principal in the second degree: a person who is actually or constructively present at the scene of the crime and does not commit the criminal act, but has agreed to render assistance to one who does.

Prison: a state or federal facility of confinement for convicted criminals, usually felons.

Privilege: a rule that excuses a witness from disclosing evidence, usually by excusing a witness from answering certain questions or producing certain physical evidence. Privileges are an exception to the general rule that all evidence must be revealed.

Probable cause: when there is a rational basis for official action.

Probation: a sentence in a criminal case in which, instead of confinement, the defendant is allowed to remain in or is released back into the community.

Prosecution's case in chief: the evidence presented by the prosecutor between the time the prosecutor calls his first witness and the time the prosecutor rests his case.

Pro se defendant: a defendant who represents himself.

Putative defendant: person against whom the government already possesses incriminating evidence at the time of his appearance before a tribunal, or upon whom the government has focused as having committed a crime.

Real property: land and anything permanently affixed to the land, such as a building.

Recognizance bond: a type of bail bond that does not require a defendant to post cash or property as a condition of being released from custody.

Re-direct examination: the questioning of a witness after cross-examination.

Scienter: the unlawful intent or design necessary to any criminal act that is not a strict liability offense. The term is interchangeable with the term *"mens rea."*

Special conditions of probation: conditions that are imposed on a sentence of probation by a judge that the probationer must satisfy.

Statute of limitations: in criminal law, a statute that establishes a fixed period of time following the occurrence of a criminal act within which a person may be prosecuted. An act of grace through which the sovereign surrenders its right to prosecute.

Statutory conditions of probation: conditions imposed by statute on all sentences of probation that the probationer must satisfy.

Street crime: a crime usually directed at a person in public, such as robbery or mugging.

Substantive criminal law: the law that declares what forms of conduct are crimes and states what the punishment is for engaging in that conduct.

Tangible personal property: property that is visible and corporeal and has substance and body.

Target: a person as to whom the prosecutor or the grand jury has substantial evidence linking him to a crime and who in the judgment of the prosecutor is a putative defendant.

Tort: a legal wrong other than a breach of contract that causes harm for which courts will impose civil liability.

Trial *in absentia*: a trial conducted when the defendant is not present.

Turpitude: contrary to justice, honesty, or good morals.

Ultimate fact: in a criminal case a fact that pertains to an issue the prosecution must prove beyond a reasonable doubt.

Venue: the place where a criminal case may be tried.

Voir dire: the preliminary examination by a judge or lawyers of prospective jurors for the purpose of exposing any bias or prejudice the potential jurors may have.

White collar crime: a crime in which the illegal act is characterized by deceit, concealment, or a violation of trust and that is not dependent upon the application or threat of physical force or violence.

Work release: a sentence in a criminal case in which the defendant is confined to jail for a specified period of time, during which he is allowed to leave the jail to go to work and required return to jail at the end of his work day.

Writ of habeas corpus: a legal device available to individual to raise constitutional challenges to their imprisonment.

Table of Cases

Principal cases are indicated by italics of case name and page numbers.

Index

Boxes and figures are indicated by b and f following page numbers.